THE PROPHETS
OF PARIS

55
60¢

harper **⚜** to

A reference-list of Harper
by subjects, is printed at t

D1201846

THE PROPHETS OF PARIS

Turgot, Condorcet, Saint-Simon, Fourier, and Comte

Frank E. Manuel

HARPER TORCHBOOKS ▼ *The Academy Library*
Harper & Row, Publishers, New York

To Fritzie

66-7359

THE PROPHETS OF PARIS

© Copyright 1962 by the President and Fellows of
Harvard College

Printed in the United States of America.

This book was originally published in 1962 by Harvard
University Press, and is here reprinted by arrangement.

First HARPER TORCHBOOK edition published 1965 by
Harper & Row, Publishers, Incorporated
49 East 33rd Street
New York, New York 10016

Library of Congress catalog card number: 62-8182

194
M319

Soc. Sci, Harper 2.25

Contents

CONTENTS

Illustrations

Preface

This is part of a continuing study of modern concepts of man, not only what he is — a poor specimen to the naked eye — but what he might become. In time these French knowers of the human condition should be followed by a German series and perhaps an English one.

Since the book belongs to the genre known as the history of ideas, purists may bridle at the intrusion of flesh-and-blood personages and occasional reflections on economic and social reality. The tracing of disembodied moral and philosophical traditions, an art which has many eminent practitioners, is not my method. I still feel the need to introduce the bearer of the idea even when he disturbs the flow of abstractions. Thus the attempt has been made to combine portraiture with historical commentary. This should not be interpreted as a commitment to psychological determinism, though I must confess to a failing in that direction, along with a penchant for sociological determinants — in fact for any elements which throw a light or cast a shadow. Because one of my purposes in this volume was the establishment of a chain of intellectual transmission in France, the omission of Saint-Simon was unthinkable; I hope the reader will excuse the plagiarism of my earlier work on his life and thought.

My interest in the manuscripts of the thinkers presented here derives largely from a romantic view of history-writing. The scribbled *brouillons*, the casual notes, the personal letters give me a sense of intimacy with these men which their published works somehow withhold. I therefore am especially grateful to the keepers of their manuscripts: the Turgot family in the Château de Lantheuil, the archivists of the Bibliothèque Nationale, the Bibliothèque de l'Arsenal, the Bibliothèque de l'Institut, the Archives Nationales, and the Archives Positivistes. For their many kindnesses in making available printed materials I owe a growing debt through the years to the librarians of Harvard College Library and the Boston Athenaeum. And last though not least — after three decades of relations in peace and war, a word of thanks to Paris itself.

Frank E. Manuel

Boston

THE PROPHETS
OF PARIS

Turgot, Baron de l'Aulne
Pastel by Ducreux

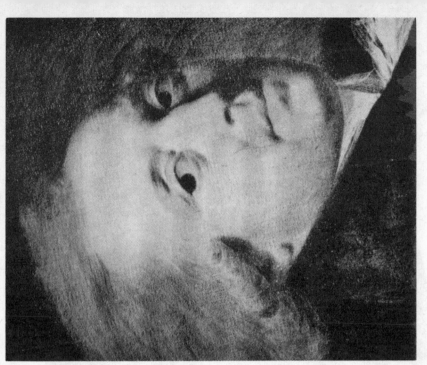

Painting by anonymous artist

Marquis de Condorcet

Lithograph by Bordes, after A. de Saint-Aubin

Comte de Saint-Simon
Pastel by Mme. Labille-Guiard, ca. 1796

Comte de Saint-Simon
Lithograph by Engelmann, 1825

Barthélemy-Prosper Enfantin
Lithograph by Grévedon

Barthélemy-Prosper Enfantin

Painting by anonymous artist

Charles Fourier
Lithograph by Cisneros

Auguste Comte
Lithograph by Tony Toullion

Prolegomenon

THIS is a book about five thinkers and a school who lived in Paris during the period from the middle of the eighteenth through the middle of the nineteenth century. They are introduced in the order in which they attracted public notice, though a number of them described in succession are members of the same generation — Saint-Simon and Fourier, the Saint-Simonians and Auguste Comte. It is difficult to designate the particular branch of thought to which they belong. Turgot would probably have to be classified as a *philosophe*, with all the ambiguities the title involved in the eighteenth century. The treatment here is limited to his work as a philosophical historian and a moralist, to the neglect of his role as an economist and an administrator. Condorcet the mathematician and Girondist politician is subordinated to the visionary of a utopia of science. Saint-Simon and Fourier are among the first of a long line of system-builders, and a system in the nineteenth century was by definition an attempt to encompass all knowledge and to dictate the rules for a new order; it would therefore be cruel to force them into the procrustean bed of any single intellectual category. Auguste Comte founded and named the science of sociology, but he surely would have bridled at the idea that he was a "sociologist," a title that would cut down his stature as the High Priest of Humanity. In uniting them all as prophets the title implies no denigration; these men are being likened to the sorely tried Judeans who were the great moral teachers of their city, sparing neither kings nor commoners, as well as revealers of a divine historical design.

Though the new age of prophecy spanned more than a century of French spiritual life, the group wrestled with common problems and there is a recognizable continuity in the preparation of their sacred remedies. As men they were tied to one another with the iron bonds of discipleship, friendship, or bitter mutual enmity. Condorcet was the devoted admirer of Turgot — he was called his chevalier — and in many respects his own work was a fulfillment and a development of the unpublished sketches of his revered predecessor. Saint-Simon was an "original," but even if his own testimony that he had met his fellow-Picard Condorcet during the Revolution is fanciful, the closeness of intellectual relationship is attested by numerous references in Saint-Simon's works and by a manuscript in which Condorcet's *Esquisse* was analyzed under explicit headings — "ideas to be adopted" and "ideas to be rejected." Comte's denial of his master Saint-Simon and the acrimonious denunciations of both his person and his writings are notorious; he preferred to establish an intellectual filiation with Condorcet and Turgot and to forget Père Simon, a betrayal which brought down upon him the mighty indignation of the Saint-Simonians. He was the Judas among the apostles. Though Fourier never met his contemporary Saint-Simon and read few of his works, he was not deterred from launching virulent attacks against his rival.

The only disciples who are awarded separate status are the Saint-Simonians, despite the fact that the adherents of Fourier and Auguste Comte also formed themselves into schools and movements. This discrimination is justified by the consideration that the Saint-Simonians, whose identity was established only after the death of their master, introduced appreciable variations in historical, social, and religious thought beyond the ideas of the man from whom they had originally drawn their inspiration. The Fourierists were obedient acolytes — though they chafed in secret — as long as their spiritual father lived, and when the doctrine spread after his death their innovations were not significant; indeed, they constricted rather than expanded his theories. Followers of Auguste Comte differed from him on pain of instant excommunication.

The contest between the Fourierists and the Saint-Simonians for the alienated souls of Europe and America is one of the unwritten secret histories of the nineteenth century. The passionate debates occasioned by these competitive systems have been forgotten, like the battles of the mystery cults in the Roman Empire; they were dwarfed by the appearance of the triumphant Marxist ideology. In their day, however, "the possessed" of Russia were torn by these alternative moral ways, and so were the more respectable idealists of New England. Positivists were late comers to the fray and hardly made as profound an impact, though Comte had his disciples in England, in the United States, in Russia, and above all in Latin America.

It occasionally happened, as one moved away from the seat of prophecy in Paris, that the distinctions between the doctrines which seemed so crucial to rival disciples — like the struggle of adjacent plants fighting for nutriment from the same soil — became blurred, especially when knowledge of the theories was derived from hearsay or secondary sources. During the early eighteen-thirties, Alexander Herzen and his friends turned to both Saint-Simon and Fourier for sustenance. The poet Ogarev, who was a member of the group, has recreated the religious atmosphere of the vague romantic Russian socialism of 1833:

> I remember a small room five *arshin* long
> The bed and the chair and the table with
>   the tallow candle
> And here three of us, children of the Decembrists
> Disciples of the new world
> Disciples of Fourier and Saint-Simon
> We swore to dedicate our whole lives
> To the people and their liberation.

But for the most part such syncretism was frowned upon, and acrid discussions among the standard-bearers of rival cults lasted far into the night.

The coteries of the great prophets were a mobile group. Once committed to the quest for an absolute system, young men moved from one to another; it was not rare for the truth-seekers to run through two and three systems in the course of a lifetime. There were the usual cries of treachery, the same bitter gnashing of teeth that had been heard fifteen hundred years before among the early Christian sectaries and would be heard again among the communists and socialists of the third and fourth decades of the twentieth century. Gustave d'Eichthal, Comte's first disciple, abandoned him for the Saint-Simonians and received the traditional pen-lashing; Jules Le Chevalier and Abel Transon left the Saint-

Simonians for Fourier, who was particularly pleased with these stolen souls. John Stuart Mill at one time flirted with the Saint-Simonians, moved into the Comtean orbit, and then broke away abruptly, marked with the anathema of the High Priest of Humanity.

There were of course a host of minor prophets in the eighteenth century, many of whom are treated in André Lichtenberger's *Le Socialisme au XVIIIe siècle*; Nicolas Boulanger and Court de Gébelin surely deserve a place as eminent predecessors, but I have dealt with them elsewhere. If one intended to complete the roster for the nineteenth century one would have to recognize Hoëné-Wronski, the Polish mathematician, philosopher of a *Réforme du savoir humain* and a *Historiosophie*; Pierre Leroux, the discoverer of the sentiment of *Homme-Humanité*; Coëssin, whose voluminous *Neuf Livres* converted spiritual families in Paris and Lyons; Ballanche, author of *L'Homme sans nom*, the *Palingénésie sociale*, and the *Ville des expiations*; Hyacinthe Azaïs, who corresponded with Saint-Simon but at the last moment shied away from a direct confrontation which would have determined once and for all whether or not his *Bases du système universel* were true; and many other sons of prophets the record of whose activities can readily be found in that curious mid-nineteenth-century compendium, *La France mistique, Tableau des excentricités religieuses de ce tems*. Its author, Alexandre Erdan, had made it his life's work to track down the prophets in their hovels and in the public squares of Paris, reporting on them in a style and with an orthography which is as bizarre as the personages whom he intended to ridicule. Though there may be occasion to mention these lesser persons as they move among the giants, this book is devoted almost exclusively to the magnificent obsessives. The works of the forgotten "mystics" often seem to be caricatures of the great systems; their authors crossed the boundary of communicability, a line which has been rather flexible in the history of human thought, but which nevertheless exists. The voice of Ganneau, Le Mapah, founder of the *religion évadienne*, raising his arms to the sky and shrieking to the crowd on the Place de la Concorde on the eve of June 13, 1849, "Take heed! my friends, take heed! Love each other and in loving you will conquer all! The force of democracy lies not in the strength of your arms and of your guns but in your hearts!" was lost; but somehow the major prophets managed to stay within the pale of relative rationality, and they survived. A process of natural selection was operative among the seers.

The prophets are dyed-in-the-wool Parisians. They remind one of nineteenth-century hostelries called *Hôtel de Paris et de l'Univers*. In their wildest dreams they never doubted for a moment that Europe was the chosen continent, France the chosen people, and Paris the mount from which the new gospel had to be delivered. Ganneau's leaflets were always addressed *à Paris, à l'Univers*. Their writings were all prepared in the city, not many streets away from one another. Though separated in time, these philosophers belonged to neighboring *quartiers*. Turgot's discourses were drawn up on the rue St. Jacques, Condorcet's *Esquisse* on the rue Servandoni; Saint-Simon lived across the river on the right bank, on the rue Richelieu, not far from the Bibliothèque Royale. The Saint-Simonians migrated: they were men of the Bourse and Montmartre. With Auguste Comte the Idea moved back again to the left bank, to rue Monsieur-le-Prince, where the religion of humanity finally established a seat which has remained the headquarters of the Positivist movement to this day. Fourier was the outsider, a provincial from Besançon, and he really does not belong. His intrusion cannot be justified on geographic grounds alone. After his denial by the newspapers of the capital he became an archenemy of Paris, and if his phalansteries were ever established the Holy City would be destroyed. He would have leveled the urban center which has been the heart of European civilization and sown the equal green patches of the phalanstery over the whole face of the earth. But even he conducted his major propaganda campaigns in Paris, and he died there. When he refuses Paris the omniarchy of the new society and spitefully settles it on Constantinople, the pique of the rejected lover is apparent.

The prophets have individual idiosyncrasies — in the hundred years of prophecy the official costume of the seer under-went marked changes, from Baron Turgot's lace ruffles to Auguste Comte's black frock coat — but there are uniform elements among them which can be readily abstracted.

They were all crisis philosophers. Mankind stood at the crossroads: since they were prophets with a historical sense, they invariably rehearsed the annals of mankind from the beginning of time to demonstrate that the moment of their speech was the instant of the great divide. There may have been other crucial happenings in the past, other troublous times, but somehow the gravity of the hour was qualitatively different from everything which had gone before both in its intensity and in its pivotal significance for world history. A great event was about to transpire. After the travail of new birth had passed, mankind would emerge — or would be catapulted — into a new world. The tonal effects of these crisis-crying prophets have been assimilated so thoroughly by modern man that they are today the inevitable hackneyed accompaniment of even the most casual social or political utterance. A century and a half ago the warning calls still had a poignancy which, it is hoped, may be preserved in the retelling of their story.

In Paris studies or garrets, depending upon their condition, they unveiled the future and in the same anxious breath tried to give it direction by persuading their contemporaries to adopt willingly and without bloodshed the course which they were inevitably destined to follow anyway. They were intoxicated with the future: they looked into what was about to be and they found it good. The past was a mere prologue and the present a spiritual and moral, even a physical, burden which at times was well nigh unendurable. They would destroy the present as fast as possible in order to usher in the longed-for future, to hasten the end. To an almost pathetic degree they were victims of what Montaigne had called "the frantic curiosity of our nature which is pleased to become absorbed with future things as if it did not have enough to do in digesting the present ones," or of that incapacity to live without the metaphysical anguish of futurity which Pascal described in the *Pensées*: "The present is never an end, the past and the present are our means. Only the future is our end. Thus we never live; but we hope to live. . . ." There are times when the writings of the Parisian prophets appear painfully adolescent; they are panting to grow up; their transitional stage of being is a source of constant uneasiness. They take no delight in the society of the most pleasure-loving city in western civilization in one of the most tumultuous centuries of its existence, when it was queen of the world. The prophets lived in eternal philosophical negation of what they were experiencing every day.

Theirs was a dream of beatitude in this world, but alas not in their time. A certain sadness pervades their prophesying, for like Moses they may only gaze upon the promised land from afar, knowing that they themselves shall never set foot upon it. The tragic fate of having been born too soon was made bearable by the philosophical reflection that they were heralding the future, inaugurating the dawn of real humanity. Like the great Prodromos, they appeared in the wilderness of corrupt Paris to announce the coming. In a confusion of roles they sometimes imagined that in their person the Messiah himself had already arrived. Saint-Simon thought that he was the reincarnation of Socrates and of Charlemagne; the disciples evoked the analogy with Jesus; Fourier, though not given to historical learning, demonstrated from Scripture that his appearance had been foretold. Auguste Comte, at the end of the line, preferred to relate himself to Saint Paul, the organizer of the Christian order whom he exalted above Christ. The eighteenth-century precursors were generally too sensible to play with such fantasies, though Condorcet in the shadow of death assumed a Stoic posture and identified himself with Socrates.

On the sociological level one is arrested by the deflection of their primary concern from the state and the definition of power to social relationships and religion. Amid the complex diplomatic intrigues and wars of the dynastic states of the West and a succession of bloody political revolutions in which men fought and died for liberty and dominion, these philosophical moralists turned their backs on the state as a superannuated institution. It is a comprehensible repudiation in a society which witnessed the promulgation and annulment of political constitutions at regular intervals. No basic metamorphosis seemed to take place during the frequent transfers of power from one regime to another. Authentic human relationships as they envisaged them for their ideal societies were not dependent upon evanescent political forms. The history of politics described nothing more than the changing of the guard. They were determined to discover the core of human nature and to build a social structure with the hard blocks of reality — man's instincts, his desires, his needs, his capacities. Each prophet might draw his plan and manipulate his materials differently in setting up the model of a good society, but the problem of the state apparatus and the overpowering role it has assumed in fostering and inhibiting satisfactions escaped them completely. The state was a scaffolding, a tool, a superstructure, a covering — not the heart of the human condition. The political order was looked down upon as a residue of the past which had to be circumvented — they did not say destroyed because they were peace-loving prophets — so that men might come face to face with their authentic problems which were moral, social, and religious. The prophets would gladly avail themselves of the services of political leaders to inaugurate the new order if the aid was proferred to them, but such intervention was considered merely auxiliary. Turgot and Condorcet thought that man was potentially a rational-scientific animal, the Saint-Simonians and Comte made him into a religious animal, Fourier into a passionate animal — but none of them would ever have regarded him as primarily a political animal. The state was a badly attached mask incapable of hiding profound conflicts which raged within the social organism.

The levity with which the prophets may sometimes be treated in this book is not meant to obscure the grand creativeness of their thought. If their psychological stigmata are examined they reveal clinical symptoms familiar to the most casual visitors of mental hospitals. The nineteenth-century group in particular are schizophrenic, megalomaniac, and paranoid. Similarities between their ideological structures and the fantasies of ordinary asylum patients are easy to establish. And yet there is always a touch of genius in their wildest extravagances. Mad or not, they addressed themselves to the needs of mankind and formulated its dilemmas; they passed about their all-too-synthetic balsams without stint, and they have been understood because even in their most introspective moments they were close to humanity and its pain.

This is a frank attempt at rehabilitation, to right the balance of historical judgment and bestow new worth upon thinkers who have often been treated with superficiality. Turgot was a man of magnificent stature in whom the *politique* overshadowed the philosopher; his intellectual grandeur can be recaptured. Up to a few decades ago Saint-Simon was generally regarded as a crackpot; a reconsideration of his work has already begun. Auguste Comte too has come to fare better in contemporary French philosophical studies, though the vogue for the rival Hegelian system has eclipsed him. Fourier has suffered most grievously of all at the hands of an unknowing posterity. Among the prophets he is perhaps the greatest and the most neglected. Thirty dossiers of his manuscripts in the Archives Nationales await a heroic editor.

The discrimination between the true and the false prophet was in ancient Israel an awesome act which often shook the polity to its foundations. In retrospect a century or two after their death, some of the prophets of Paris seem to have approached nearer to the prognostic truth than others. The hypothetical timetable most of them set up in their mind's eye was almost invariably in error; the fates seem to grind more slowly than the prophets anticipated, though one should not be too exacting about defects of scheduling which in the vast aeons of time may turn out to be *de minimis*. Perhaps it is still too early to designate the true prophets among them. In some mechanical respects Condorcet and Saint-Simon with their dreams of science and professional hierarchies showed the insight of authentic seers; but who knows, their day may pass — this stage may be only a prolegomenon — and mankind may yet be ushered in to the rich world of Charles Fourier with its endless delights or, may the gods forfend, it may lapse into the ordered, successfully repressed or sublimated society of Auguste Comte. The moral alternatives of sensate expansiveness to achieve felicity or the contraction of desires to attain spiritual perfectibility were the extremes between which the French prophets wavered, a not unfamiliar choice for hapless man with his constitutional repugnance to assimilating mixed systems. The debates of the great classical schools of morality were here re-enacted on another plane with a new rhetoric.

They were prophets of universal love — even the intellectualists among them — so ravished by their vision that the problems of distributive justice paled into insignificance, for in total love men do not haggle about their portions. In contrast with the prognosticators of a bloody apocalypse who came from across the Rhine and the distant lands of the Russian Czar, the French prophets were mild and consoling preachers. They foresaw a gentle settling of the crises of the age without violence. Resembling the comforter of the Second Isaiah rather than the grim punisher of the First, they were bearers of good cheer. "The golden age is before us," said Saint-Simon. "Breathe freely and forget your ancient evils," Fourier encouraged the inhabitants of Europe in the midst of the Napoleonic slaughter. "Abandon yourselves to joy, for a fortunate invention finally brings you the social compass." "O you whose somber sadness and stubborn regrets remain obstinately bound to the debris of the past," Père Enfantin addressed the unbelievers in 1832, "O you who doubt of your victory and vainly seek joy and repose in the society which you have fashioned, dry your tears and rejoice, for I have come in the name of God, of Saint-Simon, and of my Fathers to make you see the brilliant colors which will soon burst forth before your eyes." But alas for suffering mankind, the thunderers who reveled in the spectacle of death and destruction may have known the hidden nature of man better than these sons of *la douce France*.

I

Turgot, Baron de l'Aulne
THE FUTURE OF MIND

Philosophe indulgent, ministre citoyen,
Qui ne cherchas le vrai que pour faire le bien,
Qui d'un peuple léger, et trop ingrat peut-être,
Préparais le bonheur et celui de son maître. . . .
Voilà donc ce Paris! voilà ces connaisseurs
Dont on veut captiver les suffrages trompeurs!
> "Epître à un homme" (1776),
> in *Oeuvres complètes de Voltaire*
> (1784), XIII, 283–284.

Que notre roi consulte Maurepas
Qu'il soit son mentor et son guide,
Qu'à tous les conseils il préside
Cela ne me surprend pas.
Mais qu'à Turgot ce mentor s'abandonne,
Qu'il laisse ce ministre fou,
Dont tout le public est si soûl
A notre État casser le cou,
C'est là ce qui m'étonne.

> "Les Ministres,"
> in Emile Raunié, *Chansonnier historique du xviiiᵉ siècle*
> (Paris, 1884), IX, 94.

66-7359

لم ٧٣٥٩

In 1750 a young bachelor of arts, scion of an illustrious Norman family, the Prior Anne Robert Jacques Turgot, Baron de l'Aulne, delivered two lectures in Latin before the Sorbonne at the opening and conclusion of the academic exercises called the *Sorboniques*. Together they framed a new conception of world history from remotest antiquity to the present and constituted the first important version in modern times of the ideology of progress.[1]

Turgot's theses had been born amid great personal spiritual travail, as befitted so momentous a pronouncement. For three months before the delivery of the first oration he had been profoundly disturbed — in a letter to his brother, a Knight of Malta, he described himself as in a depressed state — and only after a most flattering triumph had been assured did he completely recover.[2] The Cardinal de la Rochefoucauld himself was in attendance at the twenty-three-year-old scholar's initial performance on July 3, 1750, which to all appearances launched the idea of human perfectibility under solemn ecclesiastical auspices. The academic stronghold of the Catholic faith seems a strange podium for the propagation of a view of mankind which in its ultimate consequences was more potent than the wit of Voltaire and the mechanistic materialism of La Mettrie in deflecting Western consciousness from a religious to a utilitarian earthly morality. Since the twentieth-century Catholic Church has become progressive and oriented toward organized social amelioration, the absurdity of the mid-eighteenth-century confrontation may now seem less flagrant, but retrospective reflection on the scene is enough to make one believe in the dialectic. From the same building where the young Abbé Turgot was lodged there regularly resounded thunderous condemnations by the Faculty of Theology against heretical works of philosophy. In the very bosom of the old religion of sin, death, and salvation was born the new religion of earthly immortality.

Nominally Turgot's discourse was a eulogy of Christianity, but to extol the ancient faith he could find no more appropriate and lofty praise for the creed of his audience than an array of historical proofs positive that the Christian religion, far from being an agent of the forces of darkness — as clandestine atheists were bruiting it about — had been the moving spirit in the progress of mankind since the fall of the Roman Empire. The truth of Christianity vindicated by the idea of progress and a harangue on the "utility of religion" were dangerous apologias, but it would seem that the mid-eighteenth-century church was grateful for approval from any quarter.[3] Turgot's defense of Christianity had marked affinities with laudatory chapters on the moral truths of Catholicism in the *Esprit des lois*. Montesquieu had already anticipated a number of Turgot's arguments when he demonstrated that on balance, historically, the social virtues of religion had outweighed its iniquities — but this was a rather weak bulwark for the church militant. The singular form of approbation voiced by these aristocratic defenders of the faith robbed Christianity of transcendence and ultimately left it so enfeebled that religion was constrained to conduct the great spiritual debate on the adversary's favorite field of combat, worldly usefulness.

In no single work published during his lifetime did Turgot ever amplify the theses of his orations of 1750, but a substantial number of fragments and outlines first collated by Dupont de Nemours under the Empire, the articles prepared for the *Encyclopédie*, scattered reflections in his essays on language and economics, verbal traditions incorporated by Condorcet in his biography of 1786, and letters to philosophical contemporaries, when assembled together, constitute a grand body of doctrine with a reasonable measure of consistency. Turgot, who shed the cloth and became one of the great administrators of France, was an innovator in the study of philosophical history, however sketchy and unfinished his brief texts may be. Had he ever written the projected universal history about which he talked at length to Condorcet instead of spending himself in abortive attempts at a rehabilitation of the French state, he would have ranked with Vico as a creator of the "new science." Even during his lifetime his ideas were far more widely diffused than the meager record of his publications would indicate.[4] Though he rejected their blasphemies, Turgot was one of the great heroes of the *philosophes*. As a man of action, albeit a failure, the promulgator of the six edicts of 1776 gave daring expression to Enlightenment theory. When the dying Voltaire, on his last triumphant journey to Paris in 1778, grasped the hands of the fallen minister, kissed them, and bathed them in tears, the skeptical king of the epoch symbolically embraced the idea of progress and the Leibnizian theodicy which *Candide* had so uproariously caricatured.

Turgot, of the middle generation of the *philosophes*, younger than Voltaire and Rousseau, older than Condorcet, despite his great talents was a blocked, frustrated man, unfulfilled. Houdon's statue has caught his melancholy air; one senses a touch of genius which was never quite realized, a sort of eighteenth-century French presage of John Stuart Mill.

In April and May 1776 the "good Turgot," whose whole being was devoted to the happiness of mankind, whose ministerial edicts were intended to alleviate the sufferings of his fellows and to save the kingdom of the young Louis XVI who had called him to his side, found himself beset by widespread hunger riots, the *guerre des farines*. These popular uprisings, now considered rehearsals for the great tumults which followed twenty years later, were largely spontaneous, though the intrigues of the courtiers and of the farmers-general whose interests where threatened by the six edicts played some role in rousing the populace.[5] Turgot approved severe measures of suppression, and a number of rioters were hanged from a high gibbet "as an example." The monarchy survived the incidents, but Turgot's enemies used the opportunity to perfect a cabal, and the minister was dismissed. Turgot foresaw the doom of the monarch he served — on one occasion he recalled to his sire the fate of Charles I — but to what avail? In a youthful *pensée* Turgot had already dwelt on the curse of the power of prescience. "If a man could foresee with certainty all the events which depend upon chance and if he directed his conduct in the light of this knowledge, he would pass for a lunatic because men would not understand his motives." [6]

The papers of this enigmatic man kept in the château of Lantheuil in Normandy have not revealed his secret — if there was one. There are rare expressions of warm affection between the Abbé Turgot and the young abbés with whom he studied at school and who offered him friendly advice on the early drafts of his discourses and prize essays. Of the two chief aides during his tenure of office, Dupont de Nemours seems to have been the object of intense paternal feeling (there are three hundred letters covering a period of twenty years); with Condorcet the relationship was more philosophical. Both worshiped him as a heroic model. "If ever friendship deigned to inhabit a temple on earth it was the heart of M. Turgot," Dupont de Nemours wrote in the introduction to the first edition of Turgot's works. "He joined the sensitivity of a young man and the modesty of a respectable woman to the character of a legislator for whom the administration of an empire was not above his capabilities, a man worthy of influencing the destinies of the world." [7] In the salons of the great ladies of the *ancien régime* Turgot was a brilliant star, but not even a breath of scandal about him can be detected in the memoir writers. During the crisis of 1776 when attacks rained upon him, a false catalogue of imaginary books in the Abbé Baudeau's library was circulated: along with run-of-the-mill titles like *L'Homme au masque, Consultation de médecine sur les délires de M. Turgot,* and *Le Nouveau Machiavel,* there was listed an *Antigunaika, ouvrage composé par M. Turgot, avec une préface du frère orateur Diderot,* a crude attempt, in the manner of contemporary libels, to cast doubt upon his interest in women. There is a tradition that Turgot had once asked for the hand of Mlle. de Ligniville, who presumably rejected him in favor of Helvétius. This scion of the great Turgot family — named from the god Thor, according to one etymology — was a shy man with a tendency to obesity whose reticence was often mistaken for arrogance. His dedication to the life of reason sometimes made incomprehensible to him the ways of men who were differently motivated.

The Baron Turgot would no doubt have resented being included as the first of the prophets of Paris. A man of orderly administration in the provinces and in the ministries, a frequenter of the great Paris drawing rooms where nothing was more alien than enthusiasm, he was worlds away from the spluttering prophets of London of 1707, those refugees from the Cévennes who foretold the doom. But, for all that, he was the true initiator of the rationalist prophetic tradition. Dismayed as he would have been by the end of the catena, by the rigid dogmatism of an Auguste Comte or the more fanciful hallucinations of a Fourier, Turgot despite his per-

sonal diffidence must take his place at the head of the procession.
First among moderns he foretold the future of reason.

NOVELTY OR THE RUT OF SAMENESS

TURGOT's philosophy of progress is firmly rooted in the current
sensationalist theory of knowledge. The capacity of man to receive
new impressions from the outside world, to combine them, and to
reflect upon them was an ultimate assurance of the inevitable and
indefinite advancement of the human mind. Sheer accumulation of
experience in time was the underlying process of the education of
mankind, as it was for the child. In the primordial stages of historical development the motives of human beings are nakedly
passionate and they partake of almost no reflective elements. Men
are goaded into action by their pains and their pleasures, their
lusts and their necessities, their hunger, their thirst for power and
conquest. Only in the latter days of Enlightenment have rational
forces begun to assume direction of world history.

This recognition of the predominance of the passionate rather
than the rational element in the history of mankind raised for Turgot a problem common to most exponents of temporal teleologies:
how could a being who to the ordinary observer has acted primarily, if not solely, out of passion, whose conduits open to the
external world are mere sensation, ever achieve a transcendent
destiny called Reason? Turgot's man, though created by God, is
bound by the laws of the Locke-Condillac epistemology, and within this framework he must accomplish his historic mission — become a civilized moral being living up to the standards of eighteenth-century Christian Stoicism; exert ever greater control over
nature through technology; acquire and preserve beyond the possibilities of destruction an increasing body of knowledge about himself and about the physical world; achieve and sustain a measure
of artistic creativity.

In most of their writings the *philosophes*, and Turgot among
them, prided themselves on their emancipation from the *esprit de
système* which they associated with scholasticism and the secular
philosophical system-builders of the seventeenth century. They
were confident of the purity of their empirical method; they looked

only at the facts. But often enough the categorical denial of innate ideas or a priori axioms was only a preparatory device which preceded a dogmatic affirmation of innate sentiments or principles of behavior. Western thought has experienced its greatest difficulties in driving out the demon of the absolute; if he was exorcised from the mind he sought refuge in feelings. Thus Rousseau, for example, in his *Discourse on Inequality*, invented the tragic "instinct" of perfectibility to explain man's unfortunate emergence from the lowest stage of the state of nature. Turgot posited a similar principle, which, though he shunned the word rendered odious by Locke, was virtually "innate." There is for Turgot a basic drive in human nature to innovate, to create novelty, to bring into being new combinations of sensations. And once this novelty-making impulse has been assumed, rock-bottom has been reached. One either accepts or rejects it.

Simultaneously Turgot identified in civilized society a hostile negating principle which, through the operation of institutions, had always sought to stall man in the rut of sameness, in a routine, in a state of treadmill repetitiveness. World history turned into a war eternal between these polar principles. In depicting the struggle, Turgot was of course no indifferent bystander, for the battle between the spirit of novelty and the spirit of routine, between the desire for movement and the tendency toward quiescence, was the underlying conflict of human destiny, a new philosophical version of the religious war between good and evil.

This idea of innovation remained the basic new concept in Turgot's view of the historical world. Traditional society had accepted a changeless state of being as the greatest good. In the most ancient documents of Near Eastern civilization the plea to the gods for an enduring order was the prayer behind the quest for peace. When Messianism with its foretelling of a great transformation appeared in Judaic and Christian history its promise of a radical metamorphosis had invariably been considered a dangerous disruptive agent by the rulers of society. With an acute sense of self-preservation institutionalized religions have always fought the millenarians. Change of the earthly order and a prediction of the change were equally disturbing. Was not the proclamation of the Jubilee of 1300 an attempt to smother under an official garment the strange stadial prognostications of the followers of Joachim of Flora? Even in war and in conquest traditionalist societies invariably aimed at establishing a stable, enduring, even immutable order. Turgot may have considered himself a devoted servant of the French monarchy, but no principle was more inimical to its preservation than his absolute commitment to eternal change and perfectibility.

By raising the spirit of novelty to the level of a major passion of human nature, Turgot established a fundamental distinction between the physical and the moral sciences, one which was increasingly emphasized as the eighteenth century passed its halfway mark. In this Socratic age, along with deep respect for the new physics there were real misgivings about man's complete immersion in the universe of the natural philosophers. The eighteenth-century moralist, though fascinated by the Newtonian world-machine, a model he longed to imitate, was not without hidden doubts about its applicability to the social sciences. The facile analogy between the movement of the spheres obeying the law of gravity and a harmony in human relationships that would reflect the natural order, a frequent correspondence, was not always convincing. A number of major eighteenth-century thinkers, though committed to the principle of the existence of moral scientific laws, dwelt upon the differences as well as the similarities between the two orders of nature and of man. Vico's *Scienza Nuova* was a deliberate attack upon preoccupation with the laws of matter, the lesser element, to the neglect and abandonment of the laws of men and nations which had their own peculiar character. Vico had made a great show of contrasting the loftier, nobler truths of his new science of history and human experience with the more limited certainty of the mathematical world of the Cartesians — a paradox to the average intellectual of the age. Rousseau, following up his earlier attack on the arts and sciences, had shouted a challenge in his *Second Discourse*: "It is of Man that I shall speak" — and he meant that he was again dealing with human problems, not the laws of nature and the achievements of technology, even though in the next breath he rendered obeisance to the Newtonian image. By contrast, Montesquieu's great masterpiece of mid-century Enlightenment was still written in the shadow of the old subservience to Newtonian physics, and his model was basically mechanistic; the good polity was subject to technical breakdown because of a failure to operate in accordance with its true character, and the genius legislator by fathoming the spirit of a nation's laws could effect a restoration, set the machine working once more so that it might continue its orderly revolutions. "Ed io anche son pittore," Montesquieu had affirmed without modesty before the unveiling of his fundamental law of climate, the equivalent of universal gravity in physics. Turgot drew upon Montesquieu for factual information, but he abjured the slavish patterning of the science of man after the science of physics. Though far from emancipated from mechanical imagery, he introduced another dimension: if the physical order expressed its innermost being in the principle of recurrence, the human order had a unique principle all its own, an antithetic principle — Progress. While Turgot rarely used organismic similes, he was already affirming the intrinsically different nature of the world of men, in which the repetitive movements were far outstripped by the novelties.

The order of men was an endless innovation. But the new was not a mere fortuitous alignment and realignment of elements in the Epicurean manner. In human events real, lasting, and enduring novelty was being created. The new configuration brought about by each successive age was not merely a replacement of one set of forms by another, nor was it only a rectification of an old structure. There was a process of eternal transmission, an ever-growing accumulation, an increasing inheritance, a sort of vast worldly repository of intellectual merit. The variations brought forth in history were additive, and the piling up of new experience was the law of mankind. Civilized man was distinguished from the savage and from the child precisely because he had recorded more diverse and complex combinations — the language of Locke's epistemology.

The constancy of the physical order had so ravished men's minds in the eighteenth century that the apparently accidental and chaotic human order had begun to appear inferior. Turgot's idea of progress, by sharply distinguishing the human order and discovering in it a relative superiority, re-established its faltering status. In this discovery there was an admixture of Christian apology and humanism. Mankind was vindicated, was restored to a central position in a separate historical world, and was granted a quality which no other part of the natural order could pretend to possess. Man was also rescued from the Epicurean view of the world, which had many somber attractions for the eighteenth-century philosophical historian. While Turgot's historical universe could not boast the obvious constancy of physical nature where events repeated themselves, it was blessed with a more sublime rule of constancy, the extraordinary law of steady perfectibility. Sameness and repetition, the very attributes which men contemplated with admiration in nature, were evil if they long endured in the world of men. Constant inconstancy, eternal change and progress, were the true distinctions of mankind.

The opening periods of the *Tableau philosophique des progrès successifs de l'esprit humain*, the second Sorbonique, contrasted the rival virtues of the two orders: "The phenomena of nature, subject to constant laws, are enclosed in a circle of revolutions which are always the same. Everything is reborn, everything perishes, and through successive generations in which vegetation and animal life reproduce themselves time merely restores at each instant the image which it has caused to disappear.

"The succession of men, however, presents a changing spectacle from century to century. Reason, the passions, liberty, produce new events without end. All ages are linked to each other by a series of causes and effects which binds the present state of the world with all those which have preceded it. The conventional signs of language and writing, affording men the means of assuring the possession of their ideas and of communicating them to others, have fashioned of all detailed forms of knowledge a common treasury, which one generation transmits to another like a legacy that is ever being augmented with the discoveries of each century, and thus the human race, considered from its beginnings, appears to the eyes of a philosopher to be one immense whole which, like every individual, has its infancy and its progress." [8]

Turgot's conception of the progressive accumulation of knowledge through time, particularly in the physical sciences, was hardly an unheralded novelty by the mid-eighteenth century. Roger Bacon probably had at least an inkling of the idea. Francis Bacon's *Novum Organum* and Bernard Fontenelle's *Digression sur les anciens et les modernes,* written incident to the famous literary "quarrel," have been recognized as respectworthy antecedents. Passages in Descartes and particularly Pascal's *Fragment de préface sur le traité du vide* [9] were forerunners insofar as they conceived of the accretion of scientific truth through the mere performance and recording of new experiments over the centuries. Turgot's theory rested upon a far broader concept. In contrast to Pascal's severe restriction of the idea to the physical sciences, accompanied by tortured doubts about the meaning of this progress to man's moral and religious nature, Turgot extended progress to virtually the whole realm of being and implanted it as the central shaft of a system of worldly morality.

Turgot's theory mirrored a profound revolution in man's attitude toward change which in the eighteenth century imposed itself with ever greater force in western European society and was soon to conquer the world. He had a pervasive psychological horror of the static, his friends have reported, and in public office he was always impatient of any curbs on his zeal to reform and rearrange whatever ancient practices came within his jurisdiction. In a playful couplet Voltaire said that Turgot did not quite know what he wanted but he was sure it would be something different. In violent rebellion against traditionalist society, as chief minister of Louis XVI he spearheaded its disruption with new ways of thought and new methods of action. He seemed to revel in its break-up. Turgot had an almost twentieth-century sense of the rapid flux of events, a succession of changes so fast that it was almost impossible to grasp the meaning of a stable structure. In the "Plan d'un ouvrage sur la géographie politique" he expressed this feeling in a brilliant *aperçu.* "Before we have learned that things are in a given situation they have already been altered several times. Thus we always become aware of events when it is too late, and politics has to foresee the present, so to speak." [10]

In the plan of the second discourse at the Sorbonne, *movement* was described as the primordial force which dispelled chaos. Only through movement had men acquired ideas of distinctiveness and of unity. If an innate sense of movement were not an aspect of human nature, men would have contented themselves with mere sensation and they would never have established differences. If they did not synthesize new combinations of feelings to yield novel reflections, they would have gone on perceiving the same things without change forever throughout history. Fortunately movement had always thrust objects into fresh relationships. Wars, migrations, catastrophes, had made discoveries possible by allowing for unprecedented confluences of events. If man were not submitted to such violent stimuli, Turgot saw him lapsing into a state of somnolence and barren decay followed by death. In Vico's doctrine the energizing drive had to be roused by necessity. Surely Turgot's early man — and perhaps man in all ages — has to be provoked and excited to produce new ideas, to assimilate new juxtapositions of phenomena. Any mutation — and he used the word — was desirable, even if it should temporarily lead men astray, because something was to be learned from any occurrence.[11] It was preferable to allow men to wander into dangerous pathways and break their legs rather than to limit experience and to promote the false belief that perfection had already been attained. Error was more salutary than imitation, he declared with an almost romantic defiance, anticipating Schiller's defense of a similar paradox. Turgot sanctioned the free exercise of caprice as long as it did not harm other persons. In a fragment on morals written when he was a young man he attacked the "sheeplike conformity" which society calls "good sense." [12] His belief in the right to error expressed itself in an absolute intellectual openness. "He tolerated equally," wrote Condorcet, "both pyrrhonism and the staunchest belief in opinions opposed to his own." [13] Since mere repetition added nothing to the total acquisitions of mankind, *to progress*, in one of its nuclear definitions, came to mean simply to innovate, to make the new, without an implied judgment of worth and excellence, and in this crude form the idea has often been adopted in Western society.

Turgot's disrespect for the dead weight of the past was dramatically set forth in his *Encyclopédie* article on Foundations. If all the graves that had ever been dug had been preserved, it would be necessary in order to cultivate the soil to overturn "these sterile monuments and to stir the ashes of the dead to nourish the living." [14] He was prepared to violate the wishes of ancestors if their endowments, their ancient wills, usurped the needs of their descendants and barred them from access to the tremendous hoards of wealth controlled by monasteries. If past generations impeded the free enjoyment of liberty, the wills of the ancestors should be annulled. The past had to be overcome, brushed aside, lest it gain a stranglehold on the unborn. Living meant an eternal breaking out of old forms, an emancipation, a liberation. When Turgot tried to refashion the traditionalist monarchy of France he was acting out his own philosophy of history. In the edict of 1776 suppressing the jurands he proclaimed the "right to work" as the possession of every man, an "inalienable right" of humanity [15] — familiar language that year, but his words should not be interpreted with the socialist overtones of 1848. Work was eulogized as the creative act of man cleansed of the stigma of original sin; and even though rooted in necessity it was the key instrument of liberty. Since any activity was potentially productive of innovation, it contained the germ of progress. To shackle work with the restrictions of the feudal system, with prohibitions and tariffs, was to smother the possibilities of change. Limitations on the movement of grain among the provinces, on the free circulation of ideas, on the mobility of labor, on the accessibility of knowledge, were kindred antiprogressive regulations. Whatever was fixed, set, hardened, a religious dogma or an economic restriction, literally anything that might block new combinations of ideas, was a source of evil, deadly.[16] Turgot's prognostication of the independence of the American colonies was the expression of a libertarian desire of the philosopher of progress, even though his analysis preserved the form of a cold diplomatic state paper.[17] Turgot favored all freedom from tutelage, any independence, because these political acts of liberty were conditions precedent to creative innovation. The very term liberty lost its medieval connotation of a privilege and became the right to bring into being what had not existed before. Turgot knew that the present and the future were locked in a sequence of relationships with the past, but there are few thinkers who have respected its survival less.

The archenemy of progress, the sickly tendency toward repetition and sameness, had historically sunk whole societies in a rut where they languished and died. "It is not error which is opposed to the progress of truth; it is not wars and revolutions which retard the progress of governments; it is softness, stubbornness, routine, and everything which leads to inaction." [18] The spirit of routine tended to become the controlling force in any intellectual elite which managed to seize power before it was permeated with a full consciousness of the morality of progress. Turgot's favorite illustration was the mandarin class and his evidence the well-nourished eighteenth-century debate on the character of the despotism of China. Here was a classic example of a society in which rational scientific progress had so far outstripped the spirit of liberty and moral progress that the rulers created a monopoly for themselves, froze education, and insisted upon mere traditional reiteration. Though the scientific level the Chinese mandarins had attained was high, their whole intellectual world became desiccated because it was static. Sects of every kind, philosophical as well as religious, faced the debilitating influence of the spirit of routine when they enjoyed power for long. Turgot was so wary of this pernicious proclivity of sects to stereotype their ideas that he even abandoned the *philosophes* on the *Encyclopédie*, repelled by their dogmatism. Only with great reluctance did he concede to his friend Condorcet, the Permanent Secretary of the Academy of Sciences, that academies might conceivably serve a useful purpose during a brief transitional period. In the bright future of mankind he saw no more need for these learned assemblies than for other corporate bodies tainted with the stigmas of feudalism. The *esprit de corps* was in itself a stultifying evil. A few common projects of direct benefit to the participants he was willing to tolerate, though not without misgivings. His historical appreciation of the sects and ancient priesthoods of Babylon and Egypt was barbed with an antagonism which derived from his hostility toward the theologians who had trained him. The definition of a priesthood as a conspiracy to withhold religious truth in order to maintain uncontested sway over the people was common enough in eighteenth-century Europe. Turgot added the further reflection that in time these intellectual monopolists lost the capacity to understand their own traditional learning; and whatever scientific treasure they had amassed soon either evaporated or was destroyed by a superior force. The accumulation of scientific knowledge required absolute freedom of inquiry — a Turgot conception which became a cornerstone of liberalism in modern times, a highly controversial contention that has often proved itself to be an article of the new faith rather than a historical proposition that is universally applicable. Hume, Turgot's friend, doubted it when the idea was first propounded.

Turgot was openly dissatisfied with the great Montesquieu's typology of polities based on climate or geography. He posed a fundamental dichotomy between those societies which featured a maximum of mobility in all branches of human activity and those which were hostile to movement. Montesquieu had betrayed a strong preference for a political configuration in a state of balance, perhaps with tension in the atmosphere, but with equilibrium maintained. Turgot extolled every manifestation of expansiveness and condemned every form of self-containment as deadening. A precondition of progress was that a society be wide open to the spirit of change, that it welcome energy and action. Progress required a climate in which novelty was passionately sought after, not only tolerated. Turgot's philosophy of history set the tone for the Revolution.

GENIUS THE DYNAMIC AGENT

IN TURGOT the idea of progress had not yet become completely dehumanized. There was a unique being, the Genius, who played a crucial role as its dynamic agent. There were continually new encounters, new contingencies, unprecedented relationships in the world, but most of them passed unperceived, leaving no lasting imprint on a human mind, and they were gone forever. A living intermediary was necessary for the consummation of the progressive act; a human being had to experience the sensations, make the proper combinations, and after reflection create a new truth. The genius was that receptive mediator who grasped novelty, who was unbound by previous modes of perception, and who dared to articulate what he saw. History functioned through genius — the new Logos — and if unfavorable circumstances prevented him from exercising his superb talents on the novel play of events, progress was temporarily arrested. Turgot, unlike Montesquieu, was in search of a human moral force, rather than a physical force such as the challenge of the environment, to spark the movement of world history. In his theory of genius and its relation to the dynamics of progress Turgot discovered a uniform single principle that was operative everywhere which could account for diversity in the tempo and character of progress in time and place without abandoning the whole mechanism to Epicurean chance.

Though Turgot recognized only minor differences in the natural physical equipment of men, he did establish a "real inequality" in the character of their souls, and though he confessed to his inability to define the causes of genius, he was convinced of its qualitative superiority. His appreciation of genius was in the romantic spirit of one segment of eighteenth-century thought and has its parallel in Diderot, though Turgot introduced none of the psychological complexities which were raised by *Le Neveu de Rameau*. Turgot's genius was a more old-fashioned respectable figure, one who could still be admitted into Fontenelle's academic society. But Turgot created the type in the philosophy of history and he grew in stature until he ultimately became Hegel's daemonic world-historical hero-monster, the embodiment of Spirit at a crucial *Moment*.

Turgot still dealt with his genius as a mechanical principle, since the most important thing about him was the mathematical frequency of his appearance in the world. The problem of the relative number of geniuses emerging in various historical periods had been debated in the course of the late-seventeenth-century quarrel between the ancients and the moderns. In their zeal to prove that it was possible for contemporary literature to be as great as the creations of the classical world, the moderns had steadfastly maintained that nature was equally prolific of genius in all times and in all places. For evidence of this constancy in the fertility of nature they used homely analogies. Since trees were obviously no thicker in antiquity than in modern times, why should genius then have been more plentiful or more sublime? The eighteenth century tended to regard an increase in the population of a society as an absolute good. For Turgot, who believed in a fixed ratio of genius births to ordinary natalities at any historic moment, the modern increase in the number of inhabitants was especially felicitous, for it presaged a greater yield of geniuses. "Genius is spread among mankind like gold in a mine. The more ore you take out the more metal you will get." [19]

Turgot introduced a new twist into the old conception of genius. To be sure, the extraordinary man was a natural phenomenon which appeared at more or less equal intervals throughout history, the same natural potential being present in an identical amount, but the crux of the problem of genius lay elsewhere. Circumstances in the world of political reality and in the accidental world of the natural genius either fostered his development or crushed him. Therefore the first task which Turgot posed for humanity was to actualize genius more frequently and to minimize the instances when a born genius was lost to mankind and to progress. If under favorable conditions in a given society many potential geniuses were trained to their full capacity, progress was assured. If only a few were suitably perfected, at best the age might become an epoch of conservation. And should genius be generally suffocated by external conditions, a temporary decline might set in. Thus the preservation of the genius and the maximization of his talents became the central function of the good society, for he held the power of the keys of progress. A whole moral system was involved in this rather simple idea. Those forces which stifled genius were evil and those which fostered it, allowed it to attain fruition, were good. During the long historic past the central role of genius had not been recognized, with the result that mankind had benefited from only a small proportion of the geniuses whom nature had proffered to civilization. This waste of genius in the world economy of knowledge had retarded progress.

All of the utopian projects for the subsidization of genius drafted by Condorcet and Saint-Simon at the turn of the century were direct outgrowths of Turgot's stress upon the critical role of genius in the historic process. The rather fanciful and complicated mechanical schemes they devised were specific responses to the problem of how to salvage more geniuses and how to increase their productivity, since both of these heirs to the Turgot conception were convinced that genius set the pace of development for progress. The rate of the fulfillment of genius established the over-all rate of progress in an absolute sense.

TURGOT, BARON DE L'AULNE

LANGUAGE THE VESSEL

ONE factor above all others determined whether the perceptions of genius were destined to become part of the main stream of universal progress or whether they were fated to be forgotten in the darkness of time: the ready accessibility of an appropriate vessel for the containment of ideas, an orderly language.[20] If for reasons related to the political life of nations — wars, conquests, turmoils — no proper language was fashioned, novelty would have sprouted in vain. Normally in the great civilizations the genius had available adequate symbols for the preservation of his thoughts and their transmission to posterity. In the future language was destined to become an even superior instrument; it would be stripped of its rhetoric, cleansed of its ambiguities, so that the only means of communication for true knowledge would be the mathematical symbol, verifiable, unchanging, eternal. The ideal of Descartes's clear and distinct ideas, terminological economy, would become a reality.

In the past one of the unfortunate consequences of the conquest of a decadent higher civilization by vigorous barbarians had been the linguistic confusion which followed the disaster. A long period of time elapsed before the victors and the vanquished merged their different forms of speech, and during the interval language, the only receptacle for the storing of scientific progress then available, was lacking. Geniuses continued to perceive new phenomena, but since they were deprived of a stable body of rational linguistic symbols their observations were stillborn. During the barbarian invasions of western Europe the Latin language, which previously had diffused works of speculative science, was adulterated by admixture with primitive tongues. The Babel of languages resulted in a protracted period of intellectual sterility during which it was impossible for a creative genius to express himself because there was no settled linguistic medium for scientific thought.[21] Turgot compared this historical situation to the pouring of two different liquids into a bottle; a passage of time was required before their fusion could be effected, before the murky color was dissipated and a new homogeneous fluid appeared. The Middle Ages were that long interval during which favorable linguistic conditions were created for the Renaissance emergence of genius. In the Byzantine Empire a stultification like that in the medieval West had occurred, but there at least the speculative science which the ancients had accumulated could be preserved intact, for in this isolated society continuity of language with the source of knowledge in Greece had never been severed.

Language was not only a means of communication for new ideas, it was also a repository for the history of progress. In an article on Languages which Turgot had projected for the *Encyclopédie* but which, like so many of his plans, never came to fruition, he intended to show that throughout the ages language was an index of the stadial development of nations, since words were invented only when there were ideas demanding utterance. The mere existence of certain words was witness to a complex civilization.[22] Should two nations "unequally advanced in their progress" intermingle, the more highly civilized people, even if defeated, would predominantly color the new language fusion because they alone possessed words corresponding to the more complicated ideas of a rich social fabric. Thus even when a decadent civilization succumbed before young barbarians its idea structure would survive. Language recorded the triumph of real progress in science even amid the ruins of once glorious empires. This conception of the history of language and literature as the embodiment of the successive stages of human development had of course been more copiously presented in the axioms of Vico's *Scienza Nuova*, but there is no evidence of any direct influence. In his *Réflexions sur les langues*, a youthful polemic against Maupertuis written about 1751, Turgot proposed historical semantic studies as the clue to mythology and to the illumination of prehistoric traditions. "The study of language, if well done, would perhaps be the best of logics. In analyzing, in comparing the words of which they are fashioned, in tracing from the beginning the different meanings which they acquired, in following the thread of ideas, we will see through which stages, through which metamorphoses men passed. . . . This kind of experimental metaphysics would be at one and the same time the history of the human mind and the history of the progress of its thoughts, always fitted to the needs which gave birth to them. Languages are at once their expression and their measure."[23] Like so many of Turgot's insights, the formula is so laconic, so apparently casual, that it would pass unnoticed were we not already sensitized to the ideas by parallel themes in other eighteenth-century thinkers.

The primitive language structure of each nation was developed independently but along similar lines, because the sensations from which speech derived were the same. While Turgot was not as militantly antidiffusionist as Vico, he had broken completely with the traditional theory of language. By mid-century there was already widespread disbelief in the orthodox notion that language was born a complete and perfect rational instrument, a fully developed means of communication which Adam already possessed in the Garden of Eden. Though still utilizing subterfuges necessitated by censorship, the weight of opinion tended to establish a hypothetical historical pattern for the growth of language, from the first emotive grunts of man in the state of nature, through a period of sentence structure, to the highest form of expression in a mathematical formula. This ideal history of the origins and development of language had roots in Locke, was repeated in Condillac, in Adam Smith, in Monboddo, in the *Encyclopédie*, in Rousseau, in Hume, and could count even respectable English bishops among its adherents. Language had become the record of the human intelligence as it passed from a stage in which man, like a child or a savage, could only record the concrete to the highest levels of abstraction, those mathematical symbols in which neither human feelings nor concrete objects obtruded. Along the way men had resorted to images, similes, poetic metaphors, admixtures of ideas and sensations. There were transitional stages during which both language and thought lacked the precision and the conciseness of the French spoken in Mlle. de L'Espinasse's salon; but even the most philosophical language was vastly inferior to a theorem as a method of rational discourse.

In all of these stadial views of human development, whether the mirror of mankind was the history of language, of writing, of religion, of civilization, of perception itself, there was one recurrent theme: the record revealed a steady rationalization of man at the expense of his emotional and imaginative faculties, a constant movement toward greater abstraction. Like Vico, Turgot's fragments also recognized a stage of human consciousness which was so primitive that man could only give voice to his ideas in myth, in metaphor, in pictorial images. And for Turgot, as for Hume, there is a manifest superiority in the abstract attitude over the concrete. Turgot was ultimately led by his worship of reason to prefer the purest mathematical abstraction over all other forms of knowledge and to look upon the metaphors and images in which the ancients communicated their ideas as a sort of baby-talk, expressive perhaps, but a form which had to be outgrown. Eighteenth-century French thinkers like Turgot were conscious of the death of the poetic spirit in their society, and they did not regret it.

In his theory of language Turgot was skirting along the borders of one of the commonest and yet most controversial conceptions in modern philosophies of history, the idea that there has been an evolvement of human modes of perception, that the differences between the primitive and the civilized are qualitative, and that they could be defined as different mentalities. Thinkers from a wide variety of disciplines seemed to be groping in this general direction throughout the eighteenth and early nineteenth centuries until the idea culminated in Comte's law of the three states, a source from which it was diffused throughout modern psychology and anthropology — though by no means without challenge. It has often been pointed out that a number of passages in Turgot already contain this positivist law in embryo.[24] Knowledge had once been exclusively theological, then it turned metaphysical, and finally it was becoming positive. By the theological stage Turgot — writing in the tradition of Fontenelle and paralleling the works of his friends Hume and de Brosses on the natural history of primitive religion — meant the propensity of men to project intelligent divine power into all manner of objects and forces in nature. The metaphysical described a stage when knowledge was thought of and expressed in terms of essences. The final, third stage was one in which men recognized the real objective nature of things and were beginning to formulate their relationships in mathematical terms. Language had recorded this growth of human modes of perception, and in their normal development all peoples would have to pass from one stage to another. In a general historico-philosophical sense Turgot conceived of progress as the ascent of mankind from one state of perception to another, each leap accompanied by the introduction of new signs and symbols.

This aspect of Turgot's theory of progress can be interpreted as an extension to the historical process of Condillac's epistemology as presented in the *Essai sur l'origine des connaissances humaines*. Those conditions which Condillac found necessary for the original acquisition of abstract thought in an individual were discovered to be the motive drives in the progress of the species throughout time. The stimulating effects of intricate and numerous social communications, the existence of a language whose symbols were clear and distinct rather than blurred, a sense of the fragility and susceptibility to error of even the greatest intellects, the importance of chance, are all ideas he drew directly from Condillac. What Turgot did was to translate the investigation from an abstract inquiry into how human knowledge should be acquired under the direction of a philosophical tutor by an ideal pupil to the vast canvas of the history of mankind, and thus to fill in with empirical detail that ancient analogy between phylogeny and ontogeny. Mankind did in fact amass its knowledge in precisely the same way as every newborn child. Its mistakes have been numerous but it has learned from experience, and in the future it may be able to minimize error by perfecting its geniuses, the men who have special talents for the manipulation of symbols and the combination of ideas. Condillac's "operations of the soul and the causes of its progressions" [25] was transmuted by Turgot into the operations of the human mind or mankind and its progressions.

ETHNOLOGY THE RECORD

Universal progress has left a record of its movement from one stage to another that is far more complete and circumstantial than written historical documents and even language; this is the living record of ethnology, the actual existence of aboriginal tribes and nations dispersed over the face of the globe, each on a different level of culture.[26] The travel literature and the missionary reports on primitive, barbaric, semibarbaric, and heathen civilized societies had come to constitute an indisputable body of data, there for any scholar to examine and for any intrepid explorer to verify, proving without recourse to conjecture that there had in fact been a stadial development of mankind. Contemporary barbaric societies were vestiges of previous stages; primarily because of their isolation, they had become frozen at a given moment in time or they were developing more slowly. "In the over-all progress of the human mind, all nations start from the same point, proceed to the same goal, follow more or less the same path, but at a very uneven pace," Turgot wrote in the article "Etymologie" in the sixth volume of the *Encyclopédie*.[27]

The idea that savage societies were exemplars of what the more advanced civilizations had once been was by the mid-eighteenth century no longer startling, but not until the writings of Turgot and de Brosses [28] in the 1750's did this momentous hypothesis become the springboard for grandiose conceptions of stadial progress. For Turgot the ethnographic record contained the whole history of the species, so that by moving throughout the world from one primitive society to another the philosopher could — if he wisely chose appropriate examples — establish the true historical series from the most barbaric through the most enlightened. Turgot defined the quintessential nature of the series as it advanced from one stage to another in terms of a history of changing capacities of perception, or at least different ways of confronting the external world, transformations in the human mind which were by no means accidental but were clearly ranged in an order of being from the less to the more perfect. The societies which exemplified the stadial development were a historical roster of excellences in which the primitive savage was the inferior and the civilized Frenchman the most recent expression of the superior.[29]

Political geography, as Turgot outlined the discipline in one of his unfinished sketches, became the description of world areas in the light of his one central theme: how proximate was each society, barbaric or civil, to the bellwether nation leading the movement of progress. Or was a people perhaps veering in the opposite direction, toward decadence, and eliminating itself from world history? When Turgot propounded his conception of progress he never implied that all nations were progressing regularly in a straight line and at an even tempo. He was neither so simple nor so obtuse as to envisage simultaneous unchecked development, though this has sometimes been inferred in crude distillations of his theory. On the contrary, in the spirit of Vico and Montesquieu and Gibbon, he was acutely conscious of the phenomenon of grandeur and decadence, of growth, maturity, fall, and decline.[30] What he intended to demonstrate from the record of world historical geography was that some society was always carrying the torch of progress forward; when it was about to be extinguished in one area the sacred fire was seized by another. As one haven of science crumbled there was always another polity which inherited the discoveries and, after an interval necessary for assimilation, advanced still further. "Thus it has happened that in alternating periods of agitation and calm, of good and evil, the total mass of the human species has moved ceaselessly toward its perfection." [31] Turgot was not precise in his definition of the societal unit in which progress was incorporated; most often he drew examples from large areas like the Greek world, the Roman Empire, Christendom, or China, though sometimes he used an individual dynastic state or even an American tribe. This vagueness in the establishment of the unit of discourse makes it difficult to relate the cyclical patterns of individual societies with the world development of progress which, *mutatis mutandis*, assumes a role analogous to Hegel's World Spirit triumphing amid the tragic death of cultures. The linking of individual instances of growth and decay with the central thread of world development has been the rock on which the most magnificent constructs of philosophical history have foundered, and Turgot was often hard put to document the transmissions, particularly from Rome to medieval Europe, though he managed to squeak through with a felicitous use of metaphor.

Political geography endowed with a time dimension became universal history. At most a few names had to be added, the key inventive geniuses and the towering political figures. History, almost entirely divested of its heroic qualities, became a record of the relations of societies to one another spatially and temporally. The images with which Turgot tried to communicate these relationships remained predominantly spatial.[32] There was distance in time as there was distance in space, and each people, nation, and tribe could be located in time on some rung of the ladder of progress with the same precision that it could be fixed in space on a world map.

The "Plan d'un ouvrage sur la géographie politique" was an outline of history demonstrating in schematic form how from a diversity of peoples on different levels of civilization one enlightened world with a uniform culture would inevitably result. The whole process was depicted in a set of geometric images. In the beginning there were numerous isolated units; with time, in any world area, the nation which had surpassed others in progress became the center of a group of political satellites. The same process was repeated in various parts of the globe which had no contact with one another. Ultimately the independent constellations extended their circles until they collided and established relations through war and commerce. In the end of the days the major political areas would coalesce, and one world whose boundaries were coterminous with the physical world would be created. Turgot extolled this ideal of one political world not only because it would unite men but because it would provide an opportunity for the maximum interpenetration of diverse perceptions among the greatest number of human beings, the necessary prerequisite for accelerated progress. The uniformity and insipidity of one world was an idea remote from his imagination.

ANATOMY OF THE FOUR PROGRESSIONS

PROGRESS naturally divided itself into four subsidiary progressions, and Turgot anatomized them, established their mutual relationships, and derived from them a law of unequal development. These types of progress were identified with distinct areas of human creative activity: speculative science, technology, moral behavior, and artistic expression. The "inequality of the progressions" was a central thesis, for he had discovered in each progression a different pattern of growth, and when referring to them as a group he constantly used the term in the plural, *les progrès*, a form which Condorcet retained in the *Esquisse*. Thus there was uneven development of progressions *within* a society as there was among various geographic entities throughout the world, a law which accounted for the extraordinary diversity of human experience despite the identity of mankind's underlying historic destiny. What conditions, asked Turgot the philosophical historian, had in the past furthered one or more progressions, and what had been the negative elements destructive of progress or blocking its path? Since progress is the integrating concept which bestows meaning upon the history of man, since it is virtually the sole historical subject, this experience of the progressions in the past will enlighten mankind about its future prospect. The diagnosis of the progressions is preliminary to a prognosis.

Of all the progressions, the technological had been the hardiest growth of man's genius, the least evanescent, for mechanical capacities were common, shared by a vast number of human beings, and it would be impossible to destroy totally the productive techniques of artisans even during periods when the political framework of society was shattered. Because the body of men who practiced mechanical arts was large, the chance of novelty was greater than in other forms of progress, for the incidence of genius was the same in all fields. Since artisans dealt with elementary needs of life, were plentiful and yet indispensable, the mechanical arts were perfected by the "mere fact that time passed." [33] Once a new device had been invented and accepted by the artisans it was hard to envisage its abandonment, because the advantages of the innovation were so manifest to utilitarian common sense. Since the preservation and transmission of technology were not dependent upon language, it could even survive a barbarian conquest. No tyrannical power had a special interest in interfering with the artisan's processes of cloth manufacture. As a consequence, technological discoveries had accumulated throughout history at a relatively even tempo; and during long epochs progress in the mechanical arts had continued without interruption even while science and artistic creativity had suffered a total eclipse. Turgot appreciated the technical progress achieved in medieval Europe, a rare insight for an eighteenth-century *philosophe*, and he was one of the first to suggest that the regeneration of speculative science in the Renaissance had been facilitated by an antecedent succession of mechanical inventions during the Middle Ages: the introduction of maritime instruments, the magnifying glass, and, most important of all, the art of printing, which diffused scientific knowledge over a wide area, made the discoveries of the ancient Greeks generally available and stimulated potential geniuses by making them aware of the achievements of their predecessors. Up to the eighteenth century, science owed more to technology than technology to science, a relationship which Turgot was prepared to see reversed by the imminent revolutionary explosion of speculative science.[34] Whatever the past interdependence of science and technology, for the future the scientists were the unchallenged vanguard of the battalions of progress.

The fine arts was one area of creativity where Turgot modified his theory of limitless infinite progress. In the literary quarrel of the ancients and the moderns he still found for the giants of antiquity. Aesthetic achievement was the tenderest plant of human genius, sensitive to political contingencies. Good taste, which had to prevail in a society before genius in the fine arts could be honored, was fragile and delicate, and it could be easily corrupted by decree throughout a whole civilization if a capricious ruling prince were imbued with bizarre or fantastic notions of the beautiful. Of all forms of human expression, art was the most vulnerable to the influence of a hostile environment. Turgot clung to the neoclassic idea that the Augustan age had reached the artistic zenith, a level that might perhaps be equaled again under proper guidance but could never be surpassed. Knowledge of the fine arts, unlike knowledge in the mechanical arts and in speculative science, was not cumulative; hence the very concept of progress was not, strictly speaking, applicable in this sphere. Atrociously bad taste could predominate in the same age when mechanical arts were accomplishing marvels of engineering. The Gothic cathedral which Turgot, in conformity with the prevailing judgment of the eighteenth century, considered a monstrosity, was a superb expression of man's ingenuity in the mechanical arts. Men still had not learned how these structures had been raised by the medieval artisans, but there was no doubt about their hideousness.

Turgot had no conception of the high seriousness of art. While discovery in mechanical arts and speculative science was part of an infinite movement, the fine arts aimed only to please. Once the philosophical canon of the pleasurable had been established on the basis of a knowledge of human psychology — which was uniform

— a specific art object either obeyed and conformed to the rules or violated them. While other branches of human endeavor were infinitely expansible, progress in the arts of poetry, painting, and music was bound by intrinsic natural limitations. Since our artistic sensibilities were restricted by the nature and sensitivity of our organs, once perfection had been attained in the Augustan age later generations were reduced to mere imitation of these models. At most there might conceivably be an improvement in the technical media of artistic production, never progress in art itself. Turgot the poetaster and translator of Vergil and Horace was unable to extol the creations of eighteenth-century France above those of the Romans, and he expressed a measure of contempt for those who deluded themselves that they were perfecting the arts when they were only rendering the artistic object more complex. "The knowledge of nature and of truth is as infinite as they are," he wrote in the second Sorbonique. "The arts whose purpose it is to please are as limited as we are. Time continually brings forth new discoveries in science, but poetry, painting, music, have a fixed limit which the genius of language, the imitation of nature, and the sensibilities of our organs determine. . . ." [35]

By contrast moral behavior was clearly subject to improvement, though what he meant by the moral implied a set of fixed criteria, ideals common to the wise philosophers of his age, universally accepted by Hume and Montesquieu, Beccaria, Lessing, and Kant. The moral was a combination of Stoic virtues and rules of general conduct with a measure of utility, the whole suffused with Christian love and charity. Future moral progress signified the end of war, cruelty, and crime, and the extension of virtues throughout all strata of European society and among all the nations of the world. It entailed the general practice of tolerance and leniency and obedience to reason, acceptance of law out of rational conviction rather than any dread of worldly punishment or superstitious fear of torments in Hell. If men acted solely on grounds of utility and reason, if they extended free inquiry and assimilated its scientific findings into the practical sphere of everyday action, then they were progressing. To the degree that man became mild, gentle, loving, tranquil, his moral behavior was improving.

Turgot never fell in with the rabid anticlericalism of some of his Encyclopedist friends, even after he had left the Church. He retained a profound respect for the moral virtues of Christianity, which he considered a further purification and not a corruption of natural religion. Under the canopy of the medieval church the bestial nature of the northern barbarians had been tamed and in time they had been transformed into polite, reasonable, well-behaved, compassionate members of society.[36] Christianity had abolished slavery, prohibited infanticide, established asylums for the sick and the weak, preached brotherhood and love. The church had been one of the great civilizing and moralizing forces in the history of mankind. His friend and loyal disciple Condorcet, alive to bloody religious persecutions, inquisitions, massacres, and crusades, was unable to stomach this summation of the historical evidence.

About the future moral progress of mankind, however, Condorcet and Turgot were in agreement. The reduction of morals to a science of observation would inevitably lead to the wider prevalence of those ways of conduct which every *philosophe* appreciated and whose essence was an extension of altruism, "contributing to the happiness of others." [37]

THE DEMONSTRATION OF INEVITABILITY

Turgot's doctrine supported itself on two central arguments: an empirical proof that progress had in fact occurred in the past from the dark primitive stage of humanity's origins through the enlightened present; and a demonstration that since retrogression was no longer possible future progress was inevitable. The past history of progress had been proved by ethnology. The prediction of its future was based upon an evaluation of the increasing momentum of progress, its accelerating tempo; upon an estimate of the global diffusion of enlightenment; and finally upon the observation that all knowledge was actually in the process of becoming encased in mathematical symbols which granted it certitude. Historical reflections in the grand manner of a Bossuet illustrated these bold and novel ideas in the Sorbonne discourses, refuting both pessimist Christian theologians and antihistorical *philosophes* who tended to regard the past as a meaningless parade of crimes and cruel accidents. Hitherto, Turgot conceded, progress had been consistently waylaid by two enemies: either barbarian invasions overwhelmed societies that had attained a high level of civilization and temporarily stifled the progress of science; or advanced societies became corroded by an equally vicious internal disease in their own bodies politic, that spirit of routine, the rut, which was always for him the very incarnation of evil. In the future, however, these two dread enemies of progress would be powerless, since the eighteenth-century reality of a unified world civilization had rendered it impossible for mankind as a whole ever again to suffer stagnation or catastrophic relapse. Knowledge of science was now so widely diffused among societies throughout the world that even the irruption of a barbarian horde intent upon devastation, even suppression by an obscurantist tyrant, could not wholly extinguish the light of progress. In the past the isolation of political societies had rendered them peculiarly susceptible to internal putrescence, but henceforward if a nation tended to fall into a stagnant state, either it would be forcibly awakened, shaken out of its torpor by commercial stimuli from abroad, or it would be conquered by a more vigorous nation which would ultimately inherit its progress. To the extent that war had kept humanity alert and constantly aroused it had not been an unmitigated evil. In the future this terrible remedy might not be necessary, but it was always available to assure humanity's forward movement.

Turgot tended to evaluate progress in two dimensions. One was intensive, vertical so to speak, the accretion of units of scientific truth in time; the other was extensive, horizontal, and entailed the gradual sowing of these scientific truths throughout the world until ultimately no area would remain barren. During his retirement Turgot toyed with inventions of cheap processes for the reproduction of writing, in order to multiply communications and extend progress among those elements in society which were still beyond its pale. The extension of the communications network became a crucial practical measure for the acceleration of the progressive process and was in harmony with the other elements in his theory. Increase communications and an ever greater number and variety of new idea combinations are transmitted to an ever larger number of human beings. Among those exposed to the new configurations would be a new quota of geniuses who would grasp the meaning of novel contingencies, formalize them, and make them a part of the accumulating body of world knowledge. To learn truth and to spread it was the essential social mission of man bequeathed by Turgot to his disciple Condorcet. "To know the truth in order to make the social order conform to it, that is the sole source of public happiness. It is therefore useful, even necessary, to extend the limits of knowledge. . . ." [38] To gather new peoples under the protection of science was from the beginning a vital element in the idea of progress. When no spot on earth was excluded from the illumination of science, then and only then was it safe from an attack by the forces of evil and ignorance, free of the threat of submersion by waves of darkness from beyond the pale of the civilized world. Only thereafter would intensive scientific progress be accelerated indefinitely, without setback or impediment. Europe's mission to civilize the world was for Turgot, as it was later for Condorcet and Saint-Simon, a necessary requirement for its own development. No region of the globe, however enlightened, could enjoy perfect tranquillity as long as savages lurked on the rim of civility. Since temporarily at least barbarians throttled a more advanced culture when they took possession, the mere existence of an uncivilized penumbra endangered civilization. The function of enlightenment was to draw the whole of the world into the orbit of civilization as an absolute insurance against retrogression. Turgot's rational belief in the inevitability of future progress was bolstered by his confidence that eighteenth-century Europeans were in manifest control of the savage world and had only to disseminate their teachings to eradicate the last remnants of the historic dread of barbarian invasions which hung over them. Intensive and extensive progress were thus interrelated; they fortified each other and were dependent upon each other.

Turgot's optimism derived from the realization that the growth of science had by now gathered so great a momentum that interruption of the process had been rendered impossible. *Vires acquirit eundo.* In the early stages of history the plant of civilization could be trampled down by outsiders, the horde, or it could be shriveled from within by sloth, luxury, an absence of challenge. But the strength and the speed of movement achieved in modern times made every progression easier and every backward lapse more improbable. An accelerating wheel became the image of progress.[39]

Finally, the richest source of confidence for the believer in the inevitability of progress lay in the special mathematical character of all forms of scientific knowledge in recent ages. Mathematics, of which Turgot had only an amateur's smattering, was for him the loftiest expression of human thought, at the summit of intellectuality. In mathematics and only in mathematics did Turgot feel an absolute sense of security about the survival of acquired knowledge. Throughout his life he had toyed with fantasies about devoting himself to science, and he was always wistfully contrasting the turbulent, ungrateful, political world in which, alas, he had expended his energies as an administrator with the peaceful, finite, enduring world of science from which the rhetoric and the prejudice that governed the politics of men had been expunged. On August 24, 1761, he had written to Voltaire: "I have the misfortune to be an Intendant. I say misfortune because in this century of quarrels there is no happiness but in living philosophically among one's studies and one's friends." [40] Science to Turgot connoted the mathematical world, the realm of the purest of the sciences, the ideal form of knowledge. Here was certainty for this uneasy intellectual.

The progress of speculative science was now solidly safeguarded by the new symbolic forms which knowledge had assumed since the Renaissance. Once mathematics had become the universal language of science, intellectual progress was emancipated from the historical vicissitudes to which the ordinary spoken vernaculars were subject. Mathematical language would soon set up an impregnable barrier against retrogression. To reduce all knowledge to mathematical symbols would become the highest achievement of mankind. For the moment only the social sciences seemed to be standing apart; but their mathematicization was the inevitable next stage of intellectual progress. In the formula no room was left for the vague, for the exaggeration of enthusiasts, for superstition — the great vices of mankind. The mathematicization of the study of man would become a double security against antiprogressive forces, for moral knowledge would find itself protected by the armor of numbers and equations, and moral problems would be removed from the disputes of the marketplace where they always provoked destructive violence. In his last years Turgot, wracked with the pains of illness, drew consolation from the vision of humanity on the threshold of this wondrous transmutation of knowledge, a leap comparable in his mind to the passage of human speech from a myth-ridden, metaphoric, poetic language to the relatively rational style of the contemporary European world. As long as mankind relied upon language and rhetoric to express its truths, knowledge would inevitably become polluted with chimeras of the imagination, with personal prejudice. Even civilized languages, rational instruments of communication though they were, had never succeeded in freeing themselves from their primitive origins and remained encumbered with similes and images which obfuscated rational thought. There was always something suspect about an idea that was not mathematicized because it was subject to passion, to political influences, to the weaknesses of the imaginative faculty. In the past scientific knowledge had been acquired rather haphazardly, and as a consequence of unpropitious external circumstances it had been stagnant for long periods at a time. Only since the regeneration of the sciences through mathematics had a long succession of geniuses been steadfastly adding to this body of knowledge and at the same time extending the dominion of science over new peoples who had once been victims of superstitious belief or obscure theological reasoning. In technical terms the new vista opening before Turgot was the imminent application of the calculus of probabilities to human behavior, thus the invasion of a whole moral world from which mathematics had previously been excluded.

Turgot is in a long tradition of French thinkers ranging from Descartes through Paul Valéry who have sought refuge in mathematics as an ultimate haven. When all other arguments in support of the inevitability of future progress were momentarily weakened by the spectacle of the real world with its oppressive stupidity and irrationality, the triumph of the mathematical spirit was a last resort. As long as the knowledge of abstract relationships in the mathematical world was growing there was progress. The final consolation lay in the existence of the equation. Princes might prove weak and false, but nothing could assail one's confidence in a theorem.

As a result of the manifold demonstrations of inevitability the burden of proof was shifted to the shoulders of the antiprogressists. Wherefrom was the antiscientific destructive storm to blow if enlightenment became universal? To impede the natural impetus of scientific progress a countervailing force equally potent was required. Since there was no such power on the historical horizon, progress would be "indefinite" or without limit, like an infinite progression in mathematics.[41]

PROGRESS A THEODICY

THE progressists have sometimes been read and interpreted as if they were continually mouthing optimist shibboleths. Turgot, whose half-smile sometimes disturbed contemporaries, was not immune to moments of disenchantment and even despair. Declarations of war by the philosophical monarchs of the Enlightenment evoked from him a cry of horror. "Poor humans!" he exclaimed in a letter of March 19, 1778, reporting to his friend Dupont de Nemours the imminent outbreak of hostilities in Germany and in Turkey.[42] He sighed when he contemplated the enduring stupidity of his race. Few of the eighteenth-century *philosophes* were naive or blissfully unconscious of contradictions in their own optimist posture. Turgot was gnawed by a deep sense of the persistence of tragedy in the human condition. In a letter to Condorcet in 1772, four years before the failure of his attempt to rescue the monarchy from collapse, Turgot revealed his feeling of futility about administrative reforms and confided a secret conviction that men would probably never overcome the evils which they inflicted upon themselves, that physical ills and moral grief would always be with us. Progress would therefore have to limit itself to the eradication of "artificial evils" generated by ignorance.[43] Turgot's optimism was rarely without qualms. His economic theory had led him to rather gloomy conclusions about any possible improvement of the lot of the ordinary worker, who was bound by a law which limited him to a subsistence level of wages — an antecedent of Marx's iron law.[44] Turgot's version of the idea of progress did not involve any utopian total elimination of evil, error, or misery from an empirical view of human experience. The Turgot who at the height of his powers was rejected by the King and ousted by a palace cabal was not the simplistic unquestioning believer in progress which some of the popularizers of his ideas have made him out to be; and neither was Condorcet, who after overthrowing the king found himself condemned to the guillotine in absentia; and neither was Saint-Simon, the perennial failure who cried out with anguish at the sight of the terrible harvest of death during the Napoleonic wars; and neither was Comte, who saw the Europe of 1848 bathed in a bloody fratricidal class war. None of these men were starry-eyed fools repeating stereotyped formulas about progress and the betterment of mankind. They all saw progress as an overcoming of contrary forces in organized society, in physical nature, in man himself. They were wrestling with the problem of evil which reappeared in a new mask in each generation, its most recent embodiment the forces of antiprogress. The war of good and evil, of Christ and anti-Christ, became the war of progressive history and antihistory. Process, movement, social dynamics, did not lose their Christian moral overtones. The doctrine of progress was born in the bosom of Christianity, and Saint-Simon and Comte even tried to retain the epithet "religious" as a key descriptive word for their new progressist systems. Turgot was aware of the overwhelming potency of the deadening forces of tradition and routine, Condorcet of the power of tyranny, sect, and lust for dominion, Saint-Simon and Comte of the divisive forces of anarchy which endangered the cohesion of the social fabric. The evil passions and even the dissolving demons of madness were not unknown to the philosophers of progress.

In the last analysis their systems were fervent attempts to solve the theodicy problem and to give meaning to historical experience once the sanctions of future rewards and punishments were removed. If Providence was a source of goodness, why the long chronicle of wars and devastations, the spectacle of crimes and barbarities perpetrated throughout the ages? The answer is common to most eighteenth-century philosophers of history — in this respect Turgot's concept is only one offshoot of a general theme. Without the impetus of the aggressive, evil passions, without the ambitions of individuals, the "leading strings" of nature, there would have been no progress in the early stages of history and man would have been doomed to peace and mediocrity. "The ambitious ones themselves in forming the great nations have contributed to the views of Providence, to the progress of enlightenment, and consequently to the increase of the happiness of the human species, a thing which did not at all interest them. Their passions, their very rages, have led them without their knowing where they were going. I seem to see an immense army all of whose movements are directed by a great genius. At the sight of the military signals, at the tumultuous noise of the trumpets and the drums, the squadrons move forward, the horses themselves are driven by a fire which has no purpose. Each section makes its way over obstacles without knowing what may result. Only the chief sees the effect of so many related steps. Thus the passions multiplied ideas, extended knowledge, perfected minds, in default of the reason whose day had not yet dawned and which would have been less potent if it had reigned earlier.

"Reason, which is justice itself, would never have carried away what belonged to another, would have forever banished war and usurpation, would have left men divided into a mob of nations, isolated from one another, speaking different languages.

"Limited, as a result, in their ideas, incapable of progress in any branch of knowledge, of science, of art, of civility, which is born of the meeting of geniuses assembled from different provinces, the human species would have forever remained in a state of mediocrity. Reason and justice, had they been hearkened to, would have fixed everything — approximately the way it happened in China." [45]

The attainment of the providential (or nature's) purpose of progress required the free play of the passions. This did not mean that individual acts of wickedness were willed by God, pleaded the former theologian Turgot. Since men committed these acts, they had to bear the moral responsibility. Progress merely utilized the opportunities created by the self-willed men who broke the moral law. And they thereby unwittingly achieved a divine purpose. The idea of progress thus comes to the rescue of the religious man who might otherwise have begun to question divine guidance of the world of men steeped in evil. Vice is enlisted in the service of Progress, and Progress in turn becomes a part of Christian apologetics.

An individual immoral deed, inspired by personal lust, can generate historical forces which lead to the perfection and humanization of the species. This theodicy, which explains the emergence of objective good for mankind from subjective evil intent, was one of the most persistent motifs in eighteenth- and early nineteenth-century philosophies of history. With variations it can be found in Vico, Herder, Kant, and Hegel as well as among the progressists of the French school. Inevitably the philosophical historians were forced into a divorcement of the will of individual morality from the unfolding of a rational purpose in history. Turgot was the first of the French group to resort to this justification of God's way in time, the equivalent of what Vico had called a civil theology. Even in its later development the secular idea of progress was never completely divested of the theological robes in which it had made its first appearance at the Sorboniques. Whatever the balance of good and evil in the world may be at any specific moment, the historic ledger always shows a credit in favor of the good. Ever since his youth Turgot, who had read Leibniz,[46] had been profoundly disturbed by the question of the origin and purpose of evil in a world that was created by a God who was perfect good. His article on Manichaeism for the *Encyclopédie* had wrestled with this, "the hardest and thorniest problem which presents itself to the mind." [47] The idea of progress provided the solution. "He saw in physical Evil, in moral Evil," Condorcet reported, "only a necessary consequence of the existence of sensitive beings capable of reason but limited. The perfectibility with which a few species, and in particular the human species, are endowed is a slow but infallible remedy to these evils." [48] And it was this insight into progress which, to the obvious annoyance of his anticlerical friend, sustained Turgot in the belief in a beneficent, providential design. "The universe viewed in its totality, in the whole range of the progressions, is a most glorious spectacle, witness to the wisdom which presides over it." [49]

Validation of the passions, however, was usually limited by

Turgot to the past. Once enlightenment had spread over the world this stimulus to progress was no longer necessary, since full-grown Reason should be able to care for its own and humanity's future development. The evil passions which were useful in the infancy of the species were superflous in man's mature rational age. Turgot recognized the complexity of the individual drives which had motivated the great discoveries of the past, and he refrained from emphasizing exclusively either love of knowledge or a quest for glory. A human desire for fame, he realized, had hitherto limited researches which required many generations to achieve fruition, but he was hopeful that in the future society, with the equalization of wealth and a diminution of the importance of political action, more men of talent would devote themselves to the pursuit of reason without the excitation of the passions.[50] With time, Turgot hoped, reason would occupy more and more space in the finite area of the spirit, casting out the disorderly passions and limiting severely the scope of the imagination. Emotion was thus progressively blotted out until in the end of the days there was only reason. The impoverishment of the spirit under the hegemony of pure reason did not trouble the eighteenth-century *philosophe*, because as he saw the world about him, the prejudice, the superstition, the ignorance, the fanaticism, he felt that mankind had only begun to fight the battle of rationality. The prospect of an undernourishment of the passions and the imaginative faculties for the sake of reason did not yet appear real to men of Turgot's generation. He was acutely aware of how young was the reign of reason — only the mathematical sciences had pursued appropriate analytic methods before the end of the seventeenth century — if measured against the background of historic time.[51] When Turgot contemplated the irrationality of the world, he derived consolation from the simple historical realization that the mathematical perception of the universe was so relatively recent an acquisition of the human spirit that its influence upon laws and morals had not as yet had an opportunity to make itself felt.[52]

At the close of the biography of his friend, Condorcet presented an Isaiahlike vision of the end of the days as it had been unfolded to him in Turgot's conversation. Most of the elements in this progressist heaven he later repeated in the last part of the tenth epoch of his own *Esquisse*, the form in which the ideas penetrated into European thought. "He [Turgot] hoped that day would come when men, disabused of the fantastic project of opposing nation to nation, power to power, passion to passion, vice to vice, would occupy themselves with hearkening to what reason would dictate for the happiness of humanity. Why should politics, based like all the other sciences on observation and reason, not be perfected in the measure that one brings to observations more subtlety and exactitude, to reasoning more precision, profundity, and good judgment? Shall we dare to fix what point could be attained in this field by minds fortified by a better education, exercised at an early age in the combination of the most varied and extensive ideas, accustomed to manipulate more general and easier methods? Let us beware of despairing of the human kind. Let us dare to envisage, in the immensity of the centuries which will follow us, a happiness and an enlightenment about which we cannot today even form a vague and indefinite idea. Let us count on that perfectibility with which nature has endowed us, on the power of genius from which long experience has taught us to expect prodigies, and let us console ourselves for the fact that we shall not witness those happier times with the pleasure of foretelling them, of enjoying them in advance, and perhaps with the even sweeter satisfaction of having accelerated that all-too-distant epoch by a few moments." [53]

In the correspondence of his last years Turgot recorded the progress of the American Revolution, the Gordon riots, the outbreak of the war with Turkey, and the ravages of the mutual passion which consumed his friends Madame Helvétius and Benjamin Franklin (who was then seventy-three). He watched these events with tender sympathy for the victims of war and civil strife and emotional excess. These were moral ills of which men had not yet been cured, and perhaps the pains were yet destined to endure for some time, like the gout with which both Turgot and the sage from Philadelphia were afflicted. Turgot's disgrace provoked no misanthropic outburst. If he was outraged at his betrayal by the King, there is no report of his indignation. The slightly skeptical smile continued to hover about the lips; it is preserved in Ducreux's pastel in the Château de Lantheuil. Not so his faithful lieutenant Condorcet. In a letter to Voltaire he gave vent to his anger with a vehemence which Turgot would never have permitted himself: "I have not written to you, my dear illustrious master, since the fatal event which has robbed all honest men of hope and courage. I waited for my wrath to cool down somewhat and for grief alone to remain. This event has changed all of nature for me. I no longer take the same pleasure in looking at the beautiful countryside where he would have spread happiness. The spectacle of the gaiety of the people makes my heart ache. They dance as if they had lost nothing. The wolves from which you delivered the country of Gex are going to invade the rest of France, and two years of abstinence have transformed their thirst for the blood of the people into a fury. Would you believe they dared demand that no writing against them be allowed and that this vile progeny of lackeys, bitches, and pimps of the past century be respected? They want to muzzle us out of fear lest the cries which our pain tears from us trouble their peace. This is where we have fallen, my dear illustrious master, and from what a lofty pinnacle! . . ." [54]

The day of the *philosophes* was drawing to a close, and the men of action were about to take over. If the conspiracy of the privileged ones ousted the last hope of France there were other means of bringing about the triumph of reason. Condorcet recovered from his dejection, girded himself for war, and flung himself into the revolutionary battle. In his turn he suffered the fate of the philosopher engaged — as had his master.

II

Marquis de Condorcet
THE TAMING OF THE FUTURE

"If the infinite perfection of our species is, as I believe, a general law of nature, man should no longer look upon himself as a being limited to a fleeting isolated moment of existence, destined to vanish after experiencing either personal happiness or misfortune or after having done good or evil to those whom chance has placed in his immediate proximity. He becomes an active part of a great whole and a cooperator in an eternal creation. In a lifetime which lasts but a moment, located at one point in space, he can through his works associate himself with all ages and continue to act for years after his memory has disappeared from the earth."

Sur l'instruction publique, in *Oeuvres de Condorcet* (1804 edition), IX, 21–22.

"Peindre le genre humain pour s'oublier lui-même."
Condorcet,
Epître d'un Polonais exilé en Sibérie à sa femme (December 1793).

A SNOW-CAPPED VOLCANO

Soon after the Marquis Jean-Antoine-Nicolas Caritat de Condorcet had turned four, his father, a dashing cavalry officer, died.[1] His fanatically devout mother, possessed with the idea of consecrating her son to the Virgin, kept him in skirts until he was eight. Finally rescued by his uncle, the Bishop of Lisieux, he was turned over to the Jesuits to be educated. "Hardly had young Condorcet opened his eyes," wrote Arago in a paper delivered before the Academy of Sciences in 1841, "than he found himself surrounded by the highest dignitaries of the church and the sword. His first guides, his first teachers, were Jesuits. What was the result of so extraordinary a confluence of circumstances? In politics a total rejection of any idea of hereditary prerogative; in matters of religion scepticism pushed to its extreme limits."[2]

Young Condorcet was quickly recognized as a mathematical genius and his geometry was much appreciated by his contemporaries, though his reputation in this branch of knowledge has not endured. After 1770 he joined the philosophical coteries, virtually abandoning his mathematical studies to become a *politique*. During Turgot's brief ministry, when the *philosophes* descended in a body upon the royal offices and were awarded sinecures, Condorcet received the mint, as Newton once had in England.

The official portrait of Condorcet depicts a man devoted to the life of reason, a mathematician, a permanent secretary of the Academy of Sciences, an exponent of the middle way in revolutionary politics, an adherent of the Girondins who broke with them in the end and died hated by all parties — in short, a *philosophe*. But Condorcet's intimate friends knew that an explosive, passionate nature was being held in check — a "snow-capped volcano" was D'Alembert's *mot*.[3] Beneath the surface Condorcet hardly resembled that image of the cool, unbiased scientist that he had set before himself as the perfect model of the man of the future. There was even a malicious streak in the official of the greatest scientific body in France. Some of the grand *éloges* of his dead colleagues, like the piece he delivered on the naturalist

Buffon, were written with tongue in cheek; he was laying on the rhetoric, he confessed to a friend, to repay the eminent Count in kind for the bombastic rodomontades of his voluminous works.

Condorcet's sentimental correspondence with Mme. Suard, the wife of a literary man of the period (the letters, now in the Bibliothèque Nationale, have been published only in inadequate extracts), spanning a period of more than two decades, reveals a complex, emotional introvert. Mme. Suard's manuscript notes on their exchange, written years after Condorcet's death, show her extraordinary perspicacity about the man, even though her remarks are sometimes tinged with venom. In the letters Condorcet the High Priest of the Temple of Reason aptly described himself as a "romanesque" character. While in the public eye he was the learned aristocrat, orderly to the point of obsession, a diligent worker in the vineyard of science, above all a calm and quiet intellectual, beneath the rather phlegmatic exterior was a frightened man who for years lived in a dream of romantic love. "I shall continue out of habit to occupy myself, but not from a desire for glory, because that would be wasting my time, and after all, if I had as much as Newton, would I be more loved?" [4]

As an eighteenth-century *philosophe* was likely to do in his private chamber, Condorcet submitted his feelings to probing psychological analysis, and was aware of his own overwhelming need for suffering in love. The philosophical historian of human progress was an anxious man, always expecting catastrophe. Commenting on his perennial uneasiness, he wrote to his confidante: "Perhaps this derives from an instinct fashioned by the habit of suffering which tells me that what is bound to hurt me will happen." Condorcet leads one to reflect on the strange paradox of a modern man whose inner emotional anguish is accompanied by a compensatory historical optimism which knows no limits. "My nerves only bother me from time to time, and what remains of my physical and moral ills is a sadness, a little imbecility, and much laziness. What you tell me of your reflections does not surprise me. Such is the misfortune of the human condition. The idea of the necessary flight of our happiness can suffice to poison it, while the idea of the flight of our miseries does not suffice to console us." The love-friendship with Mme. Suard, which remained Platonic — for seven years Condorcet lived in a chaste *ménage à trois* with the Suards — gave rise to transports in which a boyish sentimental love, almost puppy love, had banished philosophy. "If it were possible for me to believe in a god, I would be persuaded that a beneficent divinity has united itself with your body as an example to the world and for the happiness of the elect."

Mme. Suard, who had a number of *philosophes* on her string, accepted his adoration for years, and she was no doubt flattered by his devotion, though at the same time she felt a measure of disdain for his softness and servility in intimate relationships. When on two occasions during the course of their long correspondence Condorcet was struck by a passion for another woman, Mme. Suard remarked in her notes upon his abjectness, the same utter sub-missiveness, the "weakness of a slave" (his childhood in female dress had left its mark). The first object of his affections, a Mme. de Meulan, the wife of a *receveur de finances*, led him on, watched him dance attendance on her, and then dropped him. The second, to whom he succumbed at the age of forty-two, was the beautiful Sophie de Grouchy, twenty-three-year-old daughter of a noble family which had fallen on evil days. During this courtship Condorcet was beside himself. To Mme. Suard he seemed to have lost all self-respect. Condorcet had always dreamed of a perfect love to which he and his partner would surrender themselves utterly. He would give his life for six months of such a love, "qu'il aimerait d'amour," he once confessed to Mme. Suard. When he offered his hand Sophie de Grouchy was still possessed by a lover (either the Duke de la Rochefoucauld or Lafayette [sic]) who was himself married and therefore not free. It was Condorcet who had to beg Sophie's hand from her paramour. Sophie de Grouchy was in-fatuated to the point where the entreaties of her mother were un-availing, and she would not accept Condorcet until her lover had relinquished her and given his consent. The whole agitated affair is described by Mme. Suard, a participant observer and far from disinterested, for she was loath to lose the loyal admirer who could always be counted upon to turn up at ten in the evening. Mme. Suard has blamed Sophie de Grouchy for the total transformation of Condorcet's personality in succeeding years and for the revolu-tionary excesses to which he abandoned himself. She depicts Sophie de Grouchy as an intriguer who was impressed by Condorcet's income and an ambitious woman who used him as a tool.

This was pure cattiness. Sophie de Grouchy was one of the brilliant hostesses of the end of the *ancien régime* whose salon became an intellectual center for *philosophes* and *politiques* from both sides of the Atlantic. Her wit and charm are extolled by the memorialists. Michelet has written of her noble and virginal figure fit for a Raphael model of Metaphysics — for Mme. Condorcet was a lady philosopher who translated Adam Smith's works on moral sentiments and the origin of language and herself composed letters on sympathy.[5] There is some truth to the allegation that it was she who pushed her rather retiring husband into the revolutionary turmoil. She was if anything more rabid in her anticlericalism than he was. While Condorcet had a horror of tumults and a fear of the tribune and at one point wrote to Mme. Suard, "I am a royalist," at his wife's instigation he became an activist, a republican, a pamphleteer using all the tricks of the trade, a president of the Legislative Assembly. There is one opinion that Mme. Condorcet, presiding over her salon, was even more influential in directing Girondist policy than Mme. Roland. During the Great Days Mme. Condorcet demonstrated with the people in the streets. Swept along by the revolutionary tide, Condorcet framed constitutions, drafted legislation, reorganized the educational system. But these *ci-devant* aristocrats could never be radical enough for the Revolution, and at the crucial moment of the great divide, the verdict on the King, Condorcet voted for a severe penalty short of death — which led to his proscription (the specific reason in the act of accusation was his publication of an attack on the Jacobin constitution accusing its authors of an attempt to restore the monarchy — an extravagant demagogic appeal of which he was capable in the heat of controversy).

In 1793 the Marquis de Condorcet, the last of the *philosophes*, the friend of Voltaire, Turgot, and Cabanis, was hiding from Robespierre's police in the house of Mme. Vernet near Saint-Sulpice in Paris. Condemned as an enemy of the Republic, he had been received by the widow of an artist in her modest establishment when it was too dangerous for him to secrete himself in the home of more prominent friends. For months elaborate security measures were in force to alert the self-immured scientist-politi-cian-philosopher in the event of a Jacobin search for suspects. He had no illusions about his survival. "I shall perish like Socrates and Sidney, for I have served my country," reads a stray fragment.[6] In his clandestine chambers, to keep from despair and to ward off distraction, he composed an *Esquisse d'un tableau historique des progrès de l'esprit humain*, spinning out an epic from his own body of accumulated knowledge, with little recourse to books. Fore-warned of an imminent raid, he escaped through the gates of Paris in disguise, only to be captured by *sans-culottes* in an obscure tavern on the outskirts of the city. He died in their detention room in Bourg-Egalité, either from apoplexy, from an embolism, or in the Stoic manner by a self-administered poison with which Dr. Cabanis had provided him.[7] In 1795, when his last testament to humanity was posthumously published, three thousand copies were purchased for distribution by the National Assembly of the Direc-torate, symbolic recognition that his theory had become official revolutionary doctrine after the Terror.[8]

To his daughter, who Michelet claims (with a measure of poetic license) was conceived on the day the Bastille fell,[9] Condorcet bequeathed a testament of another character, an eighteenth-century man's warning against the ravages of the passions which is almost a confession. "I shall not give you useless advice to avoid the pas-sions and to beware of excessive emotionality. But I shall tell you to be sincere with yourself and not to exaggerate your emotions, either out of vanity or to flatter your imagination or to fire some-one else's imagination. Fear the false enthusiasm of the passions. It never compensates either for their dangers or their misfortunes. It may be that one is not sufficiently master of one's heart to refuse to listen to it, but one is always capable of not exciting it, and that is the only useful and practical counsel which reason can give to emotion." [10]

In the hour of the hunted philosopher's need Mme. Condorcet, the philosophical, aristocratic beauty, and the loyal friend, Mme. Suard, were both put to the test, and each comported herself in her own manner. Sophie de Condorcet, disguised as a peasant girl, mingled with the mob around the guillotine in order to make her way through Paris undetected when she paid her visits to the attic on the rue des Fossoyeurs (now rue Servandoni). To earn a living in the hard winter of '93–'94 she opened a store and sold underclothes. When the revolutionary patriots made their regular perquisitions in search of her husband she somehow preserved herself and her daughter by distracting them with quick sketches and pastel drawings. As conditions became even grimmer, she was forced to apply for a divorce — with Condorcet's secret consent — in order to evade the law against the wives of proscribed citizens and to protect the property of their child. What had once been a marriage of convenience had ripened into a profound affection. Her last letters to Condorcet show the full measure of the woman, passionate, realistic, true. "O that I could give my life for you. I am having a good vest made for you. Avoid the dampness and preserve yourself for this child. . . . Your misfortunes devour my being. My soul is in the same torment as yours. I have the same horror as you for this camouflaged rupture, but between me and this lying shadow I see the interest of our child. . . ." [11]

After Condorcet left Mme. Vernet's garret and succeeded in getting beyond the gates of Paris he sought asylum in the house of the Suards in the country, where they were outwaiting the Terror. M. Suard refused the bearded and disheveled Condorcet for the same reasons that rational men have always found to abandon or betray their tracked friends. They had a "servante patriote." "I saw this man leave," Mme. Suard later wrote in a privately printed memoir on her husband, "but I only saw his back and his posture alone filled me with the greatest pity. Without turning he was looking for something in his pockets, something he did not find. He departed and M. Suard came to tell me that it was M. de C * * * who had been so dear to us. Ah, how fortunate that he had not presented himself to me first! Seeing him in this state I would have allowed a cry of anguish to escape from my heart: it would have betrayed him and I would have been disconsolate forever." [12] The false note in this sentimental outburst still jars.

In the shadow of the guillotine Condorcet had composed a dramatic paean, a passionate affirmation of rationalist faith, the climactic expression of the eighteenth-century quest for reason in history. The temper of the times had altered the calm, majestic assurance with which his predecessor Turgot had unfolded his ideas half a century before. Condorcet was writing amid hostile forces, in defiance of them, for the enemies of mankind were lurking all about him, and at the moment the tyrant seemed to be triumphant over virtue. In the decades since 1750 the conception of progress had broadened; it had been sparked by a sense of revolutionary urgency which Turgot's mid-century philosophical reflections often lacked. During the Revolution Condorcet had experienced life situations which Turgot the philosophical states-man had only comprehended abstractly. He had witnessed the declaration of war against the chosen nation by the aristocracies and clerisies of the world. The practicing savant, secretary of the Academy of Sciences, an exemplary agent of intellectual advance-ment, had soiled his hands in the blood and dirt of the Revolution, and he spoke to posterity like a prophet who had seen the people, one who knew their refractory ways but would bend them to the inevitable yoke which was their worldly destiny.

Condorcet was profuse in acknowledgments to his predecessors, Turgot and the two Englishmen who were the subversive bêtes noires of Edmund Burke's *Reflections on the French Revolution*: "We have witnessed the development of a new doctrine which is to deliver the final blow to the already tottering structure of prejudice. It is the idea of the limitless perfectibility of the human species, a doctrine whose first and most illustrious apostles were Turgot, Price, and Priestley." [13] But the writings of his antecedents were too sketchy and dispersed ever to become popular. The *Es-quisse* was the form in which the eighteenth-century idea of prog-ress was generally assimilated by Western thought. Condorcet wrote his manifesto with full awareness of its world revolutionary significance. Those who came after him had no choice but to affirm allegiance like Godwin and Saint-Simon and Comte, or to proclaim their hostility as Malthus did on the very title page of his pessimist *Essay on Population*, which appeared as a formal refutation of the French *philosophe*.[14] When the traditionalists of the de Maistre school declared war on eighteenth-century ideology they were engaged in controverting the arguments of the *Esquisse*, even when it was not mentioned by name. De Bonald anathematized it as the "Apocalypse of the new Gospel." [15]

Condorcet's conception of progress is by no means restricted to the *Esquisse*; it is the very lifeblood of all his intellectual labors, whether he is studying laws of probability in social phenomena, drafting constitutional norms for the revolutionary state, writing popular journalism, preparing *éloges*, in the tradition of Fontenelle, for deceased academic colleagues, collecting contemporary philosophical works for a world library of knowledge, or outlining projects for universal education. To be fully appreciated, the text of the *Esquisse* must be supplemented by a set of parallel chapters that amplify three of the epochs, documents published in the Arago edition of Condorcet's works in the 1840's.[16] Particularly revealing are the often-forgotten section which parallels the fourth epoch and a commentary on the *New Atlantis* of Francis Bacon, both of which were attached to the 1804 edition of the *Esquisse* and exerted a profound influence on Saint-Simon and Comte. The variants and supplements of the *Esquisse* which are still in manuscript in the library of the Institut de France and in the Bibliothèque Nationale elucidate many obscurities and bear witness that Condorcet's historical optimism was far less banal than a casual reading of the accepted text may lead one to believe.

THE MECHANICS OF SECULAR HISTORY

The *Esquisse* set forth the historical great chain of being: "We pass by imperceptible gradations from the brute to the savage and from the savage to Euler and Newton."[17] The term *progrès* and its derivations broke through all hitherto accepted bounds of meaning and became at one and the same time a capsulated description of empirical history, a charted goal for men's activities in the present and in the future, a definition of the good at any historic moment, and an identification of the moral man. Progress was a capacity inherent in the growth of rational intelligence. Less of a philosopher than Turgot, Condorcet merely accepted and incorporated his predecessor's psychology and epistemology. In the very first stage of his spiritual existence man's ability to make "new combinations" was already fully formed, and the secret of his progressist nature resided in his natural talent and desire to innovate. The tempo of progress was not uniform throughout history, either in Condorcet's version or in Turgot's. The early stages of barbarism had witnessed only a feeble development because man, weighed down by the repetitive labors of hunting, fishing, and agriculture, did not have sufficient leisure to effect the progress-bearing "new combinations." Higher civilizations resulted from the accident of a surplus which allowed some men to devote themselves completely to observation and to meditation — a formula that should be familiar to the Marxist historians of the growth of consciousness, though no direct Condorcet influence need be traced since the idea had become commonplace by the 1840's. Unlike their more primitive necessitous forebears, read the Condorcet account of the dawn of reason, the men of civilization had the time to study the new phenomena which chance had thrown in their path. Progress was still, as with Turgot, dependent primarily upon the individual act of a man of extraordinary talent, but a different emphasis altered the role of genius. For Condorcet each invention had to fulfill a social need at a given historic moment before it could be adopted by the people. Turgot was absorbed in the personal fate of the genius, whom inimical political conditions might crush. While Condorcet honored and extolled the genius, he shifted the focus to the state of society and its general readiness to assimilate an invention once it had seen the light. Throughout Condorcet's work the crucial instant of the progressive act was not the initial discovery, but its acceptance. In filial deference to Turgot the title of the *Esquisse* retained an intellectualist and elitist bias, but in the working out of the historical process the concept was weighted heavily in the direction of the social.

Condorcet the secularist could no longer derive the idea of progress from God, making of it a new eighteenth-century attribute of divinity.[18] Vico, Turgot, and Herder had reassured themselves of the existence of historical laws in the world by fashioning arguments touched with theology and teleology. It has been rightly said that for German thought enlightenment usually meant the enlightenment of theology. Could a rational God have bestowed the reign of law upon the movement of the planets, upon organic and inorganic matter, and have abandoned human history to mere accident? Could a God who was infinite goodness have created the noblest of His creatures and then rendered his life on earth a meaningless, disorderly succession of events which would arouse disgust in a rational man? Herder's answer was a pious negative. Could Nature have endowed man with reason and afforded no opportunity for its unfolding in time, asked Immanuel Kant; for surely the half-bestial man of the present hardly represented the total fulfillment of rational and ethical capacities. Turgot's historical theodicy still reflected analogous quasi-religious reasoning. But for Condorcet the godless one, who wished to commit himself to the teleology of progress, none of these religious props was available to bolster his confidence.

From the outset Condorcet stripped the historical process bare of its ceremonial Christian elements. It was no longer a civil theology as with Vico, nor a theodicy as it had been with Turgot. Condorcet self-consciously secularized his master's world history and injected it with a virulent antireligious bias, though the dynamic forces on earth remained unchanged even after the guiding hand of God through time had been removed. History lost a transcendental sanction, but the substantive worldly goals of Turgot were preserved intact and the motive psychological drives of men were unaltered. Instead of Providence working through history, henceforward history would have to function only through itself. Progress became an autonomous human creation free from divine will or direction. Instead of pointing up a unique, divinely ordained quality in human history as distinguished from natural history, Condorcet resorted to the complete identification of history with the other sciences. Even if it were not a science of absolute prediction like physics, it could still preserve the fundamental character of science by calling its findings truths with a high degree of probability. Condorcet was willing to submit historical hypotheses to the same rigorous tests of necessity and constancy that prevailed in the other disciplines. Armed with the theory of probability, he could then integrate the historico-social sciences with the physical sciences and dispense completely with theology.

Through his disproof of the idea of "necessary connection" or simple causality, Hume as much as any philosopher had brought about a rapprochement between the social and the physical sciences; for if absolute law was denied to the physical sciences then both forms of knowledge were reduced to the level of sciences of probability. When Condorcet wrote about "general and constant facts" he meant facts of general enough a character to permit of reasonably accurate prediction. In this respect all phenomena, both human and physical, could be viewed as on the same plane. "They are equally susceptible of being calculated," he worte in a manuscript, "and all that is necessary, to reduce the whole of nature to laws similar to those which Newton discovered with the aid of the calculus, is to have a sufficient number of observations and a mathematics that is complex enough." [19]

After his traditional obeisance to scientific method in the tenth epoch of the *Esquisse*, which lacked only a formal acknowledgment to the philosophy of Chancellor Bacon for completeness, Condorcet launched into an excursus on "our hopes" for the future, by which he meant those hopes of the *philosophes* transcribed by himself which, according to the empirical evidence of history, had a reasonable probability of fulfillment. The leap from a rationalist statement of scientific methodology to wishing is not so rare in the science of society as to warrant comment, but the ingenuousness of the transition in Condorcet is truly disarming.

In Condorcet's view the study of history could accomplish for mankind most of the functions which Auguste Comte later arrogated to the science of sociology. It was "a science to foresee the progressions of the human species," [20] a science of prediction, and the capacity to foretell was a source of vast power. It made it possible "to tame the future." [21] Through the separating out of obstacles and aids, which could then be recorded on the debit or the credit side of the ledger, past history could be made to yield the key to future development, because in an old-fashioned sense it was a storehouse of moral lessons teaching humanity what to elect and what to reject, how to minimize historic pain and regulate the temporal dimension of achievement. History could indicate, by what would now be called extrapolation, the general future tendency of the evolution of the human mind; delving into the record of past transformations was no mere idle amusement, for it instructed men in the art of directing progress. "These observations on what man has been and what he is today will later lead to the means of assuring and accelerating the new progressions which human nature still permits him to hope for."

History also served as a prophylaxis against prejudice. At

moments this faithful devotee of reason called upon history to deflate the arrogance of self-complacent rationalists who imagined themselves totally emancipated from the parochial attitudes of their own age. "He who limits himself to knowing only the epoch in which he lives, even if it enjoys a marked superiority over its predecessors, exposes himself to the danger of partaking of all its superstitions; for each generation has its own, and it would be exceedingly dangerous to fancy oneself so close to the ultimate limits of reason that one no longer had to fear these prejudices." [22]

While there is a determined progressive development — absolute retrogression is impossible — whose grand sweep mankind can no longer defy, there remains a quasi-independent human force which sets the pace or the measure of progress and affects environmental conditions more or less favorably. Though the present state of knowledge guarantees a happy future for the over-all movement of world history, a human variable can alter the methods whereby felicity may be attained. "And in order that the happiness which it promises us shall be less dearly bought, in order that it may spread with greater rapidity over a very extensive area, in order that it may be more complete in its results, do we not need to study in the history of the human mind what impediments we still have to fear, what means we possess for surmounting them?" [23] Condorcet adopted Turgot's arguments demonstrating the past reality and future inevitability of progress as foregone conclusions and then reshaped the whole problem: what was the most efficient, gentle, and easy method for the attainment of perfectibility? [24] In the *Fragment de justification* of July 1793, he described his own life's mission in precisely these terms. "Long since persuaded that the human species is infinitely perfectible, and that this perfection . . . cannot be arrested but by physical revolutions of the globe, I considered the task of hastening progress to be one of my sweetest occupations, one of the first duties of a man who has strengthened his reason by study and meditation." [25]

The narration of the first nine epochs of world history in the *Esquisse* revealed the natural motivation of mankind to have been a steady agelong pursuit of utility. There are passages in which progress is called an "instinct" or a "transcendent goal"; as epoch after epoch is analyzed, as the concrete discoveries, inventions, and moral leaps are described in detail, it becomes abundantly clear that there is one fundamental utilitarian drive in man; if left to his own devices he will invariably pursue the useful and the pleasurable, Hume's *utile et dulce*, in the ordinary economic sense of the eighteenth-century Encyclopedists.[26] From the primitives upward, whenever men realized that a practice, often discovered by chance, consumed less energy, was less costly, afforded more enjoyment, they adopted it. It was this identification of the *progressus* of mankind with the law of least action which was to arouse the towering rage of Nietzsche, guardian of the Will, against these passive optimists. For Condorcet every major progress was a conclusion reached by reasonable men thoroughly imbued with the spirit of rational utility. The momentous advancement in morals depicted in the second epoch, for example, when men stopped strangling their war captives, was the direct consequence of a tidy bit of commonsensical bookkeeping which convinced the conquerors that a healthy young slave was worth more in productive labor than the cost of his subsistence. Before such rational propositions mankind had to bow. Of course, at crucial moments the intervention of genius — a genius of utility — was often required to point out the new profit before the mass of ignorant, unthinking mankind could perceive it. This principle of utility was the driving force in all times and places and led to identical institutions under like circumstances. Common needs produced similar utilitarian solutions, ran the eighteenth-century ditty. Institutions such as feudalism were not peculiar to western Europe, Condorcet argued, but a universal form "found almost everywhere in the world at all stages of civilization each time that one and the same territory was occupied by two peoples among whom victory had established an unequal heredity." [27] This type of world-historical thinking was most congenial to the monist *philosophes* of the eighteenth century. Court de Gébelin's Great Order of needs is the obvious parallel — and Condorcet knew his *Monde primitif*. If men were left to operate freely, "naturally," they would, he believed, produce a series of functional innovations which continuously increased their happiness. Condorcet was not a profound theoretician of human motives, and his historical world-view should not be over-systematized. There are times when, in the spirit of D'Alembert's

Discours préliminaire, he joined to utility an abstract concept like scientific curiosity as a progressive drive of mankind; but for the most part history was a succession of recognized needs and appeasements of needs in the course of which man was accumulating an ever greater stockpile of scientific and moral truths.

That this smooth progression had not always been the past experience of mankind was due to the intrusion of nonfunctional, false, religious ideas which confused men, disrupted and distorted the normal, "natural" operations of their utilitarianism. The injection of alien motives had resulted in the war of progress against prejudice, which had become the substance and central theme of history. Only the contemporary triumph of Locke's sensationalism, that incomparable tool for the analysis of ideas, was henceforward "an eternal barrier between mankind and the old errors of his infancy, which should prevent him from ever being returned to his former ignorance by new prejudices. . . ." [28]

In the past there had been grave setbacks. "Would anybody imagine that the whole system of human faculties in all individuals could have always made such methodical progress that in no part of the system would either disturbances or disorders ever result, that all the faculties would perfect themselves at one and the same time, in accordance with a felicitous sense of proportion, steadfastly maintaining among the parts an equilibrium most favorable to the happiness of the whole species?" [29] Such absolute balance would have been impossible, hence the variety of historical vicissitudes and the unevenness of development among peoples and individuals. History has been a worldly battleground between those forces advancing real utility and those suppressing it in the name of a religion, a philosophic system, or a tyrannical lust for domination. This is a somewhat differently accented translation of the struggle between the promoters of novelty and the adherents to routine which Turgot had described. More explicitly than in Turgot, religious bodies in all ages harbored evil antiprogressive elements and their opponents were the legions of the good. The plots of organized castes and priesthoods to maintain themselves, the deceivers, in power, and their deliberate conspiracy to keep the mass of the people, the duped, in ignorance through imposture were a hackneyed theme in eighteenth-century thought to which

Condorcet gave final expression. Ultimately the enthroned sacerdotal tyranny was undermined because the sane spirit of men, of virtuous souls, of natural utilitarians, broke through the hard crust of lies imposed by the theological conspirators and resumed the quest for truth. Falsehood could not be maintained forever, for the priests soon contradicted themselves and revealed their own inconsistencies. Throughout the historical drama there is a conviction that virtue must triumph in the end and that however oppressive may be the dominion of darkness and evil, man's dogged inquiring energy in search of the useful will finally reassert itself.

The first nine epochs of the *Esquisse* are largely a tirade against clerical enemies. Turgot had still found a respectworthy place for Christianity in the development of rational thought; unlike his predecessor, Condorcet was fighting *l'infâme*. The arraignment of priests and religious impostors of all nations grows into a tiresome harangue.[30] In refutation of his friend's appreciation of the benign role of the Church in softening the barbarians of the north, Condorcet cried out, "The blood of millions of men massacred in the name of God still steams about us. Everywhere the earth which supports us covers the bones of a barbaric intolerance."[31] The medieval *Cathari* are depicted as heroic figures, the first who dared to reject the lies of the conspirators, and the brutal subjugation of the heretics by the fanatical armies whom the priests unleashed against them is bewailed as the sad loss of brothers in progress and revolution. But happily the defeats of the righteous are always temporary, the forces of light suppressed in one area re-emerge in another, and no power or violence is mighty enough to choke off the diffusion of new ideas.

The historic, almost Zoroastrian combat between enlightenment and obscurantism was marked by a series of great technological and scientific discoveries, which became the natural benchmarks of Condorcet's world tableau. The early stages of civilization were relatively simultaneous developments in different parts of the globe, for primitive human nature was everywhere the same; only with the flowering of Greek genius was there a breakthrough of a unique course of rational progress in Europe. But, alas, the Greek system-makers, the sectarians of the schools, brought about their own downfall; Condorcet abhorred the institutionalized knowledge of Greece and Rome and of the Chinese mandarins almost as much as he did the medieval schoolmen. Metaphysicians and system-makers in all ages, men with a tendency to raise questions for which mankind would perhaps never have answers and to construct "a philosophy of words" as a response, were as inimical to progress as priests and religious enthusiasts.[32] True knowledge was restricted to what he called the "sciences réelles," [33] by which he meant precisely what Mme. de Staël and Saint-Simon did a few years later when they introduced the neologism "sciences positives": simple straightforward empirical science, preferably with a mathematical base — that alone was authentic knowledge accumulating in time. Philosophies were disguised religions and they invariably led to the decline of true science. In its hour of triumph Christianity had merely picked up the debris of twenty rival Greco-Roman sects and systems which had battled one another into a state of exhaustion under the Empire, and this was "the signal for the total decadence of the sciences and of philosophy." [34] Medieval Christianity, a dismal period of retrogression after the bloom of Greek genius, was the target of his persistent bitter eloquence. "Theological reveries, superstitious impostures are the only expressions of human genius, religious intolerance their only morality, and Europe, compressed between sacerdotal tyranny and military despotism, awaited in blood and tears the moment when new knowledge would allow it to be reborn to liberty, to humanity, and to virtue." [35] For Condorcet the world was still witnessing a death struggle irreconcilable between Christianity and progress, the great polar opposites both in scientific and in moral values.

The progressist angel of salvation appeared in the guise of the scientific Arabs, who transmitted back to Europe what the Greeks had discovered, the Romans preserved, and the Middle Ages destroyed. The anticlerical *philosophe* would naturally rather see the new illumination come from Islam than from Christendom. Condorcet was less impressed than Turgot by medieval developments in the mechanical arts as a prelude to Renaissance science. The medieval world was really a dark age. With the restoration of the arts and the sciences mankind had to resume progress where the ancients left off, expunging a whole era of human existence as sterile.

In the great revival after the Middle Ages the art of printing occupied a crucial position, for in this instrument the conspirators of evil were confronted with an invention which could spread scientific truth over so vast an expanse of territory that suppression became virtually impossible. As in Turgot, the extension of progress, the massive quantitative promulgation of the new ideas, would henceforward fundamentally alter the balance in the conflict between light and darkness. During the initial stages of the anti-religious struggle the enemies of the priestly conspiracy had been forced to be circumspect. Men but recently emancipated from superstition had not dared attack frontally; they had introduced their ideas stealthily into books read by the upper classes, had resorted to wit rather than overt invective, and had thus hoodwinked the persecutors of truth. To render the breakdown of the medieval sacerdotal system plausible, Condorcet dreamed up a counterconspiracy of truth, secret societies of philosophical adepts whose traces had been lost. He even hazarded the wild guess that the Knights Templar had been a clandestine organization of this character, sworn to the propagation of truth, and that this was the real reason for their suppression. When he asked himself what manner of men were they who risked combat with priestly authority, his rather insipid answer was that "those who had a sounder mind, a more open, elevated nature . . . fought for the cause of men against the priests." [36]

The history of the progress of the human mind became the chronicle of the princes of the intellect who at eight or nine moments set the spirit of man free. Each stage was a separate act in the drama, and the argument was a repetitive one: there was always a body of wily men, a heroic genius, a conflict of power, a moment of triumph followed by a regrouping of the agents of evil who, bloated with the new knowledge acquired through the discoveries of genius, again closed the gates of the temple of reason and practiced the wicked rites which they fashioned into a tradition. The drama was usually enacted with aristocratic characters as in classical tragedy. The people themselves played virtually no role in the historic process. Condorcet was fully conscious of the inclination toward decadence, particularly among the priestly or philosophical conspirators. In the early stages, after the infusion of a new potion of energy from the free genius, even the theological systematizers were inventive, but as time passed and they were subject to no new stimuli their works became stale and hackneyed; and in the end they could not even comprehend their own traditions. Wicked priests made use of the temporal arm of cruel tyrants, but the evil ones invariably fell out among themselves like a band of thieves. Each side summoned new forces, uncommitted men, and these aides in an internecine conflict among obscurantists grasped the opportunity to insinuate fresh ideas into the discussion. Both traditionalist rivals were constrained by their own abominable lust for power to employ the good geniuses, and in time, once they had been allowed into the city, the newcomers took possession of the ideology which had been sapped of its vital force.

Condorcet, like many modern philosophers of history prior to Hegel, made frequent use of a primitive sort of historical dialectic. Since history was a conflict of the forces of good and evil and since evil had been triumphant for many centuries, the progressist had to demonstrate how contradictory forces could arise in the bosom of an old order. One example of the process was the growth of learning in the later Middle Ages, despite society's commitment to obscurantism and sheer power-lust. The priests, in the very act of strengthening their offensive against the secret propagators of truth, had to study the liberal arguments that were being propounded against them. Similarly they were constrained to become learned in order to fabricate evidence bolstering their own position against secular rivals for power. Kings in their turn had to establish schools for jurisconsults in an effort to uphold their temporal regimes. Thus in the very ranks of the fanatics, despite the self-interest and ill will of priests and lords, learning and knowledge were diffused, and in the desperate attempt to consolidate the power of superstition a new light was kindled.

The crusades were another example of Condorcet's crude "dialectic" of history. Religious prejudice had impelled Christian Europeans to fight in the East, but from the wars there stemmed consequences disastrous to the feudal antiprogressist regimes. The crusades weakened the power of the *seigneurs*. Men were brought into close relations with the Arab peoples and their learning so that ultimately if the late medieval Christians did not surpass Arab science they at least came to equal it. "These wars undertaken for the cause of superstition served to destroy it." [37] Even scholasticism, for all its excessive subtleties and its false ideas, sharpened the human mind and became "the first origin of the philosophical analysis which has since been the fecund source of our progress. . . . This scholasticism did not lead to the discovery of truth; it did not even serve for its discussion, for a good appreciation of its proofs; but it sharpened the minds. . . ." [38]

Condorcet's treatment of the discovery of cannon and gunpowder was perhaps his most striking instance of progressist good emanating from tyrannical evil. The new weapons were retrogressive agents if evaluated in terms of eighteenth-century pacifist morality, for they increased the terrible potentialities of destruction. In its long-term effect, however, the cannon poured forth a host of salutary results. Warriors became less ferocious because gunpowder obliged them to fight at greater distances from one another. The heavy cost of military expeditions made even the most bellicose nations devote themselves to commerce and the arts of peace in order to be able to finance their wars. Finally, the discovery of gunpowder reduced the likelihood that a sudden invasion of barbarians, possessed by blind courage, would be able to crush less warlike, civilized peoples. "The great conquests and the revolutions which follow them have become almost impossible." [39] Gunpowder reduced the superiority of the mounted knight and in the long run diminished the prestige of the nobility. Thus an invention which had threatened to destroy the human species removed the last obstacles to the attainment of real liberty and equality among men. The "cunning of reason" is a perennial conception of philosophical history; virtually all the modern prophets resort to it. "The very passions of men, their interests falsely understood, lead them to spread enlightenment, liberty, happiness, to do good despite themselves," [40] was Condorcet's simplistic expression of the idea in one of his manuscripts.

In Condorcet's secular history those who denied liberty, particularly in the pursuit of science, were the wicked ones, and in this respect the rigid philosophical system-builders were thrown into the same category in progressist Hell as the theologians and priestly dogmatists. The early sections of the *Esquisse* continue the

Turgot tradition with an indissoluble association of liberty and progress. Whenever there had been decadence, a temporary blotting out of progress — as under the latter-day caliphs, in China, or in medieval Christian Europe — Condorcet found explanations almost exclusively in the imposition of tyranny and the crushing of liberty. The absolutist institutions of Christianity had been antihuman not only because of the cruelties they perpetrated upon their enemies but because they denied mankind the full measure of progress under freedom it was naturally capable of achieving after the Greek advance.

In the nineteenth century this narrative of events became the unimpeachable framework for any popular liberal anticlerical view of world history. But in his espousal of liberty as the dynamic of progress Condorcet soon encountered a dilemma, and a tension was introduced into the heart of his system, perhaps the pivotal development in the history of the concept, a still unresolved dilemma. There came to be an issue, even a contradiction, between liberty and the optimum tempo of progress. Essentially the problem was posed for the future of mankind; in the past it had not been pressing since the historic spiritual powers and their organizational embodiments had always degenerated into antiprogressive strongholds. Medieval Christianity never impressed Condorcet as the repository and preserver of the acquisitions of mankind, as it had the young Turgot, for he saw only its repressive sword cutting off genius in its prime, stifling truth. The proclamation of freedom of inquiry had hitherto been the natural rallying-cry of progressists. But what of the future? Was the rule of liberty applied with Turgot's absolutism the best way for the attainment of maximal progress as fast as humanly possible? Or was there another road? The union between liberty and progress might be rent asunder, and liberty might yield before the prospect of accelerated development under organization with its necessary restrictions. This alternative had many ramifications in Condorcet's theory, which then became more than a mere rehearsal of his admired predecessor's reflections.

MARQUIS DE CONDORCET

PROGRESS IN EQUALITY

For Turgot the diffusion of progress still resembled a benevolent act of enlightened monarchy; in the hands of Condorcet progress in equality became an intrinsic constituent element in the idea. To render men more or less equal assumed moral value and was a goal virtually independent, to be pursued in and of itself. The extension of enlightenment among the nations and a diminution of inequalities was for Turgot primarily intended to moralize the people, but there was always another purpose too, one rooted in aristocratic suspicion — to safeguard the acquisitions of humanity from a resurgence of the ignorant mob. In Condorcet there is an appreciation of the positive uses of democracy for progress which the prerevolutionary noble *philosophe* could not wholeheartedly entertain. Condorcet altered Turgot's theory of the incidence of genius, the idea that it was a fixed though infinitesimal proportion of the population in any epoch, by proposing a critically different ratio: the creative scientists were a proportion of all persons subject to the influence of rationalist education. If the state provided instruction for a vastly increased number of inhabitants, the total of productive scientists would multiply astronomically. The agent of progress was still the scientist, but in Condorcet he was less the unique genius of Turgot, less the rare colossus of the mind, and more a statistical probability of mass enlightenment.

Condorcet faced one of the central historic problems of the idea of progress — the relative worth of intensive scientific progress among the elite and of extensive progress of scientific knowledge among the masses. Which should be preferred? He was consistently opposed to the double-truth doctrines which had become current among Deists and one wing of the *philosophes*, the idea that there was one truth for the masses and another for the elite, who alone could comprehend science and the mathematical world. This was for Condorcet dangerous thinking which had served as the basis for the domination of society by a hieratic priesthood. In the Orient the exclusive concentration of truth in the hands of an elite had resulted in the desiccation of scientific creativity. Condorcet democratized the idea of progress. He was so worried that progress might be crushed by an educated class with a monopoly of knowledge that he was even willing to sacrifice to a degree the intensification of scientific knowledge among the elite — this was the critical test — in favor of its propagation among the masses. It was salutary, for example, to abolish Latin as the exclusive language of scientific communication, even at the risk of placing additional burdens upon scholars who henceforth would have to spend time learning many languages. The use of the vernacular for their publications would prevent the scientists from becoming an exclusive clique, thus creating two distinct classes and curtailing the progress of the "mass of the human species." [41] Condorcet himself was highly conscious of the distinction between the two measures of progress — one intrinsic and intensive, the other extensive — which in Turgot was only implicit. "We shall distinguish between the progress of science itself which can be measured only in terms of the totality of the truths which it has uncovered and the progress accomplished by a nation in each science, a progress which is measured both by the number of people who are acquainted with the most common and the most important truths and by the number and the nature of the truths generally known." [42] In passages of the ninth epoch Condorcet clearly reduced the prestige of pure scientific discovery and made it the handmaiden of popular well-being. Meaningful history consisted in tracing the consequences of a new scientific discovery, a new system of laws, or a political revolution, as they affected "the most numerous portion of each society. . . . For this is the real object of philosophy, since all intermediary effects of these same causes can only be considered forces ultimately working on those who truly constitute the mass of humanity." [43]

Only in the progress of the mass of mankind could there be an ultimate value judgment. Did a man really deserve his titles to glory? The people would decide. Had human reason really progressed, had there been a real perfection of mankind? Only in the mass could one judge. Progress usually starts with a scientific discovery which through a long chain of events goes back centuries, but the end of the development is popular utility. In the past the two basic forms of progress, the moral and the scientific, had not always been compatible. A high level of scientific information was once the monopoly of a sacerdotal class which used its knowledge for ends diametrically contrary to the moral progress of their society. The tragic fault lay in the very fact of exclusivity. As soon as modern science reached a "certain point" of advance among a number of nations and penetrated among the mass of people in any one nation whose language and relationships were universal (France seems the chosen one), an unbreakable bond between scientific and moral progress would be forged. The past had witnessed elite scientific progress which could be abused; the future popularization of science made its freezing into a hieratic system — the death of progress — impossible.

Inevitably progress would extend itself everywhere throughout the globe, making all nations and peoples more or less equal. Equal in what? Equal in progress.

The hopes for the future that Condorcet was able to find within himself could be reduced to three (even the sworn enemy of the Catholic Church, when driven to prophecy, was triadic), and they all dealt with the principle of equality. Before his mind's eye loomed a plateau of excellence in science and well-being which was occupied by the French and Anglo-American nations. (He was thus one of the first to conceive of an Atlantic community.) In time the other peoples of the globe would rise to a status more or less equal with this lofty plane. Similarly there was an eminence of scientific knowledge and well-being in the elite of each nation, and progress would signify the raising of all men in a polity close to this level. His third hope was a desire for the perfection of man in a biological sense. This too was a development which would affect all men more or less equally through the inheritance of acquired characteristics.

Condorcet proceeded to test the empirical validity of these desires for equality. Was there any evidence that they would be fulfilled? His response assumed the form of rhetorical questions which no son of the Revolution, whatever his party, could answer in the negative. Were there peoples on earth condemned to live forever without liberty and without reason? Was there any inherent necessity for the wide disparities in scientific knowledge and general well-being among nations — was the existence of barbarous peoples inevitable? Were gross inequalities in the enlightenment and prosperity of various classes in a nation necessary conditions of the civilized state? He could find no basis for replying affirmatively; therefore the converse was true. *Quod erat demonstrandum.*

The wide inequalities of contemporary society were due to a mechanical defect in administration, in social art. There was nothing irremediable in civilization which required the persistence of such flagrant differences. Condorcet was not free of the Rousseauist conception of a blissful state of nature, and he accepted the argument of the *Second Discourse* in a modified form: up until the Age of Enlightenment the growth of the arts and the sciences had been accompanied by an unfortunate maximization of the original natural, though slight, inequality among human beings. Before men acquired talents and the vanities of *amour-propre* and comparative morality, the inequalities of birth, the natural inequalities, had been of no great significance. Only when an individual man engrossed subsidiary powers from civilization did horrid and unnatural inequalities become the very basis of an oppressive social organization. Fortunately in the immediate future a counter tendency would make itself felt, a momentous turn in the history of human inequality on earth. While the arts and the sciences were preserved and their progress was furthered, a concomitant decrease in inequality among men would become manifest. The strengthening of this development becomes one of the main efforts of conscious future action, the practical goal of the "social art." Absolute equality would never be reached nor was it desirable, for there were benign inequalities, special excellences, unique attributes and capacities, which Condorcet's intimate friend Cabanis was to comment upon in his famous papers before the Institute in 1794–1795. These were to be fostered not for themselves but because paradoxically they accelerated general equality. The natural inequalities of Turgot's men of genius — and that is what Condorcet counted on — would, if afforded a favorable environment, spread a high measure of equality through their contributions to the general utilitarian progress of civilization. Natural inequalities would endure, but they would no longer entail dependence, impoverishment, or humiliation for the great mass of mankind.

Reaching a status of relative equality meant becoming citizens in a free society, and this presupposed minimal physical, intellectual, and moral attainments. Human beings all had a natural capacity for reason which had to be nourished with knowledge until they were capable of discerning truth from falsehood, thus emancipating themselves from traditional prejudices, foremost among them religious superstitions. Men had to be aware of their rights as citizens and to be in a position to exercise these rights freely and independently. The use of judgment demanded a certain physical ease. Natural faculties and the conveniences of living had to be sufficiently developed lest men be too wretched to fulfill their elementary citizenship obligations. A prelude to freedom and true equality was the existence of a general social climate in which stupidity and misery were accidents, the rare exceptions rather than the habitual fate and norm of mankind. Condorcet the intellectual was far from indifferent to ordinary material wants. Their gratification was a condition precedent, it was almost taken for granted, to any future evolution. He reaffirmed, like Bacon and Leibniz before him, the relationship between progress in science and technology and the raising of the general level of prosperity. At the end of the eighteenth century the utility of science, aside from its value as a search for truth, was just becoming a widespread popular notion. For Condorcet this was the point of contact between intellectual and moral progress.

Condorcet's estimate of the world political situation confirmed him in the hypothesis that the ideal of equality was in fact in the process of realization. All enlightened men on earth had already accepted the principles of the French Revolution. Their diffusion was so wide that no counterforce could prevent their eventual penetration everywhere. In the new dawn the universal values of the Declaration of the Rights of Man could not remain the monopoly of a spiritual clique. Once the truths of the French Revolution were taught in the huts of enslaved peoples, their rational capacities would be awakened and they would fight to secure for themselves the same rights enjoyed by Europeans. Condorcet drew a grim portrait of the colonial slave living in mute indigation; but he was nevertheless a man, and it required only a spark to arouse in him all his human qualities. Condorcet perhaps telescoped the periods of eighteenth-century colonialism, nineteenth-century imperialism, and twentieth-century independence, but *sub specie aeternitatis* he still deserves to retain an honorable place in the fraternity of augurers and prognosticators.

The movement toward equality would not proceed at the same tempo and in the same manner throughout the whole world. There was uneven development, to borrow Marx's later phrase. The political action of individual governments would determine the manner in which the egalitarian revolution took place. Among some nations a recognition of the inevitability of the process would bring about a peaceful transition; among others stubborn, blind resistance on the part of the tyrants who held the reins of governance would provoke outbreaks of violence. The burden of choice between a peaceful and a chaotic transition was thrust upon those who now exercised power. Revolution would be the fate of those polities which refused to accept the verdict of history. But in either event the final consequence, a world converted to the French Revolutionary ideology, was preordained.

With time all nations and peoples of the earth would climb toward the high level of civilization and enlightenment achieved along the shores of the Atlantic, the area that was the pace-setter of universal egalitarian progress. This presupposed the abolition of slavery, of colonial domination, and of the exploitation of one political society by another. The methods by which this was achieved — peaceful or violent — were less significant than the fact that total world civilization among relative equals was a necessary aspect of total progress. In one curious passage Condorcet conceded the remote possibility of an irruption of barbarians from the plateau of Tartary to cut short European and hence world progress, but it was only a passing reflection. Europeans would soon increase so rapidly that they would overflow onto other continents, civilizing and assimilating backward peoples. The horrors of the enslavement of native populations which the Abbé Raynal had depicted with indignation in the *Histoire philosophique* would then give way before a universal education program directed by altruist white Europeans bearing science. In Saint-Simon the idea later assumed the form of a white European's mission or crusade to uproot the primitive religions of Asia and Africa and impose scientificism. There was only one true form of knowledge allowable, and any other spiritual existence or culture represented a grave danger. The progressists had so absolutist a faith in the objective validity of their scientific utilitarian civilization that its universal propagation as a perfect good was never questioned for a single moment. The Europocentrism of the liberal idea of progress exemplified by Condorcet became one of its more naive though deep-rooted preconceptions.

THE SCIENTIFIC SOCIETY

THE important element introduced by Condorcet into the idea of progress was not the commonplace that the study of the past would help man in the future, a frequent variation on any moralizing history, but the sense of tempo, the belief that philosophical history, if deciphered, would teach man how to affect the historic timetable. That progress was inevitable after a certain stage of human development Turgot had already demonstrated. What then was a worthy human purpose in life and what should be a man's individual role? Condorcet's solution is a prototype for similar, nineteenth-century theories in Saint-Simon, Comte, and Marx. There was a peculiar merit in accelerating the rate of progress. Since it was defined in terms of utilitarian good, the sooner it dispensed its bounty the better. To hasten the end was a longing of medieval mystics. Worldly progress, infinite and inevitable, had no final historic moment like an apocalypse, but there was nevertheless an implied virtue in the acquisition of more felicity as fast as possible. A hypothetical maximum pace could be achieved if the total human effort were expended, and there was an inference that failure to fulfill one's progressist mission to the utmost was sinning against humanity. Once progress had become the absolute of human behavior there was an implied immorality in not bringing to fruition the complete development of which humanity was capable at any moment. A delay in the discovery of abstract truth was not an innocent failing, because progress in science could overnight — this was uncontested — be transmuted into moral progress and happiness. To decelerate the pace for whatever reason was therefore a great iniquity, for it was a refusal to bestow happiness upon fellow men. Driven one step further it became an act of treachery against humanity.

The eighteenth-century ideology of progress has long since engulfed the politics of the world, East and West. Some of the real differences between them are mechanical and organizational: how fast shall the tempo be accelerated and what price in liberty shall be paid at any given stage of development? Condorcet was one of the first modern thinkers to explore the problems entailed by the painful alternatives.

Throughout the *Esquisse* and the fragments attached to it Condorcet communicated the feeling that mankind stood at one of the great divides in history, an emotion he shared with two other philosophical geniuses, one old, the other young, who were alive at the moment of the French Revolution — Kant and Hegel. The conviction that the whole human race was on the verge of a great bound forward into another realm of social being made Condorcet a militant activist and persuaded him to venture, perhaps without full consciousness of what the decision might imply, upon a plan for the ordering of world progress. Turgot had conceived of liberty as the absolute prerequisite of progress, the very air in which it breathed most easily. Suddenly the problem of tempo intruded, raising the provocative query whether under liberty mankind was in fact achieving the maximum harvest extensively and intensively of which the species was capable at a given moment in time. Once progress became the moral absolute, then even liberty could be called upon to bend, at least a little. Throughout his description of the mechanics for the realization of his utopia, Condorcet tended to soften the contradiction between liberty and progress, to show that men would be drawn to organization freely and of their own will, to demonstrate that at this advanced stage a rational order necessarily required complete organization. At times he expressed confidence that it would be feasible to enjoy the benefits of organization and of liberty too. By introducing libertarian safeguards he hoped to avoid the more flagrant impositions and dangers of institutional control, which he had studied, examined, and inveighed against so dramatically in his universal history. He was often markedly uncomfortable with the denial of absolute liberty, but ultimately in the name of progress he allowed himself to be enticed into the new order.

A side glance at the realities of scientific organization at the turn of the eighteenth century may highlight the novelty of Condorcet's break with existing practice. Despite a few instances of international cooperation, particularly in the gathering of astronomic data, seventeenth- and eighteenth-century scientific discovery had been the work of lone individuals, men of heroic genius. During the revolutionary era learned societies of Paris and the provinces offered prizes on a heterogeneous array of research topics, and a substantial number of scientists were salaried by the state in professional schools and institutes; but in these endeavors public attention and sponsorship were always concentrated upon isolated individual performance. A deep-rooted hostility to the *esprit de système* which the *idéologues* had inherited from Condillac rendered them inaccessible to the notion of collective experimentation; it savored too much of a School which cramped initiative. Scientists were empiricists who published their discoveries as they made them, without subscribing to preconceived "metaphysical" ideas of any master, and somehow their total effort added up to human perfectibility. Free enterprise in business was paralleled by private research in the sciences, and benefits to humanity would accrue from both. In the universities, learned societies, and academies, general consciousness of a European intellectual community had been fostered over the centuries, but it had bred a zealous spirit of competition among scientists rather than any tendency toward combination or coordination. Bitter controversy over the priority of scientific discoveries was a symptom of this contentious rivalry. The republic of science was not necessarily a happy family. And not all its members considered themselves professional scientists rather than individuals who practiced science as an avocation out of sheer curiosity. After Condorcet's death, with the establishment of the Institute and the great schools, the adoption of a universal system of education, and the promulgation of Napoleon's decree demanding regular reports from the various classes of the Institute (before he reorganized the Class of Political and Moral Sciences out of existence), communication among scientists and scholars became more intimate and regular — there was a growing professional consciousness — and at formal sessions the presidents of the several classes rendered verbal obeisance to the idea of the unity of science. Despite the more frequent assemblages, however, there was no interference with the individual scientist as he chose his subject and conducted his research in private. The announcement of prize competitions by the various classes of the Institute focused attention upon specific problems in separate areas of knowledge, but there were no coordinated efforts at their solution. Nor was there any interdisciplinary body charged with the formulation of problems in accordance with a preconceived scientific scheme. In this historical environment the plans of Condorcet, and the later ones of Saint-Simon, for the universal administration of science were revolutionary proposals that went against the grain of existing mores.[44]

Drawing his inspiration from Francis Bacon's description of the activities of Salomon and his scientists on New Atlantis, Condorcet proposed a voluntary organization of world scientists acting under a common direction and in accordance with a "perpetual" plan of research. His commentary on the *New Atlantis* was one of the last things he wrote. Viewed historically the manuscript was a key work of transition between eighteenth- and nineteenth-century thought. The bulk of what Condorcet said in the *Esquisse* is readily assimilable with the conceptions of the 1700's; the new emphasis on *organization*, however, was destined to become so overpowering in its intensity that it has by now drowned out most other elements in the idea of progress. What for Bacon had been a utopia in the convention of the seventeenth century was for Condorcet, writing on the eve of his death, a realistic program of action which would surely be put into effect within the next few generations and might even be initiated in his own. The piece is what the editors of the 1840's called it, a fragment, and its tone is discursive; he is answering arguments against the feasibility of the heterodox proposal, refuting an imaginary skeptical interlocutor.

The guiding brain of Condorcet's plan was a supreme body for the direction of science, independent of all state institutions, even those operating under an egalitarian political system. While making men more or less equal was an immediate social goal, Condorcet was well aware that the spirit of equality could degenerate into low envy of excellence, that mediocrity hated dangerous rivals and feared "a penetrating and severe judge in the most modest talent."[45] For all his insistence upon equality in his social and political theory, he recognized the intellectual gulf which separated those people who had managed to acquire sufficient knowledge to carry on the ordinary functions of society from the outstanding scientists of genius for whom the acquisition of truth was the all-absorbing passion of their entire lives. What then could prevent the leveling spirit, albeit on a high plane of excellence, from interfering with the progress of new scientific investigations organized internationally, which genius alone could appreciate?

It was a precondition of Condorcet's utopia of science that the bulk of mankind would be emancipated from the grosser errors of superstition and that scientific achievement, in lieu of power, riches, and military glory, would become the channel into which men of talent naturally drove their energies. The problem for the future was less the intrusion of a stupid tyrant or mass ignorance than how to assure the superiority of the real genius over the charlatan, how to safeguard mankind from embarking upon useless projects which might attract run-of-the-mill rational men but were not the most urgent needs of science. In effect, how would elitist science, having accepted organization for the sake of accelerated development, maintain its independence and deal with democratic controls in an egalitarian society? — a not unfamiliar query in the seventh decade of the twentieth century. Ordinary men could think only in terms of their immediate needs and desires, and if they had a dominant voice in the organization of science it would be almost impossible to agree upon the support of a grandiose plan which would break through the natural limitations of time imposed upon one generation of mankind and the limitations of space imposed upon one scientist or national scientific group. Bacon had dreamed of a monarch who would undertake scientific projects beyond the capacity of any one genius, but there was no assurance for Condorcet that a great king, even if he could be interested in science rather than hunting, would further studies which served the total requirements of science and humanity rather than those which attracted his fancy or increased his power.

Since only scientists could appraise the needs of their discipline, Condorcet contrived a mechanism aimed at guaranteeing their independence from outside influences and at the same time preventing their passions from exerting deleterious effects upon the choice of projects, yet providing for a maximum coordination of all creative efforts. As a *politique* Condorcet was one of the great protectors of the absolute rights of the individual in the face of the state, but when it came to the organization of science new elements were abruptly introduced into his system of values. The individual scientists of the future, even the geniuses among them, would not be able to achieve great progress as long as they continued to operate in isolation, even if they maintained casual contacts with one another. Since the really important discoveries of the future necessitated observations in places dispersed over the whole face of the globe and over a period of many generations, an over-all plan for the collection of data, guaranteeing constancy of observation and uniformity of method, was indispensable. The lone scientist could not undertake projects of this scope because of the limitations of his mortality and of his resources. The new areas of knowledge to be explored henceforth depended upon a massive quantification of scientific experiments and observations.

Like most of his contemporaries, Condorcet was smugly convinced that problems of scientific theory had all been solved or at least were on the verge of solution. His world organization took for granted a common self-evident methodology which was easy of access; modern questions in the philosophy of science did not perturb him, and the prospect of accumulating ever more data and of establishing appropriate correlations among them seemed endlessly fruitful. With scientists agreed upon method, there was a common standard for the evaluation of the separate parts of whatever grand plan was adopted. Scientists could not, without violating their own natures, their inner sense of what was right, espouse a project which was useless or irrelevant. There persisted, to be sure, that old canker of envy and competition, especially among men in the top grades of a scientific hierarchy, and this might lead to conflicts over who should direct the supreme body of science. To mitigate these antagonisms he suggested that final judgment of rank come not from the rivals themselves but from the lower echelons, lesser men, but persons informed, impartial, and free from the passion of rivalry because they were either younger or humbler scientific workers who recognized the limitations of their status. Even if the army of scientists should err somewhat in their selection, the consequences would not be disastrous for mankind, since rough justice was all that was necessary. Quacks and fakers had to be excluded, and for this purpose the judgment of the informed corps of scientists in each discipline was adequate. The opinion even of rational, educated laymen, on the other hand, would not suffice.

Before it could be instituted, the perpetual and universal society for the progress of the sciences had to face stubborn obstacles in human wills and passions. What would persuade the scientific great to abandon the splendid autocracy of their individual laboratories and to join in the common world enterprise? Condorcet's answer was threefold: First, there was a growing consciousness in every field that the problems of science had become far too vast for any one man to aspire to solve them alone. Second, the imminent tremendous increase in the total number of creative scientists would lead to cooperation. In the tenth epoch of the *Esquisse*, by the simple process of multiplying the existing ratio of scientists to educated persons by the prospective factor of increase in the number of men with adequate schooling, he had arrived at the conjecture of an array of scientists that was staggering, at least to the imagination of an eighteenth-century man. In this multitude there would be esteem for everybody, but no single individual genius would tower above the body of science like a Newton. Therefore great scientists, more or less equal in capacity, would not hesitate to welcome one another in joint enterprises. Third, the scientists would rush to participate in the universal society out of curiosity and for the pleasure of learning new truths, passions which in the real scientist overcame and superseded the natural egotist desire for individual fame. "The love of truth assembles there the men whom the sacrifice of ordinary passions has rendered worthy of her; and enlightened nations, aware of all that she can do for the happiness of the human species, lavish upon genius the means of unfolding its activity and its strength." [46]

In his politics Condorcet had provided for frequent revisions of the French constitution. Fearful (as his friend Turgot had taught him to be) of the dangers to intellectual progress of falling into a rut, into a set pattern, he allowed for the review of his scientific grand design by each new generation. The eighteenth-century *philosophes*, possessed by the spirit of innovation, were wary of the dead hand of the past, and Condorcet would not allow the originators of the scientific plan to force future generations into fixed grooves of research. But there was an equivalent hazard if there were no continuity from one epoch to another. In answer to the argument that a partisan contentious spirit in a succeeding age might jettison the whole plan, not only amend it, he recalled that in the history of science the conservative, traditionalist, repetitive spirit had been predominant and was far more to be feared than innovation. The risk of a subsequent overturning of the apple-cart was dismissed with a reiteration of his basic premise that a scientific methodology universally agreed upon would have established general standards which no scientists in the future would dare to violate. Thus there could be revisions of the over-all plan without an interruption of the accumulative process of research from one generation to another.

Embryonic elements of the cooperative spirit destined to permeate the whole corps of world scientists were already present among contemporaries. Scientists reacted with great excitement to the announcement of every new discovery, even if it took place in the most distant land. Why would they be less moved by the annual revelation of the new harvest of truths yielded by their common labors? Science, like all human institutions and social relationships, had to be purified of its "fanaticisms," the self-interest, ambitions, and predilections of its practitioners. This was to be accomplished by a technique similar to that which Condorcet had applied to other social problems, the elaboration of an appropriate administrative device, an institutional arrangement under which it became difficult, almost impossible, for the individual passion for fame to find expression at the cost of excellence. In the end world science would be freed from the dross of personal prejudice; it would become objective.

There lurked another menace to the realization of Condorcet's collegiate body of progressive scientists, rivalry among the scientific disciplines. To offset this spirit of corps competition Condorcet preached a sermon on the unity of the scientific system and illustrated the interdependence of the social and the mathematical and physical sciences. While each scientist's natural preference for his own discipline would not disappear, Condorcet's faith resided in the diffusion of the general concepts of every branch of knowledge among all scientists. With the propagation of the idea of the universality of science, the rivalry among its branches, if not abolished, would at least abate. An exaggerated estimation of one's own science was a trait of mediocrities who were incapable of rising to the top ranks of the profession and therefore consoled themselves by trumpeting the pre-eminence of their special field.

A primary characteristic of Condorcet's scientific society was its independent voluntary nature; it was not state-directed, and scientists joined it freely because they were convinced that it fulfilled their most expansive hopes. This was his facile verbal conciliation of liberty and organization. There had been momentous individual discoveries in the past, and even if the anarchic play of scientific investigation continued, some new truths would emerge fortuitously in the course of future centuries; but "the plan" would greatly increase the quantity of discoveries, their realization would become more certain, the element of chance would be minimized, and, above all, the time factor would be sharply reduced. A rhetorical question was addressed to those men of science reluctant to join the society: by what right did they deprive whole generations of mankind of the enjoyment of the fruits of their researches because of their stubborn unwillingness to organize? It was immoral not to have given birth as soon as possible to a discovery that was potentially feasible; it was an act of perfidy against the ideal of scientific progress. To hasten the revelation of truth with its humanitarian consequences was an article of the scientist's creed. To delay it was antiscientific.

According to one version of the organizational mechanics of Condorcet's scientific society, those who subscribed to the "Fund" could participate in the election of a small number of scientists whose function it would be to draft the over-all plan of operations. On the eve of his death in 1794, after his dismal experiences in the Legislative Assembly, Condorcet was none too sanguine about the efficiency of great public bodies. He therefore advised that the election of the scientists had best be arranged in writing, without speeches. "One must in general avoid any large meeting. This is the only means of obtaining true equality, of avoiding the influence of intrigue, of charlatanism, and of verbiage; of conserving for simple truth the whole of its empire, of being led by knowledge and not by passions." [47] Condorcet the scientific expert was becoming uneasy about democratic parliamentary procedures. He died before his distrust of revolutionary assemblies was given forthright public expression; his successors Saint-Simon and Comte would no longer be bound by his populist past.

In return for a contribution to the fund, each subscriber received scientific papers and a decennial report on new discoveries (omitting those of too recent date). While a contributor might designate the particular project on which he wanted his money spent, a tenth of all collections automatically became part of the budget for the maintenance of the long-term or perpetual projects. Condorcet was still on the alert lest any one generation exercise an excessive influence on the future progress of science by abandoning certain branches of knowledge completely. In the decisions of the elected scientists, a very high majority would be required for the alteration of a basic part of the plan, a simple plurality for modifications of detail. An annual renewal of a third of the directing body — perhaps a chance recollection of the American constitution — would assure continuity without allowing scientific school prejudices to become deeply entrenched. Though state aid would not be rejected, it would be subject to the same conditions as the subscriptions of other members. The scientific society might avail itself of governmental facilities, but the character of the free relationship between a public power and an autonomous association had to be preserved. Since the "historical review" had taught him that whenever state power became the controller of science decadence invariably set in — as with the Arabs — he was opposed to direct governmental participation in his scientific society. "It is for the association alone to judge in an independent manner what it believes should be undertaken for the progress of the sciences. It is for the public power to judge, with the same independence, which of these projects appears to merit either its concurrence or its munificence." [48] A self-imposed neutrality on the part of the modern state in its relations to science was one of Condorcet's more naive illusions. The organizer of science tried to balance nicely elements of innovation and conservation, elements of freedom and constraint.

Condorcet's commentary on the *New Atlantis* was only a fragment and he never had an opportunity to iron out its inconsistencies. It is thus not quite clear whether the basic unit of the society's organization is a state or the whole world. He began by referring to the "general union of the scientists in a universal republic of the sciences." [49] and then somehow switched to a national unit. In the end he reverted to the prospect of a world scientific society and proposed among its labors the establishment of a universal language and the somewhat cryptic though at the moment highly relevant "execution of a monument which shelters the sciences even from a general revolution of the globe."

From the Institut de France manuscripts it appears that while Condorcet was confident that the spread of knowledge virtually insured mankind against any recrudescence of barbarism it could not be safeguarded from "an upheaval of the globe which, without entirely destroying the human species and without swallowing up in an eternal abyss the monuments which had been raised, would nevertheless cause the arts and sciences and their fragile repositories, including all the languages spoken today, to disappear." This was an obvious echo of the works of Nicolas Boulanger, the young engineer and member of the Holbach circle who had left a number of fantastic works based upon the hypothesis that the earth had through geological time already experienced countless deluges, each of which had destroyed a high civilization. Condorcet grappled with the idea of how progress might survive the apparently inevitable cataclysms of nature, and he finally found an answer in the lesson of the Egyptian hieroglyphs. If contemporary mankind incorporated its knowledge in symbolic forms and engraved them on steles capable of surviving the most terrible catastrophes, a future philosopher, a Plato for example, would somehow be able to divine their meaning even though he understood none of the languages. In this way even after the deluge mankind would not have to start from scratch but could move forward from a high level of scientific knowledge.[50] The theme of total destruction will occur again among the prophets, especially in Saint-Simon's early writings and in Fourier. Condorcet's solution is a poignant expression of the passionate will to render eternal the scientific treasure house of man.

WORK PROJECTS

PERHAPS the most remarkable aspect of Condorcet's theory is his blueprint of practical works for the realistic utopia of the future. This guesswork of genius actually foretold the direction of scientific inquiry in many fields for the next hundred and fifty years. Such prognostication about the prospect of science by scientists is, of course, one of the great self-fulfilling prophecies of the modern era. It does not often fail.

The second part of the fragment on the *New Atlantis* presented a catalogue of the areas of research most appropriate for a society which had burst the narrow limitations of time and space in planning for the future. Daily and perpetual observations in astronomy, meteorology, the natural history of man, and rural economy seemed the most fruitful activities. If organized on an international scale astronomical observatories could be located on optimum sites at appropriate intervals. Meteorological stations could be dispersed in the same way (he raised the possibility of using mechanical instruments to make and record observations). Most of all he concentrated on projects which assembled quantities of data relating to the science of man. Two methods were proposed, one involving the general observation of the total population of a country, another, the intensive investigation of a limited number of specimens. Vital statistics would use the former, medicine the latter technique. Together these studies would solve all medical and moral problems, would cure disease, end epidemics, increase longevity, and lead to the "limitless perfectibility of the human faculties and the social order." [51] The republic of science would undertake a study of all factors which affect the deterioration of the human mechanism: heredity, education, climate, the laws, occupations, pleasures, habits, exercises. Scientists would measure the influence of race. The relations among human physiology and intellectual powers and moral behavior presented perplexing problems to the eighteenth-century philosopher of progress, for which he expected solutions from the scientists of the future. "We know that absolute equality of aptitudes does not exist at the moment of birth, neither for any of our senses, nor for any of our faculties. But new observations alone may teach us whether there exist between the differences which one can notice in physical organization and the variations in the intellectual faculties determinable relationships or whether our knowledge must forever be limited merely to knowing that these relations exist. The same reflections apply to our moral faculties." [52]

Condorcet propounded a series of questions on the relations between physiology and psychology to which, after a century and a half of research, few answers are yet available. "Are human faculties perfectible only by the perfection of the organs which produce them? Can the faculties be perfected only by the progress of methods for the development of the organs, for directing them, strengthening them through exercise . . .?" [53] He wondered whether a state of moral virtue might not be produced in man by a combination of institutional changes and improved heredity to the point "where every action contrary to the right of another man will be as impossible physically as an act of barbarism committed in cold blood is today for most men." [54] He looked to a quantification of data for confirmation of his intuitive belief that differences in the moral and intellectual aptitudes of the two sexes had been grossly exaggerated.

Other experimental proposals ranged from mineralogy, organic chemistry, geography, to human and animal anatomy. Since world prosperity might lead to an increase in population and tax the world food supply, Condorcet advised the organized scientists to study methods for the maximum utilization of foods and fuels, to investigate the nutritional elements in various products, the feasibility of manufacturing animal and vegetable substances artificially, the utilization of substances which were wasted, the possibilities of diminishing consumption without a concomitant loss of enjoyment. The institutional and technological problems of a society devoted to the pleasure principle were discussed, but the moral absolutes of hedonism were never called into question. These practical researches might not carry much glory, but for that very reason they should be undertaken by the universal society.

In the gamut of suggestions there is a marked de-emphasis of physics and mechanics, understandable in an age which imagined that the fundamental principles of these sciences had been established forever, that the possibilities of new findings were on the verge of exhaustion. The life sciences and the social sciences had now become the focus of scholarly attention, and it was precisely these areas of knowledge that depended upon quantification of data, requiring the cooperation of a vast number of researchers. Condorcet had not broken with the dominant mathematical spirit; by utilizing the calculus of probabilities in the social sciences he proposed to "mathematicize" social phenomena and finally to introduce predictability and law into the science of man. In his famous edition of Pascal in 1776 (the *philosophes* were always itching for a confrontation with the man in whom they recognized their profound enemy), Condorcet attacked him for sharply bifurcating the world into two separate kingdoms, the mathematical and the moral, allowing certitude to the former and abandoning the latter to despair and impotent confusion. There was now a bridge between the realms, Condorcet maintained, the calculus of probabilities, and once this discovery was applied moral problems would be resolved as scientifically as geometric ones. He rejected the famous Pascalian distinction between the *esprit géométrique* and the *esprit de finesse*; their methods were similar, not contradictory. In response to Pascalian jeremiads on the feebleness of human knowledge, Condorcet countered again and again with the new panacea, the science of probabilities.

In 1785 he had written a long technical treatise entitled *Essai sur l'application de l'analyse à la probabilité des décisions rendues à la pluralité des voix* to demonstrate in a specific sociopolitical case study the feasibility of reducing moral data to mathematical terms. This had been a favorite topic of conversation with the middle-aged Turgot; even in moments of doubt it had led him to hope that the "human species would of necessity make progress toward happiness and perfection." [55] While Condorcet was not confident that all aspects of human behavior could be presented in mathematical form, he drafted an impressive list of social phenomena which were amenable to statistical calculation by governments or learned societies.[56] His technique for forecasting majority decisions, the central proposition of his work, is of more than passing interest to the contemporary public opinion analyst. Condorcet the professional mathematician, even more than his friend the great bureaucrat, remained suspicious of truths which had to be clothed in eloquence and thus suffered from an "admixture of hyperbole." His own revolutionary experiences as a politician, a pamphleteer, a committee reporter on educational projects to the National Assembly, and a framer of constitutions only fortified his skepticism about the validity of knowledge which could not be mathematicized.

A brief article published posthumously in the *Journal d'instruction sociale* set forth the first principles of a mathematical social science (*mathématique sociale*) with even greater detail than his earlier, prerevolutionary work. Since all judgments and opinions were based upon an almost automatic presumption of probability, there would always be an advantage on the side of the man who acted by scientific calculation over the one who merely responded by instinct or routine. Those truths which were impervious to calculation were in effect so vague that they were useless because they could not be applied. Truths arrived at by abstract reasoning alone could become transformed into their very opposites, into mere prejudices, when they were raised to a level of generality not appropriate to them. The "new science" would be of particular significance during the aftermath of a revolution which called for political and moral decisions based upon data computed with precision in order to establish truths beyond the realm of passion and the sophisms of self-interest. A revolution confused values, and only by invoking mathematical clarity could the dangers of the stormy period during which the passions dominated action be passed in safety.

In the same article Condorcet spelled out the theoretical justification for the application of mathematics to political and moral sciences: it was a direct derivation from the fundamental idea of equality. Our essential sensate similarity made us calculable. "Since all men who inhabit the same country have more or less the same needs and since they also generally have the same tastes and the same ideas of utility what has *value* for one of them generally has it for all." [57] By following out this postulate it would be possible for the state to estimate probabilities of desire and to legislate accordingly. In his last manuscripts there continually obtruded grave misgivings about the decisions of any public bodies which were not technically competent as experts. With the accumulation of sufficient data and the application of the calculus of probabilities the state could be run by social mathematics — without debates. With one leap the first sociologist of scientific creativity traversed the age of middle-class parliamentarism and arrived at the ideal of the all-knowing scientific technician as the ruler of society.

THE PLEASURES OF FORETELLING

MORAL progress ended up as a conditioning process, functioning through education and the exercise of the laws, which made a man identify his own interest with the common interest, constrained him to harness his immediate, direct, egotist desires and passions and to act in harmony with the dictates of universal reason and justice — alternative ways of defining the "common interest." That legitimate human rights never could be in contradiction one with another was an axiom of the optimist moralism of the age. If they appeared to be at odds, then error had crept in somewhere. Almost all social conflicts were the result of inadequate institutional and juridic mechanics, amenable to easy remedy. The contests among men which seemed at first glance to defy any possible settlement, conflicting passions for the same person, for example, were minor exceptions to the general principle, and even they were subject to institutional control; the intensity of passion in such rivalries could be reduced. "I believe," Condorcet concluded in his *Fragment de l'histoire de la xe époque*, "that I have proved the possibility and indicated the means of resolving what is perhaps the most important problem for the human species: perfectibility of the broad masses, that is to say the problem of rendering right judgment, an independent sound reason, an enlightened conscience, a habitual submission to the rules of humanity and justice, almost universal qualities, so that as a consequence the normal state of man is guided by truth even though subject to error, is subordinate in its conduct to the rules of morality even though sometimes drawn into crime, is nurtured on gentle and pure feelings which unite him to his family, to his friends, to the unfortunate, to his country, to the whole of humanity, even though he is still susceptible of being led astray by personal passions — a state in which man is as happy as he is permitted by the pains, the needs, and the losses which are the necessary consequence of the general laws of the universe." [58]

When rational conduct finally became normative behavior for all mankind (with only rare lapses into crime and injustice), then a state of society would be reached where the whole emphasis of human activity could be shifted. In this happy age the state would be administered by officials who exercised the powers of office for brief periods of time, because the minimum aptitude requirement necessary for the posts was within the common capacity of all men and offices were readily interchangeable among average citizens. There would be no special bureaucratic class trained in the operations of the state, and public office would not be sought after as a great honor, for it would merely be a commonplace function. No corps would have a vested interest in government. In this ideal state the laws would not allow for the concentration of great fortunes in a few hands. Though there would be no communism of property, the gulf between the richest and the poorest would be narrowed by abolition of the economic measures which in the past fostered the accumulation of wealth and by insurance schemes which protected all men from the miseries of unemployment and of abject poverty. The passion for riches would be diminished because great fortune would no longer be an important source of distinction — no more than would be the governing power — and it would confer no unusual privileges upon its holders.

Though glory in war had long since ceased to attract mankind after the dethronement of the tyrants who originally provoked international strife, men were still zealous for esteem and they still had a drive to surpass other men; the competitive spirit was inborn and could not be completely eradicated. As in Turgot, there is a feeling that emulation is a necessary stimulus to action and a safeguard against lethargy. What should these new men of the future, well-conditioned and well-nourished, do with themselves? What activities would then attract men of energy and zeal, since they could not excel in war, government, or wealth? Condorcet's plan for the organization of a society for the advancement of scientific research was the only possible outlet. Man was thus turned by

Condorcet into a scientific animal, the direct consequence of his being a rational animal. The whole of society would be deliberately organized for the production of scientists and science. His imagination was excited by the prospect of a vastly increased annual yield of science and technology as a direct result of the mere multiplication of science-producing educated men. The world of nature would be opened up to exploitation. The food supply could be increased virtually indefinitely. If the population problem should ever become troublesome, then rational man would know how to curtail his breeding propensities. Before Malthus' attack, Condorcet clearly foresaw many of the difficulties which a rapid increase in population would entail. His answers may not satisfy neo-Malthusians, but they have a straightforward commonsense ring which belies the caricatures that have been made of the prophets. In the end of the days he may turn out to be more realistic than his matter-of-fact critics. "If from the perfection of hygiene there results a greater life span, a greater fertility, the survival of a greater number of children; if the perfection of medicine postpones the decline of life and the death of most individuals; if this increase of population exceeds the limit which the annual production of materials of consumption can attain, will not the human race find itself unable to escape destruction . . .?" [59] Condorcet's panacea is simply contraception. Modern man can regulate his reproduction without curtailing his pleasure. In warrior societies the prevention of births was looked upon with horror because a large population was necessary for conquest. The church, which viewed all pleasure as a crime, had naturally condemned sexual gratification without intent to reproduce. When rational men of the future controlled parenthood, contraception would reduce infidelity and perversion. If the love of children is real, then an element of calculation must enter into their birth. There might come a time when a further population increase would be considered contrary to the general interest.

Condorcet was equally forthright in his manuscript discussion both of medical cures for venereal disease and of the nature of contraceptive substances. In publishing his work his executors were far more circumspect. He refuted the argument that these medicines would lead to venereal excesses. If there was a way of rendering all mushrooms less indigestible and of eliminating the poisonous ones, would anyone argue that such discoveries should be kept secret because they might lead to gluttony? He recognized that any scientists of his day who presumed to read papers on sexual diseases would be expelled from the academy. For the future he expected open treatment, without prudery, of medical questions which were of vital concern to the health and pleasure of mankind.

Condorcet also examined the complicated consequences of a hypothetical scientific discovery which might render it possible to predetermine the sex of offspring. Would males motivated by prejudice and passion tend to increase the number of women disproportionately in order to have younger girls available for their lusts? After going through an elaborate calculus of desires he reached the comforting conclusion that in the future the number of the two sexes would remain more or less equal despite the capacity to produce a given sex at will.[60] In his discussion of artificial insemination Condorcet hinted at the improvement of the species through eugenic measures. The absolute equality between the sexes which he foresaw led him to interesting psychological insights into the nature of the love relationships resulting from the new independence of women. "Everything which can contribute to rendering individuals more independent is also a good relative to the happiness which they can reciprocally bestow upon each other; their happiness will be greater when the individual action is more voluntary." [61]

But had he never foreseen the possibilities of fantastic new weapons of destruction in flying machines or balloons? "I shall not stop over the futile fear of dangers which might result from the art of traversing the air," he wrote with assurance in one manuscript, "because since it would be impossible to keep it secret, the capacity to harm cannot be increased without augmenting that of defense." [62] Nonetheless he was at times troubled by the idea that some unnamed discoveries, which could not be ruled out as possibilities, might impede the march of perfectibility. Such transient misgivings, however, remained buried in his manuscripts.[63]

Without fear of illness and starvation man would become gentle and the problem of criminality would be reduced to insignificance. Once the scientists discovered and promulgated the laws of happiness it was inconceivable that men should be so stupid as not to implement them. If chemistry found a new dye it was immediately utilized; why should sound social law not enjoy similar instantaneous application and spontaneous acquiescence? When retrogressive institutional sources, the external causes of evil, were removed, man would be left with his pristine virtue, free to further the advancement of science. Through technological improvements man's senses would receive a new extension into what Sébastien Mercier had called the two infinities, the telescopic and the microscopic worlds. This sensory progress could be achieved without altering human nature, but there was also a prospect of organic improvement in the human mechanism. That acquired characteristics were inherited was a widespread hypothesis among many eighteenth-century thinkers well before Lamarck's exposition of his evolutionist thesis in 1801. This doctrine, perhaps more than any other belief, was proof positive for Condorcet in the tenth epoch of the *Esquisse* that the intellectual and moral attainments of one generation could be passed on intact to its successor. Any possible remnant of doubt about the inevitable and infinite progress of the human spirit was dispelled once the human organism was shown to be subject to biological perfectibility. Progress was indefinite. This became its quintessential attribute. It vied with and replaced the infinity of God. Only after having reached one high level could man even conceive of the still loftier peaks which loomed ahead. The wildest visions could not foretell the ultimate capabilities of man, because it would require a far more developed mind even to imagine them. The favorite analogy in Condorcet's theory is the mathematical progression toward infinity.

The totality of nature may never be known, but that does not mean that any specific thing is unknowable. There is only the not yet known. This is another sense in which progress is infinite — the continuous acquisition of the not yet known at the same time that man recognizes his incapacity ever to possess the whole of knowledge. Man's constant struggle with refractory nature, utilizing the laws wrested from nature as the most powerful weapon leading to its subjugation — a conception later dramatized by the Saint-Simonians and Marx — was portrayed with eloquence in many of Condorcet's minor published works and in his manuscripts. In the *Mémoire sur l'instruction* he wrote of the "eternal conflict between nature and genius, between man and things." He described the assault in grand terms: "Interrogated everywhere, observed in all its aspects, attacked simultaneously by a variety of methods and instruments capable of tearing away its secrets, nature will at last be forced to let them escape." [64] In his acceptance speech before the Academy of Sciences he had announced, "Every discovery is a conquest over nature, and over chance." [65] While man is subject to the laws of nature, "he has the power of modifying these laws, of making them contribute to his well-being. This power may be feeble and insignificant in each individual, but if it is observed in the species and is exercised over a great span of many generations, ever growing with the progress of the human mind, it can ultimately balance that of nature." [66] This is the most daring manifesto of eighteenth-century *hubris* — man and nature enter the arena of the distant future equal in strength.

The movement of future progress described by Condorcet can be likened to the advance of the whole of mankind on an open plain. In the front rank, ahead of their fellow men, the scientific elite are dashing forward at a speed that is continually being augmented; behind the main body portions of humanity lag because they have been duped by Machiavellian despots and their priestly minions. But the forward thrust of the great scientists is of such Herculean power that it pulls the whole of mankind along with it. And as they advance in time men are ever healthier, happier, more acute in their sense perceptions, more precise in their reasoning power, more equal in wealth and opportunity, more humane in their moral behavior.

The vision was so compelling that judgments of worth could henceforth be expressed only in terms of the conception of perfectibility. The good of all future generations — not the individual, not the nation, not even the age — was the proper criterion for human action. Moral judgment was the verdict of all future time.

How was it possible for a materialist, a sensationalist, a believer in the rather simplistic code of the harmony of self-interests, to achieve this intense passion for progress and work? The doctrine of benevolence, the outgoing compassion of man, had come to the rescue. Natural man had sympathy for his kind — that was an innate characteristic of his emotional being, Rousseau and a long line of Scottish moralists had taught. When in his fantasy Condorcet extended sympathy from contemporary mankind to all future generations of humanity a vast new horizon was opened. *Bienveillance* was now borne aloft on the wings of infinity. Once aware of this sympathy, man in the present could enjoy the delights of the future by working toward it or by mere contemplation of the ultimate bliss. The last page of the *Esquisse* is a noble period depicting the consolations of the idea of progress even under the reign of a tyrant and an obscurantist.[67] To sustain the utilitarian martyr, Progress, the new god of the age, had arrogated to itself a tender solace of the old religion — the dream of future beatitude. "In the contemplation of this vision he receives the reward of his efforts for the progress of reason, for the defense of liberty. He then dares to join his exertions to the eternal chain of human destinies. There he finds the true recompense of virtue; it lies in the pleasure of having accomplished an enduring good, which fate will never again destroy by an unfortunate reversal restoring prejudice and slavery. This contemplation is for him an asylum where the memory of his persecutors cannot pursue him. Living in thought with man re-established in his rights as well as in the dignity of his nature, he forgets the man whom avarice, fear, or envy torments and corrupts. Then he truly is with his equals in an Elysium which his reason has been able to create and which his love for humanity embellishes with the purest joys." [68] Here the eighteenth century left its final message to the ages.

III

Comte de Saint-Simon
THE PEAR IS RIPE

J'ai vu Saint-Simon le prophète,
Riche d'abord, puis endetté,
Qui des fondements jusqu'au faîte
Refaisait la société.
Plein de son oeuvre commencée,
Vieux, pour elle il tendait la main,
Sûr qu'il embrassait la pensée
Qui doit sauver le genre humain.

"Les Fous,"
in *Chansons de Béranger*
(Paris, 1859), II, 301.

"For the past twelve days, Gentlemen, I have been busy explaining how you can best unite your efforts for our enterprise. For the past three hours I have been trying to summarize my thoughts on this subject. . . . The pear is ripe, you must pluck it. The last part of our work will perhaps be misunderstood. By attacking the religious system of the Middle Ages only one thing has been proved: that it is no longer in harmony with the progress of positive science. But it was wrong to conclude that religion itself has tended to disappear. Religion must bring itself into harmony with the progress of the sciences. I repeat to you, the pear is ripe, you must pluck it. Forty-eight hours after the appearance of our next publication we shall be a party."

Report on the death of Saint-Simon,
"Notice historique,"
in *Oeuvres*, I, 121–122.

THE GRAND SEIGNEUR SANS-CULOTTES

OF all the modern prophets the Count Claude Henri de Rouvroy de Saint-Simon was the most picaresque; he resembled a character out of *Gil Blas* more than a traditional seer. [1] But when the spirit of foretelling hovers about, it may possess the most unlikely subjects. Born in Paris on October 17, 1760, he belonged to a collateral branch of the same family as the famous Duke, author of the voluminous *Memoirs of Saint-Simon* on the court of Louis XIV and the Regency. Traditions about his youth gathered by disciples depict him as stubborn and self-willed, in such continual and bitter conflict with his father that the elder Saint-Simon once imprisoned him for his contumely. At the age of seventeen, the young Saint-Simon received his first military commission, and in 1779 he set sail from Brittany with the Touraine Regiment to fight in the War for American Independence, not as a dashing volunteer, but as a line officer obeying royal orders. After participating in a number of engagements in the Antilles, his contingent joined Washington at Yorktown. During the battle he acquitted himself creditably in command of a section of artillery and was later elected a member of the Society of Cincinnatus in recognition of his services. The French continued the war in the West Indies after Cornwallis' capitulation, and Saint-Simon saw action again at St. Kitts. In the great naval engagement — disastrous for the French — between the forces of Admirals Rodney and De Grasse in April 1782, Saint-Simon was on the flagship. Stunned by a cannon ball, he was taken prisoner in the general surrender, and was interned in Jamaica. After his liberation, he presented to the Viceroy of Mexico his first grand project, a plan for an interoceanic canal running through Lake Nicaragua — and he was rebuffed.

Back in France, Saint-Simon was promoted at regular intervals, but the life of an officer in barracks was dull, and he took leave from the army. In Holland in 1786 he involved himself in an abortive plan to join the Dutch and the French in an attempt to drive the English out of India. Then he turned up in Spain, where in cooperation with Count Cabarrus, father of the future chief mistress of Barras, he sponsored another unsuccessful canal project, to link Madrid with the sea. While in Spain he met a Saxon, Count Redern, the Prussian Ambassador, who lent him a sum of money presumably for investment in French securities — the beginning of a strange relationship.

Upon his return to France during the early months of the Revolution, Saint-Simon commenced to play a complicated role, commuting between Paris and the provinces. In Falvy, Marchéle-pot, Cambrai, Péronne, towns near his ancestral estates, he acted the enthusiastic partisan of the Revolution, helping to draft local *cahiers*, presiding at popular assemblies, delivering revolutionary speeches, and commanding the national guard at moments of crisis. Simultaneously he bought extensive church lands with small down payments, profiting from the steady drop in the value of the assignats. On September 20, 1793, when the Jacobin wave was high, Saint-Simon formally abdicated his noble name and titles and assumed an earthy peasant surname, Bonhomme. Numerous acts of republican virtue, the adoption of aged citizens and the purchase of animals for needy peasants, brought him favorable repute among the local people of his ancestral communes. In Paris, by laying out small deposits, he came into the possession of mansions of nobles who had emigrated or been guillotined. Since he had made his first investments with money given him by Count Redern, he was under the impression that they had established an informal partnership in which he was the active member. To play safe, the deals were negotiated under a host of false names. The enterprises were vast and rumor embroidered upon them; there was even a tale that he had made a bid for Notre Dame de Paris. Saint-Simon habitually resided near the Palais Royal and frequented the society of other speculators, a motley group in which international bankers, foreign spies, Dantonists of the right, and Hébertists of the extreme left were intermingled. They led licentious lives, in sharp contrast with the Incorruptible One who dominated the Committee of Public Safety. When Robespierre finally moved against the whole crew, he was able to throw their heads into a common basket by using the police agent's technique of guilt by association.

Saint-Simon was arrested, though probably in error, on No-

vember 19, 1793, during one of the roundups of international
bankers and foreign agents. The government seems to have been
looking for the Simon brothers, who were Belgian bankers. In
prison Saint-Simon protested his innocence in a long, carefully
drafted memoir to the Committee of Public Safety, and the local
patriots of Picardy, among whom Saint-Simon had shown his revolutionary zeal on more than one occasion, wrote numerous testi-
monials of civic virtue for him. He behaved most circumspectly
in the antechamber of death and cautiously avoided participation
in any of the plots against Robespierre which General Ronsin was
hatching among the desperate men in the prisons.

Saint-Simon never was tried before the revolutionary tribunal
and he survived the Terror. The original down payments on his
vast holdings in Paris and the provinces had preserved his title to
these properties even while he was in prison, and once he was
liberated he came to own them outright by paying the balance of
the price in almost worthless assignats. He led a wild life as a
member of the Barras circle, toying with Directory politics, new
constitutional schemes, and all manner of novel industrial and
commercial projects. In his salon he entertained lavishly, and
invited as his guests bankers, politicians, intellectuals, and artists.
He played the Maecenas and subsidized bright young scientists.
Learning intrigued him as much as finance, and he dabbled in all
the mathematical and physical sciences, in the psychology and
social doctrines of the *idéologues*. He was a brilliant conversationalist, witty, obscene in the fashion of the Directory, cynical, and
yet moved by a strange passion for projects to revolutionize science
and society. During this period his plans never went beyond the
animated talk of the dinner table.

Count Redern appeared in Paris in 1797 and for a while gorged
himself on the *punch aux oeufs* and truffles that Saint-Simon
served. But he was growing uneasy both about the extravagance
of his partner's expenditures and the wild financial and industrial
projects which he was promoting. Saint-Simon thought that
Redern was a philosophical soul-mate, and when the German asked
for a dissolution of their partnership he nonchalantly left the details to his discretion. Redern drew up the documents which broke
their financial union and Saint-Simon took his share, withdrew

from business, and determined henceforth to study and to work solely on projects for the betterment of mankind.

Saint-Simon was married on August 7, 1801, to Alexandrine-Sophie Goury de Champgrand, the daughter of a former comrade in arms and fellow-speculator of the Palais Royal. It appears to have been a marriage of convenience. She was penniless and he wanted an elegant hostess for his salon. Sophie was a literary lady and she brought a contingent of artists, composers, and musicians to their parties. In later life she described her embarrassment when Saint-Simon tried to go back on the chaste arrangement he had made with her. She was amused but also somewhat frightened by his philosophical projects, and on June 24, 1802, they were divorced.

There is a very strong anglophile undercurrent in all Saint-Simon's writings. On a journey to England in March 1802 after the Peace of Amiens, he learned to appreciate its laws. How deeply he had been involved earlier with the English Foreign Office remains a subject of conjecture. It is a matter of record that he acted as one of Lord Malmesbury's French informants, though probably not a paid agent, during the peace negotiations of 1797 at Lille.

In 1802 Saint-Simon traveled to Switzerland, where, according to Saint-Simonian tradition, he proposed at Coppet to Madame de Staël, recently bereaved of her husband. What was probably the first edition of the *Lettres d'un habitant de Genève* was printed at Geneva during this trip. It was addressed "à l'humanité." The edition which became more generally known was entitled *Lettres d'un habitant de Genève à ses contemporains* and was distributed if not actually published by a Paris bookseller in 1803. Both editions were anonymous and neither bore a place or date of publication. A copy was addressed to the First Consul from Geneva, accompanied by a curious letter, full of adulation, soliciting his opinion of the work. The *Lettres d'un habitant de Genève* was ignored by contemporaries, and Saint-Simon never made reference to it in later life. His disciple, the eminent mathematician Olinde Rodrigues, discovered the work in 1826 and printed it in 1832. A strange first book for a middle-aged adventurer to produce, it is the only serious writing of his prosperous period. Almost all the ideas he later developed in his streams of reiterative pamphlets are here in embryo.

During the two or three years after the appearance of the *Lettres d'un habitant de Genève*, Saint-Simon spent the rest of the fortune allotted to him by the dissolution of the Redern partnership, and by 1805 he was penniless. Then began a long succession of pleadings for money from the friends and acquaintances of his affluent days. Many of them had been assimilated by the Imperial régime and occupied cabinet posts and offices of importance in the bureaucracy. Usually Saint-Simon's begging met with stony silence, and the replies he did receive were not generous. Perhaps it was the tone of his letters which left the men in power cold. Even when he solicited aid he did so with the arrogance of a noble of the old monarchy. He had a right to their purse because he and he alone held the key to the progress of mankind. In 1807 Count Ségur obtained for him a job as copyist in the government pawn-shop at 1200 francs a year, not much more than a good day laborer's wage.

Saint-Simon's passion for knowledge grew stronger in his poverty. He spent long nights after work spinning out his philosophical projects, until he fell ill and spit blood. When he had reached the depths of misery, a savior appeared in the person of his former servant Diard, who took him under his care and provided for him. Curious scientific intuitions poured forth in an outburst of disorganized tracts: *Introduction aux travaux scientifiques du XIXe siècle* (1807); *Nouvelle encyclopédie* (1810); *Histoire de l'homme* (1810); *Mémoire sur la science de l'homme* (1813); *Travail sur la gravitation universelle* (1813). When he could not afford to print he copied in manuscript. As soon as a mere sketch of an idea was completed, he sent it around to members of the Institute, to scientific establishments, and to the Emperor. Accompanying letters asked financial aid to help him complete his projects; but he needed more than money; he wanted advice and criticism, most of all sanction and praise. Most scientists did not even deign to cut the pages of the brochures addressed to them, and copies were discovered untouched in their libraries after their death. At best, they sent formal notice of receipt. The crueler men among them mockingly expressed their lack of interest in his plans. Cut to the quick, Saint-Simon rejoined with bitterness, challenging the scientific geniuses of the age to spiritual combat. His letters became a series of wild ravings about genius, his mission, and the persecutions he endured from his enemies. Interspersed among the psychopathic tirades there are moving passages about his passion for glory, written in the grand romantic manner. A family genealogy traced the Saint-Simons back to Charlemagne, and on more than one occasion his great ancestor appeared to him in a vision. They both had the same mission, separated though they were by a thousand years — the spiritual and temporal reorganization of European society.

During this period Saint-Simon turned to a more practical solution of his financial troubles by reopening in public his final property settlement with Redern, who had in the meantime become a respectable French property-owner engaged in useful agricultural and manufacturing projects. Saint-Simon got hold of intermediaries and letters were exchanged, after which the whole Saint-Simon–Redern affair was published to the world. Saint-Simon complained that he had played the dupe in allowing Redern to control their final arrangements. His simplicity was attributable to their unique philosophico-psychological relationship, which had led him to believe that their two souls moved as one. Redern found the moral blackmail of his eccentric former partner annoying, and from time to time he tried to appease him with a pittance, but when Saint-Simon kept printing scurrilous letters on the affair, Redern grew stern and fortified himself in his legal position. Saint-Simon moved to Alençon to harass Redern in the province where he was gaining prestige, but he failed to make any headway, and during one of the journeys he fell seriously ill. Descriptions of his state sound like madness. He was put into a private hospital for the insane in Charenton and was treated by the famous Dr. Pinel.

But the man rebounds. Sometime before 1814 he recovered. To get rid of his pretensions to a portion of his ancestral estate, his own family settled a small annuity upon him. When he returned to Paris during the Hundred Days he even got a post in the library of the Arsenal. The darkness seems to have left his brain, and at fifty-four he embarked upon a new career. The scientific projects were forgotten, he never mentioned the strange

brochures of the Empire, and he became an active political polem-
icist during the Restoration period.

Apparently Saint-Simon had enough money to hire a secretary,
and he soon attracted respectable friends and collaborators. From
then on he never worked alone; there were always young men
by his side who edited his copy, joined with him in publication,
and accepted his guidance. He had an eye for brilliance. The first
of a series of secretaries was Augustin Thierry, the future historian,
with whom he published a scheme entitled *De la réorganisation
de la société européenne* during the Congress of Vienna. It was
more than an adaptation of the Abbé de Saint-Pierre's plan for
universal peace, which it resembled superficially; Saint-Simon
placed his emphasis on an integral federation of Europe, the cornerstone of which was to be an Anglo-French alliance. Another
thesis put forth in the pamphlet concerned the superiority of the
modern commercial over the military nation, an idea which Benjamin Constant was developing with greater subtlety.

The political brochures which Saint-Simon wrote during the
First Restoration and the Hundred Days won him admittance into
the circle of liberal economists and publicists identified with Jean-
Baptiste Say and Charles Dunoyer. He ceased to be treated as a
mere crackpot, though he was still considered "an original" by
his more sedate friends. His baptism of respectability was so efficacious that he was even received in the salons of the Parisian
bankers Laffitte and Ardouin. The new relationships included enterprising industrialists such as Ternaux, the great textile manufacturer. Saint-Simon became a member of a party. The *bourgeoisie*, which had grown fully conscious of its power under Napoleon
even when dominated by him, was now confronted with a serious
attempt on the part of the *émigrés* thirsting for vengeance to re-
constitute intact the ancient régime with its noble prerogatives and
disparagement of industry and commerce. There was developing
a full-blown struggle of a new ruling class against the restoration
hopes of the old, and it was being fought out in a parliamentary
régime. Saint-Simon became a more or less official propagandist
for the bourgeois. He organized a series of periodical publications:
L'Industrie (1816–1818); *Le Politique* (1819); *L'Organisateur*
(1819–1820); *Du système industriel* (1821–1822); *Catéchisme*

des industriels (1823–1824); *Opinions littéraires, philosophiques et industrielles* (1825). The issues appeared intermittently, in part to evade rules of censorship on regular serial publications, but chiefly because there were always money troubles. Each new publication was launched with great fanfare and a laborious campaign of fund solicitation from the bankers and industrialists whose interests Saint-Simon was espousing. When after a few numbers the enterprise failed to take hold — for there were many more sober and trustworthy rivals who made demands on the purse of the *bourgeoisie* — Saint-Simon formed a new organization and tried again. On more than one occasion he went beyond the polemical line that his proper banker and industrialist friends were ready to support. While they were willing to have him extol the virtues of the industrial class and its historic right to assume control of the state, they were not yet prepared to attack frontally the power of the revived Catholic Church. When Saint-Simon used such dangerous phrases as "terrestrial morality," which would not have troubled in the least an eighteenth-century bourgeois, many of the Restoration bankers dropped him cold.

In February 1820 he had an even more unfortunate experience. *L'Organisateur* had included in its very first issue a literary artifice — the famous Parable — in which Saint-Simon contrasted the possible consequences to France of the death of her foremost scientists, artists, artisans, industrialists, and bankers with the death of all the leading nobles and officials of the bureaucracy. On February 13 Louvel assassinated the Duke of Berry, and Saint-Simon was tried as one of the moral instigators of the crime. It was a profound affront to a man who abhorred revolutionary violence with a consistency which was remarkable in a figure so mercurial. He managed to escape punishment after a complicated judicial proceeding.

Augustin Thierry, a collaborator of 1814, soon left him, and in his place came a young graduate of the Ecole Polytechnique, Auguste Comte. The new secretary had a well-organized mind and a forceful, logical method of presentation. At first he allowed himself to be known as a pupil of Saint-Simon's, but he soon chafed at the subordinate position. After Comte's defection, Saint-Simon made the acquaintance of several medical men, a Dr. Bailly among them, who were fascinated by his ideas on the physiology of society. But his worldly success was far from brilliant. The infelicitous reference to "terrestrial morality" and his trial of 1820 made most respectable bourgeois shy away from him. They had more discreet plans for seizing power. He was again forced to beg for alms to support his little household, which had acquired a mistress and a dog. One day in 1823, after recommending his Julie to the industrialist Ternaux, in a fit of despair he shot himself. But he was found in time, doctors were called, and the only injury discovered was that one of the shots had penetrated an eye.

He lived for two years longer. A new group of friends appeared, among them two young Jews whose academic careers had been brusquely interrupted by the restrictions against them reimposed by the Restoration. They were Léon Halévy, father of the future playwright of the Second Empire, and Olinde Rodrigues, one of the real innovators of nineteenth-century mathematics. The young men were thirsting for a new morality to fill the emptiness of their souls, and Saint-Simon provided the gospel in the *Nouveau Christianisme* (1825). He conversed with Olinde Rodrigues for many hours during his last years, and in this manner the oral tradition of the master's ideas was transmitted to the disciples. Many of his keenest reflections never appeared in print; they either evaporated in conversation or were received and passed on by Rodrigues. During the last months before his death in 1825 the group began planning a new journal to be called *Le Producteur*.

SCIENCE DETHRONED

It was reported by the eighteenth-century memoir writer Mathieu Marais that Saint-Simon's maternal grandmother, who engaged in strange chemical experiments either to find the philosopher's stone or to prepare medicines for the poor, had died asphyxiated in her laboratory with an assistant who was also her lover. Other accounts have described his parents in attendance at amateur chemical courses where the wonders of the new science were displayed to while away the hours of the bored aristocracy. Henri Saint-Simon's own technical training in science had probably not advanced far beyond that of his ancestors. He may have acquired an interest in engineering at the military school in Mézières, where he is said to have listened to Monge, and he showed some practical knowledge of the art while he served as the Marquis de Bouillé's aide-de-camp during the Revolutionary War in America, but none of his writings betray more than an elementary or autodidact's knowledge of any science. Under the Directorate, when he was wealthy with the monies acquired through speculating in national properties and had settled down in Paris in the vicinity of the great schools, he achieved a smattering of science through osmosis.

But though he knew virtually no science, in all his writings Saint-Simon had a great deal to say about scientists and their unique role in modern society. In one of his autobiographical fragments he confessed that an understanding of the character of men of science had always been his paramount interest in listening to their conversation. During the quarter century of his creative intellectual life he adopted a wide variety of changing attitudes toward them, many of which were doubtless colored by the individual reactions of scientists and of the dominant scientific schools to his person and his doctrine. Nonetheless his conception of the role of the scientist is a fruitful vantage point from which to examine the whole body of his writings. It is one of the most persistent motifs, recurring time and again with different variations. His early works, completely in the Condorcet spirit, had raised the scientists to the apex of society; by Saint-Simon's death science had been dethroned — a revolution in the spiritual conception of the nineteenth-century French prophets which distinguishes them from their eighteenth-century predecessors. Saint-Simon still honored the scientists, though he made them share their social hegemony with others; in Auguste Comte's final phase, technical science as it had been practiced since the Renaissance would be banished.

The very first work Saint-Simon ever published, the anonymous and erratic letter *A la Société du Lycée* (1802), posed a momentous scientific question with childish naiveté. What was the key to the historical progress of mathematics from the quantitative judgment of the first animals through Newton? Primitive man's mentality was not far above that of the animal directly beneath him on the scale of intelligence, and yet man had made such impressive strides in this science. Perhaps if the secret of the history of mathematics were unraveled, then the whole future of science would be within man's control, subject to acceleration at will. Nobody bothered to answer the great query since Saint-Simon was generally regarded as a scientific buffoon.

In the *Lettres d'un habitant de Genève à ses contemporains* Saint-Simon discussed the problem of the role of the scientist as the crux of the contemporary social disarray in France. His class analysis of the French Revolution and its aftermath, in an essay whose originality Friedrich Engels admired and perhaps exaggerated, defined the underlying development of the whole epoch as a conflict between the propertied and the propertyless. As third element in the struggle, the scientists were a floating elite with no natural class alignment; they were mobile and could be recruited to one or the other side of the dichotomic conflict. Though numerically weak, the scientists held the balance of power and could therefore throw victory in the class war to the contestant they favored. In the French Revolution, Saint-Simon reminded his respectable readers, the scientists had sided with the men without property, and the consequence was upheaval, bloodshed, and chaos. It was to the interest of both hostile social classes to put an end to the crisis of the times, and this could only be achieved by neutralizing the political power of the scientists. Blandly Saint-Simon advised the rival temporal classes that the best way to reach this reasonable solution was to elevate the scientists to the summit of the social structure and to subordinate themselves to their rational commands. If scientists organized the spiritual world, social conflicts would cease and men would attain terrestrial happiness.

The intellectual origins of this conception are not hard to identify. They derive from Condorcet, from Cabanis, and from the *idéologues* who, prior to their fatal political miscalculation in sponsoring Napoleon, dreamed of such a hegemony of science under the benign tutelage of a modern Marcus Aurelius. Saint-Simon went a step further than Condorcet and the *idéologues* when he explicitly summoned all classes in world society to establish a new universal spiritual power in the form of the scientific priesthood of the Religion of Newton. Aside from the synthetic character of the ceremonials he proposed — rather creaky contrivances after

the manner of the Directorate theophilanthropic cults — his founding of the sacerdocy of science was based upon a number of rationalist and historical considerations which were current at the
time. There was a widespread consensus that a people had to have
some religious beliefs and institutions in order to preserve order
and that even if atheism was an ideal for the elite there had to be
an exoteric religious doctrine for the mass of the people. The
theory of Charles Dupuis, propounded in his *Origine de tous les
cultes*, that all ancient religions were really codifications of scientific knowledge was adapted by Saint-Simon for practical religious
purposes. The new religion which he at one point dubbed Physicism was thus merely a modern application of respectworthy time-
honored usages among mankind.

The rule of the priest-scientists would end the moral crisis of
the age and would give impetus to a vast expansion of scientific
knowledge. New sciences would become "positive" in an appropriate hierarchical succession from the less to the more complex,
culminating in the science of man. As a consequence of the creation
of this elite the men with the greatest energies and capacities
would no longer pour their efforts into wars of destruction, but
would become productive scientists — the same idea which Condorcet had already suggested in one of his manuscript elaborations
of the tenth epoch of the *Esquisse*. "No more honors for the
Alexanders! Long live the Archimedes!" [2] was Saint-Simon's hor-
tatory way of predicting this inevitable ideological metamorphosis.
In the *Lettres* he expressed confidence that both antagonistic social
classes would not fail to subscribe to the religious fund rendering
scientists absolutely independent of the temporal powers: the men
of property in order to be reassured about what they were most
interested in, possession of their property and freedom from revolution; the propertyless in order to be saved from becoming
cannon-fodder in war.

Saint-Simon's attitude toward the scientist is often an ambiguous one even in the *Lettres*; he seems at moments to parallel
Diderot's ambivalent description of genius in *Le Neveu de Rameau*
(still unpublished at the time, of course). The scientist held the
key to the salvation of mankind in his power of discovery, and he
should be supported and granted complete liberty for the develop-

ment of his precious talents. Many passages bewail the lot of the neglected and impoverished young scientist with romantic rhetoric usually reserved in the early nineteenth century for the depiction of the sufferings of poetic genius; and yet Saint-Simon is equally aware of the destructive potential of the scientist, his demonic quality. The superhuman power of scientific genius must be harnessed for social peace and progress, is Saint-Simon's ominous warning to the propertied and the propertyless alike.

Once Saint-Simon fell into penury under the Empire, his bitter personal experiences with the official scientists of the Napoleonic hierarchy roused him to a frenzy of violence against them. In his paranoid state he fixed on Laplace and Bouvard of the Bureau of Longitudes as his archenemies, the men who were preventing the sublime truths of his *Introduction aux travaux scientifiques du XIX e siècle* from being recognized. His conception of the scientist's role became more complicated. On the one hand he still held firm to the idea that the individual scientist was the seminal historical force, a thesis he demonstrated in numerous truncated *aperçus* on the history of world science; in fact historical epochs were definable primarily in terms of their scientific geniuses. But simultaneously in his scattered unfinished works of the Empire he adumbrated a kind of scientific historical determinism in which the person of the scientist was eclipsed by the absolute and anonymous rhythm of scientific evolution. According to his formula the historical process of science, like all fundamental movements both physical and spiritual, required an alternativity of analysis and synthesis. Thus in the development of modern science, the age of Descartes synthesized, Newton and Locke analyzed, and now a new synthesis was to follow, a synthetic genius of science had to arise. "Indeed, are the constitutions and conceptual power of men like Lagrange and Laplace inferior to those of Newton? I do not believe it at all. But I think that they are subject to a law of circumstances which has left them no other use for their powers than the improvements which we owe to them. At the end of the sixteenth century they would have been Bacons, at the beginning of the seventeenth Descartes, at the beginning of the eighteenth Lockes and Newtons; and if today these same men were no more than twenty I would vouch that before having finished half their careers they would alter the course of the School [of Science]." [3]

This scheme for the history of modern science was the rational kernel in his otherwise pathological attacks against the contemporary Napoleonic scientists. Instead of proceeding with the new synthesis which was their historically ordained mission in accordance with the law of alternativity which he had propounded, the school scientists were continuing to act like epigoni of eighteenth-century science and were becoming mere particularizers, detailists. "You gentlemen are anarchist scientists. You deny the existence, the supremacy of the general theory," he charged in a series of violent letters. [4] The great Napoleon had summoned them for a report on the needs and mission of science, and they continued to conduct their individual experiments oblivious of historic duty, in fact in open defiance of the true destiny of nineteenth-century science. They were thus at once traitors to science, to history, and to Napoleon. The science of the nineteenth century had to develop a unified plan, to construct a new view of the world, to oust old-fashioned religion and purge education of residual elements of superstition. Scientists had to cooperate and associate among themselves in the production of a New Encyclopedia based upon a principle of synthesis that would replace Diderot's merely destructive encyclopedia; they had to fit their individual studies into an organic whole and then to crown their labors with social physiology, the newest of the sciences, in which was hidden the secret of man's salvation. Instead scientists were piddling away their time egotistically on their own petty disordered experiments. "The philosophy of the eighteenth century was critical and revolutionary, that of the nineteenth will be inventive and organizational," was the motto of his new encyclopedia. [5] Saint-Simon knew that the synthesis of the coming century would have a single principle, and he divined a priori that the principle would be Newton's law of gravitation, an idea which was by no means limited to physics but could be extended to chemistry, physiology, and the science of man. What he desperately needed was the aid, the collaboration, of technicians and other scientists — the very men who spurned him.

During the period of Saint-Simon's gravest psychic crisis, in 1812–1813, when the slaughter in Europe was at its height, his rage against the indifference of the scientists mounted to a frenetic violence. At first he distinguished between the mathematical and the life scientists. He had quickly become disillusioned with the *brutiers*, for unlike Condorcet he saw no prospect for the solution of the social problems of mankind through the application of the calculus of probabilities. Many fragments directed against the mathematical and physical scientists hiding behind their "ramparts of X and Y," coldly indifferent to the fate of man, serving in the destructive corps of all the armies of the Continent, have a contemporary poignancy. With sarcastic contempt Saint-Simon ordered the inhuman *brutiers* from the height of the scientific eminence. He demoted them in esteem. For a while the only hope lay in the biologists, physiologists, and social scientists. Dr. Burdin, a surgeon in the armies of the Revolution, had once told him that the new science would be born when someone synthesized the writings of Vicq-d'Azyr, Cabanis, Bichat, and Condorcet, and Saint-Simon long clung to this expectation as the salvation of Europe. But there were times when even the life scientists seemed to have been engulfed in the general chaos. In his madness he cried out for the creation of a scientific papacy, for the summoning of great international councils of science to save mankind.

Saint-Simon's recuperation from his breakdown coincided with the end of the Napoleonic wars and the respite of Europe. As he emerged into the light his attitude toward the scientists underwent a drastic change. In the early years of the Restoration, when he gave ever greater prominence to the organizing role of the *industriels* in society, the scientist lost status by comparison. There are a number of different versions of his shifting sociological theory, but they all have this in common, a uniform devaluation of the role of the scientist in society. At times he thought of an ideal duumvirate with more or less equivalent status for scientists and industrialists, the one representing the spiritual, the other the temporal power, and he refashioned his whole philosophy of modern history along the lines of a novel pattern: the replacement over the centuries of the medieval priestly and military ruling classes by the scientists and the bourgeois. This historical conceptualization, which has since become a platitude of Marxist universal history, had many dialectical turns of thought: the new scientific elite did not succeed the old priesthood in a mechanical manner; in the very bosom of the medieval sacerdotal class the modern scientists occupied positions from which they were able to carry on their destructive warfare against religion. But despite this rather traditional dualism — the two swords — in which the scientists seem to represent a growing independent spiritual force, in the early Restoration writings Saint-Simon tended more and more to subordinate them to the industrialists. Sometimes he tried to use old projects, like his encyclopedia, as a device for the forging of a common militant consciousness between the scientists and the industrialists, but on many occasions he forthrightly proclaimed that it would be best for society as a whole if the industrialists would in the last analysis become the final judges of the value of what the scientists accomplished. When he was most deeply under the influence of the French liberal economists Dunoyer and Jean-Baptiste Say he found no objection to considering the achievements of the scientists as mere commodities whose worth was to be estimated by the industrialists in terms of their practical needs and desires. His disenchantment with the official scientists was so profound that he could no longer conceive of them as playing a role of primacy in society. They were not heroic leaders but mere followers. Most of them lived on sinecures and emoluments from the state, and any overt opposition to the retrograde Bourbon aristocracy was too much to expect of them. They were timid and pusillanimous. Their intellectual productions were worthwhile — and they were not to be classed with useless bureaucrats, generals, and priests — but as often as not Saint-Simon came to see them as underlings. In some writings he merely grouped the scientists along with other useful persons such as entrepreneurs and workers under the general rubric *industriels*, which came to be an over-all category of productive people in every conceivable occupation who were contrasted with the *fainéants*, the do-nothings.

Unfortunately for his material well-being, try as he might Saint-Simon could not long rest content with his limited role as a moderately successful propagandist for the bourgeois. As soon as he broke loose and propounded in *L'Industrie* the crucial need for a terrestrial morality, he was thrown back into the problem of the competitive roles of the scientists and the priests. One of his solutions, during the period when he was still eager to retain the financial support of his nonrevolutionary Restoration businessmen, was to propose a transitional stage for society during which the priests of the old religion would be taught more and more science in the seminaries, so that those who in fact controlled education would thus promote the ideology of science while still wearing clerical garb. To avoid the horror of revolution and the evils of precipitous change Saint-Simon would advise the priests to become scientists — or he would have the Papacy order them to do so. Existing conditions in the spiritual world of the Restoration were morally intolerable because the great learned organizations were in the hands of scientists, while the educational system was still under the control of priests who knew no science, a fatal division which resulted in chaos. Perhaps if the priesthood could be converted to science no class revolution in the spiritual realm would even be necessary, as a mere transition would suffice. Of one thing Saint-Simon was certain: the scientific ideas of the elite of savants were penetrating all elements of the population, even the lowest classes, and the ultimate expulsion of existing orthodox religious ideas was inevitable.

In the final stages of Saint-Simon's doctrinal development, roughly after 1822, the scientists had to share their elite position not only with the administrative directors of society but with a third ruling group, the moralist leaders of the New Christianity. Religious and scientific functions were conceived of as distinct, requiring different capacities. In this period Saint-Simon came to realize the full social implications of an idea which he had first discovered in the writings of the physiologist Bichat. There he found a separation of all men into three natural classes, psycho-physiological types so to speak, in each of which one quality predominated, the motor, the rational, or the emotive. During his last years Saint-Simon adopted this triadic division as the ideal structuring of the good society of the future as contrasted with the existing unnatural roles into which men were cast by the status of their birth and by haphazard. In the new world of Saint-Simon men would engage in motor activity either as administrators or workers, in pure rational research as scientists, or, as moralizers and inspirers of mankind, in appealing to human emotions through preaching and the arts. Since under this "industrial system" each man would be fulfilling his natural capacity to the utmost, there would be no misfits and no class conflicts. Each "capacity" would labor in its respective branch and would evince no desire to encroach upon the province of another. Perfect harmony would prevail, the power state would disappear, and men would be directed to the exploitation of nature instead of exercising dominion over one another. While Saint-Simon tended to conceive of the three capacities of acting, thinking, and feeling as mutually exclusive, he did make exceptions; in one of his works he even had a prophetic insight into the future central role of the engineer in the industrial system. In Saint-Simon's classificatory order the engineer combined the characteristics of both the administrator and the scientist, and he could therefore serve as an ideal intermediary in the implementation of the grandiose projects of the new society.

A substantial portion of Saint-Simon's writing in his final years was devoted to the drafting of blueprints for the administrative organization of the future world. Their detail is often tedious, but they have one constant element: all organs of administration — he eschewed the term government — were so arranged that each of the three fundamental natural classes was always represented in what he called the "high administration of society" in the fulfillment of its special capacities. As a rule, under the new division of labor the emotive or moralist branch tended to initiate projects, the scientific to criticize and evaluate them, and the administrators to execute them. In these ideal constitutions the scientist was thus cast in a rather uncreative rationalistic role; he was more often the emendator than the original inventor. The scientist seemed to represent the analytic spirit more and more, and Saint-Simon had come to appreciate the originality of the poet and the moralist above the talent of the scientist. In principle the three capacities were equal in worth, but if the spirit rather than the letter of Saint-Simon's last writings is considered, the scientist has somehow become the least preferred of the three brothers, and the religious leader who taught men to love one another was awarded ever greater prestige. The cynic of the Directorate was on the way to becoming a Saint-Simonian.

The final article in a collection of essays Saint-Simon published in Paris in 1825, the *Opinions littéraires, philosophiques et industrielles*, was a discussion among representatives of the triumvirate who were destined to direct the future society. It was entitled "L'Artiste, le savant et l'industriel." The mission of his profession set forth by the scientist was precise: it was another plea for a general theory to encompass all the sciences rather than allow each of them separately and in isolation to achieve a high degree of abstraction; but there was also a new emphasis in this work upon the relations of theoretical science to "practice." As a consequence of the new social philanthropic tendency of his lifework, Saint-Simon insisted upon a reorganization of both science and education for practical purposes, which meant a speedy increase in the production of goods. The scientist's utilitarian and even "proletarian" goals were set forth with simple frankness. "What are the general applications of mechanics and of all the other sciences by means of which the most numerous class of producers will be able to increase its comforts and diminish its physical exertions, with the result that the price of human muscular labor will rise in direct relationship with the perfection of scientific processes? In a word scientists will undertake a series of works directly intended to perfect industrial arts." [6] While the scientists as a corps retain their dignity, they are forced out of their isolation — pure theory in any particular science is thrust aside — and all their works are specifically applied to the needs of technology, which alone is able to bestow a new worth upon the manual laborer. Human activities are set in a new hierarchy of values: science is subordinated to technology and technology is made to serve not profit-making but the appreciation of that element in production which is not mechanical — the human component.

Two hundred years after Saint-Simon's birth his system of natural classes based upon capabilities seems to be acquiring more realistic significance than it enjoyed during the intervening period. Relations between scientists and administrators are now among the crucial internal problems of organization of the more complex civilizations, whatever their economic systems may be. The third element in the Saint-Simonian triad hardly seems to have held its own with the other two. Neither does Saint-Simon's conception of the mutual exclusiveness of the three capacities seem to have been borne out by time. If few administrators have awakened to discover themselves endowed with rare scientific talents, the scientists, at least in the American economy, have been constrained to accept administrative responsibilities of a complexity never dreamed of before. The subordination of science to technology, military and civilian, is now taken for granted despite an undertone of protest in the name of pure theory. Science is now controlled, directed, and administered by scientists themselves and by bureaucrats to a degree inconceivable in Condorcet's and Saint-Simon's wildest imaginings. The "anarchist scientists" have given way to the totally organized scientists, with results yet unforeseeable in productivity or, who knows, perhaps in sterility.

FROM EQUALITY TO ORGANICISM

SAINT-SIMON has one underlying preconception which is identical with the outlook of the philosophical egalitarians, the conviction that the ideal forms of the good society must be congruent with what is natural in man. From a cursory reading of the physiologists, however, Saint-Simon came away with a different version of the natural: the natural was inequality. He inveighed against *philosophisme* for its ignorance of the simple physiological facts, positive scientific facts, which had since been set forth by Cabanis and Bichat. Confirmed in the belief that physiology was the only sound foundation upon which to construct a social theory, he experimented with variant schemes of social classification, and the plan he devised in the final phase of his thinking was a direct adaptation of the Bichat typology. His three social functions and three mutually exclusive social classes corresponded to the physiologist's three human types. [7] First society needed scientists to discover positive laws which in turn could be translated into guides for social action. This scientific capacity — the brain type, which he sometimes called the Aristotelian capacity — if given free play would fulfill the mission which Condorcet had proposed for the leading scientific intellects. Bichat's motor capacity was transformed by Saint-Simon into the industrial class. Most of mankind, whose primary aptitude was the motor capacity, were destined to remain manual laborers, though a small elite of this class with essentially the same kind of talent would become the administrators of the temporal affairs of society — the men who organized states and directed public works and engineered vast projects for the exploitation of nature. Saint-Simon's third class, which corresponded to Bichat's sensory man, were the artists, poets, religious leaders, ethical teachers, whom he sometimes identified with the Platonic capacity. In the last years of his life, when he emphasized the religious character of his doctrine, he endowed the sensory aptitude with special worth since he considered it capable of overcoming the atomist, egoist, egalitarian propensities of the contemporary world in crisis. The men of sentiment would give the new industrial society its quality and cohesive humanitarian spirit.

The good society thus represented a harmonious association or cooperation of men fundamentally dissimilar in their most essential natures, organized in three natural classes. Together they embodied the total needs of mankind — rational-scientific, manual-administrative, sensory-religious. The eighteenth-century *philosophes*, even when they admitted human inequalities, had still insisted upon organizing the state and society around those elements which men had in common, their natural equalities and relatively equal capacity for governance and the holding of public office. Saint-Simon and all later organicist doctrines which derived from him may have taken for granted some of the equal juridical rights of the *philosophes*, but they then proceeded to fashion society out of the different clays which were the raw materials of human nature. All men were not equally capable of participating in the administration of society. The new philosopher of society approached the whole problem with the initial preconception that the physiological and psychological differences of men were the very brick and mortar of the perfect social edifice.

The presumption is overwhelming that each man seeks to express his own and not an alien nature, that he desires to live and work in the classification where he has natural endowments, be they scientific, administrative, or poetic capacities. Saint-Simon here adapted one of the major contentions of the de Maistre and de Bonald theocrats, who steadfastly maintained that men were not driven by a passion for equality with other men of higher status or great wealth, but really had a profound desire to remain in their own traditional occupations and to continue to express themselves in the traditional roles into which they were cast at birth. They wanted not equality but the expression of their true social natures. Saint-Simon merely translated this conception into "scientific" terms: men by nature desired not equality with others but the expression of their intrinsic and immutable physiological aptitudes. The Aristotelian idea that every being seeks a fulfillment of its essential character or nature has found an echo both in the theocratic and in the Saint-Simonian theories. It is a dogma that no man would be so monstrous as to desire to exercise administrative functions if he were born with a scientific capacity; at least, no good social order would allow such an anarchic misplacement of human talent. In the Saint-Simonian world outlook, organic inequality among men, inequality in the social hierarchy, and difference of social function were natural and beneficent, wholly superior to the *égalité turque* of the Jacobin revolutionaries, which was an equality of slavery beneath an omnipotent state authority. [8] Born unequal in their faculties, men required a society in which each was allotted a function. If a man operated in a social class to which he did not naturally belong, performing functions for which he was not naturally equipped, he would be wasting his own talents and reducing the total creative potential of humanity. Among Saint-Simon's last words to his favorite disciple was a definition of the quintessential goal of his doctrine and his life's work: "to afford all members of society the greatest possible opportunity for the development of their faculties." [9]

Talleyrand's image of the national workshop propounded in his report on the reorganization of public education survives in Saint-Simon's writings, where the goal of the new society is maximum production through maximum utilization of individual capacities. In Saint-Simon's vision of the golden age of plenty, the emphasis is placed upon ever more production and creation, rather than upon consumption and distribution. The banquet spread before mankind is so sumptous that dwelling upon material rewards, so characteristic of a world of scarcity, seems to be beside the point. Saint-Simon's humanitarian doctrine thus incorporated the Condorcet principle that society could be organized so that misery and ignorance became accidents rather than the norm of human experience; [10] his theory had none of the crushing pessimism associated with later Social Darwinism, even though he too was inspired by biological analogies.

Perhaps the difference between Saint-Simon's and the eighteenth-century conception has its crux in a new view of humanity. Instead of the man of reason as the most perfect expression of humanity toward which all men are striving, Saint-Simon thinks of man now and in the future as at once rational, activist, and religious, at once mind, will, and feeling. His ends are moral, intellectual, and physical, three major areas of human effort corresponding to the aptitudes of the artist, the scientist, and the industrialist. This is the whole man, whose being is paralleled in the organization of the healthy body social. If man is primarily a rational animal and the highest form of reason is mathematics, the Turgot-Condorcet egalitarian ideal of rational units behaving in accordance with mathematicized social rules is comprehensible. But if humanity is a composite whose various manifestations include the predominantly activist or religious as well as rationalist, the social structure, reflecting and embracing the variety and diversity of men, will be organismic, a harmony of complex, different, and essential parts.

The organismic society, unlike the atomist egalitarian society, which functions like mechanical clockwork, requires a "vitalist" element — some pervasive emotion, feeling, or belief to give life to the body. Though the eighteenth century had developed the concepts of benevolence and humanity as characteristics of natural men of virtue, Saint-Simon in the romantic temper infused the idea of the love of humanity with an emotional drive which it had lacked in the minds of the *philosophes*. Love was the fluid which coursed through the body social, gave it movement and energy. In Saint-Simon's judgment the equal atoms of the eighteenth-century world view were always on the verge of strife; his ideal of love created an organic harmonious whole out of society's vital parts. Men hungered for this comfort on the morrow of a quarter-century of world revolution which had loosened the very bonds of society. The need for the emotionalization of relationships if society was not to fall apart and disintegrate into its discrete elements had been dramatized by Burke and de Bonald and de

Maistre. Saint-Simon by his own testimony was communicating the same urgent longing of men for a society in which they could feel themselves integral parts, an organic society, as contrasted with a state in which isolated units competed and fought with one another. Egalitarianism had come to represent the eternal struggle of equals in a world of cold and brutal competition.

Saint-Simon's formula for the organization of society aimed to eliminate the sources of social waste, maladjustment, and friction not only through a class division based on function and ability; within each class of aptitudes provision was made for the emergence of a natural elite — an elite of real capacity — through keeping the course open to talent. There is a presumption in Saint-Simon that among men with similar or identical aptitudes superiority and excellence will automatically be recognized without jealousy or conflict. He generalized to all fields of endeavor the apparent unanimity with which the foremost mathematicians, physicists, and biologists seemed to be appreciated by men of science.

In the good society this natural elite corps (he was directly influenced by the contemporary analogy of Napoleon's *troupes d'élite*), one with authentic, proved capacities, directed the various classes. Leadership was not, as the doctrine of popular sovereignty held, a generalized capacity in which all men were more or less equal and which made it feasible and natural for offices to be elective. In the organic society, workers instinctively rendered obedience to their natural superiors, their "chiefs," in their own class. [11] The idealized image of the Napoleonic army, in which ordinary soldiers had risen to be marshals, in which rank was at least in theory the reward of talent and merit, was a prototype for Saint-Simon's civilian class society.

Since it was in the very order of the universe that men should be unequal, instead of attempting to level these differences Saint-Simon, in the spirit of Bichat's physiological doctrines, held that it would be beneficial to the whole of society to emphasize them, to nurture and develop the uncommon and extraordinary capacities in individual men. Saint-Simon denied that Negroes were equal to Europeans. [12] Among Europeans themselves there were professional and class distinctions which he called "anomalies." The corps of the nobility and the clergy in European society had originally been founded upon just such organic anomalies in the human species. Though these anomalies had become attenuated through the centuries, the egalitarian *philosophes* had made a fatal error when they proclaimed the abolition of all specialized corps simply because the existing elites in name had ceased to be elites in fact. True scientists of society would not try to minimize unique excellences, but would devote themselves to the regeneration of specialized corps, confining their membership to the men who were patently superior, those who had the most marked "anomalies."

Saint-Simon's doctrine of what he called the "great trinity" of capacities was further developed by the Saint-Simonians, but this is one area in which they remained mere emendators, adding little that was new. At most they emotionalized a problem which Saint-Simon had set forth in rationalist terms.

THE TWILIGHT OF POWER

In the *Introduction aux travaux scientifiques du XIXe siècle*, Saint-Simon had shown his awareness of the universality of the power drive. "Every man, every grouping of men, whatever its character, tends toward the increase of power. The warrior with the saber, the diplomat with his wiles, the geometer with his compass, the chemist with his retorts, the physiologist with his scalpel, the hero by his deeds, the philosopher by his combinations, all struggle to achieve command. From different sides they scale the plateau on whose height stands the fantastic being who rules all of nature and whom every man who has a strong constitution tries to replace." [13]

Saint-Simon's Restoration works established a sharp distinction between the exercise of power by ruling classes in the past and the direction of the future industrial society which would become the function of entrepreneurial and scientific chiefs. The prospect of the survival of power, with its dread military and psychological consequences, into the golden age seemed to poison the benign placidity of free labor in association in the ideal state of mankind. Struck by the ubiquity of the power lust, Saint-Simon in his later works squarely met the challenge which it represented to his entire system. In a significant passage in the ninth letter of *L'Organisateur* he dismissed as irrelevant to the discussion furious madmen like Napoleon who reveled in the exercise of arbitrary power for its own sake, for such men were monstrosities. This was a typical eighteenth-century way of dealing with the abnormal: it was eliminated from consideration. As for the rest of mankind, there was a happy way out of the contradictions with which persistent and omnipresent human aggressiveness confronted the good society: the civilizing process tended to transfer the object of the power lust from men to nature.

By power Saint-Simon meant the exercise of any force by one human being upon another, an act of dominion essentially vicious. Power would not be necessary in the future industrial society composed of men freely utilizing their capacities. The energy which had previously been wasted upon the exercise of power over men would be channeled in another direction, toward the ever more intensive exploitation of nature. ". . . The only useful action that man can perform is the action of man on things. The action of man on man is always in itself harmful to the species because of the twofold waste of energy which it entails. It can only be useful if it is subsidiary and if it supplements the performance of a greater action on nature." [14] Power injured both the man over whom it was wielded and the man who carried the rod. Men whose capacities were devoted to nothing more creative than action on other men were members of Saint-Simon's do-nothing classes. This succinct expression of a new moral ideal for the industrial society captured the imagination of later socialist theorists and found an echo in their writings.

The historic substitution of nature for man as the object of aggression, so provocatively suggestive of both Marx and Freud, nurtured Saint-Simon's optimistic belief that with time not only intellectual but moral progress was feasible. Despite the fact that the most recent embodiment of the great demon of power lust was still alive on the rock of Saint Helena, Saint-Simon forecast the ultimate quiescence of the evil:

"This love of dominion, which is certainly indestructible in man, has nevertheless been eradicated in large part by the progress of civilization, or at least its disadvantages have almost disappeared under the new system. In fact, the development of action against nature has changed the direction of this sentiment by leveling it against objects. The desire to command men has slowly transformed itself into the desire to make and remake nature in accordance with our will.

"From this time on the desire to dominate which is innate in all men has ceased to be pernicious, or at least we can foresee an epoch when it will not be harmful any longer, but will become useful. Thus civilization has perfected human morality not only in the animal sense by improving intelligence but also in the organic sense by curbing the passions.

"Though, according to the laws of man's physiology, this second order of vital functions [his organic being] is not by itself perfectible, it can be improved by the exercise of the first order of functions [the intelligence] on the second." [15]

Along with his teachings that man's body influenced his mind, Cabanis had dwelt upon the reciprocal influence of the *moral* on the *physique*, an idea Saint-Simon had always found congenial. This doctrine allowed for the possibility that, with a great development of man's scientific knowledge, his passions might be bridled. Society had already given promise of the eventual pacification of the power lust. Saint-Simon proved by homely example that the seductions of industrial civilization were becoming so potent that most men would sacrifice even the exercise of absolute power to enjoy their pleasures in the peace of the new society — *vide* the English nabob who after years of service in India preferred the simple comforts of rural England to arbitrary dominion in Bengal.

Since the natural elite of the industrial scientific society was based upon sheer capacity, talents which presumably all men could instantaneously recognize, there was no room in the society of the future for class and power conflict. Men found their way into the elite because their natural aptitudes drew them there. The prospect of jealousies and internal struggles within scientific elites did not disturb Saint-Simon. The act of appreciation of superior genius appeared to be miraculously free from the baser passions. As for conflicts among coequal bodies of the elite, such as the scientists and the industrial entrepreneurs, they were beyond the realm of possibility. The innermost desire of each member of an elite was the exercise of those aptitudes and functions in which he excelled. It would therefore be contrary to nature for a scientist, for example, a theoretician, to covet administrative powers, or for an industrialist to presume to seek membership in a scientific corps. Such capacities, Bichat had taught, were mutually exclusive, and in the good society each man would find his proper place. In the new moral order, "know thyself" read "know thy capacity."

In past epochs of civilization there had been internecine strife among the ruling classes because these classes were constituted as agencies for the exercise of superior power over all men. The medieval nobles were inflamed by a desire to control the inhabitants of ever more extensive territories, the clergy to enjoy absolute mastery over the minds of their parishioners. Such corps ambitions had to clash because they vied for exclusive power. In the industrial scientific society, basic drives would be turned outward toward the world of objects. The scientist was discovering the deepest truths of nature and the industrialist was harnessing the refractory forces of nature, two different, noncompetitive functions. The direction of men in the new society was only an ancillary phenomenon to the exploitation of nature, both in the spiritual realm and in the temporal. Dominion over men was indivisible, whereas the management of nature could be separated into specialized functions, eliminating power conflicts.

In the industrial scientific society all capacities were given free play. Saint-Simon himself did not overstress the hierarchic nature of this society. He was, of course, not completely emancipated from a classical denigration of manual labor; the scientists and the industrial chiefs were endowed with special excellence. But, for all that, no working function in society was disdained in and of itself. "All men shall work" was still the commandment of the new order. Men's labors varied with their capacities. As for their rewards, Saint-Simon was not an egalitarian. He dismissed the problem with the assurance that each member of the body politic would be recompensed in accordance with his investment, a vague formula which left room for differentials in material emoluments. "Each person enjoys a measure of importance and benefits proportionate to his capacity and to his investment. This constitutes the highest degree of equality possible and desirable." [16] Saint-

Simon always focused on production, impediments to production, methods for increasing productivity; the rules governing the distribution of rewards were reduced to issues of a secondary nature, for amid the great superfluities of the society of producers there would surely be enough for the needs of all men. The social organism was guided by the lodestar of an ideological absolute which discouraged too wide a disparity between the rewards of one man and another. The primary goal was to raise the physical and moral well-being of the poorest and most numerous classes. While he rejected Condorcet's equality as an ideal, he never raised the incentive of class divergences as the motive drive animating the social body.

The only sound system was a functioning class society in which the roles of the men who administered were mere extensions of their social occupations. The "high administration of society," that clumsy phrase which he preferred both to "state" and "government," required no special aptitudes or talents and no specialized personnel beyond those occupied in directing normal social functions. There was no need for a government expert or a man trained in administration. Before the triumph of the industrial society men had been governed, in the order of the future they would be administered. The old and the new leadership were different because they reflected this underlying transformation in the nature of human relationships. Saint-Simon was emphasizing the distinction between the exercise of power based on physical force and of direction founded on a recognition of superior capacity in the elite, between the command function and the organization of an association for the common welfare. At first sight it might seem utopian to turn society over to a group of administrators after men for centuries had accustomed themselves to the absolutes of governance, power, and dominion. Saint-Simon pointed out, however, that in his day many pivotal economic institutions already in operation had dispensed with the command function and were voluntary associations — the banks, insurance companies, savings societies, and canal construction companies. These administered societies were models for the total society of the future, and he anticipated no special difficulties incident to the enlargement of the unit of administration. Society itself was one large national workshop with more varied activities, though none essentially different from those of a canal construction company.

The transfer of political power from the noble class to the chiefs of the industrial class — "professors in administration" — who in their factories and banks and companies had already been virtually exercising civil administration, would not be perplexing to the mass of the workers, since they had long since grown accustomed on the job to an appreciation of these entrepreneurs as their natural leaders. In the new order, entrepreneurial leadership would simply be extended from individual factories to the requirements of the "high administration of society." For the proletariat such a scheme of things would involve a return to a more normal relation in which they would no longer have to deal with two leaderships, one political and one civil; the chiefs of daily work would be at the same time the chiefs of the total society. Thus there would eventually be created an organic integrated society in which men would cease to be pulled in two opposite directions by rival forces. Similarly, the unification of the spiritual power in society, ending the present division between the clergy and the scientists, would not be a disturbing novelty for the mass of the people but would represent a desirable amalgamation replacing the confusion which had hitherto bedeviled them.

Saint-Simon drew up a catalogue of distinctions governing the relations of people and their chiefs under the old feudal order and the new industrial society. Under the old the people were regimented by superiors; under the new, they were related to one another by occupational ties. Under the old they were commanded, under the new they were directed. Under the old they were subjects, under the new they were members. Above all, the great virtue of the industrial society consisted in the fact that all its members, from the simple worker to the rich manufacturer, were "collaborators." [17] In the old society there was force, in the new a "cooperation" of capacities, a true "association."

Class conflicts would be banished from the new society. Since the capacities of real classes could not overlap, what could they fight about? Since men of a class would seek to excel in their natural aptitudes, there could be only rivalry in good works, not a struggle for power. [18] When class chiefs owed their prestige to their control of men, they could fight over one another's "governed," but since there would be no governors and no subjects, from what source would class antagonism be derived? Within a class men of the same capacity would be striving to excel one another with creations whose merits all members of the class would be able to evaluate. Between classes there could only be mutual aid. There was no basis for hostility, no occasion for invading one another's territory.

In a few key paragraphs of his tract *Suite à la brochure des Bourbons et des Stuarts*, published on January 24, 1822, he expressed in capsule form his whole concept of the natural elite in a society without power. "All privileges will be abolished and never reappear since the most complete system of equality which can possibly exist will be constituted. The men who show the greatest capacity in positive sciences, in the fine arts, and in industry will be called by the new system to enter the top echelon of social prestige and will be placed in charge of public affairs — a fundamental disposition which destines all men possessing a transcendent talent to rise to the first rank, no matter in what position the chance of birth may have placed them." [19] The whole social structure thus constituted would have as its goal the implementation of a *révolution régénératrice* throughout the European continent.

The regenerated society of the future would be emancipated from the shackles and burdens of government which weighed upon his contemporaries. During the early years of the Restoration his periodicals gave a prominent place to meticulous analyses of the inflated national budget and directed harassing attacks against excessive government expenditures in all branches of the Bourbon administration. Saint-Simon laid down the principle that a government was best when it governed least and most cheaply. [20] The productive industrials were paying the rising tax levies of the Bourbon state, most of whose operations appeared to them supernumerary. The Bourbons were doling out pensions to returned émigrés, compensating them with billions of francs for their losses during the Revolution, creating new offices and sinecures after the manner of the *ancien régime*. To the industrials and their mouthpiece Saint-Simon, this was prodigious waste. France needed no army for national defense, since nobody was threatening to strike at the Bourbons, whom a coalition of European powers had just set upon the throne. The vast judicial system was overloaded with judges, a large part of whose work could have been accomplished more quickly, wisely, and economically by arbitration tribunals of industrials. If the state were run like a national workshop it would consume but a fraction of current expenditures. Only businessmen, not bureaucrats, were capable of drawing up an economical budget for the state and administering it effectively. *L'Industrie* included essays which were as thoroughgoing statements against government regulation as could be found anywhere on the continent. [21]

The more Saint-Simon analyzed the governmental functions of the state, the less use he found for its existence in such swollen dimensions. His industrial society could operate with administrative and scientific capacities alone, without men adept at wielding force. The existing governmental system, which he hoped to replace in the near future, had raised men to office not because they demonstrated special talents, but because they had cunning and knew how to acquire and to manipulate power. [22] Their evil genius would be thwarted in the productive society of the future.

In the modern world the only useful work was scientific, artistic, technological, industrial (in the broad sense of the term); everything else was parasitic. Hitherto despite the fact that society had had to squander a large proportion of its energies on struggles for power, it had nevertheless managed to achieve a high level of prosperity. *A fortiori*, what great accomplishments was humanity capable of if men ceased to spend themselves in power conflicts and devoted themselves solely to cooperative labor?

After Saint-Simon surveyed the various branches of the Bourbon government, he came to the conclusion that only the police power had some justification for existence. Though he made this grudging admission, he assigned the police a subordinate position in the industrial society, severely reducing the exalted status it enjoyed under the Bourbons. At times he even eliminated the maintenance of order as a formal attribute of the state. "This function . . .," he wrote, "can easily become almost in its entirety a duty common to all citizens. . . ." [23] His state virtually "withered away," though he did not use the phrase.

In the good society, governmental action — by which Saint-Simon understood the command function — would be "reduced to nothing, or almost nothing." Since the goal of society was general happiness and happiness was defined as the development of the arts and sciences and the diffusion of their benefits through technology and industry, only managerial action would be required. Inevitably the progress of industry would reduce poverty, idleness, and ignorance, the chief sources of public disorder, and thus the need for most governmental functions, even the police, would dissolve. The industrial society, by eradicating the causes of disorder, made it possible virtually to eliminate the state. Granted a thoroughgoing economic liberalism — free trade, no domestic governmental regulation of industry and commerce, an inevitable reduction in crime, a foreign policy committed to peace — it seemed difficult to discover any broad areas in which the state could operate. Ultimately decisions affecting the body social would be impersonal and would be reached like other positivist scientific conclusions. "Decisions can only be the result of scientific demonstrations, absolutely independent of any human will. . . ." [24]

However much Marx differed from Saint-Simon in analyzing the historical process, there was agreement between them that the new society emerging from the last conflict of systems or classes would witness the twilight of power and the cessation of power conflicts among men. Both saw power and aggressiveness not as ineradicable characteristics of man but as transient historical manifestations generated by previous, imperfect social systems and destined to perish with them. Their optimism was a corollary to their analysis of the classes designated as the agents of the last revolution. The "industrials" were by definition productive entrepreneurs to whom the spirit of war and conflict was alien; it would be contrary to their nature to become intoxicated with power. The proletarians were in their nature men who worked, not men who exploited, hence they could not engineer a proletarian revolution and thereafter exploit others. The simplicity with which socialist theory turned its head away from the realities of power was the great blind spot of its outlook.

THE NEW CHRISTIANITY

SAINT-SIMON's various religious posturings froze in a final attitude in the *Nouveau Christianisme*, published shortly before his death. The work was originally intended as an essay in the second volume of the *Opinions littéraires, philosophiques et industrielles*, but the urgency of the political and moral crisis moved him to issue it separately, and it appeared early in 1825, preceded by an unsigned introduction from the pen of Olinde Rodrigues which was an effort to smooth the transition between Saint-Simon's earlier philosophical works and the religious proclamation. The favorite disciple was only partially successful, for there is a chasm between the two careers which cannot readily be bridged in a few pages.[25]

As a manifesto of the New Christians, this last publication of Saint-Simon's is not a very pungent piece of writing. In many respects it is his dullest work. The tract has no clear plan; it is verbose and repetitive, and its occasional flights of fancy invariably fall flat. Nevertheless it was revered by his disciples as the final testament of Saint-Simon, and they strove to discover in it a hidden sense. Unfortunately for his reputation as a theorist, his name has been identified with this work above all others. [26]

Even in this tract the break with past doctrine is not absolute. Saint-Simon is still the philosopher of an industrial-scientific-artistic society organized as an "aristocracy of talent." He still is the enemy of the warrior nobility and the do-nothings. He still indulges in dialectical turns of thought, contrasts of epochs, of moral systems, of emotional drives. The heart of his whole system, however, has changed, for it is first and foremost a religion.

The *Nouveau Christianisme* is cast as a dialogue between an innovator (a New Christian) and a conservative, during the course of which the conservative is converted rather effortlessly. The opening lines announce the innovator's credo, his belief in the existence of God, in straightforward catechismic affirmations. The dialogue ends with a proof that Christianity is a religion which must have been inspired by divine revelation. Forgotten are the Physicism of the Empire and the sacrilegious Dupuis theory. In the New Christianity religion was no longer the mere expression of general science, even though scientific knowledge was a major prerequisite for the priesthood. The essence of Christianity was its moral content. Dogma and ritual in great religions were only utilitarian addenda, handmaidens of the moral principles, which were timeless and not subject to change; the philosopher who once used the phrase "nineteenth-century morality" had recanted his heretical, relativist doctrine. Only the physical sciences have had a history and there has been progress in the accumulation of their data. Since the revelation of Christ morality has had one principle and only one. The absolute perfection of this abstract moral truth could not be altered in time, even though the appropriate application of Christian morality would still be subject to the law of change and progress. In brief, the Christian moral principle was eternal; only its historical embodiment was relative.[27]

The Christian religion, said Saint-Simon, was summed up in one sublime commandment, the Golden Rule: men should behave toward one another like brothers. [28] When the conservative expressed incredulity at this succinct reduction of Christianity, he was silenced with Saint-Simon's monist dogma: "It would be blasphemy to presume that the All-Powerful One founded his religion on several principles." [29] The Christian apostles had taught this principle of brotherly love in its original simple form in the primitive catechism. [30] Preached to a society that was still divided into two classes, the Roman masters and their slaves, it was a lofty, revolutionary principle. The early Christians were thus daring moral reformers whose principles were to dominate the medieval system. In the heyday of its power, Christian papal society went a long way toward the practical application of the Christian catechism in the abolition of slavery. But the injunction of the catechism — to love one another as brothers — was not in its primitive form the ultimate embodiment of the Christian principle.

By the fifteenth century the primitive sense of the Christian principle had already become outmoded and urgently needed rejuvenation, but unfortunately the Catholic clergy, secure in their institutional powers, opposed any changes in the original expression of the moral principle. What was worse, they became inveterate enemies of its practical implementation, unlike their medieval predecessors, and they had remained so ever since. In the *Nouveau Christianisme* Saint-Simon threw caution to the winds. He arraigned the Papacy and the Catholic hierarchy before the bar of primitive Christianity and accused them of heresy. His language and tone were no longer circumspect; he labeled them Antichrists. They were heretics because for four hundred years the Christian principle had needed new raiment, and they refused to recognize its plight. It was no longer sufficient to preach brotherly love, for with the progress of science and the discovery of new worlds it was incumbent upon the church to recast Christianity into a morality which taught that to labor for the amelioration of the lot of the poorest and most numerous classes in society was man's goal on earth. The services of the New Christianity would not be concerned with disputations about dogma but would concentrate on extolling those who upheld the new principle and condemning those who opposed it. What would worship consist of in the New Christianity? A prolix passage at once defines the new religion and conveys the spirit of the cult.

"Today worship should be envisaged only as a means, during days of rest, of calling the attention of men to philanthropic considerations and sentiments, and the dogma should be conceived only as a collection of commentaries having as their object general applications of these considerations and sentiments to the great political events which may arise, or having as their object to facilitate among the faithful the applications of morality in the daily relations which exist among them." [31]

Saint-Simon repeated his earlier strictures against violence and his absolute belief in the powers of persuasion. Propagation of the Christian doctrine by force was contrary to Christianity itself. With this principle he hoped to reassure the rich, who might otherwise be terrified lest the poor, having most to gain from the New Christianity, resort to revolution to inaugurate it speedily. As he explained, he had long delayed the promulgation of the religious cult of his system because he wanted the rich first to become familiar with his scientific and industrial doctrine so as to be convinced that he was not an egalitarian subversive preaching against them. His earlier works had demonstrated the real character of the industrial society. The rich had nothing to fear from the New Christianity because the grand projects he planned, the universal exploitation of world resources, affording full employment, could be undertaken only under their direction and to their incidental enrichment. The industrial society with the New Christianity as its moral principle was a capitalist society working under a profit system. Saint-Simon saw no inconsistency between entrepreneurial activity and the moral ideal of the New Christianity. In this sense he was one of the great ideologists of modern philanthropic capitalism.

The treatment of the spiritual power of the old order of society always posed a troublesome problem for Saint-Simon. The old Christian clergy of Europe had failed in their function as an intellectual elite, and they had to disappear. But the fate of this class was more disturbing than was the destiny of the military rulers of society. There was no conceivable continuity between the functions of a warrior noble class and a new industrial class, so that the framework of the former could not be preserved to house the latter. The spiritual power seemed to have greater continuity from the Middle Ages to modern times, since in medieval Europe the Christian clergy were the repositories of whatever scientific knowledge was available and they were also the protagonists of the only moral principle in society. It would perhaps have been desirable, in the name of an orderly transition, for the Christian clergy to have assimilated the new science and the new version of the humanitarian principle of early Christianity rather than for the class of scientists to develop outside the Church. Saint-Simon was not intent on destroying the clergy, but on transforming their nature. Unfortunately the European clergy, having failed to keep abreast of scientific knowledge, had forfeited its right to function as society's intellectual elite. They had become a corps stronghold of superstition and false ideas, which they were defending against the new scientists merely out of a desire to maintain themselves in power.

The failure of the clergy to preach the moral law of Christian brotherly love was fatal to their continuance as a spiritual force. Whereas the medieval clergy as the spiritual power had pretended to supremacy over the feudal classes or at least to a status of equality with the feudal-temporal force, the modern religious leaders had resigned themselves to complete dependence upon Caesar and his heirs in all the European political societies. The need for moralists, scientists, teachers of the newly discovered truths, even theologians as formulators of the truth into religious principles, still existed, but the clergies of the formal European religious faiths were no longer capable of filling this spiritual role, and therefore they had to vanish as classes in their existing role. Perhaps a few of them would be assimilated among the leaders of the new Academy of Reasoning or the Academy of Sentiment, but the old religious organizational structures, mere shells of their former selves, would have to be divested of their spiritual power. If the Christian churches persisted in trying to hold the minds and the passions of men in their grip, they would have to be destroyed after a few individuals were integrated with the new spiritual bodies. Saint-Simon did not expect this process to be a very profound shock to the European spirit since for a number of hundreds of years the scientists had been slowly absorbing the prestige which was being lost by the clergy. Most people, even those in the lowest ranks of the industrials, no longer gave credence to the clergy's superstition-laden explanations of natural phenomena, so that the abolition of the clergy as a class involved nothing more than the continuation of a process which was already far advanced. The acceptance of the New Christianity as the religion of the scientific industrial society would be the climax of this development. The old clergy having betrayed their trust as professors of morals and guides of sentiment and teachers of progressive scientific truth, their duties would be assumed by new classes composed of artists, poets, moralists, scientists, new theologians.

In his last work Saint-Simon wrote about the "church" of the New Christianity, his "mission," and the "voice of God" speaking "through his mouth." He referred to the "revelation of Christianity" and to its "superhuman character." [32] By this time the religious phrases had probably ceased to be mere literary artifices with him, as he had truly come to believe that Christianity was a unique historical experience and that he was the messiah of the new creed. In an early passage of the *Nouveau Christianisme* he made explicit reference to the messianic belief of the Jews and implied that he was its fulfillment. But despite the grandiloquent phrases, nowhere in the whole work is there an iota of what has traditionally been described as religious sentiment or expression. The word "mystical" has a negative connotation whenever he uses it, for his New Christianity is founded upon the truths of positive science and the one absolute moral principle of all time — brotherly love. It is even difficult to identify this religion with romantic pantheism and the romantic religious posturing which was in vogue in Europe during this period. Saint-Simon took occasion to condemn in passing the tendencies toward the "vague" in contemporary German literature, where romantic religiosity had struck deepest roots. His use of the arts in the propagation of the faith is a far cry from Chateaubriand's revelation of the beauties of Christianity. Chateaubriand tried to illustrate the genius of Christianity by pointing to the sublime creations its spirit had inspired; Saint-Simon would employ the artists as mere agents, to rouse men to action in harmony with the New Christianity's philanthropic moral principles. The final rewards of his new religion were not dissimilar from the promise which Diderot extended to the moral man who by his services to science and by his philanthropy had deserved well of humanity — the preservation of his memory among posterity. The gulf between Saint-Simon and traditional faiths is so unbridgeable that it seems presumptuous to embrace his humanitarian creed and the Judeo-Christian revelations under the same rubric of religion, were it not for the fact that the actual practice of many Jewish and Christian modernists is far closer to Saint-Simon's morality religion than to orthodox belief. [33]

At the outbreak of the French Revolution Saint-Simon was already twenty-nine years old, and the basic emotional pattern of his own personal life had been set in the sensuous irreligious climate of the later eighteenth century. [34] But with the Restoration he revealed a remarkable sensitivity to the temper of the new generation born at the turn of the century and to its peculiar emotional needs. The religious and moral vacuum of post-Napoleonic France, so poignantly described by de Musset in *La Confession d'un enfant du siècle* [35] and by Stendhal in *Le Rouge et le noir*, was unbearable for many young men — the legion of Julien Sorels who had inwardly broken with traditional revealed religions, yet had found nothing to fill the emptiness. Olinde Rodrigues, the tense, emotional mathematician who became the constant companion of Saint-Simon's last days, no doubt strengthened his early intuition that a new morality and a new organic age had to assume a religious form. The Catholic revival in the romantic manner ushered in by the works of men like Chateaubriand was one of the officially approved religious solutions proffered to these young men. The *Génie du Christianisme* was an attempt to make the old religion palatable by embellishing it with the aesthetics of romanticism. But this religion of "sentiment" which passed for the revived Catholicism was rejected by many young intellectuals. Saint-Simon's New Christianity was more eclectic: in many ways it provided an ideal moral and religious syncretism. He praised the rationalist creations of the scientists and the speculations of the entrepreneurs; he dipped their ethics into a bath of moral sentiment, the love for humanity, and called it religion. Saint-Simon himself could not quite improvise the requisite romantic style and imagery for this new religion, which in his hands remained simple, amystical, at times crudely rationalist. Within a few years after his death, the young men who formed a cult in his name unabashedly drank in the metaphors and poetic conceptions of contemporary Catholic thinkers and emerged with a special cult jargon and ritual. It was a feat of exegesis to use the trite doctrinaire text of the *Nouveau Christianisme* in a public evangelism. There is none of the Saint-Simonian mysticism in the master's own written works, though he might conceivably have been swept along with his young men had he lived. Saint-Simon actually had in preparation a third dialogue which was to cover the morality, the worship, and the dogma of the new religion as well as a credo for New Christians. But he died before it was completed.

Enfantin in his Teaching of November 28, 1831, publicly confessed that for long the disciples had not fully comprehended the *Nouveau Christianisme*, particularly the profound dogmas for the cult which it contained, for the simple reason that all was not explicit in this last testament. "When Eugène and I were laying the first bases of the trinitarian dogma in its theological form, we had not yet understood how profoundly this dogma had been sensed by Saint-Simon in the *Nouveau Christianisme*. Your father Rodrigues was the only one who constantly repeated to us that this book had enclosed within it the most lofty teaching which was ever given man to receive." [36]

Intent upon effecting a fusion between Saint-Simon's theory and Catholicism, Enfantin reread the last work in the light of a trinitarian principle, and so assiduous were his researches that he found the principle of three everywhere. The good society had three capacities, fine arts, science, and industry; the true religion had three aspects, morality, dogma, ritual. [37] If read in the spirit of Enfantin, the whole history of Christianity as set forth in the *Nouveau Christianisme* was a triad of eras whose character was dialectical. In Saint-Simon's Empire writings the history of scientific development had been established as an alternativity of epochs of synthesis and generalization and epochs of analysis and particularization. The *Nouveau Christianisme* revived this terminology, extending it far beyond the limits of a scientific method, adapting it to describe the whole social and moral order. First, there was an age of generalization:

"From the establishment of Christianity until the fifteenth century the human species has principally been occupied with the coordination of its general feelings and the establishment of a universal and unique principle and with the foundation of a general institution having as its goal the superimposition of an aristocracy of talents over an aristocracy of birth, and thus with submitting all particular interests to the general interest. During this whole period direct observations on private interests, on particular facts, and on secondary principles were neglected. They were denigrated in the minds of most people and a preponderance of opinion was agreed on this point, that secondary principles should be deduced from general facts and from one universal principle. This opinion was a truth of a purely speculative character, given that the human intelligence has not the means of establishing generalities of so precise a nature that it would be possible to derive from them as direct consequences all the particulars." [38]

This was the medieval outlook with its monist absolute, one is tempted to say the "thesis." Then followed the second stage, the contrary movement of this trinity — the history of Christianity from the Reformation to the present. During this second era, a new spirit of particularization, specialization, individuation, replaced generalization. This next epoch is clearly the antithesis, the contradiction of the first.

"Since the dissolution of the European spiritual power, a consequence of the insurrection of Luther, since the fifteenth century, the human spirit has detached itself from the most general views and has given itself over to specialization. It has occupied itself with the analysis of particular facts, with the private interests of various classes of society. It has labored to establish the secondary principles which might serve as foundations for the various branches of knowledge. And during this second period the opinion prevailed that reflections on the general facts, on the general principles, and on the general interests of the human species were nothing but vague metaphysical reflections, incapable of contributing effectively to the progress of knowledge and to the perfection of civilization." [39]

Though Saint-Simon does not use any of the Hegelian dialectical language he does express the concept: "Thus the human spirit has followed, since the fifteenth century, a direction opposed to what it had followed up to this period. And surely the important and positive progress which resulted in all our fields of knowledge proves irrevocably how much our ancestors in the Middle Ages were deceived in judging the study of particular facts, of secondary principles, and the analysis of private interests to be of little utility." [40]

This second antithetic movement of Christian history bore with it spiritual faults of its own, particular to its specializing, individualizing nature. Saint-Simon described again the malady of the modern age of self-centered, egotistic, isolated units, the moral parallel to the dominant trend of scientific particularization.

"But it is equally true that a very great evil resulted for society from the state of abandonment in which since the fifteenth century the works relative to the study of general facts, of general principles, and of general interests have been left. This abandonment has given birth to a feeling of egotism which has become dominant among all classes and in all individuals. This sentiment has facilitated for Caesar the means of recovering a large part of the political power which he had lost before the fifteenth century. It is to this egotism that we should attribute the political malady of our age, a malady which makes all the workers useful to society suffer, a malady which makes the kings absorb a very large part of the wages of the poor for their personal expenditure, for that of their courtiers and of their soldiers; a malady which makes royalty and the aristocracy of birth usurp an enormous part of the esteem which is due the scientists, the artists, and the chiefs of industrial works for their services of direct and positive utility which they render to the body social." [41]

Moral deficiencies of the second movement of Christian history necessitated another reversal of the trend, away from particularization, individuation, egotism, but in this, Saint-Simon's last formula for the alternativity principle, he did not call for a complete turning back to the general. He ended with an appeal for the coexistence of the two elements of individuation and of generalization, not quite a new synthesis, but a civilization in which both antithetical elements were present. "It is therefore very desirable that the works which have as their object the perfection of our knowledge relative to general facts, general principles, and general interests, should promptly be activated and should henceforth be protected by society on a basis of equality with those works which have as their object the study of particular facts, of secondary principles, and of private interests." [42] A simultaneous advance on both fronts, the synthetic and the particularistic, was the ideal course for the new religious society.

With less warrant Enfantin and Eugène Rodrigues later read into Saint-Simon's works other trinitarian formulas such as God, Man, and World, or the Infinite, the Ego, and the Non-Ego. Their doctrine moved further and further away from his positivism and shot off into a world of sensual mysticism alien to Saint-Simon's thought. On the other hand, it would be difficult to reduce Saint-Simon to a matter-of-fact *philosophe* of the simple, *idéologue* persuasion.

Eight days before his death Saint-Simon by word of mouth communicated to Olinde Rodrigues his faith that the *Nouveau Christianisme* was the very heart of his system, despite the fact that it would at first be misconstrued. "Our last work will be the last to be understood. It is generally believed that men are not susceptible of becoming passionate in a religious direction, but this is a grave error. The Catholic system was in contradiction with the system of the sciences and modern industry, and therefore its fall was inevitable. It took place, and this fall is the signal for a new belief which is going to fill with its enthusiasm the void which criticism has left in the souls of men, for it is a belief which will draw its strength from everything that belongs to the ancient belief. . . . *The whole doctrine is there*. . . ." [43]

At another time, while conversing of their future triumph, Saint-Simon prophesied, "A passing sleep followed by a perpetual awakening." [44]

IV

Children of Saint-Simon

THE TRIUMPH OF LOVE

"Fatalism can inspire no virtue beyond a gloomy resignation, since man is ignorant of and fears the inevitable destiny which awaits him; from a belief in the providential system, on the other hand, there results great activity full of confidence and love, for the more a man is conscious of his destiny the more he works in concert with God to realize it.

"Therefore cast aside all fear, Gentlemen, and do not struggle against the flood-tide which bears you to a happy future. Put an end to the uncertainty which withers your hearts and strikes you with impotence. Embrace with love the altar of reconciliation, for the times have been fulfilled and the hour will soon ring when according to the Saint-Simonian transfiguration of the Christian word, *All shall be called and all shall be chosen.*"

Doctrine de Saint-Simon. Deuxième Séance.

"As for the new moral theories and the questions of doctrine which separate me from Père Enfantin, I cannot yet explain myself clearly because I doubt. . . . I even doubt Saint-Simon. I doubt those who have continued him. In a word I doubt everything. I am becoming a *philosophe* again. . . . I am once more alone in the world."

Jules Le Chevalier, *Religion Saint-Simonienne.*
Réunion générale de la famille.
Séance du samedi 19 Novembre (Paris, 1832).

Wʜᴇɴ the Saint-Simonian movement was founded by Olinde Rodrigues on the morrow of the master's death, it attracted a heterogeneous group of brilliant, disturbed young men — Buchez, Holstein, Arlès, Bazard, Fournel, Enfantin, d'Eichthal, the Pereires, Michel Chevalier, Duveyrier, Barrault.[1] They proselytized throughout Europe — though they usually preferred to convert in Paris — organized missions to the working classes, lectured in hired halls, contributed to newspapers and journals (*Le Producteur* and *Le Globe* became their official organs), were worshiped and denied. Soon they betrayed a characteristic common to young sects, religious and secular, Christian, Marxist, and Freudian — they fought bitterly among themselves. Violent personal rivalries for power and profound doctrinal differences developed in the church, and in the heat of the controversy the two antagonisms became inextricably confounded with each other. Enfantin, a strikingly handsome man touching thirty, an engineer graduated from the Ecole Polytechnique, the son of a bankrupt businessman, quickly rose to be head of the hierarchy in the sacred college, though he had seen Saint-Simon in the flesh only once and there is no record of the master's judgment — his dog Presto is reported to have barked his disapproval. Père Enfantin presided over a succession of heartrending schisms, melodramatic temporary reconciliations, and final excommunications, accounts of which found their way into print immediately after their occurrence. The lives of the Fathers were stenographically reported. When Buchez, Bazard, and Rodrigues himself were ultimately separated from the Saint-Simonian family and church, the surviving faithful redoubled their devotion to the new pope. They had all been committed to the rehabilitation of the flesh and to the commandment: Sanctify yourselves in work and in pleasure. They were united in their resolve to establish a new organic order in which the senses would be gratified through the flowering of art, science, and material prosperity; but Enfantin's theological postulates, his androgynous image of God, and his apparent sanction of promiscuous love relationships passed beyond the point of tolerance for some of the adepts. When Rodrigues counterattacked he charged Père Enfantin with the very vices which their religion had come to remedy in contemporary society — destructiveness and revolutionary negation.

Saint-Simonian meetings were often disrupted by hoodlums hired by prominent citizens who feared the seductions of the cult for their young. Stendhal's Lucien Leuwen, it will be remembered, threatened his banker father that he would run off and become a Saint-Simonian if his wishes were not acceded to. The noisy debates among the apostles transpired in an atmosphere of general hysteria which induced seizures and fainting spells. Men saw visions of Christ and Enfantin. Edouard Charton, a Saint-Simonian preacher, has left a description of his initial terror, followed by a flood of free associations and by a passionate evocation of his experience when in the presence of the Father the gift of tongues was upon him. "Soon I could hear myself speak. I slowly became master of myself. I felt carried away by a torrent of thoughts and I took courage. I let my memories roam slowly from one event to another. . . . If I aroused pity for the miseries of the people, I really was cold, I was hungry. If I bemoaned the grief of the isolated, betrayed man, I suddenly felt myself enveloped by the loneliness of my student room or the disdainful looks of men rejecting my entreaties. I was happy because I lived in body and soul with a greater intensity than I ever had before in my life! My whole being expanded and filled the hall. . . . Borne aloft by my emotions as if they were powerful wings, I floated beneath a mysterious sky." [2] At meetings of the Saint-Simonian family "members of the proletariat" who were one moment burning with hatred against the privileged orders found themselves overcome by love as they embraced young nobles before the whole assembly, all joined as children in Saint-Simon. [3]

The strange fascination which Enfantin exercised upon the disciples was a troublesome memory years later when most of them had resumed respectable careers and had become successful bankers, engineers, entrepreneurs, and artists of the Second Empire. The search for the Female Messiah, the emancipator of her sex, for whom Enfantin was only a precursor, the expeditions to

North Africa and the Middle East, degenerated into *opéra bouffe* and the movement petered out. The sentimental doctrines of the cult soon melted into the general romantic temper of the period. Triumphant international Victorianism put a determined stop to the easy talk of free love, but even in death Saint-Simonism remained one of the most potent emotional and intellectual influences in nineteenth-century society, inchoate, diffuse, but always there, penetrating into the most improbable places. Paradoxically enough, the Saint-Simonians exerted an enduring influence in the business world, where they provided an ideology for expansive nineteenth-century capitalism in the Catholic countries of Europe which unfortunately, *pace* Max Weber, had been deprived of a Protestant ethic. The Saint-Simonians left their mark on the projects of the Crédit Mobilier, the railway networks of the Continent, and de Lesseps' Suez Canal; their economic teachings have been traced to even more remote areas, the works of Visconde Mauá, the Brazilian entrepreneur, and of Lamanski, a pioneer of Russian industrialization. In the period between the First and Second World Wars there was talk of a neo-Saint-Simonian revival among French and German captains of industry.

Today one is more drawn to the psychological theories of the Saint-Simonians and the vivid portrayal of spiritual anguish in their public confessionals. Piercing insights into the nature of love and sexuality, which outraged the good bourgeois of the 1830's and brought down the police upon them, now have a greater appeal than economic doctrines which have become rather commonplace. Enfantin dared to discuss sexual repression with frankness in an age which had grown unaccustomed to such ideas since the Restoration reimposed a restrictive system of public moral behavior from which at least the upper classes of eighteenth-century society had felt themselves emancipated. Saint-Simonian schisms were usually provoked by quarrels over the degree of sexual emancipation allowable in the new world. The more sedate among them would countenance divorce, but insisted on monogamy. For a brief period at least Enfantin preached free love with the same unrelenting absolutism with which Turgot had once espoused freedom of thought and economic action.

In the first public exposition of their doctrine in a hall on rue

Taranne in 1828–1829, the Saint Simonians were still demonstrating the positive scientific character of their teachings in language reminiscent of both Condorcet and Saint-Simon. This was their last obeisance to reason. When they proclaimed themselves a religion, as distinguished from a movement, their orators repudiated the groveling adjustment to contemporary taste which had characterized the scientific and historical proofs of their lecture series, published as the *Doctrine de Saint-Simon*. At a ceremony on November 27, 1831, Enfantin solemnly announced, "Up to now Saint-Simonism has been a doctrine and we have been doctors. Now we are going to realize our teachings. We are going to found the religion. . . . We are now apostles." [4] As religious teachers they spoke directly to the hearts of men, to the downtrodden workers, to the enslaved women of the world, to moral men in conflict with themselves in all ranks of society. They were resolved to awaken the dormant feelings of love in mankind not by historical disquisitions and not by denunciations of the evils of the existing order, but by the beautiful example of their love for one another. Those Saint-Simonians who survived the great schisms voluntarily submitted to the discipline of the hierarchy, adored the Father, and ennobled the commonest labor by performing it with devotion in their retreat in Ménilmontant on the outskirts of Paris. Their sermons depicted the happiness of a future world where the passions were free, where both jealousy and indifference had been extirpated, where each man loved and worked according to his capacity, where the flesh was not mortified, where monogamy was not imposed but was practiced spontaneously — though only by the monogamous. In the religion of Saint-Simon dullards and sluggards in love would be aroused by the inspiration, the exhortations, and if need be the personal ministrations of the high priests and priestesses. For the nonce, alas, the seat of the Mother by side of Père Enfantin was left vacant. In this second phase — when the preachments of the Saint-Simonians became dogmatic and they abandoned demonstrations from philosophical history — ritual, drama, costume, and music were introduced to fire the imagination of prospective converts. More and more they sought to pattern their actions after those of the early Christians. Enfantin's vest, a relic which has been preserved in the Bibliothèque de l'Arsenal, was a symbolic garment: since it could only be laced in back, to don it required the assistance of another human being — a witness to the unity and brotherhood of man.

The religion turned its light on man's sexual nature and its relation to his intellect, on the psychic debasement of women, on the nature of love and God. On November 19, 1831, in a lesson to the Saint-Simonian assembly, Enfantin developed a complex theory of love and proposed a new sexual order based on the realities of human affections to replace the monogamous marriage which recognized no divorce. First he distinguished between two types of love, expressive of fundamentally different psychic natures, the constant and the fickle. "There are beings with profound durable affections which time only knits more closely. There are other affections which are lively, quick, passing but nonetheless strong, for which time is a painful, sometimes an insupportable, trial." [5] To subject both characters to the legal arrangements which conformed only to the passionate desires of the monogamous entailed emotional misery and inevitably resulted in social chaos. Enfantin identified three forms of love relationship instead of one, and he sanctioned them all without praise or blame: the intimate, the convenient, and the religious. Intimate affections could be equally profound whether they were enduring or fleeting, as long as they were consummated among characters of the same type. When on occasion two contradictory personalities established relationships, the love was to be labeled convenient or casual. A third love, which he called religious, was the unique attribute of the Saint-Simonian sacerdocy — the priest's love for the two natures, which he understood equally well. "Thus with respect to morality the temple is divided into three parts, which correspond to the three faces of love — casual affection, profound affection, and calm or sacerdotal affection which knows how to combine them one with another." [6] What Enfantin meant by free love was the freedom to love in accordance with one's psychic nature, not universal promiscuity or universal evasion of the moral order through fornication and adultery. "How can one give both psychological types satisfaction and a rule at the same time? How can one safeguard exclusive love from the abnormal exaltation which renders it vicious and also protect it from the disruptive influence which the character of the other series, the Don Juan, exercises on the person of its choice? How preserve (no less important, despite what Christian prejudice has been able to do and still does to favor exclusive love) the individual who has this progressive love, who does not stop at one because he has loved one, but can, after having loved one, move toward another if the second is greater than the first — how preserve such a person from the anathema, condemnation, and contempt which Christianity hurls against him and from the impositions of persons endowed with exclusive affections sanctified by Christian law?" The solutions lay in the Saint-Simonian doctrines of the rehabilitation of the flesh, the emancipation of women, and the hierarchic priesthood of love, whose guidance was essential to avoid emotional abuses. [7]

The Saint-Simonian rebuttal of the bourgeois defenders of the family was full of scorn for the moralists whose hypocritical code was preserved only by the acceptance of prostitution and by the social toleration of adultery — the bourgeois safeguarded the chastity of their own daughters by "levying a tribute upon the daughters of the poor who walked the streets." Abel Transon's sermon on the *Affranchissement des femmes* on January 1, 1832, was a tender defense of the prostitutes of Paris, the modern Magdalens. [8] Later Marxist derision of bourgeois morality and Victorian spirituality drew heavily from Saint-Simonian and Fourierist sources. If progress came to signify the liberation and full expression of the whole man, his total personality, then sexual actualization had to be recognized as good, sexual repression as an illness which affected man's rational capacities adversely. Progress should not be restricted to the advancement of reason at the cost of a drying up of the fonts of love. As long as one vital drive in man's nature was curbed there could be no true happiness. For a brief period the Saint-Simonians, at Enfantin's command, attempted what would now be called sublimation in their retreat in Ménilmontant, in denial of the popular interpretation of their religion as gross sensuality. They were preaching the triumph of love, not mere carnal passion, but the distinction was difficult to communicate in nineteenth-century Christian bourgeois society, and when the rehabilitation of the flesh became a central dogma of the new religion, a rich vein of crude humor was discovered by contemporary journalists, who exploited it to the utmost. Enfantin's truth was not understood at the time by his revilers; the Saint-Simonians were expressing profound psychological realities which could not be assimilated by even the most perceptive *idéologue* observers of the human drama — men like Stendhal, for example, who wrote a witty though superficial pasquinade against them, joining the pack whose inner corrosion he knew so well. Sometimes it is difficult to believe in the authenticity of the Saint-Simonian love experience, and there is much that seems artificial in their aping of Christian models. Enfantin's withdrawal with a party of forty disciples to a house in the district where he had spent his childhood, the resurrection of the image of the Father and the bestowal of the august title upon a young man with a "childish" name, the quest for the Mother in distant lands, the reliance upon adolescent forms like an "initiation," all bear witness to their perturbed affective natures. On June 6, 1832, before assuming the Saint-Simonian dress, Retouret ceremoniously turned to Enfantin: "Father, once I told you that I saw in you the majesty of an emperor . . . the goodness of a Messiah. You appeared formidable to me. Today I have felt how profoundly tender and gentle you are. Father, I am ready." [9] Yet, for all these tinsel trappings, the Saint-Simonians voiced subconscious longings whose very existence the bourgeois of Paris dared not admit.

Simultaneously the Saint-Simonians, Fourier, and Auguste Comte made a momentous discovery. They came to realize that women, one half of humanity, with their unique capacity for feeling, tenderness, and passion, had been suppressed for centuries because the Judeo-Christian tradition had identified them with evil, with the flesh, and with the grosser parts of human nature. The Saint-Simonian proclamation of the emancipation of women, Fourier's masterful depictions of their real needs and wants, and Comte's idealization of his beloved angel broke not only with Catholicism but with the eighteenth-century tradition of many *philosophes*, who even in their most expansive moods had regarded women as either frivolous or lesser human beings. This superior attitude had still been Père Simon's. For the Saint-Simonians and for Fourier the emancipation of women became the symbol of the liberation of bodily desires. If capacities were to be expressed in all their wholeness, the sexual desires of men, and women too, would have to be fully appeased, not as inferior but as noble, integral functions of the body. Once the Saint-Simonians denied the Christian dichotomy of the body and the soul (and Saint-Simon himself in a number of passages had already pointed in this direction) a pronouncement of instinctual emancipation had to follow. The Saint-Simonians and Fourier drew back from the position which the Marquis de Sade had defended earlier in the century when his sensationalism *à outrance* demanded forbidden gratifications, but they were accepting the consequences of their view of man as a feeling or instinctual being as well as an intellectual and active one. Condorcet had approved of women voters and women scientists, but he still thought of sexual passions in somewhat pejorative terms. While the desires were natural, they had to be regulated. Condorcet the materialist was absorbed with the body — physical ailments were a field in which man could brilliantly exercise his scientific genius by preventing disease and by increasing longevity — but he was never as direct and wholehearted as the Saint-Simonians in demanding respect and honor for the passions He retained a hierarchy of values among the expressions of man's nature: the mind was still on top, an order which the Saint-Simonians and Fourier abandoned.

THE MALADY OF THE AGE

THE Saint-Simonians startled the intellectuals of Europe with a cry of despair, "Progress is in danger!" Civilization itself was threatened with total dissolution. The crisis of the times which Saint-Simon had diagnosed earlier in the century had been prolonged for decades; continually aggravated, it was undermining the whole social structure. The elementary bonds of human relations were being loosened. Faith in the eventual restoration of sanity and in the progress of humanity was unshaken among the Saint-Simonians, but what a terrible moral toll was being exacted from their generation, living in a twilight world when that-which-had-been no longer held men's allegiance and that-which-would-be was not yet believed. "Gentlemen," began the lecturer at the opening session of the exposition of the *Doctrine de Saint-Simon* on December 17, 1828, "Viewed as a whole, society today presents the spectacle of two warring camps. In one are entrenched the few remaining defenders of the religious and political organization of the Middle Ages; in the other, drawn up under the rather inappropriate name of *partisans of the new ideas*, are all those who either cooperated in or applauded the overthrow of the ancient edifice. We come to bring peace to these two armies by proclaiming a doctrine which preaches not only its horror of blood but its horror of strife under whatever name it may disguise itself. *Antagonism* between a spiritual and a temporal power, *opposition* in honor of liberty, *competition* for the greatest good of all — we do not believe in the everlasting need for any of these war machines. We do not allow to civilized humanity any *natural right* which obliges it to tear its own entrails." [10]

The degradation of the age was described by the Saint-Simonians in images less powerful than Balzac's but with the same moralist intent. Love relations were false; young girls were decked out by their parents to increase their value like slaves on the auction block. Since egotism colored all human relationships, in order to get people to perform an act of charity one had to invite them to a ball. The Greeks were being oppressed by the Turks, but no European nation rose to their defense and Christians traded with the persecutors. Fashionable atheism was proof that there were no ties, either to God or among men. An act of devotion or love was met with a sneer. Indignation at the persistence of social conflict was dismissed with the cynical reflection that such had always been the nature of man. "We have spared you the grief one experiences in penetrating into the intimacy of those families without faith and without belief which, turned in upon themselves, are linked to society only by the bond of taxation." [11] The malady of the age was an atrophy of love and association. "If one takes away the sympathies which unite men to their fellows, which cause them to suffer of their sufferings, take pleasure in their joys, in a word live their lives, it is impossible to see anything else in society but an aggregate of individuals without ties or relationships, having nothing to motivate their conduct but the impulses of egotism." [12]

THE PROPHETS OF PARIS

A passionate indictment of their selfish generation was the leitmotiv of everything the Saint-Simonians wrote and taught. It struck a responsive note in the audience of the Salle Taitbout and among correspondents throughout the world who recognized that the disease was their own. "Yes, my friend," wrote a gentleman from New York to *Le Globe*, "for twenty years I have been a Saint-Simonian in my inner being." [13] The Saint-Simonians brought to a reconsideration of the problem of progress their own anxieties, their thirst for faith, their fear in the face of a moral vacuum, their self-disgust with indifference and verbal atheism, above all, horror of their incapacity to love. Though they were not acquainted with the Hegelian idea of alienation, they described many of the symptoms of the spiritual *malaise* which Marx dwelt upon a decade later.

The Saint-Simonian inquiry into the state and destiny of economic production, science, and art in a world of disorder and confusion, of political and moral anarchy, drew a bleak picture. Industry was in a state of chaos. The cutthroat competition among entrepreneurs had brought about a haphazard distribution of productive forces accompanied by periodic crises during which competent managers lost their fortunes in bankruptcies and masses of workers starved. The common people refused to be comforted by the assurance of the economists that free enterprise and the introduction of machinery would ultimately lead to increased employment. The disorder, secrecy, and monopoly which interfered with technological improvement, the incompetent direction of industry by men who had nothing to recommend them but inherited wealth, the sufferings of the proletariat, the indifference of the economists who devoted their studies to a description of competitive antagonisms rather than to devising means for their alleviation, the absence of a central direction to industrial life which would allocate instruments of production in accordance with need and capacity — these were both the symptoms and the causes of the prevailing industrial anarchy. The possessors of capital were idlers, merit went unrewarded, gains were distributed in a chance manner. *Laissez faire* had resulted in a colossal waste of human energy: technological potentialities were not fulfilled and material production was only a fraction of capacity. The physical misery of fellow humans left most men cold. Economic antagonism was the rule of industrial relations between workers and employers, when the true nature of man was pacific, cooperative, loving, and associative. "What is unbridled competition but murderous war, which perpetuates itself in a new form, of individual against individual, nation against nation? All the theories which this dogma tends to foster are based only on hostility." [14]

The Saint-Simonians developed their attack against Malthus and the liberal economists with a vigor unknown to their master, who had once been close to Jean-Baptiste Say and Charles Dunoyer. "They say the present distribution of property condemns the *proletarian* . . . to wretchedness if he marries; therefore he should live isolated in the world without a companion to share his sufferings, without children who would make him understand hope and would attach him to the future." The Saint-Simonians had read the arguments of the school economists who demonstrated that the introduction of machinery created only temporary unemployment, that in the end supply and demand would be balanced. But what about the human beings involved? "Will our reasonings console them? Will they accept their misery patiently because statistical calculations prove that in a number of years they will have bread?" [15]

Science was in the same sorry state. Here the disciples repeated Saint-Simon's strictures against the piddling practitioners who were content with their anarchic laboratory observations and kept amassing insignificant details without a general theory, without a unified direction, smug in their little niches, callous to the woes of the rest of the world and the fate of humanity, cold *brutiers*. The competition which raged among the industrialists was paralleled among the scientists; they were absorbed in precedence of discovery, and in the absence of a general allocation of scientific resources they repeated one another's experiments, squandering their own and humanity's genius. In academies they convened in the same room, but that was the extent of their association. There was no over-all scientific plan. Teaching and research were two separate compartments and what one branch knew was hardly ever communicated to the other. There were hundreds of analytic scientists, no synthesis. There were isolated discoveries, but no concerted attempt to apply them for the good of mankind through technology. Again, *laissez faire* in science was dissipating energies upon useless projects.

Most pitiable was the state of the fine arts, a form of expression which in every age faithfully mirrored the moral nature of man. Unlike the creative geniuses of Greece and medieval Europe, contemporary artists had been reduced to the role of satirists who mocked their society or elegists who bewailed the state of mankind. They represented no great affirmations. Unless men believed in something, whether it was war or religion or humanity, there could be no grandeur in the arts. In the absence of a common ideal, the fine arts were mere evocations and reflections of the prevailing anarchy.

When the Saint-Simonians reached maturity a new generation of poets and dramatists had begun issuing manifestoes against the classical spirit and proclaiming the rebirth of poetry. The outburst of romanticism bestowed new worth upon aesthetic genius and gave the lie to those pessimists of the previous generation who had maintained that science could achieve victories only at the expense of the poetic spirit. The regeneration of the fine arts — though devoid of the wished-for vital spirit — convinced the Saint-Simonians that man could develop a more fertile imagination along with a more productive intellect and a vast material expansion of civilization. The fine arts, instead of being doomed — a common eighteenth-century attitude — might even become the most magnificent embodiment of human creative capacity. By comparison with masterpieces of beauty, the sciences appeared cold and lifeless; the passion for science which Condorcet had extolled so eloquently in his fragment on the *New Atlantis* was surpassed by a new enthusiasm for literature, painting, and music. Within a decade Saint-Simonian doctrines were absorbed by poets and artists throughout Europe who established no formal ties with the church, but who gave voice to its ideology. In this sense writers as widely dispersed as Alfred de Vigny, Ogarev, Carlyle, Heine, and the poets of young Germany were Saint-Simonians; even Victor Hugo paid his debt to Enfantin in a famous letter. Progressive humanity, the idealization of love, of association, of brotherly feeling, of outgoing emotion, appeared as new subjects capable of inspiring an artist to accomplishments superior to the work of the *Grand*

Siècle with its exaltation of military glory. The notion of socially conscious art and literature, which has in the last hundred and fifty years spawned so many worthless documents and a few works of genius, was born among the Saint-Simonians. To sing of productive humanity and not of warriors would be the artistic ideal of the new order. To warm men's hearts grown frigid in the contemplation of neoclassic forms was the poetic mission. Poetry was no longer condemned to a repetition of the ancient myths; it had acquired a vast corpus of novel situations drawn from human history in all times and places, the whole gamut of human emotions, not the few permissible ones presented on the traditional stage. There were new feelings to be experienced and new priests of sentiment to be ordained.

While the Saint-Simonian ideology of love and humanity as a cure for the *mal du siècle* evoked a widespread emotional response, the purely religious doctrine of the cult was a dismal failure: it was a manufactured religion whose raw materials were easily recognizable. When they called religion "the synthesis of all conceptions of humanity, of all ways of being," and preached that "not only will religion dominate the political order but the political order will be in its ensemble a religious institution, for nothing can be conceived outside of God or developed outside of his law . . . ," [16] it all sounded as artificial and rusty as the writings of Saint-Simon himself when he concocted rituals for the Religion of Newton, expounded Physicism, or taught the New Christianity. One group of Saint-Simonians had been exposed to German intellectual influences, particularly Gustave d'Eichthal and Eugène Rodrigues, and through them the amorphous pantheism of eighteenth-century German religious thought infiltrated France. The young Rodrigues had translated Lessing's aphorisms on the *Erziehung des Menschengeschlechts*, which are redolent with a romantic Spinozism that has little or nothing to do with the hard geometric propositions of which Spinoza's ethical system was originally constructed. The Germanic *Schwärmerei* invariably fell flat when it was presented in Cartesian French; it lacked authenticity. The Saint-Simonians' talk of a unitary law and of a providential plan, of the inevitable religious revival — for by definition all organic periods had to be religious — is deficient in feeling-tone. After

Enfantin made the image of God androgynous a few loyal Saint-Simonians died with the "Father-Mother" on their lips, but though the Saint-Simonian religion may have for a fleeting moment inspired the adepts at Ménilmontant to ecstasy, its sermons sound imitative, mechanical, and stereotyped. No doubt some of them had religious experiences in William James's sense of the term, felt newborn upon conversion, and at least for a time were in a state of love which they identified with God; but a mere handful, perhaps only Holstein, Enfantin's oldest friend, were sustained in this emotion to the very end. Their historic proof that a new religion must be born after the incredulity of their own generation was nothing more than the threadbare analogy — worn even thinner since — between the contemporary world and the latter days of the Roman Empire. If the taste of their cynical age was bitter on their parched lips, there is little evidence that their thirst for a new religion was ever quenched by the ceremonies which Enfantin and Chevalier contrived — perhaps to stimulate themselves as much as their disciples. "Let us be prepared, as de Maistre has said," the lecturer of the thirteenth séance concluded, "for a great event in the divine order, one toward which we are moving with an accelerated pace, one which must strike all observers: let us say with him, there is no more religion on earth and a human being cannot remain in this state; but we are more fortunate than de Maistre, we no longer have to await the man of genius whose coming he prophesied, who was destined, according to him, to reveal the natural affinity of religion and science. Saint-Simon has appeared." [17] The heavy draughts of Joseph de Maistre's revived papal Catholicism with which they buoyed their drooping spirits never really touched more than a few of the most susceptible, the conversion-prone. Saint-Simonism remained a social doctrine with a religious aura; it was never a religion.

THE SOCIAL TRINITY

ASIDE from the religious beliefs and paraphernalia of the cult, which rendered them notorious, the Saint-Simonians bequeathed to Western civilization a solid, relatively systematic body of social thought. Many of their ideas penetrated European socialist party programs in the form of slogans; others were more widely if more thinly disseminated. Since the original writings of Saint-Simon were almost impossible to come by, his ideas were generally fused with those of the school in the commentaries of the thirties and the forties. As a "progressive" theory, Saint-Simonism had no inhibitions against putting into Saint-Simon's mouth words he had never uttered, if these were considered necessary developments of his thought. In general the rationalist and historical doctrines, which antedated the religious phase, found readier acceptance than Enfantin's mystical lucubrations in the *Physiologie religieuse*, but the two periods are to be distinguished more by the views they accented and the style of preaching than by any fundamental cleavage in ideas.

The very definition of man had been changed by the Saint-Simonians; hence the nature of his evolution — the term became common — had to be reinterpreted. In one of his aspects man was still a rationalist, scientific, calculating utilitarian, who through time was fulfilling his needs; but what a feeble, one-sided identification of his glorious self this Turgot-Condorcet man had become in the eyes of the romantic Saint-Simonians of the thirties. They never outrightly denounced their spiritual ancestors, the eighteenth-century French forerunners. They paid them due homage, but they also adopted additional fathers in progress from across the Rhine, Kant and Herder and Lessing, and introduced that lone Neapolitan, Vico. The foreign thinkers endowed the Saint-Simonian image of man with moral and emotional depth. The eighteenth-century progressists knew well enough that man in their age was not yet a rational utilitarian, but they firmly believed that he would become one, for that was his destiny. The Saint-Simonians invoked Saint-Simon and Vico and ultimately Plato to reveal a different man, a tripartite man, a being who was at once a rational scientist, a practical industrial activist, and a man of feeling and moral drives, a creature of emotion. Since this was the real total man, any theory which limited him to one aspect of his triadic nature was a false representation of his sacred personality. In Turgot and Condorcet and the early Saint-Simon the conclusion is inescapable that the history of mankind since primitive times had demonstrated the flowering of rational capacities at the expense of imaginative and passionate nature and that they deemed this one-sided evolution good in an absolute sense. For the Saint-Simonians progress was never encased within the relatively finite compartment which a rationalist view pre-established, a world in which you withdrew from the passions what you bestowed upon reason, a closed economy with a fixed quantum of energy. Saint-Simonian man had infinite capacities in all directions; he could at one and the same time progress in power over nature, in expansive feeling, and in the endless accumulation of knowledge.

The redefinition of the nature of man by the Saint-Simonians had moved far away from the rather mechanical Bichat typology. The three cardinal capacities were present in all men, and in the good society they would all be nurtured and developed. The Saint-Simonians recognized that men were not equal and tended to excel in one or another talent, that each man had a specialized capacity which would require separate training; but while Bichat seemed to posit a finite store of energy which was concentrated among different people in uneven proportions, for the Saint-Simonians capacities were all endlessly expansive. What the Saint-Simonians rejected were the exclusivity and limitations of all previous definitions of man. Man was at once utilitarian and religious and activist: morality had a sanction in use, in God, and in nature all at the same time. The Christian duality of the spiritual and the corporeal, the contempt for the body and its desires, the eighteenth century's hypertrophy of reason and its implied denigration of the creative imagination, and the Stoic repression of feeling were all banished. Man appeared with both his body and his soul, loving, with an insatiable thirst for learning, boundlessly dynamic in his conquests of nature. In the hundred years of prophecy Turgot's "progress of the human mind" became the Saint-Simonian "progress of the general emancipation of humanity."

As in all triadic systems ancient and modern, the role, relative potency, and position of excellence of the three elements composing the unity was a harassing problem. It invariably led to disputations. Saint-Simon himself had wrestled with the three capacities and had offered his alternative, often contradictory, solutions; and the great heresiarch Comte struggled with the new trinity, producing complex, subtle responses worthy of a latter-day Greek

Father of the Church. The relations among the capacity to reason, to act, and to feel became central to Saint-Simonian theology. The ideal of equivalence among the three has always been difficult to maintain (Christianity with its trinitarian definition of God had a similarly irksome intellectual problem which found expression in thousands of volumes and cost hundreds of thousands of lives). What was man, after all, was he *primarily* a rational, a sentient, or an activist being? Which psychological type should rule the world? Which should lead in the march of progress and which should docilely accept subordination? The eighteenth-century rationalists faced none of these prickly questions because the reign of reason as an ideal was virtually unchallenged. Saint-Simon and his disciples, the true and the dissident, had to make a configuration out of the different natures which comprised the human soul, and however much they pleaded for the parallel worth of knowing, feeling, and acting, discoursed on their common interdependence, praised their mutual indispensability, the very idea of hierarchy raised questions of precedence, and the worm of rivalry among the three equally noble parts crept into the bosom of the doctrine. Though Plato's triad was always in the background of the Saint-Simonian system, the outright subordination of the nonrational capacities in the ancient myth made direct references to him uncongenial.

The Saint-Simonians accentuated the final phase of the tradition of their master and elevated to pre-eminence the *artists* — their generic name for what he had called the Platonic capacity — a category that extends far beyond painters, poets, and musicians, and embraces all moral teachers, whatever may be their instruments of instruction. If man was tripartite his emotional being was the most developed side of his nature in the good, healthy, organic periods of human existence. The crisis of modern times was primarily an emotional one and the malady of the age a morbidity of the sentient capacity. Mankind's talent for love had shriveled. The scientific capacity, if left to itself, would become glacial, merely critical; science was always useful, but it would be dangerous if allowed to dominate society. Since the sentient capacity was the clue to man's religious future — the major problem of human existence — clearly the man of feeling was the ideal personality type, before whom his brothers in humanity had to incline slightly, even if they did not quite genuflect. The man of moral capacity set goals and inspired his brethren with the desire to achieve them. By his side the scientist who merely accumulated observations was a frigid analytic agent, indispensable for progress, but surely not to be ensconced on the throne. The Saint-Simonians were among the first to voice their horror of the neutrality of science.

The appeal of this idealized artist-poet-priest type to the romantics who listened to the exposition of the *Doctrine de Saint-Simon* was overwhelming. A fusion of religious and aesthetic enthusiasm had been achieved by eighteenth-century German writers; it was an underlying tenet of Chateaubriand's religiosity in France; Saint-Simonism was thus sowing in well-ploughed fields. Even before the Saint-Simonian preachers mounted the rostrum the young poets of Europe had already arrogated to themselves the emotional direction of mankind which the clergies of all nations were allowing to slip from their grasp. Since feeling was all, the artist-poet-musician with the most acute sensitivities could best express man's moral nature and reawaken dormant moral sentiments. The romantic genius was *Obermann*, Vigny's *Chatterton*, Hölderlin, Beethoven — all Christlike martyrs — not the rationalist scientist-geniuses of Turgot and Condorcet. It was most flattering to the poets of Western romanticism to find themselves raised to the pinnacle of society — albeit the society of the future — at a time when they were disdained by the successful activist philistine bourgeois and treated with cold indifference by the rationalist men of letters and science in the academies.

FROM ANTAGONISM TO ASSOCIATION

THE whole of past history had only been provisional or transitional. The "new man" had not yet come into being. The first century of progressist thinkers — and even Marx can be cast among them, despite the fact that he would hold his nose in this company — were all conscious that history was bifurcated by their generation. With the revelation of Saint-Simon there had transpired a qualitative change in man's historic destiny. The prime distinction between the past and the future hinged on the transformation of one dominant moral characteristic of the "old man" — Antagonism.

Unlike their autodidact master, the Saint-Simonians incorporated philosophical history from beyond the boundaries of France. In addition to members of the school the principal agents of transmission were Victor Cousin, who had popularized Kant and Hegel in his lectures, and Michelet, who had translated Vico a year after Saint-Simon's death. When Edgar Quinet adapted Herder, the chain was complete. The Kantian theory of history, developed in a brilliant little essay published in 1784 in the *Berliner Monatschrift*, the "Idea for a Universal History with Cosmopolitan Intent," provided the Saint-Simonians with a key formula that explained the historical process. Two elements in man, sociability and asociability, were the forces whose interplay and tension, Antagonism (Kant used the term in the original German text), had brought about the novelty of moral progress. Kant's was a more subtle form of the good-out-of-evil theory, rational consequences from irrational passions. It was an answer to the query whence came the dynamic impulse for change, and it purported to show how the historical panorama of conflicting desires, destructive outbursts of heroic figures, battles of religions and peoples, violent expressions of bestiality, inevitably resulted in the ethicization of man. Offhand it seemed contrary to commonsense that the vices of tyrants, the sacking of cities, the egotistical striving for power, the warring for possession among the states, could further a rational purpose. Manifest history showed no examples of deliberate ethical acts; to the observer it was nothing more than a succession of unrelated cruelties without purpose, mere sound and fury. And yet Kant proved that in the very pursuit of his anarchic asocial desires man was creating a rational order.

The word and the concept of Antagonism introduced into the cult from Kant's essay was endowed by the Saint-Simonians with an easy optimism which the philosopher of Königsberg never expressed. The history of mankind became the record of the evolution of this primary immoral passion and of the variegated forms that it had assumed through time. The Saint-Simonians were rectilinear progressists, for whom the feeling of antagonism was subject to modal changes in a continuous series — to adopt their language for a moment; in the large they contemplated history as a temporal process in which the quantity of overt antagonism in the world underwent a steady diminution as the result of a salutary transformation of human institutions. In the beginning, ran the Saint-Simonian account of Genesis, there had been only isolated families, each of them held together by enmity toward all other families on the globe — the maximum possible extension of the hostile feeling. Only within the confined orbit of this primeval human association did even a glimmer of harmony and love prevail. With time, as the organizational forms of society encompassed ever greater numbers of persons, advancing in a series from the family to the tribe to the city to the nation to the multinational religion, the sum total of possible antagonisms among persons decreased arithmetically and the love relationships within the broader social unit increased in a like proportion.

"Let us conclude from what has gone before that properly speaking there have in the past been real associations only in opposition to other rival associations, so that the whole of the past can with respect to the future be envisaged as one vast state of systematic war. . . .

"Order, peace, love, are for the future. The past has always sought, studied, and practiced war, hate, and antagonism. And nevertheless the human species always advanced toward its pacific destiny, moving in turn from an imperfect to a better order, from a weak and narrow association to a stronger and more extended one." [18]

World history thus became the study of the general diffusion of love and the contraction of antagonism, a new adaptation of the geographic analogies which Turgot and Condorcet had once used to describe the spread of scientific enlightenment and the gradual blotting out of obscurantism. A history of the progressions of love replaced the successive advances of mind.

In its detail Saint-Simonian history is not quite as simple as this image at first implies. While antagonism assumed new shapes — city wars, national wars, religious wars — the old conflicts were not completely eradicated within the inflated structures of association, so that even after international religious societies were organized the spirit of hostility within the family based upon age and sex differences, within the city based upon families, and within the nation based upon cities tenaciously persisted. Love had never taken complete possession of even the most intimate associations of the older "in-groups" — to employ a contemporary barbarism. A Saint-Simonian view of the world as it stood on the threshold of association and love gave rise to the paradoxical reflection that there was still pervasive antagonism throughout human society both on an international and on an intimate personal level; on the verge of universal love, the world was riddled with hates. The conflicts might be said to have diminished within the limits of the smaller associations only in the sense that they had become attenuated and milder in their overt expressions. Men were no longer commonly anthropophagous.

Another facet of antagonism which had undergone a series of quantitative, measurable changes was manifested in the economic exploitation of one man by another, in the treatment of men as objects rather than persons (here the Saint-Simonians clearly drew on Beccaria and Kant). In the earliest times men devoured their captives, then with progress they merely killed them, and finally they enslaved them. The first modes of the series were lost in prehistory, but the later forms of exploitation were known and recorded in the successive institutions of slavery, serfdom, and free labor. Legally, at every one of the stages, there had been some further limitation upon the absolute power of the exploitation of man by man. The progress of love was thus demonstrable, though complete freedom had not yet been achieved and in the condition of the modern proletariat — the indignity of the term, connoting the status of workers as a mere child-bearing mass, made it repugnant to Saint-Simonians — remnants of the ancient forms of exploitation had survived. There were vital respects in which modern workers were still slaves and serfs — a common theme in the contemporary literature depicting the wretchedness of the laboring classes in Western society. But though exploitation was an abominable reality of the organization of work, a review of its history proved that in long terms it was a waning form and that association and sociability were steadily gaining the upper hand. "Today, gentlemen, we have to consult history to learn what a master really was like and to comprehend what a vast distance separated the seigneur from the serf attached to the soil. Man today has a horror of blood, when for long ages it was one of his delights. The whole apparatus of barbarous tortures has disappeared even in the punishment of the guilty. National hatreds are diminishing every day and the peoples of the earth who are ready for a total and definitive alliance present us with the beautiful spectacle of humanity gravitating toward *universal association*." [19]

The Saint-Simonians had still another way of interpreting the past, one derived directly from Saint-Simon, which involved the introduction of an alternating rhythm into world history, a heartbeat of the historical process. As Toynbee has shown, this concept is one of the most ancient historico-philosophical generalizations. Among the Saint-Simonians it took shape as a succession of organic and critical epochs; they fixed the terminology, though Saint-Simon had already described the phenomenon. The organic was a period in which individuals were tied together by some common bond — be it war or religious faith — in which there was at least a harmony between spiritual and secular powers, education trained men to a set of common values, the moral and material forces in the society were not in flagrant contradiction with each other, there was organization and order. The order may have been rooted in false scientific assumptions, as it was in the Middle Ages, and the moral level of an organic epoch may have been relatively low, as it was in the Greek world; but these ages were sound, healthy, human, harmonious, social, integrated — they merited the positive adjectives in the Saint-Simonian vocabulary. It was unfortunately the nature of the historic process for these organic epochs to become disturbed and ultimately to disintegrate. The causes of the disruption could be found in the inadequate level of moral, scientific, and activist achievement of previous societies, in the internecine rivalry among the leading capacities, and in the persistence of superannuated organizational forms. The organic epochs were invariably followed by critical epochs which had a deplorable, even a tragic, historic function to perform, for it was their mission to criticize and to destroy the old organic institutions which once held a society together, to mock and to attack its values, to annihilate its ruling groups, an ugly thankless task which had usually brought to the fore analytic character-types, men who could dissect and anatomize but not create. At this point the Saint-Simonians modified somewhat their master's conception. He had depicted the alternativity of the organic and the critical almost exclusively in class terms, the version in which the doctrine penetrated Marxist thought. His new classes, both spiritual and temporal, had grown in the very bosom of the old order and had secretly waxed powerful beneath the surface of the overt political institutions until they were mighty enough to overthrow the dominant forces and assume control themselves. The initial period of class revolt was drawn by Saint-Simon in heroic terms: his most elaborately developed illustration, the combat of the modern industrial-scientific powers against the medieval military-theological ones, was marked by a strong Condorcetlike jubilation at the triumph of rational good over superstitious evil. The Saint-Simonians were consistently pejorative toward critical epochs. Destruction was a necessary clinical operation, and they occasionally recognized the force and the vitality of those engaged in wiping out antiquated scientific and moral ideas and decrepit temporal rulers whose day had passed, but once the ancient beliefs had lost their sway over men's hearts and minds, there followed a most terrible period of human history, an age of nothingness, of the void, of indifference, of isolation, of egotism, of loneliness, of psychic suffering, of longing. The Saint-Simonians were describing the Roman empire before the triumph of Christianity and their own miserable century. The portrayal of the darkness before the dawn in the Saint-Simonian sermons made them documents of spiritual self-revelation, *mutatis mutandis* like the writings of the early Church Fathers.

From de Maistre, Bonald, and Ballanche they drew an idealized image of medieval Europe, the last great organic epoch of history, an age of love, devotion, and duty, when men had faith, when they belonged, when society had unity and order. Their romantic medievalism was transparent. In destroying the abstract values of Condorcet's progressist school — the ideals of equality, rational science, and liberty — they also turned his philosophical history topsy-turvy. The good ages were those in which spiritual and religious authority were spontaneously respected, in which there was no conflict, no opposition, no contradiction, no dissension.

Saint-Simonians had one rational method for the propagation

of the new doctrine, the demonstration through an array of empirical evidence that the attainment of a society of universal love was historically inevitable. Their theme was not novel; the idea of a historical series, prevalent enough in eighteenth-century thought, was continued on into the nineteenth, strengthened by the addition of analogies from biological growth. The mathematical series never lost its fascination even after organic concepts describing evolution had been introduced, since the organic metaphors could not render the idea of infinity as convincingly as an arithmetic progression without end. In the organic image the fear of death or the notion of mere cyclical recurrence always lurked in the background, and at moments the most ardent of the progressists like Saint-Simon and Fourier succumbed to the prospect of inevitable degeneration. Infinite organic growth was hard to conceive, while a long series moving in one direction and begging for extrapolation was irresistible. Why should the course be reversed? If in the past there had been temporary stoppages and even brief setbacks, the Saint-Simonians' theory of progress improvised specific *ad hoc* excuses to explain away the insignificant deviations from the main current of history. "The law of perfectibility is absolute. It is a condition so intimately related to the existence of our species that whenever a people placed at the head of humanity has become static the seeds of progress which had been compressed within its bosom were immediately transferred elsewhere to a soil where they could develop. . . . Civilization has moved, like those migrant birds who seek in a distant land a more favorable climate and atmosphere. . . . Today everything leads to the conclusion that with the cessation of wars, with the establishment of a regime which will put an end to violent crises, no retrogression, not even a partial one, will ever again take place. There will be continuity and acceleration of the progressions among the whole of mankind, because peoples will teach one another and will support one another." [20] The rhetoric has changed somewhat, but the ideas of inevitability and indefinite progress were in the direct tradition of Turgot and Condorcet.

CHILDREN OF SAINT-SIMON

EACH ACCORDING TO HIS CAPACITY

THE only solution to the crisis of the times was the moral transformation of mankind through the religion of Saint-Simon. To join the Saint-Simonian movement was an act of commitment to the future progress of man, an act of faith in his potential development. It involved a spiritual conversion from egotism, the dominant morality of the age, to humanity, the moral law of the future. The dawn of a new religious epoch was inevitable because the law of progress foretold another synthesis after the atheism and emotional barrenness of the second stage of the critical epoch. But the process could be delayed or hastened, and it was the mission of the Saint-Simonians to put an end to an age of disbelief and anarchy and to inaugurate the new world, to regenerate mankind. The leaders of the cult knew their historic role well — they were the Fathers of the Church, come after Saint-Simon to spread the new doctrine. The renovation of man would now be total; this was the last stage of provisional history and mankind was about to make the leap into definitive history, a world of order, limitless progress in the flowering of all capacities, a world without antagonism, virtually without pain, a world of love, unity, and cohesiveness.

The members of the movement practiced those virtues which would become normal among all mankind in the future. The movement, the religion, was the new world in miniature.

The prevailing chaos resulted from the repression of true capacity and excellence among industrialists, artists, and scientists and the haphazard disposition of human energies in accordance with hereditary privileges and antiquated legislation. The principle of the new order would be antithetical: "Each according to his capacity! Each capacity according to its works!" became the Saint-Simonian motto. In the social organism there was an optimum spot for every individual, and its discovery was the end of the social art. It is an unquestioned presupposition of Saint-Simonism that each man's capacity is clearly definable by a hierarchy of experts whose authority culminates in the priests and priestesses of the new religion, and that each man will willingly crawl into his appointed cubbyhole in the perfect system. This did not involve a destruction of personality or liberty — the Saint-Simonian preachers thus quieted the qualms of their audience of romantic individualists — but a genuine fulfillment. "Our religion does not stifle liberty," Père Barrault assured his listeners on November 27, 1831, "it does not absorb sacred personality. It holds each individual to be saintly and sacred. Since it promises classification according to capacity, does this not guarantee each man the preservation and development of his own native physiognomy, his own particular attitude, under a name which belongs only to him?" [21]

In order to achieve the proper distribution of capacities two profound changes had to be effectuated in the order of Western society. First the property system had to be reorganized, and then a new educational system introduced. The transmission of property through inheritance had to be abolished, even though private property was preserved as an institutional instrument to reward merit. Inheritance had become the vicious mechanism for the induction of incompetents into the administration of society, where they created anarchy and stifled progress. Their posts rightfully belonged to men of capacity. Order required the reward of each according to his works, and the intrusion of inherited wealth rendered any such allotment for merit impossible. The Saint-Simonians, who always thought of themselves as men of moderation, sharply distinguishable from the revolutionaries, drew the attention of their listeners to the numerous transformations which property had undergone in historic times in order to present the abolition of inheritance as a mere step in a long series — the final metamorphosis.

Absolute equality in property would entail equal awards for unequal merit, and such communism was contrary to human nature. "We must foresee that some people will confound this system with what is known under the name of *community of goods*. There is nevertheless no relationship between them. In the social organization of the future each one, we have said, will find himself *classified* in accordance with his capacity, rewarded in accordance with his works; this should sufficiently indicate the inequality of the division." [22] But while capacities and works and rewards were all unequal in the new society, the dimensions of differences were not conceived of in our contemporary terms and the pursuit of inequality, the desire to outstrip one's fellows, was never envisaged as an energizing drive of society. Inequality resulting from rewards according to works was a consequence, not a goal. Like Condorcet, the Saint-Simonians knew that in the new distribution of functions in accordance with technical capacity partiality would sully the purity of the moral world, but that was not the issue, they maintained, anticipating the arguments of their opponents; in their day there was chaos and misery in a society of misfits, in the future "errors, accidents, and injustices will only be exceptions." [23]

In the economic realm Saint-Simonism became a utopia of finance capital. The whole industrial mechanism was conceived of as one vast enterprise presided over by a unitary directing bank which dominated the rest and was able to weigh accurately the various credit needs of all branches of industry. "Let us transport ourselves to a new world. There proprietors and isolated capitalists whose habits are alien to industrial labors no longer control the choice of enterprises and the destiny of the workers. A social institution is invested with these functions which are so badly filled today. It presides over all exploitation of materials. Thus it has a general view of the process which allows it to comprehend all parts of the industrial workshop at the same time. . . ." [24] There would be a central budget which on the credit side consisted of the "totality of the annual products of industry," [25] the gross national product of present-day parlance. On the debit side were the requirements of the various subsidiary credit institutions and the banks of the specialized industrial branches. In this bankers' dream world the demands of centralized supervision and of local special institutions were delicately balanced — in a way, the contemporary practice, though not the theory, of all highly organized economies of the "capitalist" or "communist" variety. The Saint-Simonians recognized that there would be competitive claims from various branches of industry, a thorny problem verbally resolved with the slogan that allocations would be made "in the interests of all." [26] In the last analysis decisions on individual demands were evaluated by the experts, or "competent chiefs," prototypes of our contemporary planning commissioners.

Of late there has been some attempt to fit the Saint-Simonians into a history of totalitarianism. Their contempt for liberalism and the franchise gives a semblance of verisimilitude to the charge that they were precursors of fascism, though a hierarchical conception of order is not necessarily totalitarian. In many respects they proposed to run the capitalist economic and social order the way it actually is run today in the welfare state. Heavy death duties are virtually the equivalent of a Saint-Simonian abolition of inheritance, and the central financial institutions of most governments exert no less power over the distribution of credit to industry than the central banks projected by the Saint-Simonians. Business, the army, and the university are run as hierarchical structures in which directives are issued from the top and diffused through various echelons, despite the continued existence of residual democratic forms and the occasional influence of a groundswell of opinion from below. In the most advanced societies the course is open to scientific and artistic and industrial talent, and sheer incompetence even when buttressed by hereditary wealth is no longer generally tolerated. Women are moving toward real as contrasted with theoretical equality, and the greatest good of the greatest number is universally accepted by all nations in solemn assembly.

Perhaps the only tenet of Saint-Simonian doctrine that has not fared well in the modern world is their proclamation of the triumph of love. While the necessity for its existence has been preached often enough in the church and in the university, love seems to have bumped up against almost insurmountable obstacles. Ours is an orderly, hierarchical society, open to capacity which is rewarded according to its works, but it is hardly a loving society. The "lonely crowd" of Mr. David Riesman would fit into any Saint-Simonian course of lectures diagnosing the ills of their world.

EDUCATION FOR LOVE

Since a whole aspect of man's instinctual nature, his capacity to love, had atrophied, leaving him only a part-man, a totally reshaped educational system was urgently required to rectify the basic failings of the old order. The progress of science and industry had so far outstripped man's emotional development that there was a grave imbalance in the human condition. Mankind had to be taught to feel again. Nourishment of the moral sentiment became the paramount objective of the Saint-Simonian educational system. Teaching the love of humanity would warm all relationships grown tepid in the critical epoch and rescue a society which had lapsed into emotional sterility. If the capacity of love were developed among all men a state would ultimately be reached where each individual spontaneously subordinated his particular interest to the good of mankind. Men would be conditioned to love as they were now trained to selfseeking, self-interest, and antisocial behavior.

The Saint-Simonians were adroit in refashioning the educational techniques of Catholicism to fit the new religion. "This does not mean," the Saint-Simonian lecturer explained to his audience of unbelievers, "that the same practices and the same forms would be perpetuated, that the catechism and the rituals, the stories which once inspired the faithful had to be preserved intact. . . . Analogous though improved methods would be utilized to prolong the education of man throughout the whole course of his life." [27] The confessional, far from being scorned as an instrument of clerical domination, was praised as an ideal way of instilling moral values. The Saint-Simonians revamped it into a "consultation" — shades of the psychoanalytic couch — and extolled it as a health-giving agency which during moments of acute personal crisis could be used to bind men's souls to the service of humanity. In the confessional-consultation "less moral and less enlightened men seek the knowledge and the strength they lack from their superiors in intelligence and in order." [28] Preaching would have the same function as in the Catholic church, and prayers would be directed to a humanitarian God and Father-Mother. In their public utterances the Saint-Simonians invariably treated Catholicism with the respect due a worthy departed ancestor — an attitude which the official ecclesiastical hierarchy failed to appreciate. Enfantin went so far in adapting Catholic theological terminology that the Pope was constrained to place the *Physiologie religieuse* on the Index lest confusion be sown among the faithful.

Since all moral truths were not rationally demonstrable, the bulk of mankind would have to accept religious teachings on authority, as they had in the old church. While the *philosophes* had always relied on the logical proof of their ideas in a popular, easily presentable form which rendered them self-evident, and had looked forward to the time when all men were amenable to reason, Saint-Simonian doctrine was heavily dosed with elitist snobbery. The attitude toward the proletariat was loving but paternalistic; hence the frank recourse to preaching *ex cathedra*: "The results of social science can be presented to most men only in a dogmatic form." [29]

In practice Saint-Simonian education would take place on two levels, the general and the special. The physiologist Bichat had stressed the specialized inborn character of human capacities, a view which favored a highly professionalized system of education. Since the Saint-Simonians agreed with his theory in its broad technical outlines, they were committed to the training of specialists in three separate departments. "There will be three kinds of education, or rather education will be divided into three branches which will have as their object the development of, one, sympathy, the source of the fine arts, two, the rational faculty, the instrument of science, and finally material activity, the instrument of industry." But the Saint-Simonians recognized grave dangers of disunity if this specialized education were allowed to dominate society exclusively. "Since each individual, whatever his aptitude may be, is nonetheless also loving, endowed with intelligence and with physical activity, it follows that all men will be subject to the same triplex education from their childhood until their classification into one of the three great divisions of the social order." [30] Under the Saint-Simonians education would thus be at once particular and common. The simultaneous capacity for both the specific and the general was a unique characteristic of the new age and distinguished it from all past organic periods; in the future men would be able to live as specialists and yet would not be cut off and isolated from the totality of their fellows. The curriculum fabricators of the American university in the fifth and sixth decades of the twentieth century, with their "general education" neologisms, may be surprised to learn that they have been unconscious disciples of the Saint-Simonians. Like Molière's *bourgeois gentilhomme*, they have been speaking prose without knowing it.

The Saint-Simonians would have been antagonistic to the easy liberalism and skepticism which underlies some American general education programs. There is, however, a substantial body of American educators who would be quite at home among the Saint-Simonian preachers determined in the face of engulfing moral chaos to hold back the flood and stop up the dike with their didactic index fingers. "To inculcate in each one the sentiment, the love of all, to unite all wills into a single will, all efforts toward the same goal, the social goal, that is what one can call *general education* or morality." [31] Out of fear of *anomie* and moral rootlessness they may yet end up subscribing to the Saint-Simonian unitary law. "Every system of moral ideas presupposes a goal that is loved, known, and clearly defined. . . ."

Despite the Saint-Simonians' roseate and comforting portrayal of the future, the passage from the egotist to the altruist society presented almost insurmountable hurdles to the educators of mankind in Balzac's France. As long as the contemporary world was steeped in blind self-love and carping negation, how could the organic society with its cohesive morality ever come into being? Marxism later introduced the idea of a total destructive revolution to clear away the debris of the old society and permit a fresh start in the industrial, scientific, and moral spheres. But since the Saint-Simonians steadfastly denied the creativity of violence and of the revolutionary act, how could mankind ever escape from its impasse? "The word upheaval is always associated with a blind and brutal force having as its goal destruction. Now these characteristics are alien to those of the doctrine of Saint-Simon. This doctrine does not itself possess or recognize for the direction of men any other power but that of persuasion and conviction; its end is to construct and not to destroy; it has always placed itself in the ranks of order, harmony, edification. . . ." [32] In imitation of Christ they ended by identifying the means with the end. Only the preaching of love was capable of arousing feelings of love and of leading to the establishment of a society in which love would blossom. They rejected social revolution because love could not be born out of the hatred of class conflict. Their apostles to the proletariat taught them to love their superiors in the social hierarchy and promised that a paternal love would embrace them in return. To add yet another form of antagonism — class conflict — to a society riddled with hatreds would only delay the dawn of the age of love. In the Saint-Simonian world the concept of hier-archic order assumed a transcendent value and became associated with love. Turgot's grand affirmations of absolute liberty and the quest for novelty as the guarantees of progress were reversed. An-archy, unguided action, revolutionary movements, were now the hidden forces of antiprogress. The Saint-Simonians went far in the denunciation of liberty of conscience, and their mockery of the weakness of individual reason had a Maistrian flavor. Free will suddenly emerged as a cover for caprice, threatening society with dissolution. The liberals' conception of order as an equilibrium of contrary forces, a derivative from Montesquieu's division of pow-ers, was censured as merely negative. Order preserved by naked power, by the hangman, was equally unpalatable. Instead the Saint-Simonians tried to envisage order as a creative force, the spon-taneous expression of love enlisted under the banner of progress. The general will turned loving — named without benefit of Rous-seau — was eulogized as the highest good, preservative of order.

But what about the inhibition and punishment of malefactors? How was the illegal defined in a society educated to love? Like Fourier and Comte the Saint-Simonians, who had many lawyers among them, never managed to arrive at a satisfactory solution to the penal problem. They either hedged or dismissed the issue as unimportant. There was an underlying presumption that if all men were allowed to follow the inclinations of their natural capa-cities in love, reason, and action there would be no great need for legal restraints, since everybody would be satisfied. At worst a few isolated abnormalities might have to be repressed. Often they re-peated the view of the eighteenth-century rationalists who con-sidered crime in the good society of the future a rare monstrosity or an illness that could be treated as a concern of social hygiene. The Saint-Simonians categorically affirmed that the existence of repressive penal laws was proof of serious defects in the educa-tional system — a fault they would quickly remedy. Montesquieu had already said that condemning a man to death was a symptom of a sick society. Saint-Simonism provided for no elaborate state apparatus; there were merely a religion and an administrative mechanism under which it was easy for the elite in each section of society to evaluate human action in terms of its contribution to social welfare and to remunerate individuals in accordance with their works. The "liberties" of the *philosophes*, the English liberties, were not considered as abstract inalienable rights; they were judged only in terms of their social consequences. In the organic society of the future there was no liberty to support the forces of retrogression, of social illness, of indifference, of destruction and conflict, of aggressiveness, and of human exploitation. There was the positive liberty to express one's creative love, to exercise scientific reason, and to exploit nature in association with other men. Legislation, insofar as it was necessary, rewarded the altruistic social virtues and penalized the egotist vices, though, they were quick to add, punishments would not be severe. They meant never to employ the death penalty, long prison terms, or police bayonets in the streets. In the new world the mere announcement of the moral law would exert a potency hitherto unknown. Judges would not be moved by vengeance and the purpose of punishment would be the rehabilitation and the regeneration of the felon. "The penalties inflicted on the propagators of antisocial doctrines will above all serve to protect them from public wrath," [33] an insidious argument that has become all too familiar in the modern communist state to justify severe punishments, though the Saint-Simonians did not echo Rousseau's summary and brutal condemnation of the violators of the general will in the *Second Discourse*. The ideals of leniency and clemency advanced by the great eighteenth-century lawgivers Montesquieu and Beccaria were incorporated into Saint-Simonian doctrine, a saving grace.

At this point one is confronted with difficulties in conveying the general tenor of their future society. In theory at least the Saint-Simonians extended the area in which crime would be punishable far beyond the carefully fixed boundaries of liberal constitutional jurisprudence. They departed from the traditions most nobly represented by Montesquieu and Mill, who staunchly rejected vague and sentimental criteria in constructing a system of law. For the Saint-Simonians there would be crimes against science as well as industrial crimes, and, to round out the trinity, moral crimes which impeded the progress of sympathy and love. They failed to provide their listeners with specific examples of these new types of wrongdoing, and their amorphous nature itself renders them suspect. They inevitably evoke the memory of wholesale accusations of disloyalty to the state and crimes against society for which twentieth-century men have been tried and condemned. The specter of emotional and moral as well as scientific and industrial control hovers over the Saint-Simonian system, and Rousseau's censor rears his ugly head. Nevertheless it seems farfetched to relate the Saint-Simonians on these grounds to the monster states of Hitler and Stalin. True, the Saint-Simonian political formulae emphasized emotion rather than reason, plus the hierarchy, an elite, the organic, and in this respect their theories bear superficial resemblance to the lucubrations of twentieth-century fascism. The ecclesiastical nonsense of the cult, however, should not obscure the fact that their image of society was founded first and foremost upon the expectation that there would be an upsurge of Eros in the world, that men would become more loving — a rather dubious assumption, though one that is not to be laughed out of court by the true skeptic. The totalitarians, and sometimes nominally libertarian democracies, have operated against their opponents with an apparatus of terror — this has been the heart of their power system. The Saint-Simonian society was founded upon relations of love among members of a hierarchy. This may be ridiculous, unfeasible, nonrational humbug, but it is totalitarian only in the sense that love may be. The Saint-Simonians were committed to the winning of converts solely through preaching and persuasion. To relate all the images of "authoritarianism" and "totalitarianism" to these tender failures of the 1830's entails driving their ideas to conclusions they never entertained. Saint-Simonians talked and quarreled far more about love, all sorts of love, than they did about authority. They never spilled a drop of blood in their lives and in middle age they became respectable bourgeois. There was something unique about the German experience under the Third Reich. Remembrance of it should not be diluted by the discovery of antecedents that are of a qualitatively different character. The Saint-Simonians may be cast into liberal hell, but there they will probably encounter as many lovers and passionately fixated men as Dante did in Christian hell.

THE TRIAL

At Ménilmontant the Saint-Simonians had labored and gotten callouses on their hands. Their master had commanded, "All men must work." Daily life was regulated by a monastic rule: at set hours there were parades, recitations, songs, symbolic acts celebrating the virtues of work. In later years the poet Maxime du Camp gathered recollections of their magnificent costumes from former members of the cult. "The trouser was white, the vest red, and the tunic blue-violet. White is the color of love, red that of labor, and blue that of faith. The costume signified that Saint-Simonism was founded on love, that it fortified its heart with labor, and that it was enveloped in faith. The headdress and the sash were left to individual choice. Since all men both in this world and in the hereafter are responsible for their own lives, the name of every Saint-Simonian had to be inscribed in large letters on his breast." [34] Watching the Saint-Simonian spectacle became the object of Parisian outings to the country; on holidays there were as many as ten thousand persons in attendance, separated off from the performing priests, priestesses, and their acolytes by a colored ribbon. The outrageous lectures of the Salle Taitbout and the goings-on in the outskirts of Paris had turned Saint-Simonism into a public scandal, but it was difficult for the government to decide upon the grounds for prosecution. Were they a subversive political movement or were they a religion, whose assemblies were protected by the laws, or were they common embezzlers who had hoodwinked the simple-minded into placing their patrimony in the hands of the church? After protracted investigation the Saint-Simonians were indicted for various felonies — some for violating article 291 of the penal code, others for outrages against public morals. The embezzlement charge was at first held in abeyance; it was never proved in court.

When they were brought to trial on August 27 and 28, 1832, the faithful ranged themselves in a hierarchical order and paraded from their retreat all the way through Paris to the Palais de Justice. The heroic moment of Saint-Simonism had arrived. [35] From the instant the colorfully bedecked adepts entered the courtroom until their final condemnation the trial was repeatedly disrupted by dramatic incidents. The advocate-general, M. Delapalme, used the case as an opportunity to rally opinion in defense of the state and its moral system, both of which had been rather shaken by the uprising of the Lyons proletariat. "We have a society, we have a social order, good or bad we must preserve it." [36] He terrified the members of the jury by raising the specter of a revolution at their very doorstep. Evidence that the Saint-Simonians had divided up their Paris propaganda organization by *faubourgs* was conclusive proof that an insurrection was being plotted. For the moral and sexual doctrines of the Saint-Simonians he expressed revulsion and contempt. The accused had rejected legal aid, insisting on the conduct of their own defense or the appointment of female Saint-Simonians as counsel. When Charles Duveyrier became obstreperous, the presiding officer threatened to appoint a spokesman for them against their will; whereupon Duveyrier had a fit of temper and pointed to an array of legal talent that was sitting in the visitors' section watching the show. "A lawyer! I told them when I came in that I am being charged with saying that everyone was living in a state of prostitution and adultery, but you are in fact all living in that state. Well, have the courage to say so out loud. That is the only way you can defend us." [37]

The first day, in his defense against the accusation that the Saint-Simonian doctrine preached an orgiastic indulgence which would sap the moral foundations of society, Enfantin distinguished between the "rehabilitation of the flesh" which he espoused and the "disorder of the flesh" prevalent in existing society. He turned the tables on the proper bourgeois who had found an ideal mouthpiece in the advocate-general. The Saint-Simonians recognized different kinds of love, he explained, and provided for their regulation through the sacerdotal office. Failure to concede the existence of variations in love had resulted in the deceptions and evasions of contemporary marriage, the great moral lie. As he developed his argument, it became apparent that the reorganization of the love-life of mankind was the major concern of the age, to which the organization of property and industry were subordinate. The evils of inheritance and the miseries of the working classes had further confused sexual relations by forcing girls into prostitution. By refusing to admit the legitimate demands of the body and the sacred rights of beauty, which should not be subject to the economic power of property, Christian society had deformed and crucified love. When free and natural relations were suppressed, love itself was rendered ugly. The Saint-Simonians condemned prostitution and adultery in the name of amorous compacts entered into only by free mutual consent. The bourgeois, they charged, were preserving these vicious human institutions in the name of the property system, the monogamous family which was its adjunct, and Christian asceticism. It was the Saint-Simonians who upheld purity in love, who espoused an ideal love based upon the equality of the sexes and the free expression of true desire, while the defenders of the existing moral order were furthering promiscuity, the purchased and enslaved love of prostitutes, and the uneducated, unregulated loves of men and women who, for want of a priesthood to guide them, were wallowing in degraded affections which were bought or clandestine.

"We wish to rehabilitate the flesh and to sanctify physical beauty by bestowing upon it a social importance which . . . it must today obtain through fraud. All your acts bear witness that our claims are not false, for you all recognize in secret and often against your will what you deny in public, the influence of beauty. Yes, truly, the flesh repressed and martyred by the Church for so long is today free from this heavy burden; but since it has been abandoned and set adrift from any religious faith it is in a state of disorder. Today the flesh still causes destruction as it did at the time of the appearance of Christ, and it is still the shame of the world. The flesh which has been crucified for so many centuries by the Christian anathema and which on this cross of malediction and suffering has at least expiated many faults, today possesses everything and covers the world with adultery and prostitution. . . ." [38]

Enfantin adverted once again to the intimate connection between the disorders of love and the anarchy of private property relations in existing society. His graphic, sometimes crude, imagery depicting the alienation of both human force and human beauty did not spare the sensitivities of his audience. "I have devoted myself to a religion unfurling the banner of universal association. How could I not be moved by the spectacle of a struggle which divides all classes? Look at the people. They sell their bodies to labor; they sell their blood to war; they sell their daughters' flesh to pleasure and to shame. For a piece of bread the world contorts them, commits them to toil and to the appeasement of passion; it prostitutes the people both in their strength and in their beauty. Then when they are wrinkled, old, and beaten, it tosses them onto a heap of straw, it throws them out and passes on. Or, if the world pities their misfortunes, if it pardons their vices, then there is the hospital — that is the paradise which it opens for them. . . . What moved me even more than the wretchedness of the people was the fraudulent, gross and immoral relations between men and women. And since I am charged with trying to raise a new society in the midst of the old one, it is necessary that I reveal to you the picture of your world which the advocate-general is so jealously anxious to safeguard. . . .[39]

"The young and old, the beautiful and distorted, the elegant and boorish, all take part in the orgy. They squeeze and they tread upon the flesh of these women as if they were grapes of the vine — women glowing with freshness or already stained with mud, women plucked before their time or savory and mature — they bring them all to their lips only in order to cast them away with contempt. . . . All in this great Babylon drink the wine of a frenzied prostitution."[40]

The president, who had showed signs of ill-contained impatience during the long speech, postponed the session to the following morning with the remark: "The defense is degenerating into a scandal."

The next day Enfantin took a quite different tack. In a self-conscious manner, whose motives he openly explained to the court, he taught the audience a lesson in the superiority of emotions and of tactile values over reason. While the advocate-general ranted about the violation of articles in the penal code, Enfantin with majestic calm extolled the power of beauty. He slowly surveyed the judge, the jury, and the prosecutor with his magnetic eye, forcing them into uncontrollable outbursts of rage as he lingered over every one of them, caressing them, thus demonstrating by example the greater strength of his moral being expressed in the eye over their rationalistic juridical arguments. He was the Father

preaching, not defending himself. At a signal, the slightest movement of his brow, members of the cult spoke or were silent. The
protracted pauses charged the atmosphere in the courtroom. When
the judge tried to break the tension by asking, "Do you want to
compose yourself?" Enfantin replied "I need to see all that surrounds me. . . . I want to teach the advocate-general the potent
influence of form, of the flesh, of the senses, and for that reason
I want him to feel the eye." "You have nothing to teach me, neither
about looking nor anything else," was Delapalme's exasperated
retort. Enfantin was unperturbed. "I believe that I can reveal the
whole of my thoughts on my face alone. . . . I want to make
everyone feel and understand how great is the moral force of
beauty in order to cleanse it of the stains with which your contempt
has caused it to be sullied." [41] Despairing of ever getting this romantic hero, who used the techniques of Mesmer popularized in
the *feuilleton* novels everyone was devouring, to return to the
well-trodden paths of legal procedure, the president closed the
session and the good bourgeois on the jury proceeded to find them
guilty.

THIRTY YEARS AFTER

THE sentence of the court, a year in jail, was generally condemned as harsh by the press — but it served the purpose of the
July Monarchy. The Saint-Simonian world of illusion was dissipated in Sainte-Pélagie — the same prison where Saint-Simon
had once been incarcerated during the Revolution — not through
cruel treatment but by leisure, good feeding, and the constant
mutual proximity of the elect. Michel Chevalier, who had been
the great activist of the movement, controlling the funds, editing
the publications, administering the affairs of the church, answering
a voluminous correspondence, finally became alienated from the
Father.

The July Monarchy liberated them both after they had served
seven and one-half months of their term, but the movement and
the religion never recovered. Chevalier was accepted back into
society almost immediately, and he effected his rehabilitation by
conducting an official mission of inquiry into the administration

of public works in the United States and Mexico. He ended up as one of the more prominent senators of the Second Empire, an official economist, though he never quite divested himself of the social ideology of the cult. There was a Saint-Simonian flavor to everything the worthy Senator Chevalier accomplished for the Napoleonic economy; even the trade treaty with Cobden was swaddled in slogans about universal brotherhood among nations. In a letter of February 20, 1832, he had called himself one of those "hierarchical men" — we would now say organization men. [42] The change from Enfantin to Napoleon III was profitable.

Père Enfantin's "return to the world" was not quite so easy. After he dropped his sacerdotal manner he eked out an existence in various jobs, a long series of fiascos. He finally was named an administrator of the Paris-Lyons-Marseilles railroad, a merger of smaller companies which he had been instrumental in effecting. This was in his eyes no mere mundane economic transaction but a presage of the great communications networks of the future which would unite all mankind. He lived on for thirty-two years after his release from prison, and even after his formal abdication he remained the Father for some of the followers. The cloud of make-believe was not suddenly dispelled for all of them at a single moment: Saint-Simonian fantasies lingered on even after they had become respectable bourgeois seemingly undifferentiated from other successful businessmen of the July Monarchy and the Empire. Not that the dissolution of the sect went smoothly; there were ugly contests about the disposition of the funds of the new religion, and Enfantin found himself denied more than thrice by the closest of his sons, Michel Chevalier. Though most of the Saint-Simonians who re-entered the world carried the old views with them, the doctrine was diluted. They completely abandoned the sexual theories of the cult. The more acceptable ideas about banking, credit, and the financing of grand projects for science and economic development cropped up in the chancelleries of Napoleon III. The fates were not equally kind to all the rehabilitated Saint-Simonians. Many died of the fever in Egypt, where Enfantin had pursued the Suez canal project with his customary tenacity. The Pereires were the most successful: their titanic struggle with the Rothschilds for the domination of the French banking system became the most important single episode in the financial history of the nineteenth century. In all their multifarious activities the Pereires clung to the illusion that their temple of Mammon had been sanctified by the commandment to improve the lot of the most numerous and poorest classes. To his dying day Enfantin, the ambiguous seer who could write treatises on railroads one day and mystic outpourings on the true nature of love the next, freely expressed the two sides of his nature. His flirtation with Napoleon III did not sit too well with some of the faithful, but since it was not successful his incorrigible activism was forgiven. His last project of the 1860's, the opening of a vast "intellectual credit" for brilliant young university graduates with only their brains as security, was rejected by his former sons, who began to find his name embarrassing in any association. A plan for a new encyclopedia, which Chevalier and the Pereires supported, was the occasion for an act of public repudiation from which Enfantin never recovered.

Some members of the cult remained loyal to the end, as did Arlès and Lambert. Most of them forgot their sectarian quarrels, and as aged men with flowing white beards they confessed to each other that the period of the rue de Monsigny and Ménilmontant had been the peak experience of their lives. The fascination Enfantin exerted upon men and women alike remains something of a mystery, hard to explain solely in terms of his beauty and his charm. He surely was not a towering intellect. There was a craving for a new translation of the concept of love, and he seems to have provided it for the disciples both in the gentleness of his person and in the mystic outpourings of his works. The *Physiologie religieuse* (1858) sounds today like sheer balderdash because he really was a mediocre writer, but he did manage to arouse enthusiasm when he preached of man's all-consuming need to love. He was a mystic *manqué*. His interpretation of the symbols of the Eucharist in human terms, describing the universal community of flesh and blood, outraged Catholics. The extended eulogies of the senses and of the various parts of the human body have a Whitmanesque flavor. To an extraordinary degree he felt communion with all living men even when the verbiage in which he clothed his sentiment was trite and wooden. Like Feuerbach's parallel system, Enfantin's theology transformed the worship of a God who allowed His son to become a man into an adoration of man who was God. Perhaps most appealing was Enfantin's conception of existence as an eternal giving of the self to others in the myriad relationships of everyday life until in the end of the days a man had transferred his whole being to mankind. No man dies because with the exhaustion of age there is nothing left to die, and all that was once part of a man lives on transmuted in others, in humanity. "I affirm," he wrote in his last testament, *La Vie éternelle*, "that I live outside of myself as certainly as I live in myself. I feel this as much in what I am as in what I hate; I feel myself live wherever I love, absent and dead in whatever I condemn; whatever I love increases my life, whatever I hate deprives me of life, robs me of it, defiles it." [43] As the medieval mystics invented a vocabulary to communicate the sentiment of merging with the godhead, Enfantin tried to render into words his sense of fusion with all persons living and dead. It was a manifesto against the sensationalist *philosophes* who had introduced into the world the image of the individual as a hard-knit little body, preferably made of marble, which stands in splendid isolation ready to receive specific stimuli from the outside. "Man does not give himself life, he receives it; one does not lose it, one gives it. This is what I call being born and dying. . . . This absolute individualization of a being whose destiny is essentially collective establishes among beings a disunion, a dissociation, a disaffection, and hence a radical absolute egotism against which all the faculties of my soul are in revolt. . . . I wish to feel my life penetrate into the life of those I love, whom I teach, as well as into this work which I am writing at this moment and for which I desire an eternal life. But this is only one side of the question. I believe myself loved. I have been and I am always being taught. I am myself the creation of another, worked upon, cultivated, nourished, fashioned by the friendly hands of my brothers and of the whole of nature." [44]

The Saint-Simonians help us to comprehend that total loss of identity, that oceanic feeling (to borrow from Freud), which men of the nineteenth and twentieth century experienced when they successfully lost self-awareness in the ardent periods of nationalist, socialist, and communist movements. They were swimming in the infinite, in universal brotherhood. Both Mazzini and the Socialists could read the Saint-Simonians and feel that their emotions were being faithfully reported. But humanist mysticism of this character can only be practiced by a select group; it is no more a popular manifestation than was Christian mysticism in the Church. The more effective organizers of the international communist movement and the militant nationalisms of every stripe have usually been endowed with claws as well as arms outstretched in brotherly love. The vision of the Saint-Simonians implied the possibility that a great mass of mankind could actually live for long periods in a state of loving so intense that the boundaries between the ego and the outside world would become blurred. Perhaps the Saint-Simonians at Ménilmontant did in fact experience this state for a brief moment — but then followed the cool awakening, as on that terrible day when Delaporte the true disciple realized that the Father was "neither Moses nor Christ, neither Charlemagne nor Napoleon — that he was only Enfantin, only Enfantin." [45]

V

Charles Fourier

THE BURGEONING OF INSTINCT

"Among them was a sect which pretended to endow humanity with a tail and a supplementary eye. This is how it happened. Toward the end of the last century there was born in Lyons one of those illustrious men who are predestined to die of hunger during their lifetime and to receive the honors of an apotheosis after their death. . . . All one knows about his beginnings is that when he was still a young man he was able to form an opinion about the wickedness of mankind. Grain hoarders had thrown a whole shipment into the sea while his back was turned. Whereupon he had a sudden revelation. 'If I had had a tail with an eye at its end,' he cried, 'I would have been able to use it to advantage on this occasion. Man lacks a sense. Man is incomplete.'"

> Louis Reybaud,
> *Jérôme Paturot à la recherche de la meilleure des républiques*
> (Paris, 1949), p. 89.

"Il est claire qu'on ne s'en est pas remis au régime gastrosophique
Dont l'établissement devait aller de pair avec la légalisation des moeurs
    phanérogames
On a préféré la bonne vieille méthode
Qui consiste à pratiquer des coupes sombres dans la multitude fantôme
Sous l'anesthésique à toute épreuve des drapeaux
Fourier est par trop sombre de les voir émerger d'un des pires cloaques de
    l'histoire
Epris du dédale qui y ramène
Impatients de recommencer pour mieux sauter."

> André Breton,
> *Ode à Charles Fourier*
> (Paris, 1947), pp. 17–18.

François Marie Charles Fourier was born in Besançon in 1772, the son of a prosperous cloth merchant.[1] Traditions about his childhood preserved among disciples document the history of the great neurotic in the making. At five he was unjustly punished by his parents for telling the truth and he took the oath of Hannibal against commerce. There followed a period of religious terror — dread of the cauldrons of Hell for having committed all the sins in the catechism. At the age of seven he confessed to fornication and simony. During the Revolution he participated in the Lyons uprising against the Convention and conceived a horror of social turmoil. His patrimony, which at one time had been considerable, was confiscated in the siege; imprisoned, he barely escaped being included in a convoy of counterrevolutionary victims who were executed en masse. For a brief period he was drafted into the cavalry, and the image of Fourier on horseback rekindles one's admiration for the French revolutionary organizers of victory.

In 1799 he became a traveling salesman. On one of his business trips to Paris that year the young provincial from the Franche-Comté saw an apple in Février's Restaurant. Its price on the bill of fare was fourteen sous; in his home town a hundred pieces of superior fruit could be bought for the same cost. Clearly something was wrong with a state of society that tolerated such differentials. When in later years he recollected the dining-room scene he placed the event in its true historical perspective. There had been four apples in the world: two were destined to sow discord and two to create concord. While Adam and Paris had brought misery to mankind, Newton's apple had inspired the discovery of the basic law of attraction which governs physical motion, and its complement, Fourier's apple, had moved him to formulate the law of passionate attraction which would inaugurate universal happiness. Such contemplative episodes made up the drama of his life. There were no heroic actions, no grand love affairs, perhaps no amorous relationships at all. Once he perceived that civilization was corroded with vice, Fourier retired into his private world and to remain pure held himself aloof from society. Only the few disciples whom he acquired in the last decades of his life believed that he would ultimately be recognized as the greatest man in history.

Fourier the bachelor lived alone in a garret and ate table d'hôte in the poorer Lyons restaurants, disliked children and spiders, loved flowers and cats, had a mania for measuring things with a yardstick cane, had a sweet tooth, could not digest bread, adored spectacles and parades, loathed the *philosophes* and their Revolution as much as he did rigid Catholicism. From all accounts he was a queer duck. Men called him mad, but no evidence has been adduced to sustain this clinical diagnosis; his autopsy revealed no signs of brain damage. Of course he talked to himself, worked in fits of excitement, could go without sleep for a week, was incapable of concentrating on any one job for long (the butterfly temperament of his own description), was quarrelsome, especially with members of his family. His writings emanated from the madhouses of Charenton, was the verdict of contemporary journalists, though this was a far less derogatory judgment than they imagined. Under Napoleon these institutions were inhabited by no mean knowers of man: in 1813 the former convent of the nuns of Picpus in Charenton, transformed during the Revolution into Belhomme's asylum, harbored at one and the same moment both the Marquis de Sade and the Comte de Saint-Simon.

Fourier's habits were meticulous, his manner frigid. One sometimes wonders whether this inventor of the system of passionate attraction ever experienced one. He could be a great hater, violently suspicious, and he showed mild symptoms of paranoia, but he also felt infinite pity for mankind, was acutely sensitive to the sufferings of the hungry and to the monotony of their lives. Acquaintances have described Fourier's fixed and abstracted gaze as if he were in a continual state of ecstasy; but he had an excellent memory, which he nourished with an endless supply of facts seemingly gathered at random. Once the idea of the phalanstery had taken shape, every chance bit of information was assimilated into the infinitely detailed and complicated system of living and working arrangements which he projected. Fourier was constantly collecting, counting, cataloguing, and analyzing. If he took a walk in Paris and a small hotel appealed to him, its proportions became the basis for the architectural framework of a phalanstery building. He seemed indifferent to the seasons and the temperature. His disciples realized that he was incapable of adapting himself to his environment and for the sake of the system tried to protect him from the sharper blows of fortune, but was he for that reason to be labeled daft? Quite on the contrary, the world and civilization were mad and he could prove it. "Only in attraction," he wrote in "La Nouvelle Isabelle," a manuscript published by his followers in volume IX of *La Phalange*, "should men have sought the interpretation of the social laws of God and of our common destiny. Despite this our planet is twenty-five centuries late in studying attraction. After such flightiness, after such insanity, is it not reasonable to maintain that there are crazy planets as there are individuals, and that if there were insane asylums for crazy planets one should send ours there for having wasted twenty-five hundred years. . . ." [2]

The initial major formulation of Fourier's doctrine, the *Théorie des quatre mouvements et des destinées générales*, appeared in 1808, about the same date as Saint-Simon's first signed publication and Hegel's *Phenomenology*. Pierre-Joseph Proudhon, a young printer in Lyons, remembered setting it up in type; the prophets had a way of rubbing elbows with one another. For three decades Fourier kept repeating what was essentially the first draft of his theory, issuing amplifications, abridgments, and summaries. The *Nouveau monde industriel* of 1827, the only version which excluded the annoying cosmogony, was probably the most successful (Fourier wrote in his own hand on many copies that anyone who understood chapters V and VI of this work had grasped his true meaning). The previous year he had moved to Paris, where he was employed as a correspondence clerk in the wholesale house of Messrs. Curtis and Lamb of New York on the rue du Mail.

During the last period of his life Fourier spent a great deal of time alleviating the specific pains of civilization among individuals: he would intervene to get overworked servant girls better jobs and he would wait on petty bureaucrats for hours to arrange for the pensions of war veterans. In his decline he seems to have found especial pleasure in the company of Madame Louise Courvoisier, *veuve* Lacombe, a sister of the Keeper of the Seals under Charles

X. Just Muiron, his first and most loyal disciple, was deaf, and since they communicated in writing even when they were together many direct solutions to the problems of phalanstery have been preserved. On October 9, 1837, Fourier died in his flat on rue Saint-Pierre Montmartre. Victor Considérant, who took over control of the school, was a man of different stripe. Under his direction Fourierism became a political and social movement involved in the subversion of the July Monarchy, and there was far greater emphasis on the structure of capitalism than on the anatomy of love, which for Fourier had always been the central problem of man in civilization. [3]

For the half-million volumes on morals and philosophy which had accumulated through the ages Fourier had nothing but contempt. Since he consulted few books after the rather stereotyped classical education of his youth, whatever he knew about the world was drawn from three primary sources: from introspection into his own desires and fantasies, from the newspapers which he read avidly, and from talk. As a traveling salesman he had observed men in all ranks of society, had noted their conversation; as a resident of pensions he had listened attentively to the local scandalmongers. These people showed him what men and women really longed for and what they loathed. Of the scabrous side of family life he learned in the coaches of the commercial travelers and at dinner in their cheap restaurants. Of the cheats of commercial civilization he was amply informed in the business houses where he worked long hours. His understanding of industrial relations came from inside the shops of Lyons, not from treatises on political economy. "I am a child of the marketplace, born and brought up in mercantile establishments," he wrote in *Le Nouveau monde industriel*, "I have witnessed the infamies of commerce with my own eyes, and I shall not describe them from hearsay as our moralists do." [4] Long before the uprisings of 1831 and 1834 when for the first time threatening banners of the proletariat were borne aloft, "To live working or to die fighting," he had known of the perennial war between the great merchant-manufacturers and the silkworkers who depended upon them for their livelihood. In Lyons he had seen cutthroat competition, social hypocrisy, prostitution. What did he need books for? The moralists had written dissertations about what men ought to desire, how they ought to behave; he knew directly what passions men yearned to gratify. To afford them total fulfillment was the simple, obvious solution to the problem of man's happiness — the creation of a society without repression. It was Fourier's mission to convince mankind that the system which he had laboriously spun out was preferable to the tawdry world of civilization depicted in the daily press. To his dying day he failed to understand how any man could refuse the happiness of his post in phalanstery and continue to endure the wretchedness, the chaos, and the frustrations of the life every man knew.

The works in which Fourier phrased and rephrased the system he had invented are full of neologisms, repetitions *ad nauseam*, and plain nonsense. There is an eccentric pagination, numerous digressions and interpolations break the argument, and references to minor events of early nineteenth-century history can have meaning only to a scholar of the period. The neologisms are particularly irritating because they require interpretation, a guess at his meaning, and are virtually untranslatable. Silberling's *Dictionnaire de sociologie phalanstérienne* is useful only to those who have already been initiated into the secret world.[5] Fourier was conscious of the fact that he was pouring forth a torrent of newfangled words, and in his manuscripts he occasionally indulged in light self-mockery on this account. "Hola, another neologism! Haro on the guilty one! but is this any worse than *doctrinaire*?"[6] Readers of the works published during his lifetime and of the extracts from his manuscripts gleaned by members of the *Ecole sociétaire* after his death generally put him down as turgid, incomprehensible, confused, and boring. Examination of the thirty-odd dossiers of his papers in the Archives Nationales leaves a surprisingly different impression. Fourier could write succinctly, with straightforward logic; he had a mordant wit and his style flowed freely. One approaches these documents expecting a cramped minuscule hand as in the columns of an obsessive accountant. Instead one finds that his handwriting has a gay swing to it and is remarkably clear. Fourier's insights came out best in brief aphorisms, in a few pungent formulae. Throughout his life he kept jotting down catch phrases in notebooks and on stray sheets, all too many of which have been preserved. "We must have something new. Fruitless attempts for

3000 years. Ergo absolute denial. Integral exploration. New sciences. Doubt everything." [7] This was the system in shorthand set down in moments of illumination, lest he forget. But the system-maker in him had to put these flashes together, and then the trouble began. He strung his individual pieces on a chain and forced them into a mechanical order. A single page or a paragraph, when the original inspiration was let alone, stands out like a life-giving spring in the desert. When he mulled over the texts preparatory to publication he usually smothered them with an avalanche of detail. Recourse to the manuscripts, even when the same ideas lie buried in his printed works, restores to his conceptions a vitality which the published writings have often lost.

Fourier's frequent and often successful play on words can hardly ever be rendered into another language, and his peculiar brand of humor is not readily comprehensible. The closest friends of this lonely man never heard him laugh; his analyses of existing social institutions betray an awareness of the ironic beneath the ponderous didactic mask, but the irony is always searing and the jokes are chastisements.

The detail of Fourier's descriptions, the endless minutiae of arrangements covering every aspect of life in the state of harmony, mark the obsessive. The style is often jerky. Each point is a hammer blow, delivered with violence. Fourier was voicing the common pain of an age confronted by the breakdown of traditional forms, an anguish which he perhaps felt with greater sharpness than did others. The longing for order which he depicted with such poignancy was a cry from the soul of early industrial society. His fantasy world of unfulfilled desires, unlike the imaginings of countless other isolated men, was somehow transmuted into an ideal system of social organization which came to exert a strange fascination upon small groups of people throughout the civilized world from the depths of czarist Russia to the wilds of transcendentalist New England. If the higher mental systems are sublimations of ungratified desire, Fourier's obsessional structure is a type-case, for virtually every pattern of labor and of love proposed for the phalanstery can be traced back to the unappeased needs of this sequestered man. Whatever the satisfaction which Fourier derived from this subtle delusional system, it has meaning to us across the

CHARLES FOURIER

decades because the everyday horrors he painted are still ours and
the infantile fantasies those of most of us who are not yet resigned
to the reality principle. The system has many virtues, above all
its humanity. Since Fourier read himself into the whole keyboard
of psychological types and endeavored to find solutions to all their
problems he was embracing the totality of mankind with its manifold woes, its secret desires, and its obstinate fixations. No one,
not even the child Fourier, was rejected.

And who can say whether his system is not the true balsam
for our pains? Who knows whether the phalansterian formula does
not hold within it the secret of future happiness? Has it ever been
tried precisely as Fourier prescribed? The abortive nineteenth-
century experiments, the Brook Farms and the New Harmonies,
were not conclusive, for in none of them was Fourier's requirement
that each phalanstery include every one of the 810 possible combinations of psychological character punctiliously observed. Fourier's phalanstery has no more been disproved than Plato's republic.

From the very beginning Fourier, like Saint-Simon, was convinced of the imminent acceptance of his projects for the transformation of mankind. If France could waste blood and treasure
on the false systems of the Revolution and the Empire, why should
it not invest the paltry funds necessary for the implementation of
the true one? This born enemy of rationalism could not understand
unreason in others, a not infrequent failing. Throughout his life,
the salesman of Lyons was on the lookout for a powerful client
who would buy his system. If only a potentate or a millionaire
would try out the plan on one square league of territory, mankind
would be overwhelmed by the sight of real human happiness under
harmony, the whole world would have to accept an irrefutable
scientific demonstration, and everybody would flock to phalansteries to taste of their delights. Every day on the stroke of twelve
he made a point of returning to his lodgings to wait for the appearance of the Maecenas who would somehow, of his own accord,
arrive to consult with him on the practical details for the establishment of a model. Fourier never stopped writing letters to prospective patrons and scheming to receive some notice, however paltry.
He sent his work to Mr. John Barnet, the American consul in Paris,
assuring him that his system was a better way of winning the

savage Creeks and Cherokees to the United States than waging war against them, an assertion that cannot be readily disproved. In Aberdeen, Scotland, a prize competition was announced for the best work demonstrating the goodness of God — precisely what Fourier's doctrine of the passions had done. Confident that the reward was his he was eager to despatch his proofs to the committee, but a little paranoid imp prevented him, insisting that the august Scottish judges should formally request a copy of his essay so that his authorship might be publicly established in advance, a reasonable precaution in case he should die in the interim and his work fall into the hands of plagiarists. In 1817 Fourier turned to the Russian Czar, offering him the tetrarchate of the world if he instituted the new system and promising him that under the influence of phalansterian labors the climate of his empire would become as pleasant as Italy's. On another occasion he tried to bribe the Rothschilds with the Kingdom of Jerusalem if they would finance his projects. If only the King of France would order the founding of an experimental phalanstery! Once admitted to a three-minute interview, he was certain to convince him. The archives of the July Monarchy are laden with Fourier's repeated efforts to reduce his system to a brief memorandum fit for hasty ministerial consumption.

Even though their conversion would immensely facilitate the transition to the new society, Fourier's appeals were not limited to the great and the powerful. In the second and third decades of the nineteenth century the popular journal with its glaring advertisements began beating upon the consciousness of Europe with a drum-like persistence hitherto unknown, and he adopted its techniques in his writings. Since results alone counted, his style often lapsed into turns of phrase that sounded like newspaper copy. He wanted to shock, to startle, to cajole, and any mechanism that drew attention served. The printing of key words in block letters, the frequent capitalization, the repetition of stock phrases, are symptoms of Fourier's neurosis, but they also mirrored a new social aspect of modern existence. He was a forerunner of the great advertising heroes. The Saint-Simonians, who were sharply attuned to the psychic tendencies of their society, were equally confirmed believers in publicity — the word was becoming common — and they employed the same oratorical rhythms which the French Revolution had insinuated into European speech. To bring happiness to mankind Fourier had to break through the barrier of public silence and ignorance, to acquaint men with the reality of the phalanstery so patently superior to civilization. And paradoxically the tools he was constrained to use were the very newspapers which reflected the falsehoods of contemporary civilization. Fourier dreamed of performing some dramatic act which would be reported and would attract attention to himself. Though he had been imprisoned under the Terror, in later years the state did not favor him with a public prosecution as it had Saint-Simon, and he never achieved notoriety. The press usually passed over his books in silence and they remained piled up in the back rooms of his printer and bookseller.

In practice the grand neurotics cannot abide by their absolutist resolves, and while proclaiming the indivisibility of truth in the system of phalanstery as contrasted with contemporary deceptions, Fourier used methods to hoodwink people into the new order as one would entice children with candy. But his lies were not comparable to the lies of civilization, because once within the gates of Eden men would see with their own eyes that happiness was prepared for them. Fourier frequently tried to pass off his total revaluation of morals and society as a mere "industrial reform." It was as if he hoped to introduce phalansteries and drag mankind to harmony while it was unaware of what was happening. His purpose was clear, to arouse little or no political and religious controversy while he turned the world topsy-turvy. "What is Fourierism?" he asked in a disingenuous letter to the *Gazette de France*. "I do not know. My theory is the continuation of Newton's on attraction. In this new mine he exploited only the material vein, I exploit the industrial. I am a continuator and I have never countenanced the name *Fouriériste*. My theory of society is not concerned with any religious, political, or administrative reform, but solely with industrial reform applied to the functions of agronomy, manufacturing, housekeeping, commerce, and general studies. If any of my disciples touches on prohibited subjects it is outside of my doctrine and concerns me no more than the divergent opinions of royalists and republicans. My discovery serves everybody without distinction of opinion — king or shepherd, the prodigal and the miserly. I have disciples from among various religions, Catholics, Protestants, Greeks, Jews. and so on. I ask of them no account of their religious beliefs because the societal mechanism of which I am the inventor is applicable to all religions, with the exception of the bloody ones which immolate human victims and the coercive ones which persecute for differences of opinion or which accept the slavery of workers and the sale and confinement of women." [8]

To reassure the religious, Fourier loudly proclaimed his belief in God; his most bombastic charge against critics was that they were atheists because they condemned the passions which God had created. Fourier's theology was not the most sophisticated part of his system. His God did not intervene in the details of this planet's operations, because He had millions of other worlds to look after; He had provided men with the instrumentalities for happiness and it was for them to divine the secret of their use. There were no individual rewards and punishments, only global ones. Because of the backwardness of the planet in discovering the key to the true system, deceased humans were now in a sort of limbo waiting expectantly for the triumph of attraction on earth so that they might be free to join universal materiality and thus have a chance to reappear on some more fortunate globe.

Toward the end of his life Fourier experienced a grave disappointment as he saw the rival sects of Owen and Saint-Simon winning adherents, or at least notoriety. The spectacle was doubly painful: on the one hand they were disseminating false doctrines and misleading humanity; on the other hand they were stealing his ideas and distorting them. The public interest which the rival sects aroused was a sign that mankind was ripe for a new system; the errors they propagated were therefore all the more vicious. Finally his rage against them overflowed in a brochure entitled *Pièges et charlatanisme des deux Sectes Saint-Simon et Owen, qui promettent l'association et le progrès*; voluminous manuscripts and letters show that plagiarism became the devouring obsession of his declining years. The Owenites were usually fought with *ad hominem* arguments against the person of Robert Owen and his dictatorial ways, but since the American experiments had already discredited him the Saint-Simonians became Fourier's chief target.

He was acute enough to put his finger on a fundamental divergence between his system and theirs. The Saint-Simonians were principally preoccupied with a moral revolution, presuming to inaugurate the new era by preaching against idleness and hereditary wealth, by instructing the workers in the ways of obedience to their hierarchical superiors, by sermonizing about universal love. They were trying to change human nature. Fourier on the contrary took man as he was, a creature of passions and desires, and by combining the passions rendered him happy. "I am the only reformer who has rallied round human nature by accepting it as it is and devising the means of utilizing it with all the defects which are inseparable from man," he wrote to his disciple Victor Considérant on October 3, 1831. "All the sophists who pretend to change it are working *in denial of man*, and what is more, in denial of God since they want to change or stifle the passions which God has bestowed on us as our fundamental drives. . . ." The Saint-Simonians were always talking about a hierarchy of functions in the good society — precisely what he had been preaching since 1800 in his doctrine of the ordered series. "You see that in this question of hierarchy, as in everything else, the Saint-Simonians take the skeleton or the shadow of my method and denature it by changing the name. . . . They want no hierarchy except in the ranks and degrees of their priests who rule arbitrarily over the whole social system, especially in the evaluation of capacities." [9] The Saint-Simonians pretended to make everybody love all mankind; this was an impossibility since amorous sympathies were selective. Their tripartite division of capacities into physical, moral, and intellectual merely vulgarized his more complex series. "These scientific pirates" stole his concepts of talent and labor and transformed them into "capacities" and "works." When a M. de Corcelle brought Fourier to one of the sessions of the Saint-Simonians, he was demonstrably jealous of the vogue they enjoyed, and after the meeting he exploded, "What a pitiful thing it is! Their dogmas are like hatchet blows and yet they have an audience and subscribers." [10] Fourier sent Enfantin a copy of his *Nouveau monde industriel* and vainly implored the Saint-Simonians to make an experiment of his system.

There is an extraordinary chronological parallel between the fortunes of Saint-Simon and Fourier in the dates of their first conceptions, their first printed works, and their first acquisition of disciples. The ideas germinated as the eighteenth century drew to a close; in 1807–1808 they both published their initial drafts; and about 1825 they both began to attract followers. Despite the angry denunciations of Fourier, the Saint-Simonians obviously did not plagiarize from him, any more than did the ancient prophets from one another. They were tuned in on the same celestial stations and listened to the sighs of the same wretched humanity. Saint-Simon had had the good fortune to die in time and to become immortalized among disciples who fought over the true interpretation of his message. Fourier with bad grace survived for about twelve years after a school and a movement had been founded, and the Fourierist journals and public lecturers were constrained to propound the doctrine under the hawk-eye of the master. It was an embarrassment for his followers when the old man lived on, criticizing their every move, snarling at them, monopolizing their periodicals with his writings, carping at every proposal that did not emanate from him. They wished that he were dead, if only for the sake of Fourierism. After their original message has been delivered, Messiahs must die.

The first phalanstery was finally organized in — of all places — Rumania, where a journalist who had returned from Paris persuaded a noble landowner to experiment with the system among his own serfs in Scâeni (then Bulgaria).[11] Unfortunately the phalanstery aroused the enmity of surrounding landowners who feared the contagion of such dangerous practices, and they invaded, crushing the society of labor and love with firearms. The phalansterians are said to have been valiant in defense of their system and there remains a wall, now honored as a historic monument by the new Rumanian Soviet state, where the Fourierist peasants took their last stand. The commune of Scâeni is today the seat of a cooperative dominated by an intrinsically un-Fourierist emotional atmosphere. When Mikhail Vasilevich Petrashevsky, the Russian revolutionary of 1848, tried to practice his Fourierism among the peasants of his own poverty-stricken estate in the region of St. Petersburg, he inspired less enthusiasm among the occupants of the communal house. "One night he found it in ashes," writes Professor Franco Venturi. "It had probably been burnt down by the peasants themselves." [12] In 1865, in a hilarious short story, Dostoevsky poked fun at the petty bureaucrat Ivan Matveitch, who, having been accidentally swallowed by a crocodile at an exposition in Saint Petersburg, had resolved in the depths of the beast's bowels to "refute everything and be a new Fourier"; but some sixteen years before Dostoevsky had stood before a firing squad sentenced to death for adherence to the Petrashevsky Fourierists. In 1841 Elizabeth P. Peabody enthusiastically announced glad tidings to the readers of the Boston *Dial*, "We understand that Brook Farm has become a Fourierist establishment. We rejoice in this, because such persons as form that association will give it fair experiment. We wish it God-speed. May it become a University where the young American shall learn his duties and become worthy of this broad land of his inheritance." For more than a year the *New York Tribune* was used by Albert Brisbane to advance the cause of Fourierism in his regular column — he had been initiated into the system in Paris by its inventor, at five francs a lesson. An authentic and complete history of Fourierism and its influence would have to cover much territory, settlements ranging from the prairies of mid-nineteenth-century America to the *kibbutzim* of modern Israel. One thing is certain, the Master would have rejected each and every one of them as vicious falsifications of the doctrine.

DEATH TO PHILOSOPHY AND ITS CIVILIZATION

FOURIER's basic method involved a deliberate total denial of all past philosophical and moralist schools. *Ecart absolu*, he called it. Its definition came early in the *Théorie des quatre mouvements*, a methodological addendum to the Cartesian doubt. "I assumed that the most certain means of arriving at useful discoveries was to remove oneself in every sense from the methods followed by the dubious sciences which never contributed an invention that was of the remotest utility to society and which, despite the immense progress of industry, had not even succeeded in preventing poverty; I therefore undertook to stand in constant opposition to these sciences." [13] The accumulation of hundreds of thousands of volumes had taught mankind nothing. Libraries of tomes by pompous and sententious thinkers had not brought man one inch closer to happiness. His own theory of the passions occupied a position of unique importance in the history of scientific discoveries. It had not really mattered that men were ignorant of the movements of the planets before Copernicus, of the sexual system of plants before Linnaeus, of the circulation of the blood before Harvey, of the existence of America before Columbus; but every delay in the proof and inauguration of the system of passionate attraction was felt in the flesh of mankind. Each year wars destroyed a million lives and poverty at least twenty million more — procrastination took a heavy toll. Since most great revolutionary geniuses had been forced to pursue mean occupations, Fourier's own humble condition was no test of the merit of his system. Metastasio had been a porter, Rousseau a menial worker, Newton a clerk in the markets (*sic*).[14] He now joined this august company by adopting the same underlying dialectical principle of *écart absolu* which had guided them — a complete reversal of the philosophical ideas which had held mankind enchained for three thousand years. "He isolated himself from all known pathways." [15] *Ecart absolu* was developed independently later in the century by Nietzsche in quest of a new moral system, and the same formula reappeared again in Rimbaud. In recent years André Breton has correctly recognized in Fourier an important predecessor of his own surrealist school and has filially composed an *Ode à Fourier*.

The two abstract concepts of philosophy and morality could vie for supremacy as the blackest of Fourier's many bêtes noires. When the *Revue encyclopédique* finally deigned to publish an article on his works they were classified under the hated rubric "philosophy," much to the dismay of the loyal disciple Just Muiron, who on May 12, 1832, wrote to Clarisse Vigoureux: "Philosophy!! Oh! did the Master hit the ceiling? I am terribly afraid." [16] And now in the second century after his death Fourier is again ill used by the fates — called a moralist and joined with his mortal enemies in a single volume. The respectworthy general ideas of eighteenth- and early nineteenth-century thought — virtue, enlightenment, emancipation, rationalism, positivism, industrialism — were for Fourier empty shibboleths, words instead of things. Progress, the grandest concept of them all, the crowning glory of Turgot and Condorcet, Saint-Simon and Comte, was an iniquitous deception because it pretended to improve civilization and this was patently impossible. Civilization had to be destroyed, it could not be amended. For Fourier civilized society was a prison: the *philosophes* were trying to ameliorate conditions in the prison, he to break its bars and escape.

In Fourier's imagery the historical world was at once stadial and cyclical. It was mankind's destiny to climb upward through a series of sixteen or so fixed epochs from the depths of savagery until the zenith was reached in harmony. Never at a loss when nomenclature had to be invented, Fourier's brain, junglelike in the fertility of its private language, devised a terminology for each of the stages in the series up the ladder and back again. The progression is not infinite, for after the passing of harmony man is ordained to trudge laboriously down sixteen steps to a societal form even more primitive than savagery, at which point he fortunately will disappear in a general dissolution of the earth. In the Fourierist dream a striving for progress in happiness is intimately associated with a vision of final destruction. Mankind was summoned to the worldly pleasures of the phalanstery but was offered no promise of eternity. The earth's delights were real but necessarily transitory: therefore *carpe diem*. With meticulous care Fourier estimated the approximate time periods originally allotted each of the sixteen successive upward stages in the historic calendar, but since the schedule was not inflexible it was possible to abbreviate intermediate periods and to accelerate the process from savagery to harmony. A heightened tempo of change was even more urgent in the Fourierist order than in Condorcet's, because man's total destiny on earth was so pathetically finite. Hastening to the felicity of harmony would lengthen the duration of the period of perfect happiness mankind might enjoy. To the degree that man was left to languish in a state of "civilization" or in preharmony interludes such as "guarantism" or "sociantism," whole generations were being robbed of their portion. The quantum of history was fixed; it could be passed either in misery or in supreme happiness. This was a human choice. Fundamentally the successful speeding-up of the pace of evolution depended upon the propagation of the correct theory, as it had with Condorcet and as it would with the major ideologists of the nineteenth century.

Fourier singled out the Jacobins as the historic archenemies of the human race, the misleaders of humanity into the blind alleys of false doctrine. They were the reactionaries who stood for the perfection of the purported moral values of civilization when its complete abolition was required. They preached the Stoic ethic of self-denial and the merits of competitive commerce when mankind craved pleasure and order; their cult of virtue was the essence of antiharmonious evil. Futile political revolution shed blood without even the redeeming feature of Napoleonic carnage — the prospect of the unification of mankind. In its pretense of discovering happiness in liberty, equality, fraternity, and the moderation of desire the Jacobin philosophy was the embodiment of anti-Fourier.

A counterpoint between the emotional and physical sufferings of man in the state of civilization and the perfect happiness attainable in the phalanstery runs through all of Fourier's works. As Burke well knew when he attempted to combat the French "reign of virtue," there is no way to refute a utopia. Try as you may to demonstrate that the ideal structure is impossible of realization, that evils will inevitably crop up to poison the harmony, that the proposed system is contrary to powerful interests, that it violates our knowledge of human nature and contradicts the wisdom of the ages, utopians like Fourier insistently direct you to take another look at the cheats of contemporary civilization, at the falsehoods which contaminate all human relationships in society as it is now constituted, and you recoil with horror, shouting as you join the movement, "Take me to the phalanstery!" The spirit of Jean-Jacques, the enemy of the *philosophes*, hovers over every line that Fourier wrote. The play of contrast between natural man and artificial man of the *Discourse on Inequality* is reflected in the antithesis of the happy man in the phalanstery and the wretched man of civilization.

Man's desire to fulfill the totality of his passionate nature was the will of God. Since nature and nature's God had bestowed passions upon man, they must be afforded absolute free expression. Even Rousseau usually avoided an extreme naturalist position by stopping at the bar of Stoic moderation. In Fourier's vocabulary moderation, along with liberty and equality, was a gross, pejorative word: to curb, to restrain, to repress a desire, was contrary to nature, hence the source of corruption. Nature never decreed moderation for everybody; surely nature never ordained moderation in all things for everybody. Fourier derided the philosophical moralists for their betrayal of the much-vaunted empirical method when they argued about what men *should* be like, what they *ought* to do, what sentiments they *ought* to have. Their discussions were chimerical nonsense, their morality high-flown dicta whose hypocritical authors never practiced their own preachments. Fourier began not with the rational principles of natural law but with an inquiry into what men actually wanted, their basic drives and passions. Despite the historical movement of mankind through the thirty-two stages up and down the ladder of progress, basic human passions had remained the same in all times and places and could be identified and described. Only the opportunities for the expression of the passions had differed from epoch to epoch. Since the passions were constant, human history was a study in varying degrees of repression.

Ever since the dawn of civilization three thousand years before, the external physical forces of nature had been sufficiently harnessed by man to allow for the total fulfillment of all the desires of all human beings on the planet; it had been theoretically possible during all those centuries for miserable mankind to leap out of civilization into harmony. The crisis of passionate man was thus not a novelty of the recent epoch of transition between feudal and industrial society. Gratuitous evil had been the lot of mankind ever since an equilibrium between desires and satisfactions had become abstractly possible. In the recent period, following the development of science and the wide extension of commercial relations, the gap between society's potential capacity to appease desires and the restrictive self-denials imposed by civilization had become ever wider, not narrower. The progress of the arts and sciences had not been paralleled by an increase in gratification. The state of civilization had been protracted far beyond its allotted span of time — the period when it was extending human capacities; it had multiplied artificial restrictions, curtailed pleasure, extended repressions. Under civilization neither rich nor poor had realized their full measure of potential enjoyment.

Fourier had been advised by his more cautious disciples to withdraw his reflections on love in order to make his ideas on the organization of labor more palatable to philosophers, less outrageous to rational civilized society. But this was the very heart of the system of harmony. "Love in phalanstery is no longer, as it is with us, a recreation which detracts from work; on the contrary it is the soul and the vehicle, the mainspring, of all works and of the whole of universal attraction." Imagine asking Praxiteles to disfigure his Venus. "I'd rather break the arms of all the *philosophes* than those of my Venus; if they do not know how to appreciate her, I'll bury her rather than mutilate her." [17] Let philosophy go to the depths of the Hell from which it came. Fourier would prefer to commit his theory to oblivion rather "than alter a single syllable" to please this nefarious clique. In his absolutism and his obsessions he was a worthy successor of Jean-Jacques. The philosophers must either accept the whole theory down to its minutest detail, the arrangement of the last mechanism of the passionate series — or nothing. There would be no compromise with philosophy and civilization. The system was a total truth which had to be preserved entire; modify its slightest aspect and it would be destroyed.

The *philosophes* were the infamous ones to be crushed; Fourier was the anti-Voltaire. Contemporary followers of the pretentious eighteenth-century moralists who believed in the perfectibility of reason had formed a cabal — he sounds Burkean in his imagining of the plot — to suppress invention in general and the one inventor in particular who could assure the happiness of mankind. The new philosophical superstition, the exaltation of reason at the expense of the passions, had to be obliterated to make way for the Fourierist truth. The morality preached by the philosophers of all ages had always been a hypocritical mask. Paris and London were the principal "volcanoes of morality" which each year poured forth on the civilized world veritable torrents of moral systems, and yet these two cities were the bastions of depravity. Athens and Sparta, the ancient centers of philosophy, had espoused pederasty as the path of virtue.

In the divine designation of insignificant Fourier as the bearer of the new doctrine of salvation there was a symbol, a correspondence with the ancient choice of a poor carpenter to defeat the scribes. "Finally to complete the humiliation of these modern titans," he wrote in the *Théorie des quatre mouvements*, "God decreed that they should be beaten by an inventor who is a stranger to the sciences and that the theory of universal movement should fall to the lot of an almost illiterate man; it is a store-clerk who is going to confound these libraries of politics and morals, the shameful fruit of ancient and modern charlatanism. Well! It is not the first time that God has used a lowly man to humble the great and has chosen an obscure man to bring to the world the most important message." [18]

The works of Fourier leveled the most circumstantial attack on the uses of civilization since Rousseau. What he lacked in style he made up in a profusion of detail. The cheats of ordinary commercial arrangements, the boredom of family life, the deceits of marriage, the hardships of the one-family farm and the miseries of pauperism in the great cities, the evils of naked competition, the neglect of genius, the sufferings of children and old people, the wastefulness of economic crises and wars, added up to a total rejection of civilization as a human epoch. Proof positive that it was quintessentially unnatural lay in the fact that children and savages, who were closest to nature, would have none of the ways of civilization until they were violently forced into its toils. The coercive mechanisms of society disguised as reason, duty, moderation, morality, necessity, or resignation did not work. In order to maintain its dominion the apparatus of mercantile trickery and morality called civilization had been constrained to rely upon more terrible contrivances: the executioner and his accessories the prisons and the bastilles. "Try to suppress these instruments of torture and the next day you will see the whole people in revolt abandoning work and returning to the savage state. Civilization is therefore a society that is contrary to nature, a reign of violence and cunning, and political science and morality, which have taken three thousand years to create this monstrosity, are sciences that are contrary to nature and worthy of profound contempt." [19] The natural goal of man was an affluence of pleasures and riches, not penury, chastity, and self-sufficiency; order and free choice, not individualistic anarchy; instead of the negative philosophy of repression, the positive one of attraction. Civilized doctrines of "the wealth of nations" had merely succeeded in covering the immense majority of laborers with rags. The lot of ordinary people under civilization was worse than that of animals.

In *La Seconde boussole* Fourier arraigned the supposed achievements of the industrial revolution. "Men have been more wretched since the introduction of the steam engine and railroads than before." The steam carriage and the steam boat which rival the grasshoppers and the salmon in their velocity are beyond doubt fine trophies for man, but these prodigies are premature. Under existing conditions of civilized society they do not lead to the goal of augmenting in steady proportions the well-being of all social classes — rich, comfortable, middle, and poor. There is a gulf between our progress in material industry and our backwardness in industrial politics or the art of increasing the happiness of nations in proportion with the progress of their labors. We are retrogressing in the very branch of knowledge which is the most useful to man. Among the hardest-working nations, England, Ireland, and Belgium, the poverty-stricken class includes as many as thirty out of a hundred; in areas that are not industrialized, Russia, Portugal, the number of indigents is three out of a hundred, ten times less than in industrialized countries. In terms of genuine progress our social system is therefore a contradiction, an essentially absurd mechanism whose elements of potential good only result in evil. This is the art of transforming gold into copper, the fate of any business in which philosophical science has become involved. Philosophy has tried to direct monarchs and peoples. Where has it led them? We see sovereigns falling into debt, running to usurers, and vying with each other in ruining their states while the peoples who have been promised happiness experience a hard time getting work and bread and are never sure of having it on the morrow. These are the fruits of the science of deception called political and business economics. Let us therefore recognize false progress for what it is, mere nonsensical social change. "It has reached an impasse; it is in a vicious circle like a horse moving round and round without getting anywhere. . . ."

Fourier's writings became the *locus classicus* for descriptions of the evils of capitalism, the thievery of the stock market, the "corruption of commerce," the miseries of economic crises, the hoarding, the speculation. The civilized order was like a dinner table at which the guests fought with one another over every morsel, while if they lived amid the abundance of the phalanstery each man would graciously serve his neighbor. How could moralists pretend to be shocked by the intricate love relations in the state of harmony when they tolerated with equanimity the crowding of men and women into the attics of Lyons as if they were herrings in a barrel? Of all the consequences of industrial and commercial anarchy Fourier was most profoundly shocked by the squandering of natural resources and the products of the earth, because this represented an absolute diminution of potential pleasure for mankind. His witness of the dumping of boatloads of rice during a famine in order to sustain high prices assumed the same symbolic significance as his vision of the costly apple. The intermediaries in the contemporary social mechanism who were not directly related to production — housekeepers, soldiers, bureaucrats, merchants, lawyers, prisoners, philosophers, Jews, and the unemployed — were useless and parasitic; they lived at the expense of producers, savages, barbarians, and children.

Fourier's critique of civilization concentrated on the portrayal of its pervasive poverty. Virtually all men — not only the proletariat — are poor, because their passions are unfulfilled, their senses are not appeased, their amorous emotions are curbed, and their naturally complex social sensibilities can find outlets only in pitifully limited channels. As a consequence all men are bored. In civilization the distinction between the rich and the poor remains an important one because among the rich a small minority may even today enjoy a measure of satisfaction, while the poor are almost totally deprived. If the gastronomy of the rich is mediocre, the poor suffer hunger in an absolute sense. If the rich can at least partially alleviate their ennui by changing women and occupations and by satisfying their senses with music and beautiful sights, the poor man bound to his small agricultural plot is condemned to long hours of repetitive labor and is almost completely bereft of pleasures. A holding based on the organization of the family is far too circumscribed a unit for the contentment of man. While the most obvious distinction between the rich and the poor is economic, the concepts of richness and *luxe* (and its opposite poverty) acquired far broader connotations in Fourier. The idea of luxury has no pejorative overtones; richness is one of the basic desires of all men; it identifies a way of life in which there is a continual experience of a wide variety of sensations and in which the opportunities for gratification are ample. Real passionate richness is what Fourier is extolling, not mere richness of wish or fantasy; being rich implies active indulgence in sensuous delights. Fourier cleansed luxury of its Christian theological stigma and demoted poverty from its ideal position as a crowning virtue. "Poverty is worse than vice," he quoted from his Franche-Comtois peasant compatriots. In the state of civilization class conflict has become endemic because the poor who are ungratified hate the rich who seem to be fulfilled (though in reality they are not) and the rich are fearful of the poor who might deprive them of their pleasures. The view of the class system of domination as a form of instinctual repression — which Freud hinted at in his last works — was developed extensively by Fourier.

Family life, the key social institution of the civilized state, was Fourier's most compelling example of an unnatural institution holding men in its iron grip, bringing misery to all its members. While upon casual inspection the patriarchal monogamous family of the French appeared to establish a system under which the males were free to satisfy their sexual passions outside of the marital bond without suffering derogation and only the females were enslaved, the realities of contemporary marriage were oppressive to men and women alike. The legal fettering of women's desires had resulted in the invention of countless subterfuges to evade the law and in the diffusion of a general hypocritical spirit throughout society. Cuckoldry was rampant. Fourier's anatomy of modern adultery with its intricate categories and typologies — he identified some sixty-odd ideal situations, varying subtly with the temperaments of the threesome involved and their social status — is a triumph of psychological analysis which earned the plaudits of no less an observer of the human comedy than Honoré de Balzac. The husband is by no means the only sufferer and ridiculous figure in the drama, for the adulterers never appease their real passions and have to pay dearly for the mere semblance of contentment.

From his conversation with men boasting about their conquests,

Fourier, not yet equipped with the delicate statistical techniques of contemporary sexologists from Indiana, arrived at the gross estimate that on the average each member of the female sex contracted six liaisons of fornication before marriage and six of adultery after marriage. But what about the exceptions, he asked rhetorically in a section of the *Traité de l'association domestique-agricole* piquantly entitled "Equilibre subversif." There goes a man who claims that he has taken a virgin to wife. He has, he says, good proofs. Maybe, if he married her young enough. But if she has not, before marriage, provided her quota of illicit loves to maintain the "subversive equilibrium," she will have to compensate by twelve liaisons of adulterous commerce after marriage. "No, says the husband, she will be chaste. I shall see to it. In that case it is necessary that her neighbor compensate by twenty-four infractions, twelve in fornication and twelve in adultery, since the general equilibrium requires twelve times as many illicit liaisons as there are men." [20] Granted the relative accuracy of his informants, Fourier's computations were impeccable.

Fourier's mordant descriptions of supposedly monogamous marital relations in a state of civilization were designed to silence those critics of free love in the state of harmony who had denounced its bestial materialism. Marriage in contemporary society, he wrote in the *Théorie de l'unité universelle*, is "pure brutality, a casual pairing off provoked by the domestic bond without any illusion of mind or heart. This is the normal way of life among the mass of the people. Dullened, morose couples who quarrel all day long are reconciled to each other on the bolster because they cannot afford two beds, and contact, the sudden pin-prick of the senses, triumphs for a moment over conjugal satiety. If this is love it is the most material and the most trivial." [21]

The desires of most people are polygamous, witness the secret bacchanalia which take place in small villages and the virtual community of women which prevails among the rich. The great "passionate" lie of love in the state of civilization is rooted in the philosophical dogma that all men and women are the same in their wants. This is simply not true. Men and women have different love needs at various periods in their life cycle. Even persons of the same age group have widely divergent amorous tendencies ranging from the extreme of inconstancy — the Don Juan type among men — to the rare extreme of monogamy. To subject them equally to the same rigid law must inevitably yield a harvest of unhappiness for all.

The gospel of Fourier was the ultimate triumph of the expansive romantic ideal. True happiness consisted of plenitude and the enjoyment of an ever-increasing abundance of pleasure. Man's goal was not the attainment of illusory juridical rights but the flowering of the passions. Though civilization was originally an advance over savagery, patriarchy, and barbarism, in its present decadent state its superiority was not marked enough to attract either savages or barbarians. In the civilized world anarchic competition, monopoly, commercial feudalism, business speculation, were despoiling the earth, spreading misery, fostering thievery in the guise of commerce. Men with diverse passionate natures were constricted within the bonds of monogamous marriage, forcing them to seek other sexual pleasures clandestinely. Man had a progressive need for ever more multifarious luxuries of the table; such gastronomic pleasures were now denied to the vast bulk of the population and the destiny of a substantial portion was hunger. Men were bored by a dull family life under civilization, and at their parties and in their clubs there was a frantic though vain attempt to escape tedium, the corrosive enemy of the species.

THE TWELVE PASSIONS

"Passionate attraction" was defined by Fourier at the opening of *Le Nouveau monde industriel* as "the drive given us by nature prior to any reflection, persistent despite the opposition of reason, of duty, and of prejudice. . . ." [22] At the core of his system was the identification of the passions of man — his fundamental instinctual drives — which like the signs of the zodiac, the gods of Olympus, and the apostles were twelve in number. Unfortunately he changed his nomenclature from time to time, introducing neologisms in "-ism" and "-ique" — about which he himself occasionally jested in his manuscripts. Nevertheless the passions can be described and rendered into English. The whole system is an organic one, conceived as analogous to a tree — Saint-Simon's favorite simile too. From the trunk, which is labeled *unityism*, stem the three main branches of the passions, the luxurious, the group, and the serial. When unityism is treated as a distinct passion it is the one which links a man's happiness with all that surrounds him, with the rest of mankind. Sometimes it is another name for that general outgoing feeling which contemporaries translated as philanthropy and which Saint-Pierre had called *bienveillance*; it is not alien to the benevolence of the Scottish moralists. When Fourier was at a loss for positive ways to communicate his meaning he defined unityism as the polar opposite of egotism, the all-pervasive emotion of the state of civilization. Unityism set the dominant tone of the state of harmony; it integrated all other passions, and therefore was appropriately the trunk of the tree.

The first branch of the passions was the luxurious one, a category designating the desires of the five senses. Every passion in this branch had an internal and an external manifestation. The internal signified the mere healthy physical capacity to give the sense great development, a respect in which human beings by nature varied. In the state of civilization the external luxurious fulfillment of the passions of the senses was dependent upon wealth; hence the anomaly, characteristic of this vicious human condition, that persons with fine appetites and vigorous stomachs capable of grand gastronomic feats were starving, that men with the subtlest musical sensibilities could never hear an opera, while those who were tone-deaf attended concerts for mere show. By virtually abolishing the barrier of penury, harmony would allow for the flowering of any inner sense. Fourier would enrich sight with the elegant structures of careful city planning, hearing with fine music; he would open up unexplored opportunities for the development of the sense of taste — on one journey this poor clerk, the inmate of provincial boardinghouses, had met Brillat-Savarin himself.

The four group passions, another branch, were called also the affective passions and comprised the desires for respect (my translation of the passion for honor), for friendship, for love, and for parenthood. Like the passions of the senses, they not only differ in intensity among individuals but their actualization assumes divergent forms in each of the thirty-two basic epochs of social movement through time, from Edenism up the scale to harmony and down again to dissolution. While the familial passion, for example, may linger on during the transition period from civilization to harmony, it would finally disappear in the perfect order of free love. In civilization parenthood is one of the most frustrated forms of affection because the intensity of feeling which flows from the superior to the inferior is never balanced by an equal reciprocal emotion on the part of the inferior. A father loves his child at least three times more than his love is returned; in harmony no father will be repressive since the educational system allows for pampering and therefore no child can resist loving his father (though the love relationship may never be equal, the discrepancy will be narrowed to at least a ratio of three to two).[23] Everything in civilization is upside down; since the familial passion has been elevated to primacy at the expense of the other affections, the whole emotional system has become gangrenous with falsehood.

Three passions of another branch, called the serial or distributive, were the most difficult to describe because in the state of civilization they were either unknown or frustrated. These were the passion to make arrangements, the concordant or the composite, the passion for intrigue, the discordant or the cabalist, and the passion for variety, the changeling or the butterfly. The existence of these passions had once been recognized by the primitives, but only in harmony would they be satisfied. "Here lies the secret of the lost happiness which has to be rediscovered," Fourier wrote in the *Quatre mouvements*.[24] The serial passions were the drives of the socializing mechanism; their intervention, which led to the creation of multifarious forms of association, made it possible for the sensory and the affective passions to achieve realization. Since these crucial instrumental — perhaps catalytic — passions were suppressed in civilization, this state could never allow for the harmonious expression of any passion.

While the *philosophes* and the Saint-Simonians, as well as Comte, were prophesying an eternal sabbath, a peace in which the elements of conflict were eliminated from human relationships, Fourier was analyzing the benign effects of the passion for discord, a notion which Georg Simmel elaborated later in the century in his sociology of conflict. The cabalistic spirit was an excellent mechanism with which to electrify the mass of workers and cause them to perform miracles. The passion for intrigue which stimulated men to a great variety of combinations, kept them alert, interested, informed about the affairs of others in old age (in the passive cabalistic sense), had to spend itself in civilization in card-playing and gambling, substitute "intrigues" to which bored people resorted because there were no opportunities for real ones. Fourier knew that some men, the cabalistic types, loved complex relationships, and he provided conditions in phalanstery under which they would be able to exercise their imaginative capacity for effecting novel combinations. The passion to emulate would not be stifled but heightened; there would be all manner of contests in phalanstery among age groups and work crews on the same project, but since these parties were not fixed organizations the competition would never continue between the same groups, and it would have none of the destructive qualities of rivalry in a state of civilization. It was of the English playing-field type, without acrimony or excessive hostility. For the performance of various functions during the course of a day in phalanstery the same individuals would be opponents and loving associates. Those who in the morning might belong to rival cabbage-growing teams would by evening be co-operating with each other in an orchestral performance that vied with another group. The plurality of associations took the sting out of competition; the emphasis was always on the relations of love and friendship within the work unit, not on the hostility to a rival group; but the stimulus of emulation was recognized as an indispensable ingredient.

The order of the phalanstery took cognizance of the reality that many men, like butterflies, would, if they could, flit from one occupation to another, from one woman to another. These "papillon" desires would be appeased by allowing for frequent changes of occupations and of loves. At present men were almost universally condemned to labor inhumanly long hours fettered to the hoe or to the industrial machine. The most remarkable aspect of the organization of labor in harmony was the regularity of the shift of work from one job to another; sessions of labor or of entertainment rarely lasted longer than an hour even among the poorer members of the phalanstery. This helped combat boredom, which for Fourier was always one of the most painful consequences of civilization.

A major vice of civilization, the desire for domination, was transformed in phalanstery. Men changed their occupations frequently during a day, work groups were composed of rich and poor alike, all age groups and both sexes were represented, the members had different talents and pursued their tasks with varying degrees of assiduity, and no one man was always the leader — he might be a captain one hour, a lieutenant the next, and a mere private the third. Thus no classes of superiors and inferiors that endured for a whole day could ever be established, and the problem of power was resolved. There were numerous honorific offices in the world of phalanstery, and men, women, and children were always being awarded posts of honor and respect (the two were virtually identical), graduated up to the world throne of omniarchy. Everybody received some honor and respect. Ambition permeated the social order; the need for respect was wholesome; it was destructive only if it was exclusive and manifested itself as an all-consuming lust for power. Since affections were always allowed free play in phalanstery there was no shame attached to being subordinate or passive in love, friendship, or organized activity.

All passions created by God were naturally good and harmonious if they were afforded maximal expression. The order of harmony was ever vigilant that every one of the twelve basic passions be well nourished. Man was by nature cooperative, loving, philanthropic, a creature with expansive capacities for enjoyment — he only needed an appropriate order based on a recognition of the mechanism of the passions. This order had to await the inventive genius of Fourier, the Columbus of the social world, as he liked to call himself. The object of the phalanstery was not regimentation for its own sake; the order had to be complex because it was the only true way to provide for the intricacy of human emotions.

Fourier's determination of the size of the phalansterian unit which in harmony was to replace the family was made by an analysis of the passions. He arrived at a minimal figure of twice 810 persons. There were in reality an infinite number of human character combinations, since any man was a composite of twelve passions each of which had a wide range, not counting the manias which were rare distortions of the passions but were present in every man to some degree. Nevertheless, for purposes of the economy of the phalanstery, he was willing to reduce men to 810 fundamental passionate combinations. For a rich life in the phalanstery all of the types in both sexes would have to be represented; usually he felt that a random sample of about 1700 to 1800 persons would yield the required full quota. The phalanstery would thus be a meeting place of diverse types who because of their very diversity could fashion by their own will a multiplicity of relationships of love and labor.

While most choices in phalanstery would be spontaneous, on occasion gifted psychological directors might intervene with advice. There would be a sort of card catalogue where each of the basic 810 types was identified, and if a weary traveler arrived in a phalanstery he could approach the proper bureau, be interviewed, have his character determined, and within a few hours find himself in the presence of a partner with whom he would be able to establish immediate amorous relations. (This is the fantasy of the traveling salesman who spent restless lonely nights in grubby provincial hotels.) Typologizing was to be an intrinsic part of the system, and the wise men who intuitively recognized psychological types would be highly paid in phalanstery because they could suggest perfect work-love combinations.

Passions could be enjoyed vicariously as well as actively, and older people in particular were not deprived of detailed information about the newest amorous intrigues in the haylofts of phalanstery, because each age group had a right to all possible pleasures. The mood of the phalanstery was peaceful, nondestructive, and nonviolent, and yet it was lively, rich, and joyous, an uninterrupted Saturday-night party, one grand weekend of horticulture and arboriculture, operas, parades, banquets, and love-making. Only the destroyers of life, insipidity and dullness, were banished.

A revolutionary educational policy was the heart of the phalansterian system. Whereas civilized education repressed and denatured the faculties of the child, the new education was aimed at what would now be called "self-actualization," the development of *all* the physical and intellectual faculties, especially the capacities for love and pleasure.[25] While the deathbed message of Saint-

Simon to his disciples also committed them to this ideal, different spirits permeate the two systems. The Saint-Simonians tended to categorize men into fixed professional types and to build their society out of gigantic corporate blocks; Fourier composed his harmonious phalansterian worlds out of psychological elements which happened to have individual embodiments. If in both systems the end was the creation of a new social being, Fourier's individuals were allowed to fulfill themselves passionately to a degree that the Saint-Simonians would not have conceived of. Their doctrine was fundamentally sociological and his psychological. Both systems were expansive in contrast with Owen's rather barrackslike monastic communism which created equality by decreasing consumption, and both valued physical as well as moral passions, at least in theory; but the Saint-Simonians often opted for the sublimation of desires as a high level of existence, while Fourier accepted gross oral and genital gratifications, if they were not harmful to others, as legitimate, desirable expressions of the real man.

Once modern moralists had become acutely conscious of the cultural relativity of customs and manners, they set out in quest of some new Petrine rock on which to raise their edifice. The eighteenth-century prophets chose reason as the only sure haven, even though aware that it was subject to the violent buffetings of emotion and to massive tidal waves of passion. Fourier's relativism forced him to seek out the passions as the only secure foundations because in common experience they alone counted: their potency was in a ratio of twelve to one if compared with reason, and nothing could be done to alter the relationship. "Since customs and morality are conventions which vary in accordance with each century, each country, and each legislator, there is only one way to arrive at moral stability: rallying customs around the desires of the passions, for these are invariable. In what century, in what place, have they bent before our systems? They march triumphant and unperturbed along the road which the Author of their movement has laid out for them. They overturn all obstacles, and reason will not prevail against them. What is the use of beating against this rock?"[26] For Christianity and for its eighteenth-century opponents the passions were shifting sands, their essential definition was change-

CHARLES FOURIER

ability and transience. Fourier's paradoxical transvaluation made
them the only authentic stable force throughout time.

Love in the state of harmony recognized the simple truth that
in any coupling a great number of different amorous modes could
prevail: it might be purely physical or purely spiritual, a combination of physical and spiritual elements on the part of both persons,
or physical alone on one side and spiritual alone on the other. A
delicate yet frank examination of the characteristics involved in
a love relationship would bring about optimum fulfillment in the
state of harmony — a condition which was rarely possible in civilization. Fourier was aware of a dialectical quality in most passionate
relations. In some, as in ambition, there was a natural submission
of the weaker to the stronger; in others, as in love and the family,
a contrapuntal submission of the stronger to the weaker.

Of the various "ways" toward the pursuit of happiness which
Freud outlined in a famous passage of *Civilization and Its Discon-
tents* Fourier would choose the path leading to substantial and
immediate gratifications. To Freud's argument that in the nature
of things pleasure can only follow upon the tension of deprivation
Fourier would reply that there was room enough in most people's
lives for a great increase in direct and varied pleasures because men
were in fact in a grave state of deprivation. Fourier is on principle
not opposed to what Freud called sublimation, but he leaves this
effort for those who desire it. As for the uses of tension in creating
the possibility of pleasure, this involved the very heart of the
mechanism of attraction for Fourier. He made use of an arsenal
of "distributive" and "affective" passions in order to maximize
pleasure and to prevent the intrusion of that state of boredom which
kills passion. The Fourierist system has been likened to a bordello
where various stimulants are administered to provoke the capacity
for pleasure. Fourier would contend that in a state of harmony
there was nothing intrinsically wrong about pleasures aroused in
this manner. They were vicious in civilization only because the
labors were not free and voluntary.

The attempt to reduce the laws governing the passions of man
to a handful, the adaptation of Newtonian terminology, and the
frequent use of mathematical-physical analogies were characteristic

of the quest for certainty in the science of man during this period. Saint-Simon's early writings had seized on the monist principle of gravity as the key to the universal system. Fourier's four "movements" of the passions were similar imitations of science. "For passionate attraction is as fixed as physical. If there are seven colors in the rainbow there are seven primitive passions in the soul. If there are four curves in the cone there are four groups of passionate attraction whose properties are the same as those of conic sections. Nothing can vary in my theory," he had written in the first fragmentary exposition of the doctrine.[27] The analogy between the psychological world and the Newtonian physical universe, this new version of the ancient comparison of the microcosm with the macrocosm, could not be driven further. Perhaps the manifesto of the whole system had already been issued in the *Lettre au grand juge*, a strange communication which Fourier had addressed to the Attorney-General under Napoleon back in 1799. "What does happiness consist of but in experiencing and satisfying an immense quantity of passions which are not harmful? That will be the fortune of men when they are delivered from the civilized, barbarous, and savage states. Their passions will be so numerous, so fiery, so varied, that the rich man will spend his life in a sort of permanent frenzy and the days which are today twenty-four hours long will pass as if they were one." [28] Fourier's works on the future happiness of mankind were an attempt to communicate a state of permanent orgasm. If the passions were good, then eternal convulsion was bliss itself.

The aims of the phalanstery were the attainment of riches and pleasures; or both could be combined to describe the common goal as the expansive enjoyment of rich pleasures. This would be achieved by uniting pleasure with work, making work attractive, establishing an accord in the distribution of rewards to three "faculties" (capital, labor, and talent), and spontaneously amalgamating unequal classes. Work in phalanstery is attractive because it is never mere labor out of necessity but is always related to one or more of the fundamental passions with which all men are endowed. Primarily men proceed to satisfy their passions; in the course of this delightful pastime they labor. The Biblical curse has been lifted.

The ideal society was not a grouping together of people who were more or less similar and hence compatible with one another. In phalanstery there would be an assembly of dissimilar character types and ages. Instead of conformities and identities Fourier maximized differences and created as many novel combinations as possible while still keeping his basic societal unit within manageable limits. He inquired into the unique characteristics of each age group and instead of subjecting all human beings to the uniformity of family life he made them happy by allowing for the particular social arrangements which were most passionately attractive at each stage in life. Children love to move about in hordes, to parade and display emblems; with appropriate organization and incentive he could even make the dirty-work of the phalanstery attractive to this age group. Work on the manure piles, which had so disturbed Nathaniel Hawthorne during his stay at Brook Farm,[29] had been amply provided for by Fourier. "The natural penchant of children for filth becomes the charm and the bond of the series. God gave children these strange tastes to provide for the execution of various repulsive tasks. If manure has to be spread over a field, youths will find it a repugnant job but groups of children will devote themselves to it with greater zeal than to clean work." [30] Among the young and the middle-aged he recognized love as the dominant passion, and the major labors of society would be organized around their manifold love relationships. Work performed by groups bound together by amorous ties would be far more productive than the labors of competitive civilization. Only the aged tended to be naturally familial, and there was room for the appeasement of this desire too. None of the age-group relations of love and labor were stereotyped. Allowance was made for the mutual passions of older men and young girls, older women and young boys. All human beings could be fitted into some symbiotic love relation; there were no absolute misfits in the fantasy world of lonely Charles Fourier. In and of itself work was neither a blessing nor a curse, but men drawn to labor in common by the attraction of sexual passion would find even work pleasurable.

In rebellion against scholastic theology and the intricacies of the royal administration of France, the *philosophes* and their revolutionary followers had eulogized sacred simplicity and a mechanical order in which all the parts were virtually interchangeable. Fourier rejected the simple as false and evil, and insisted on complexity, variety, contrast, multiplicity. His denunciations of the metaphysical order of the philosophers are reminiscent of Burke, though he never read him. Since man was a psychologically complex creature he needed an intricate social order to fulfill the design of his nature.

REPRESSIONS AND MANIAS

"Nature driven out through the door comes back through the window," Fourier wrote to the *Gazette de France*.[31] The whole system of repression is, according to Fourier, based on the assumption that man is free to choose between succumbing to the so-called destructive impulses or resisting them. The premise is false. Nothing can be done to curb the natural passions under civilization short of the use of inhuman instruments of oppression. Man's only alternative is a choice between a vicious civilized state and a virtuous phalansterian one. Once they are thrust into civilization most men cannot resist the forces which lead them to what is known as evil. "Perhaps a few individuals with weak passions seem to be less driven and they give the appearance of having the faculty to repress their passions" — shades of Nietzsche — "but the mass will never repress theirs." What happens in civilization is that the repressed passions assume a different external form. "Hence the development which, after Horace and Lafontaine, I have called the countermovement (*contremarche*) and recurrence of the passions deprived of expression. These produce a double evil instead of the double good which might have been born of their direct development."[32] The pivotal social science was the analysis of the twelve "recurrent" passions or counterpassions, the malignant transformations of the benign. If, for example, the normal desires for fame and for love do not have natural outlets, they are turned into prostitutions of the passions: the ambitious ones become *philosophes* and the amorous ones prostitutes. "It is then that one realizes the stupidity of the *philosophes* who want to repress, compress, and suppress nature and the passions."[33] The same theme was repeated in *Le Nouveau monde industriel*: "It is easy to compress the passions with violence. Philosophy suppresses them with a stroke of the pen. Prison-bolts and the saber come to the aid of gentle morality. But nature appeals from these judgments. It recaptures its rights in secret. Passion stifled at one point reappears in another, like nature contained by a dike; it is driven in like the humour of an ulcer closed too soon." [34]

In the state of harmony the patently destructive passions are not sublimated, they are merely channelized and used in a salutary manner by being appropriately combined with others. Fourier's employment of the little hordes of boys that love to wallow in dirt is a classic example of the technique; as disposers of filth, they contribute to the mechanism of harmony. Moreover, Fourier the eternal bookkeeper added, they are economical agents since they are paid only in *fumées de gloire* (clearly a pun on *fumier*).[35] His treatment of a potential Nero is equally well known, a device often adopted by Eugène Sue in effectuating a sudden reformation of the characters in his novels. The rehabilitation of Slasher in *Les Mystères de Paris* is completely in the Fourier spirit. If a Nero is harassed and repressed up to the age of sixteen, at twenty he becomes like a powerful torrent that breaks the dike and ravages the countryside. "This is the effect of morality which while trying to repress and to change the passions merely irritates them and treats them as infamous in order to excuse its ignorance of the proper method of employing them." The remedy for Nero is simple: "From an early age he will be attracted to work in the butcheries." [36]

The distortion of salutary passions into vices as a direct consequence of repression is one of the more original psychological reflections of Fourier. To describe the dynamics of the phenomenon he invented a special vocabulary which is perhaps neither better nor worse than the one that has come to dominate our common modes of expression, and he garnered a few case histories to support his abstract system. In volume IX of *La Phalange* the disciples rescued the following strange passage from the debris of his manuscripts:

"Every passion that is suffocated produces its counterpassion, which is as malignant as the natural passion would have been benign.

The same holds true for manias. Let us give an example of their suffocation.

"Lady Strogonoff, a Moscow princess, seeing herself grow old, became jealous of the beauty of one of her young slaves. She had her tortured; she herself pricked her with pins. What was the real motive behind these cruelties? Was it really jealousy? No. Without knowing it the woman was in love with the beautiful slave in whose torture she participated. If someone had presented this idea to Madame Strogonoff and arranged a conciliation between her and her victim, they would have become very passionate friends. But instead of thinking of it, the princess fell into a counterpassion of a subversive character. She persecuted the person whom she should have cherished, and her fury was all the greater since the suffocation derived from a prejudice which, in hiding the veritable object of her passion from this lady, did not even leave her the possibility of an ideal development. A violent suffocation, which is the nature of all forced privations, leads to such furies. Others have exercised in a collective sense the atrocities which Madame Strogonoff practiced individually. Nero loved collective cruelties or their general application. Odin had made of them a religious system and de Sade a moral system. This taste for atrocities is nothing but a counterpassion, the effect of a suffocation of the passions." [37] (Fourier's appreciation of the nature of primitive religious ritual and of the character of de Sade's writings is rare in this period.) It is an axiom of the system that virtually all sadistic passions could be turned into wholesome expressions. In Fourier this is accomplished without sublimation into the higher mental systems; and the newly directed passions lose nothing of their vivacity and intensity — a proposition which Freud generally denied.

With a sense of compassion hitherto unknown in psychological literature Fourier confronted the problem of hidden manias, and when they were not harmful to others he defended their right to existence as a part of man's nature. "After the many insults which have been heaped upon the self-love of civilized men, I am finally going to rehabilitate them in their own eyes and become the champion of every one of their manias. I am going to teach them to be proud of all the ludicrous secret feelings which bewilder

them and which everyone conceals, even the amorous extravagances which readily lend themselves to jokes. . . ." [38] Though his
definition is somewhat cryptic, the notion of a mania as a secondary
passion should attract the interest of sexologists. "Manias are dimin-
utive passions, the result of man's need to create stimulants for
himself. This can give rise to superstition and is, so to speak, the
root of spiritual manias. In love, especially when one seeks an ideal
happiness in a habit that is in itself often indifferent, manias develop
very actively." [39] Normally the twelve passions in their various
combinations grouped themselves into 810 types; but the manias
were outside the keyboard of the passions. If they were as frequent
as 1 in 810 they were still intramanias; if as rare as 1 in 100,000
clearly extramanias. "The passionate manias, both *intra* and *extra*
keyboard, are innumerable, for each person can have many in
relation to each passion, many in love, many in friendship, in
ambition, and even in the passions of the senses." Fourier's formal
definition of a mania in his manuscripts was not very satisfactory.
"I call deviation or mania in passion every fantasy which is considered unreasonable and outside of the circle of the passion, outside of its admissible development." [40] The rare manias arrested
Fourier's particular attention; if they were infinitesimal in number
in the world, they would be especially significant in the study of
psychological prognoses called horoscopes, for the very infrequency
of a mania made its effect the more readily calculable. All manias
were to be investigated with respect: men were without prudery
in harmony. Fourier was conscious of the prejudices he would
have to overcome in rehabilitating manias that were seemingly
useless and extremely bizarre, especially since the amorous passion
itself was not yet recognized in its own full rights.

The ultimate purpose of conducting psychological studies was
the prediction of human character by the establishment of physical
and psychic correspondences. Calculations based on his 810 basic
types would be extended through many generations with the
purpose of foretelling the appearance of manias in an active, passive
(we would now say latent), or mixed state — social hygiene. If
at an early age a child showed the identifiable manias of a future
monster men would know soon enough to keep him away from
the throne. In this respect Fourier differentiated his system not

only from the rival sects of Owen and Saint-Simon but from the phrenologists with whose character typologies he had certain marked affinities. The phrenologists were only willing, on physiological grounds, to indicate the psychological propensities of an individual; they would never hazard a guess about what circumstances might do to alter them. Fourier's system, on the contrary, not only analyzed character but so fashioned the external circumstances of society that a sound development of natural tendencies was predetermined.

In proclaiming absolute freedom from repression Fourier had to face the problem of sexual perversions. He certainly would protect the young from them. In the case of older people, he seems to have hedged. In general he solved the problem by asserting dogmatically that virtually all perversions and vices were the direct consequence of repression. If the banquet of nature were free, he maintained in a passage reminiscent of Montesquieu's *Spirit of the Laws*, pederasty and sapphism would disappear. Alcoholism too was a consequence of deprivation, and if liquors were available in abundance there would be few addicts. Moralists preached their doctrines of repression in order to preserve society — at least that was the pretense — but Fourier doubted profoundly whether moral sermons had ever repressed anything. The real agencies of repression were other, he repeatedly affirmed in crisp language that is a strange echo of de Maistre's defense of the executioner. "It is not morality but the bayonet which represses the weak; and supposing it were a good to repress the passions, is the whole thing not illusory as long as this repression cannot be extended to the powerful, to Nero and Tiberius, to Genghis and Attila, who still have the capacity to persecute a hundred million men? As for the common people whom one pretends to repress, in all countries they abandon themselves to every vice which force cannot reach, such as embezzlement and adultery. . . . Morality is impotent in repression without the gibbet and bayonets, the pivots around which all human legislation revolves." [41]

But what about murder and robbery, are these not malevolent passions which have to be repressed? Here again Fourier stuck by his contention that in and of themselves there are no evil passions; there are only corrupted developments of originally salutary passions, for in the perfect harmony of God's creation there were no qualities which did not serve a purpose. Fourier's system merely drove to their absolute conclusion the arguments which seventeenth and eighteenth-century Christian virtuosi had used to demonstrate God's perfection from a contemplation of rational purposiveness in the most minute physical and biological phenomena in the world. "God had to create bloodthirsty characters. Without them there would be neither hunters nor butchers in harmony. It is therefore necessary that there be among the 810 character types a certain number of naturally ferocious ones, who are actually very wicked in the present order where everything suffocates and irritates the passions; but in harmony where the passions find an easy expression the bloodthirsty man, having no cause to hate his fellows, will be drawn to exercise himself on animals. . . . Thus ferocity, the spirit of conquest, robbery, concupiscence, and many other unsavory passions are not vicious in the seed; only in growth are they rendered vicious by the civilization that poisons the mainsprings of the passions, which were all considered useful by God, who created none of them without assigning to it a place and a purpose in the vast harmonious mechanism. As soon as we wish to repress a single passion we are engaged in an act of insurrection against God. By that very act we accuse Him of stupidity in having created it." [42] Little did Leibniz reckon where his philosophy of universal harmony could lead.

THE DELIGHTS OF PHALANSTERY

FOURIER's treatment of the education of the young in phalanstery has attracted special attention because he dissolved traditional family relationships. Any coercion in the process of upbringing would be prohibited. Methods would be found for giving free expression to the unruly as well as to the docile child, and teachers chosen whose characters harmonized with the various types of children. They would be enticed by ruses to perform unpleasant yet necessary tasks such as reading and writing. Instead of the nightmare of howling children in a state of civilization, Fourier opened up the prospect of cooperative young ones engaged in contests, marching in parades, working, and learning what every good phalansterian should know through actual practice, taught by professors who were well paid and had achieved a new dignity in society. If children broke the rules, they would be subject to the reproof of their comrades, a sort of gentle mockery rather than punishment, and when the child returned to the bosom of his parents at night they could overwhelm him with love and affection without endangering the educational process or spoiling him.

Amorous adolescents and young people would be allowed to contract a wide variety of relationships, some constant, others promiscuous, depending upon their innate character structures, the reality of their passions. This would end hypocrisy in love. One partner would not be condemned to monogamy while the other was free to love at will — the common practice of the rich man in civilization. Contracts of work and love would somehow be supervised, but the punishments for their breach are not always clearly defined. Group opinion, it seems, would exercise its pressure by making the delinquents feel ashamed. With Fourier, as with the Saint-Simonians, penal problems do not loom large, because there is an underlying assumption that once opportunities were open for passionate expression, no one would feel that the contract freely entered into was onerous. Since the dissolution of relationships would be easy, men would tend to abide by those they accepted without the imposition of external force — a highly dubious assumption.

Fourier preserved private property in his system; he rewarded purchasers of shares in phalanstery according to their investment. He railed against the Saint-Simonian abolition of inheritance and against any preachments of communistic economic egalitarianism as unnatural. This was no follower of Babeuf; a passion for equality is somehow not recognized in the keyboard. There would be disparities of income in the phalanstery and therefore distinctions in the degree of pleasure attainable by those who had greater or fewer economic resources. When he described a typical day's program of work and pleasure for a rich man and for a poor man there turned out to be substantial differences in the refinement of the pleasures available to them. Members of the Fourierist movement later tended to minimize these distinctions and to emphasize economic communism, but they were probably not as far wrong in interpreting the master's ultimate goal as a superficial reading might indicate. In phalanstery every one was so gloriously rich in a psychic and in an emotional sense that the variations in degrees of enjoyment measured in accordance with wealth became insignificant. Wines, for example — and his receipted bills in the Archives Nationales indicate that Fourier was quite interested in the subject as a major source of gastronomic pleasure — that were served at the poorest table in phalanstery would be of a quality superior to the finest Romanée-Conti reserved in civilization for only a few of the richest men in France. With the prevalence of such real luxury everywhere there could be no class alignments on the basis of wealth. While the differences existed, they did not matter. Moreover, there was great social mobility, and men and women would shift easily from one economic category to another because passions, not money, would dictate amorous alliances. Fourier's preservation of a rudimentary economic hierarchy at times seems a mere stratagem to win rich adherents in a blinded world of civilization where men do not recognize true values — their own desires.

Fourier took a similar position with respect to the family. He did not abolish it outright; but in phalanstery there were so many other ways of achieving passionate fulfillment that with time this antiquated institutional form would just drop by the wayside — vanish without anyone's noticing its disappearance.

Superior creative talents in any branch of activity would be rewarded with astronomic royalties which made the contemporary compensation of a writer or a composer appear puny by contrast. The expansion of creative talents among phalansterians would assume gigantic proportions; under instinctual freedom geniuses would proliferate like rabbits. Fourier's obscurantism was directed against moralists and philosophers, not against mathematical scientists and artists. "When the globe shall have been organized and brought to a total of three billion inhabitants, there will normally be on earth thirty-seven million poets the equal of Homer, thirty-seven million mathematicians the equal of Newton, thirty-seven million authors of comedies the equal of Molière, and the same number in all other conceivable talents (these are estimates). It is a great error to believe that nature is miserly in talents; it is far more prodigal than our desires and our needs. But one must know

how to discover and develop the seed. About this you are as ignorant as a savage is about the discovery and the exploitation of
mines." [43]

In the choice of his ideal unit of about seventeen hundred
persons he was in the ancient Platonic tradition which could only
conceive of good societies as small. In making the basic work form
agricultural he was giving voice to the small townsman's horror
of the vast agglomerations of Lyons and Paris. But Fourier did
not abandon his phalansteries to peasant idiocy and isolation. There
would be traveling groups of artists who knitted phalansteries together not only in one nation but in different parts of the world;
extraordinary excellence in any field was universally shared, not
monopolized. There was even a vague hierarchical set of international political powers, culminating in an omniarch — a position
which he offered Napoleon in his first work. Through its combined
efforts the world union of phalansteries would change the physical
face of the earth so drastically that the weather would everywhere
be affected and the very polar regions of the earth made habitable
— no longer as absurd a notion as it appeared to the short-sighted
journalists of Fourier's France.

Fourier knew that he had aroused great enmity among the
respectable middle-aged defenders of the family; after one year
in phalanstery the rigorous moralists would become the most ardent
admirers of the system of free love. The corps spirit of the vestal
virgins would defend the chastity of young girls — those who chose
this way of life — far more effectively than the watchful eyes of
bourgeois parents. Aging men and women would find young lovers
without losing their self-respect, because the organized groups of
bayaderes, female fakirs, bacchants, and magicians would appease
all desires and be paid by society, not the individual. Fourier was
one of the first to dwell on the psychic isolation of the aged, condemned to the company of babies for conversation. The new
medical science of geriatrics would have much to learn from his
reflections.

Fourier always maintained that his theories of love had been
completely misunderstood by his critics because they were applied
to the present debased state of civilization, whereas they were
intended for a purified humanity. "People keep judging the innova-

tions I have proclaimed in accordance with the results they would bring forth if amalgamated with civilization, a condition in which they would only produce material and spiritual infamies." [44] How could the existence of corporations of voluptuaries be reconciled with a civilized order which is infected with venereal diseases? How could such corporations be organized before mankind had been cleansed by a universal quarantine — somewhat difficult to implement, to be sure — one of the first public measures of the unitary order? The same incompatibility existed in the moral sphere. Would not the bayaderes willing to devote themselves to the service of the contemporary vulgar rabble be even more crapulous than they? "All the arrangements of free love are reserved for a period when the physical and moral being of people shall have been transformed, and it is ridiculous to think that I ever had the notion of fully applying this new system to the present-day mob. But our great minds do not want to wait until an inventor has explained his plan to them; they anticipate his reasoning and know better than he does what he has not yet communicated. . . . To condemn without listening, that is the rule of the modern philosophers who brag that they have perfected the perfection of perfectibility." [45]

In the stage called *Sériosophie*, which precedes harmony, when men are still in the process of developing the passionate series, great sensitivity would have to be exercised during the ritual of choosing among partners to make certain that no pain was inflicted on rejected suitors. At a ball no individual invitations would be extended from a man to a woman; instead there would be multiple requests signalized by the deposition of symbolic torches before each woman, and when she finally made her selection the refusal would be "composite"; it would never be given directly and verbally and thus would not wound any one individual. Should there only be two requests, the woman must accept them both lest a singular refusal result. Fourier's psychology was founded upon the premise that in plurality and complexity there was salvation and happiness; in multiplicity there was freedom. The dangerous relationships were the limited ones, because in exclusivity there lurked disasters — an idea Freud recognized on more than one occasion.

Ordinary services would be performed by special corps who were paid as a unit, and their choice of a person to serve was dependent on mutual friendship and inclination, a relationship in which pleasure on both sides would grace every minor act of attention. Division of the emoluments of the service corps was directed by a group council who were easily informed of the relative devotion of the various members. Their judgments would never be unfair, for though passion might blind an individual to prefer his favorite, it could not mislead ten to twelve persons, pronouncing a collective judgment on the assiduity and the dexterity of one. "In short, the complex is always just and true, the simple always false. . . ." [46]

Without a passionate mechanism there was emotional chaos. Civilized institutions created universal frustration, the false mechanism. The social art consisted of skill in manipulation — this was the Fourier doctrine with which, much to his dismay, the *philosophe* Condorcet might have been in abstract agreement. But there was also a profound difference between them. Condorcet saw the passions as disruptions of an ideal Stoic calm; while one could not do without them, they had to be moderated. They were the winds that gave movement to the sailboat, but they also dashed it against the rocks. Fourier's passions all served a noble purpose; they were numerous and good. Man could do nothing about their God-given nature; what he could do was to provide for their burgeoning and to establish appropriate social institutions for their guidance.

No projects combined the expansive potentialities of the union of labor and love more felicitously than the "harmonious armies" which Fourier described in his books and manuscripts (the still unpublished grey notebook series). [47] These vast enterprises would come into being only after harmony was well established and therefore prepared to undertake the colossal public works necessary to reforest the mountain chains of the world, to force rivers back into their proper channels, and to repair the ravages of nature caused by the negligence of the civilized stage of mankind. Industrial armies might comprise as much as 2 or 3 per cent of the total population; an empire the size of Britain could recruit 600,000 a year and disperse them over various parts of the globe. "Harmonious armies" would not be condemned to arduous labors alone.

Women would be attached to them, and besides cooking and performing fine arts in the evening, each one of them would provide for the sexual needs of three to four men. "Most women of twenty-five have a temperament suited to this role, which will then become a noble one." The honored ladies who had contempt for that "egotist love called fidelity" [48] would be consecrated to the service of the fatherland in order to charm young men into working in the armies without pay. This counting-clerk prophet was always intent upon running his grand projects as economically as possible.

The bacchantes would in no way resemble modern courtesans or camp followers. They would have ranks bestowed upon them in accordance with their capacities, and a lady marshal would command cohorts of fifty to a hundred thousand women whose feats would be reported in phalansterian newspapers throughout the world. There would be wars in harmony, but what delightful wars! Armies composed of men and women in equal numbers would do combat with each other, but no one would be killed. Positional warfare, as in a game of chess, would dominate the field and neutral judges award the palms of victory. Prisoners would belong to the conquerors for a period of one to three days. A battalion of men divided up among a battalion of women would have to follow their orders, and the young women warriors might, out of sympathy, occasionally lend their young captives to older women. If the fellows did not behave gallantly with the aged and satisfy them, their imprisonment would be prolonged. Similar fates awaited young female captives, who would be awarded to venerable old men. Since the only real vices recognized in harmony were lying and deception, couples contractually committed to fidelity would by agreement be allowed to grant each other periods of sexual liberty, especially when the "harmonious armies" came marching through their territory. Time and again Fourier reiterated that all this would become feasible only when the last generation of civilization — the generation of the wilderness — had disappeared and reason dominated love relations.

The term reason at first sounds incongruous in a Fourier manuscript. Was this not the shameful hallmark of the philosophical enemies of mankind? But Fourier endowed reason with new attributes. "What is reason in the state of harmony? It is the employment of any method which multiplies relationships and satisfies a great number of individuals without injuring anybody. A beautiful woman operates in contradiction of this rule if she wants to remain faithful and to belong exclusively to one man all her life. She might have contributed to the happiness of ten thousand men in thirty years of philanthropic service, leaving fond memories behind among these ten thousand."

In harmony punishments for secret infidelity were inflicted by courts of love. A young woman culprit, for example, might be ordered to keep herself at the disposition of a worthy member of the phalanstery for a day or two. In general Fourier was not too disturbed by such infidelities, because no real evil had been committed. After all, amorous relationships had been multiplied, and that was a good in and of itself. The young man who was condemned must perform his corvée for an old crone with courtesy "because the old lady is free to grant or to refuse the certificate of good conduct upon which his absolution depends." Failure to obey a *cour d'amour* led to exclusion from pleasures and employment, hence the young persons would obey with alacrity. The system is so arranged that "no age capable of love is frustrated in its desire." [49]

Many of the facile objections which have since been raised against the system were already answered by Fourier somewhere in his voluminous manuscripts. What happens in phalanstery when two men are in love with one woman? How is the rejected suitor treated? Fourier was not at all fazed by this unfortunate circumstance. In the state of civilization the fellow would probably become a misanthropist, but nothing of the sort occurs in the state of harmony, because a special corps of fairies (*fées*) take hold of him, women skilled in playing on a man's accidental sympathies. Using techniques based upon passionate identities and contrasts they divert him from his fixed attraction. This type of magnetism is a recognized positive science in the phalanstery, a branch of medicine. [50]

When it came to elaborating the details of the system of harmony, Fourier the structure-builder was never at a loss. The printed word has not caught up with his manuscript plans for the architecture of buildings in phalanstery, for the regulation of the complex free labor exchange with its myriad contractual forms, for the celebration of banquets and fêtes, for the pyramidal grouping of phalansteries on various levels from the individual unit through the caliphate, the empire, the caesarate, to the omniarchy of the world (his relentless vengeance against Paris expressed itself in reducing the capital to a mere caliphate while Nevers [!] became the center of the French empire).

In final defense of Fourier it should be remembered that some of the wildest reveries imputed to him, such as the prognostication that men of the future would grow tails with an eye in them, were the inventions of his detractors. Since our recent experiments with interplanetary instruments and our manipulation of the weather, cosmological fantasies have become somewhat less ridiculous. The idea that under certain conditions the ocean would change from its present saline state into a not unpleasant lemonade may not bear immediate conviction, but a reasonable skeptic would hardly be willing to assert the stable character of the sea for all future geological time. When Fourier described the copulation of the planets he was difficult to follow, though many of his more respectable philosophical predecessors had heard the music of the spheres. The cautious may suspend judgment on his prospect of an aromatic revolution generated by the harmonious labors organized in the new industrial society. But we have no right to dismiss him for these conceits. His reflections on the relationship between love and work, the ideal of total self-fulfillment, ought not to be treated lightly by an age which has swallowed the values of the new psychology. If Freud transformed into a permissive father becomes the savior, Fourier will have to be revered as a respectworthy forerunner.

THE MASK OF HARLEQUIN

OF all the nineteenth-century system-makers Fourier has left behind the most complete documentation for a study of his character structure. The published works, the manuscripts which members of the Fourierist movement issued posthumously, and the unpublished dossiers in the Archives Nationales respond to any sounding with a rush of evidence. But the *meaning* of this profusion of evidence is, as Hume would say, "exposed to some more difficulty."

In a manuscript entitled "Le Sphinx sans Oedipe ou l'énigme des quatre mouvements" Fourier wove a fantasy describing how he had deceived the *philosophes*. Like Saint-Simon he conceived of his system as an act of aggression against the philosophical authorities; and in his war with "them," the all-powerful fathers, only stratagems and guile could prevail. Because he knew his theory would clash with accepted opinion, would be ridiculed by the "philosophical cabal," and would be covertly plagiarized, he had to devise a way of presenting his ideas so that nobody should doubt his title to them even though they long remained hidden and came to light only generations later. Since men were incapable of reasoning when their prejudices were shocked too profoundly, he had schemed to catch them off their guard. Introspective Fourier was well aware that bizarre forms came naturally to him, but on this occasion he had deliberately assumed a peculiar habit. It was a ruse to sound out the age, to see how contemporaries would react to his ideas. Or it was a trap set for the pretentious, cunning Parisians. Surely his first book and its title were strange, but they were less strange than its judges were obtuse when they failed to detect the masquerade which had been dictated by prudence.[51] The cosmogonic theories were the sections of his work which attracted the eye and called forth the sneers of reviewers in the 1820's, while virtually nothing was said about his social system. Precisely what he had wanted. The artifice had been successful — he had purposely included these sensational fancies to distract attention from his two revolutionary attacks, one directed against the family, the other against the economic system. His cosmogony had convinced men that he was a visionary, and nobody prosecuted visionaries; in the meantime his ideas on the family and the economy, on love and on labor, had been allowed to insinuate themselves slowly into the consciousness of his contemporaries. He had intentionally assumed the mask of Harlequin;[52] playing the court fool, he had been allowed to say things which would otherwise have been prohibited.[53] Another way of putting it was even more involuted: knowing that all philosophers were intolerant of new ideas, he had adopted a trick from the confessional: just as the canny penitent slips a major sin among a host of venial ones, in the *Quatre mouvements* Fourier had concealed his reflections on free love among a mass of notions on planetary changes which he touched up with obscenity — "the pearl in the mud." [54]

Fourier had triumphed in his contest with the philosophers; he had successfully outfoxed the potential plagiarists; they had been repelled by his undemonstrated cosmogonies and had turned away. Despite the jeering reception in the newspapers, it was not he who had been rejected and mocked; grand strategist of society, he had outwitted all his enemies. Nobody, none of the smart Frenchmen, had guessed the riddle. The laugh was on them, the wiseacres of Paris who wrote witty *feuilletons* about him, *le fou du Palais Royal*. It was they who were mad, they who were fools. He had planned it all that way in 1806, when he first surveyed the social scene where he would have to sow his doctrine. His book was a scout sent out beyond the front lines to observe the enemy. The newspapers said the work lacked method: it had the method of an enigma.

One of his manuscripts described an imaginary dialogue between an inventor of the compass and the philosophers of Athens, who treated him as a madman and sent him to the asylum to be cured. In the course of the conversation, in order to humor him, they publicly conceded the one point that he was intent upon — they admitted that he had discovered the needle and that any benefits which derived from it were henceforth traceable to him alone. Fourier did not care that they considered him daft as long as his authorship of the system was recognized for all eternity. If Fourier's explanation of the secret of the *Quatre mouvements* were accepted, many of his extravagances would have to be interpreted in a different spirit. Actually, much of this is a later rationalization constructed to steel himself against ridicule; this divided man may have believed in his cosmogonies at some moments and at others have been so ashamed of them that he chose to deny them and to pass them off as mere window-dressing. Like other neurotic geniuses, Fourier was shrewd when he played the fool, and at times he really was the credulous fool. The ambiguity remains.

There was a sadistic element in this builder of a utopia of love. He feasted on dreams of glorious vengeance against his generation, against the philosophers, against Frenchmen, especially Parisians —

against all those who had mocked him. The punishments he meted out to his detractors were terrible. Paranoid elements are almost always latent in the great structure-builders; in Fourier they rise to the surface — nothing is hidden. Fourier proclaimed his resolve "to punish his century." [55] Ultimately he might relent and publish his latest findings, but only in bits and pieces, tantalizing his contemporaries, making them suffer for their doubts about his truth. In later writings he demonstrated that the decision to wreak his wrath upon his compatriots had been fully realized in the final stages of the Napoleonic wars. Suppose the inventor of the physical compass had kept his discovery secret, what shipwrecks, what destruction would have been visited upon mankind — "he would have punished the whole world." [56] The Frenchmen had suffered a similar chastisement for their refusal of the social compass. "More than any other people, they have been victims of the protraction of the state of civilization from which I could show them a release. The fates have pursued them and their chief since 1808. They have been punished." Frenchmen had missed a historic opportunity by making fun of him in 1808. If they had accepted the system straightway they would have been able to grasp the initiative in the diffusion of uniform communications, signs, and measures. Eventually a new international language would be invented, but for an interim transitional period French would have been used and Frenchmen would have been in great demand throughout the phalansteries of the world. They lost their chance. Fourier recounted the punishment of France for the neglect of his first work in terms that evoke de Maistre's divine scourge, the Revolution visited on the land for its abandonment of the true religion. The chronological coincidence is perfect: in 1808 the *Quatre mouvements* was published and in 1808 the war in Spain broke out, the beginning of the defeats of France. "Opprobrium, ruin, public servitude, finally all the calamities which have assailed and devoured her, date from the period when she disdained the discovery of the calculus of attraction. The capital where this discovery was derided has been invaded twice, sullied by the outrages of its enemies. France thought she would rule the world; she has become its plaything. I repeat: if I had had any power over destiny, would I have been able to demand of it a more remarkable vengeance?" [57]

Fourier's megalomaniac fantasies were vivid and bloody. It was he who condemned France to a horrible retribution, he who had secretly resolved to wait until France had lost another million heads in combat before he published further details on the operation of the system. "Finally the year 1813 amply paid this tribute of a million heads which I had imposed on France. There is today even a surplus of three to four hundred thousand heads in the massacre." [58]

Paris was Fourier's immediate adversary because there the false, lying monopoly of philosophical journalists reigned supreme. In Paris opinion had to be bought and he was no Croesus. What did they expect, that he who had discovered the secret of human happiness should come to them — who by right should be his suppliants — on bended knee? Fourier hated Paris with the passion of a provincial unrecognized, disdained by the coteries among whom he could make no headway. In the end of the days he would be avenged: the capital of the world would be set up in Constantinople, and Paris would be humbled even as Paris had humiliated him.

At the conclusion of the manuscript of *Annonce d'une nouvelle publication*, to throw his contemporaries into utter turmoil, he slyly raised the prospect of his own death — what if he died in the interim before the printing, and his invention were lost forever? Then indeed they would have cause to wail. Fourier shot out sibylline utterances, refusing to tell his ungrateful generation on what evidence they had been based. Let them be tormented with curiosity while he kept his secret; he wanted them to be sorry, to grieve over having missed the opportunity to learn the truths of the new science. He acted out childish fantasies; how they, the civilization of the nineteenth century, would regret him when he was gone, how they would miss his theories, mourn the loss of the clue to mankind's happiness.

But what really was there beneath this mask of Harlequin which Fourier was so anxious to display? Like many of the great neurotics, there was some measure of everything in him. Many of his descriptions of life in phalanstery are the obvious daydreams of the deprived; the gastronomical bouts and jolly companies are the wish-fulfillments of a poverty-stricken man condemned to lonely 25-sous meals, and the amorous feats he depicted with such obvious relish the longings of one who was probably impotent.

When one moves from this realm of simple frustration to look deeper, the waters become troubled. There are passages in Fourier's writings which more than hint at masochist and perhaps homosexual elements that are not infrequent accompaniments of sadism. After denouncing the overlordship imposed by males in civilization and hailing Catherine the Great for having "crushed the masculine sex underfoot," Fourier let a fantasy escape in the *Théorie des quatre mouvements*: "To confound the tyranny of men there should exist for a century a third sex, male and female, one stronger than man. This new sex would prove with a beating of rods that men as well as women are made for its pleasure; then one would hear men protest against the tyranny of the hermaphroditic sex and admit that force should not be the sole rule of right." [59]

If Fourier's descriptions of the destructiveness of children mirror his own suppressed desires — his wrecking of an orchard at the age of three was a persistent childhood memory [60] — if his threats to France are reflections of his massive sadism, then the transformation of the daydream of total annihilation into a utopia of love follows the rule of his own system. The extremes touched, and what he called a counterpassion became operative. Similarly, a Freudian might interpret Fourier's overflowing love for all humanity as a transmuted fear of punishment for its opposite, the hidden wish for universal destruction. That a vision of total love was born of fantasies of hate would surely not have astonished Nietzsche, the analyst of *ressentiment*.

VI

Auguste Comte

EMBODIMENT IN THE GREAT BEING

"We have so often said to one another: one tires of thought and even of action, but one never tires of loving."

Auguste Comte, *Testament.*
Confession Annuelle, October 4, 1846, p. 109.

"The strangest part of the matter is, that this doctrine seems to M. Comte to be axiomatic. That all perfection consists in unity, he apparently considers to be a maxim which no sane man thinks of questioning. It never seems to enter into his conceptions that any one could object *ab initio*, and ask, why this universal systematizing, systematizing, systematizing? Why is it necessary that all human life should point to one object, and be cultivated into a system of means to a single end?"

John Stuart Mill,
Auguste Comte and Positivism
(London, 1865), p. 141.

In the person of Auguste Comte the age of prophecy reached a pathetic climax.[1] His was at once the most abstract and the most intimate vision. In no other modern philosopher was the rationalist fantasy so inextricably bound up with private life.

In 1817 the former Polytechnician Auguste Comte, then only nineteen, was wandering about Paris at loose ends with no particular occupation, when a friend introduced him to the aging Saint-Simon. The impecunious petty bourgeois from the south was at first dazzled by the philosopher who had preserved the buoyancy of a young man and the elegant manners of an aristocrat. When Comte became his secretary and "adopted son," Saint-Simon presented him to the circle of liberal economists, paid him whenever the rich industrialists and bankers sent money, and in long conversations expounded his scientific and social system. The letters which Comte addressed to his friend Valat during this period bear witness to the young man's enthusiasm for his master. Saint-Simon was a remarkable conversationalist, and like many other men with the gift of volubility he was incapable of formulating his ideas in long, structured treatises. In contrast, Comte was not an autodidact with a volatile temperament like *père Simon*; a rigorous scientific training at the Ecole Polytechnique had even further strengthened his extraordinary native powers of systematization. At the beginning it seemed that their geniuses complemented each other and that the relationship would yield a rich intellectual harvest. Unfortunately two obstacles, one of a theoretical and the other of a psychological nature, stood in the way of any lasting collaboration. In his very first independent pamphlets, *Séparation générale entre les opinions et les désirs* (July 1819), *Sommaire appréciation de l'ensemble du passé moderne* (April 1820), and *Prospectus des travaux scientifiques nécessaires pour réorganiser la société* (May 1822), Comte revealed his fundamental disagreement with Saint-Simon's plans; he was again bringing to the fore the philosophy of the sciences which had troubled Saint-Simon in the brochures of the Empire, but had since been abandoned for practical considerations. Believing it vain to attempt the solution of the social problem before mankind had for guidance in the wilderness the steady light of a settled comprehensive philosophy, Comte continued his mathematical studies and engaged in researches in the other sciences, with the aim of actually creating that synthesis of all knowledge which Saint-Simon had merely sketched in a page of the *Mémoire sur la science de l'homme*. Only after the synthesis was achieved would the temporal world end its internecine struggles, because it would then have before its eyes, in detail, the elaborated system of positive science and positive politics. Before the grandiose revelation of the true laws of the polity, the forces of anarchy would give way. Comte criticized Saint-Simon's policy of the Restoration as absurdly premature, when the old philosopher pretended to instill positive political notions into the minds of his contemporaries before the full exposition of the philosophy of science had been finished. Saint-Simon, on the contrary, stood firmly by his industrialists, espousing their cause against the nobility even after he had added a tinge of religious sentimentality to his doctrine. Formulated in a simple manner, the theoretical controversy was concentrated in one problem: could scientific truth alone force men to act in accordance with its precepts, as Comte then thought, or should practical men of action forge ahead, allowing scientists to trail after them with advice, as Saint-Simon had come to feel after his disillusioning experiences with the savants of the Empire.

In the spring of 1824 a quarrel which had long been smoldering flared up. The final rupture ended an uneasy communion between two of the most extraordinary thinkers in modern times. Their friendship degenerated into a fishwives' squabble which, as might be expected among philosophers, had a universal resonance. During the early years of their relationship Auguste Comte had played it safe. He avoided signing his articles, and Saint-Simon assumed complete legal responsibility for the opinions expressed in the periodicals which in effect they had edited together. This arrangement seemed to be one of common consent. It would have been no consolation for Saint-Simon to have his "pupil" hanged along with him. As for young Comte, he would have been delighted to proclaim his authorship of various articles, if only for reasons of *amour-propre*, and the public trials did not scare him, but he was afraid lest his parents down in Montpellier learn that he was getting himself enmeshed in subversive politics. In the twenties, however, he reached a point of philosophical maturity where he could no longer endure Saint-Simon's tutelage, and he became less concerned about shocking his family than about his subordinate position with respect to the old philosopher. When the break finally occurred Comte announced it in long analytical letters to his friends, for he had to retract his old enthusiasm for his master. At first the young man was calm and perceptive enough to view the relation with Saint-Simon with a certain detachment, as he would a historical process. Like metropolitan countries toward their colonies, Comte explained, Saint-Simon revealed a fundamental physiological — we would now say psychological — fault; since Comte had once been his pupil he expected him to remain his pupil indefinitely, even after his "beard had begun to grow." As long as Comte needed to complete his education, he had been able to tolerate Saint-Simon's "regulation" of his works, but as he matured, the imposition became unbearable. By 1824 Comte had come to believe that for the past four years not only had Saint-Simon taught him virtually nothing new, but, what was more serious, the supervision of the master had tended to fetter and to stifle his philosophical talents.[2]

After a long period of disturbance and vexation during which they had tried to conceal their mounting mutual annoyance with each other, the issue came to a head over the publication of Comte's essay, the *Système de politique positive*, as a cahier in Saint-Simon's *Catéchisme des industriels*. In the course of their protracted arguments Comte became convinced that Saint-Simon was madly jealous of his rising fame, that he wanted to "hold him under cover," to make a mere instrument of him. In one climactic outburst Comte bluntly told Saint-Simon that only dullards could endure such a status. It had previously been decided that Saint-Simon should sponsor a work by Comte which was to appear in two parts, one a systematic presentation of their common doctrine and the other a history of civilization illustrating the doctrine. After months of delay it was agreed to publish the theoretical part separately, and they were about to go to press when Saint-Simon came forward with the proposal that the treatise should appear anonymously in the *Catéchisme des industriels*, which to Comte meant assigning the authorship to Saint-Simon. Moreover, Saint-Simon, who disagreed with some of the principles enunciated by Comte, wanted to preface it with an introduction in his own manner. Comte flatly refused, belaboring Saint-Simon with grievances which he had long borne secretly in his heart. Saint-Simon finally consented, though with reluctance, to a separate title page for Comte and to the omission of any alien introduction; their understanding was formalized in a written agreement. After the bitter wrangling Saint-Simon curtly informed his pupil that their association was at an end.

Disinheritance was a crushing blow to Auguste Comte, because it was only through Saint-Simon that he had maintained contact with the liberal Paris journals which could afford to pay honoraria to their contributors. This source of income would dry up and he would have to seek other means of subsistence. Incensed, he wrote his friend Tabarié on April 5, 1824, "I shall never pardon M. de Saint-Simon for this, because it is pure vengeance, motivated by nothing and leading to nothing. . . ." [3] Comte felt that his part in their collaboration had always been at least as fruitful as Saint-Simon's, that for seven years he had been strung along with promises of financial independence once their publications succeeded, and that now, abruptly, he had been cut off. Saint-Simon had agreed to send the *Système de politique positive* to the subscribers of the *Catéchisme des industriels* and to give Comte a hundred copies for his own distribution, but for the rest, there was to be nothing further between them. To Comte this meant that he would be obliged to toady to "influential people" in order to earn a living, an odious prospect.

According to Comte's version of what happened next — the only explanation available, but quite plausible — Saint Simon broke his word. He published a hundred copies in the agreed manner with a separate title page bearing Comte's name and without reference to the *Catéchisme des industriels*; these copies were delivered to Comte for his private distribution. But in addition Saint-Simon printed a thousand copies with only *Catéchisme des industriels* on the flyleaf and with his own special introduction, which were

distributed to the regular subscribers of the periodical. In retaliation, before Comte sent around his allotment of copies of the
Système de politique positive, he tore off his own lavish acknowledgment of discipleship. As far as Comte was concerned there
had been a clear breach of faith, and he took the position that no
formal publication of the work had occurred. Whenever Saint-
Simon questioned him about the second part, he lied, on his own
admission, pretending that he was occupying himself with revisions. He was planning a one-volume edition of both parts under
his own title and with his own name, a format which never appeared.[4] A quarter of a century passed before the *Système de politique positive* was republished — by which time it had grown into
four massive tomes.

In a letter to young Gustave d'Eichthal on May 1, 1824, Comte,
outraged by Saint-Simon's deception, gave full vent to his bitter
anger. He no longer rationalized the enmity between them on
grounds of simple envy and jealousy alone. His earlier psychological explanation, which proved that the fight was inevitable, inherent in the very nature of their physiological "organizations,"
was now barbed with contempt and sometimes with hate. The
trouble with Saint-Simon was that no real collaboration with him
was possible unless one resigned oneself to being his tool, since
Saint-Simon was convinced that only he was the discoverer of
great new ideas and that at most others could contribute to the
perfection of his original insights in some minor respect. Saint-
Simon considered himself an exception to the ordinary rules of
physiology, immune to the deterioration of age. He believed that
his mind was sharper than it had ever been. With the brutality of
youth Comte wrote his friend that Saint-Simon had grown senile
and ought to retire forthwith from the philosophical profession.

After Saint-Simon's death, though Comte at first disdained
any part of the Saint-Simonian *Le Producteur*, his need for money
induced him to become a collaborator — *à contre-coeur* because
he anticipated the irksome censorship of "Rodrigues et compagnie."
In the end Comte's association with the disciples was short-lived.
He could not stomach their deification of the master, and by 1828
he was already poking fun at their plan to found a new religion,
a "sort of incarnation of the divinity in Saint-Simon." [5] Bitter was

his disillusionment when he found that Gustave d'Eichthal, his one disciple, to whom he had freely unburdened himself of his grievances against Saint-Simon, to whom he had confided his most intimate philosophical and psychological reflections, was swept along by the religious wave of the Saint-Simonian school. On December 7, 1829, he sent d'Eichthal a biting, sarcastic letter, enclosing an entrance card to the reopening of his course on positive philosophy: "Since the change of direction which your mind has just taken, I must admit to you that I no longer count on you for anything. You are on so sublime a summit that you must, even against your will, pity our wretched positive studies, which you no longer need and which on the contrary would trouble your theological labors." [6]

When the Saint-Simonians transformed themselves into a religious cult and their meetings became a public scandal which ultimately brought them before the King's Bench, Auguste Comte took himself off. His erstwhile colleagues charged that he had stolen all his doctrines from them, a contention which drew from Comte a nasty letter to Michel Chevalier, then editor of their new organ *Le Globe*. "For a number of years, Sir, I had a very intimate association with Saint-Simon, and this was a good deal earlier than the relations which any of the chiefs of your society could have had with him. This relationship had entirely ceased about two years [sic] before the death of the philosopher, consequently at a time when there was not yet the slightest question in the world of Saint-Simonians. I must, moreover, have you take note that M. de Saint-Simon had not as yet adopted a theological coloration and that our rupture might even be attributed in part to the fact that I began to discern in him a theological tendency profoundly incompatible with the philosophical direction which is characteristic of my thought." [7] Chevalier was not daunted by Comte's testiness. With an admixture of acrimony and apostolic zeal, he exhorted him to return to the master's teachings. "For seven years you were by Saint-Simon's side and you were loved as a son. While under his fruitful influence you wrote the *Système de politique positive* which assures you a high rank among the thinkers of our time. All that you have since written is only a commentary on this work, even as the *Système* itself is the elaboration of a work written by Saint-Simon while you were still in the cradle, under the title *Lettres d'un habitant de Genève à ses contemporains*." With passionate irony the young Chevalier attacked the ingrate: "Tell me, sir, ever since you carefully struck from the third pamphlet of the *Catéchisme des industriels* the name of the master of all of us . . . have you been happier?" [8]

For almost twenty years Comte abided by his resolution never again to refer to his relationship with Saint-Simon, but attention was drawn to it by other men. When in the fifties some international notice was finally given to Comte's works, both critics and disciples began to question him about the influence of Saint-Simon. Comte was acutely sensitive on the point and believed that his enemies had resurrected his old friend only to plague him and to accuse him of having plagiarized his major ideas. With the publication of George Lewes' *Comte's Philosophy of the Sciences*, which casually noted the connection of the two men, the whole affair became known to Comte's American correspondents [9] and to followers throughout the world. In answer to the charges of his adversaries, Comte fought furiously for his claim to originality in all the ideas which he had developed, and in his letters of this period the repudiation of Saint-Simon's effect upon his doctrine became an *idée fixe*. He freely admitted their association during a brief period, but he steadfastly maintained that he had learned nothing from the befuddled old philosopher. Far from attributing any dominant role to the obfuscated ideas of Saint-Simon, Comte was convinced that any one of the other friends of his youth — such as Jean-Baptiste Say and Charles Dunoyer — had been of far greater importance to him. His spiritual antecedents were Hume, Kant, Condorcet, and de Maistre, Gall and Bichat, not the venal and corrupt Saint-Simon.[10] When in order to torment him Comte's detractors revived the idea that his profound law of the three states had been borrowed, he could find no epithet violent enough to hurl back at them. In the introduction to the *Système de politique positive* he mentioned the foolish old philosopher of the Restoration with disdain, and in one of his last letters he called him a "depraved juggler." [11]

After Comte's death, friends and disciples of both "positivist messiahs" aligned themselves into two forces, proclaiming or denying the influence of Saint-Simon on Comte.[12] Of those who have written on the problem, Deroisin, a rather heretical Positivist, who heard Comte harangue against Saint-Simon in the fifties, had keen insight into the nature of the High Priest of Humanity's feelings toward the founder of the New Christianity. "Comte had become possessed by hatred for the memory of Saint-Simon. I always heard him speak of him without restraint. Even in his courses he treated him severely. . . . Comte's hostility toward the Jesus Christ type can be explained by his assimilating Christ's usurpation of St. Paul's title of founder of the new religion to the attempt to usurp his own brevet as the initiator of the positive philosophy in favor of Saint-Simon." [13]

A re-examination of the manuscripts and published works of both Saint-Simon and Comte during the early twenties cannot settle the controversy, but it helps to understand it. The key work is Comte's *Prospectus des travaux scientifiques nécessaires pour réorganiser la société*, which appeared in April 1822 in conjunction with Saint-Simon's inconsequential little essay *Du contrat social*. Comte himself considered this *Prospectus*, which was issued in only fifty copies marked *Epreuve*, to be the first draft of his positive philosophy and positive polity. Begun when he was twenty-four and still a close collaborator of Saint-Simon, it already included the law of the three states and adumbrated the basic positivist classification of the sciences. The act of composition for Comte had been a momentous one. He was so self-conscious about its significance that he noted the precise hour and minute of writing at the head of each section.[14] The draft did not flow smoothly, and there was much writing and rewriting. One half-page is filled with a doodle of his name and his first initial. The young man was asserting himself. A reworking of this opuscule became the controversial April 1824 *Système de politique positive, t. I, première partie*, and with some changes Comte later reprinted it as the *Plan des travaux scientifiques nécessaires pour réorganiser la société*.

Comte was preparing for the April 1822 essay during the time that he participated in the writing and editing of *L'Organisateur* and *Du système industriel*, from 1819 through the first half of 1822. The cover of Comte's 1822 manuscript bore the title *Suite des travaux ayant pour objet le système industriel*; thus he proclaimed that his work was part of the general theory of Saint-Simon's *système industriel*, and a textual analysis reveals many parallel passages and ideas in the cahiers of *Du système industriel* and Comte's essay. Does this indicate that Comte was merely utilizing his own contributions, that he was borrowing from Saint-Simon, or, what is more probable, that he was combining his own ideas with those of Saint-Simon? During this formative period it is no more possible to separate the proprietary rights of Saint-Simon or Comte from their common store of ideas than it would be to perform the same task for Marx and Engels. Manuscript notes of Comte and Saint-Simon are therefore not conclusive. Saint-Simon was the man of the spoken word and his writing was far inferior to Comte's in organization. The flashes of insight, however, were Saint-Simon's surely as often as they were Comte's.

Comte believed that he was making revolutionary discoveries in *physique sociale*, that he was laying down fundamental laws of social science. No doubt he experienced sudden moments of scientific illumination when the facts ordered themselves in a pattern which he called a law. Saint-Simon had had these moments of intuitive ecstasy under the Empire. Both of Comte's fundamental conceptions, the law of the three states and the hierarchic classification of the sciences, were present in embryonic form in Saint-Simon's writings long before he knew Comte and in more developed versions during the years of their collaboration. To maintain that all the original ideas of *L'Industrie*, *L'Organisateur*, and *Du système industriel* were the products of Comte's genius and to dismiss Saint-Simon as nothing more than a "magnetic personality," as Professor Gouhier does in *La Jeunesse d'Auguste Comte*, is somewhat offhand. Such a thesis must gloss over Saint-Simon's writings of the Empire and reduce to nullity his part in the works of the Restoration.

Undoubtedly Saint-Simon felt rancor toward the fledglings who drifted off on their own. On the other hand he was among the first to announce Comte's part in their common work — he advertised Comte's talent in the salons, introduced him to the journalists of Paris, enthused about him to his own patron Ternaux, granted him status on their editorial boards. After Comte had assimilated Saint-Simon's insights, he realized the intrinsic superiority of his own organizational powers, he chafed at the bit, he wanted to break loose, to realize his potentialities. He saw only the weakness of the old philosopher, particularly after the suicide attempt, and he rebelled against his domination.

For Saint-Simon Comte's defection was a personal tragedy. He knew that he had neither the solid scientific training nor the capacity to formulate grand conceptions with which his young assistant was gifted. Comte not only deprived his master of the use of his talents; when he proceeded to write in an independent direction he was challenging the essential nature of Saint-Simon's "system," which was unitary. The whole purpose of the industrial philosophy was to call a halt to the battle of systems, to achieve integral unanimity in the spiritual and in the temporal world. The young man who left to work in isolation was not simply producing a variant on the truth, which might be tolerated; he was a traitor to the unity of the system, an egotist whose vile deed would protract the chaos of contemporary society. Saint-Simon could no more endure this subversion of his monist principle, though garbed in the magic word positivist, than he could brook the false and misleading ideologies of theologians and metaphysicians. The inevitable counterpart of Saint-Simon's philosophical monism had to be personal absolutism in his relations with Comte.

As for Comte, a strange destiny awaited him — a recapitulation of the life of Saint-Simon, with all its grand delusions of universal love, black despair, and drives toward self-destruction. He who had denied the master was in turn spurned by his own disciples.

WICKED WIFE AND GOOD ANGEL

In 1822 Auguste Comte walked into a bookstore and recognized behind the counter a girl whom he had once picked up in the Palais Royal. The prominent lawyer Cerclet, her original seducer, a privilege for which he had paid a thousand *écus*, had set up the establishment. Comte renewed the acquaintance, and within a year they merged their living quarters. The common-law marriage had to be formalized at the city hall when a policeman threatened to arrest her in a public restaurant where she and Comte were eating, because she had failed to report regularly to the authorities on whose register she was entered as a prostitute. Through the intervention of Cerclet her name was erased and the ménage seemed on the road to respectability. Comte had academic aspirations.

The opening lectures of his course on positive philosophy which he conducted privately in his apartment in 1826 had a small but illustrious audience; but before the thirteenth session Comte suffered his first psychic breakdown. For the next fifteen years Mme. Comte wrangled with this mad genius; while no succeeding outburst was as wild as the first one, he never completely recovered. At the height of an attack scenes of violence were frequent. In between crises his smoldering fury spent itself on his wife and on academic colleagues. In 1842 Mme. Comte left his bed and board for the last time — there had been intermittent separations — but this strange tenacious woman kept turning up again, and in 1850 it was her intervention with the Ministry of Education which made it possible for Comte to continue the popular lectures to which he clung so desperately — rare moments of public recognition.

The vengeance with which Comte pursued his wife in later years was monstrous. To the disciples he left a secret testament setting forth in detail the facts of her life as a prostitute along with a dismal rehearsal of his marital complaints. In the first attack of madness in 1826 it was this woman who kept him at home behind barred windows after the famous psychiatrist Dr. Esquirol had surrendered him with the notation "No cure," suffered his flinging of knives, his ravings, his acted-out fantasies of Homeric grandeur, and nursed him back to a state of relative equilibrium. It was she who went through that macabre religious marriage ceremony on which Comte's mother had insisted — a guard from Esquirol's clinic in attendance, a priest prolonging the sacrament while Comte ranted on against the church, his mother on bended knees calling for the transfer of God's punishment from her son to herself. (The groom had ended the performance by signing the contract Brutus Napoleon Comte.)

The history of Comte's academic life was a record of defeats whenever he was proposed for a full chair either at the Polytechnique or in the university. Public denunciations of his perfidious colleagues were accompanied by vain appeals to the ministries, outbursts of wild paranoia against detractors, calls to the world to avenge the wrongs perpetrated against him. The accusations he leveled against the academic intriguers were true enough; and the more he reviled his adversaries the more convinced they became that they did not want him in their company. For most of his adult career he eked out an existence as an entrance examiner at the Polytechnique, and in his last years even this was denied him.

In 1844, after the definitive estrangement from his wife, Auguste Comte fell in love with Mme. Clothilde de Vaux, a woman of about thirty abandoned by her husband, a petty official and a gambler who had absconded with government funds. Comte first met "his angel" at the home of a young disciple, and from the outset this was the proverbial *coup de foudre* for the man in his mid-forties. At first the young lady took his attentions lightly, and the philosopher's letters, read aloud, were objects of merriment in the family circle. Soon the intensity of his passion enveloped her. While their affections began on a lofty spiritual plane, Comte importuned her with his physical needs, and when entreaties failed he was not beyond using the threat that her denials were endangering his health and upsetting his cerebral hygiene. At one point Clothilde de Vaux succumbed to the epistolary barrage and sent him a written consent, but the consummation proved more difficult and the fiasco of what was to have been their amorous meeting unloosed the floodgates of grand emotions. There was sincere self-analysis upon the part of the woman whose flesh was still bound to her ne'er-do-well husband, noble self-abnegation on the part of the philosopher who promised to wait and yet never completely abandoned his sly insistence. Crises were frequent, and the whole affair resulted in an exchange of admirable letters in the romantic vein. Clothilde de Vaux had literary talent, extraordinary sensitivity, a rare candor. Their emotional tug-of-war ended in tragedy — Comte was again on the verge of madness and his beloved became afflicted with a disease, probably tubercular, which brought on her death. The last months of her life were tormented with the contradictory advice of rival physicians, Comte's maniacal pretension to supervise personally the direction of the cure, violent quarrels between Comte and the dying young woman's family, which at one point led to his expulsion from the sickroom. When he was called back toward the very end he bolted the door of the death chamber, excluding her parents so that Clothilde died in his presence alone.

THE TWO CAREERS

THE first series of private lectures on the positive philosophy had been attended by Blainville the physiologist, Dunoyer the economist, and the naturalist Alexander von Humboldt. When the course was resumed in 1829 after the attack of insanity and the attempts at suicide Broussais the phrenologist, Dr. Esquirol, and Fourier the mathematician were in the audience. But during that long and troubled period from 1830 to 1842 — years of tremendous intellectual concentration, plagued by marital difficulties, mental aberrations, poverty, and a vain search for some academic position which would be worthy of him — the brilliant reputation of his youth gave way to ridicule in official learned circles. A contemporary bibliography listed him as already dead.[15]

The six volumes of the *Cours de philosophie positive* (1830–1842), composed in isolation during these years of wretchedness, were an attempt to synthesize the particular studies of individual scientists by sharply marking the bounds of every form of knowledge and drawing from each the essence of its philosophic generality. It involved writing a history of science — which is still worth reading for its extraordinary flashes of insight — as well as arranging the sciences in a hierarchy of complexity which would prove that each had in turn progressed first from a theological into a metaphysical and then into a positive state. The drama of the work was the struggle of positivist, nonmetaphysical, and nontheological truth with the remnants of antiquated intellectual forms which still sought to corrupt it. Religion and sentiment were banished as the handmaidens of theologians and metaphysicians; the *Cours* was at once a new *Organon*, a new *Methodus*, and a new philosophy of history.

The *Cours* gained the approval of a few philosophers and scientists. In 1837 John Stuart Mill was won over by many of Comte's methodological principles, and a group of physiologists headed by Blainville listened attentively as Comte set their science into the general framework of human knowledge. Hitherto scientists had been working independently, making their minute and precious discoveries without any feeling for the whole of human thought. They had accepted as absolute truths the specific results of their laboratory experiments, but had also found a place in their lives for the existing institutions of religion, for a divine will, and for some metaphysical system. Comte sharpened spiritual distinctions: the scientists could no longer continue the cant of their old procedure, tinkering with the particular tools of their special discipline and at the same time worshiping at the shrine of final causes. He demanded that they be thoroughly consistent, that they abide by the philosophical implications of their scientific endeavors, and that they recognize in every particular experiment some additional element to the great structure of positive science. The philosophy of each science which he formulated showed exactly what part the individual investigator was playing in the passage of human thought from the metaphysical into the final positive stage. Social physics, because it was the most complex of the sciences and was dependent on the others for sustenance, was the last to become positive, and with this new science the work culminated — though he did not yet reveal all its possibilities in social action.

The *Cours* had a style that was dull, dry, and lumbering. While the positive philosophy did not help many scientists in their labors, it was adopted by a few littérateurs who needed an over-all pattern for their popular scientific notions. These men were impressed with the hard rationality of each Comtean formula. The long, involved sentences of the *Cours*, which strove so mightily to be exact and concrete, left no ambiguities once their full meaning had been unraveled. Comte was ordinarily classified as the ultimate fulfillment of the eighteenth-century ideal of materialism. He had left few traces of his turbulent emotional existence in these volumes. To those foreign readers who did not know his life history he appeared to be the archenemy of all enthusiasm, imagination, and mysticism. Emile Littré later summarized the elements in the positive philosophy which had originally appealed to him: "Positive philosophy is the only one which can explain the connexities between these three things: the order of immanent properties, the order of the successive constitution of the sciences, the order of their hierarchical teaching." [16]

Inevitably, the appearance of the *Système de politique positive* from 1851 through 1854, which proclaimed love as the motive force of mankind, was a violent shock to the select group of Comte's rationalist admirers. As he laboriously evolved a special calendar for his church and multiplied ritual observances for the Religion of Humanity, he seemed to be denying the very spirit of his previous works. Many considered his change of front a treacherous defection to those forces of darkness which he had driven forth from the positive system. Between the *Cours* and the *Système de politique positive* he had risen from the depths of misery to a mystical love so overpowering that true disciples looked on in dismay and outsiders scoffed. The publication of the correspondence of Clothilde de Vaux and Comte, his annual written confessions after her death, and his prayers to her memory have not added to his philosophical stature, though they reveal a complex emotional being. There was something pathetic if not ridiculous about this forty-six-year-old man on his knees before an empty red plush chair — his altar — holding a medallion in which a lock of hair was preserved, a relic which reawakened in him what he named primitive fetishistic emotion. When the middle-aged philosopher calls his beloved an angel and protests in volume after volume the innocent purity of their relationship, despite his numerous unsuccessful attempts to render their union physical, it is difficult to restrain a smirk.

After Clothilde's death Comte's whole life became devoted to a religious worship of her image. Those disciples who had admired his powerful mind watched with troubled spirits as he embarked upon a system which was deeply colored by elements of religious mania. Yet to Auguste Comte the positive church seemed the natural fruition of an original plan which he had developed in his earliest pamphlets in the 1820's. The scientific synthesis of the *Cours* had only been a foundation. His friends knew nothing of the youthful writings in which he had expatiated on the power of the sentiments and of the imagination in moving mankind to action and had praised spontaneous religious faith as the force which would again bring intellectual and moral unity to humanity. They had never read those passages in which he had extolled the organic unity of medieval Catholicism in the language of de Maistre. Even before Comte had met Clothilde de Vaux he wrote to Mme. Austin on April 4, 1844, complaining that she was unjust in interpreting positivism as antiemotional: "Believe me, I know how to cry, not only in admiration but also out of sorrow, above all sympathetic sorrow. As for prayer, it is really only a particular form in the old order of ecstatic emotions, or general emotions, whose indestructible core will always be a part of human nature, whatever its mental habits may become." [17] Comte himself recognized that there was a difference of emphasis in what came to be called his two careers. In the first period he considered himself primarily an Aristotle, and in the second he had become a St. Paul, but the elements of the second period had already existed in embryo in the first. The social opuscules of his youth support his contention. As conclusive proof of the unity of his work Comte reprinted six of these brochures as a general appendix to the fourth volume of the *Système de politique positive* (1854).

When the committed rationalists in his circle realized the new turn in his thought, they slowly withdrew. The head of the French group was Littré, and the leaders of the English were Mill and Lewes, three men who had been among the first to call the world's attention to the positive philosophy. Littré and Mill, who in the beginning had been fascinated by the broad generalizations of the system and had felt it their duty to subordinate criticisms of detail to a favorable exposition of his general view,[18] were now repelled by Comte's religious pretensions; and he in turn did not hide his animosity toward "Mill, Lewes, Carlyle & Co." when they tried to stifle social positivism beneath intellectual positivism.[19] Littré, the son of a Jacobin, could not long stomach Comte's reactionary political position, which became ever more marked as he advanced into the Religion of Humanity. Comte had prepared poisoned darts for Littré, especially when he ventured to involve himself in Comte's marital quarrels. Sometime in the summer of 1852, he announced to his disciples Segond and Deroisin, "You know that my break with M. Littré is definitive. Along with Mme. Comte, the Reds, and the Institute he is the adversary. M. Littré is the lover of Mme. Comte, so that now the battle is on between the angel who will always be thirty-two and the demon who has just turned fifty-two." [20] In order definitively to annihilate the pseudo-positivists, Comte wrote to M. Hadéry on July 7, 1857, that he would in the future sign all his circulars "Le Fondateur de la religion universelle, Grand Prêtre de l'Humanité," [21] and he let it be known that his being would become more sacred than the Catholic pontiff's. The Pope was only a minister, but he, Auguste Comte, who had discovered the fundamental laws of human evolution, was the very personification of the Great Being. Thereafter all the supposed expositions of positivism by Mill, Littré, and Lewes could be considered null and void in the face of the practical application of the positive philosophy in the positive church. Comte came to prefer a Napoleon III or a Henry V, who would at least preserve order in the midst of the world's spiritual anarchy, to Mill, Littré, and Lewes, who with their "dose of positivist theorems" had become the chief Occidental disturbers. Heretics have invariably been treated with more severity by religious leaders than those who have not yet seen the light.

Littré was profoundly upset by his inability to accept the positive polity with the same passion that he had espoused Comte's philosophy, and he was particularly grieved at being cast in the role of the Judas of positivism. In order to justify his own infidelity he fell upon the notion that only a serious mental strain, the consequence of some organic illness, could have produced the positivist church and its ritual.[22] Littré's manipulations did not end with Comte's death; while proclaiming their love for Comte, Littré and Mme. Comte tried to have the *Testament* legally annulled and sought to eradicate the memory of the second period of Comte's writing, embalming the founder of the positive philosophy as a figure dissociated from the worshiper of Clothilde de Vaux. They joined in a formal declaration that Comte had been mad, but in a final trial in 1870, after many years of litigation, the true disciples won their case, and Comte's Religion of Humanity was not mutilated.[23] "Positivism consists essentially of a philosophy and a polity. These can never be dissevered," maintained the English disciple Dr. Bridges, and most scholars of Auguste Comte have acquiesced in this view.

THE PROPHETS OF PARIS

THE HIGH PRIEST OF HUMANITY

Wʜᴇɴ Comte apotheosized Clothilde de Vaux as the spiritual symbol of the Virgin-Mother, superior even to himself, who was only the High Priest of Humanity, and established her grave as a place of sacred pilgrimage, his cult suffered the ridicule of all fabricated ceremonials that fail of acceptance by a sufficient body of believers to become sanctioned vehicles for the expression of religion emotion. For Comte it was now science and excessive absorption in rationalist analysis that became suspect, dangerous for the spiritual well-being of mankind. The philosopher of positivism ended up rejecting a large proportion of the works of science as futile. As his view of the good life became ever more restrictive, ever more cramped, less expansive and sensate, modern science and technology which provided great abundance and riches became distracting superfluities. Comte accepted a social system based upon a division between the rich and the poor, but neither grouping was of fundamental importance since the end of man was the training of his emotional being to sublimated love. A mania for regulation possessed him and he set up rules of conduct to govern each epoch in a man's life; the transitions from one to another stage of being were marked by rigid sacramental performances. Order became more vital than progress. The multiplication of new artifacts of any nature — scientific or industrial — became an anarchic impediment to good disposition and arrangement. The positivist law of family life demanded a vow of eternal widowhood, and divorce was refused. The world would be made continent and puritanical. The commandments preached, "Love your neighbor. Live for others" — but a cold chill came to pervade the chambers of the Comtean mansion.

From the chair of the High Priest of Humanity in his apartment on rue Monsieur-le-Prince, Auguste Comte contemplated the Revolution of 1848, the bloody June days, and the rise of the dictator Napoleon III. These misfortunes had been visited upon the Occident because it was ignorant of its true historic destiny. The epoch of the positive polity had arrived, but instead of reading its laws as they had been expounded in Comte's writings, humanity was wasting its divine forces in material conflicts and civil strife.

AUGUSTE COMTE

There was warfare of diverse doctrines at a time when the essence of humanity should be unity; there was revolutionary antagonism to the religious principle when the very being of mankind was religious — in the positivist sense. All past history had been a battleground for partisan spirits. Revolutionaries of the gospel of 1789 (the first year of anarchy) and their philosophers were besmirching the noble morality of the Middle Ages, when all men should have realized that medieval civilization was one of the most progressive forms of social synthesis. Men of religion were in their turn denouncing the great cultural productions of classical antiquity and decrying the achievements of science, when these were necessary prolegomena to the new state of postivism. If the warring factions accepted that world-historical outlook which Comte had revealed to them while lying on his philosophic sofa, they would understand that all history has borne good fruits, and that whoever would act with wisdom in the future had to preserve for mankind the creations of past civilizations and incorporate them into his being, without rancor and without hatred for any age. So violent were the emotions stirred in him by the subjective resurrection of the past that after anniversaries of Clothilde de Vaux's death Comte was incapable of working for a month at a time. In the High Priest all previous human existence had come to life again. The positivist calendar commemorated saints and scientists, musicians and poets, territorial organizers and philosophers of different ages, on successive days.

There was but one power in the world capable of judging history with justice, a power embodied in the High Priest of Humanity who, while synthesizing the past, would impart to the annals of mankind a unity of movement and purpose which it would be difficult to violate in petty quarrels of the moment. As long as men were engaged in material struggles and foolhardy theorists and pamphleteers were pretending to solve the social problem by writing brochures on the organization of labor and the rights of one class as opposed to another, there would be no coherence and no salvation for mankind. In the eleventh century, Hildebrand had for a moment imposed his spiritual power over the conflicting forces of the West, but because of the scientific backwardness of his age the Catholic civilization could not endure.

The Catholic Church, Comte's only serious competitor in the mission of achieving spiritual unity for the Occidental Positivist Republic, having proved itself a failure after a thousand years of striving, should now relinquish its hold upon mankind to its historically ordained successor.

In the Revolution of 1848 Comte saw the Occidental world at a point of final crisis, and only he could save it from the chaos and anarchy in which it was seething. The Positivist Society, which had formed itself about Comte, formulated a pretentious plan of action for the Provisional Government, and Comte was willing to establish contact with the most violent of the revolutionaries, even Barbès and Blanqui, if only their movement could be diverted into a positivist channel.[24] But Paris was a city of barricades, strewn with the corpses of the proletariat. Comte called the spirits of social peace, but alas they would not answer. The *coup d'état* of December 2 caused disruption in the Positivist Society. Littré and Robin were terrified because of their relations with the democratic newspapers. A positivist lawyer, Lejeune, died in jail. Ribbentrop, the German disciple who had also been associated with the communists, was arrested. Lucas, the Lyons pharmacist, who had organized a positivist workers' group, was thrown into prison and his correspondence with Comte was seized. During the troubles Comte remained calm, expecting positivist results from the dictatorship after the years of vain wrangling over what he considered a metaphysical constitution. So great was his faith in an ultimate victory that any event, however contrary it might at first appear to the purposes of his propaganda for positivism, could always be reinterpreted as intrinsically beneficial to the new religion. When Lucas' papers were confiscated by the police, Comte assured Deroisin, "They will read my letters; they will draw some ideas from them." [25]

The belief of the High Priest of Humanity in the power of the idea, of the true philosophic and religious system, was so all-absorbing that the nature of the political régime became a matter of indifference. The state was but a subject ready to take on the coloration of the positive religion once the executive power was enlightened. A disorganized revolutionary government which presents the spectacle of warring factions is less amenable to the propaganda of the idea than a dictatorship which is concentrated in one man. Convert this man and the cause of positivism is won. Saint-Simon and Fourier had addressed their early memoirs to Napoleon I; Comte was willing to accept Napoleon III if only he would become a positivist.

Comte's political identification with the Empire and his growing arrogance divided the Positivist Society. One group called the *claqueurs* remained blindly faithful and accepted all his excursions into religion together with his vituperation; others retained their reverence for his philosophic intelligence but, while they never dared criticize him to his face, had mental reservations and mocked him when his back was turned. They were the *rieurs*. As for most scholars and scientists, they did not deign to notice his works and they formed against him a dread conspiracy of silence.

Though secretly tormented by this indifference, Comte continued to mount giant block upon block in the construction of his great pyramid. After the *Cours de philosophie positive* and the *Système de politique positive*, there appeared in 1856 the first volume of the *Synthèse subjective*, also called the *Système de logique positive*. Works for the next few years were planned and announced in advance: for 1859 the *Système de morale positive* or the *Traité de l'éducation universelle*, and for 1861 the *Système d'industrie positive* or the *Traité de l'action totale de l'humanité sur sa planète*. Comte was writing for the future, for the men of 1927 perhaps, when, as he analyzed the course of events, the positivist regeneration of the Occident would be accomplished, at least among the souls of the elite. Few men have had a more poignant sense of their historical mission. "Living in an anticipated tomb, I must henceforth speak a posthumous language to the living, a form of speech which is as free from all manner of prejudices, above all the theoretical ones, as our descendants will be. Up to now I have always had to speak in the name of the past, though I was continually aspiring toward the future. Now I must interest the public of the West in the future state — which irrevocably follows from the totality of the various anterior modes — in order to discipline them at the same time that I consecrate them." [26]

Toward the end of his life, Comte was deeply involved in spreading the doctrine among the noblest members of all classes of society. He was aware that neither of his two major works could reach broad masses of people. Therefore he undertook positivist propaganda (the word is Comte's) by composing in 1852 a *Catéchisme positiviste* for the use of women and workers, and in 1855 an *Appel aux conservateurs* for the education of contemporary political leaders. And there was some response: in the fifties a heterogeneous group of disciples from all over the world came to pay homage to the founder of positivism. Each new adherent to the Positivist Society was carefully examined by the High Priest, was required to read the most important positivist pamphlets and to express his doubts in writing in order that the doctrine might be fully explained to him before his adherence to the faith. Disciples brought their moral dilemmas to Comte, and some, Henry Edger of Long Island among them, even burdened the philosopher with clinical descriptions of their sexual problems.

As Comte regulated his own diet and arranged hours for prayer and work with obsessive punctuality, so he multiplied ritualistic details for the Religion of Humanity. The positive sacraments became the manifest symbols of the new educational process: the presentation of the infant, initiation at fourteen, admission at twenty-one, destination at twenty-eight, marriage before thirty-five, maturity at forty-two, retirement at sixty-two, and finally the sacrament of transformation.[27] In the end the evil ones, the suicides and the executed, or those who had failed in their duty to humanity, were relegated to the field of the forgotten, while those upon whom the final judgment of Incorporation was favorable were transferred to the Holy Wood which surrounded the Temple of Humanity. The last judgment was brought down from heaven to rue Monsieur-le-Prince. As his priestly character grew upon him, Comte became ever more irascible and intolerant of contradiction. In 1850 Comte prepared a funeral oration for his old friend Blainville (who was still alive) in which he attacked the learned doctor as an egoist filled with theological opinions and all but consigned him to the positivist hell where Mme. Comte was destined to burn. Comte celebrated two positivist marriages, one in 1848 and the other two years later. In the midst of tears, both women swore eternal widowhood. Marriage became an even stronger tie than in the Catholic Church, for this was the establishment of final monogamy. It was a portent that one of the marriages emanated from the "pure proletariat," as Comte put it, and another from the more comfortable classes.

No one escaped Comte's proselytizing zeal. The general of the Jesuits, the Czar of Russia, and Mehemet Ali were all addressed by the sovereign pontiff and invited to institute the true Religion of Humanity. He hoped that Notre Dame would become the central church of the Occidental Republic, and that there, in the midst of the tombs of the elect of humanity, he would conduct his ceremonies. In the meantime, Comte had his two flags: one religious and one political, one white and one green, both of them avoiding the "fatal red flag" of communism.[28] Comte exaggerated the importance of each new convert, and listed a man among the faithful as soon as he revealed the vaguest interest. Living in dismal isolation, he became oversanguine in the hope of mass conversions whenever he attracted the slightest notice. Even when he was criticized by American clerics and philosophers, their harsh words were more pleasant to his ears than the stony silence of the official French academicians. The positivist subsidy had been rising since its establishment on November 12, 1848, but the accounts of the free gifts of the faithful, which Comte published in regular circulars, show how precarious his material existence continued to be. In these financial contributions Comte saw a symbol of positivism, the great church within whose bosom both of the contending classes, the capitalists and the workers, were to find peace. If additional conservatives and workers would begin to send regular donations to the pontifical fund, the institution of the organic civilization would not be long delayed.

In France Comte was not read during his lifetime. Ridicule was heaped upon him and he was just one of numerous religious messiahs who had come forth with a panacea for universal peace and happiness. His aloofness from the class struggle made his writings meaningless to the revolutionaries who were organizing the workers with the slogans of communism and socialism. To sectors of the middle class who were seeking parliamentary reform in the Revolution of 1848 his philosophy was of no importance. For those who were trying to defend the existing property system his teachings were quite superfluous, because they had no need of his theocracy to ensure their domination. Many of the leaders of the Second Empire were Saint-Simonians, some of whom were still giving lip service to the humanitarian ideals of their master. The hierarchy of Auguste Comte and his spiritual tyranny were not consonant with their expansive activism.

Ultimately positivism, like many of the other great dogmatic structures of modern times, exerted its greatest influence in those countries which were comparatively backward in their cultural and economic development. Its attractions for the intelligentsia of Russia in the sixties and seventies has recently been studied.[29] In South America it became the ideal formula among those members of the upper classes who had abandoned the Catholic Church and yet did not wish to grope in the darkness of skepticism. Positivism was acceptable to them as an organic philosophy of life which provided for the status quo of class relationships and demanded only that order and progress become the general ideological principles of political and social action. Brazil has inscribed the motto of Comte's church, *Ordem e Progresso*, on its national flag and has accepted Comte as its official philosopher.[30]

Positivism in England was a movement of some strength, especially after Mill briefly espoused its cause; but in the long run the English felt no need for it, for Herbert Spencer had provided them with essentially the same doctrine in a native mixture that rivaled the original in pomposity and long-windedness.[31] There were stray groups of positivists in Holland, Italy, Sweden, and the United States. When on January 1, 1881, Edward Spencer Beesly celebrated the Festival of Humanity in London, he could speak of a union of all Positivists, comprised of members in Havre, Rouen, Mons, Rio de Janeiro, Dublin, New York, and Stockholm, who were at that moment turning toward Paris, where Pierre Laffitte, the successor of Comte as the head of the Positivist Society, was conducting the ceremonials in the very abode of the Master.[32]

ORDER AND PROGRESS

WITH Auguste Comte the fount of original inspiration has all but dried up. The earlier prophets stammered, uttered sibylline or ambiguous phrases, contradicted themselves when buffeted about by winds of doctrine from different directions. With Comte everything has become organized and reasoned. Only positivist neophytes might think they found discrepancies between one part of the system and another; in fact everything is consistent down to the most trivial detail. Comte was at once the St. Paul and the Aquinas of the new religion, and he interrelated all its parts even as he presumed to regulate the lives of all its adherents. The names which religious founders assume are often telling self-revelations. When Auguste Comte bestowed upon himself the title of "High Priest of Humanity" he was symbolically closing the anarchic period of prophecy and instituting the sacerdotal office. The priests were taking over from the prophets.

By temperament Comte was a theologian, and he planned each tome of his *Summa* with a view to its function in the architectonic whole. French social thought and philosophical history culminated in the four massive volumes of the *Système de politique positive*. None of Comte's predecessors had elaborated their conceptions with a detail and a rich complexity that is even remotely comparable. The design of the work is of heroic proportions, though some formulas do reappear with obsessive frequency. The style is forbidding; it has a Germanic turgidity despite his invocation of the spirit of Aristotle and his summons to the great eighteenth-century masters of prose, Hume and Diderot, as patrons of his doctrine. Comte has an annoying way of making reference to political figures and eminent scientists periphrastically, without any direct mention of their names; cryptic allusions to ideas and accomplishments are enveloped in his own private language, so that the identification of his historical heroes and villains becomes an intellectual guessing game. Ideas which Saint-Simon had passed off as reflections of philosophical history and the Saint-Simonians had arranged in orderly oratorical propositions fit for teaching, Auguste Comte embodied in grandiose positive laws of sociology and morality. While Saint-Simon had died in search of collaborators for the system of his dreams, Auguste Comte actually fixed the hard and sharp lines, laid out the boxes, established ironclad categories. Though the main argument is sometimes obscured by a profusion of corollaries, anyone who takes the trouble to fathom the full meaning of a Comtean paragraph will find in it a balanced combination of the particular and the general. Far more learned than his predecessors, Comte was capable of drawing pertinent analogies from any field of scientific knowledge without committing the gaucheries of the autodidact.

Progress became the definition of Social Dynamics — we have been propelled into the jargon-world of sociology by its founder — as Order was the key to Social Statics. "Progress is the development of Order," or Progress is the dynamic form of the static concept of Order. The social series, another way of identifying the philosophy of history, was an extension of the animal hierarchy and was governed throughout by the same fundamental principle: a simultaneous evolution toward the complex, the harmonious, and the unified. As one passed from the lowest inorganic state to Humanity, Comte's hypostatization of the highest state of social being, forms became ever more complicated and more tightly integrated. Saint-Simon had toyed with this new version of the great chain of being; Auguste Comte spelled it out.

Historical progress dealt with the evolution of the higher forms of social dynamics, but it was rooted in a psychology of human nature that was enduring and unchangeable. From the early nineteenth-century physiologist Bichat, who had already influenced Saint-Simon, and the phrenologists Gall and Broussais, who had dissected Saint-Simon's brain, Comte adopted the tripartite division of man and the geography of the cerebral areas governing the various capacities. From Broussais he also derived the conception of mental illness as a mere intensification of the normal, an idea to which he lent historical wings by relating the primitive to the normal of the future on one extended evolutionary chain. The Comtean laws of social dynamics were so closely interrelated that they could be expressed as one, three, or four fundamental principles, depending upon the level of discourse on which one was engaged. The law of the three states, the law of the encyclopedic hierarchy of the sciences, the law of the transformations of activity, and the law of the growth of sentiment were merely different aspects of the single dynamic law of progress.

The most comprehensive way of formulating the totality of the historical process was the law of the three states, even though in the narrow sense it referred primarily to the evolution of

human intelligence. To accept one of Comte's own windy definitions of a "state of intelligence" would not be very illuminating.
Since he expounded his doctrine a century after Turgot's embryonic statement of the same concept and after Vico's meaty description of the three types of human nature — *tre spezie di nature* —
which followed each other in every revolution of the historical
cycle, the Comtean "state of intelligence" had absorbed meaning
from both sources. A "state of intelligence" was a particular type
of psychological perception of the world, a language of the mind
and a logic; above all it was a stage in the evolving relationship
between man's subjective images and the external objective world.
Comte was heir to Turgot's idea that a higher stage of mind was
achieved at the expense of a diminution of subjective imaginative
fancy, and to Hume's definition of man's primitive religious feeling
in *The Natural History of Religion* as a total immersion in primary
passions of fear and hope accompanied by little or no capacity for
abstraction. Following Vico, Saint-Simon, and the Saint-Simonians,
Auguste Comte fixed on the nature of man's religion as the most
characteristic index of human mentality in any epoch, and thus
the history of human intelligence became for him, as it had been
for his predecessors, a history of religion.

To define the first and most primitive state of man Comte
employed a variety of terms which require translation; he called
it spontaneous and fictitious — we might today say that it was
freely creative and subjective, that it had relatively little to do
with the outside object world. Fetishism, a term he borrowed from
de Brosses' little essay *Du culte des dieux fétiches*, was the first,
totally subjective explanation of man's relationship with external
reality. Theologism, with its subsidiaries polytheism and monotheism, though it had a separate name, was still a part of the
primary state, the provisional pattern of human intelligence which
was inevitably destined to be superseded not only for historical
reasons but because man's perception bore within itself the inherent
necessity of evolution into a new form. The logic of history had
psychological foundations. Comte's descriptions of the passing
from one phase of development to another within theologism were
circumstantial and ingenious, replete with illustrative materials
his predecessors were ignorant of, since his prodigious memory had

assimilated and stored the contents of new works of erudition. The second or transitional state he labeled metaphysicism; its essential character was abstraction. The medieval theologians were the major intellects of the metaphysical and their monotheism was typical of the tail end of theologism merging into metaphysicism. Using metaphysicism to define medieval philosophy was bewildering, but it served to fill a pressing psychic need on Comte's part, to differentiate his categories from those of Saint-Simon, who had stuck to commonsensical nomenclature, theology as the spiritual expression of the medieval mind and metaphysics as the intermediary form between theology and positive science. Needless to say, Comte's verbal switch did not profoundly alter the nature of the evolution both of them described. Positivism, whose characteristic was demonstration, was the third and definitive stage of human evolution. It was only a few centuries old, it had not yet eradicated the remnants of metaphysicism, and many ages lay before it. A high degree of subordination of subjectivity to the objective world was its most noteworthy attribute. Mankind had thus moved in a direction that was polar opposite to primitive fetishism, it had passed from subjectivity to objectivity; but here Comte raised an ominous warning: there was grave danger in the total elimination of creative subjectivity; merely objective perception could lead to idiocy.

Pursuing another parallel which Saint-Simon had already explored, Comte correlated the three stages of progressive intelligence with three forms of social activity (Saint-Simon had still referred to spiritual and temporal powers). The ancients had been military and aggressive conquerors who organized labor as slavery; the medievals were also committed to warfare, but unlike the peoples of antiquity their military tactics tended to be primarily defensive — they locked themselves behind the ramparts of their castles — and this slackening of the offensive warrior spirit gave birth to a transitional form of activity which allowed for the growth of industrial labor. In the positivist epoch a free proletariat became the dominant pattern for the organization of labor. "These three successive modes of action — conquest, defense, and labor — correspond precisely to the three successive stages of intelligence — the fictitious, the abstract, and the demonstrable. From

this fundamental correlation there also results the general explanation of the three natural ages of humanity. Its long infancy, which
fills the whole of antiquity, had to be essentially theological and
military; its adolescence in the Middle Ages was metaphysical and
feudal; finally its maturity, which has only begun to be appreciated
in the last few centuries, is necessarily positive and industrial." [33]
With variations in vocabulary — modern sociology has come by
its terminology legitimately, from the father — this theme had
been constant in French philosophical history since Turgot. Comte
explained the conflict between the activists and the intellectuals
in the first two stages of social dynamics on the ground that these
elements were competitive with one another — as Saint-Simon had
— and he forecast the elimination of the conflict in the third and
final stage because scientific positivism in intelligence and industrialism as a method of work organization would be compatible,
not rival.

Usually there was a third law (sometimes it was expressed not
as a separate law but merely as a derivation of the two preceding
ones) which illustrated moral or emotional progress. The third
series fitted perfectly with the other two — all the gears of social
dynamics mesh. The progress of sentiment, which the Saint-Simonians had described as the growth of love in an almost identical
form, could be traced in the extension of the area of consciousness
over which affects of sympathy had power. The higher stages of
this development were the direct moral consequence of progress
in activity and intelligence: growth in love was thus a derivative
form. The ancients recognized only civic sentiments, the medievals
a wider sphere designated as collective European consciousness,
and the moderns under positivism were destined to render sympathy universal, the loftiest moral ideal, at once the most complicated and the most unified. The same moral progression of
sentiment could also be expressed conversely as a decreasing egotism, a condition marked by a steady weakening of nutritive and
sexual instincts and an increase of altruism. Comte too had undergone the influence of Kant's concept of antagonism and had set
up a world history of progress around the idea of decreasing rivalries and increasing love relationships among humans. As a characteristic index of this development he pointed to the growing

social and moral role of women, who symbolized the affectionate element. As a final, fourth law of social dynamics Comte included the philosophical key to the history of scientific development which had already been expounded in the *Cours*, the idea that the sciences progressed in chronological order from the simplest to the most complex, culminating in sociology — an idea which is directly traceable to Saint-Simon's earliest works and which he in turn owed, on his own testimony, to a Doctor Burdin, a surgeon in the armies of the Republic.

Comte faced the problem of the boundlessness of future progress and of the geographic areas in which his laws of social dynamics operated with more forthrightness than some of his predecessors. Similar to Fourier in this respect, he entertained the possibility of ultimate decline and death, carrying out the ontogenetic analogy, though he was quick to reassure his contemporaries that it was far too early to determine the shape of the downward stadial course of mankind. While Saint-Simon's theory was Europocentric and its universalization depended upon the conquest of other continents by the industrial-scientific ideology, and the Saint-Simonians felt that scholarship was not yet sufficiently advanced to document their thesis with Asian analogies, Comte made his law of three states equally applicable throughout the world. Ultimately every region would have to pass through the same stages, but — and here was the escape clause — the evolution could be accelerated by a more intense rate of progress in non-European areas. Like children, the savages might be able to leap over the metaphysical stage and emerge as full-fledged positivists; only fetishism was a necessary condition. He even allowed for slight variations — he called them "oscillations" — apparent minor movements of retrogression, though in universal terms the over-all development was inevitable and absolute.

Comte's vision diverges fundamentally from Saint-Simon's less in the nomenclature of the historical periods than in the complete abandonment of individual self-realization for a new emphasis on the total absorption in social statics and social dynamics. Saint-Simon in his last words to his disciple Olinde Rodrigues had still insisted on the development of individual capacities. Men were to be joined in association and love, but the individual would not be lost — this was a Saint-Simonian pledge to prospective converts. With Auguste Comte the Great Being became the time-bearing ocean in which all men were engulfed. The individual found his true fulfillment only by subordinating his subjectivity. The impression is inescapable that in the positivist religion there is a total loss of personality as man is merged in the perfect transcendent unity of Humanity. The late Teilhard de Chardin, the eminent paleontologist and theoretician of human evolution who prognosticated a similar development for the species, was fully aware of the affinities between his own philosophy and Comte's.

The other unique element in the Comtean doctrine is the richness of the psychological characterization of the three stages of consciousness. In a most revealing excursus in the third volume of the *Système de politique positive* Comte reported that during the course of his madness in 1826 he had acquired a personal conviction of the truth of the law of three states. Under the impact of mental strain he had felt himself regress backward through various stages of metaphysics, monotheism, and polytheism to fetishism, and then, in the process of recuperation, he had watched himself mount again through the progressive changes of human consciousness, at once historical and individual, to positivism and health.[34] This was a far more profound conception than the rather commonplace analogy between phylogeny and ontogeny to which Saint-Simon had regularly adverted. Comte experienced these stages as distinct states of consciousness fundamentally different from one another. When a man went mad and there was a derangement of psychic processes he naturally fell back along the same historic path of development. This embryonic Comtean version of Jung's idea of a collective consciousness, its origins and growth, and the view of regression as at once a return to the infantile and to the primitive had many eighteenth-century roots, but never before in the literature of psychology or sociology had these conceptions been developed with comparable vigor. His own tragic disease had bestowed psychic depth upon an intellectualist conception. The very content and tone of his law of the three states made it qualitatively different from previous theories of this character, relating it more to the writings of Vico, Hume, and de Brosses than to those of Turgot, Condorcet, and Saint-Simon. For all their progressist theories, Comte's immediate French predecessors still believed that a baby emerging from the womb in the future would be fundamentally the same kind of psychological creature as babies had been in the past and that it would remain so throughout its life. Changes in the social order would in time alter man's affective responses; but even if his acquired moral characteristics, as Condorcet believed, were inherited, the transformations would represent no more than a perfection of known rational faculties and sensory organs. Nothing as psychologically revolutionary as what Comte meant by spontaneous, fictitious, or abstract perception was generally indicated by the *philosophes*. Comte raised the theory of progress to a new level when in addition to technological, scientific, intellectual, and moral progress he envisaged a progressive growth of consciousness and proceeded to define its constituent historical elements. At the same time he had the extraordinary insight that as mankind advanced, the earlier stages of consciousness would not be completely sloughed off and forgotten forever, but on the contrary every child born in the new humanity would re-experience the history of the race and pass through the successive orders of intelligence in the course of its education. In previous stadial theories there is an impression of completeness in each stage: once man has achieved a higher level the old forms are abandoned. For Comte, who had known madness, the fetishist world was an ever-present reality, and in his religious philosophy he wrestled with the problem of preserving the direct and immediate emotional responses which characterized primitive religion even in the positive polity of the future.

Auguste Comte's predilection for the institution-bound priest was reflected everywhere in his philosophical review of history. Whenever a sacerdotal body appeared upon the scene mankind was at least temporarily in secure hands. From the lying trickster priest of Condorcet to Comte's benign ecclesiastical authorities who at every crucial moment in history ordered human intelligence and feeling, there had been a complete *volte face*. Even the fetishist priests, about whom de Brosses had written in 1760 with mixed horror and contempt as the heart of primitive darkness, in Comte's analysis became wise leaders who turned the subjective cause-seeking of savages to a moral purpose, the creation of communal sentiment among primitive mankind. The fetishists were not merely superstition-ridden; the spontaneous projections of their own passions onto the external world had ultimately led to a form of inquiry about objective existence. Both de Maistre and Saint-Simon had early taught Comte to acknowledge the worth of the medieval clergy, under whom theologism reached its zenith, because they had introduced elements of universality into human consciousness and had strengthened the feminine loving quality in mankind. The later metaphysicians who directed the transitional stage from theologism to positivism were the spiritual leaders who earned the least praise in the whole history of mankind; they had in fact given no general institutional direction to human endeavors. The anarchic potentialities of metaphysicism were always so powerful that it colored their works, and whatever was sound and progressive in their epoch was to be credited to the secret undercover operations of the positivist spirit at work in their midst and not to the abstractions of philosophy. The positivist priesthood which Comte was initiating was destined to resume the direct creative tradition of mankind which ran from the *fetisseros*, through the Catholic Church, to the high sacerdotal authority of the new religion.

Embryonic dialectical elements have been noted before in eighteenth-century philosophers of history like Condorcet. With Comte this mode of thought came to pervade the whole process of historical knowledge. No event, political, scientific, or artistic, but could be subjected to a historicophilosophical dissection, in the course of which the negative, retrogressive elements were distinguished from the positive, progressive ones. Occurrences were rarely appreciated as wholes. The Comtean method of absolute relativism made it impossible to comprehend any historical happening except as a combination of positive and negative elements, because in some respects the event was still clinging to previous forms of existence and in others it was bearing novelty. Historical personages were symbols of the conflict between the old and the new, and amid their manifold activities the two contrary facets of existence could be identified by the philosopher of history probing with his scalpel. Some historic roles were more purely positive, others more clearly negative, still others were patent conciliations of the contradictory forces. The truly great men were invariably the order seekers, the consolidators of new scientific and politico-industrial forces. Comte's favorite modern heroes were Richelieu, Louis XIV, and Frederick the Great. Diderot the *philosophe* who destroyed the values of medieval Catholicism was appreciated less than Diderot the synthesizing genius who foresaw the need for an in-gathering of the disparate elements of science into an encyclopedia, a presage of the scientific synthesis which Comte at long last was able to achieve in all its fullness.

Historical crises occurred when there was a grave imbalance among the progressions and in the arrangement of the various human creative capacities, when the industrial-political or the ideological maturation of a new epoch was either too sluggish or too precipitous. In the third volume of the *Politique positive*, Comte's interpretation of the outbreak of the French Revolution is characteristic of his thinking and expression. He descends from a dogmatic statement of the grand laws of social dynamics in the opening chapter to illustrate their workings in the "facts" of history. "This fatal inversion was above all the result of the inadequate harmony between the two evolutions, negative and positive, one of which then required a renewal which the other could not direct. All beliefs had been dissolved, and the regressive dictatorship, which held together the wreckage of the *ancien régime*, found itself irrevocably discredited. At the same time, feelings, which alone support that kind of society, already had undergone an intimate transformation as a result of the anarchy of thoughts, as shown by the steady diminution of feminine influence and the growing insurrection of the mind against the heart. On the other hand, science remained limited to inert nature and even tended toward academic degeneration. Philosophy, for lack of an objective base, spent itself in thin aspirations toward a subjective synthesis. Since organic evolution was incapable of satisfying the needs manifested by the critical movement, a social upheaval then became inevitable. . . ." [35] The providence of the Great Being could not be demonstrated more conclusively.

Comte had a keen awareness that ideological maxims and antiquated political forms often outlasted their usefulness and brought on upheavals by their very protracted survival; as an uncom-

promising historical relativist he was continually on the lookout
to detect the flaws in past spiritual doctrines which had pretended
to define the "final type of human order" when they were merely
preparatory, perhaps leading up to the positivist synthesis but in
themselves only partial improvements. Whenever an epoch steeped
in chaos, as a consequence of the mutual negation of powerful
forces, seemed to condemn mankind to definitive retrogression,
a "spontaneous emergence" of a new organizing force had set
humanity on the right path again. In his description of the powers
which imposed cohesion on society Comte frequently used the
term dictatorship, but not always with the same emotive significance: the dictatorship could be regressive (like Napoleon's) or
progressive (like Louis XIV's). There was always a conscious
avoidance of any ahistorical commitment to the libertarian slogans
of the French Revolution. All was relative. Liberty was a good in
the destruction of superannuated feudal economic forms; it was
an evil when it led to the intellectual and emotional anarchy of
the nineteenth century. The remedy of one epoch was the deadly
poison of another.

While the broad lines of the development of the Great Being
were fixed by the laws of social dynamics, there was a sense in
which human "modificability" played a role, albeit a restricted one.
There was sometimes choice between serving a positive or a
negative force, even though the over-all course itself was objectively determined. Much as Comte dwelt upon the "spontaneous
emergence" of new aspects of the Great Being in the historical
process, he was, perhaps more than any other thinker before the
triumph of depth psychology, aware of the tremendous weight of
the generations of the past in delimiting the scope of any novel
action. The new, if it was to be more than a mere expression of
caprice and anarchy doomed at the very moment of birth, had to
take its properly ordained place in the historic queue. No disorderly breakthroughs could be countenanced; if they occurred they
had no real, that is, lasting, existence. The past determined the
future so overwhelmingly that every action, every sprout of intellectual and moral growth, was relative to what had gone before.

Since harmonious unity — the Saint-Simonians would have said
an organic synthesis — is the only good society, Comte's historical

enemies were those intellectual, activist, or emotional forces which failed to contribute to social integration on an ever-higher plane of existence — the destructive critics, the revolutionaries, in a word, the anarchists. Saint-Simon's attack against the "liberals" became Comtean tirades against the "revolutionary anarchists" who had initiated the "great crisis," the men of 1789. Traditionalists like de Maistre were less dangerous to progress than the revolutionaries because they at least understood the need for the creation of a collective consciousness. The theocratic school's utopia of the organic society was the great divide in this respect between the two eighteenth-century progressists Turgot and Condorcet and their nineteenth-century followers Saint-Simon and Auguste Comte. Whereas Turgot had been almost pathologically afraid of sameness and its deadening effect on man, Saint-Simon and Comte saw in those who desired novelty and innovation for their own sake an even greater danger. Both of them raised the specter of formlessness as the dread antiprogressist force, a French sociological tradition which culminated in Durkheim's conception of *anomie*. A change in politics or science which was not organically integrated was for Comte destructive of the good order — it was like an act of historical regression either in an individual or in humanity. Throughout his historical presentation Comte was ever vigilant to apprehend the violators of the preordained historical timetable and to censure them retroactively. Condorcet's flogging of science and technology into ever-faster accomplishments was not the part of the *Esquisse* Comte admired. The progressions of intelligence, activity, and emotion ideally should march in step, three abreast, and any attempt of the intellectuals or the activists to be precocious in the introduction of their wares, especially if they neglected mankind's emotional maturity, only meant that they were breaking up the parade of order and progress. "In every normal existence, affects always dominate over speculation and action, although their intervention is indispensable to emotion in order that it may undergo the effect of and modify external impressions. But it is to feeling that each theoretical and practical step must be related. Since at bottom our evolution consists in the development of our unity, any progression in intelligence and activity which does not influence sentiment, the sole source of such a harmony, must be treated as abortive or regarded as purely preparatory." [36] Untimely revolutions were in their consequences retrogressive. The worst political catastrophes of the past were laid to a defect in this sense of timing; for the future the problem was less grave because fortunately there was now a High Priest of Humanity. He and his successors were the watchful ones, the leaders who would beat out the measure of progress with their sacerdotal batons, not too slow, not too fast, ever mindful of the optimum tempo for the emotive advance of mankind.

MORAL LOVE AND GAY SCIENCE

WHILE of late there has been a renaissance of Hegelian philosophy in France, the works of the native son Auguste Comte lie virtually neglected. And yet the parallels between the two mammoth systematizations evolved in absolute independence on either side of the Rhine are becoming more strikingly evident as time sets them both in perspective. Stripped of the thick hide of their private language these philosophical dinosaurs stand revealed as belonging to the same species. Nineteenth-century European thought had a penchant for total systems at once grand in scope and minute in their detail, full of generalities and particularities. Hegel and Comte are two nation-culture versions of idealist historical philosophies of spirit. Hegel's *Weltgeist* moved from civilization to civilization east to west, from China to Germany, passing through an organic life-cycle from birth to death in each temporal embodiment only to awaken anew in the next proximate locale and to resume its struggle for freedom on a higher level. Comte's Great Being possessed in turn each of the sciences in the encyclopedic hierarchy from astronomy to physics, chemistry, biology, sociology, and finally morality.[37] In each one of these sciences the Great Being had gone through theological and metaphysical stages before it became positive, and the total experience in one science had to be completed before the process could be initiated in its successor, a development that was about to be completed with the writing of Comte's treatise on morality. Both systems, the Hegelian and the Comtean, are at once logics and philosophies of history. Both deal with the epistemological relationship between subject and object and resolve it by temporalizing the problem.

But there is one fundamental respect in which Hegel and Comte differed. Hegel had baffled his commentators by a refusal to don the prophetic robes; the astute have been able to glean hints here and there in his writings about the future state of man, but the image is blurred. Comte, on the other hand, was not so diffident: his descriptions were circumstantial; the future was, after all, the whole purpose of his colossal labors — *savoir pour prévoir*. The detail with which he prophesied about calendars, holidays, and sacraments has repelled the skeptical though it should not have, because in his capacity as High Priest of Humanity he was actually instituting the future which he depicted, the perfect model of a self-fulfilling prophet. After long travail, having become successfully identified with the Great Being, he had only to interrogate himself about his own spontaneous desires to know what the future would be — a procedure which has been followed unconsciously by many dissenters from the positivist religion.

In the temporal order the rulers of the future Comtean society would remain the capitalists, and he was not afraid to flaunt the name in the face of the revolutionary radicals of 1848. These men would remain responsible for the material arrangements of the world because they controlled its wealth and were by nature gifted in the activist art of manipulation. In effect they would be more like economic administrators than domineering potentates. Comte had in mind men such as the philanthropic textile manufacturer of the Restoration, Baron Ternaux, who had befriended him during the lean period when he lived in Saint-Simon's shadow. He saw no reason to alter the satisfactory existing order under which the capitalists controlled the instruments of production. Though there would be no legal or institutional checks upon the free utilization of their talents, there were other restraints of far greater potency than mere state legislation. Rational scientists, no longer supreme but influential in their own sphere, were a complementary force engaged in ordering society through their control of the educational system. Once the moral goal was set and made explicit, capitalists and scientists would operate harmoniously without conflict. Since Comte's utopia was not an expansive sensuous society, the production of novelties which appealed to the senses and the conduct of researches such as astronomic investigations of distant planets would be frowned upon as futile. In his popular works when he was proselytizing "conservatives" and "proletarians" Comte never outrightly condemned the luxuries of capitalists; they were allowed their excesses without censure; theirs were peccadilloes which he tolerated, not ways of life establishing the moral tone of the society. His description of the really distant future leads one to surmise, however, that the forbearance of the Great Being in this respect would not be of long duration. Comte's extreme personal asceticism during the second phase of his philosophical career was projected onto the whole of society. The preservation of a stable temporal order was far more important than the intrusion into the system of new artifacts which would disrupt the fixed spiritual arrangements which he planned for mankind. Though the Saint-Simonian goal which dedicated the whole of society to the improvement of the moral and physical lot of the poorest and most numerous classes was not accepted, Comte did take for granted that capitalists who had adopted the device of the positive religion, *To live for others*, would provide for the fulfillment of the indispensable material needs of all human beings. In addition he relied upon the new dignity which would be achieved by the two most oppressed classes of existing society to infuse a totally different spirit into the contemporary egotistic industrial-scientific order. Women and proletarians were the classes whose elevation Comte, along with most other reformers of the thirties and forties, predicted. Both had similar natures: they represented the simple, tender, loving element in mankind whose true force consisted not in ruling but in modifying the selfish character of the rulers in the very process of being ruled. The proletarians who had the power of numbers would not use their brute strength to achieve a false equality contrary to human nature, Comte preached on the morrow of the June Days. Instead, the moral influence they exerted on the capitalists would put an end to class conflicts and persuade the economic directors of society to behave toward their proletarians as loving parents would to children. In the family — the central unit of existence, absorbing many emotions now dissipated on public bodies — women would exercise a similar paramount influence. They would be universally recognized as morally superior to men — as Clothilde de Vaux was to Comte — and though they were dominated and enjoyed no independent existence, either in life or in death (for even their positivist immortality was bound up with the fate of their husbands), they suffused the whole of society with a gentle warmth.

After the provisional period of theologism and the transitional period of metaphysicism the positivist priesthood would inaugurate definitive history. The new religion from which God was banished would consciously reorient social relationships by locating the focus of existence in the Great Being, the source of moral judgment in the future as it had been the end of moral and psychic development in the past. "Happiness as well as duty consists in uniting oneself more closely with the Great Being which epitomizes the universal order." [38] With the triumph of the positive religion, sociology, a political science, would be superseded in the hierarchy of knowledge by morality.

Relations among the sciences in the encyclopedic hierarchy were not conceived of simply as a mechanical succession in which the lower forms served as a mere base for the higher ones. As in the Marxist relationship of substructure and superstructure there was a reciprocal interplay of forms among the various echelons in the ladder. The final transformation of man's moral being was dependent upon the perfection of the biological sciences, primarily through the development and extension of the ideas of Gall and Broussais, whose phrenological discoveries Comte considered pivotal in the science of man since they established specific connections between physical brain areas and intellectual, emotional, and activist expressions. Toward the end of the first volume of the *Système de politique positive*, he defined the moral problem in an adaptation of their physiopsychological jargon: "how to make the three social instincts, assisted by the five intellectual organs, surmount as a matter of habit the impulses resulting from the seven personal tendencies, by reducing these to the minimum of indispensable satisfactions in order to consecrate the three active organs in the service of sociability." [39] Moral education metamorphosed the nature of biological functions by developing some and atrophying others. Man the agent could be perfected through a complex educational mechanism which supervised every age group in the life cycle through the successive ministrations of mothers, teachers, and priests, leading to a total improvement in spontaneous biological action-responses which could be measured in terms of the growth of love, altruism, living for others. Personality, an odious word in the Comtean vocabulary reminiscent of the anarchy of late metaphysicism, was not meant to flower but to merge in the totality of existence, past, present, and future.

All sciences on the lower levels of the encyclopedic scale would be affected by the moralization of man because the loving sentiment would pervade the scientific experiment and enrich it. Comte had a full awareness of the gap which separated a mere intellectual comprehension of a phenomenon and an emotional experience of the same event — an idea which has often been touted as a discovery of late nineteenth-century German sociology. Comte repeatedly protested to those of his disciples who maximized the distinction between his two careers that in the essays of the 1820's he had already announced a revolution of sentiment and the institution of a new moral authority as the inevitable development of the present epoch, only at that time his understanding of the necessity had been chiefly intellectual. Not until his first profound experience of love, when he had felt in his own soul (the word was allowable to connote a combination of mind and feeling) the moral effects of a sublime selfless passion for another person, was he able to institute a new religion which would operate through love and metamorphose those who lived in the Great Being from self-loving into other-loving. On March 11, 1846, in his one hundred and seventy-ninth letter to Clothilde de Vaux, Comte had written in a similar vein, "To become a perfect philosopher I lacked above all else a passion at once profound and pure that would make me appreciate sufficiently the emotional side of humanity. Its explicit consideration, which could only be accessory in my first great work, must, on the contrary, now dominate my second. . . . The great nervous crisis which was at first inherent in the invasion of this sacred love might have momentarily retarded the direct execution of my new philosophical operation. But you cannot, dear angel, feel as I do how profoundly its general conception has been improved. If you only knew what progress I have made in the last year, in the midst of these apparent perturbations, toward my principal philosophical goal, the final systematization of the whole of human existence around its true universal center: love." [40] In the new moral world there would be no objective scientific experiments unrelated to the needs of affection.

The temporal order of the future did not occupy a central place in Comte's considerations because in the end this was the lesser order. If capitalists were allowed their profits and the direction of the economy were entrusted to their hands they would not be encouraged to produce material objects with which man could readily dispense. The sensuous desires to which modern industry caters were destined to become ever weaker manifestations of human existence; with the enfeeblement of the nutritive and sexual passions there really was no wide field open for the expression of capitalist productivity. The boundless exploitation of nature in which the Saint-Simonians reveled was not a part of the Comtean dream. In bowdlerized language which spared the sensitivities of his Victorian readers Auguste Comte foretold the end of sex in the fourth volume of the *Politique positive*.

"The rational analysis of the problem is based on the determination of the real function of the masculine apparatus, which is meant to furnish the blood with a stimulating fluid and is capable of fortifying all vital operations, animal as well as organic. Compared to this general service the impregnating stimulation becomes a particular case, of a more and more secondary character to the degree that the organism evolves. One can thus imagine that in the noblest species this liquid might stop being indispensable to the awakening of the seed, an operation which might result artificially from various other sources, even material ones, and above all from a better reaction of the nervous on the vascular system. Such a perfection is presaged by the growing development of chastity, which, proper to the human race, at least among males, shows the physical, intellectual, and moral efficacy of a sound employment of the vivifying fluid. . . . Thus one conceives that civilization not only disposes man to appreciate woman more but continually increases the participation of the female sex in human reproduction, ultimately reaching a point where birth would emanate from woman alone." [41]

Indispensable sustenance of the body — but no more — was the restriction imposed upon the appetites. From the time of his first mental crisis through the climax of his love for Clothilde de Vaux Comte established a relationship in his own life between the curtailment of a sumptuary superfluity or extravagance and the unveiling of new philosophical vistas — he had in turn denied himself tobacco, coffee, and wine at each point in the progression. And since Comte conceived of himself as a symbolic embodiment of the man of the future, what was good for Comte was good for mankind. Time and again there are hints in his writings that sensual gratification denied was transmutable into vast resources of spiritual power of an intellectual or an emotional character. The direct connection between his sublimated love for Clothilde de Vaux and the massive outpourings of his last years was the most conclusive evidence of his theory. The period of the *Système de politique positive* and the *Synthèse subjective* can hardly be looked upon as a creative decline, however little one may be attracted by the prospects which the High Priest held out for humanity.

Natural science had been a necessary introduction to the final science of morality; but knowing physical relationships was not an end in itself. Comte's parsimonious system allowed for the expansion of technical science only insofar as it was related to the ordering of human relationships and the stimulation of progress in love. Beyond that point professional virtuosity was wasteful, and Comte was prepared to decree a breaking of the chemists' retorts and the biologists' test tubes as well as a burning of the books if sheer curiosity multiplied information beyond the point where it was assimilable by the study of man. Comte and Fourier would have lighted the firebrand together and both would be preaching eternal love — and yet what different faces of love — as they destroyed the intellectual accumulation of the ages in its name.

Comte's vision of the future moral life of man — for there is no other — at times seems unbearably dull, but there is another aspect to the man and his doctrine which is often obscured by the dark austerity of his mien. The second volume of the *Système de politique positive* extrapolated lines of human development which, though they may not suit the taste of contemporary sybarites or the men of action engaged in a struggle for power, cannot be lightly dismissed as baseless conjecture. In the hypothetical distant future state man is virtually liberated from work and the subsidiary intellectual occupations which have been dependent upon labor as a necessity. Not every type of work enjoyed Comte's moral sanction. "Activity dictated by our physical needs exerts an influence that is doubly corrupting, directly on the heart, indirectly on the mind." Freedom from work, whose only real justification is the biological need to keep the body alive, would be easily achieved. "It will only be necessary that the preparation of solid food habitually require as little trouble as our liquid or gaseous nutrition does today." [42] After the ages of slavery and labor there would follow an epoch in which man's intellectual and emotional nature — as Comte defined it — would enjoy free play. During the course of his historical review of human activity Comte referred to the "destructive instinct" which he sometimes called more energetic than the constructive one,[43] but all this was forgotten when he turned to the future. The destructive instinct had been stimulated by necessity, but once man is emancipated from physical needs and abandons his meat diet he will become spontaneously loving and his altruist nature will express itself in all its fullness. The parallel to Marx's utopia in the *German Ideology* is arresting. For the first time in the history of man freedom from necessity will allow for the development of pure consciousness, the essential human nature. Perhaps with Marx the image is more intellectualist (though he had his Fourierist moments too) and with Comte the emotive capacity tends to prevail, but in the end of the days the inhabitants of the Comtean and the Marxist worlds would recognize one another and perhaps become reconciled.

"We must now evaluate what our intellectual existence will be like," Comte begins blandly in the second chapter of the social statics, when he allows himself to be catapulted into a fantasy world which is one of the most charming of the rationalistic utopias. For once the dry, obsessively precise mathematics teacher seems to have thrown his textbooks out of the celestial windows and abandoned himself to the Italian operas whose delights he relished but could not always afford. There would be virtually no development in technological thought because such practical speculations were always sparked by physical needs, and these, as he has shown, would be appeased with the expenditure of little or no work. Scientific culture itself, which had once been bound to industrial activity, would thus find itself free. The passion for pure theory and the quest for the explanation of phenomena for their own sake are "instincts" too feeble to sustain man in these arduous labors. If technical science is not stimulated either by practical needs or by love it will soon be abandoned as sterile. Perhaps the free intellect will still occasionally erect scientific models which derive from simple analogies. But science will not be the main channel into which human intelligence flows. Aesthetic works will attract the energies formerly spent upon scientific and technical labors, since this is a natural predilection of the human desire for expression and is not born out of mere necessity. Instead of devoting himself to the elaboration of scientific constructs which are remote and complicated, man will seek the most direct means of self-expression and he will find them both in art and in the expansion of his emotive vocabulary. Intelligence will thus become bound up with love and sympathy to a degree that was never feasible under the reign of technical science. Man's need for activity will not disappear even though he is freed from the burdens of labor, only the nature of action will be profoundly changed. Domestic animals, all of whose needs are provided for, do not cease to express themselves; instead of being scavengers they become playful. "In a word, acts would essentially be transformed into games, which instead of being preparations for active existence would constitute pure means of exercise and expansiveness." No longer absorbed by work enterprises of an external character, action will apply itself to the organization of *fêtes* which develop the mutual affections — chaste ones of course — of the participants. The aesthetic will prevail because it lies in a more direct physiological relationship with the emotions than either science or industry. "We shall then exercise no other activity but the perfection of our special means for expressing affection, as we shall cultivate no other science but the *gaie science* naively preferred by our chivalrous ancestors." [44] Nietzsche's *Gaya Scienza!*

In the end Comte's Great Being has turned out to be even more cunning than Hegel's Reason. In the early stages of mankind the primitive was forced to labor and to discover scientific facts which might alleviate the pains of his arduous tasks; finally in the course of expanding both his knowledge and his activity he reached a point where both labor and science were transcended and free human nature could express itself directly in beauty and in love. "In blessing a fatality which has become the principal source of our real grandeur we express our debt for all these benefits to the active providence, first spontaneous, then systematic, whereby the true Great Being rendered a naturally oppressive yoke more and more beneficent." [45]

Epilogue

REFLECTIONS ON THE NEW PROPHECY

Tᴜʀɢᴏᴛ and Condorcet wrote plans and sketches for universal history, delivered academic discourses, prepared tableaux and *esquisses*. Their aperçus were meant to be tentative—almost dialogues in which the interlocutors are convincing themselves as well as their friends. When on the eve of the Revolution it was rumored that Garat was composing a grand work on the progress of the human mind—he already used the phrase—but one that was afflicted with the *esprit de système*, his friend Condorcet let loose his caustic tongue in a letter to Mme. Suard: "The poor human mind already has so many natural impediments to overcome that one should not erect new ones for it."[1] Turgot had been even more deprecatory about closed systems: "Like a mausoleum, a monument to the arrogance of the great and the wretchedness of man, which seems to make us more aware of the emptiness of human affairs and of the death which it tries to hide, a system only serves to cover the shame of our ignorance. It is a bier in which a cadaver is contained and which itself becomes a sign of death."[2] By the turn of the century casualness of intellectual form was no longer fashionable; everything had to be an integrated part of an organic system, and the prophets of the new age built mammoth structures in which past, present, and future in every domain of knowledge were synthesized in a mystical unity. The eighteenth-century men still wrote reflections on history; by the nineteenth century the voices of the prophets had become strident and absolutist; they were fanatically certain of every last detail of their visions.

While Turgot was not one of the great wits of the age, he had a sense of humor: on the false bookcase front of his elegant library at Limoges he stamped such fanciful titles as *Délices du gouvernement turc, dédiées au Kislar-Aga, par S. N. H. Linguet*; *Véritable*

*utilité de la guerre, ouvrage posthume des fr. Paris; Art de com-
pliquer les questions simples, par l'Abbé Gagliano; and L'Art de
faire des glaces, par un buvetier de l'Inquisition.*[3] Condorcet was
more sarcastic than jocular, but he knew the art of *double-entendre.*
Saint-Simon had a light, skeptical turn of phrase in private conversation, though only rare traces of it can be discovered in his published works. The Saint-Simonians were divided personalities, who
might indulge in a measure of self-mockery on occasion but in general were unbearably pompous in their ceremonials. Where the
doctrine was concerned, Fourier was heavy and deadly serious; he
was capable of brutal irony but not laughter. With Auguste Comte
one enters the dark caverns of unrelieved solemnity.

But much as they differed in their style and rhetoric, the prophets made pronouncements on the same overwhelming questions
confronting Western man: on the nature of love and the institution
of the family, on the uses of philosophical history and its relation to
social action, on the property system and the ideal mode of compensation for work, on the future of man's religious predicament,
on the relative virtues of reason and the imaginative faculty, on the
merits of violent political revolution and the power of persuasion.
If the prophets did not agree among themselves, they bequeathed a
spectrum of moral alternatives, many of which have been revived
— in modified form, to be sure — in the course of the last century.
This rich body of teaching on the social, moral, and religious dilemmas of man has not been lost, even though the works themselves
are now rarely read outside of an academic context. A summary reflection upon the intellectual fabric of this French age of prophecy
may serve to illuminate its brilliance and complexity.

The French prophets had a rival — of whose works only the
Saint-Simonians[4] and Auguste Comte[5] were vaguely aware — in
Professor Georg Wilhelm Friedrich Hegel, whose philosophy of
history was sketchily outlined in 1820 and then amplified in regular
lectures at Berlin in the decade that followed. Perhaps nothing can
better serve to sharpen the contrast between intellectual tempers on
opposite sides of the Rhine than a passage in the preface to his
*Grundlinien der Philosophie des Rechts oder Naturrecht und Staats-
wissenschaft im Grundrisse* (1820): "A word on preaching about
how the world should be. For that, philosophy always arrives too

late. As the *thought* of the world, it only makes its appearance after actuality has finished its process of development and is over. What the conception teaches, history also shows to be necessary. Only in the maturation of actuality does the ideal appear to confront the real. Then the ideal reconstructs this world for itself in the form of an intellectual realm comprehending it in its substance. When philosophy paints its gray in gray then the form of life has grown old, and this gray in gray is not capable of rejuvenating it, merely of understanding it. The owl of Minerva only begins its flight when twilight falls."[6] Unlike their German counterparts, none of the prophets of Paris were closeted academic philosophers, and for them action was always bound up with theory. They were all committed men; they knew what they wanted the future world to be like, often down to the minutest social arrangement. They were of the dawn, not the twilight. Philosophical history was for them a prerequisite for sound prophecy, and prophecy was necessary for right conduct. In this respect the Marx of the theses on Feuerbach — "philosophers have hitherto merely interpreted the world variously, the issue is to change it"[7] — derived from them rather than from Hegel.

Sometimes this passion for the active life, for taming the future, for dominating history, diverted intellectual energies away from philosophy to politics. Turgot's grand projects of reform when he was Intendant at Limoges and Comptroller-General of the realm of France were elaborated at the expense of philosophical contemplation. Condorcet, the professional scientist-philosopher, in the conclusion of a famous letter to Voltaire, expressed his frank preference for the moral pleasures of direct action on behalf of humanity that he had experienced while working as Turgot's assistant during their brief tenure of office over the "glories" of geometry and philosophy.[8] Saint-Simon was by nature an entrepreneur turned philosopher. The nineteenth-century system-builders and projectors were prototypes of the organizers of schools, movements, and churches. No mere contemplators of the course of history after the fact, they were dedicated to its immediate control and direction.

As philosophical historians the French prophets were both determinists and activists. The grand design was ordained by Providence for Turgot, by nature for Condorcet and Saint-Simon, by the

Great Being for Comte; but this did not minimize the importance of either philosophy or action. "The philosopher places himself at the summit of thought. From there he views the world as it has been and as it must become. He is not only an observer. He is an actor. He is an actor of the first rank in the moral world because his opinions on what the world must become regulate human society," Saint-Simon wrote in the *Travail sur la gravitation universelle*.[9] Man's influence on what Saint-Simon called "secondary effects" made him no mean figure in the historical process.[10] The massive, Latinate, periodic sentences of Turgot's discourses affirming the doctrine of progress in the face of a widely held belief that decadence was inevitable should not blind one to the fact that in the analysis of particular situations this great bureaucrat always sought a multiplicity of causes, and that he believed in the importance of contingencies, divergences, the crucial role of individual genius, the "flux and reflux" of the revolutions of nations and peoples — a phrase he used independently of Vico and Hume.[11] When his friend and schoolmate, the Abbé Lebon, sent him a list of causes for the decay of the arts and sciences in certain epochs — to be used in his competition for the essay prize offered by the Soissons Academy — young Turgot marked the letter up with marginalia that show the elasticity of his historical conceptions: "truer, but not always," "perhaps?" "some truth and some falsehood in the idea," "depending on the circumstances."[12] The minister who experienced the vicissitudes of public life in the dying days of the *ancien régime* and was not above trying his hand at an occasional cabal — though he was inept at it — never forced all human events into a single mold. The "plan" was a vast loose garment and did not presume to account for a multitude of human foibles and stupidities. Condorcet has often been cited as an illustration of the naive believer in simple, rectilinear progress. And yet the notes for his *Esquisse* in the Bibliothèque Nationale give the lie to this image. "It would be absurd to think that nothing can change the regular march of these progressions, that liberty may not suffer passing eclipses in a nation, that perfectibility will not be stopped by an unfortunate return to some old errors or even by the temporarily usurped rule of some new prejudices. It is virtually impossible that great obstacles should be quickly overcome by a union of enlightenment and force, of reason and passion, without having the movements which aroused mass opinion produce various kinds of oscillations."[13] Auguste Comte, who reduced historical evolution to "laws," was, as we have seen, also willing to allow for "oscillations" in the inevitable trend — "modifiable fatality."

But once the prophets were convinced, by their study of philosophical history and their prognosis of the next element in the series, that the hour of mankind's delivery was at hand, they had no choice but to act, for they and they alone could end the crisis of the times, hasten the coming of the future. If only mankind heeded them, they were each profoundly convinced, and drove the false prophets away, the travail of new birth would come to a happy conclusion.

Of the whole group only Condorcet made a temporary commitment to violent political revolution as a means of bringing about the reign of reason. Though Turgot's edicts were radical enough in their day and contemporary song-writers made fun of the utopia he and his *compagnons* presumed to inaugurate overnight, Turgot always operated within the institutional framework of the French monarchy and he was no lover of tumults. Even Condorcet's position was ambivalent. At the beginning of the Revolution he expressed in his private correspondence grave, almost prophetic, misgivings about the turbulent course of events; and yet for a long time he allowed himself to be publicly identified with the men of blood. This reticent, excitable man, thrust into the political maelstrom of '92–'93, was the archetype of the hesitant revolutionary, beset by moral scruples and remorse. At moments in the heat of partisan battle he eulogized force, and he did not openly condemn the September massacres — though he did refuse to approve the proscription of Robespierre and he cast his vote against the death penalty for the King. Privately he justified his continued association with the *bavards* on the ground that he exerted a moderating influence upon them, the voice of reason among the *enragés*. But in the solitude of his room in Mme. Vernet's house, the problem of revolutionary violence as a means of bringing about felicity gnawed at him. In his notes for the *Esquisse* he expressed more than passing doubt about the intrinsic worth of sudden revolutionary triumphs in the overthrow of "prejudices." "They give way to enthusiasm and not to conviction, and soon ignorance reclaims its own. A system of truths carefully developed, based on truths that have been closely analyzed, does not replace in vulgar heads the vague doctrines, the dubious ideas, upon which they were nourished. Soon these vague doctrines either find their way back or the vacuum which they left is filled with errors more favorable to the passions of the moment. These passions may well have supported the effects of enlightenment by destroying the obstacles which prevented the progress of truth, but only the slow, certain hand of reason can engrave truth on the minds of men in a durable manner." [14] The union of reason with force and passion could well lead to temporary retrogression. In a moving poem which he wrote in his very last days, this hunted man posed for himself the stark moral problem of revolutionary crime: if faced with the alternatives of committing a crime or suffering misfortune he would have to accept the latter fate. "Ils m'ont dis: Choisis, d'être oppresseur ou victime / J'embrassai le malheur et leur laissai le crime." [15]

To the other prophets from Saint-Simon through Comte, political revolutions of the type which they or their parents had lived through were anathema. Revolutions distorted and confused the basic social, moral, and religious issues. They led men into a labyrinth of metaphysics: revolutionary oratory obfuscated positive truths about human nature. New conflicts were engendered before old ones were resolved, and men became habituated to crime. In the revolutionary jails Saint-Simon and Fourier had known indescribable anguish anticipating death on the scaffold. The Saint-Simonians made a great point of abstaining from participation in the July days of 1830, and in 1848 the High Priest of Humanity could only bewail the stupidity of his contemporaries locked in fratricidal strife. For Comte political revolutionaries were madmen, the chief agents of retrogression, and in grand defiance of the liberals he dated his works from the year of "the great crisis," 1789.

If the prophets abhorred revolutionary violence, they placed no great confidence in the efficacy of parliamentary procedures. Only in Turgot and in Condorcet can one still discover a traditional interest in the organs of government, in constitutions, and in voting procedures. Turgot analyzed the newborn American system, and Condorcet, in his revolutionary period at least, was an assiduous drafter of constitutions. But the papers of Condorcet show that as the Revolution wore on he began to wonder whether rational wisdom really presided over the deliberations of elected assemblies. As for the nineteenth-century prophets, they had little use either for popular representative bodies or for other democratic forms. Saint-Simon and the cult respected the dignity of the ordinary man, not his legislative capacity. The dangers of popular democracy represented by Jacobinism were real to Condorcet, to Saint-Simon and the Saint-Simonians, and above all to Auguste Comte. In his utopia of science Condorcet devised special techniques to prevent the masses from interfering with expenditures for scientific experiments whose utility they could not conceivably grasp. Comte and the Saint-Simonians were hierarchical men, not believers in the right judgment of the people. Majority rule rather than the reign of the wise and the most competent appalled them.

Since Fourier regarded relationships in the ideal society as individual arrangements freely entered upon without the administrative intervention of a bureaucracy — except to record desires — his politics verged on anarchism and he has always had a great appeal for anarchist theoreticians — Proudhon, for example.

Barring political action as a panacea, the prophets believed that the word and the word alone could save mankind. For Turgot and Condorcet it was the word of reason cleansed of enthusiasm. For the nineteenth-century thinkers it was the spontaneous word of moral truth, not devoid of reason, above all historical reason, but drawing its strength from another font of human capacity, the power to love. In the face of both the traditional Christian concept of love and its popular libertine usage, the nineteenth-century moralists essayed a new definition of love, probably their most ambitious creative attempt. And along with this redefinition of love, the rehabilitation of the flesh, the emancipation of women, and the burgeoning of instinct, the institution of the monogamous family came to be questioned.

In the writings of Turgot, Condorcet, and Saint-Simon, while the orbit of human affections was enlarged, there was no tampering with the traditional form of the family, though even the eighteenth-century *philosophes* were moving in the direction of equal rights for men and women. Turgot's youthful manuscript reflections deplore the attitude toward women in contemporary society, where they were displayed like chattels. Condorcet, husband of a lady philosopher, granted to women equality of rights in many constitutional schemes, and he made the point that increasing the independence of women would heighten the delights of love for both partners. Saint-Simon, whose profligate ways during the Revolution were notorious, never said anything significant on the subject of the sexes, though he did allow women to serve as members of the ruling Council of Newton.[16] The problem becomes really paramount with Fourier, the Saint-Simonians, and Comte, for all of whom the contemporary "egotist" family was an obstacle to the development of sympathies and love for larger social units. They had to wrestle with the alternatives of either reconstituting or abolishing it. In the end both the Saint-Simonians and Comte retained the family as the basic unit of society, though they proposed changes in its emotional and juridical character. Enfantin and Comte, loathing isolated anarchic individualism, established the pair as the exclusive nucleus of social existence. They differed, however, in their conceptions of the permanence of the marital bond. Enfantin countenanced a variety of unions of greater or less durability depending upon the temperaments of the persons involved — which led to charges that he favored promiscuity. For Comte marriage was an indissoluble tie which even outlasted the death of one of the partners, imposing eternal fidelity.

Despite their emphasis on the pair, the Saint-Simonians and Comte taught that a full human existence required the growth of affections embracing all of humanity. This created an enduring problem: would there be a conflict between the intensity of love within the pair and the love of mankind? When Freud later faced this question his reply was clear-cut: there was a finite store of libidinous energy, and in this closed economy the love which was diffused among the broader units of society and served to cement the relationships of civilization was inevitably withdrawn from the woman's hearth, arousing her antagonism. For the Saint-Simonians and Comte love is "progressive": it can tap ever greater sources of energy; it needs only the framework and atmosphere of an appropriate system in order to expand infinitely on both levels. The love of humanity, the macrocosm, somehow does not subtract from the love of the pair, the microcosm; they coexist and grow ever stronger through time. Most of the early internal crises of the Saint-Simonians were centered around conflicting views of the two loves — the love of the private family and its stability and the love of the brotherhood in Saint-Simon. In Enfantin's version of Saint-Simonian theology the religious Father and Mother, the priest and the priestess, served as mediators between the two loves, fashioning them into a harmonious unity, rousing either one whenever it showed signs of flagging. Comte's High Priest of Humanity would ultimately play a similar role, though his influence would always be exerted on the side of the Great Being. In their own anarchic civilization, the prophets agreed, neither love was true and both were sullied with antagonism. There were of course perspicacious Saint-Simonians like Gustave d'Eichthal, who at the very outset of the heated discussions which took place within the closed circle of the apostles arrived at the private conclusion that in the future the emotional ties of the family would not last much beyond the period when the child needed parental protection. From then on affection would be transferred to the greater family of the Saint-Simonians, who were humanity.

Fourier, permissive in all things, allowed for the pair and its children to continue a familial existence if they so desired. When he was cautious and defensive in expounding his system he even indicated that this would be the normal practice during the transitional stages. In the true state of harmony, however, few except the very old would opt for such a tedious social relationship. Fourier's man has many loves, numerous and diverse, and the love of unity and totality which is the love of all mankind is certainly one of them. If afforded free expression it circulates through every fiber of the phalansterian system, an indispensable fluid in the world of harmony. It would never have occurred to Fourier that there was a contradiction between the universal love which binds mankind together and the multifarious individual loves.

Comte and the Saint-Simonians rejected intermediate loyalties or loves expressed in spatial or temporal terms — there was no provision for the love of a locality, a professional corps, a nation, or even one's own generation. For the purpose of propagating the new faith they organized their churches along national lines, but these divisions had solely administrative significance. On occasion Comte made passing reflections on the character of the major nations composing Occidental civilization, but he did not think of the enduring nature of man in national terms. The Saint-Simonian and Comtean religions were universal — though it was taken for granted, of course, that the Mother Church would always be located in Paris. Fourier the amateur geographer has left hundreds of sheets of paper grouping the phalansteries of the world in all manner of territorial combinations, and he was far from averse to the cultivation of intermediate loyalties — to the work group in which one labored for an hour, to the phalanstery in which one lived, to the nation, the continent, the planet — but how different these were from the ordinary fixations of men in civilization. The loyalties might be intense but they were usually fleeting; they were like team spirit in the best sportsmen's tradition, and left behind no rancor in defeat, no arrogance in victory.

For Turgot and Condorcet the future expansion of mind involved a parallel impoverishment of the imagination. Fantasy, error, and superstition were linked with imagination and their common decline was awaited with satisfaction. In his early writings Saint-Simon accepted Madame de Staël's prognostication of the death of the poetic and the triumph of the positive, but in his second period he related imagination to the enthusiastic, moral, and religious faculties, and prophesied a glorious future for this capacity revived, though he still bridled at the extravagant forms of contemporary German romanticism. Comte went through a similar development, ending his life in a total reversal of the positions of Turgot and Condorcet, whom he had once proclaimed his mentors. The rational-scientific capacity will atrophy, he foretold, while the spontaneous free play of the imagination will flourish as the most natural human activity. The Saint-Simonians held by the final word of their master, proclaimed the renascence of poetry and the arts — which was already taking place — and gave special prominence to the imminent flowering of the religious imagination. "The reign of the imagination is not past," wrote Eugène Rodrigues in a letter of December 21, 1828, "It will be reborn more brilliant than ever. No, the human species has not been disinherited of this noble faculty." [17]

In their diverging attitudes toward religion and the religious imagination the breach between the eighteenth- and the nineteenth-century moralists is sharpest. When the Abbé Turgot abandoned his clerical vocation he stopped going to mass, though he did not join in the antireligious crusade of the Holbachians and he died in the bosom of the Church. His was a reasonable Christian Deism. His friend Condorcet was an intransigent atheist, and though in revolutionary politics he was willing to compromise on issues involving the Christian clergy, he never imagined that religion would play a role in the future history of mankind.

The prophets of the nineteenth century came to concentrate upon the nature of religion as the most critical and the all-embracing problem of man. Here again Saint-Simon was the pivotal figure of the transition from French thought of the previous century. Himself a libertine and an atheist, he became convinced that before humanity lay the prospect of a new religion to fill the vacuum of contemporary disbelief. But how define the new religion — what dogmas and doctrines, what ceremonials, would it have? In his early period the religion of the future was for Saint-Simon nothing more than "generalized science"; toward the end of his life this religion of science was infused with emotional and moral elements. Religious love, expressed in philanthropic aid to the poorest and most numerous classes, was usually conceived of in sensate utilitarian terms and the primary goal was universal physical well-being; but even Saint-Simon recognized that psychic elements were interwoven with the religious love of one's brothers. In his last works the moral dignity of the manual laborer was appreciated, and the fulfillment of all human capacities in society became the supreme religious duty.

In the Pereire papers now in the Bibliothèque Nationale, it is possible to follow in detail the evolution of the religious doctrine from Saint-Simon to the Saint-Simonians. The act of association of the first journal they founded, *Le Producteur*, though it vested control in the hands of the future "fathers" Enfantin and Olinde Rodrigues, still included as shareholders the Voltaireans in Saint-Simon's circle, men like Léon Halévy and Dr. Bailly; Laffitte, the most important financial figure in France, essentially a secularist, bought ten shares for a periodical that was committed to increasing respect for producers. But the progression away from the rationalist doctrines of the system was rapid.[18] The Saint-Simonians first called the society of the future *le système industriel*, as Saint-Simon had, then the *Nouveau Christianisme* after his last work, then the Saint-Simonian School, and finally the Saint-Simonian Religion. They embarked in earnest upon the quest for a new vocabulary to articulate sentiments of love and faith which had not been experienced before. The Fathers and the Apostles of the Mother Church in Paris were highly self-conscious about creating a dogma and a ritual for their new religion. Rather artificially those ordained for the task, particularly Eugène Rodrigues and Charles Duveyrier, studied the Christian mystics to draw inspiration from the past. They were eager to establish ties with their religious antecedents, above all with primitive Christianity. The emotions engendered by Saint-Simonism were novel, but the language of their religion could not easily free itself from the accretion of past meanings. The symbols Eugène Rodrigues adopted from Biblical history at times failed of their mark, and he was chided by the Fathers, who worried lest their "formulae" be considered "vieux style." [19] Unfortunately, the ex-bank clerks, engineers, and future financiers who controlled the movement were not blessed with the power of the word. There was not a real poet among them, and the cult produced only religious ditties.[20] When Enfantin is groping for phrases in which to render the hitherto unfelt love of humanity he picks up echoes of German idealist philosophy. He was attempting to create a religious amalgam of the *moi* and the *non-moi* in Saint-Simonian love, to define religious love, not as the Christian spiritualists had before him nor as the pagan materialists had, but as love both of the body and the spirit. While eschewing a concept of the soul, Enfantin skirted around the idea of an inner being as the bearer of this Saint-Simonian religious love. He could not fashion appropriate speech for its expression, and often as not he lapsed into romantic pantheism.[21]

In retrospect the experience of the Saint-Simonians remains one of the most curious and fertile sources for the study of religious phenomena in a century that spawned hundreds of new sects. A dictatorial streak in Enfantin's character was responsible, at least in part, for many of the Saint-Simonian schisms, and yet it would be wrong to shove him into the pigeonhole reserved for the authoritarian personality. To be sure, the retreat at Ménilmontant was run like an army barracks — lights out at nine-thirty and on at four-fifteen, work duties allotted by order — but there are other far more complex aspects to the relations among the members of the Saint-Simonian family which Sébastien Charléty's classic though matter-of-fact study did not venture to explore. In a half-conscious manner Enfantin was experimenting with techniques for tne cure of souls hallowed by practitioners ancient and modern. He had the notion that if the Saint-Simonian priest developed in his charge a strong attachment of love for his person he would through this means be able to direct the sentiments of his devotee and the "progressive" development of his character. A letter of Enfantin's to his mother confirms the accusation that in his view a priestess might on occasion be called upon to practice all the arts of love spiritual and physical in order to return to health those who had despaired of life.[22] In this intimate role she would be acting like a second mother, a moral mother. Enfantin inspired passions in both men and women which are amply attested by voluminous files of letters in the Bibliothèque Nationale and the Bibliothèque de l'Arsenal.[23] Under the eye of the Father there were frequent crises, abrupt departures, denials by the resistant, equally sudden returns followed by violent outpourings of love. At the height of his power Enfantin never chided, however flagrant the sins of his children; he only loved and comforted, called for a reconsideration, warned the devotee that his suffering would be greater away from the Father than in his presence.[24] Auguste Comte later tried to arrogate to himself the same functions; but unfortunately this desiccated little man, so pitifully aware of his ugliness, could not emit the appropriate effluvia.

In Fourier and Comte the religion of love assumed guises in flagrant contradiction of each other. Fourier insisted on the preservation of the idea of God in his system of the passions; it was a religious duty to treasure the whims and desires of every man as a manifestation of the divine, and those who would suppress a human instinct were atheistic philosophers. Comte abandoned the idea and name of God for a love of humanity so general that it led to a total absorption in the Great Being. Arid and syncretistic, his ritual was even more imitative of Catholicism than was the Saint-Simonian. That men of intellect in far-flung parts of the world have been moved to recite his dry positivistic prayers is witness to the persistence of the "thirst for the sacred," as Eugène Rodrigues felicitously described the religious predicament.

Turgot and Condorcet are separated from the other prophets by the French Revolution and the novel historical and religious conceptions introduced by the traditionalists, above all by de Maistre. But this divide, important as it may be, is less absolute than has sometimes been imagined. Organicist doctrines antedated the Revolution and so did romantic sensibility. Perhaps of greater significance was the growing awareness of the conflicts of economic classes and the dramatic realities of what the economist Adolphe Blanqui in 1837 called the "industrial revolution." In quantitative terms the industrialization of France was insignificant in the first half of the nineteenth century, but the spotty developments and the small-scale economic crises raised all the social problems of a full-grown industrial society. Though even here it can hardly be said that the Turgot of the *guerre des farines* and Condorcet, the author of the article "Que toutes les classes de la société n'ont qu'un même intérêt," were wholly unaware of potential social clashes.

With respect to views on the nature of the property system and the distribution of the products of labor there was a marked transformation in the course of the century from 1750 to 1850. While Turgot would have abolished the medieval economic restrictions on the movement of grain which caused famine to ravage the land, and would have allowed the free choice of occupation, he did not envisage drastic alterations in the institutional system of private property relations once the remnants of feudalism had been extirpated. As an economist he was skeptical and pessimistic about the possibilities of significant amelioration in the standard of living of the ordinary worker.

Condorcet made the revolutionary leap when he posed as a realistic ideal for the not-too-distant future a system of relative economic equality among nations and among persons of various classes within nations. A minimum level of well-being for all was assumed, and the hazards of the usurpation of power by the rich were eliminated by establishing a benign scientific hegemony over society. The property system as such was allowed to stand.

Saint-Simon, who was highly conscious of the potentialities of destructive conflict between men of property and the propertyless, erected a hierarchical pyramid of control on the apex of which the industrialists would be both the economic and the political administrators. But since his society would be directed by an ideal — the improvement of the physical and moral condition of the poorest and most numerous classes — by definition class wars disappeared. In the spirit of the Napoleonic armies, the road was open to talent and remuneration was relative to productive performance. Absolute equality was rejected as illusory. Saint-Simon allowed for returns on private investment as an element in the economy, and his doctrine is "socialist" chiefly in the sense that there is a sector of collective social enterprise — vast engineering projects, for example, which are run by technical experts. Problems of the equitable distribution of goods are minimized by a boundless production which not only appeases needs but creates superfluities. Technological innovation is recognized as the means for raising the worth of the manual laborer, because paradoxically his skills will be more appreciated when machines assume most of the burden of heavy work. Private property is maintained, but it is no longer subject to the anarchic will of its owner since it is governed by laws dictating a total utilization of resources. The economy still operates as a profit system, but it is responsive to the demands of an expansive society dedicated to the public welfare.

The Saint-Simonians made the first real break with the system of private property by proclaiming outright the abolition of inheritance, a vicious impediment to the free operation of an order based on natural capacities, though at the same time they steadfastly denied, at least in their rationalist expositions of the doctrine, any community of property or equality of compensation for all work. They were usually willing to accept the epithet "socialist," first coming into general usage in England and France in the early 1830's, but they rejected communism. "To each according to his capacity" was the ultimate version of their slogan (there had been previous variants such as "to each according to his vocation" and "classification according to capacity").[25] The second part of their rule read "to each capacity according to its works," which clearly implied differentials in remuneration because, as the Pereires insisted in the classical manner, men needed incentives in order to be stimulated to labor for others.[26] Among Saint-Simonians the "works" formula retained overtones of a religious reward for virtuous action — it was not mere economic compensation.

Even in Fourier's phalanstery investors were allowed a return in accordance with the number of shares held, and consequently there were distinctions in the consumptive pleasures of the very wealthy and the relatively poor; but accumulated riches did not matter much because the passions freely dictated love relationships, and bountiful nature organized in the state of harmony had an endless storehouse of delights for all, including the very poorest. Penury was abolished because even in the transition period Fourier would guarantee a human minimum to all persons, as he wrote to Enfantin in his demonstration of the superiority of his own system over the Saint-Simonian.[27]

Comte allowed his capitalists to direct enterprises and to exert paternal controls over the proletariat, but on closer inspection their power turns out to be rather nominal, though for a different reason than in the worlds of Saint-Simon and Fourier. Since Comte's future is spiritualist and sensuous excesses are rigidly suppressed, property ownership beyond the provision of basic necessities ceases to be a major preoccupation. In both the Fourierist and the Comtean societies goods will be available to each according to his needs, though the conception of needs will be progressively sensuous (at least for most people) in Fourier's vision and dynamically spiritualized and rendered more and more immaterial in Comte's. In their interpretation of needs the Saint-Simonians represented a middle way, balancing physical and spiritual elements, since they were neither ascetics nor sybarites.

Though they differed in their systems of compensation, a new valuation of the worth of manual labor and work in general characterized both the Saint-Simonians and Fourier. The eighteenth-century *philosophes* had respected all arts and sciences equally — there could no longer be a traditional hierarchy of knowledge and activity after the publication of the alphabetical *Encyclopédie* — but Saint-Simon raised labor to a new height when he pronounced the commandment: "All men must work." Fourier could not conceive of a man who would refuse to work if labor ceased to be drudgery and were skilfully associated with the passions, for he would then be abandoned to boredom. The cultivated Saint-Simonian apostles in their retreat in Ménilmontant shocked Parisian wits by sanctifying manual labor. In this respect as in many others

Comte deviated from the rest of the prophets. While affording the proletarians a respectable position alongside of women, he saw no absolute or intrinsic merit in work. Labor was part of the transitional world of necessity from whose fetters the man of the future would ultimately be freed.

The prophets were staunch in their belief that a metamorphosis in the idea and the organization of work would end the exploitation of man by man and initiate the epoch of the boundless exploitation of nature through the united efforts of men. In Turgot this conception is not yet ripe because he was still engaged in a preliminary skirmish, the emancipation of labor from feudal restrictions; in Condorcet's manuscripts it assumes a heroic, almost mythic form: by joining forces in the conquest of nature's secrets, men become the equal of nature in power and capable of dominating her. For Saint-Simon and the Saint-Simonians this deflection of man's aggressiveness from his fellows to outward physical reality is the clue to the transformation of his bellicose nature into benevolence. Simultaneously labor as a crucial fulfillment of personality is established. Fourier is perhaps the most brilliant in devising techniques for channeling the hostile instincts which characterize human relationships into types of labor dealing with objects and animals which call for a measure of bloodthirsty violence. Comte alone was sceptical of the meaningfulness of this outer-directed activity in changing man's inner being.

It was the social doctrines of the nineteenth-century prophets which exerted the most profound and direct influence upon modern political thought and diction. The joint commitment to the emancipation of women and of the proletariat was taken over by virtually all socialist and communist movements, however they varied in their plans for the implementation of the doctrines. Descriptions of the thralldom of women and the sufferings of the working classes in the writings of Fourier and the Saint-Simonians created a dramatic image of a civilization ruthless, cruel, and anarchic in its relations of love and labor. Their mordant phrases have pervaded the literature of protest and revolt, and echoes of their words still reverberate.

In a famous letter, the *Critique of the Gotha Programme* (1875), which has had an enduring influence on communist thought, Marx wrote of the higher phase of communist society: ". . . After the enslaving subordination of individuals to the division of labor has disappeared, and with it the contradiction between intellectual and physical work; after labor has become not only a means for life, but itself the prime necessity of living; after the forces of production have grown, along with the many-sided development of the individual, and all the wellsprings of communal riches flow more plentifully — only then can the narrow, bourgeois horizon of rights be completely transcended, and society inscribe on its banners: from each according to his abilities, to each according to his needs!"[28] This oft-quoted formulation of the communist ideal is clearly a syncretism of ideas and phrases garnered from the French age of prophecy, particularly from the Saint-Simonians and the Fourierists.[29] Of course, Marx's historical analysis of "needs," intimately related to the Hegelian problem of alienation, is an extraordinarily complex conceptualization, in many ways far more subtle philosophically than anything the Frenchmen propounded. None the less, all of them were aiming their arrows in the same direction.[30] Marx's "self-actualization of the individual,"[31] Saint-Simon's "development of faculties," and Fourier's plea for the "burgeoning of instinct," moral ideals with a long past history, in our time have come to be articulate, almost universal demands. While need still retains a simple alimentary meaning for starving hundreds of millions, the more expansive definition of needs essayed by the French prophets and by Marx follows fast upon the appeasement of hunger.

One final word. Broad as was the horizon of their inquiry and understanding, there is a blind spot among the prophets of Paris, the absence of a tragic sense. Whatever they wrote in their philosophies, Turgot and Condorcet in their style of life are essentially Stoic-Epicurean — for the eighteenth century often combined these two ancient moralities with adroitness. Their strong sense of civic duty was Roman touched with an aristocratic *noblesse oblige*. Both of them died clutching their Horaces (Turgot was translating the *Aequam memento*; the odes were found on Condorcet's person in the prison of Bourg-Egalité). The haggard Condorcet, tracked like an animal, hiding in ditches, wandering in the fields around Paris, cannot rail against the gods or the fates or the demons, for there are none. There is only history. Such events as political defeat at the hands of a king or an assembly were but passing accidents, and in the end the philosophers would be vindicated by the historical process, in its grand sweep the incarnation of reason. A melancholy air befits this historical faith — a residue from Lucretius. The unsuccessful suicide attempts of Saint-Simon and Comte are pathetic but, again, hardly tragic. What more pitiable than a former officer who could not shoot a bullet through his head and a scientist who could not drown and had to be fished out of the Seine! Charles Fourier was perhaps the most fortunate — he rarely awakened from his dream of glory, while Saint-Simon and Comte had moments of terrible lucidity and despair.

But despite the sadness which pervades the lives of the prophets, they failed to recognize and confront in their writings the blind, meaningless destructiveness of fate which can overwhelm a man, for the prophets could always escape to that other world of the future, the "blue heaven" where there was compensation enough. If rejected by their contemporaries, they are redeemed by history. Their life drama ends happily. In their fantasies they become the immortals, the smiling gods who usher in an eternity of peace and happiness for all mankind. It is not their wild impractical utopianism which at times makes these lovers of humanity appear so inhumanly optimistic in their published works. In retrospect their predictions seem far more realistic than those of their down-to-earth contemporaries. Their man of the future has self-actualizing work and love, play and pleasure, ease, order, and even a measure of freedom. Barring total annihilation, an irrelevant hypothesis, all these bounties and more are in prospect. Yet something is lacking in their vision of man. It is their refusal (or was this perhaps the secret lie of the prophets of Paris?) to contemplate the inherently tragic aspect of life itself, beyond the consolations of philosophy and history, that reduces their humanity to philanthropy.

Notes

CHAPTER I

TURGOT, BARON DE L'AULNE

1. There are three editions of the works of Turgot: the first, by Dupont de Nemours, 9 vols. (Paris, 1808–1811), secularized the religious tone of the Sorbonne discourses; the second was by Eugène Daire and Hippolyte Dussard, 2 vols. (Paris, 1844); the third and probably definitive edition was by Gustave Schelle, 5 vols. (Paris, 1913–1922). Fragments of Turgot's work were translated into English in W. Walker Stephens, *The Life and Writings of Turgot, Comptroller General of France, 1774–1776* (London and New York, 1895); and there is a translation titled *On the Progress of the Human Mind*, with notes and an appendix by McQuilkin de Grange (Hanover, New Hampshire, 1928). The *Textes choisis* by Pierre Vigreux (Paris, 1947) emphasizes economic thought. A collection of texts on Turgot's theory of progress has appeared in Spanish, *El progresso en la historia universal; traducción del francés por María Vergara* (Madrid, 1941).

Of the major works on Turgot, two appeared in the eighteenth century, written by devoted admirers and disciples: Dupont de Nemours, *Mémoires sur la vie et les ouvrages de M. Turgot* (Philadelphia [Paris], 1782), and Condorcet, *Vie de Turgot* (London, 1786). These really constitute the oral tradition and cannot be separated from the writings themselves. Most of the mid-nineteenth-century works are slight: A. Bouchot, *Eloge*, at the Académie française (1846); G. Kellner, *Zur Geschichte des Physiokratismus. Quesnay, Gournay, Turgot* (Göttingen, 1847); S. Murav'ev, *Turgot* [in Russian] (Moscow, 1858); Anselme Batbie, *Turgot philosophe, économiste et administrateur* (Paris, 1861); W. B. Hodgson, *Turgot: his life, times, and opinions* (London, 1870); Félix Cadet, *Turgot* (Paris, 1873). C. J. Tissot, *Turgot, sa vie, son administration, ses ouvrages*, Mémoire couronné par l'Académie des sciences morales et politiques (Paris, 1862), is by far the best of the group. Later nineteenth-century works are Alfred Neymarck, *Turgot et ses doctrines* (Paris, 1885), 2 vols., the most complete study of his thought; S. Feilbogen, *Smith und Turgot. Ein Beitrag zur Geschichte und Theorie der Nationalökonomie* (1892); and James M. Barnard, *A Sketch of Anne Robert Jacques Turgot* (Boston, 1899). In the twentieth century there have been two books in English, both of which concentrate almost exclusively on Turgot as a statesman: R. P. Shepherd, *Turgot and the Six Edicts* (New York, 1903), and Douglas Dakin, *Turgot and the Ancient Régime in France* (London, 1939), which has a good bibliography (pp. 307–316). Claude Joseph Gignoux, *Turgot* (Paris, 1945), is insignificant. The article by Dino Fiorot, "Sul pensiero filosofico e politico di Jacques Robert Turgot," *Nuova Rivista Storica*, XXXV (1952), 398–441, does not treat his historical philosophy extensively.

General works on the history of the philosophy of history and on the idea of progress usually include Turgot: Robert Flint, *The Philosophy of History in France and Germany* (London, 1875); Jules Delvaille, *Essai sur l'histoire de l'idée de progrès jusqu'à la fin du xviii* siècle* (Paris, 1910); John Bagnell Bury, *The Idea of Progress* (London, 1920); René Hubert, "Histoire de l'idée de progrès," in *La notion de progrès devant la science*

actuelle. Sixième semaine internationale de synthèse (Paris, 1938); Magal-
hães Vilhena, *Progresso; história breve de uma idéia* (Lisbon, 1939); R. G.
Collingwood, *The Idea of History* (Oxford, 1946); Charles Frankel, *The
Faith of Reason: The Idea of Progress in the French Enlightenment* (New
York, 1948); Frederick John Teggart, editor, *The Idea of Progress: A
Collection of Readings* (Berkeley, 1949), where an excerpt from Turgot
is translated (pp. 242–259); John Baillie, *The Belief in Progress* (London,
1950); Morris Ginsberg, *The Idea of Progress: A Revaluation* (London,
1953). There is an interesting treatment of antecedents to the eighteenth-
century idea in Ernest Lee Tuveson, *Millennium and Utopia: A Study in
the Background of the Idea of Progress* (Berkeley, 1949), and significant
reflections on the whole problem in Arthur O. Lovejoy and George Boas,
Primitivism and Related Ideas in Antiquity (Baltimore, 1937). The most
recent treatment of Turgot, in R. V. Sampson, *Progress in the Age of
Reason* (London, 1956), pp. 163–168, is rather offhand.

2. Turgot to the Chevalier Turgot at Malta, July 31, 1750, in Schelle
edition, I, 184.

3. Turgot, the man of taste, was sometimes self-conscious about the
apologetics. On one draft of the discourse he wrote, "All this has a didactic
air." MS in the Turgot archives, Château de Lantheuil.

4. Condorcet, a jealous disciple, would not have agreed. "His real
opinions were not known. There existed in Europe only a very few men
in a position to comprehend them in their totality and to judge them."
Condorcet, *Vie de Turgot*, p. 287.

5. The recent studies have been summarized in Edgar Faure, *La Dis-
grâce de Turgot* (Paris, 1961).

6. MS in the Turgot archives, Château de Lantheuil.

7. Dupont de Nemours edition, I, 417–418.

8. Schelle edition, I, 214–215.

9. Charles Frankel, whose *The Faith of Reason*, pp. 29–38, correctly
appreciates the brilliance of Pascal's fragment of ca. 1647, might have indicated that it was not published until the Bossut edition of 1779 (see
Oeuvres de Blaise Pascal, published by Léon Brunschvigg and Pierre Bou-
troux, Paris, 1923, II, 129fn). By that time Turgot's ideas were completely
fashioned.

10. "Pensées diverses," Schelle edition, I, 321.

11. "No mutation has taken place without producing experience, and
without spreading or ameliorating or preparing education." "Plan de deux
discours sur l'histoire universelle" (ca. 1751), Schelle edition, I, 285.

12. MS note in the Turgot archives, Château de Lantheuil.

13. Condorcet, *Vie de Turgot*, p. 220.

14. Schelle edition, I, 593.

15. Schelle edition, V, 242–243.

16. *Tableau philosophique des progrès successifs de l'esprit humain*
(1750), Schelle edition, I, 222.

17. *Réflexions rédigées à l'occasion d'un Mémoire remis de Vergennes
au Roi sur la manière dont la France et l'Espagne doivent envisager les
suites de la querelle entre la Grande-Bretagne et ses colonies*, Schelle edition,
V, 416.

18. *Recherches sur les causes des progrès et de la décadence des sciences*

et des arts ou réflexions sur l'histoire des progrès de l'esprit humain, Schelle edition, I, 133.

19. "Plan du second discours sur les progrès de l'esprit humain," Schelle edition, I, 302–303.

20. Abbé Etienne Bonnot de Condillac had already treated of the dependence of genius on the availability of appropriate language forms. "Circumstances favorable to the development of geniuses are found in a nation at the time when its language begins to have fixed principles and set character. This is the epoch of the great men." *Essai sur l'origine des connaissances humaines*, in *Oeuvres* (edition of 1798), I, 437.

21. Turgot's whole discussion of language is clearly derivative from Condillac. "Besides, it would show little understanding of the genius of language to imagine that one could cause to be transmuted all of a sudden the most perfect forms from the most crude. This can only be the work of time." *Ibid.*, I, 440. "The success of the best organized geniuses depends completely on the progress of language in the century when they live." *Ibid.*, I, 439. This held equally true for literary and scientific genius: "The success of Newton was prepared by the choice of symbols which had been made before him. . . ." *Ibid.*, I, 438–439.

22. Similar ideas are expressed in the *Tableau philosophique*, I, 223. Condillac in Chapter XV, "Du génie des langues," of the *Essai sur l'origine des connaissances humaines*, had already used language as the embodiment of the character of nations; Turgot transferred the idea directly to historical stages. In this instance, as in many others, he historicized Condillac.

23. Schelle edition, I, 347.

24. The following passage from Turgot is usually quoted (by Robert Flint, *The Philosophy of History*, p. 113, for example) to illustrate the origins of the Comtean law: "Before knowing the connection of physical facts with one another, nothing was more natural than to suppose that they were produced by beings intelligent, invisible, and like to ourselves. Everything which happened without man's own intervention had its god, to which fear or hope caused a worship to be paid conforming to the respect accorded to powerful men — the gods being only men more or less powerful in proportion as the age which originated them was more or less enlightened as to what constitutes the true perfections of humanity. But when philosophers perceived the absurdity of these fables, without having attained to a real acquaintance with the history of nature, they fancifully accounted for phenomena by abstract expressions, by essences and faculties, which indeed explained nothing, but were reasoned from as if they were real existences. It was only very late that, from observing the mechanical action of bodies on one another, other hypotheses were inferred, which mathematics could develop and experience verify." Dupont de Nemours edition, II, 294–295. P. J. B. Buchez, *Introduction à la science de l'histoire* (Paris, 1842), I, 121, had already noted this similarity of ideas; it has been accepted by Delvaille, *L'Histoire de l'idée de progrès*, pp. 398–399. Auguste Comte acknowledged "the wise Turgot" as a predecessor, in the *Cours de philosophie positive*, IV, 201. Wilhelm Dilthey, in *Sitzungsberichte der Berliner Akademie*, 1890, p. 979, classified Turgot as a precursor of Positivism.

25. Condillac, *Essai sur l'origine des connaissances humaines*, in *Oeuvres* (edition of 1798), I, 457.

26. Charles Frankel, *The Faith of Reason*, p. 125, has tended to exaggerate the abstract teleological elements in Turgot to the complete neglect of his attempt to demonstrate the reality of progress empirically through the evidence of world history, ethnography, the history of science, of languages, and of literatures. "By observing the present one can see all the forms that barbarism has assumed spread over the face of the earth and thus, so to speak, the historical monuments of every age." MS notes, Turgot archives, Château de Lantheuil.

27. Schelle edition, I, 495.

28. Charles de Brosses, *Du culte des dieux fétiches* (Geneva, 1760).

29. In a very early work, the *Lettre à Madame de Graffigny sur les Lettres d'une Péruvienne* (1751), Turgot already expressed sharp divergence from the primitivists; there is no appreciation of man in the state of nature, and the primitive world is dark, ignorant, and cruel. Schelle edition, I, 243.

30. "Plan du premier discours sur la formation des gouvernements et le mélange des nations," Schelle edition, I, 289.

31. "Plan de deux discours sur l'histoire universelle," Schelle edition, I, 285.

32. "Plan d'un ouvrage sur la géographie politique" (1751), Schelle edition, I, 257.

33. *Tableau philosophique des progrès successifs de l'esprit humain*, Schelle edition, I, 231.

34. In a letter to Abbé Cicé (only a part of which Schelle, I, 108–109, reproduced) Turgot emphasized the dependence of seventeenth-century speculative science upon a prior development of the mechanical arts. "At all times men have studied for their needs, and there have in all ages been workers who have known the physics of their jobs better than the physicists of their time." MS in the Turgot archives, Château de Lantheuil.

35. *Tableau philosophique des progrès successifs de l'esprit humain*, Schelle edition, I, 227.

36. Schelle edition, I, 199–200.

37. Condorcet, *Vie de Turgot*, p. 240.

38. *Ibid.*, p. 251.

39. On the other side of the channel Richard Price was expressing a cognate idea in somewhat different similes at about the same time: "Such are the nature of things that this progress must continue. During particular intervals it may be interrupted, but it cannot be destroyed. Every present advance prepares the way for farther advances; and a single experiment or discovery may sometimes give rise to so many more as suddenly to raise the species higher, and to resemble the effects of opening a new sense, or of the fall of a spark on a train that springs a mine." *Observations on the Importance of the American Revolution and the Means of Making It a Benefit to the World* (London, 1785), pp. 3–4.

40. Dupont de Nemours edition, III, 448.

41. This definition is attributed to Turgot by Condorcet, *Vie de Turgot*, in *Oeuvres*, V, 14.

42. By no means did he always sustain the youthful ecstasy of his 1750 *Tableau philosophique des progrès successifs de l'esprit humain*, where he thus described the age of enlightenment: "Finally, all the shadows have

been dissipated. What light shines in all directions! What a perfection of human reason!" Schelle edition, I, 234. Turgot's mature writing is perhaps not quite as simplistic in its emotional tone as Ronald Grimsley has summarized it in "Turgot's Article 'Existence' in the *Encyclopédie*": "The 'existentialist' inadequacy of the article 'Existence' would be the optimism of the eighteenth-century thinker who, with his faith in nature, reason, and humanity, had no occasion to experience the 'anguish' of our own age. Since man was separated from happiness only by his ignorance and stupidity, there seemed no reason why, in Turgot's words, 'the very foundations of philosophy' should not be uncovered by means of the intellectual tools which were at the disposal of every 'enlightened' thinker." *The French Mind: Studies in Honor of Gustave Rudler* (Oxford, 1952), p. 151.

43. Turgot to Condorcet, Ussel, June 20, 1772, *Correspondance inédite de Condorcet et de Turgot, 1770–1779.* Publiée avec des notes et une introduction par M. Charles Henry (Paris, 1883), p. 88.

44. *Réflexions sur la formation et la distribution des richesses* (1776), Schelle edition, II, 537.

45. "Plan du premier discours sur la formation des gouvernements et le mélange des nations," Schelle edition, I, 283. Kant, without referring to Turgot, developed a similar conception in his *Ideen.* This theme had been the heart of Vico's civil theology.

46. "The *Théodicée* of Leibniz should serve as a model for anyone who would put a vast erudition to use. . . ." *Pensées*, Schelle edition, I, 340. The Leibnizian influence is obvious throughout in Turgot. "I have also shown," wrote Leibniz, "that it is this Harmony which establishes the ties both of the future with the past as well as of the present and what is absent." *Essais de Théodicée*, in *Opera Philosophica* (Berlin, 1840), p. 477.

47. *Encyclopédie*, X, 22.

48. Condorcet, *Vie de Turgot*, p. 212.

49. "Plan de deux discours sur l'histoire universelle," Schelle edition, I, 285.

50. Condorcet, *Vie de Turgot*, p. 279.

51. *Ibid.*, p. 249.

52. *Ibid.*, p. 249.

53. *Ibid.*, pp. 276–277. See the last passage of Condorcet's *Esquisse*, written as a consolation of philosophy, Genoa edition of 1798, p. 359.

54. *Oeuvres de Condorcet* (Paris, 1847–1849), I, 113–114.

CHAPTER II

MARQUIS DE CONDORCET

1. The original edition of Condorcet's *Esquisse* was published by P. C.-F. Daunou and Mme. M.-L. S. de Condorcet in 1795. An *Oeuvres complètes* in 21 volumes appeared in Brunswick and Paris, 1804, edited by Mme. Condorcet with the assistance of A. A. Barbier, Dr. Pierre Cabanis, and D. J. Garat; the standard edition of the *Oeuvres de Condorcet*, published by A. Condorcet O'Connor and M. F. Arago, appeared in 12 volumes in

Paris, 1847–1849. An English translation of the *Esquisse* by Thomas Churchill was published in London, 1795 (also in Philadelphia, 1796, and Baltimore, 1802); the recent rendering by J. Barraclough (London, 1955) corrects many obvious mistakes but sometimes loses the flavor of the original. There is a "Table alphabétique des oeuvres de Condorcet," I, 641–646, and a "Table chronologique des oeuvres de Condorcet," I, 647–652, in the 1847–1849 edition.

The bulk of the Condorcet manuscripts is in the Bibliothèque de l'Institut de France; there are also papers relating to the *Esquisse* and his amorous life in the Bibliothèque Nationale. The edition of the *Esquisse* by O. H. Prior (Paris, 1933) has by no means clarified the numerous technical problems relating to the composition of this work, nor has it classified the many supplementary pieces. Since the edition of Condorcet's works in 1847–1849, his manuscripts have been studied for a variety of purposes: R. Doumic published a summary of his love letters to Mme. Suard in the *Revue des Deux Mondes*, V (1911), 302–325, 835–860, and VI (1912), 128–176; Léon Cahen published supplements to the *Esquisse* as "Condorcet Inédit. Notes pour le tableau des progrès de l'esprit humain" in *La Révolution française*, LXXV (1922), 199–212; Alberto Cento's inventory of the *Esquisse* manuscripts in "Dei Manoscritti del 'Tableau' de Condorcet" in *Istituto lombardo di scienze e lettere. Estratto dai Rendiconti. Classe di Lettere*, LXXXVII (1955), 312–324, leaves much to be desired; Gilles-Gaston Granger, in *La Mathématique sociale du Marquis de Condorcet*, utilized the scientific manuscripts with perspicacity. Léon Cahen, *Condorcet et la révolution française* (Paris, 1904), is the classical dissertation on his political career; it can be supplemented by Franck Alengry, *Condorcet guide de la Révolution française* (Paris, 1904), and Jacob Salwyn Schapiro, *Condorcet and the rise of liberalism* (New York, 1934). See also A. de Montfort, *Les Idées de Condorcet sur le suffrage* (Paris, 1925); C. Caillaud, *Les Idées économiques de Condorcet* (Paris, 1908); Hélène Delsaux, *Condorcet journaliste* (Paris, 1931). Cahen's work has a section entitled "Bibliographie," pp. xi–xxi, which covers the location of manuscripts, primary and secondary sources. Since both Alengry and Cahen appeared in the same year there was some contest at the time about who had priority in the discovery of certain manuscript sources. These works completely superseded Jean François Eugène Robinet, *Condorcet. Sa vie, son oeuvre* (Paris, 1893).

In recent years there has been substantial interest in Condorcet's "social mathematics"; see M. J. Laboulle, "La Mathématique sociale: Condorcet et ses prédécesseurs," in *Revue d'histoire littéraire de la France*, XXXVI (1939); but especially the writings of Gilles-Gaston Granger, "Langue universelle et formalisation des sciences," in *Revue d'histoire des sciences*, VII (1954), 197–219, and *La Mathématique sociale du marquis de Condorcet* (Paris, 1956).

The best commentaries on Condorcet the *philosophe* are A. Koyré, "Condorcet," in *Revue de Métaphysique et de Morale*, LIII (1948), 166–189; Pierre Sergescu, "La Contribution de Condorcet à l'Encyclopédie," *Revue d'histoire des sciences et de leurs applications*, IV (1951), 233–237; Alberto Cento, *Condorcet e l'idea di progresso* (Florence, 1956), whose "Nota Bibliografica," pp. 135–143, lists recent secondary literature and reports on the present status of the manuscripts; and Michelangelo Ghio, "Condorcet," in *Filosofia*, VI (1955), 227–263.

Of interest are the older memoirs on Condorcet: Antoine Diannyère, *Notice sur la vie et les ouvrages de Condorcet* (Leipzig, 1796); S. F. Lacroix, *Notice historique sur la vie et les ouvrages de Condorcet* (Paris, 1813); Mme. Suard, *Dernier écrit de Condorcet, précédé d'une notice sur ses derniers momens* (Paris, 1825). Among recent books on Condorcet of a miscellaneous character are Torau-Boyle, *Condorcet: marquis et philosophe, organisateur du monde moderne* (Paris, 1938); Robert Alt, *Erziehungsprogramme der Französischen Revolution. Mirabeau. Condorcet. Lepeletier* (Berlin, 1949); Condorcet, *Choix de textes*, introduction by J.-B. Séverac (Paris, 1930).

2. Condorcet, *Oeuvres*, I (Paris, 1847), viii.

3. The classical portrait by Mlle. de l'Espinasse is in *Oeuvres*, I, 626–635.

4. Correspondence of Condorcet with Mme. Amélie Suard, Bibliothèque Nationale, N.a.fr. 23639.

5. Marie-Louise-Sophie de Grouchy, *Théorie des sentimens moraux ou Essai analytique sur les principes des jugemens que portent naturellement les hommes . . . suivi d'une dissertation sur l'origine des langues. Huit lettres sur la sympathie*, 2 vols. (Paris, 1798). The most recent work on Mme. Condorcet is Henri Valentino, *Madame de Condorcet* (Paris, 1950). Jules Michelet's description is in *Les Femmes de la révolution* (Paris, 1883), pp. 92–93.

6. Condorcet, *Oeuvres*, I, 608.

7. Dr. Augustin Cabanès, *Les Indiscretions de l'histoire*, fifth series (Paris, 1903–1909), pp. 339ff., on the basis of documents published by Marius Barroux in *La Révolution française*, IX (1889), 173–185, concluded that he died of a cerebral hemorrhage. For a rectification of details in Michelet's account of Condorcet's death, which most historians have followed, see Gérard Walter's notes to his edition of Jules Michelet, *Histoire de la révolution française* (Paris, 1952), II, 1304–1306.

8. Condorcet, *Oeuvres*, VI, 5.

9. Michelet, *Les Femmes de la révolution*, p. 94.

10. Condorcet, "Conseil de Condorcet à sa fille," in *Oeuvres*, I, 617–618.

11. Valentino, *Madame de Condorcet*, p. 63.

12. Mme. Amélie Suard, *Essais de mémoire sur M. Suard* (Paris, 1820), p. 197.

13. Condorcet, *Esquisse* (Genoa, 1798), p. 250.

14. Thomas Robert Malthus, *An Essay on the Principles of Population, as it affects the future improvement of society. With remarks on the speculations of Mr. Godwin, M. Condorcet, and other writers* (London, 1798).

15. La Harpe and Chateaubriand spread the *canard* that Condorcet believed progress in science could render man immortal. François Picavet, *Les Idéologues* (Paris, 1891), p. 116fn.

16. Epochs I, V, and X.

17. Condorcet, *Oeuvres*, VI, 346.

18. Condorcet's atheism was outspoken. The contention of O. H. Prior in his edition of the *Esquisse* (Paris, 1933), pp. xi–xii, "He was certainly not an atheist," cannot be supported.

19. Quoted in Alberto Cento, *Condorcet e l'idea di progresso*, p. 84, from Institut de France, MS. 885, fasc. B, fol. 109.

20. Condorcet, *Esquisse* (Genoa, 1798), p. 24.

21. Quoted in Cento, *Condorcet*, p. 164.

22. Condorcet, *Mémoire sur l'instruction publique*, in *Oeuvres*, VII, 355.

23. Condorcet, *Esquisse* (Genoa, 1798), p. 26.

24. In his discourse of reception at the Académie Française, February 21, 1782, he had already made his commitment: "Each century will add new knowledge to the century which has preceded it, and these progressions, which nothing henceforth can either arrest or suspend, will have no other limits but those of the duration of the universe." *Oeuvres*, I, 390–391.

25. Condorcet, *Oeuvres*, I, 594.

26. Condorcet, *Fragment de l'histoire de la Xe époque*, in *Oeuvres*, VI, 516.

27. Condorcet, *Esquisse* (Genoa, 1798), p. 58.

28. *Ibid.*, pp. 236–237.

29. Condorcet, *Fragment de l'histoire de la première époque*, in *Oeuvres*, VI, 378–379.

30. James G. Frazer, in his essay on *Condorcet on the Progress of the Human Mind* (Oxford, 1933), p. 17, commented with characteristic understatement that he probably exaggerated "the moral obliquity of the class of men whom he criticized."

31. Condorcet, *Vie de Turgot*, p. 10.

32. Condorcet, *Esquisse* (Genoa, 1798), p. 128.

33. *Ibid.*, p. 88.

34. *Ibid.*, p. 129.

35. *Ibid.*, p. 129.

36. *Ibid.*, p. 162.

37. *Ibid.*, p. 164.

38. *Ibid.*, p. 168

39. *Ibid.*, p. 171.

40. Bibliothèque Nationale, N.a.fr. 4586, fol. 214.

41. Condorcet, *Esquisse* (Genoa, 1798), p. 210. A good deal of Condorcet's concern with the mass of the people was still of course quite abstract and remote. His articles on workers' education were quite patronizing: since they would still have to labor six days a week he would limit himself to the inculcation of a few simple moral precepts and the teaching of elementary laws of science. He seems to have been particularly annoyed by the religious ditties they sang while they worked; for these he would substitute moralizing rhymes, of which he left a few unfortunate examples.

> Le travail est souvent le père du plaisir
> Plaignons l'homme accablé du poids de son loisir

or

> Les mortels sont égaux. Ce n'est pas la naissance
> C'est la seule vertu qui fait leur différence.

Bibliothèque Nationale, N.a.fr. 23639.

42. *Esquisse* (Genoa, 1798), pp. 213–214.

43. *Ibid.*, p. 302.

44. The idea of cooperative scientific ventures had already been mentioned a number of times by Condorcet in the course of his *éloges* of deceased colleagues. *Eloge de Haller*, in *Oeuvres*, II, 307: "The successive progressions of these sciences can be the result of the combined works of a great number of men." *Eloge de Linnaeus*, in *Oeuvres*, II, 342, described the worldwide cooperation between Linnaeus and his admirers in reporting new specimens.

45. Condorcet, *Fragment sur l'Atlantide*, in *Oeuvres*, VI, 600.

46. *Ibid.*, VI, 598.

47. *Ibid.*, VI, 652.

48. *Ibid.*, VI, 657.

49. *Ibid.*, VI, 603.

50. Institut de France, MS. 885, fasc. C, fols. 9–10.

51. Condorcet, *Fragment sur l'Atlantide*, in *Oeuvres*, VI, 618.

52. *Ibid.*, VI, 600.

53. *Ibid.*, VI, 626.

54. *Ibid.*, VI, 628.

55. Condorcet, *Essai sur l'application de l'analyse à la probabilité des décisions rendues à la pluralité des voix* (Paris, 1785), p. i.

56. *Ibid.*, pp. clxxxvi-clxxxix.

57. Condorcet, "Tableau général de la Science, qui a pour objet l'application du calcul aux sciences politiques et morales," *Journal d'instruction sociale*, June 22 and July 6, 1795, in *Oeuvres*, I, 558.

58. Condorcet, *Fragment de l'histoire de la Xe époque*, in *Oeuvres*, VI, 595.

59. Bibliothèque Nationale, N.a.fr. 4586, fol. 190.

60. Léon Cahen, in "Condorcet Inédit. Notes pour le tableau des progrès de l'esprit humain," published fragments from N.a.fr. 4586 entitled "Effet, dans l'état moral et politique de l'espèce humaine, de quelques découvertes physiques comme du moyen de produire avec une certaine probabilité des enfants mâles ou femelles à son choix." These notes have never been published in their entirety. When first deposited at the Bibliothèque Nationale on February 12, 1812, they were described as "Manuscrits de M. Condorcet sur les connaissances humaines."

61. Bibliothèque Nationale, N.a.fr. 4586, fol. 207.

62. Léon Cahen, "Condorcet Inédit. Notes pour le tableau des progrès de l'esprit humain," p. 210.

63. Bibliothèque Nationale, N.a.fr. 4586, fol. 189.

64. Condorcet, *Oeuvres*, VII, 433.

65. Condorcet, "Discours lu à l'Académie des Sciences," in *Oeuvres*, I, 470.

66. Institut de France, MS 885, fasc. A, fol. 4.4°.

67. The *idéologues* of the *Décade philosophique* considered these last paragraphs as sublime as anything the philosophers of antiquity had written. Picavet, *Les Idéologues*, pp. 92–93.

68. Condorcet, *Esquisse* (Genoa, 1798), p. 339. After the sacking of Priestley's laboratory by a mob, Condorcet had written him in a similar vein from Paris, July 30, 1791: "The beautiful day of universal liberty will shine for our descendants; but we at least shall have witnessed the

dawn, we shall have enjoyed the hope, and you, sir, you have accelerated the moment by your works, by the example of your virtues. . . ." *Oeuvres*, I, 333-334.

CHAPTER III

COMTE DE SAINT-SIMON

1. The pioneer scholarly work on Saint-Simon was Georges Weill, *Un Précurseur du socialisme, Saint-Simon et son oeuvre* (Paris, 1896); the first to use archival materials was Maxime Leroy, *La Vie véritable du Comte Henri de Saint-Simon* (Paris, 1925); the second volume of Henri Gouhier, *La Jeunesse d'Auguste Comte* (Paris, 1933–1941) is largely devoted to Saint-Simon; the most recent general work is Frank E. Manuel, *The New World of Henri Saint-Simon* (Cambridge, Massachusetts, 1956), where bibliographical references are included in the section of notes, pp. 371-423. Mathurin Dondo, *The French Faust Henri Saint-Simon* (New York, 1955), is largely biographical.

Olinde Rodrigues first attempted to collect Saint-Simon's works in *Oeuvres complètes de Saint-Simon* (Paris, 1832). The *Oeuvres choisies de C. H. Saint-Simon, précédées d'un essai sur sa doctrine*, by Lemonnier, 3 vols. (Brussels, 1859), and the *Oeuvres de Saint-Simon et d'Enfantin*, 47 vols. (Paris, 1865–1878), cited as *Oeuvres*, are two collections which complement each other. *Selected Writings* have been edited and translated into English by F. M. H. Markham (Oxford, 1952). Jean Dautry's *Saint-Simon, Textes choisis* (Paris, 1951) includes excerpts from manuscripts in the Bibliothèque Nationale and in the La Sicotière Collection which had not previously been published.

In addition to the works mentioned above, interesting commentaries from a variety of different viewpoints are: Maxime Leroy, *Le Socialisme des producteurs* (Paris, 1924); V. Volgin, "Über die historische Stellung St. Simons," *Marx-Engels Archiv, Zeitschrift des Marx-Engels Institut*, II (1929), 82–119; E. Troeltsch, *Die Dynamik der Geschichte nach der Geschichtsphilosophie des Positivismus* (Berlin, 1919); Heinrich Cunow, "Saint-Simon als Geschichtstheoretiker," *Neue Zeit*, XXXVIII (1919), 281–287; Georges Dumas, *Psychologie de deux messies positivistes* (Paris, 1905); Alfred Pereire, *Autour de Saint-Simon* (Paris, 1912); Emile Durkheim, *Le Socialisme, sa définition, ses débuts, la doctrine saint-simonienne* (Paris, 1928), which is largely devoted to Saint-Simon. See also Viacheslav Petrovich Volgin, *Frantsuzskii Utopicheskii Kommunizm* (Moscow, 1960) and *Sen-Simon i Sen-Simonism* (Moscow, 1961).

Four sections of this chapter have appeared in print earlier in a more extensive form in: "The Role of the Scientist in Saint-Simon," *Revue internationale de philosophie*, XIV (1960), 344–356; "From Equality to Organicism," *Journal of the History of Ideas*, XVII (1956), 54–69; chaps. 26 and 31 of *The New World of Henri Saint-Simon*.

2. *Lettres d'un habitant de Genève*, in *Oeuvres de Saint-Simon et d'Enfantin*, XV, 22.

3. *Oeuvres choisies*, I, 141.

4. *Lettres de C.-H. Saint-Simon, 1ʳᵉ correspondance* (Paris, 1808), p. 74.

5. *Esquisse d'une nouvelle encyclopédie* (Paris, n.d.), p. 5.

6. *Opinions littéraires, philosophiques et industrielles* (Paris, 1825), pp. 374–375.

7. The "immortal physiologist" Bichat was by Saint-Simon's own testimony the source of his conception of mutually exclusive capacities, a theory which in *Du système industriel* he called a law of human organization. *Oeuvres*, XXII, 56. Xavier Bichat, *Physiological Researches upon Life and Death*, transl. by Tobias Watkins (Philadelphia, 1809), pp. 112–113. The work was originally published in France in the Year VIII (1799–1800).

8. *Oeuvres*, XXII, 17fn.

9. *Notice historique*, in *Oeuvres*, I, 122.

10. Condorcet, *Esquisse d'un tableau historique*, in *Oeuvres*, VI, 238.

11. The idea of the natural elite was developed by Saint-Simon in *L'Industrie*, in *Oeuvres*, XVIII, 142–145. The same conception had been adumbrated earlier in the fragment entitled "Sur la capacité de l'Empereur," in the *Introduction aux travaux scientifiques du XIX* siècle, in *Oeuvres choisies*.

12. *Oeuvres choisies*, I, 173.

13. *Introduction aux travaux scientifiques du XIX* siècle, in *Oeuvres choisies*, I, 143.

14. *L'Organisateur*, in *Oeuvres*, XX, 192.

15. *Oeuvres*, XX, 126–127fn.

16. *Oeuvres*, XX, 151.

17. *Oeuvres*, XX, 150.

18. Saint-Simon's solution of the problem of internecine conflict within the elite is reminiscent of Condorcet's treatment of jealousy among the scientists called upon to collaborate on grand international projects. "Once the true methods for studying the sciences, for making progress in them, are known, there cannot fail to exist among those who cultivate some one science with success a common opinion, accepted principles which they would not be able to transgress without violating an inner feeling, without giving themselves either a reputation for ignorance or for bad faith.

"These men are doubtless not exempt from the pettiness of self-love. They are not alien to jealousy. But they will not sacrifice to the impulses of these wretched passions the very object which inspires them." *Fragment sur l'Atlantide*, in *Oeuvres*, VI, 604.

19. *Suite à la brochure des Bourbons et des Stuarts*, in *Oeuvres choisies*, II, 444–445.

20. "Governments will no longer lead men. Their functions will be limited to preventing useful labors from being disturbed. They will have at their disposal but few powers and little money, because limited powers and little money should suffice to attain this end." *L'Industrie*, in *Oeuvres*, XVIII, 168.

21. The function of government was "to protect the men who work from the unproductive action of the idle, to maintain security and liberty in production." *Oeuvres*, XIX, 36.

22. *L'Organisateur*, in *Oeuvres*, XX, 200.

23. *Oeuvres*, XX, 202.

24. *Oeuvres*, XX, 199.

25. The belief that Olinde Rodrigues wrote the introduction is based

upon a manuscript note in a copy of the *Nouveau Christianisme* in the Bibliothèque de l'Arsenal, Fonds Enfantin 7802 (132) 8. Hoëné Wroński once told Frédéric de Rougemont that the *Nouveau Christianisme* was not written by Saint-Simon. Frédéric de Rougemont, *Les Deux cités. La philosophie de l'histoire aux différents âges de l'humanité*, 2 vols. (Paris, 1874), II, 439. This evidence by a rival Messiah is naturally suspect.

26. In a letter to John Stuart Mill on December 1, 1829, Gustave d'Eichthal, who was a close friend of Olinde Rodrigues, thus described the new religious orientation of Saint-Simon's last period: "Saint-Simon, after having in his early writings tried to reorganize society in the name of Science, after having later renewed the same attempt in the name of Industry, realized that he had mistaken the *means* for the *end*; that it is in the name of their *sympathies* that one must speak to men, and above all, in the name of their *religious sympathies*, which should summarize all others." J. S. Mill, *Correspondance inédite avec Gustave d'Eichthal* (Paris, 1898), pp. 75–76. D'Eichthal had written in his letter of November 23, 1829, that for two years none of the disciples was able to grasp the full meaning of the *Nouveau Christianisme. Correspondance*, p. 57fn. By December 1, 1829, the key had been discovered and the religion of Saint-Simon had been clothed in the language of romanticized Spinozism: "The religious doctrine of Saint-Simon has this *unitary* character which should gather about it all the men of the future. It puts neither *spirit* above *matter*, nor *matter* above *spirit*. It considers them as intimately united one with another, as being the condition one of the other, as being the two modes in which *being* is manifest, *living* being, *sympathetic* being." *Correspondance*, p. 74.

27. "But there is a science which is more important for society than physical and mathematical knowledge. It is the science which constitutes society, which serves as its base. It is morals. Now morals have followed a path absolutely contrary to that of the physical and mathematical sciences. More than eighteen hundred years have elapsed since its fundamental principle was produced, and since that time all the researches of men of the greatest genius have not been able to discover a principle superior in its generality or in its precision to the one formulated at that epoch by the founder of Christianity." *Nouveau Christianisme*, in *Oeuvres choisies*, III, 378–379.

28. "Les hommes doivent se conduire en frères à l'égard les uns des autres." *Oeuvres choisies*, III, 322. It is not absolutely clear to which New Testament text he refers. It could be the King James version equivalent in Romans xiii: "In love of the brethren be tenderly affectioned one to another." The epigraph of the *Nouveau Christianisme* was derived from passages in the French version of Romans xiii: "for he that loveth his neighbor hath fulfilled the law . . . and if there be any other commandment, it is summed up in this word, namely, Thou shalt love thy neighbor as thyself."

29. *Nouveau Christianisme*, in *Oeuvres choisies*, III, 322.

30. The primitive catechism to which Saint-Simon referred expressed the Golden Rule in a negative rather than a positive form.

31. *Oeuvres choisies*, III, 363–364.

32. *Oeuvres choisies*, III, 379.

33. Saint-Simon's limitation of Christianity to a set of moral principles, discarding all its dogmas, never sat well with religious thinkers. J. Régnier, "Les idées morales et religieuses de Saint-Simon," *Nouvelle Revue*, new series, XX (1903), 229–238; Rudolf Stammler, *Sozialismus und Christentum* (Leipzig, 1920), p. 83. De Lépine, *Le Dieu malgré lui*, p. 24, says that Saint-Simon sent a copy of the *Nouveau Christianisme* to the Pope. The romantic Catholic K. W. Schiebler, one of the first Germans to write about the new morality of Saint-Simon sympathetically, was of course repelled by the religious heresies; see his *Der Saint-Simonismus oder die Lehre Saint-Simon's und seiner Anhänger* (Leipzig, 1831).

34. C. Lemonnier, in the *Revue des cours littéraires*, XXI (1876), 383, was of the opinion that a total view of Saint-Simon's works could, despite the contradictions, only lead to the conclusion that "he died as he lived, that he remained to the end in the ranks of the free-thinkers." Professor Henri Gouhier's judgment is categoric: "The Saint-Simonism of Saint-Simon is not a religion, but a social philosophy disguised as a religion." *La Jeunesse d'Auguste Comte* (Paris, 1933–1941), III, 231.

35. Alfred de Musset's description of his generation in *La Confession d'un enfant du siècle* (Paris, 1937), pp. 19, 24: "Alas! Alas! Religion is vanishing. . . . We no longer have either hope or expectation, not even two little pieces of black wood in a cross before which to wring our hands. . . . Everything that was is no more. All that will be is not yet."

36. *Enseignements d'Enfantin*, in *Oeuvres*, XIV, 4. Rodrigues's speech of December 31, 1829, confirms this. "The *Christianisme*, thanks to my perseverance, was read, reread, and each day more and more understood." Bibliothèque de l'Arsenal, Fonds Enfantin, 7644.

37. *Enseignements d'Enfantin*, in *Oeuvres*, XIV, 5, 9–10.

38. *Nouveau Christianisme*, in *Oeuvres*, XXIII, 182–183.

39. *Oeuvres*, XXIII, 183.

40. *Oeuvres*, XXIII, 184

41. *Oeuvres*, XXIII, 184–185.

42. *Oeuvres*, XXIII, 185.

43. *Notice historique*, in *Oeuvres*, II, 115, 116. Rodrigues quoted Saint-Simon in a speech delivered on December 31, 1829, when he resigned the direction of the school. Bibliothèque de l'Arsenal, Fonds Enfantin, 7644.

44. *Oeuvres*, XXXVII, p. xxxvi.

45. *Oeuvres*, XXII, 248.

46. *Oeuvres*, XXII, 250–251.

47. *Oeuvres*, XXII, 132.

CHAPTER IV

CHILDREN OF SAINT-SIMON

1. The classical scholarly work on the Saint-Simonians remains Sébastien Camille Gustave Charléty, *Histoire du Saint-Simonisme* (Paris, 1931), which superseded the pioneer study by Georges Weill, *L'Ecole saint-simonienne: son histoire, son influence jusqu'à nos jours* (Paris, 1896).

Henry-René d'Allemagne, *Les Saint-Simoniens* (Paris, 1930), is noteworthy primarily for its illustrations. Georg G. Iggers, *The Cult of Authority. The Political Philosophy of the Saint-Simonians. A Chapter in the History of Totalitarianism* (The Hague, 1958), the most recent general work, identifies its orientation in the title. Both Charléty, pp. 365–379, and Iggers, pp. 195–203, have bibliographies. Charléty expanded Henry Fournel's meticulous *Bibliographie Saint-Simonienne* (Paris, 1833) to include the secondary literature up to 1931; Iggers has covered the literature of the last quarter century in the major European languages, though in his zeal for completeness he has sometimes erroneously included items which refer to the Duke de Saint-Simon and not to the founder of Saint-Simonism. For a study of the ideas of the Saint-Simonians the *Doctrine de Saint-Simon. Exposition. Première année, 1829*, edited by C. Bouglé and Elie Halévy (Paris, 1924), is the key work, profusely and brilliantly annotated. The *Doctrine* has been translated into English by Iggers (Boston, 1958).

Enfantin's works were published in the eccentrically edited *Oeuvres de Saint-Simon et d'Enfantin* (Paris, 1865–1878); his writings appear as vols. XIV, XVI, XVII, XXIV–XXXVI, XLVI. The two principal Saint-Simonian journals were *Le Producteur, journal philosophique de l'industrie, des sciences et des beaux-arts* (Paris, 1825–1826), 5 vols., and *Le Globe* (Paris, 1830–1832), vols. IX-XII.

A number of studies of the thirties and forties merit special notice because the ideas of the Saint-Simonians were often transmitted to European intellectuals through their summaries rather than in the original writings of the school. Karl Gottlieb Bretschneider, *Der Saint-Simonismus und das Christentum* (Leipzig, 1832); Moritz Veit, *Saint-Simon und der Saint-Simonismus* (Leipzig, 1834); Louis Reybaud, *Etudes sur les réformateurs ou socialistes modernes* (Paris, 1840); Lorenz von Stein, *Der Sozialismus und Communismus des heutigen Frankreichs* (Leipzig, 1842); Karl Grün, *Die soziale Bewegung in Frankreich und Belgien* (Darmstadt, 1845).

Charléty was the first to use the rich Saint-Simonian archives in the Bibliothèque de l'Arsenal, though he did not exhaust the materials. Within the last decade a number of articles have again turned to manuscript sources: G. D. Zioutos, "Le Saint-Simonisme hors de France: quelques cahiers inédits sur l'expédition à l'Egypte," *Revue d'histoire économique et sociale*, XXXI (1953), 23–49; F. B. Duroselle, "Michel Chevalier, saint-simonien," *Revue historique*, LXXXII (1956), 292–306. The Pereire Collection in the Bibliothèque Nationale is now catalogued and available.

The literary influence of the Saint-Simonians has been studied in numerous books and articles: E. M. Butler, *The Saint-Simonian Religion in Germany* (Cambridge, 1926); Margaret A. Clarke, *Heine et la Monarchie de Juillet: étude critique sur les Französische Zustände suivie d'une étude sur le Saint-Simonisme chez Heine* (Paris, 1927); D. C. Evans, "Vigny and the Doctrine de Saint-Simon," *Romanic Review*, XXXIX (1948), 22–29; Fritz Gerathewohl, *Saint-Simonistische Ideen in der deutschen Literatur* (Munich, 1920); Paul Hazard, "Saint-Simonisme et littérature," *Néophilologue*, XXIII (1937–38), 129–134; Maxime Leroy, "Le Saint-Simonisme de Sainte-Beuve," *Zeitschrift für Sozialforschung*, VII (1938), nos. 1–2; Hill Shine, *Carlyle and the Saint-Simonians: The Conception of Historical Peri-*

10. Charles Pellarin, *Fourier, sa vie et sa théorie* (Paris, 1849), p. 104.

11. Emile Poulat, *Les manuscrits de Fourier* (Paris, 1957), pp. 14-15.

12. Franco Venturi, *Roots of Revolution: A History of the Populist and Socialist Movements in Nineteenth Century Russia* (New York, 1960), 83.

13. *Théorie des quatre mouvements et des destinées générales. Prospectus et annonce de la découverte* (1808), in *Oeuvres complètes*, I, 7-8.

14. Archives Nationales, 10 AS 20.

15. Archives Nationales, 10 AS 20.

16. Archives Nationales, 10 AS 40, letter of Just Muiron to Mme. Clarisse Vigoureux, May 12, 1832.

17. *La Phalange*, IX (1849), 200.

18. *Théorie des quatre mouvements, Oeuvres complètes*, I, 143-144.

19. Archives Nationales, 10 AS 20 (3).

20. *Traité de l'association domestique-agricole* (1822), *Oeuvres complètes*, II, 413.

21. *Théorie de l'unité universelle, Oeuvres complètes*, IV, 462.

22. *Oeuvres complètes*, VI, 47.

23. *Du Garantisme*, in *La Phalange*, IX (1849), 328.

24. *Théorie des quatre mouvements, Oeuvres complètes*, I, 115.

25. Archives Nationales, 10 AS 8.

26. Archives Nationales, 10 AS 8 (4).

27. Charles Pellarin, *Lettre de Fourier au grand juge, 4 nivôse an XII* (Paris, 1874), pp. 24-25.

28. *Lettre de Fourier au grand juge*, p. 22.

29. Hawthorne started out enthusiastic about his labors with the dung pile of Brook Farm. ". . . There is nothing so unseemly and disagreeable in this sort of toil as thou wouldst think. It defiles the hands, indeed, but not the soul. This gold ore is a pure and wholesome substance; else our Mother Nature would not devour it so readily, and derive so much nourishment from it, and return such a rich abundance of good grain and roots in requital of it," Nathaniel Hawthorne wrote to his wife on May 4, 1841 (p. 73 in *The Heart of Hawthorne's Journal*, edited by Newton Arvin, Boston, 1929). By the beginning of June the tune had changed. "It is my opinion, dearest, that a man's soul may be buried and perish under a dung-heap or in a furrow of the field, just as well as under a pile of money" (p. 74).

30. *Notions préliminaires sur les Séries et l'éducation naturelle*, in *La Phalange*, VII (1848), 138.

31. MS letter to the *Gazette de France*, Archives Nationales, 10 AS (7).

32. MS letter to the *Gazette de France*, Archives Nationales, 10 AS (7).

33. *La Fausse industrie morcelée, répugnante, mensongère et l'antidote, l'industrie naturelle, combinée, attrayante, véridique, donnant quadruple produit* (Paris, 1835), pp. 360-361.

34. *Oeuvres complètes*, VI, 403.

35. MS letter to the *Gazette de France*, Archives Nationales, 10 AS (7).

odicity (Baltimore, 1941); Marguérite Thibert, "Le rôle social de l'art d'après les Saint-Simoniens," *Revue d'histoire économique et sociale*, XIII (1925), 181-195; Ella M. Murphy, "Carlyle and the Saint-Simonians," *Studies in Philology*, XXXIII (1936), 93-118; Werner Suhge, *Saint-Simonismus und Junges Deutschland; das saint-simonistische System in der deutschen Literatur des ersten hälfte des 19. Jahrhunderts* (Berlin, 1935); Paul Bonnefon, "Maxime du Camp et les Saint-Simoniens," *Revue d'histoire littéraire de la France*, XVII (1910), 709-835.

The economic doctrines and activities of the Saint-Simonians have received special treatment in Henry René d'Allemagne, *Prosper Enfantin et les grandes entreprises du XIX* siècle* (Paris, 1935); Rondo E. Cameron, "The Crédit Mobilier and the Economic Development of Europe," *Journal of Political Economy*, LXI (1953), 461-488; E. S. Mason, "The Rationalization of Industry," *Quarterly Journal of Economics*, XLV (1930), 640-685; and Johann Plenge, *Gründung und Geschichte des Crédit Mobilier* (Tübingen, 1903). The problems of the diffusion of Saint-Simonism have been studied in H. Hauser, "Problèmes d'influences. Le Saint-Simonisme au Brésil," *Annales d'histoire économique et sociale*, IX (1937), 1-7; O. Noordenbosch, "Le Saint-Simonisme in Nederland," *Nederlands Archief*, n.s. XXIII (ca. 1931-1932), 281-283; Richard K. P. Pankhurst, "Saint-Simonism in England," *Twentieth Century*, CLII (1952), 499-512, and CLIII (1953), 47-58; Louis Paoli, "Le Saint-Simonisme en Italie," *Revue d'économie politique*, XII (1898), 689-710.

2. Edouard Charton, *Mémoires d'un prédicateur Saint-Simonien* (Paris, 1831), pp. 22-23.

3. *Enseignement des ouvriers, séance du 25 déc. 1831* (Paris, 1832), pp. 16-17.

4. *Religion Saint-Simonienne. Cérémonie du 27 novembre* (Paris, 1831), p. 4.

5. *Procès en la cour d'assises de la Seine, les 27 et 28 août 1832* (Paris, 1832). Extract from an *Enseignement* of November 19, 1831, p. 75.

6. *Procès en la cour d'assises*, p. 76.

7. *Procès en la cour d'assises*, p. 78.

8. Abel Transon, *Affranchissement des femmes; prédication du 1ᵉʳ janvier* (Paris, 1832).

9. *Retraite de Ménilmontant* (Paris, 1832), p. 15.

10. *Doctrine de Saint-Simon*, ed. Bouglé and Halévy, pp. 121-122.

11. *Doctrine de Saint-Simon*, pp. 157-158.

12. *Doctrine de Saint-Simon*, p. 340.

13. *Correspondance. Articles extraits du Globe* (Paris, 1831), p. 53.

14. *Doctrine de Saint-Simon*, p. 267.

15. *Doctrine de Saint-Simon*, p. 141.

16. *Doctrine de Saint-Simon*, pp. 404-405.

17. *Doctrine de Saint-Simon*, pp. 418-419.

18. *Doctrine de Saint-Simon*, pp. 211, 193.

19. *Doctrine de Saint-Simon*, p. 164.

20. *Doctrine de Saint-Simon*, pp. 166-167.

21. *Religion Saint-Simonienne. Cérémonie du 27 novembre* (Paris, 1831), p. 17.

22. *Doctrine de Saint-Simon*, p. 248.
23. *Doctrine de Saint-Simon*, p. 353.
24. *Doctrine de Saint-Simon*, p. 261.
25. *Doctrine de Saint-Simon*, p. 274.
26. *Doctrine de Saint-Simon*, p. 276.
27. *Doctrine de Saint-Simon*, p. 347.
28. *Doctrine de Saint-Simon*, p. 346.
29. *Doctrine de Saint-Simon*, p. 343.
30. *Doctrine de Saint-Simon*, p. 320.
31. *Doctrine de Saint-Simon*, p. 323.
32. *Doctrine de Saint-Simon*, pp. 278-279.
33. *Doctrine de Saint-Simon*, pp. 382-383.
34. Maxime du Camp, *Souvenirs littéraires* (Paris, 1883), II, 124.
35. For descriptions of the trial see Charléty, *Histoire du Saint-Simonisme*, pp. 175-185; *Oeuvres de Saint-Simon et d'Enfantin*, VII, 197-256; d'Allemagne, *Les Saint-Simoniens*, pp. 294-302.
36. *Procès en la cour d'assises*, p. 63.
37. *Procès en la cour d'assises*, p. 194.
38. *Procès en la cour d'assises*, p. 221.
39. *Procès en la cour d'assises*, pp. 206-207.
40. *Procès en la cour d'assises*, p. 212.
41. *Procès en la cour d'assises*, p. 218.
42. Duroselle, "Michel Chevalier saint-simonien," p. 240.
43. Prosper Enfantin, *La Vie Eternelle, passée, présente, future* (Paris, 1861), p. 49.
44. Enfantin, *La Vie Eternelle*, p. 79.
45. Quoted in Charléty, *Histoire du Saint-Simonisme*, p. 324.

CHAPTER V

CHARLES FOURIER

1. The most recent summary of the present state of Fourierist studies may be found in the introduction by Henri Desroche, "Fouriérisme écrit et Fouriérisme pratiqué. Notes sur les études fouriéristes contemporaines," to Emile Poulat, *Les Cahiers manuscrits de Fourier. Etude historique et inventaire raisonné* (Paris, 1957), pp. 6-36. The bibliographical emphasis in this introduction is on the Fourierist school and the diffusion of Fourierism throughout the world rather than on the works of Fourier himself. Hubert Bourgin, *Fourier* (Paris, 1905), still remains the most comprehensive scholarly study of the man and his works; its bibliography, pp. 17-45, is an excellent presentation of primary and secondary sources published before 1905. M. Lansac, *Les conceptions méthodologiques et sociales de Charles Fourier* (Paris, 1926), has not superseded Bourgin's work. Charles Gide, *Fourier précurseur de la coopération* (Paris, 1922-1923); C. Bouglé, *Socialismes Français* (Paris, 1932); and H. Louvancour, *De Henri Saint-Simon à Fourier. Etude sur le socialisme romantique français de 1830* (Chartres, 1913), are significant studies of Fourier himself. Despite the fact

that the Fourier manuscripts were available to both Bour[g] no study of Fourier has significantly explored the materi Archives Nationales, for which Emile Poulat prepared his ventaire raisonné." The manuscript inventory in the Arch by Edith Thomas is more detailed, but it does not indica[t] manuscripts has been published, as Poulat does. Hubert Bo[ ] of these manuscript sources (p. 24) is one of the major ina[ ] classic work.

The most significant bibliography of Fourierist lite[ ] ing separate chronological sections on the works of Fouri[ ] school, periodicals, and books on Fourierism, is the invento[ ] erist collection in the Biblioteca Feltrinelli (Milan) firs[ ] Giuseppe del Bo in the *Movimento Operaio*, N.S. I (1953), and expanded in 1957 as *Il Socialismo Utopistico. Charles Fo[ ] Societaria (1801-1922). Saggio Bibliografico* (Milan, 1957)[ ] *Oeuvres complètes* appeared in Paris, 1841-1845, 6 vols., bu[ ] does not include Fourier's manuscripts published in *La Phal[ ]*

There is a thesis in the Faculté de Droit at the University by M. Buchs entitled "Le Fouriérisme aux Etats-Unis; contr[ ] du socialisme américain"; the most extensive published gui[ ] Fourierism is J. W. Eaton and S. M. Katz, *Research Guide [ ] Group Farming* (New York, 1942). The standard work [ ] rierism is G. Sourine, *Le Fouriérisme en Russie* (Paris, [ ] many respects it has been superseded by Franco Venturi'[s] the second edition of Louis Reybaud, *Etudes sur les réform[ ] istes modernes* won the prix Monthyon of the Académie F[ ] most of the nineteenth century his treatment of Saint-Sim[ ] Owen as "utopian socialists" became canonical. Among mo[ ] al histories of socialism the section on Fourier in H. P. *Socialisten Personen en Stelsels* (Amsterdam, 1921), II, 113[ ] Ramm, *Die Grossen Sozialisten als Rechts- und Sozialphiloso[ ]* 1955), are worthy of note. Ramm's selective bibliograph[ ] includes the most recent international literature on Fourier. bibliography the extensive index work of E. Silberling, *sociologie phalanstérienne. Guide des oeuvres complètes de [ ]* (Paris, 1911; 459 pp.), deserves special mention.

2. "La Nouvelle Isabelle," in *La Phalange*, IX (1849), 2[ ]
3. See Victor Considérant, *Exposition abrégée du systè[ ] de Fourier* (Paris, 1846), 3rd edition of his lectures of 184[ ] and simplification of Fourier in which the whole system i[ ] organization of labor.
4. *Oeuvres complètes*, VI, 398-399.
5. E. Silberling, *Dictionnaire de sociologie phalanstéri[ ] oeuvres complètes de Charles Fourier* (Paris, 1911).
6. Archives Nationales, 10 AS 20.
7. Archives Nationales, 10 AS 20: notebooks.
8. Archives Nationales, 10 AS 20.
9. Archives Nationales, 10 AS 21 (13), letter of F[o] Considérant, Paris, October 3, 1831.

36. MS letter to the *Gazette de France*, Archives Nationales, 10 AS 20 (7).

37. "Fragments," *La Phalange*, IX (1849), 456–457.

38. "Fragments," *La Phalange*, IX (1849), 453–454.

39. "Fragments," *La Phalange*, IX (1849), 454.

40. "Fragments," *La Phalange*, IX (1849), 455.

41. Archives Nationales, 10 AS 8 (4).

42. Archives Nationales, 10 AS 8 (4).

43. *Théorie des quatre mouvements, Oeuvres complètes*, I, 117.

44. *La Phalange*, IX (1849), 204.

45. Archives Nationales, 10 AS 8.

46. *De la sériosophie*, in *La Phalange*, IX, 48.

47. Archives Nationales, 10 AS 8.

48. Archives Nationales, 10 AS 8.

49. Archives Nationales, 10 AS 8.

50. Archives Nationales, 10 AS 8.

51. *La Phalange*, IX (1849), 195.

52. *La Phalange*, IX (1849), 194.

53. *La Phalange*, IX (1849), 197.

54. *La Phalange*, IX (1849), 202.

55. "Le Sphinx sans Oedipe ou l'énigme des quatre mouvements," in *La Phalange*, IX (1849), 204.

56. "Le Sphinx sans Oedipe," *La Phalange*, IX (1849), 214.

57. *La Phalange*, IX (1849), 223.

58. *La Phalange*, IX (1849), 224.

59. *Oeuvres complètes*, I, 219.

60. After the incident he was called a "petit massacre, enragé d'enfant." *Théorie de l'unité universelle*, in *Oeuvres complètes*, V, 41–42.

CHAPTER VI

AUGUSTE COMTE

1. There is no critical edition of Comte's works. His most important writings and collections of his letters are here presented in the chronological order of their initial publication: *Système de politique positive. Tome premier. Première partie* (Paris, 1824), an essay; *Cours de philosophie positive* (Paris, 1830–1842), 6 vols. — a condensation by Harriet Martineau in 2 vols. appeared in London in 1853 and won Comte's approval; *Traité élémentaire de géométrie analytique à deux et à trois dimensions* (Paris, 1843); *Discours sur l'esprit positif*, prefixed to the *Traité philosophique d'astronomie populaire* (Paris, 1844) — an English translation of the *Discours* appeared in London in 1883; *Discours sur l'ensemble du positivisme, ou Exposition sommaire de la doctrine sociale . . . à la grande république occidentale composée des cinq populations avancées, française, italienne, germanique, britannique, et espagnole* (Paris, 1848), English transl., London, 1865; *Calendrier positiviste, ou Système général de commémoration publique, destiné surtout à la transition finale de la grande République occidentale*

(Paris, 1849), English transl., London, 1894; *Système de politique positive, ou Traité de sociologie instituant la religion de l'humanité* (Paris, 1851–1854), 4 vols., English transl. by J. H. Bridges, Frederic Harrison, and others, London, 1875–1877; *Catéchisme positiviste, ou Sommaire exposition de la religion universelle en onze entretiens systématiques entre une femme et un prêtre de l'humanité* (Paris, 1852), English transl., London, 1858; *Bibliothèque du prolétaire au dix neuvième siècle, conseillée par l'auteur du Système de philosophie positive et du Système de politique positive* (Paris, 1852), English transl., London, 1886; *Appel aux conservateurs* (Paris, 1855), English transl., London, 1889; *Synthèse subjective, ou Système universel des conceptions propres à l'état normal de l'humanité. Tome premier, contenant le Système de logique positive, ou Traité de philosophie mathématique* (Paris, 1856), English transl., London, 1891; *Lettres . . . à M. Valat . . . 1815–1844*, ed. by P. Valat (Paris, 1870); *Lettres . . . à John Stuart Mill, 1841–1844* (Paris, 1877); *Essais de philosophie mathématique*, ed. from unpublished papers by Pierre Laffitte (Paris, 1878); *Testament d'Auguste Comte, avec les documents qui s'y rapportent; pièces justificatives, prières quotidiennes, confessions annuelles, correspondance avec Mme. de Vaux. Publié par ses exécuteurs testamentaires* (Paris, 1884), English transl., Liverpool, 1910; *Lettres à Richard Congreve* (London, 1889); *Lettres à des positivistes anglais* (London, 1889); *Lettres à Henry Edger et à John Metcalf*, ed. by J. Lagarrigue (Paris, 1889); *Lettres à Henry Dix Hutton* (Dublin, 1890); *Correspondance inédite d'Auguste Comte*, 4 sér. (Paris, 1903, 1904); *Lettres inédites à C. de Blignières. Présentées par Paul Arbousse-Bastide* (Paris, 1932); *Nouvelles lettres inédites. Textes présentés par Paulo E. de Berredo-Carneiro* (Paris, 1939).

The only significant scholarly works written on Auguste Comte in recent years have been done by three French scholars. Henri Gouhier, *La vie d'Auguste Comte* (Paris, 1931), is still the best biography; *La jeunesse d'Auguste Comte et la formation du positivisme*, 3 vols. (Paris, 1933, 1936, 1941), is the most complete work on Comte's intellectual origins and early development. Pierre Ducassé, *Méthode et intuition chez Auguste Comte* (Paris, 1939), is a brilliant philosophical analysis from the viewpoint indicated in the title; he is also the author of *La méthode positive et l'intuition comtienne* (Paris, 1940). The recent work by Paul Arbousse-Bastide, *La doctrine de l'éducation universelle dans la philosophie d'Auguste Comte* (Paris, 1957), 2 vols., is more comprehensive than its name seems to imply; it also has a bibliography (II, 717–724) which supplements the work by Ducassé. Among noteworthy older treatments outside of those in the standard histories of philosophy are George Dumas, *Psychologie de deux messies positivistes: Saint-Simon et Auguste Comte* (Paris, 1905); L. Lévy-Bruhl, *La philosophie d'Auguste Comte* (Paris, 1900); E. de Seillière, *Auguste Comte* (Paris, 1924); J. Delvolvé, *Réflexions sur la pensée comtienne* (Paris, 1908). M. Uta, *La loi des trois états dans la philosophie d'Auguste Comte* (Paris, 1928) is a good summary of this controversial theory. Two articles on Comte as a historian of science deserve special mention: Paul Tannery, "Comte et l'histoire des sciences," *Revue générale des sciences*, XVI (1905), 410–417, and George Sarton, "Auguste Comte, Historian of Science," *Osiris*, X (1952), 328–357. See also Donald Geoffrey Charlton,

Positivist Thought in France During the Second Empire (Oxford, 1959).

2. The long letter to M. Emile Tabarié *fils* of April 5, 1824, contains Comte's fullest account of his quarrel with Saint-Simon. Comte, *Lettres à divers* (Paris, 1905), II, 3–7.

3. *Lettres à divers*, II, 6: Comte to Tabarié *fils*, April 5, 1824.

4. *Lettres à divers*, II, 35–36; Comte to Gustave d'Eichthal, May 1, 1824.

5. *Lettres à divers*, II, 104; Comte to Gustave d'Eichthal, December 9, 1828.

6. *Lettres à divers*, II, 107: Comte to Gustave d'Eichthal, December 7, 1829.

7. *Lettres à divers*, II, 169–170: Comte to Michel Chevalier, January 5, 1832.

8. *Notice historique*, in *Oeuvres de Saint-Simon et d'Enfantin* (Paris, 1865–1878), V, 115, 117: Michel Chevalier to Comte.

9. Richard L. Hawkins, *Auguste Comte and the United States* (Cambridge, Mass., 1936), pp. 81–82.

10. Hawkins, *Auguste Comte*, pp. 115–116: Auguste Comte to George F. Holmes, September 18, 1852.

11. Comte, *Correspondance inédite*, II, 255: Comte to M. Hadéry, August 8, 1853.

12. For a résumé of the controversy see Frank E. Manuel, *The New World of Henri Saint-Simon* (Cambridge, Mass., 1956), p. 419, note 29.

13. H.-P. Deroisin, *Notes sur Auguste Comte par un de ses disciples* (Paris, 1909), pp. 20–21.

14. The manuscripts of the *Prospectus* in the Archives Positivistes, Paris. See also Laffitte, "Matériaux pour servir à la biographie d'Auguste Comte," *Revue occidentale*, VIII (1882), 315–324.

15. Deroisin offered striking proof of the obscurity which began to envelop Comte after his attack of insanity: "In 1828 the bibliographer Quérard gave him as having already died in the beginning of 1827." *Notes sur Auguste Comte*, p. 27.

16. Emile Littré, *Principes de philosophie positive par Auguste Comte, précédés de la préface d'un disciple* (Paris, 1868), p. 14.

17. Auguste Comte to Mme. Austin, April 4, 1844, *Lettres à divers* (Paris, 1905), II, 276.

18. Emile Littré, *De la philosophie positive* (Paris, 1845), p. 102.

19. Auguste Comte to Pierre Laffitte, August 30, 1855, *Correspondance inédite*, II, 183.

20. Deroisin, *Notes sur Auguste Comte*, p. 57.

21. Auguste Comte to Hadéry, July 7, 1857, *Correspondance inédite*, II, 390.

22. E. Caro, *M. Littré et le positivisme* (Paris, 1883), p. 120.

23. André Poëy, *M. Littré et Auguste Comte* (Paris, 1880), pp. 8, 9.

24. *Rapport de la Société positiviste par la Commission chargée d'examiner la nature et le plan du nouveau Gouvernement révolutionnaire de la République Française* (Paris, 1848).

25. Deroisin, *Notes sur Auguste Comte*, p. 52.

26. Quoted by Henri Gouhier, *La vie d'Auguste Comte*, p. 277.

27. See Charles de Rouvre, *Auguste Comte et le Catholicisme* (Paris, 1928).

28. Auguste Comte to Dr. Audiffrent, January 29, 1851, *Lettres à divers*, I², 21.

29. James H. Billington, "The Intelligentsia and the Religion of Humanity," *American Historical Review*, LXV (1960), 807–821.

30. On Positivism in Brazil see Antonio Gomes d'Azevedo Sampaïo, *Essai sur l'histoire du positivisme au Brésil* (Paris, 1899); Clovis Bevilaqua, *A philosophia positiva no Brasil* (Recife, 1883); Hermann Dohms, *Der Positivismus in Brazilien* (São Leopoldo, 1931); Sylvio Roméro, *O evolucionismo e o positivismo no Brasil* (Rio de Janeiro, 1895).

31. On Positivism in England see John Edwin McGee, *A Crusade for Humanity: The History of Organized Positivism in England* (London, 1931).

32. See Hermann Gruber, *Der Positivismus vom Tode Auguste Comte's bis auf unsere Tage* (Freiburg, 1891).

33. Comte, *Système de politique positive*, III, 63.

34. Comte, *Système de politique positive*, III, 75.

35. Comte, *Système de politique positive*, III, 595–596.

36. Comte, *Système de politique positive*, III, 67.

37. Henri Gouhier, "La Philosophie de l'histoire d'Auguste Comte," *Journal of World History*, II (1955), 507, called it "a philosophy of history of the spirit via the sciences." See also F. A. Hayek, "Comte and Hegel," *Measure*, II (1951), 324–341.

38. Comte, *Système de politique positive*, II, 466.

39. Comte, *Système de politique positive*, I, 733.

40. Auguste Comte to Clothilde de Vaux, March 11, 1846, *Testament*, p. 551.

41. Comte, *Système de politique positive*, IV, 276–277.

42. Comte, *Système de politique positive*, II, 141.

43. Comte, *Système de politique positive*, II, 57.

44. Comte, *Système de politique positive*, II, 145.

45. Comte, *Système de politique positive*, II, 168–169.

EPILOGUE

REFLECTIONS ON THE NEW PROPHECY

1. Correspondence of Condorcet with Mme. Suard, Bibliothèque Nationale, N.a.fr. 23639 (55).

2. Schelle edition, I, 340–341.

3. Schelle edition, III, 683–686: "Catalogue des livres imaginaires dont les dos figuraient dans une fausse bibliothèque du cabinet de Turgot."

4. Gustave d'Eichthal knew of Hegel from his stay in Berlin. During Saint-Simonian discussions, to accuse a man of agreeing with Hegel, as d'Eichthal accused Michel Chevalier on one occasion when he grew too subtle, was to charge him with uttering metaphysical nonsense. "Hegel would not have disavowed him," was d'Eichthal's parting shot at the conclu-

sion of a heated controversy on June 15, 1830. Bibliothèque Nationale, Collection Alfred Pereire, N.a.fr. 24609.

5. In the *Calendrier Positiviste*, Hegel Day was the twenty-seventh of Descartes, the eleventh month of the year, consecrated to modern philosophy (Comte, *Système de politique positive*, V, insert between pp. 402 and 403), but there is no serious discussion of Hegel in Comte's works.

6. Hegel, *Grundlinien der Philosophie des Rechts oder Naturrecht und Staatswissenschaft im Grundrisse*, 3rd ed. (Berlin, 1854), p. 20.

7. Karl Marx, *Marx über Feuerbach*, in *Gesamtausgabe*, part I, vol. V (Berlin, 1932), p. 535.

8. Condorcet, *Oeuvres*, I, 114.

9. Saint-Simon put these words into Socrates' mouth in an imaginary discourse delivered to his pupils. *Travail sur la gravitation universelle*, in *Oeuvres*, XL, 254.

10. The idea is developed in *L'Organisateur*, in *Oeuvres*, XX, 118–119, and in stray papers which ended up in the Léon Duchesne de la Sicotière Collection and were sold at auction in Paris, November 30, 1959.

11. "Pensées diverses," manuscript in the Turgot archives, Château de Lantheuil.

12. Schelle edition, I, 102–104.

13. Condorcet's notes for the *Esquisse*, Bibliothèque Nationale, N.a.fr. 4586.

14. Condorcet's notes for the *Esquisse*, Bibliothèque Nationale, N.a.fr. 4586.

15. Condorcet, "Epître d'un polonais exilé en Sibérie à sa femme," in *Oeuvres*, I, 606.

16. In his 1832 edition of Saint-Simon's *Lettres d'un habitant de Genève*, Olinde Rodrigues capitalized the sentence, "Les femmes seront admises, elles pourront être nommées," in order to cite the authority of the master for the "emancipation of women" (*Oeuvres*, XVI, 11).

17. Bibliothèque Nationale, Collection Alfred Pereire, N.a.fr. 24608.

18. In the transition period the Saint-Simonians held intimate "doctrinal dinners" to make important converts. When they once encountered a scientist who had worked with Arago, Poisson, and Clouet in Saint-Simon's "scientific institute" of his wild Directorate days, they were at first nonplussed by the realistic and hardly flattering portrait of their master which he painted. Then, recovering, they turned the tables on the skeptic as they called upon him to contemplate the miracle of "an immoral madman producing scholarly and moral disciples." Bibliothèque Nationale, Collection Alfred Pereire, N.a.fr. 24608 (284).

19. Eugène Rodrigues saw in the symbol of Jacob's dream "the history of humanity becoming all love by the transfiguration of God in it." Enfantin was critical: "One should relate the future to the past but beware of finding all the future in the past." Bibliothèque Nationale, Collection Alfred Pereire, N.a.fr. 24608 (274).

20. Charles Duveyrier's canticles are characteristic of the prosaic, if fervent, character of their literary expression: "I should like to paint this future which I see as if it were there, with all its celebrations, its scientific and industrial inventions, its hierarchy, its works, on land and sea, in the air, every-

where movement, a crowd and the most perfect order, the monuments, the convents, the shops, the wonders of art, the blaze of colors, the perfumes, the concerts, the dances, the religious performances, and the moral well-being, social and individual love which grows, grows, grows always, always!" Bibliothèque Nationale, Collection Alfred Pereire, N.a.fr. 24609 (457 verso).

21. "My life is one. It manifests itself in me, outside of me, and in the *union* of the me and the non-me. This last respect is, properly speaking, the unity of my being, but all three are indispensable for me to love, to understand, and to protect life. Microcosm and macrocosm, union of the little and the great worlds, that is life.

"I must be as much in you as in myself because my life is only complete at the moment when I kiss you, at the moment when your mouth has united the two halves of me. Your kiss is the mysterious emblem of life.

"Yes, Charles, you live in me but you do not live alone. I am a world.

"A union of love, a union of spirit, a union of matter. Such is the life of man. Such are the phenomena Divine unity is constantly revealing to him, toward which he can advance only if he has a love coitus (the word is too beautiful to be avoided) of intellect and matter with all that is.

"My life is eternal. Your death will not prevent me from feeling you in me, me in you." Enfantin to Duveyrier, Bibliothèque Nationale, Collection Alfred Pereire, N.a.fr. 24608 (128, 132).

22. Enfantin wrote to his mother: "I can imagine circumstances when my wife alone would be capable of bestowing happiness, health, life on one of my sons in St. Simon, of reawakening in him the social sympathies that are about to leave him, of warming him in her caressing arms at the moment when some profound unhappiness would require a powerful diversion, at the moment when his heart, broken and crushed, would be bleeding in disgust of life. O Mother, has it not been said: what is not a mother's heart capable of? Now the mother of whom I speak is not the mother by birth but a mother by adoption, a mother who through moral direction has the power of giving birth not once but forever, for her word and her caresses give life. This mother can love and allow herself to be loved without fear because her love saves the child who suffers and calms the one who is distraught." Bibliothèque Nationale, Collection Alfred Pereire, N.a.fr. 24608.

23. Total subordination in love to the Father assumed ecstatic forms, an experience not unknown to modern analysts. See, for example, a letter from Moïse Retouret to Enfantin (undated): "When you will it I shall be your servant. At any hour of the day and at any hour of the night. Dispose of my waking and of my sleep. I shall love whatever you love in me. I love today the idea that you think that I belong wholly to you. Father, may the love of your son, the love he gives to you, flow in your blood and bring you the same delight which your love flowing in his blood brings to him, and may the heart of our divine Father rejoice in his children and in the children of his children." Bibliothèque Nationale, Collection Alfred Pereire, N.a.fr. 24610 (415).

24. Enfantin to Veturé, March 1832: "You have fled! . . . My dear child, I say this to you again: You are weaker doubting our love for you than you would have been had our will and not your own directed you to

Metz. Do therefore immediately ask for an authorization, explaining your motives, to remain away from us for a while or return here in the midst of your proletarians, of your children, and of all of us, because you are loved by all our children and by him who is their father and yours." Bibliothèque Nationale, Collection Alfred Pereire, N.a.fr. 24608 (140–141).

25. In a letter of February 12, 1829, Eugène Rodrigues used the formula: "Il faut que chacun soît récompensé selon ses oeuvres." Bibliothèque Nationale, Collection Alfred Pereire, N.a.fr. 24611 (45). Variants of the Saint-Simonian formula were "le classement selon la capacité, la rétribution selon les oeuvres" and "à chacun selon sa vocation." Bibliothèque Nationale, Collection Alfred Pereire, N.a.fr. 24612 (426).

26. "Any community conceived as the equal division of the instruments or the products of labor is and will always be nothing but a utopia. . . . In the distribution of products into equal portions all men would be lowered to the same level and would be deprived of the stimulus which causes them to work for the amelioration of the existence of their fellows." Pereire *jeune*, April 28, 1828, Bibliothèque Nationale, Collection Alfred Pereire, N.a.fr. 24610 (241).

27. Fourier's remark on the need to guarantee a decent minimum standard was made in a letter to Enfantin, May 21, 1829. Bibliothèque Nationale, Collection Alfred Pereire, N.a.fr. 24614.

28. Karl Marx, *Kritik des Gothaer Programms* (Berlin, 1946), p. 21.

29. Marx had already adopted similar formulae as early as *Die Deutsche Ideologie* of the forties: "Now one of the most substantive principles of communism, which distinguishes it from every form of reactionary socialism, consists in the view, based on an empirical observation of man, that differences in the mind and in intellectual capacities involve no differences in the stomach and in physical needs; that therefore the dictum "To each according to his abilities," which is based upon existing false relationships, must, insofar as pleasure in the narrower sense is concerned, be transformed into the dictum "To each according to need"; so that, in other words, variation in activity, in work, entitles one to no inequality or privilege insofar as ownership and enjoyment are involved." *Gesamtausgabe*, Part I, Volume V, p. 526.

30. Pierre Naville, in *De l'aliénation à la jouissance, la genèse de la sociologie du travail chez Marx et Engels* (Paris, 1957), has begun to unravel the intricacies of Marx's conceptions of work and need.

31. The phrase "Selbstverwirklichung des Individuums" occurs in Marx's manuscripts of the fifties which have come to be known as *Grundrisse der Politischen Ökonomie. Rohentwurf 1857–1859* (Berlin, 1953), p. 505.

INDEX OF NAMES AND TITLES

INDEX

INDEX

INDEX

Revised February 1966

harper ⚜ torchbooks

HUMANITIES AND SOCIAL SCIENCES

American Studies: General

American Studies: Colonial

American Studies: From the Revolution to 1860

---

† The New American Nation Series, edited by Henry Steele Commager and Richard B. Morris.
‡ American Perspectives series, edited by Bernard Wishy and William E. Leuchtenburg.
* The Rise of Modern Europe series, edited by William L. Langer.
‖ Researches in the Social, Cultural, and Behavioral Sciences, edited by Benjamin Nelson.
§ The Library of Religion and Culture, edited by Benjamin Nelson.
Z Harper Modern Science Series, edited by James R. Newman.
° Not for sale in Canada.

1

Business, Economics & Economic History

REINHARD BENDIX: Work and Authority in Industry: *Ideologies of Management in the Course of Industrialization* TB/3035
GILBERT BURCK & EDITORS OF FORTUNE: The Computer Age: *And Its Potential for Management* TB/1179
THOMAS C. COCHRAN: The American Business System: *A Historical Perspective, 1900-1955* TB/1080
THOMAS C. COCHRAN: The Inner Revolution: *Essays on the Social Sciences in History* TB/1140
THOMAS C. COCHRAN & WILLIAM MILLER: The Age of Enterprise: *A Social History of Industrial America* TB/1054
ROBERT DAHL & CHARLES E. LINDBLOM: Politics, Economics, and Welfare: *Planning & Politico-Economic Systems Resolved into Basic Social Processes* TB/3037
PETER F. DRUCKER: The New Society: *The Anatomy of Industrial Order* TB/1082
EDITORS OF FORTUNE: America in the Sixties: *The Economy and the Society* TB/1015
ROBERT L. HEILBRONER: The Great Ascent: *The Struggle for Economic Development in Our Time* TB/3030
FRANK H. KNIGHT: The Economic Organization TB/1214
FRANK H. KNIGHT: Risk, Uncertainty and Profit TB/1215
ABBA P. LERNER: Everybody's Business: *Current Assumptions in Economics and Public Policy* TB/3051
ROBERT GREEN MC CLOSKEY: American Conservatism in the Age of Enterprise, 1865-1910 TB/1137
PAUL MANTOUX: The Industrial Revolution in the Eighteenth Century: *The Beginnings of the Modern Factory System in England* ° TB/1079
WILLIAM MILLER, Ed.: Men in Business: *Essays on the Historical Role of the Entrepreneur* TB/1081
RICHARD B. MORRIS: Government and Labor in Early America TB/1244
HERBERT SIMON: The Shape of Automation: *For Men and Management* TB/1245
PERRIN STRYKER: The Character of the Executive: *Eleven Studies in Managerial Qualities* TB/1041
PIERRE URI: Partnership for Progress: *A Program for Transatlantic Action* TB/3036

Contemporary Culture

JACQUES BARZUN: The House of Intellect TB/1051
JOHN U. NEF: Cultural Foundations of Industrial Civilization TB/1024
NATHAN M. PUSEY: The Age of the Scholar: *Observations on Education in a Troubled Decade* TB/1157
PAUL VALÉRY: The Outlook for Intelligence TB/2016

Historiography & Philosophy of History

JACOB BURCKHARDT: On History and Historians. *Intro. by H. R. Trevor-Roper* TB/1216
WILHELM DILTHEY: Pattern and Meaning in History: *Thoughts on History and Society.* ° *Edited with an Introduction by H. P. Rickman* TB/1075
J. H. HEXTER: Reappraisals in History: *New Views on History & Society in Early Modern Europe* TB/1100
H. STUART HUGHES: History as Art and as Science: *Twin Vistas on the Past* TB/1207
RAYMOND KLIBANSKY & H. J. PATON, Eds.: Philosophy and History: *The Ernst Cassirer Festschrift. Illus.* TB/1115
GEORGE H. NADEL, Ed.: Studies in the Philosophy of History: *Selected Essays from History and Theory* TB/1208
JOSE ORTEGA Y GASSET: The Modern Theme. *Introduction by Jose Ferrater Mora* TB/1038
KARL R. POPPER: The Open Society and Its Enemies
Vol. I: The Spell of Plato TB/1101
Vol. II: The High Tide of Prophecy: Hegel, Marx and the Aftermath TB/1102
KARL R. POPPER: The Poverty of Historicism ° TB/1126

G. J. RENIER: History: Its Purpose and Method TB/1209
W. H. WALSH: Philosophy of History: *An Introduction* TB/1020

History: General

L. CARRINGTON GOODRICH: A Short History of the Chinese People. *Illus.* TB/3015
DAN N. JACOBS & HANS H. BAERWALD: Chinese Communism: *Selected Documents* TB/3031
BERNARD LEWIS: The Arabs in History TB/1029

History: Ancient

A. ANDREWES: The Greek Tyrants TB/1103
ADOLF ERMAN, Ed.: The Ancient Egyptians: *A Sourcebook of Their Writings. New material and Introduction by William Kelly Simpson* TB/1233
MICHAEL GRANT: Ancient History ° TB/1190
SAMUEL NOAH KRAMER: Sumerian Mythology TB/1055
NAPHTALI LEWIS & MEYER REINHOLD, Eds.: Roman Civilization. *Sourcebook I: The Republic* TB/1231
NAPHTALI LEWIS & MEYER REINHOLD, Eds.: Roman Civilization. *Sourcebook II: The Empire* TB/1232

History: Medieval

P. BOISSONNADE: Life and Work in Medieval Europe: *The Evolution of the Medieval Economy, the 5th to the 15th Century.* ° *Preface by Lynn White, Jr.* TB/1141
HELEN CAM: England before Elizabeth TB/1026
NORMAN COHN: The Pursuit of the Millennium: *Revolutionary Messianism in Medieval and Reformation Europe* TB/1037
G. G. COULTON: Medieval Village, Manor, and Monastery TB/1022
HEINRICH FICHTENAU: The Carolingian Empire: *The Age of Charlemagne* TB/1142
F. L. GANSHOF: Feudalism TB/1058
EDWARD GIBBON: The Triumph of Christendom in the Roman Empire (Chaps. XV-XX of "Decline and Fall," J. B. Bury edition). § *Illus.* TB/46
W. O. HASSALL, Ed.: Medieval England: *As Viewed by Contemporaries* TB/1205
DENYS HAY: The Medieval Centuries ° TB/1192
J. M. HUSSEY: The Byzantine World TB/1057
FERDINAND LOT: The End of the Ancient World and the Beginnings of the Middle Ages. *Introduction by Glanville Downey* TB/1044
G. MOLLAT: The Popes at Avignon: 1305-1378 TB/308
CHARLES PETIT-DUTAILLIS: The Feudal Monarchy in France and England: *From the Tenth to the Thirteenth Century* ° TB/1165
HENRI PIRENNE: Early Democracies in the Low Countries: *Urban Society and Political Conflict in the Middle Ages and the Renaissance. Introduction by John H. Mundy* TB/1110
STEVEN RUNCIMAN: A History of the Crusades.
Volume I: The First Crusade and the Foundation of the Kingdom of Jerusalem. Illus. TB/1143
Volume II: The Kingdom of Jerusalem and the Frankish East, 1100-1187. Illus. TB/1243
FERDINAND SCHEVILL: Siena: *The History of a Medieval Commune. Intro. by William M. Bowsky* TB/1164
SULPICIUS SEVERUS et al.: The Western Fathers: *Being the Lives of Martin of Tours, Ambrose, Augustine of Hippo, Honoratus of Arles and Germanus of Auxerre. Edited and translated by F. R. Hoare* TB/309
HENRY OSBORN TAYLOR: The Classical Heritage of the Middle Ages. *Foreword and Biblio. by Kenneth M. Setton* TB/1117
F. VAN DER MEER: Augustine the Bishop: *Church and Society at the Dawn of the Middle Ages* TB/304
J. M. WALLACE-HADRILL: The Barbarian West: *The Early Middle Ages, A.D. 400-1000* TB/1061

3

4

Intellectual History & History of Ideas

Literature, Poetry, The Novel & Criticism

Myth, Symbol & Folklore

Christianity: The Roman and Eastern Traditions

Oriental Religions: Far Eastern, Near Eastern

Philosophy of Religion

Religion, Culture & Society

NATURAL SCIENCES AND MATHEMATICS

Biological Sciences

LUDWIG VON BERTALANFFY: Modern Theories of Development: *An Introduction to Theoretical Biology* TB/554
LUDWIG VON BERTALANFFY: Problems of Life: *An Evaluation of Modern Biological and Scientific Thought* TB/521
HAROLD F. BLUM: Time's Arrow and Evolution TB/555
JOHN TYLER BONNER: The Ideas of Biology. Σ *Illus.* TB/570
A. J. CAIN: Animal Species and their Evolution. *Illus.* TB/519
WALTER B. CANNON: Bodily Changes in Pain, Hunger, Fear and Rage. *Illus.* TB/562
W. E. LE GROS CLARK: The Antecedents of Man: *Intro. to Evolution of the Primates.* º *Illus.* TB/559
W. H. DOWDESWELL: Animal Ecology. *Illus.* TB/543
W. H. DOWDESWELL: The Mechanism of Evolution. *Illus.* TB/527
R. W. GERARD: Unresting Cells. *Illus.* TB/541
DAVID LACK: Darwin's Finches. *Illus.* TB/544
J. E. MORTON: Molluscs: *An Introduction to their Form and Functions. Illus.* TB/529
ADOLF PORTMANN: Animals as Social Beings. º *Illus.* TB/572
O. W. RICHARDS: The Social Insects. *Illus.* TB/542
P. M. SHEPPARD: Natural Selection and Heredity. *Illus.* TB/528
EDMUND W. SINNOTT: Cell and Psyche: *The Biology of Purpose* TB/546
C. H. WADDINGTON: How Animals Develop. *Illus.* TB/553
C. H. WADDINGTON: The Nature of Life: *The Main Problems and Trends in Modern Biology* TB/580

Chemistry

J. R. PARTINGTON: A Short History of Chemistry. *Illus.* TB/522
J. READ: A Direct Entry to Organic Chemistry. *Illus.* TB/523
J. READ: Through Alchemy to Chemistry. *Illus.* TB/561

Communication Theory

J. R. PIERCE: Symbols, Signals and Noise: *The Nature and Process of Communication* TB/574

Geography

R. E. COKER: This Great and Wide Sea: *An Introduction to Oceanography and Marine Biology. Illus.* TB/551
F. K. HARE: The Restless Atmosphere TB/560

History of Science

W. DAMPIER, Ed.: Readings in the Literature of Science. *Illus.* TB/512
A. HUNTER DUPREE: Science in the Federal Government: *A History of Policies and Activities to 1940* TB/573
ALEXANDRE KOYRÉ: From the Closed World to the Infinite Universe: *Copernicus, Kepler, Galileo, Newton, etc.* TB/31
A. G. VAN MELSEN: From Atomos to Atom: *A History of the Concept Atom* TB/517
O. NEUGEBAUER: The Exact Sciences in Antiquity TB/552
H. T. PLEDGE: Science Since 1500: *A Short History of Mathematics, Physics, Chemistry and Biology. Illus.* TB/506
HANS THIRRING: Energy for Man: *From Windmills to Nuclear Power* TB/556
LANCELOT LAW WHYTE: Essay on Atomism: *From Democritus to 1960* TB/565
A. WOLF: A History of Science, Technology and Philosophy in the 16th and 17th Centuries. º *Illus.*
Vol. I TB/508; Vol. II TB/509

A. WOLF: A History of Science, Technology, and Philosophy in the Eighteenth Century. º *Illus.*
Vol. I TB/539; Vol. II TB/540

Mathematics

E. W. BETH: The Foundations of Mathematics: *A Study in the Philosophy of Science* TB/581
H. DAVENPORT: The Higher Arithmetic: *An Introduction to the Theory of Numbers* TB/526
H. G. FORDER: Geometry: An Introduction TB/548
GOTTLOB FREGE: The Foundations of Arithmetic: *A Logico-Mathematical Enquiry* TB/534
S. KÖRNER: The Philosophy of Mathematics: *An Introduction* TB/547
D. E. LITTLEWOOD: Skeleton Key of Mathematics: *A Simple Account of Complex Algebraic Problems* TB/525
GEORGE E. OWEN: Fundamentals of Scientific Mathematics TB/569
WILLARD VAN ORMAN QUINE: Mathematical Logic TB/558
O. G. SUTTON: Mathematics in Action. º *Foreword by James R. Newman. Illus.* TB/518
FREDERICK WAISMANN: Introduction to Mathematical Thinking. *Foreword by Karl Menger* TB/511

Philosophy of Science

R. B. BRAITHWAITE: Scientific Explanation TB/515
J. BRONOWSKI: Science and Human Values. *Revised and Enlarged Edition* TB/505
ALBERT EINSTEIN et al.: Albert Einstein: Philosopher-Scientist. *Edited by Paul A. Schilpp* Vol. I TB/502
Vol. II TB/503
WERNER HEISENBERG: Physics and Philosophy: *The Revolution in Modern Science* TB/549
JOHN MAYNARD KEYNES: A Treatise on Probability. º *Introduction by N. R. Hanson* TB/557
KARL R. POPPER: The Logic of Scientific Discovery TB/576
STEPHEN TOULMIN: Foresight and Understanding: *An Enquiry into the Aims of Science. Foreword by Jacques Barzun* TB/564
STEPHEN TOULMIN: The Philosophy of Science: *An Introduction* TB/513
G. J. WHITROW: The Natural Philosophy of Time º TB/563

Physics and Cosmology

STEPHEN TOULMIN & JUNE GOODFIELD: The Fabric of the Heavens: *The Development of Astronomy and Dynamics. Illus.* TB/579
DAVID BOHM: Causality and Chance in Modern Physics. *Foreword by Louis de Broglie* TB/536
P. W. BRIDGMAN: The Nature of Thermodynamics TB/537
P. W. BRIDGMAN: A Sophisticate's Primer of Relativity TB/575
A. C. CROMBIE, Ed.: Turning Point in Physics TB/535
C. V. DURELL: Readable Relativity. *Foreword by Freeman J. Dyson* TB/530
ARTHUR EDDINGTON: Space, Time and Gravitation: *An Outline of the General Relativity Theory* TB/510
GEORGE GAMOW: Biography of Physics Σ TB/567
MAX JAMMER: Concepts of Force: *A Study in the Foundation of Dynamics* TB/550
MAX JAMMER: Concepts of Mass *in Classical and Modern Physics* TB/571
MAX JAMMER: Concepts of Space: *The History of Theories of Space in Physics. Foreword by Albert Einstein* TB/533
EDMUND WHITTAKER: History of the Theories of Aether and Electricity
Volume I: *The Classical Theories* TB/531
Volume II: *The Modern Theories* TB/532
G. J. WHITROW: The Structure and Evolution of the Universe: *An Introduction to Cosmology. Illus.* TB/504

The Craft of Bureaucratic Neutrality

Interests and Influence in Governmental Regulation of Occupational Safety

GREGORY A. HUBER
Yale University

CAMBRIDGE
UNIVERSITY PRESS

JF
1501
.H83
2007

CAMBRIDGE UNIVERSITY PRESS
Cambridge, New York, Melbourne, Madrid, Cape Town, Singapore, São Paulo

Cambridge University Press
32 Avenue of the Americas, New York, NY 10013-2473, USA

www.cambridge.org
Information on this title: www.cambridge.org/9780521872799

© Gregory A. Huber 2007

This publication is in copyright. Subject to statutory exception
and to the provisions of relevant collective licensing agreements,
no reproduction of any part may take place without
the written permission of Cambridge University Press.

First published 2007

Printed in the United States of America

A catalog record for this publication is available from the British Library.

Library of Congress Cataloging in Publication Data

Huber, Gregory Alain, 1973–
The Craft of bureaucratic neutrality : interests and influence in governmental
regulation of occupational safety / Gregory A. Huber.
    p.   cm.
Includes bibliographical references and index.
ISBN-13: 978-0-521-87279-9
1. Bureaucracy.   2. Industrial safety – Government policy – United States.
3. United States. Occupational Safety and Health Act of 1970.   I. Title.
JF1501.H83   2007
363.1'10684 – dc22   2006031967

ISBN   978-0-521-87279-9 hardback

Cambridge University Press has no responsibility for
the persistence or accuracy of URLs for external or
third-party Internet Web sites referred to in this publication
and does not guarantee that any content on such
Web sites is, or will remain, accurate or appropriate.

Contents

University Libraries
Carnegie Mellon University
Pittsburgh, PA 15213-3890

Acknowledgments

This book originated in my long-standing interest in the discretionary application of the state's coercive powers. Its completion would not have been possible, however, without the assistance of the numerous federal and state officials who aided my research. As a group, they readily answered my innumerable questions about the interactions between politics and work inside their respective agencies. They also provided many of the internal agency reports, and much of the unpublished data, used in the analyses that follow. In deference to their collective candor and the wishes of Princeton University's Human Subjects Review Board, however, their individual contributions must remain anonymous.

The Politics Department at Princeton University proved to be an ideal environment for transforming my research interest into scholarship. Doug Arnold, Tom Romer, and Howard Rosenthal comprised an extraordinary dissertation committee. Each entertained my musings on this topic from the earliest stages, pressed me to improve my arguments, and facilitated the timely completion of the dissertation. Doug served as my primary advisor throughout graduate school, and I thank him for both his friendship and his sage advice about how, as well as what, to write. Larry Bartels, Jim Doig, Fred Greenstein, Jeff Lewis, Nolan McCarty, Tali Mendelberg, Eric Oliver, and other participants in Princeton's American Politics Research Seminar offered useful guidance throughout the course of the project. In chronological order, the Association of Princeton Graduate Alumni, the Center for Domestic and Comparative Policy Studies at Princeton University, the Environmental Protection Agency, the Woodrow Wilson Society of Fellows at Princeton University, the National Science Foundation (SES Grant #9818668), and the Brookings Institution provided financial support during my dissertation research. I am grateful to these groups for facilitating my data gathering, providing forums for constructive feedback, and leaving me with uninterrupted time to write. Of course, my arguments may not reflect their views.

I had the good fortune to leave Princeton for Yale's equally supportive Political Science Department. While revising my dissertation into this book, I benefited from the comments of Alan Gerber, Don Green, Anna Grzymala-Busse, Jacob Hacker, Herbert Kaufman, David Mayhew, Fiona McGillivray, Rose Razaghian, Andrew Schrank, Ken Scheve, Stephen Skowronek, Alastair Smith, and James Vreeland. Leila Afshar, Stephen Engel, and Matthew Green provided superior research assistance. Barb Dozier, Ella Futrell, Pam Greene, and Pam Lamonaca helped make Yale's Institution for Social and Policy Studies the ideal work environment. Invitations to present the nearly complete manuscript at the University of Connecticut and the University of Virginia proved especially timely. Brandice Canes-Wrone's insightful reading of the final manuscript allowed me to both improve and shorten what follows.

Anonymous readers for Cambridge University Press, as well as conference participants and other anonymous reviewers, offered valuable suggestions that led me to rework substantial portions of the manuscript. I am especially grateful to Sandy Gordon, David Lewis, and Debbie Schildkraut for their support and assistance during this revision process. Sandy and Debbie observed this project at its inception and, along with Amanda Dickins and Tomoharu Nishino, have long tolerated my interest in government regulation. Their friendship has helped to preserve my sanity and generally cheerful demeanor over the years. I am also indebted to the staff at Cambridge University Press, and particularly to my editor, Lewis Bateman, for shepherding the manuscript to publication. Many of the useful insights in the pages that follow originated in the comments of others, and I am thankful to all those individuals who have helped me in this regard. Alas, the remaining failings are mine alone.

Finally, I wish to thank my family. My parents, to whom this book is dedicated, cultivated my interest in learning early on and embraced my decision to pursue a Ph.D. later. As a further testament to their love and support, my sister has also followed this path. Caitlin Simon has made this journey altogether worthwhile and, along with Caroline and Nicholas, has filled my days with joy. For them, as well as for their friendship over the last decade, I also thank my in-laws, Susan and Lin Simon.

Introduction

How can one reconcile the apparent conflict between political understandings of bureaucracy and Weberian conceptions of administrative
neutrality? As universal explanations, neither claim – that administration
is intrinsically political or that it is purely impartial – is satisfactory. Government agencies at times implement the law in ways that seem rife with
political considerations, while at other times the machinations of administration seem largely technocratic and above the political fray. What,
however, are the appropriate boundaries of, and interactions between,
each characterization?

The argument advanced here is that the stark dichotomy between
political and bureaucratic understandings of administrative behavior is
a false one. By adopting the language of neutrality and efficiency at the
core of the Weberian account of neutrally competent modern bureaucracy,
administrative agencies can serve political ends. Agency leaders guide
how the law is implemented through internal management practices that
seek to minimize both agency inefficiency and the susceptibility of lower-
level bureaucrats to outside influences. In critical ways, then, subordinate
bureaucrats exemplify Weber's description of "[t]he 'objective' discharge
of business . . . according to calculable rules and 'without regard for persons'" (1946: 215). At the same time, centralized administrative decisions
move implementation away from "pure" neutrality to something more
strategically valuable for agency leaders.

In sum, "strategic neutrality" is an implementation practice that simultaneously serves agency leaders' management and political needs. It helps
guide public policy toward desired ends while minimizing the likelihood
that outsiders will gain sufficient political strength to overrule agency

decisions. Strategic neutrality therefore allows unelected agency officials to become limited, but important, independent political actors capable of shaping policy and subsequent political conflict.

That the language of neutrality and efficiency is used for political ends does not mean that these are empty concepts, however. Government implementation decisions are rarely "purely" neutral, in that they often incorporate important political calculations for differentiating among the recipients of government benefits and costs. (Moreover, even objectively neutral policy can produce disparate outcomes because of preexisting differences in society.) At the same time, the strategic neutrality that emerges is hardly either random or solely targeted to reward the powerful. Instead, it serves to limit particularism by routinizing and centralizing throughout entire agencies decisions about who is worthy of "special treatment." Likewise, efficiency provides a benchmark against which to compare the relative cost of different political achievements. Agencies that can provide desirable outcomes in return for the least political investment (in terms of money and the time spent placating opponents) are more likely to survive than those that require greater attention.

The idea that bureaucracies adopt policies that are "strategically neutral" and then implement them through effective control of subordinates has important implications for political science and public administration alike. Most significantly, it suggests that the combination of internal administrative concerns and external political considerations together affect public policy. How the law is written makes little difference if agencies are unable to implement it; nor will administrators be able to generate support for sound policy ideas if they are unable to bring them to fruition. By contrast, agencies without the discretion to shape public policy have little ability to guide political conflict. When agencies have the authority and means to effectively alter how the law is implemented, however, these administrative machinations matter. Not only does this administratively directed policy immediately influence how the law is carried out, it also mediates external political pressure and alters the nature of subsequent political conflict about agency behavior. Public administration and political science are therefore inseparable.

1. Political Science, Public Administration, and Political Influence on Bureaucracy

There is long-standing scholarly interest in the relationship between political influence and how government agencies implement the law. Normative scholarship on this topic is concerned with the appropriate operation of American government. For instance, Lowi (1979) criticizes the delegation of policy-making authority to the bureaucracy, arguing that it inevitably entrenches organized interests, is contrary to the public good, and subverts the rule of law. Other scholars (e.g., Wood and Waterman 1994) claim, however, that the ongoing influence of interest groups and elected leaders on how the law is enforced demonstrates the health of American democracy itself. Roughly, they argue that because delegation is inevitable, control of implementation is a legitimate form of governance.

This debate suggests that two additional forms of inquiry are in order. The first is theoretical, the second empirical. On the theoretical side, do government agencies change how they implement the law in response to the influence of their elected overseers and powerful interest groups? If so, when? If the bureaucracy is ungovernable or if administrative decisions are purely apolitical applications of the law to the facts at hand, one would expect agencies to be largely unresponsive to outside pressures. On the other hand, the real world of politics is messy. Agencies operate with broad and uncertain mandates, and their decisions substantially shape the implementation of public policy. Given bureaucratic discretion, bureaus may very well look to the political realm for guidance in choosing how to enforce the law. Not surprisingly, therefore, political scientists have variously hypothesized that agencies are "dominated" by powerful congressional committees (Weingast and Moran 1983); that bureaucratic structures and procedures advantage certain groups but not others (Moe 1989); that powerful interest groups are able to influence directly how subordinate bureaucrats implement the law (Scholz et al. 1991); and that interest groups "capture" the agencies tasked to oversee them (Huntington 1952).

At the same time, public administration scholars and those studying the sociology of organizations have pointed to factors internal to the bureaucracy in explaining administrative performance. In this view, the ideology of bureaucratic leaders (and their commitment to neutral and effective policy implementation), the recruitment and socialization of professional experts, and simple management routines are the primary sources of bureaucratic outputs. In practice, it is argued, many bureaucratic agencies implement public policy in a way that resembles the neutral competence ideal advocated in Weber's account of a professionalized bureaucracy.

1.1 *The Political Power of Neutrality*

Seemingly apolitical bureaucratic decisions about policy implementation nonetheless have significant political implications. As early as the 1960s, for instance, examinations of the practices of urban service bureaucracies revealed the distributional consequences of internally generated bureaucratic decision rules for "who gets what and how." The "neutral" practice of forgoing street repaving in areas slated for utility work or of assigning library resources based on patterns of use can create service delivery patterns that mirror important political divisions (Levy et al. 1974). Similarly, basing city trash collection or environmental enforcement on "neutral" measures of, respectively, waste production or citizen complaints produces a distribution of government action that is politically relevant (Jones et al. 1977; 1978). Administratively focused scholars, however, often argue against interpreting these implementation decisions as overtly political. Rather, they are merely unforeseen consequences of professional management decisions by control-, expertise-, and routine-oriented managers as manifested in politically relevant policy decisions.

I argue that these seemingly incompatible visions of bureaucracy – externally constrained by the political environment or internally driven by bureaucratic preferences about appropriate behavior and the need to control subordinates – are in fact manifestations of the same reality. Of course, this is not an entirely new statement. Others have suggested that how bureaucracies are managed internally is linked to the external political environment (Moe 1987) and that internal management has important implications for efforts by outsiders to control the bureaucracy (Carpenter 2001). But are the central Weberian attributes of professional neutrality and efficiency incompatible with political visions of contemporary public bureaucracy? The answer suggested here is not at all.

Rather, adopting the language of efficiency and the practice of "neutral" implementation can itself be a political strategy. This practice of strategic neutrality is driven simultaneously by internal management needs of bureaucratic leaders and the linkages between external political support and an agency's behavior. Therefore, the observation that bureaucracies at times develop and sustain patterns of policy implementation that are "neutral" along some given dimension of political conflict should not lead one to reject the notion of political control. Nor, however, should one infer from bureaucratic responsiveness along a given dimension that bureaucracies are politically impotent. Rather, the language of efficiency allows an agency to defend itself against certain efforts to "politicize" dimensions of its behavior. Additionally, by implementing policy that is "strategically neutral," an agency can attempt to prevent the formation of political coalitions that might otherwise garner the support necessary to change agency behavior. This is a limited form of political power, but it is power that nonetheless has important implications for understanding the contours of public policy outcomes and the external governance of the bureaucracy.

Existing theories of political control – congressional dominance, agency design, and direct and indirect interest group influence – are therefore best understood as potential constraints on bureaucratic power. Bureaucratic leaders, when imbued with discretion, make policy choices with significant implications for how the law is carried out. Agency leaders' decisions are limited, however, by both internal management concerns and the need to secure political support. One important strategy that achieves these twin ends in the area of regulation is strategic neutrality. An important contribution of this perspective is to identify the reasons why some dimensions of policy choice become subject to larger political conflict (e.g., the appropriate level of spending on government safety regulation) whereas others do not (e.g., whether federal inspectors should be more aggressive in one state than in another). Thus, the theory helps to explain how the strategic construction of administrative neutrality is in fact a political choice with significant implications for political conflict.

The dissonance among existing theoretical perspectives on bureaucratic behavior is echoed in the uncertainty surrounding empirical work on the relationship among interest groups, elected officials, and how agencies implement the law. Writing about grant allocation, for instance, Arnold reports that "bureaucrats appear to allocate benefits strategically in an effort both to maintain and to expand their supporting coalitions" (1979: 207). In examining a broader set of grant programs, however, Rich concludes that "political influence . . . accounted for very little in the distribution of program funds. . . . [Economic Development Agency] officials do a relatively good job of targeting grant allocations to the neediest places" (1989: 207–208).

1.2 *The Need for Holism in Understanding Bureaucratic Power*
Perhaps this inquiry will help us to understand how these seemingly irreconcilable characterizations of bureaucracy persist. In general, neither bureaucratic choice nor real political conflict is readily reducible to a single measure. Therefore, finding that changes in some aspect of bureaucratic performance correlate with external political stimuli does not prove that all bureaucratic decisions will respond similarly to, for instance, changes in the preferences of the relevant congressional oversight committee. Likewise, merely identifying some pattern of bureaucratic decision making that seems unresponsive to the wishes of powerful actors does not mean

that bureaucrats are immune to political pressure. In general, some of the persistent disagreement about the nature of political control may simply reflect the fact that different scholars have taken different cuts at what an agency does, thereby presenting divergent pictures of a unified political animal.

Given these concerns, it is perhaps more useful to examine holistically, rather than piecemeal, bureaucratic choices in the implementation of the law. This approach serves two ends. First, it helps to illuminate how and when bureaucratic choices about implementation are constrained by external political pressures. Significantly, when external political threats exist, bureaucratic leaders may choose to heed these pressures in order to avoid being compelled to do so. These external threats are best seen as constraints, however, and not as immutable external mandates. Despite persistent external political pressure, bureaucratic leaders can still make discretionary choices about policy implementation that affect the likelihood of garnering support or opposition.

Second, examining all aspects of implementation helps to clarify the interactions among the multiple dimensions of policy choice at stake in the execution of the law. Strategic choices along one dimension of policy choice – for instance, which businesses a regulatory agency should target for inspection – may alter the support an agency receives for enforcement more generally. An agency may therefore make and sustain unpopular targeting decisions because this allows it to sustain political support elsewhere. But analyzing aggregate agency behavior along a single dimension – for example, how many inspections it conducts or the number of citations it issues – will miss these critical machinations. The interactions between external politics and internal management efforts to direct subordinate bureaucrats along the many dimensions of choice in policy implementation may not be clear without a wholesale consideration of how an agency implements the law.

2. The OSH Act Case

My general theoretical argument is advanced in the context of an investigation of federal law governing occupational safety. In order to better understand how unelected officials affect the enforcement of the law and when they adjust their implementation decisions in response to political pressure, I examine how the Occupational Safety and Health Administration (OSHA), in cooperation with state agencies, enforces the Occupational Safety and Health Act of 1970 (OSH Act).

This is a fruitful case for understanding the nature and limits of bureaucratic power for several reasons. First, OSHA is widely perceived as highly constrained by its political environment. The OSH Act was enacted during the Nixon presidency and came into force in a political environment that was already increasingly hostile to government regulation. Despite limited funding and near constant attacks from the businesses community and conservative Republicans, however, the agency has persisted in supporting a credible enforcement presence. This perseverance, even in the face of unified Republican control of the executive and legislative branches, suggests that an agency that would otherwise be characterized as a political football caught between liberal and conservative extremes has managed to defuse a substantial portion of the conservative opposition that initially fought for the agency's abolition. It has done so without becoming aligned with business interests, becoming hamstrung by the red tape originally imposed on it (Moe 1987), or simply responding reflexively to the contemporaneous power of business and labor groups. OSHA is therefore a tough case; if one can establish that it embraced strategic neutrality to become an independent (albeit limited) policymaker, then many less-constrained agencies should be similarly empowered.

The second reason this is a useful case for inquiry is that enforcement of the OSH Act involves numerous decisions made by actors in different political environments at different levels within OSHA's hierarchy. When OSHA issues a citation to an employer, it is the culmination of a complex chain of events involving the choice of an inspection target, a visit by an inspector to a workplace, the interpretation of OSHA standards, and the subsequent drafting and review of a citation. OSHA and state inspectors are in this way similar to forest rangers (Kaufman 1960), Environmental Protection Agency enforcement personnel (Gordon 1999), and numerous other government agents who perform tasks in the field, away from the direct review of agency leaders. The structure of OSHA's field enforcement program is therefore critical in shaping how the law is enforced and directly links internal administrative decisions to the political conflict surrounding the OSH Act. If OSHA's leaders are to pursue a strategically neutral enforcement strategy, they must overcome these centrifugal tendencies.

Previous scholarship, however, has characterized OSHA's enforcement posture as highly responsive to local political concerns. Scholz and colleagues (1991), for example, conclude that local political actors (interest groups and elected officials) affect the vigor with which OSHA's field-level bureaucrats enforce the law by changing how the agency behaves in different localities. By this account, perhaps OSHA has survived by engaging in enforcement that is calibrated to appease different local constituencies. Such an explanation, while enticing, seems inconsonant with business and labor concerns about the competitive costs of regulation. Businesses subject to more aggressive regulation than their competitors are at a competitive disadvantage. It therefore seems unlikely that this sort of discernment would have saved OSHA from its political opponents.

In this respect, studying OSHA is ideal because it is possible to disaggregate the regulatory process. At OSHA, the routine of choosing and inspecting workplaces is repeated thousands of times per year, and the result of every inspection is recorded in thorough detail. This makes it possible to diagnose the means of political influence on enforcement outcomes and related management efforts to mitigate or encourage this responsiveness. By examining variation in OSHA's treatment of similar regulated employers, one can assess whether inequality is related to differences in regulatory effort (the number of inspectors an agency deploys or the number of inspections that these inspectors conduct), fair treatment (more aggressive enforcement in politically supportive areas), or perhaps even behavior by workers or employers at regulated firms (e.g., whether or not workers complain about workplace hazards and whether or not employers make efforts to alleviate workplace hazards).[1] This diagnosis is essential for understanding whether and how external influences affect bureaucratic decisions.

To give a brief sense of my findings in this regard, the analysis in the following pages confirms this empirical pattern – more aggressive and persistent enforcement in some areas than in others – but disputes the attribution of influence. OSHA does not appear to tailor enforcement to appease local constituencies. Instead, OSHA's allocation of staff, choice of workplaces to inspect, inspector effort, and stringency of inspections are largely consistent across geographic areas. Enforcement variation does persist, however, both because of variation in the geographic distribution of the businesses OSHA targets for frequent inspections – large businesses in unsafe industries – and because of variation in the behavior of employers and workers – their willingness to exercise their statutory right to complain to OSHA and participate in workplace inspections. Attributing this variation to political influence on discretionary OSHA decisions in the field is therefore incorrect.

---

[1] The terms "employer," "business," and "firm" are used interchangeably throughout this book. This simplification glosses over differences between nonprofit employers (e.g., universities) and private businesses.

Clearly, this does not demonstrate that politics per se is irrelevant. Rather, OSHA's leadership has made a political choice to undertake a geographically neutral inspection strategy while discriminating among businesses on the basis of size, industry of operation, and compliance history. Recast in this light, political scientists are correct to doubt claims of absolute neutrality in enforcement, but perhaps too quick to reject evidence of successful efforts by national agency leaders to insulate field enforcement efforts from local political influences.

Furthermore, the bifurcated federal and state enforcement of OSHA standards provides a window into how different bureaucracies implement the same task. In twenty-one states, OSHA has granted primary enforcement authority to a state agency.[2] Examining variation in how the law is enforced across each of these agencies allows one to assess whether differences in state politics affect the generic imperative for bureaucratic leaders to build supportive coalitions and control their subordinates. Additionally, understanding variation in the shared federal and state enforcement of a federal statute is important because one of the principal justifications for federal action is the claim that the states are subject to competitive pressures that deter aggressive regulation and redistribution (Fesler 1949). A uniform federal statute, according to this argument, is supposed to alleviate these pressures. If allowing the states to participate in the enforcement process re-creates the pressures for a "race to the bottom," however, it calls into question both the reason for allowing state enforcement of federal law in the first place and whether aggressive federal enforcement is politically feasible when states are also active in enforcing the law.

Finally, beyond this focus on the nature of bureaucratic choice, governance of OSHA is important because enforcement of the OSH Act has a large effect on workers, individual businesses, and the national economy. As Table I.1. shows, 12 percent of the nation's employees, and 25 percent of workers in the manufacturing sector, work at establishments that are inspected by OSHA or the states in a given year.[3] In 1992 alone, OSHA imposed $77 million in penalties for violations of the OSH

---

[2] The states are Alaska, Arizona, California, Hawaii, Indiana, Iowa, Kentucky, Maryland, Michigan, Minnesota, Nevada, New Mexico, North Carolina, Oregon, South Carolina, Tennessee, Utah, Vermont, Virginia, Washington, and Wyoming. Additionally, Connecticut, New Jersey, and New York have programs restricted to state and local public employees. In all states, federal OSHA retains enforcement authority for federal employees and most maritime activity.

[3] Thus, the fact that OSHA and the states inspect only 2 percent of the nation's businesses every year dramatically understates the scope of OSH Act enforcement.

TABLE I.I. *OSH Act inspection rates, 1995*

	Overall	Manufacturing
Number of private sector establishments	6,660,864	402,030
Number inspected[a]	96,847	25,119
Percent inspected	1.45%	6.25%
Number of private sector employees	103,573,156	19,939,124
Number of employees whose workplace was inspected	12,218,376	4,962,924
Percent subject to inspection	11.80%	24.89%

[a] Includes state and federal inspections. All figures are for calendar year 1995.
Source: OSHA IMIS database and Bureau of the Census County Business Patterns data.

Act and conducted forty-eight thousand inspections.[4] These inspections and penalties are associated with substantial improvements in workplace safety (Gray and Scholz 1993). But this worker protection is not without its costs. Gray (1987) estimates that OSHA regulations accounted for about 20 percent of the decline in manufacturing productivity in the 1970s, and critics charge that OSHA's ergonomics standard would have imposed annual costs in excess of $18 billion dollars on private employers had it not been repealed by Congress (Dreazen 2000).

3. Research Approach

The idea of strategic neutrality suggests that bureaucratic leaders are not merely acted upon by external political forces, but can also proactively shape the nature of their political environment. Simultaneously, the limits of this power are demarcated both by agency leaders' management concerns and their need to secure political support from elected leaders and powerful groups. Establishing the power of strategic neutrality therefore requires demonstrating, first, that agency leaders act to shape their political environment and, second, that their choices are bound by these internal and external constraints. Theoretically, this approach therefore impinges upon arguments about the power of interest groups, the preferences and powers of elected officials, and the management and operation of bureaucracies.

Empirically, I employ diverse methodological approaches to establish the power and limits of strategic neutrality. In addition to detailed

---

[4] Source: OSHA IMIS database.

examinations of public interactions between OSHA and elected officials, I consider the malleability of the interest group environment the agency faces, study the lobbying and advocacy behavior of labor and business groups and their individual members, and rely on detailed histories of OSHA's founding and evolution in policy implementation. These external sources are supplemented by internal agency documents and interviews I conducted with select business and labor groups and more than one hundred field-level bureaucrats, their supervisors, and regional and head-quarters administrators. These interviews place my conclusions within the nuances and complexity of real organizations.

This qualitative evidence is supplemented by a series of quantitative analyses of federal and state OSH Act enforcement efforts. By disaggregating federal and state enforcement activities and examining separately (1) the allocation of inspectors to local field offices, (2) the choice of inspection targets, (3) inspector effort, and (4) inspector stringency, I am able to identify how the OSH Act and internal management decisions combine to alter actual enforcement outcomes. In sum, violations are not simply and uniformly produced, but result from a sequence of actions that culminate in an inspector choosing whether or not to issue a citation (Diver 1980). By taking these "multiple cuts" at the way in which the law is enforced it becomes possible to understand which actors within the bureaucracy make individual decisions and how these individuals are influenced by outside political pressure in carrying out their jobs. It is therefore feasible to adjudicate among competing theories that posit different causal mechanisms for the linkage between political pressure and variation in bureaucratic performance. Additionally, by getting "inside" the bureaucracy, one can understand how bureaucrats are influenced by their superiors and constrained by the law itself. Finally, the combination of these data sources allows for more effective use of counterfactuals in theory testing and a greater understanding of the causal mechanisms at work in directing bureaucratic behavior. Overall, I hope that this diverse approach improves the overall probity and quality of the inquiry.

This short introduction has provided a taste of what is to follow. The remainder of this book is organized as follows. Chapter 1 develops more fully the idea of strategic neutrality as a way for bureaucratic leaders to exercise political power and positions this argument vis-à-vis existing perspectives. Chapter 2 introduces the book's primarily empirical focus, namely, state and federal enforcement of the OSH Act; discusses the nature of political conflict over OSHA's enforcement of the OSH Act; and specifies the particular strategic choices that OSHA's leaders have made about how to shape the agency's field efforts to garner political support. Chapters 3 and 4 are applications of the theory to different facets of OSH Act implementation. Chapter 3 examines the allocation and consistency of federal enforcement efforts across different political environments and individual firms, while Chapter 4 explores both the effect of state participation in OSH Act enforcement on regulatory enforcement throughout the country and OSHA's response to the potential for weak state enforcement to upset support for its geographically neutral enforcement posture. Finally, Chapter 5 considers the consequences for public policy of efforts to move away from the strong centralized control of subordinates at the core of the notion of strategic neutrality and also examines the limits of bureaucratic leadership both by exploring efforts to move OSHA away from its traditionally pro-labor posture and then by applying the theory to other agencies.

I

Bureaucratic Power and Strategic Neutrality

One of the core questions of governance is whether citizens and their elected representatives can control the apparatus of the state. In the contemporary era, where administrative agencies staffed by unelected bureaucrats must implement broad and uncertain mandates, control of how agencies execute the law has gained even greater significance. At the same time, extensive political "meddling" in the details of policy implementation threatens to yield agencies so hamstrung by external intervention that they are incapable of effectively executing policy. Political control, in short, may come at the cost of capable public administration.

This chapter examines the dominant accounts within political science and public administration of whether and how elected officials and interest groups shape bureaucratic decisions. These perspectives include the assertion that the bureaucracy is ungovernable or guided by bureaucrats' professional training and beliefs, theories of congressional dominance and agency design, and claims of direct and indirect interest group capture. These viewpoints are used, in both academic and common discourse, to explain "why government agencies act the way they do." They highlight, among other factors, internal bureaucratic norms, the influence of congressional committees and legislative statutes, and interest group power in explaining how agencies enforce the law. They do little to explain regulatory enforcement and implementation, however, because they understate the linkages between the internal management of bureaucracy and external political conflict. Consequently, when these theories recognize the potential for bureaucratic power, they fail to identify the contingent nature of this bureaucratic leadership, which is critically affected by internal management concerns and conflict among elected officials and interest groups.

13

A desirable theory of bureaucratic power should therefore have three features. First, it should allow for "agency" by acknowledging not just that bureaucracies are acted upon by outside forces, but also that they have the power to initiate and alter policy of their own accord. Second, it should disaggregate the bureaucracy by recognizing that government agencies are not unitary actors. Rather, they are hierarchical organizations in which agency leaders must concern themselves with how their ideal policies are implemented by their subordinates. Finally, in addition to identifying these internal limits on bureaucratic leadership, a theory of bureaucratic power must account for the interaction between bureaucratic decisions and the external political environment. While that environment may be pliable, the potential for unitary or coordinated action by elected officials (perhaps at the behest of interest groups) may be sufficient to compel bureaucratic quiescence.

In seeking to meet these standards, I propose a theory that identifies the conditions under which bureaucratic leaders can exercise political power by manipulating implementation to shape support for and opposition to an agency. In this perspective, outside opportunities to influence agency decisions are mediated through bureaucratic structures, which are shaped by bureaucratic leaders' choices in light of their political preferences and the difficulty of managing their subordinates. At the agency level, bureaucratic leaders may choose different enforcement patterns to serve both their management and political needs, but one particularly attractive tack is "strategic neutrality." Strategic neutrality means practicing uniform implementation with regard to factors outside the direct control of centralized bureaucratic superiors while nonetheless allowing agency-wide decisions to vary according to centralized directives. It is, in other words, centralized partiality. Strategic neutrality minimizes both opportunities for damaging subordinate malfeasance and dangerous external political opposition. In this perspective, agency leaders' decisions about policy affect subsequent dimensions of political conflict. Agency leaders therefore have a substantial, if limited, power to alter political conflict.

In developing this argument, this chapter first discusses the dominant theories of bureaucratic influence and decision making and then turns its attention to specifying the conditions of bureaucratic power through the pursuit of strategic neutrality.

1. Existing Perspectives on Bureaucratic Power and Political Influence

Existing accounts of the nature of bureaucratic power and external influence on bureaucratic decisions are usefully grouped into five broad categories: (1) the bureaucracy as ungovernable, (2) congressional or committee dominance, (3) structural or design constraints, (4) interest group influence, and (5) multiple impulses.

1.1. The Ungovernable Bureaucracy

The strong form of the ungovernable bureaucracy perspective argues that bureaucracies are largely immune to political control. This autonomy may arise because expert bureaucrats hold private information that is too costly for elected officials to reveal through oversight (Niskanen 1971). Alternatively, otherwise powerful constituencies may be left out of critical subgovernment arrangements. Groups that do challenge the bureaucracy may still become entangled in the quagmire of administrative decision making; agencies may thereby absorb the furor of political advocates while yielding little substantive change (Katznelson 1981).

There are several difficulties, however, with theories positing that bureaucratic autonomy is intrinsic to administration. Foremost, a lack of vigorous oversight activities by elected officials (e.g., Ogul 1976; Dodd and Schott 1979) is also consistent with complete bureaucratic subservience to the whims of elected officials alert to potential agency missteps (McCubbins and Schwartz 1984). There exists, in short, a problem of "observational equivalence." Nor does deference to the bureaucracy on certain issues indicate that all bureaucratic deviations from the preferences of these officials would be tolerated. Additionally, contrary to characterizations of the bureaucracy as ungovernable, politicians are in fact often highly informed about internal bureaucratic machinations and willing to challenge agency claims of expertise, and agency leaders are usually highly attentive to the wishes of their elected overseers and important constituencies (Kaufman 1981). Furthermore, numerous scholars have documented the influence of presidents, Congress, and the courts on specific aspects of agency behavior (see Krause 1999 for a comprehensive review).

If bureaucracies are not intrinsically independent, alternatives theories suggest that bureaucratic autonomy may be a contingent phenomenon. One conception of bureaucratic autonomy, advocated by Carpenter (2001), is that bureaucracies become autonomous when they are able to enact policies that elected officials do not like but that are too politically costly to overturn. In Carpenter's perspective, agencies become powerful by developing reputations for trustworthiness (built on policy expertise and skill in implementation) and then using these reputations to craft policies that attract political support independent of traditional party cleavages. This perspective therefore qualifies existing work that suggests that bureaucratic expertise leads to deference to agency decisions, or claims that agencies are powerful when they initiate policies that generate supportive constituencies (e.g., Rourke 1984). Still, few agencies have the initial administrative authority, resources, and expertise necessary to develop a reputation for policy development that leads to subsequent independence. (In the words of Moe [1989], new agencies may be "designed to fail.") Nonetheless, agencies that are not autonomous – in Carpenter's sense – are clearly still capable of independent political action. What remains uncertain is how agencies that are neither totally autonomous nor completely subservient choose to behave.

A second characterization of the contingent nature of bureaucratic power focuses on the agenda-setting power of administrative action. By guiding policy, bureaucracies may create constituencies that support agency decisions (Rourke 1984). An agency imbued with discretionary authority can, in this perspective, manipulate policy so long as outsiders cannot work together to overrule it. In formal expositions of agenda setting in the one-dimensional spatial model setting, agency decisions persist so long as policy outcomes remain within the "gridlock" region in which the president and members of the House and Senate cannot agree to work together to overrule the bureaucracy's decisions (e.g., Volden 2002; Shipan 2004).[1] In the more robust multidimensional setting, agencies do not simply move policy left or right in a single existing dimension, but instead propose policy bundles that structure the dimensions of political conflict (Calvert, McCubbins, and Weingast 1989).

The strength of this perspective is the acknowledgement that bureaucratic power is not purely anticipatory (e.g., Arnold 1979) in nature; bureaucracies also have an independent ability to direct policy toward their own goals. At the same time, the notion that agencies simply pick policy bundles from an abstract multidimensional space ignores the real details of policy implementation. Agencies, real hierarchies with their concomitant problems of management, may not be able to effectively implement all potential groupings of policy.

1.2. Congressional (Committee) Dominance

The theory of congressional (committee) dominance contrasts starkly with the image of the bureaucracy as powerful. This theory suggests that

---

[1] For example, suppose a bare majority in the House and the entire Senate seek to overrule an agency's decision. If the president prefers the bureaucracy's position to the legislative alternative, a presidential veto will protect the agency's decision because there are insufficient votes in the House to override it.

agencies, rather than being autonomous, are largely subservient to the wishes of their congressional overseers (e.g., Weingast and Moran 1982; McCubbins and Schwartz 1984). The foundation of this perspective is twofold. First, members of Congress have extensive power over agencies because of their control of agency appropriations, enabling statutes, and the confirmation of agency appointees. Second, the congressional committee system allows members to specialize in different policy domains and to distribute benefits to locally relevant constituencies. Consequently, members of programmatic and budgetary committees have great influence over agencies within their jurisdiction. Overall, "rewards go to those agencies that pursue policies of interest to the current committee members; those agencies that fail to do so are confronted with sanctions" (Weingast and Moran 1983: 768).

This theoretical claim serves as the basis for two distinct sets of arguments about the influence of members of Congress on bureaucratic decision making. On the one hand, the theory of congressional dominance is an argument about the importance of congressional preferences in the design of agency structures. This perspective will be discussed in greater detail later in this chapter. On the other hand, the theory is more commonly understood as an explanation for the continuing influence of committee members in Congress on how bureaucratic agencies implement the law.[2]

The dominance theory may overstate the capacity for continuing congressional control, however, by presuming that the remaining members of Congress and other political actors will allow committees to shape agency policy. More specifically, members of Congress might be expected to restrict committee power when committee members use their oversight authority to advantage themselves at the expense of other members (Krehbiel 1991). Congress may allow a committee wide latitude to shape policy, but it is under no obligation to respect a committee's recommendations. Thus, not all committee threats to an agency are equally viable. A committee backed by majorities sufficient to pass legislation can credibly pressure a recalcitrant agency, but many threats are hollow because the committee lacks sufficient support in Congress and from the president to carry them out (Moe 1987).

Overall, committees are likely to have more real power in some circumstances than in others. What is missing in the traditional congressional dominance setup, however, is an understanding of the conditions under

---

[2] See, for example, Weingast and Moran 1983, Wood 1988, and Scholz and Wood 1998.

which committees are left alone to make policy decisions and bureaucracies respond to their enticements. Ultimately, committee power does not exist in a vacuum, but is shaped by other political actors and the strategic actions of the bureaucracy itself.

1.3. The Politics of Bureaucratic Structure and Procedure

In contrast to the focus on contemporaneous congressional intervention in the congressional dominance perspective, the structural explanation for bureaucratic behavior highlights the politics of agency design. In this perspective, agency behavior in the present is a product of historical political struggles that are manifested in structures and procedures that advantage some interests but not others (Moe 1989). Statutory constraints matter because they determine the degree of administrative discretion (what an agency can and cannot do; Epstein and O'Halloran 1994), the relative influence of presidential appointees and congressional overseers (Lewis 2003), and the procedures agencies must follow in implementing the law (McCubbins et al. 1987; McNollgast 1990).[3]

This theory predicts that *ex ante* agencies are likely to enjoy greater independence when bureaucrats possess technical expertise to deal with policy questions that legislators cannot resolve (Bawn 1995), when elected officials want to shield themselves from making potentially unpopular decisions,[4] and when crafting compromise legislation requires making concrete decisions about divisive issues. Accordingly, conflict between Congress and the president and uncertainty about the future shape the nature of administrative discretion. If groups that are in power when agencies are designed fear they may lose power in the future, they have an

---

[3] These models therefore include courts as interpreters of whether statutes and the Constitution prohibit particular bureaucratic choices.

[4] Fiorina (1986) instead argues that interest groups are readily deceived by adverse decisions made within the bureaucracy. In his model of delegation to the bureaucracy, when legislators wish to serve the "public interest" they delegate to avoid being blamed by organized interests for not serving their needs. It seems unlikely, however, that active interest groups would be fooled by this ruse or that the public would reward it. Active interest groups are likely to recognize a move to delegate authority that is contrary to their interests, and latent groups are unlikely to do so. When Congress and the president enact a law that allocates money to a particular constituency, it is highly visible even to relatively inattentive voters. By contrast, active interest groups are more likely than atomistic citizens to discern the political effects of decisions made within the bureaucracy. It is far more probable that elected officials would delegate in order to serve an active group, because the active group would recognize that its interests are being served, while elected officials could avoid taking readily observable steps that might evoke the ire of any latent opposition.

incentive to design agencies that protect their gains over the long run by restricting the ability of future officeholders to direct policy (Moe 1989; see also de Figueiredo 2002).

A focus on structure and procedures provides insights into the basic workings of bureaucratic decision making. Bureaucratic discretion is a necessary prerequisite of administrative choice. Similarly, agency structures and procedures alter the influence of different officials and groups in administrative proceedings (Moe 1989). But politics does not end with statutory construction. While a great deal of attention has been devoted to explaining when bureaucracies have discretion (e.g., Huber and Shipan 2002), this perspective gives comparatively little attention to how bureaucrats choose to use the discretion they are given. These choices in turn shape contemporaneous policy and the subsequent political struggles among different groups. Consequently, bureaucratic structure alone cannot explain how bureaucrats make discretionary implementation choices or the likely effects of these choices on the political standing of the bureaucracy itself.

1.4. Direct and Indirect Interest Group Influence

Scholars of interest group influence eschew a primary focus on elected officials and agency design in explaining bureaucratic behavior. Instead, they highlight the direct and indirect powers of advocacy groups to shape bureaucratic decisions (e.g., Lowi 1979; Gormley 1983). The direct interest group perspective posits that individual bureaucrats respond to the wishes of powerful groups (Scholz et al. 1991). The theory assumes that individual bureaucrats care about the support of powerful groups and act on behalf of these groups without any actual or threatened legislative or presidential involvement.

Interest groups are hypothesized to shape bureaucrats' decisions directly because of their control over social and material rewards of interest to individual bureaucrats. According to this argument, in cases where discretion is greatest and centralized oversight is weakest, bureaucrats have good reason to seek material and nonmaterial support from appropriate powerful groups. In some cases, groups are hypothesized to be powerful simply because they dominate a bureaucrat's work environment (Blau 1955; Hutter 1989). Social rewards outside of work may also become important if bureaucrats have ties to the community (Selznick 1949) or are recruited from the constituencies they serve (Carpenter 2001). In addition to these social benefits, interest groups are also hypothesized to have material rewards they can use to shape bureaucrats' decisions. Apart from direct (and usually illegal) material incentives like bribes, interest groups may hold sway over future employment opportunities and local support for an agency (Scholz et al. 1991).

This perspective may overstate the capacity for groups to influence bureaucratic decisions, however, by ignoring the processes that shapes bureaucrats' responsiveness to outside pressures. Bureaucratic leaders are generally cognizant of outside efforts to influence the behavior of their subordinates and may act to diminish agency responsiveness to these pressures. Indeed, Kaufman's (1960) classic study of the Forest Service describes an agency where a central concern of the headquarters staff is to prevent rangers from falling under the influence of local constituencies by consciously hiring rangers professionalized in the norms of responsible forestry and carefully monitoring their behavior in the field. In general, an individual bureaucrat is likely to respond to outside pressures only so long as there is some basis for exchange between the outside group and the bureaucrat. This requires both bureaucratic discretion and the opportunity for an exchange. For direct interest group influence to occur, groups must therefore be able to allocate the benefits that individual bureaucrats seek in sufficient quantities to overcome agency leaders' (and policymakers') efforts to prevent this responsiveness. Overall, rather than attributing responsiveness to opportunities for influence, a more complete explanation must account for the circumstances that lead agencies to encourage or allow responsiveness to particular outside influences.

By contrast, the indirect interest group influence perspective, often called the theory of agency capture, is broadly understood to predict that agencies become beholden to the interests of the groups they regulate or are themselves the product of interest group influence.[5] (On the influence of groups in agency design, see section 1.3.) Whereas the theory of direct interest group influence focuses on the ties between the enticements outside groups offer to individual bureaucrats and bureaucratic behavior, the theory of indirect interest group influence argues that bureaucracies respond to the wishes of powerful groups because these groups hold sway with elected officials who control an agency's political fortunes. Agency officials are therefore inclined to direct policy in ways that can garner the support of, and avoid the opposition of, groups with ties to elected officials (Arnold 1979).

---

[5] Others have characterized the close ties among interest groups, agencies, and congressional officials as iron triangles or subgovernments (e.g., Lowi 1979). The nature of congressional power was discussed earlier. Here the examination focuses on the interest group component of these (potentially) tripartite relationships.

This perspective has two interdependent lineages.[6] One begins with work by Huntington (1952) and Bernstein (1955) that tries to understand why regulatory agencies may come to ally themselves with the groups they are supposed to oversee on behalf of the "public interest." In their formulations, this shift occurs because the public, although mobilized at a critical moment to create a regulatory apparatus, is inattentive to ongoing policy decisions and is therefore replaced by the regulated community as an agency's political patron. The other begins with work by Stigler (1971) that seeks to explain the rise of regulation. Whereas Bernstein and Huntington focus on industry influence under an existing regulatory apparatus, Stigler argues that industry groups may actually seek regulation to prevent competition and extract cartel rents from consumers via entry restrictions (e.g., licensing rules for attorneys), pricing rules (e.g., the Civil Aeronautics Board's control of airline rates), and cost-raising measures like pollution controls. Both lineages are built on assumptions about the sources of group power. One is the mobilizing advantage of concentrated producer groups in which members individually have much at stake (Olson 1965). The other is the capability of groups to reward supportive elected officials (and punish opponents) through votes and campaign contributions.

Subsequent work builds on this twin foundation by suggesting the limitations and sources of group influence. First, group power is circumscribed because one group's gains are likely to encourage the countermobilization of other groups that would otherwise remain disorganized or unwilling to invest in influencing elected leaders (Peltzman 1976; see also Arnold's [1990] notion of "potential publics"). Overall, there are likely to be equilibrating effects such that few groups can sustain extreme gains and politicians will have the incentive to seek politically efficient solutions (Romer and Rosenthal 1987).[7] Strategies that minimize opposition include sharing the benefits of regulation with other potentially hostile groups.[8] Second, group power is shaped by the nature of the ties

---

[6] Posner (1974) and others stress the differences between the "pressure group" approach of Bernstein (and other political scientists) and the "economic theory" of Stigler. Nonetheless, both approaches rely on the assumption that certain groups will be privileged in organizing and shaping policy. In practice, contemporary political economy builds on both traditions.

[7] This perspective is therefore similar to "systems" theories that identify equilibrating effects among competing groups and forces in society.

[8] For instance, cross-subsidization occurs when the rents derived from regulation are not retained exclusively by the group seeking state protection but are used instead to placate potentially powerful opponents of the original group's policy efforts. The more general phenomenon of strategic compromise is discussed in greater detail later in this chapter.

between elected officials and groups. Thus, geographically defined legislative districts (Arnold 1979) and the different electoral rules for members of each chamber of Congress (Lee 2004) and the executive mediate group influence.

The contributions provided by the theory of instrumental group influence are significant. And yet the answers provided by this body of theory remain unsatisfying in several respects. Most significantly, while scholars regularly identify *ex post* the conditions that facilitated a group's success, rarely can they predict *ex ante* which groups will form and what advocacy strategies they will adopt.[9] For instance, in lobbying over farm policy one sometimes observes a united farm lobby, advocacy by geographic area (California versus Florida), organization by commodity (sugar versus soybeans), and even lobbying by farm size (industrial versus family-owned farms). Similarly, consumer mobilization occurs in certain policy domains and at particular times, but seemingly without any regular pattern related simply to group characteristics. What explains the observed variation in group activation and lobbying strategies?

Clearly, group advocacy strategies can be endogenous to the current political environment. Consequently, focusing on "which groups win now" ignores the way in which other political actors' decisions shape group strategy (Rothenberg 1994).[10] (An added difficulty of this approach, emphasized by Carpenter [2004], is that bureaucratic policies may advantage some groups even though those beneficiaries had little to do with policy creation. It is therefore dangerous to infer power from current advantage.) Thus, independent bureaucratic decisions may matter

---

[9] A notable exception to this characterization is work in comparative politics on the nature of trade protections for domestic industries (e.g., McGillivray 2004). Existing scholarship does recognize that certain latent groups will have an easier time overcoming the collective action problems associated with organization. Groups are more likely to form when their potential members share common goals, are few in number, have much at stake, include an entrepreneur willing to bear group start-up costs, and belong to existing communication networks. Groups with these characteristics are mobilized more easily both because the transaction costs associated with organization are lower and because it is easier for them to monitor and prevent the free-riding problems accompanying the creation of public goods. These factors, however, overlook strategic concerns that would affect group creation and advocacy. This oversight is important, since political success demands that a group must do more than organize; it must secure policy that advantages its members.

[10] Note that this point is different from the assertion that "history matters" (intrinsically) or that "policies create constituencies." Rather, strategic choices by elected officials and bureaucrats alter present political bargaining by varying the likely outcomes of adopting different advocacy strategies (see, e.g., Pierson 2000).

because they can alter groups' opportunities for and payoffs from pursuing different influence strategies. Overall, by reifying group identity and advocacy patterns, existing theories fail to consider the dynamic relationship between the interest group environment and bureaucratic decisions (Carpenter and Whittington 2003). A more accurate understanding of the capacity for group influence must therefore account for how bureaucrats choose to use the discretion they are given and how these choices alter the political calculations surrounding interest group strategies.

1.5. Multiple Impulses and Bureaucratic Behavior

Finally, empirical work on external control of the bureaucracy often encompasses many of the mechanisms specified by the theories discussed here into a unified framework in which multiple impulses act on the bureaucracy (see, for example, Wood and Waterman 1994; for a comprehensive review, see Krause 1999). Using the language of agency (Moe 1984), these analyses generally specify a hierarchical relationship between multiple political principals (Congress as a whole, key committees, the president, interest groups, etc.) and a bureaucratic agent. In this framework, bureaucracies respond to signals, ranging from budgetary changes to political appointments, sent by their political overseers.

As an empirical approach, this line of scholarship has produced many significant findings documenting political influence over bureaucratic behavior and strongly undercutting claims about intrinsic bureaucratic power. These findings have generally been confined to a few readily measured elements of bureaucratic choice (e.g., inspections, citations, and fines), however. It remains uncertain, therefore, whether important elements of bureaucratic choice are concealed in these aggregate counts of agency behavior.[11] As a theoretical model, this approach raises several more fundamental questions. Most significantly, applications often posit numerous potential political principals capable of sending signals to the bureaucracy without reconciling the underlying differences between the component theories that suppose different actors are powerful. Is it the locally elected member of Congress, the committee, or Congress as a whole that is powerful? If these actors disagree, who wins? Without a clearer delineation of why, for instance, an agency should respond to pressure applied by a committee given the preferences and powers of other political actors, the model mostly provides a prediction of occasional

---

[11] For example, Olson (1995) documents that the FDA substituted low-cost inspections for high-cost inspections to placate external political demands.

responsiveness. Additionally, this theoretical framework ignores the true spirit of agency models in which agents have preferences and act to achieve them. By focusing solely on bureaucratic responsiveness to externally generated signals, the model never makes clear what bureaucrats' care about or how bureaucratic choices affect external efforts to control them. How much, for example, do agencies "give in" when external demands are made of them?

2. Strategic Neutrality and the Conditions of Bureaucratic Leadership

What is the capacity for citizens and elected officials to control bureaucratic implementation of the law? Here I propose a new theory that highlights the uncertain link between interests and policy. This theory identifies the conditions under which bureaucratic leaders become capable of independently shaping how the law is implemented. The primary difference between this perspective and existing work is that it places bureaucratic leaders as primary actors in shaping political conflict while simultaneously recognizing their intrinsic problems as agency managers. Policy-motivated bureaucrats who are concerned about external political intervention and the need to control their subordinates mediate external efforts to alter bureaucratic decisions. While interest groups and elected officials are important in this model, they are not the only actors behaving strategically to shape government policy.

The critical features of this perspective are threefold. The first is the claim that bureaucratic leaders can use their existing authority to substantially shape policy when they do so in a way that prevents politicians from coordinating to overrule their decisions. When this discretion extends to the details of policy formulation and implementation, it may allow bureaucratic leaders to concoct policy agendas that become difficult for outsiders to upset. This perspective therefore extends notions of bureaucratic anticipation (Canes-Wrone 2003) by suggesting that bureaucratic power is manifested when agencies manipulate policy to remain in the "gridlock region." In other words, by moving first, bureaucrats alter the status quo policy over which external political bargaining takes place (Calvert et al. 1989). Of course, agency leaders do need to garner outside political support to obtain the resources and authority necessary for bureaucratic action. Thus, they must constantly concern themselves with whether political coalitions sufficient to compel alternative bureaucratic action are likely to form and succeed in their efforts to undo bureaucratic choices.

The second is the argument that feasible bureaucratic strategies are intrinsically intermeshed with the concerns agency leaders have about the control of their subordinates. While bureaucratic leaders may hold any set of policy preferences, the pursuit of a particular end is fundamentally limited by their need to control their subordinates, who might otherwise act in pursuit of their own ends and thereby impede the policy goals of bureaucratic leaders or imperil an agency's political standing (Brehm and Gates 1997). These internal management concerns eliminate certain policy options that, in the absence of the risk of subordinate malfeasance, might otherwise serve bureaucratic leaders' larger political ends.

Finally, the third is the assertion that interest group advocacy strategies and influence are both shaped by bureaucratic decisions (Rothenberg 1994). External groups are able to influence policy only if they can use existing procedural tools to compel bureaucratic action, build (or threaten to build) a majority sufficient to nominate newly supportive officials or enact new legislation compelling bureaucratic action, or find allies in the bureaucracy who have the discretion to act on their behalf. Bureaucratic action that independently shapes policy may alter the payoffs to potential group members of seeking change through these means. Through the careful construction of policy, agency leaders may therefore shape the nature of the support they garner and the opposition they face.

Given these features of the interaction between agency leaders, their subordinates, and the political environment, bureaucratic leaders have strong incentives to *limit subordinate discretion* and *demonstrate political efficiency*. An ideal way to achieve these ends is to engage in the *strategically neutral* implementation of the law. By limiting subordinate discretion – through direct administrative decree, monitoring, or self-policing norms (e.g., professionalism) – agency leaders minimize both generic losses to subordinate shirking and the political risks associated with malfeasance by subordinate bureaucrats.

Achieving *political efficiency*, defined as agency competence in implementing public policy that supportive politicians and groups desire while minimizing the costs for potential opponents, allows agencies to secure support and short-circuit potential opposition. Political efficiency differs from true "social welfare" efficiency in that politically efficient agencies are worthy of support from politicians and groups after accounting for the costs to them that an agency generates in both real dollars and political opposition. Political inefficiency, either agency wastefulness or political opposition to agency decisions, makes investments of support (in dollars, time, or other political capital) less likely. Politically efficient agencies, by contrast, do not imperil their supporters and are therefore more likely to be considered worthy of the investment of support from these allies.

Strategic neutrality, impartial implementation of the law given important centrally managed priorities, helps bureaucratic leaders to control their subordinates and allows them to demonstrate political efficiency given important political constraints. Strategic neutrality differs from true or naïve neutrality because it means agency leaders can embrace the language of fairness while simultaneously tailoring policy so as to achieve their own policy ends and improve their agency's political fortunes. Centrally directed and largely uniform field implementation provides an additional benefit over many alternative strategies given bureaucratic leaders' management needs because it enhances centralized management. It thereby lessens the risk of subordinate malfeasance. Strategic neutrality therefore brings together the Weberian ideal of neutral and professional implementation of the law by subordinate bureaucrats and the strategic manipulation of overall agency behavior by policy-minded bureaucrats.

In more fully fleshing out this argument, I proceed as follows. First, I introduce assumptions about the actors at the core of this model: bureaucrats, interest groups, and elected officials. Second, I diagnose the effects of the internal organization of bureaucracy on opportunities for political influence to be translated into policy. The strategic decisions of bureaucratic leaders about agency policy are motivated by their own policy preferences, but the pursuit of these ends is circumscribed by concerns about managing the bureaucracy and building political support. Bureaucratic leaders therefore have strong incentives to control their subordinates and seek politically efficient outcomes. Given these constraints, a policy of strategic neutrality often advantages bureaucratic leaders. This gives bureaucratic leaders a substantial, albeit limited, independent policy-making power best characterized as one of agenda setting. The theory is then applied to the case of EPA leadership during the Reagan years. Finally, the last section identifies the necessary conditions for bureaucratic leadership and the conditions under which this leadership may be circumscribed. Here I also contrast the predictions offered by this integrated theory of bureaucratic decision making and implementation with earlier perspectives.

2.1. Assumptions

Analyzing the complex interactions among government agencies, interest groups, and elected officials requires first identifying the goals and powers of these political actors.

2.1.1. bureaucrats: preferences and position. Bureaucrats have preferences about both their personal condition and public policy. Bureaucrats' preferences about their personal condition may include many different goals – for instance, self-promotion, power, prestige, financial reward, and an enjoyable work environment (Wilson 1989). In further specifying bureaucratic preferences, it is useful to distinguish between managers and lower-level subordinates.[12] Managers give orders and subordinates receive them. Technically, only the lowest-level bureaucrats are purely subordinates because they give orders to no one, while middle managers both give and receive orders. Still, it is useful to differentiate between those bureaucrats at the top of agencies who make policies that others must follow and those who mostly implement or oversee direct implementation.[13] Obviously, all managers may not agree about the appropriate course of public policy. For example, careerists may disagree substantially with presidential appointees.

Overall, bureaucrats must balance between conflicting goals in making decisions about how to implement public policy as well as with regard to narrower components of bureaucratic performance – for instance, how hard to work. As a result, elected officials and bureaucratic superiors can manipulate, at least to a degree, how subordinate bureaucrats make

[12] Wilson (1989) distinguishes among careerists, politicians, and professionals in explaining the motivations of different classes of bureaucrats. The difficulty with this trichotomization is that many managers and lower-level bureaucrats are both professionals and careerists. In other words, they must consider both their allegiance to an agency and their ties to like-minded professionals. Likewise, most high-level managers recognize the political nature of their positions, even if they are not explicitly chosen for their political beliefs. Alternatively, Downs (1967) identifies five "ideal-type" bureaucrats based on assumptions about how much weight individuals assign to nine different underlying goals. These five types are further divided into two classes who consider their self-interest and political goals in making decisions, "purely self-interested officials" and "mixed-motive officials." As will be explained later, I assume (roughly) that managers are more likely to behave like mixed-motive officials than are their subordinates. Finally, Niskanen (1971) and others propose as a simplifying assumption that bureaucrats are simply "budget maximizers" concerned with inflating their agency's gross (or slack) budget. Given that the officials with the most control over budgetary requests are also those bureaucrats most likely to hold strong beliefs about appropriate public policy outcomes, ignoring their preferences about agency policy seems inappropriate if one is trying to explain their behavior. Depending on how a manager wants to change policy, a smaller budget may be just as much a means to an end as a larger one.

[13] Carpenter (2001) labels these crucial midlevel managers, who both design and oversee the implementation of policy, as the "mezzo" level. In my perspective, these bureaucrats who have the authority to shape broader implementation are managers.

decisions.[14] Bureaucrats who refuse to perform the basic tasks listed in their job assignment may be terminated; those who violate federal ethics laws or conspire to commit fraud may face criminal prosecution; and those who perform poorly may be assigned undesirable tasks with little opportunity for personal reward or hope for promotion (Brehm and Gates 1997).

2.1.2. interest groups: preferences, activity, and strategy.
Interest groups desire to shape public policy. An interest group is composed of those nongovernmental actors who have formed an organization to advance their common interests (Olson 1965). Interest groups can pursue a variety of policy ends. They may try to abolish an agency, expand or contract the scope of its power, or shape how it behaves in particular situations. Whatever the source of their motivation, interest groups are politically relevant when they try to influence public policy.

In the larger class of "interested parties" – those actors with some common concern affected by government policy – interest groups are those coalitions that have succeeded in forming active advocacy groups. Alternatively, interested parties may include both latent and active interest groups.[15] Politically, active interest groups have a pair of important advantages over latent groups. Because active interest groups have already underwritten the costs of organization, they are more likely to join the political fray whenever an issue that affects their members arises, while latent groups must overcome free-riding and start-up costs. Additionally, active interest groups are less readily deceived than "diffuse publics" and other atomized groups because they can invest resources in developing mechanisms for monitoring government.[16] Active interest groups are therefore more likely than latent groups to be able to attribute blame for actions contrary to their interests and to reward their supporters.

A further assumption is that interest groups are not static entities with predetermined lobbying agendas. Rather, both group membership and

---

[14] On the generic effects of control by superiors, see Lipsky 1980. On the strengths and limits of this control, see Padgett 1981.

[15] I use the term "interest group" to refer exclusively to active interest groups.

[16] In Arnold's terms, active groups are far less likely to be deceived by legislators' efforts to diminish the traceability of their actions, regardless of whether they improve or impair a group's members' positions. It may also be the case, however, that latent groups can rely on the stewardship of a third party to alert them to the losses they face. For instance, opportunist members of Congress may take steps to make visible the costs being imposed on the diffuse public (Arnold 1990). Still, contingent on being made aware of the stakes in a given policy conflict, members of a latent group must still overcome their lethargy in order to participate as anything other than atomistic voters.

advocacy strategies are strategic choices, such that the coalitions of actors that come together to form an active interest group and the advocacy strategy this group pursues are themselves products of the political environment. Interest groups must then make two decisions in deciding how to pursue their members' interests. First, a group must decide what position it will it take. That is, it must decide whether to advocate and, if it does, what particular policy outcome it will seek. Second, a group must decide how it will go about trying to achieve this end. Will it try to influence directly how the law is implemented, take advantage of existing procedural routes to direct bureaucratic decisions, or will it seek to change the law itself? Overall, in choosing how to advocate, interest group leaders have to consider two interrelated factors: the gain from successful advocacy and the likelihood of success. These are interconnected questions because the policy a group pursues and the means it uses to achieve this end affect the opposition it faces and the allies it attracts.

The first interest group decision is which policy position to pursue. A group must weigh the potential gain offered by a lobbying strategy and the probability that this strategy will succeed. Significantly, an advocacy strategy that increases a group's potential gain from lobbying may be less likely to succeed than a strategy that, if successful, would yield more modest gains. This is because a more moderate strategy may allow a group to attract more allies (and make fewer enemies) than a more selfish one. The second interest group decision is how to go about changing policy. In particular, in trying to shape bureaucratic decisions, a group must choose among the formal lawmaking process, taking advantage of existing procedural protections, and direct efforts to influence bureaucratic behavior. In making this decision, an interest group must once again weigh the gains from a given lobbying strategy and the probability that it will succeed. Here, two questions are most important.[17] The first is whether different efforts to alter policy are likely to become visible and therefore mobilize latent opponents. More specifically, it may be the case that efforts to alter the law in Congress would engender opposition from latent groups that equally efficacious sub rosa efforts to lobby the bureaucracy directly would not. The second is how the efficacy of different tools for changing policy is affected by existing constraints on the bureaucracy and the preferences of elected officials and bureaucrats. In other words, which strategy will succeed in a given circumstance depends on where

---

[17] In addition to these concerns, groups may also consider their relative performance over the long term. See the earlier discussion of agency design.

(and if) the group is able to locate allies with the discretion to act on its behalf.

In sum, different policy positions promise different dividends if successful, but may also differ substantially in their probability of success. If successful, a targeted legislative enactment favoring a single group might offer it more than a broad coalition generally attacking an agency. However, the latter strategy might be more desirable because the overall probability of success is higher. Likewise, the group might forgo legislative action altogether and attempt to use direct interaction with the bureaucracy, but whether this tactic succeeds depends on bureaucratic discretion and sufficient bureaucratic support (or fear).[18] When groups do turn to elected officials to act on their behalf, they must consider the concerns of those actors. The following section explores how and when elected officials may work on behalf of interest groups, with particular attention to the powers and limits of the tools available to different officials to influence policy.

2.1.3. elected officials: preferences and tools. Elected officials have preferences about bureaucratic actions and can act to influence bureaucratic decisions. Elected officials' preferences may be rooted in many sources, including ideological beliefs, interest group support, constituency service, and a desire for good public policy. Interest groups, however, are particularly important in shaping officials' preferences. Interest groups are powerful because their greater attention to politics allows them to affect who is elected directly through the votes of their members and indirectly through endorsements and campaign contributions (Jacobson 1997). For these reasons, larger and wealthier groups are advantaged vis-à-vis smaller and poorer ones.[19]

Elected officials can try to influence bureaucratic decisions – whether on behalf of an interest group or not – either during periods of agency design

---

[18] Not discussed in this example is the use of procedural protections to influence bureaucratic behavior. Procedural approaches offer some of the advantages and disadvantages of both direct and legislative influence strategies. Procedural rights usually require bureaucratic action, but the scope of the necessary bureaucratic response is usually limited such that the degree of bureaucratic support within the bureaucracy and the power of a group's allies outside the bureaucracy affect the responsiveness of agencies to the use of procedural tools. Also, different procedures vary substantially in their visibility and thus in their likelihood of generating opposition from a group's opponents. For instance, successfully challenging an agency's decisions in court is far more likely to be noticed by a group's opponents than achieving the same end through less-visible participation in rule making.

[19] Groups representing an official's ideological and geographic constituency are also likely to be more powerful because serving them will be less likely to alienate other supporters and may attract more relevant votes.

or as part of their ongoing oversight of the bureaucracy. This discussion focuses on the latter case, recognizing that agency governance takes place in light of existing statutes that are likely to encompass previous strategic decisions by these officials when agencies were created anew. Broadly speaking, elected officials can choose between using formal and informal means to influence bureaucratic decisions during ongoing oversight of the bureaucracy. Formal actions are direct and include passing laws, such as appropriations riders, and appointing and confirming officials. Informal actions provide guidance to agencies and include contacting agency officials, conducting oversight hearings, and using extra-organizational apparatus, like the Office of Management and Budget, to shape agency policy. Formal actions are more likely to change policy in the face of bureaucratic resistance, but they are both more difficult to undertake and more likely to arouse the opposition of policy opponents. Informal actions are less visible, more flexible, and less subject to majority review, but are simultaneously vulnerable to bureaucratic resistance (Gormley 1989). Elected officials' choices of tools for pressuring administrative agencies are affected in important ways by the interest group environment and the support of other elected officials and the bureaucracy.

First, the interest group environment alters the relative risks and rewards of different types of group-serving activity. As explained earlier, active interest groups are likely to detect either informal or formal actions affecting their interests. Consequently, elected officials can claim credit with (or be blamed by) active constituencies through either method of policy manipulation. Inactive constituencies are poorly served through informal means, however, because elected officials are unlikely to be able to undertake credit claiming without a visible public action necessary to demonstrate their success. For the same reason, formal policy making raises greater risks for elected officials who wish to serve an active group without their actions being detected, and potentially punished, by an inactive or latent group. Thus, ceteris paribus, elected officials are more likely to prefer informal efforts to direct policy when these efforts serve an active group at the expense of a latent group.

Second, an elected official's choice of how to manipulate policy is shaped by the relative support the official enjoys in the bureaucracy and from other elected officials. Conflict among elected leaders impedes the use of formal policy tools, while informal efforts to change policy are subject to bureaucratic resistance and can be overruled by formal policy making. If there is sufficient conflict among elected leaders, the bureaucracy can resist external pressure without fear of being compelled to change its behavior through formal policy making (Calvert et al. 1989). Alternatively, the bureaucracy may resist even in the face of credible threats to compel changes in its behavior if it prefers public rebuke to demurring privately.

Two types of conflict among elected leaders are most important in affecting the strategies of politicians acting to control agency decisions. The first is conflict between the president and Congress. The second is conflict among members of Congress, particularly between committee members and the remaining members of Congress.[20] While in theory all members of Congress share the power to control the bureaucracy, only certain members sit on the oversight and appropriations committees responsible for agency policy. Thus, day-to-day agency oversight is the responsibility of only a subset of all members of Congress, and these committee members may seek to shape policy in a way that is contrary to other members' preferences. Conflict among elected officials is therefore likely to make different strategies for controlling agencies more attractive to these officials. When the president, congressional committees, and the remainder of the congressional majority are in agreement about policy, or when the remaining actors are willing to defer to each other, elected officials may rely on either formal or informal means to shape agency decisions.[21]

When the president and Congress are in disagreement, however, each actor's appropriate powers take on special significance and policy outcomes are more uncertain. For instance, the president can nominate anyone he sees fit to head an agency, but cannot compel the Senate to confirm her. Likewise, the Congress can pass legislation, but this legislation is subject to presidential veto. A similar uncertainty prevails when the remaining members of Congress are unwilling to defer to committees. In general, the difficulty of exercising formal means of control in the face of opposition is likely to diminish the responsiveness of the bureaucracy to threats to

[20] Two other potential dimensions of disagreement within the Congress are not discussed here: conflict between the Senate and House and conflict between the majority and the minority.

[21] All else being equal, elected officials are more likely to try informal means to direct agency decisions on behalf of active interest groups, because they are less time-consuming, more flexible, and less likely to engender significant opposition. If existing institutional arrangements prevent agencies from acting as Congress and the president desire, however, elected officials can turn to their entire range of formal tools. Similarly, if an agency rebuffs a united Congress and president, either party can undertake formal proceedings to rein in the bureaucracy subject to the concerns about mobilizing a previously inactive interest group discussed earlier.

enact these changes. This is not to suggest that conflict is entirely emasculating. Presidents can still use their discretionary authority as head of the executive branch to direct policy (Howell 2003). Likewise, committees can use their negative power to prevent legislation from coming to the floor to manipulate the legislative agenda (Snyder 1992). Both presidential and committee activism, however, are subject to being trumped by the coordinated actions of other elected officials or undone by bureaucratic resistance. When elected officials disagree, it affects both whether informal oversight actions are challenged and whether formal policy changes, or the threat thereof, succeed. It follows that the next important topic is to identify the circumstances under which bureaucrats will use their discretion in response to external pressures. This requires an examination of the dual pressures facing bureaucratic leaders as agency managers and strategic political actors.

2.2. The Fundamental Intertwining of Management and Political Needs: Controlling Subordinates and Seeking Political Efficiency

The preceding discussion of actors' preferences and tools for influencing policy lays the groundwork for the exposition of the claim that strategic neutrality is an ideal bureaucratic posture. A central focus on bureaucratic choice necessitates, however, an additional understanding of how internal management considerations and external political needs are intertwined. The nature of outside influence on the bureaucracy is linked with problems of internal management because agency leaders' political strategies are "constrained by internal organizational considerations" (Moe 1987: 481).

Concerns about management and control of subordinates arise for several reasons. Generally, task complexity and the division of authority force bureaucratic leaders to delegate authority to their subordinates. This is particularly true in the field of regulation, where enforcement outcomes result from a stream of decisions about how to identify, evaluate, and punish those who violate the law (Diver 1980). This task complexity exacerbates the division of authority that raises further concerns about the management of subordinates.[22] Unfortunately for bureaucratic leaders,

---

[22] Authority is divided for several reasons. First, because the number of parties to be regulated is very large, bureaucratic leaders must devolve authority to those who actually conduct enforcement activities. Second, when a government agency must oversee a geographically dispersed set of actors, it is infeasible to have a single person accomplish these tasks. Third, the skills and training necessary to detect violations of the law differ substantially from those that are necessary to prosecute and handle the legal challenges surrounding the punishment of noncompliance.

subordinates imbued with authority may "shirk" by avoiding difficult work, wasting government resources, or otherwise undercutting the efficient implementation of the law. This is a basic problem of agency – as long as monitoring and incentives are imperfect, subordinates may not behave as their superiors desire (Moe 1984). In the political arena, however, shirking has important additional implications for how bureaucrats can go about pursuing their personal and policy goals.

Generally, the possibility that subordinates might engage in untoward behavior creates incentives for government managers to engage in greater and more effective control of their subordinates. Subordinates who shirk consume resources that could otherwise serve managers' needs. But being lazy is not the worst that a government employee can do. Like their private sector counterparts, government bureaucrats can engage in "sabotage," taking actions that are not simply inefficient or ineffective, but destructive (Brehm and Gates 1997). For bureaucrats who are concerned about policy, shirking and sabotage are particularly damaging because government agencies, as purely derivative creations of their political overseers, have no inherent claim of legitimacy. In other words, unlike a private group, they depend on the explicit and continuing support of elected officials to maintain their existence. Thus, the management needs of bureaucratic leaders are tied directly to their political needs. If agency leaders want to make demands for continued authority or financial support, they must demonstrate that government authority and resources are not misused. Inefficiency is damaging because it undercuts the weight others give to agency demands for resources. Sabotage is even more dangerous, however. Subordinate malfeasance can both frustrate the achievement of a leader's policy goals and endanger an agency's external political coalition.

This tie between internal management and external political considerations creates an inherent bias among managers toward effective control of their subordinates. Because bureaucratic leaders care about policy and their personal position, they worry that if their subordinates are left to their own devices, they may shirk or sabotage.[23] Control is necessary to overcome these centrifugal tendencies. (Note that it is not necessary that control be exercised only through direct limits on subordinate discretion or extensive monitoring. As others have noted, bureaucracies constructed

---

[23] It is reasonable to note that some agency leaders actually oppose their agency's own mission (however defined). Consequently, they might seem to have an incentive to weaken control in order to undercut the agency's performance. The case of the Environmental Protection Agency (EPA), discussed later in this chapter, demonstrates how the impetus for control applies across the ideological spectrum.

around strong professional or cultural norms [e.g., Kaufman 1960; Miller 1992] can yield especially effective control of subordinates.)

The second implication of the intertwining of management and political needs is the strong incentive for agency leaders who seek to direct an agency to their own ends to produce politically efficient policy. To reiterate, political efficiency is the ability of agency leaders to produce benefits that supportive politicians and groups desire while minimizing the real and opposition-induced costs of directing policy in this manner. Generically, "apolitical" economic efficiency is desirable because it shows that agencies are worth the resources politicians invest in them. Regardless of the political climate, those managers who seek an agency's survival have a generic incentive to demonstrate to elected officials that agency resources are being used efficaciously. But why is political efficiency desirable in all circumstances? If an agency faces a supportive political climate, inefficiency demonstrates that an agency cannot be trusted. Thus, shirking and sabotage undercut claims that additional resources (which politicians can presumably invest elsewhere) will be used appropriately. Efficiency, by contrast, shows that an agency can be trusted and will not abuse its power. Perhaps somewhat counterintuitively, however, the same incentives prevail if an agency faces a hostile political climate. In this case, agency opponents are already inclined to cut agency budgets, scale back bureaucratic authority, or constrain agency choices. Inefficiency and the misuse of authority only further demonstrate that these moves are warranted. Efficiency, however, maintains an agency's reputation for effective governance (see Carpenter 2001).[24] It also demonstrates to those individuals who may be unsure of an agency's value that agency expenditures are worthwhile.

Political efficiency, however, also binds agencies to do more than maximize outputs per dollar of invested resources. Specifically, it requires agencies to take account of the support and opposition they attract. This group calculus is therefore interwoven with the generic incentive to implement

---

[24] One might object to this argument by claiming that inefficiency, by making an agency less threatening, would help it survive in the face of a hostile cadre of elected officials. Inefficiency, however, would do little to placate a truly powerful opponent. If the opponent could gut the agency, inefficiency would not protect it or encourage supportive elected officials to sustain it. Additionally, "temporary inefficiency" serves neither side over the long run. If they could, agency opponents would rather secure protection from a resurgent agency over the long run by decreasing agency appropriations and curtailing its authority. For an agency that is hoping its allies will regain power in the future, inefficiency would damage its reputation for effectiveness and thus weaken future efforts to justify restoring funding and authority.

effective policy. Policies that attract more support are, ceteris paribus, no more efficient politically if they simultaneously attract substantial opposition from powerful groups (Romer and Rosenthal 1987). If, on the other hand, an agency can tailor policy to generate similar support without any increase in opposition, it is more politically efficient. Not only does minimizing opposition decrease the chances that outsiders will overrule agency decisions directly, it also diminishes the costs to agency supporters of defending the agency rather than devoting scarce political capital to other endeavors.[25] In practical terms, as Rourke (1984: 60) argues, minimizing countermobilization encourages agencies to engage in the same careful calibration of policy through cross-subsidization and other means that scholars of interest group influence have attributed to legislatures in regulatory design (e.g., Gilligan et al. 1989).

Note that claiming that agencies have an incentive to manage toward political efficiency does not mean that agencies will enact policy that is socially optimal. Agency leaders may choose to direct their subordinates in a way that is politically desirable but disadvantages society as a whole. The core claim is that agencies will make efforts to appear necessary and efficient *as far as their supporters are concerned* while minimizing unnecessary costs to viable political opponents. Shirking and sabotage are thus measured relative to the goals of agency leaders and their allies and not relative to some external and contested reference of social good.

2.3. Strategic Neutrality

The interlinked imperatives of controlling subordinates and demonstrating political efficiency restrict the range of options from which bureaucratic leaders can feasibly choose in seeking to shape policy. In light of these concerns and the larger political environment in which outside actors seek to alter bureaucratic decisions, leaders of complex bureaucratic organizations have an incentive to pursue strategic neutrality. Strategic neutrality limits the opportunities for outsiders to compel bureaucratic action by minimizing the probability that outside coalitions sufficiently powerful to overturn bureaucratic decisions will form.

What is strategic neutrality? As noted earlier, strategic neutrality means practicing uniform implementation with regard to factors outside the

---

[25] For example, Republicans attacked the Internal Revenue Service (IRS) after their takeover of the House in 1994 with the claim that the IRS was auditing too many individuals who had properly represented their income. A higher "yield" in audits, however, would have helped the agency to refute claims that it was politically motivated to target certain law-abiding citizens.

direct control of centralized bureaucratic superiors while nonetheless allowing agencywide decisions to vary according to centralized directives. That is, at the micro level, local and particularized decision making is consistent, while aggregate and macro agencywide implementation varies according to centralized directives. In other words, strategic neutrality requires treating similar parties similarly, but allows centralized and uniform decisions to dictate what will constitute both "like" parties and suitable treatment of these parties. Unlike true neutrality, these centralized decisions about appropriate categorizations of similarity (as transmitted to and implemented by field-level bureaucrats) will reflect strategic political decisions about how to build agency support (by demonstrating political efficiency) while still accomplishing bureaucratic leaders' personal and political ends.[26]

So an enforcement agency might, for instance, step back from enforcing against one class of regulated party in order to avoid political conflict, or aggressively pursue another type in order to build political support. Significantly, however, these strategic decisions will be made at the upper levels of the agency and implemented uniformly – neutrally – throughout the agency. In other words, while agencywide enforcement might reflect targeted variation, bureaucratic leaders will nonetheless make efforts to isolate bureaucratic subordinates from making decisions of this sort on the basis of their own readings of the political and work environment. This centralized partiality but lower-level consistency allows bureaucratic leaders the best of both worlds. They can tailor macro-agency decisions to build political support while also controlling their subordinates who might otherwise enforce the law differently (for their own personal or political reasons) to the detriment of agency leaders' personal and political goals. Strategic neutrality can therefore blend together subordinate professionalism and neutrality with political maneuvering by agency heads.

The linkage between the notion of strategic neutrality and Weber's conception of the power of modern bureaucracy is clear. Weber defined a

---

[26] Redford (1969) suggests that there is a generic imperative for bureaucratic leaders to encourage subordinate consistency and neutrality because of the pressure on lower-level bureaucrats to tailor implementation to the political power of, among other things, individual businesses and communities. By contrast, I argue that the structuring of subordinate decision making will be shaped by important political considerations, rather than by a simple desire to achieve objective neutrality.

This discussion also sidesteps the question of whether there might be a normative benchmark for neutral treatment (see Gordon 1999). At the extreme, one might argue that the only legitimate bases for differentiation are those explicitly recognized by statute. Of course, there are often nontrivial disagreements about the meaning of statutory language.

central characteristic of bureaucracy as subordinate enforcement of "general rules, which are more or less stable, more or less exhaustive, and which can be learned" (1946: 198). "The 'objective' discharge of business primarily means a discharge of business according to *calculable rules* and 'without regard for persons' " (215). This routinized enforcement serves to promote efficiency by systematizing the exercise of state power in a way that is not possible in pre-bureaucratic government. Rule-boundedness therefore serves an internal function within bureaucracy, guiding subordinates to a single coherent end and promoting organizational efficiency.

But Weber also goes further, noting that neutrality serves the bureaucracy in its interactions with others in society. "The more complicated and specialized modern culture becomes, the more its external supporting apparatus demands the personally detached and strictly 'objective' *expert*. . . . As a rule, only bureaucracy has established the foundation for the administration of a [conceptually systemized] rational law" (216). Thus, bureaucracy is a symbol of the rule of law and fairness against which charismatic or particularistic implementation should be compared. A similar power persists even now: Claims of fairness and consistency allow bureaucracies to appear "above politics" (see, e.g., Lind and Tyler 1988; but see Chapter 5 for a discussion of the conflict between fairness and reasonableness).

Weber was of course not so naïve as to accept bureaucratic reasoning as devoid of political concerns (of the political instincts of bureaucratic leaders, he writes, "[A]bove all, the sure instincts of the bureaucracy for the conditions of maintaining its power in its own state . . . are inseparably fused with the canonization of the abstract and 'objective' idea of 'reasons of state' " [220].) Thus, strategic neutrality is perhaps the full exposition of the idea of the construction of neutrality for political reasons. Where I diverge from Weber is in specifying the limits of this power, because contemporary political actors, when allied, are clearly able to overcome the "[overtowering] power position of a fully developed bureaucracy" (232).

In some ways, this examination of bureaucratic decision making has so far left unanswered the central question of this inquiry: Under what circumstances do bureaucrats respond to the pressures exerted by interest groups and elected officials acting on behalf of those groups? So far, I have suggested that bureaucratic leaders have a generic incentive to control their subordinates and to seek politically efficient solutions and that strategic neutrality is a beneficial strategy for achieving these ends. Within these general confines, however, I have left unspecified the particular direction in which bureaucrats will choose to direct policy. In large part, that is because the answer posed here is that bureaucratic leaders facing external pressures make choices about how to direct policy, but that these choices are not preordained.

A bureaucratic leader's range of feasible choices is limited by formal constraints on the bureaucracy and credible indirect political constraints. Within these confines, bureaucrats nonetheless exercise some power over policy. Consequently, insofar as bureaucratic leaders make decisions, it is impossible to understand their actions without identifying their preferences or the central influence their choices have on the likelihood that their decisions will subsequently be overruled. The net result of this power is that bureaucratic leaders are transformed from simple agents of external political pressures to limited shapers of policy who make strategic decisions about how to navigate and shape their political environment.

Perhaps the best way to characterize the power bureaucratic leaders have to shape policy is as agenda setters, albeit limited ones. Policy changes initiated by the bureaucracy are subject to subsequently being overruled by other actors. But, insofar as compelling the bureaucracy to change policy is difficult, the status quo created by bureaucratic action is a privileged "reversion point" (Romer and Rosenthal 1979; Calvert, McCubbins, and Weingast 1989). Absent external action, the bureaucracy's position will endure. As an agenda setter, the bureaucracy can move policy in one direction or another along existing dimensions of observed conflict if it can avoid being overruled (for example, see Volden 2002 and Shipan 2004). But more fundamentally, an agency can reconfigure the packaging of policy choices so as to alter the dimensions of political conflict. That is, rather than making a choice about more or less A (enforcement in large businesses) and B (enforcement in small businesses), a bureaucratically initiated move can make the choice about more or less A (enforcement in large businesses) alone. This ability to generate policy initiatives that alter the choices outsiders face in trying to overrule bureaucratic decisions is an important component of setting an agenda. It is the power not only to make choices, but also to structure the choices outsiders can subsequently act upon.

The Environmental Protection Agency's experience during the Reagan administration provides a concrete demonstration of the generic importance of controlling subordinates and demonstrating political efficiency, as well as of the potential power of strategic neutrality. In sharp contrast with the agency's reputation during the Carter administration for "filing first, negotiating later," Reagan's first appointee to head the agency, Anne (Burford) Gorsuch, was largely opposed to this confrontational enforcement posture (Mintz 1995: 42). How did an administrator hostile to her agency's traditionally understood mission go about her job? First, she sought greater control of EPA's enforcement apparatus. This was achieved through a variety of means, including internal reorganizations, staff reassignments, and, perhaps most critically, greater review at headquarters (by newly hired and ideologically supportive attorneys) of all legal proceedings and negotiations (Mintz 1995: 49). This move undercut the power of lower-level career EPA staff, who were also told that confrontational enforcement, failure to support state enforcement decisions, and an inability to reach negotiated settlements would be grounds for negative evaluation (Mintz 1995: 46). To reiterate, despite her hostility to the EPA's traditional enforcement mission, Gorsuch did not promote discretion within the bureaucracy but instead sought to control her subordinates.

In terms of demonstrating political efficiency, Gorsuch's leadership was far less successful. Moving the EPA away from traditional "legalistic" enforcement toward more cooperative regulation might have allowed the agency to reorient its basis of support from liberals and environmentalists to conservatives and business interests. However, the near total collapse of EPA enforcement activities, allegations that EPA political appointees were negotiating "sweetheart" deals with politically well-connected polluters, and a sharp cutback in Superfund remediation efforts made it appear that the agency was giving up on enforcement rather than simply altering its means for protecting the environment (Mintz 1995: 51). Democrats and environmental groups mobilized in opposition to Gorsuch's leadership, but far more damaging were criticisms by moderate Republicans and many members of the business community. Under pressure from Congress, Gorsuch was ultimately forced to resign and was replaced by William Ruckelshaus, a moderate Republican who had headed the EPA during the Nixon administration. In sum,

[T]he EPA managers of the early 1980s failed from the outset to enunciate a clear and defensible approach to EPA's enforcement work. In this respect, their efforts stand in sharp contrast not only to the litigious EPA enforcement strategies of the Carter administration but also to enforcement regimes of the Nixon and Ford administrations, as well as the EPA enforcement programs of the past ten years. (Mintz 1995: 57–58)

Overall, Gorsuch achieved the first tenet of strategic neutrality, garnering control of subordinates, but failed in the second, demonstrating political efficiency. Was a strategically neutral policy feasible? It seems clear that if Gorsuch's primary goal was reducing the burden of government regulation for private firms over the long term, she could have tried to adjust policy to reward those "high compliance" businesses that still faced extensive enforcement costs and hostile interactions with the agency. Alternatively, there might have been more support for reducing government regulation in those industries most endangered by costly and aggressive regulation (for example, rules requiring heavy industry to remediate, rather than contain, polluted soil). But the wholesale abandonment of enforcement left a still costly agency that did little to satisfy the majority coalition demanding some regulatory enforcement.

More generally, environmental protection is a policy area in which there are active interest groups on both sides of the issue and substantial heterogeneity in the goals of apparent allies. An EPA enforcement posture that did not anger all pro-regulation groups as well as many of those opposed to aggressive regulation was clearly feasible. Gorsuch did not find such a strategy, however. Ruckelshaus's policy of encouraging cooperative compliance and working with state agencies while simultaneously using Superfund resources aggressively to clean up polluted areas was more successful, although Congress continued to press the EPA to demonstrate its worth by bringing additional enforcement actions and also gave the agency little leeway because of ongoing suspicion about haphazard enforcement of rules for solid waste disposal (Mintz 1995: 70).

2.4. The Conditions of Bureaucratic Power

This argument advanced here qualifies existing theories about the nature of bureaucratic power and decision making in several critical respects. Unlike the theory of congressional dominance or interest group capture, this perspective suggests that bureaucratic leaders are active policymakers. Given discretion, they make choices that other actors must in turn respond to. This agenda-setting power means that bureaucrats make strategic decisions that alter the nature of subsequent political conflict and that allow them to take advantage of conflict among elected officials and the potential fragility of advocacy coalitions. This argument does not mean, however, that one must accept the proposition that the bureaucracy is ungovernable. Rather, bureaucrats make decisions that direct policy, recognizing that these decisions may be overruled by coalitions of elected leaders acting on behalf of interest groups. Bureaucratic leaders are also constrained in important ways by their need to control their subordinates. In sum, external political control is conditional – on being able to create coalitions to enact legislation or use other formal actions or procedural tools to direct policy, on being able to credibly threaten bureaucratic leaders with advocacy by elected officials, and on finding bureaucratic allies with sufficient discretion to act on a group's demands (and who will not subsequently be overruled).[27]

More broadly, this argument suggests that political visions of agency particularism are not incompatible with bureaucratic professionalism. One way for agency leaders to achieve strategic neutrality is to recruit and oversee professional bureaucrats who will competently implement the law. Agency leaders will simultaneously tailor the tasks these subordinate bureaucrats are given, however, so that competent implementation does not come at the cost of the agency's political standing. Several conditions must be met for bureaucrats to be able to exercise political power in this way. For bureaucratic leaders to enjoy agenda-setting power, they must have some initial discretion to direct policy. Without the authority to alter policy – because of statutory rules prohibiting some type of behavior or court intervention, for example – bureaucratic leaders lack the ability to guide policy in a way that will persist absent external intervention. Put another way, in order for bureaucrats to compel outsiders to respond to their efforts to shape policy, they must be able to take actions that will change the status quo.

Second, not all bureaucratic efforts to set the agenda are sustainable because managers need to control implementation by their subordinates and because their decisions are occasionally subject to being overruled immediately by outsiders. Agency leaders might change policy, but if these moves allow subordinate bureaucrats to subvert them, there will be no real policy change. Likewise, weak bureaucracies may prove immune to even politically astute leadership. Similarly, agency leaders imbued with discretion may try to change policy only to find that members of Congress and the president work together to undo their handiwork. More generally,

---

[27] Nor is my argument informational in nature – bureaucrats are not powerful because they can deceive politicians. Instead, bureaucratic leaders are powerful because they can direct policy, and in order to override these decisions elected officials have to create coalitions sufficient to move policy from this newly (and bureaucratically) created "reversion point." Information clearly matters, in that inactive groups are less likely to detect decisions internal to the bureaucracy, but this is of concern to interest groups and not to elected officials. It is useful to contrast this perspective with that posed by Lafont and Tirole (1991), who incorporate assumptions about asymmetric information between the bureaucracy and Congress into a model in which agencies can collude with regulated groups. In my model, groups are also able to collude with supportive bureaucracies if inactive groups remain unaware. Consequently, there is no reason for elected officials to become informed or involved.

although bureaucrats may succeed in repackaging the nature of political conflict, the agency reauthorization and funding processes may expose an agency to externally mandated reconfiguration of political conflict. Conflicts over agency funding in committee, for instance, provide an ideal way for enterprising members of Congress to introduce appropriations riders that either build or cut into an agency's interest group support.

The degree to which bureaucratic leaders have the capacity to direct policy is therefore influenced by the nature of the policy under consideration – how easily centralized control can achieve a leader's agenda without encouraging bureaucratic resistance – and the nature of the interest group environment (and the related level of agreement among elected officials). When strategic policy direction would require extensive subordinate discretion, bureaucratic leaders must find means to shape this discretion or risk being undone from within. Policy that can be directed centrally – where resources are sent, which staff are hired, and how agency rules are crafted – is, by contrast, an ideal means for directing an agency.

The final key condition for bureaucratic leadership is therefore sufficient flexibility in the interest group environment. A policy area dominated by a single interest group leaves bureaucratic leaders with little choice about whom to serve, but the presence of potential competing groups and variation in their possible activities gives bureaucratic leaders important leverage in choosing policy goals and the means to achieve them. Consider separately a political environment dominated by a single powerful interest group, one characterized by multiple groups where one group is presently more active, and finally an environment in which there are multiple active interest groups.[28] If the interest group environment is dominated by a single well-organized and politically powerful advocacy coalition, bureaucratic leaders are unlikely to have any real choice about whether or not to serve this group's wishes. Lacking substantial

---

[28] Wilson instead identifies four types of interest-agency relations: client, entrepreneurial, interest group, and majoritarian. Client agencies are those allied with a supportive dominant interest group, while entrepreneurial agencies face a dominant hostile interest group. Instead, I differentiate between agencies that face active groups on both sides of an issue and those that confront an active group on only one side of an issue. The distinction between client and entrepreneurial agencies depends largely on the preferences of individual bureaucrats about what role an agency should play, while my typology focuses instead on interest group strength and activity. Wilson further differentiates interest group agencies from majoritarian agencies by arguing that interest group agencies confront both active supporters and opponents, while majoritarian agencies do not face any interest groups at all. I group these cases together, since all agencies confront potential opponents and supporters, even if they are presently inactive.

opposition, this group is likely to have the support of nearly all elected officials, and an agency is ripe for capture. Although bureaucratic leaders are unlikely to be able to resist a unilaterally powerful group, they nonetheless must choose whether to "give in" or to fight the good fight before losing.[29]

By contrast, when a potentially powerful but inactive countervailing coalition exists, bureaucratic leaders have a more viable chance to resist the currently active group. On the one extreme, the bureaucratic leader can serve the already powerful group with little chance of reprisal because the well-mobilized group is likely to understand that its interests are being met, while the disparate group will not. On the other extreme, the bureaucrat can choose to resist the informal pressure to serve the mobilized group if she can reasonably expect that the latent group can be made to come to her defense. So, for instance, she could publicize the pressure to shape policy or force Congress and the president to take formal action to compel bureaucratic compliance if either move would cause the latent group to become active and potentially apply pressure to elected officials.

Between the extremes of giving in and outright resistance, however, are the more interesting areas of bureaucratic choice in which bureaucratic leaders can try to co-opt an active group, altering policy so as to placate a portion of an advocacy coalition without giving in completely. For instance, in the area of airline regulation, the Civil Aeronautics Board (CAB) was able to build support for regulation by restricting carriers from cutting service to smaller communities (see McCraw 1984 for a concise history). Because regulation raised the price of flights over potentially competitive routes, it could have generated substantial consumer ire. Instead, the CAB gained the support of smaller communities by requiring the airlines to serve these cities, fracturing and preempting the formation of a potential antiregulation consumer coalition. Thus, despite the fact that it was unprofitable for the airlines to serve these routes, they tolerated the move because it built support for a regulatory regime that allowed them to charge above-market rates on other routes.[30] To put this point

[29] Additionally, because there is uncertainty about the responsiveness of outside actors to bureaucratically initiated policy changes, one may observe the bureaucracy "losing" when bureaucratic leaders either misread the political environment or chance a political loss. It is also important to recognize that despite the historical concern with agency capture among political scientists and pundits, this circumstance is actually quite rare. In most cases, a credible opposition exists, even if it is presently inactive and uninformed.

[30] During the early 1970s this coalition began to unravel, and the CAB's position shifted. For a full accounting, see Derthick and Quirk 1985, as well as Behrman 1980 for an alternate explanation.

more strongly: Bureaucratic leaders can sometimes shape the nature of opposing advocacy coalitions. In either refusing outright or co-opting the opposition, all that bureaucratic leaders must do to direct policy independently is find sufficient allies in Congress and the White House to prevent their actions from being overruled.

Similarly, in the final case in which the interest group environment contains roughly equally powerful groups, bureaucratic leaders have potential room for making strategic decisions in response to external political threats. By altering policy to placate a subset of an opposition group (as in the CAB case just mentioned), a bureaucrat may undercut an opposition coalition's unity.

3. Conclusion: The Theory Revisited

Overall, bureaucratic leaders play an important role that affects which interests are able to influence implementation. Bureaucratic leaders' actions are shaped by their preferences, but are constrained by formal limits placed on their discretion, their need to control their subordinates, and the support the agency enjoys from elected officials and interest groups. Consequently, in choosing whether and how to respond to external pressures, bureaucratic leaders will consider both their internal management needs and their external political goals. Their strategic choices are therefore neither purely administrative nor purely political. Rather, as bureaucratic leaders direct policy from within the bureaucracy, they must consider how their decisions will fare both within the bureaucracy and outside it. These choices alter policy and the nature of political conflict itself.

This theoretical perspective expands the scope of factors necessary to explain bureaucratic decisions. Congressional committees and highly motivated interest groups are important players in this perspective, but neither is determinative of agency performance. In this model, both interest group strength and the powers of elected leaders are dynamic quantities. Politics is also a dynamic process incorporating fluid interest group strategies and conflict and bargaining among elected leaders. This interaction is in turn shaped by strategic bureaucratic decisions. All of these abstract pressures for policy change are therefore mediated through agencies that are organized and managed by bureaucrats who are concerned with policy, their personal positions, and control of their subordinates.

Significantly, this theoretical perspective acknowledges the uncertainty of political conflict. This is both a strength and a weakness. It is a weakness because it lacks the parsimonious explanations of extant theories that "committees dominate" or "producer groups win." It is a strength, however, because the loss of parsimony provides a gain in empirical validity. Real political conflict is uncertain, complicated, and messy. Moreover, it depends on previous political conflicts and the vagaries of alliances and tactics. Predicting agency decisions is not so simple that a singular focus on congressional committees or the nature of regulated groups can always provide an accurate understanding of the real political world. Overall, in the trade-off between parsimony and accuracy, some increase in complexity seems a worthwhile burden.

2

Political Conflict and the Occupational Safety and Health Act

The primary empirical focus of this book is federal and state enforcement of the Occupational Safety and Health Act of 1970 (OSH Act).[1] The OSH Act sets out as its purpose "[t]o assure safe and healthful working conditions for working men and women," and to attain this goal it authorizes the promulgation and enforcement of rules for employers governing working conditions.[2] The enforcement of these rules is the shared responsibility of a federal agency, the Occupational Safety and Health Administration (OSHA), and the states. After introducing this case, this chapter tests the claim that bureaucratic leaders can often respond to both external political pressure and the need to control their subordinates by adopting a "strategically neutral" enforcement posture. This examination therefore links this specific inquiry with my more general interest in assessing the theories of bureaucratic power and decision making introduced in the previous chapter.

OSHA's embrace of strategic neutrality has allowed the agency's leaders to direct policy, to a substantial degree, toward their own ends despite opposition to aggressive government regulation of working conditions. By systemically discriminating among businesses based on their size, safety history, and industry of operation, OSHA has demobilized specific components of the business lobby, particularly small businesses in safe industries, that would otherwise incline politicians to act against the agency. At the same time, by persistently enforcing the law neutrally across

---

[1] Public Law 91–596.
[2] OSH Act, Preamble.

geographic areas and individual firms, OSHA has assured supporters that it is necessary and effective.

This strategy, the combination of (largely) geographically impartial enforcement and centrally directed particularism, is tenable in the OSH Act case because of the nature of the interest group environment OSHA faces (in light of how enforcing the OSH Act affects businesses and labor). Consequently, understanding the value of, and potential for, such a strategy requires identifying what is at stake, and for whom, in OSH Act regulation. Additionally, to describe OSHA as having chosen this enforcement posture necessitates demonstrating both that OSHA's leaders could have adopted other approaches (but that this one best served their personal and political needs) and that they saw the move as improving their political standing. That is, there must exist other feasible implementation strategies that agency leaders could have pursued but did not for reasons of their own choosing.

In developing the claim that OSHA's leaders chose the posture of strategic neutrality because it served their policy and political goals, the remainder of this chapter is divided into four parts. The first provides an overview of the regulatory structure in which OSHA and state enforcement agencies operate. This review includes a brief history of OSHA's founding and an introduction to the contemporary inspection process that OSHA and the states use to detect and penalize violations of workplace safety and health standards. Readers familiar with the OSH Act can skip this section. The second section explores political conflict over matters of OSH Act policy. In light of evidence about the OSH Act's real and potential costs for businesses and workers, it identifies the strategies and strengths of the potential interest group coalitions that seek to shape OSHA policy.

The third section draws these topics together by identifying how OSHA has chosen to implement the OSH Act given the preferences and powers of concerned interest groups and elected officials. Here I detail how, in light of important management and political pressures, OSHA has chosen to engage in strategically neutral enforcement of the OSH Act. I show why OSHA chose this centralized and geographically neutral approach to enforcement that nonetheless systematically differentiates among small and large businesses and safe and unsafe industries. Additionally, I discuss the differences between this strategic neutrality and alternative implementation plans, including "pure" neutrality. The fourth section concludes.

1. The Occupational Safety and Health Act and the Structure of Regulatory Enforcement

The Occupational Safety and Health Act of 1970 was passed by a Democratic Congress and signed by a Republican president. OSHA is permanently authorized, which shields the agency from efforts to amend or repeal the OSH Act otherwise afforded by the congressional reauthorization process. The overall structure of the OSH Act reflects significant compromises between labor and business interests (Moe 1989: 301–303). Specifically, the law created the Occupational Safety and Health Administration in the union-friendly Department of Labor and empowered the agency to develop standards for worker protection and to issue (with the states) citations and penalties for violations of these standards. Disputes about the validity of these citations are heard, however, by the Occupational Safety Health and Review Commission (hereinafter the Review Commission), and upon further appeal by the federal courts.[3] The Review Commission is an independent body whose members are appointed by the president and confirmed by the Senate. OSHA issues standards following a period of public comment and enforces them through workplace inspections. Overall, the OSH Act rejected both more radical efforts to alter the basic structure of market capitalism and the use of marketlike mechanisms to protect workers through, for instance, the nationalization of workers' compensation.

Despite significant compromises, the powers granted to OSHA are substantial. The agency is authorized to issue standards for working conditions such that "to the extent feasible...no employee will suffer material impairment of health or functional capacity even if such employee has regular exposure to the hazard...for the period of his working life."[4] This choice of wording rejects the analysis of the relative costs and benefits of regulation in favor of protecting as many workers as is feasible (Mendeloff 1979; Noble 1986). In cooperation with the states, OSHA has the authority to inspect "any factory, plant, establishment, construction site, or other area, workplace or environment where work is performed"[5]

---

[3] In states granted primacy for enforcement, citations and penalties are reviewed in a variety of different ways. In some cases, a Review Commission–like independent board exists (AK); in others, the state workers' compensation apparatus is used (WA); and in still others there is direct review in state court (VA).

[4] OSH Act, section 6, subsection B, part 5.

[5] OSH Act, section 8, subsection A, part 1.

and to issue citations that carry civil penalties to employers for violations of OSHA standards detected during these inspections.[6] These penalties are imposed without any civil or criminal hearing. Criminal prosecution of an employer is authorized when the employer willfully violates an OSHA standard and this violation causes the death of an employee. OSHA is also empowered to seek an injunction from a federal district judge to force an employer to rectify situations of imminent danger prior to OSHA taking independent enforcement action. This injunction may prohibit employees from working if doing so is necessary to prevent a hazard "which could reasonably be expected to cause death or serious physical harm ... before ... such danger can be eliminated through ... [OSHA] enforcement procedures."[7]

The OSH Act also provides employees significant rights and protections. Foremost, any employee "who believes that a violation of a safety or health standard exists that threatens physical harm, or that an imminent danger exists"[8] may initiate an OSHA inspection by filing a complaint with OSHA. OSHA, without releasing the name of the complaining employee, is required to perform an inspection in response to a properly filed complaint so long as "there are reasonable grounds to believe that such violation or danger exists."[9] Additionally, workers (and employers) have the right to accompany the OSHA inspector during an inspection, "for the purpose of aiding such inspection."[10] Significantly, the OSHA inspector may also question any employee privately and away from the supervision of his or her employer.[11] These procedural rights are enhanced by the protections given to any employee who complains to OSHA or cooperates with an OSHA inspector: "No person shall discharge or in any manner discriminate against any employee because such employee has filed any complaint or instituted ... any proceeding under or related

---

[6] Where a specific OSHA standard is not applicable, OSHA can also resort to the "general duty clause" to issue a citation with penalties when a workplace is not "free from recognized hazards that are causing or are likely to cause death or serious physical harm to his employees" (OSH Act, section 5, subsection A, part 1).

[7] OSH Act, section 13, subsection A. This provision is a compromise that allows only a temporary injunction when the danger is imminent.

[8] OSH Act, section 8, subsection F, part 1.

[9] Ibid.

[10] OSH Act, section 8, subsection E. This right is first extended to "a representative authorized by his employees," and in cases where no authorized representative exists, the inspector is obliged to interview "a reasonable number of employees" during the inspection. OSH Act, section 8, subsection E.

[11] OSH Act, section 8, subsection A, part 2.

to this Act . . . or because of the exercise . . . of any right afforded by this Act."[12] An employee who alleges retaliation or discrimination can seek redress by filing a complaint with OSHA.[13]

Yet, in what is generally regarded as a significant victory for business interests, the final regulatory structure set forth in the OSH Act also gives states a significant role in enforcing standards for worker protection. Specifically, the OSH Act allows any state to assume responsibility for enforcement of the OSH Act within its boundaries if the state submits a plan showing that the state program "will be at least as effective in providing safe and healthful employment as the standards promulgated under [this Act]"[14] and "devote[s] adequate funds to the administration and enforcement [of OSHA standards.]"[15] Chapter 4 examines federal oversight of state enforcement programs and state agency performance.

1.1. OSHA's Implementation of the OSH Act

Over the three decades since the passage of the OSH Act, OSHA's implementation of the act has matured into the system described here. The primary emphasis in this description is on the enforcement process whereby OSHA deploys inspectors throughout the country, selects workplaces for inspection, inspects these workplaces to detect violation of OSHA standards, and subsequently issues and litigates citations and penalties for violations of OSHA standards. This description, which draws from my interviews with OSHA personnel and internal OSHA documents, characterizes the enforcement practices that were in place by 1990 and that continued through the aborted Clinton administration reforms discussed in the next chapter.

OSHA's obligation to actually inspect workplaces for violations of OSHA standards, set forth in the text of the OSH Act, has substantially shaped the agency's organization. While setting standards and other activities are easily centralized in Washington, inspecting workplaces requires the physical presence of inspectors at workplaces throughout the United States. OSHA's response to this need for a local inspection force is the division of the country into ten geographic regions. Within each region

---

[12] OSH Act, section 11, subsection C, part 1.

[13] OSHA has wide latitude, however, in deciding whether or not to investigate the employee claim ("the Secretary shall cause such investigation to be made as he deems appropriate" [OSH Act, section 11, subsection C, part 2]), and the employee must rely on OSHA to bring an action for relief in federal court.

[14] OSH Act, section 18, subsection C, part 2.

[15] OSH Act, section 18, subsection C, part 5.

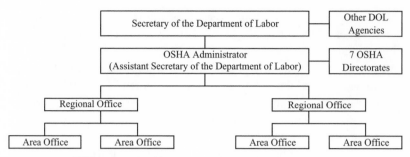

FIGURE 2.1. OSHA organization.

the territory is further divided, and oversight of employers in a selection of geographically proximate counties is assigned to one of approximately seventy-five local area offices. The assignment of a group of inspectors to the local area office balances the productivity gain derived from limiting the time lost traveling to workplaces and the weakening of centralized control and coordination resulting from dividing the agency's workforce. Each area office director reports to a representative of the appropriate regional administrator, and the regional administrators in turn report to a deputy to the head of OSHA. The regional offices provide day-to-day support for the area offices – for instance, assisting in rule interpretation and on questions of protocol. Figure 2.1 details OSHA's organization.

This arrangement has two important characteristics. First, although OSHA is located within the Department of Labor, and even though OSHA's regional structure mirrors that of other bureaus within the Department of Labor, OSHA retains direct oversight of agency field activities. Second, OSHA's regional structure, in which the regional administrators report to the assistant secretary, bypasses the internal organizational and programmatic divisions within OSHA. OSHA is divided into seven directorates (policy, health standards, safety standards, administrative programs, federal and state operations, technical support, and compliance programs), and these offices have an obvious role in both developing and interpreting OSHA standards and in assisting and evaluating field operations. But the offices do not have a direct means for controlling field operations. According to OSHA administrators, this arrangement improves the assistant secretary's coordination of OSHA policy and prevents any single directorate from dominating field office decisions.

To overcome the centrifugal tendencies present in any large and complicated organization, OSHA has written policies and rules formalizing expected practices. These "preformed decisions" (Kaufman 1960), issued as OSHA directives, cover the full gamut of issues in day-to-day bureau-cratic life (e.g., compliance, personnel management, procurement, public information, and standards). For the field enforcement program, the Field Inspection Reference Manual (hereinafter the Field Manual or FIRM) is the primary source of guidance.[16] Supplemented by the Field Operations Manual, the OSHA Technical Manual, and directives and letters inter-preting specific standards, the Field Manual guides OSHA's regions, area offices, and inspectors through the entire enforcement process.

The locus of the enforcement process is the area office where individual inspectors are assigned inspection targets, prepare inspection reports, and propose citations. Safety and health supervisors, in cooperation with the area office director, oversee the assignment of inspectors to inspections and the documentation and preparation of proposed OSHA citations. These managers also conduct the informal settlement conferences in which a majority of contested OSHA citations and penalties are resolved. Most area offices have between fifteen and thirty inspectors. In all but the small-est offices, the inspectors are divided into safety and health teams, and each team is overseen by, respectively, a safety or health supervisor.[17] Many area office directors and supervisors are themselves former field inspectors.

The OSHA inspector is a trained professional with a primary specialty in the area of occupational safety or occupational health.[18] Most inspec-tors have college degrees or significant experience in their area of special-ization (e.g., construction or high-voltage electrical transmission). Safety inspectors outnumber health inspectors at OSHA, but health inspectors are becoming more common and are generally better paid, as greater train-ing is needed to perform the testing and analysis used to identify occupa-tional health hazards.[19] After being hired by OSHA, a new inspector is put through a three-year training and apprenticeship program that begins with classes at OSHA's central training facility in Illinois. New inspectors

---

[16] The FIRM is compliance directive 2.103.

[17] In 1995, as part of the Clinton administration reinvention program in the Department of Labor, OSHA began reorganizing its field offices. Among the changes enacted was the replacement of the traditional division between safety and health inspectors with a division based on the impetus for an OSHA inspection. I discuss these and other details of this reorganization more fully in Chapter 3.

[18] OSHA refers to an inspector as a CSHO (Compliance Safety and Health Officer).

[19] Among the occupational health specialists I interviewed, most held degrees in industrial hygiene. According to agency officials, many inspectors with a specialty in occupational health are also trained as safety inspectors, although the converse is not as common. For this reason, the trend at OSHA is toward hiring individuals with health training.

then accompany more experienced inspectors on inspections and later perform their first independent inspections. New inspectors conduct inspections while being observed by a supervisor, a practice that OSHA continues (albeit far less frequently) even for the most senior enforcement personnel. Furthermore, classroom training continues throughout an OSHA inspector's career.

So far, this section has described the details of OSHA's organizational design without actually explaining the practice of regulatory enforcement. Roughly, the enforcement process can be broken into three steps: (1) the selection of workplaces for inspection, (2) the inspection of these workplaces and the (possible) subsequent issuance of citations and penalties, and (3) the negotiation and litigation of these citations and penalties. Each is now described in greater detail.

1.1.1. SELECTING WORKPLACES FOR INSPECTION. The first step in the enforcement of OSHA standards is the selection of workplaces for inspection. OSHA inspections are broadly classified into two categories: planned and unplanned.[20] Planned inspections are conducted according to an OSHA-wide targeting system that allocates inspectors to workplaces in proportion to the likely dangers to workers at those facilities. Unplanned inspections, by contrast, are initiated in response to outside events, including worker complaints, third-party referrals, fatalities and catastrophes, and employer requests for variances (exceptions) from an OSHA standard. Chapter 3 details how OSHA prioritizes among and implements these different classes of inspections. Significantly, Congress, through frequent appropriations riders, has intervened directly to limit OSHA's authority to select certain types of workplaces for planned inspections. In particular, Congress has restricted OSHA activity directed toward most farms and has prevented the agency from performing planned safety inspections in workplaces with ten or fewer employees in industries with an injury rate below the national average.[21]

1.1.2. CONDUCTING INSPECTIONS AND ISSUING CITATIONS AND PENALTIES. The second step in the enforcement process encompasses the trip by an inspector to a workplace, the inspection of the workplace, and the subsequent drafting and issuance of citations and penalties for discovered violations of OSHA standards. An OSHA inspection begins when an inspector arrives at a workplace, presents his or her OSHA credentials, and requests entry to perform an inspection. In most cases, the inspector's

---

[20] OSHA uses, respectively, the labels "programmed" and "unprogrammed."
[21] See OSHA CPL 2–0.51J and earlier directives.

arrival is a surprise, and the employer will not have been warned that the workplace has been selected for inspection.[22]

After the inspector has been granted access to the workplace, he or she conducts an opening conference with the employer and an employee representative to describe the upcoming inspection. At this conference the inspector explains why the workplace was selected for inspection, employer obligations under the OSH Act, employee rights, and how the remainder of the inspection will proceed. At the conclusion of the conference, the inspector will usually review the employer's required accident and injury records to identify any areas for extra attention.[23]

The physical inspection of the workplace is the next stage in the enforcement process.[24] Walking through the workplace allows the inspector to identify violations of OSHA standards – for instance, an unguarded machine tool or an employee working above a specified height without fall protection. The inspector will note any identified hazards and may also videotape or photograph them. If necessary, the inspector may also test the concentration of regulated chemicals and substances. At the conclusion of the physical inspection, a closing conference is held in which the inspector tells the employer of identified or potential violations of OSHA standards. The employer is advised of possible remedies for these hazards, that penalties may be forthcoming, and that he or she has the right to contest any OSHA citation. If an employee representative is present, he or she is also told how employees can participate in the adjudication and contesting of OSHA citations.

The compliance officer then returns to the area office to prepare the case file, which may include proposed citations and penalties. In most cases a citation must document a violation of an OSHA standard, occurring

---

[22] According to agency officials, if the employer refuses entry to the inspector, then the OSHA inspector will leave and initiate proceedings to obtain a warrant. However, in cases where OSHA anticipates that an employer will refuse entry without a warrant (e.g., because of corporate policy), OSHA usually obtains a warrant before sending an inspector to the workplace.

[23] The inspectors I interviewed noted that both the content of the records and the care with which they were maintained was informative.

[24] Planned inspections are generally comprehensive, covering all aspects of an employer's business. For unplanned inspections, the inspection is usually limited to the hazards that led to the inspection, although OSHA's Field Manual states that the inspector may at his or her discretion expand the scope of the inspection "[based on] professional judgment...[and] information gathered during records...review and [the] walkaround inspection" (OSHA FIRM, Chapter 2, (A)(1)(b)). OSHA officials reported that by far the most frequent grounds for expanding an inspection's scope was when the inspector observed other potential hazards during the course of the inspection.

in the last six months, to which employees were exposed. Penalties are calculated within statutory guidelines according to formulas published in the Field Manual and take into account the gravity of a violation. Gravity is a combination of the severity and probability of employee impairment arising from an OSHA violation. So, for example, a hazard that is less likely to result in injury but that would be highly damaging if it did so might have the same gravity score as a hazard that is more likely to lead to injury but that would be less damaging if it did so. Penalties may then be reduced by up to 95 percent according to OSHA-generated guidelines in the Field Manual for the size of the business (60 percent), the good faith of the employer (25 percent), and the employer's compliance history (10 percent). The Field Manual also prescribes increased penalties for repeat and willful violations, as well as for the failure to abate a cited hazard.

The appropriate supervisor and/or the area office director then review the case file before transmitting any citations to the employer. If an inspection reveals violations that may be prosecuted criminally, or if the value of the proposed penalties in a case is likely to exceed $100,000, then the case file is also forwarded to the regional office for internal agency review. Copies of any citation are also forwarded to any employee representative or complaining employee. Finally, the employer is also required to post any citations in a location accessible to his or her employees.

1.1.3. NEGOTIATING AND LITIGATING CITATIONS. The last phase of the enforcement process is the informal negotiation and formal adjudication of OSHA citations and penalties. By statute, employers can challenge an OSHA citation and any penalties before the Review Commission within fifteen days of receiving the citation. Prior to this formal contest, however, OSHA also offers employers the opportunity to reach an informal settlement with OSHA. In an informal settlement conference, the employer meets with the OSHA area office director (or one of the team leaders) and (usually) the inspector who conducted the inspection. An employee representative is also invited to participate in this meeting and to comment on any proposed settlement.

In the course of the informal settlement process, the Field Manual authorizes the area office director to rectify any errors present in the original citation, to adjust the proposed penalties and violations to account for employer willingness to take other corrective action (e.g., to adopt a safety and health program), or to make changes "if the employer presents evidence during the informal conference which convinces the Area Director that the changes are justified."[25] This broadly worded mandate encourages area office directors to settle cases, often after a substantial reduction in penalties and violations, because many cases that are formally contested are litigated over several years, are ultimately settled anyway, or are dropped altogether because of insufficient resources to prosecute them.

If OSHA and an employer cannot reach an informal settlement, the employer can go forward with a formal contest. The Department of Labor's Office of the Solicitor represents OSHA in all cases before the Review Commission. An administrative law judge first hears contested cases. Either party may appeal these decisions to the full Review Commission, whose decisions may in turn be challenged in federal court. A case that is contested formally may still be settled, but unlike settlements reached before a formal contest is filed, these settlements are subject to review by the Review Commission. Employees also have the right to contest any Review Commission decision that modifies a requirement for the abatement of a hazard.

2. Coalitions of Interests and OSH Act Enforcement

The enforcement apparatus described in the previous section allows the government to play an important role in regulating private working conditions. Not surprisingly, the business and labor groups involved in conflicts over OSHA's initial design remain among the most active participants seeking to shape contemporary OSHA policy. This section examines the nature of political conflict over the OSH Act and its implementation, identifying what is actually at stake, and for whom, in these disagreements. This discussion moves beyond a simple description of observed patterns of political conflict to consider potential political alliances in battles about the OSH Act. This discussion lays the groundwork for understanding both how OSHA is constrained by its political environment and the potential malleability of that environment.

In its broadest terms, conflict over the OSH Act and its implementation is another manifestation of liberal-conservative conflict over the appropriate role of the state (Poole and Daniels 1985). Liberals, often aligned with labor groups, desire greater government intervention in the workplace. Conservatives, aligned with business groups, usually seek a smaller government role in the private labor market. But active conflict

---

[25] OSHA FIRM, Chapter 4, (D)(4)(a)(2).

over implementation of the OSH Act is not intrinsically characterized as uniform labor support for OSHA versus cohesive business opposition to the agency. Rather, some businesses may be relatively unaffected by enforcement of the act, and enforcement may improve the position of businesses vis-à-vis their competitors. Likewise, workers' support for OSH Act enforcement may be moderated by concerns about unemployment associated with increasing production costs. How, then, are these varied interests transformed into actual political conflict, and which advocacy coalitions are most viable? The first step in answering these questions is to understand how the OSH Act affects different workers and businesses.

2.1. The Effects of OSH Act Enforcement on Business and Labor

The OSH Act provides a mechanism for the state to impose costs on private employers for hazards in the workplace. Potential enforcement of OSHA standards may cause businesses to take costly actions to protect workers and imposes additional penalties on businesses that do not comply prior to a state or federal inspection. There are two primary mechanisms by which enforcement of the OSH Act can alter business behavior: deterrence and awareness. Deterrence occurs when a business alters its behavior to comply with the law in response to the threat of government sanctions for noncompliance. Deterrence is specific when a business changes its behavior in response to enforcement activities at that particular business, and general when the generic threat of sanctions leads an employer to alter its behavior. Awareness leads to changes in employer behavior when government regulations and their enforcement lead employers to remedy hazards for reasons other than the threat of being punished for failing to do so.

There is a strong evidence of the specific deterrent effect of OSHA inspections accompanied by sanctions (Gray and Scholz 1993), while the data supporting OSHA's general deterrent effect are more mixed. (For those with greater interest, chapter appendix 2.1 examines the difficulties associated with measuring workplace safety and health, while appendix 2.2 discusses in greater detail both the mechanisms by which OSH Act enforcement can affect workplace safety and health and the empirical evidence supporting these effects.) Similarly, the research supporting the claim that OSHA causes changes in employer behavior via awareness is also more circumscribed, in part because it is difficult to disentangle whether changes in employer behavior occur because of OSHA's threat of sanctions or because OSHA causes employers to pay more attention to workplace conditions for reasons unrelated to potential punishment.

Overall, because enforcement of OSH Act standards causes (some) businesses to undertake costly compliance efforts, it increases business costs and decreases the competitiveness of American business vis-à-vis foreign competitors. Not surprisingly, therefore, business groups have regularly attacked OSHA's standards and enforcement program as inefficient, overbearing, and unnecessary. Nonetheless, there is significant variation in the real costs that OSHA imposes on employers, and this variation can alter the strategies businesses pursue in their efforts to lobby elected officials and during their direct interactions with OSHA.

There are several sources of variation in the real costs imposed by OSH Act enforcement. These arise primarily because the OSH Act did not initiate employer attention to workplace conditions de novo. Instead, the OSH Act's standard-setting and enforcement apparatus supplements existing systems that shape working conditions. The two primary systems onto which the OSH Act was grafted are the private labor market (the liability system) and workers' compensation. The private labor market provides employees, individually or collectively as union members, an opportunity to bargain with employers over working conditions and compensation. Extensive workers' compensation systems in all fifty states and the District of Columbia impose costs on employers for workplace injuries and compensate injured workers. These systems generate variation in whether or not employers would have to take costly action to remedy workplace dangers even in the absence of OSH Act enforcement. (For readers with more interest, appendix 2.3 provides greater details about how these systems independently shape working conditions and employer costs.)

The union status of an employer's workforce is the most significant source of non–OSH Act related variation in labor market–induced employer costs. If an employer's workforce is unionized, the employer is more likely to have to remove workplace hazards or pay a greater "risk premium" to compensate workers for workplace hazards (Dickens 1984). Unionized workers demand safer workplaces and greater compensation for working in dangerous conditions both because they are more informed about workplace dangers than nonunion workers and because bargaining collectively means that negotiations take place between the employer and the median worker rather than with the more risk-seeking marginal worker. Absent OSH Act enforcement, employers with a unionized labor force are therefore at a competitive disadvantage relative to other employers who produce the same product but whose employees are not unionized. Put simply, it costs more to employ union workers than nonunion workers.[26]

Additionally, the direct and indirect costs of compliance with OSH Act standards vary. Two significant sources of differences in the direct costs of compliance are the nature of a firm's production process and its size. Certain industries necessarily involve equipment and practices that expose workers to more potential violations of OSHA rules. For a bowling alley, standards relating to toxic chemicals and construction are largely irrelevant. By contrast, an oil refinery presents numerous opportunities for costly noncompliance. Similarly, larger firms have the advantage of economies of scale in complying with OSH Act standards, while for smaller firms the administrative costs of compliance are proportionately larger (Bartel and Thomas 1987). Hiring a safety and health manager, for example, is a proportionally large cost for a business with twenty employees, but it is trivial for a company employing five thousand.

Businesses also vary in the degree to which the indirect costs of OSH Act enforcement generated by increasing production costs are threatening. These costs may substantially diminish the profits of businesses that produce goods that are also produced by less-regulated foreign competitors. More generally, if consumption of a business's products is highly sensitive to price, increasing production costs are more threatening for that firm than for businesses that produce goods for which demand is relatively inelastic, for which few substitutes exist, and for which foreign production is less relevant.

2.2. *Labor's Potential Lobbying Strategies*
OSH Act enforcement offers different costs and benefits for union and nonunion workers. Unique to labor's maneuvering, however, is the vast disparity between nonunion workers and organized labor in both worker knowledge of OSH Act issues and advocacy strength. Union workers are members of explicitly political organizations designed to inform and harness their membership's political power. Nonunion workers, by contrast, are largely atomized individual participants in the labor market

---

[26] Employers in industries that are subject to oversight by other regulatory agencies (e.g., the Nuclear Regulatory Commission) or liability litigation for workplace hazards (e.g., asbestos companies) have similar incentives to remedy workplace hazards, as do businesses in states with higher workers' compensation premiums where those premiums are experience-rated (scaled to an employer's accident history).

and uninvolved in most national debates over matters of OSH Act policy.[27]

Enforcement of the OSH Act offers all workers the opportunity to decrease the frequency and severity of workplace hazards. But more aggressive enforcement is not without its potential costs. If enforcement increases a business's costs above those of its competitors, it may lay off workers or move abroad in search of lower production costs. Generally, the OSH Act may make workplaces safer at the cost of unemployment. For nonunion workers, for whom the labor market is less likely to guarantee a safer workplace, the potential unemployment effects of vigorous enforcement may therefore temper support for the OSH Act. These cost-raising effects of OSH Act enforcement are particularly important for nonunion workers because they have a difficult time competing with more productive, but also more expensive, unionized labor. But because these workers are also unlikely to be aware of these policy concerns or to become active in seeking to influence elected officials and policy, their strategic concerns are nearly irrelevant in describing the expressed political strategy of labor groups. Nonunion workers are simply not active participants in national policymaking surrounding the OSH Act.

In stark contrast, union workers already enjoy many of the protections the OSH Act provides. They are both better informed about workplace hazards and more effective in bargaining for the removal of these hazards (or for larger compensating "risk premiums").[28] Union workers nonetheless have a strong stake in enforcement of the OSH Act. First, although union workers are relatively better informed about workplace dangers, it is still difficult for them to identify every hazard. OSH Act inspections therefore help union workers audit whether or not employers are keeping their promises to protect workers (Scholz and Gray 1997). Significantly, the potential short-term unemployment effects of OSH Act enforcement are less threatening for union workers because they are often protected from being laid off or have generous severance packages as part of their collective bargaining agreements (Abraham and Medoff 1984).

---

[27] One piece of evidence in support of the dominance of union workers in national political conflict is the high proportion of individual participants in rule making who are associated with a union. More generally, on the atomization of nonunion workers in wage negotiations relative to the collective power of unionized workers, see Kahn 1987 and Moore and Viscusi 1990.

[28] Union contracts also often provide many of the procedural protections found in the OSH Act, including the right to complain without being fired and to refuse to work in hazardous circumstances.

Second, and more significantly, union workers have an additional stake in aggressive OSH Act enforcement because it improves the competitiveness of union workers vis-à-vis other laborers. Providing a safe and healthful working environment is costly. On average, however, nonunion workers recognize fewer workplace hazards and demand less "hazard pay" than union workers. In the absence of OSH Act enforcement, nonunion workers are therefore less expensive to employ than union workers. Uniform enforcement of OSHA standards imposes some of the same costs for providing a safe workplace on nonunion businesses that unionized employers already bear (Krizan 1994). Union workers have the strongest incentive to pursue the cost-raising strategy within their industry because it improves their competitive position within an industrial labor market where nonunion labor may make untenable union workers' demands for wage premiums. The same incentive also applies generically. Rising labor costs throughout the local and national economy make more highly skilled union labor comparatively less expensive and enhance union workers' demands for skill and experience premiums.[29]

With this basic set of incentives, union workers are likely to support vigorous enforcement of the OSH Act during direct interactions with an enforcement agency. During formal policymaking in the national political arena, however, union workers must make explicit choices about how to advocate on matters of OSH Act policy. Given union concerns with OSHA enforcement, not only in union workplaces but also elsewhere in the country, two national advocacy strategies seem most favorable. On the one hand, union workers can band together with all other union workers to seek aggressive enforcement of the OSH Act. Although labor-employer bargaining in the United States is highly decentralized, the AFL-CIO aggregates trade and industrial unions nationwide for unified political advocacy and provides a convenient mechanism for coordinated lobbying across geographic areas and economic sectors. Such a strategy allows unions to support the OSH Act for the direct benefit of their members and to improve organized labor's competitive position in the economy, although it does risk inviting general opposition from the business community.

On the other hand, unions can focus on strengthening enforcement in industries where they face competition from domestic nonunion labor.

---

[29] Similarly, industrial unions support the minimum wage because it raises the relative cost of employing less skilled nonunion workers, even though few of their members have traditionally worked in jobs affected by the law (Krehbiel and Rivers 1988; Burkhauser and Finegan 1989).

Such a strategy also provides direct safety benefits for union workers and indirectly improves the competitiveness of union labor in partially unionized industries. It does little to improve union labor's competitiveness within the larger labor market, but it may mitigate opposition to OSH Act enforcement from employers in other industries while still advantaging union workers in the given industry.

2.3. *Business's Potential Lobbying Strategies*

Every business has a generic incentive to minimize the costs incurred during its direct interactions with OSHA or a state enforcement agency. In individual enforcement proceedings all firms therefore have a desire to minimize the costs of this interaction by reducing penalty amounts. This naïve preference, however, does not predict whether or how businesses will act collectively to shape OSH Act enforcement. For businesses largely unaffected by enforcement, advocacy may not be worth the cost. By contrast, for businesses with competition from less-regulated foreign firms or for whom the demand for their product is highly elastic to price increases, any enforcement is threatening. Finally, for businesses competing with other domestic employers with different costs in the face of OSH Act enforcement, lobbying on OSH Act matters can provide strategic opportunities to raise competitors' relative costs.

Uniform enforcement of OSHA regulations may advantage larger businesses at the expense of their smaller competitors and improve the competitiveness of unionized employers relative to nonunion firms in the same industry. Generically, regulation is a nonmarket mechanism for employers to discourage competitive entry and raise competitors' costs (see Stigler 1971; Maloney and McCormick 1982; Salop and Scheffman 1987). In the OSHA case, Viscusi argues that this dynamic affects lobbying over existing rules:

> The prospect of any change in the [OSHA cotton dust] standard, however, is not great. Now that the large firms in the industry are in compliance, they no longer advocate changes in the regulation. Presumably, the reason is that the capital costs of achieving compliance represent a barrier to the entry of newcomers into the industry (1992: 177).

More generally, Carpenter (2004) has suggested that any regulatory system can advantage those parties that first undertake compliance with the law because their subsequent compliance costs are smaller. For this reason, regulatory regimes may create "winners" and "losers" despite those eventual winners having had little to do with the design of the regulatory system that yielded their advantage. In sum, within a given industry, no employer wants to be the only one to bear the costs of complying with OSH Act rules, but businesses vary in whether or not aggressive enforcement of the OSH Act improves their competitive position relative to nonunion and smaller employers.

In light of these underlying differences, businesses (and their advocacy groups) have to choose whether to actively seek changes in OSH Act enforcement and, if so, how to do so. Assuming a business becomes active, three natural advocacy coalitions and strategies are most viable.[30] First, all employers might join together as the "business lobby" to shape OSH Act policy. A united business community is clearly a potent political force, although it may engender substantial unified labor opposition (Smith 2000). Weakening OSH Act enforcement generally may most advantage low-compliance businesses, but even businesses likely to comply absent strong enforcement may see important advantages in continued opposition to government intervention in the workplace. A business that is currently aided by the enforcement of one standard might face high costs from the enforcement of other standards or the issuance of new ones. Generically, the threat of OSH Act enforcement and increasing production costs may be larger than the potential benefits of using the state to gain advantage over domestic competitors.

Second, employers in a particular industry might join together to influence OSH Act policy. Industry groups can lobby against the application of new rules to an industry, seek outright exemption from enforcement, or participate in rule making to shape proposed standards. Industry advocacy groups, while not as politically powerful as business as a whole, nonetheless offer several advantages. For one, the similarity of business practices suggests greater homogeneity of preferences and similar concerns about matters of OSH Act policy. Additionally, advocacy by sector takes advantage of existing formal organizations and may be less likely to encourage unified union opposition.

---

[30] This discussion ignores other national lobbying strategies on the grounds that they are likely to be ineffective politically. These include lobbying by individual firms for singular exemptions from OSH Act enforcement (likely to face opposition from both other businesses and labor groups and also unlikely to garner the support of a substantial number of legislators) and lobbying by geographic area for geographic preferences (likely to face opposition both from labor groups and from other geographic areas and their legislators). In the following chapters, I also consider whether individual businesses or groups of businesses (and their allied legislators and interest groups) are successful in influencing enforcement through direct lobbying of local agency officials.

Finally, businesses might organize around some other shared characteristic. Unlike advocacy by industrial sector, this strategy allows groups to take positions that advantage their members relative to domestic competitors in the same industry. For example, small business owners in safe industries have succeeded in gaining exemptions from certain inspections through their advocacy (and ongoing threat of advocacy). In these industries, smaller businesses can therefore more easily avoid incurring the costs of complying with OSH Act rules than their larger competitors. Of course, for this reason, such advocacy efforts are also likely to risk substantial opposition from more regulated competitors within the same industry. While small businesses are politically influential because they are numerous and spread throughout the country in many congressional districts, they are in many respects politically weaker than the larger businesses they are competing with because they have relatively few resources to commit to national lobbying efforts (Hart 2001: 1232).

More generally, other potential groupings of businesses (e.g., minority-owned businesses or a hypothetical grouping of businesses owned by left-handed people) have not succeeded in influencing aggregate OSH Act enforcement. In part, this is probably because these groups do not share preferences about how to use OSH Act enforcement to advantage themselves vis-à-vis their domestic competitors. It may also be because these groups of businesses are not as politically powerful or as easily mobilized.

2.4. *Patterns of National Political Conflict*

Given the consequences of OSH Act enforcement for labor and business, how have workers and businesses actually organized and sought to shape OSH Act implementation in the arena of national policymaking? The answer here is deceptively simple: In large part, labor and business have simply advocated against each another. Workers, nearly always represented by organized labor, have sought new rules and more aggressive enforcement of the act. The business community has advocated with nearly the same unanimity against new OSHA rules and for weaker enforcement of the act, although business activism clearly varies across individual businesses and although there also appear to be limitations in the willingness of certain high-compliance firms to support great reductions in OSH Act enforcement.

Evidence of labor's generally pro–OSH Act and business's anti–OSH Act stances is available from several independent sources. Impressionistic and historical accounts of the passage of the OSH Act, for one, suggest that the OSH Act was strongly supported by organized labor and opposed by business (see Mendeloff 1979; Kelman 1980; Mintz 1984; Noble 1986; Moe 1989). This general pattern of conflict continued throughout the 1970s in matters of OSH Act policy and regulation more generally (Salisbury et al. 1987). In particular, in the face of the threat of additional regulation and a weakening economy, the business community came together throughout the 1970s to lobby against most forms of federal regulation, although this unity declined after 1981 (Akard 1992). Interestingly, Akard argues that, in part, the mechanism by which this unity was achieved was the use of existing advocacy organizations by large businesses to harness the political clout of the small business community (Akard 1992: 603). This suggests that there was natural room for OSHA to weaken business opposition by demobilizing this important constituency.

Analyses of congressional voting also demonstrate that debates about enforcement of the OSH Act, whether for business as a whole or directed toward small business, have also mapped well into general left-right patterns of ideological conflict (Romer and Rosenthal 1987; see also Chapter 3). Liberal Democrats are OSHA's most strident supporters, while conservative Republicans are the most vocal opponents. Presidential support for aggressive enforcement of the OSH Act is likewise arrayed along readily identifiable ideological lines, with the greatest opposition observed in conservative Republican administrations (Reagan) and the greatest support during moderate Republican (Bush I) and Democratic (Clinton and Carter) administrations.

While this evidence seems to suggest relatively uniform pro- and anti–OSH Act coalitions, it is difficult to identify the involvement of individual businesses and workers from these aggregate data. For example, our earlier discussion might suggest that organized labor's position may not be representative of the positions of all workers. To address this concern, I investigated labor's and business's expressed political positions on matters of OSH Act rule making and legislation. Specifically, I identified the positions taken in a representative selection of rule-making proceedings and during congressional hearings on those proposed rules by labor and business groups and individual workers and businesses. My selection of proposed OSHA rules covered the period 1976–99 and includes "new" and "old" rules and also rules that would apply to specific types of businesses (and their workers) or to business and labor more generally. The six proposed rules are listed in Table 2.1. I then coded the positions and affiliations of participants in relevant congressional hearings and in

TABLE 2.1. *Labor and business positions during OSHA rule making*

Rule	Scope: General or Industry-Specific	Year Rule First Proposed (or Draft Proposal Circulated)	Any Labor Opposition?[a]	Any Employer Support?[b]
Cotton dust	Specific	1976	No	No
Medical records	General	1978	No	Yes: 1 business association (3%)
Grain handling	Specific	1984	No	Yes: 1 business association (3%)
Fall protection	Specific	1986	Yes: 1 union (17%)	Yes: 1 individual business (5%)
Safety and health programs	General	1996	No	No
Ergonomics	General	1999	No	Yes: 11 individual businesses (7.5%)

[a] Percentages are of all labor participants taking a clear pro/anti position in congressional hearings or rule-making proceedings.

[b] Percentages are of all business participants, except those supplying goods or services necessary to comply with a proposed rule, taking a clear pro/anti position in congressional hearings or rule-making proceedings.

published Federal Register rule-making proceedings.[31] This coding distinguished between individual participants and labor/business groups and, for the specific rules, between participants in the affected industry and those in other industries.

The relative uniformity of business and labor positions on these issues is shown in the last two columns of Table 2.1. Specifically, they list the frequency with which labor opposed a proposed OSHA rule or business supported it.[32] Labor, represented by unions or their self-identified members more than two-thirds of the time, is nearly uniform in its support

---

[31] Analyzing these data separately to account for the strategies associated with inviting participants to congressional hearings did not alter these basic results.

[32] In my calculations of business support I exclude those businesses that make equipment or provide services necessary to comply with the rule.

for new OSHA rules.[33] In only a single case, involving OSHA's proposed fall protection rule, did a union oppose OSHA. Business groups are similarly uniform in their opposition to OSHA rules. In only one case did a business association affected by a rule come out in support of it, and this case involved only 3 percent of the business associations active in deliberations surrounding the 1978 medical records rule. Individual businesses occasionally come out in support of OSHA rules, but these cases are still relatively rare (on average only about 2 percent of all business participants). These patterns are also stable across the period studied.

Additionally, two other significant patterns emerge in these data. First, labor and business groups affected by a given rule dominate participation in rule-making and congressional hearings. For the three rules that affect only particular types of businesses (cotton dust, grain handling, and fall protection), unaffected workers and labor groups are never active, and unaffected businesses are active only twice (and this activity is less than 3 percent of all business participation). This hints that OSHA policy is not a constant area of focus for individual labor and business groups, but becomes so only when the actions of the agency affect specific employers (industries) or employees. Second, just as unions dominate labor participation, large businesses and their allied advocacy groups dominate business advocacy.[34] Overall, less than 10 percent of all business participation in rule-making and congressional hearings is by small businesses or explicitly small business advocacy groups. This suggests that large businesses remain important for both continued monitoring of OSH Act implementation and advocacy on these matters.

For proposed legislation, I examined labor and business groups' positions as reported in the trade press for the period 1992–98. In this search I was unable to locate a single case in which unions supported legislation to weaken the OSH Act or opposed proposals to strengthen it. Among the business community, however, there were two interesting cases in which businesses opposed weakening the OSH Act. First, the Chemical Manufacturers Association's (CMA) opposed 1995 legislation that would have substantially weakened OSHA's enforcement powers (*Chemical Week* 1995). The CMA, which primarily represents large and well-regulated

---

[33] The two-thirds figure probably understates union participation, because individual union members may not have advertised their union affiliation when testifying or submitting comments.

[34] These business groups may also include small businesses as members.

chemical manufacturers (who also often employ union workers), opposed the bill introduced by Republican Representative Cass Ballenger that would have both dramatically expanded the planned inspection exemption for small businesses and allowed businesses to correct detected violations during an inspection to avoid penalties.[35]

Second, the Voluntary Protection Programs Participants' Association (VPPPA) opposed legislation proposed by Republican Representative Jim Talent and others that would have allowed businesses to use third party consultants' recommendations to indemnify themselves against future OSHA penalties (Fairley 1998). VPPPA's membership is composed of unions and businesses involved in OSHA's voluntary compliance program (discussed in greater detail in Chapter 5). The employers in this group have already agreed to take extensive measures to comply with OSHA rules in return for exemptions from planned OSHA inspections. The businesses opposed to each piece of legislation (neither of which advanced) were likely to have complied with many OSHA rules already. At least in the short run, they therefore would not have benefited from legislation allowing other businesses to avoid complying with OSHA rules. (Additionally, in the former case, large chemical manufacturers were opposed to the unequal protection given to small businesses.)

Overall, OSHA's political environment is best characterized as relatively coherent support for aggressive OSH Act enforcement by organized labor and intermittent and variable opposition to aggressive enforcement from the business community. Industry opposition and advocacy is linked to the costs individual businesses face and is most uniform on matters that would affect all businesses, such as the issuance of new broad-ranging rules. On particular policy proposals that would alter the distribution of OSH Act enforcement costs across individual businesses, however, unaffected businesses are rarely involved, and one occasionally observes opposition to measures that would advantage subsets of industry relative to their competitors. Thus, this pattern suggests that OSHA might be able to succeed in demobilizing some of the business opposition to enforcement of the OSH Act if it could move employers from the class likely to face persistent costs from OSHA to the class largely unaffected by the agency. This potential positioning opens the way for OSHA to shape its political environment through the pursuit of strategic neutrality.

[35] Additionally, the bill failed to garner support from the American Petroleum Institute and the Synthetic Organic Chemical Manufacturers Association. Like the CMA, these groups primarily represent large, heavily unionized, and otherwise well-regulated employers.

3. OSHA's "Strategic Neutrality"

How has OSHA's leadership acted in light of the constraints imposed by its political environment and the statutory foundations of the OSH Act discussed earlier? The central claim advanced here is that OSHA has chosen "strategic neutrality" in the enforcement of the OSH Act and that this strategy has allowed the agency's leaders to achieve many of their policy goals while accommodating political pressures.

What is meant by strategic neutrality? Earlier, I defined the concept as "the impartial implementation of the law given important centrally managed priorities." In the OSHA case, the agency has embraced neutrality by rejecting opportunities to vary how it enforces the law to advantage particular geographic areas or individual businesses. Rather, OSHA has chosen to construct its enforcement program to overtly (and strategically) discriminate among regulated employers on the basis of three factors: firm size, danger in an industry, and the previous compliance history of individual firms. While these factors are justified by the agency as naturally related to the allocation of scarce enforcement resources, this enforcement posture is also more fundamentally related to agency leaders' political and management needs.

In particular, this centrally managed enforcement strategy has allowed the agency to become more politically efficient. By focusing discretionary agency resources on manifestly unsafe businesses where violations are readily detectable, OSHA's field inspectors are more likely to generate regular streams of serious violations that agency leaders can use to persuade agency supporters of both the need for continued enforcement and OSHA's ability to detect and penalize employers who violate the law.[36] Cutting back on enforcement (inspections and penalties) in smaller and safer businesses has simultaneously allowed OSHA to demobilize important components of the business lobby. Internal to the agency, this strategy has allowed agency leaders to embrace professional norms among inspectors that encourage aggressive enforcement of the OSH Act in the field while minimizing inspector discretion about who is worthy of equal treatment. This field-level consistency combined with centralized particularism allows aggressive enforcement in the field to coexist with a diminished

---

[36] This argument assumes that enforcement of the OSH Act will never be sufficient to deter all employers from violating the law. If this were not the case, OSHA could find itself in a position where too-aggressive enforcement, by deterring noncompliance, would decrease the number of violations the agency could find. Given the statutory constraints on OSHA's imposed penalties and the agency's limited inspection resources, OSHA is unlikely ever to face this dilemma.

likelihood of political opposition arising on the grounds of inconsistent treatment.

This strategy is politically sustainable because it has made it harder for outside coalitions to come together to overrule choices that OSHA's leadership has made about how to enforce the OSH Act. Thus, it is not that business has grown to support OSHA, but instead that the way OSHA has used its enforcement powers has altered the nature of the coalitions that form in support of and in opposition to the agency. Business continues to be able to work to oppose expansion of the agency's powers and the issuance of new rules that would increase costs for all businesses, but individual businesses, especially small and safe employers, are less active simply because they are not as likely to face costs imposed by the agency.[37] Similarly, geographic neutrality has helped the agency to avoid opposition from business and labor groups in, respectively, more and less aggressively regulated geographic areas.

In further developing this argument, three interrelated questions remain. They are: First, did OSHA choose this enforcement strategy, or did external pressures dictate it? Second, did OSHA actually benefit from its strategy of discriminating among businesses on the basis of firm size, danger in an industry, and individual compliance history while simultaneously rejecting the use of geography and other characteristics to shape enforcement? And third, how is OSHA's "strategically neutral" enforcement posture, which I argue was deeply shaped by political and management concerns, different from a truly neutral or depoliticized implementation of the OSH Act?

3.1. Choosing Strategic Neutrality

Why and how did OSHA's leadership choose the strategically neutral enforcement posture described here? While it was politically beneficial, the real advantage of this approach over other politically feasible approaches

---

[37] Interesting anecdotal support for this proposition is found in comparing the National Federation of Independent Business's (NFIB, the primary lobbying group solely aligned with small business) posture toward new OSHA rules to its stance on continued OSH Act enforcement matters. After the Republican takeover of the House in 1994, most analysts acknowledge that the NFIB was in a newly powerful position to secure small business interests. OSHA officials acknowledged that this would likely preclude the agency from issuing new rules affecting this important constituency ("Small business may get a partial or complete exemption [from the proposed safety plan rule]" [Hosansky 1998]). But the NFIB, with the notable exception of the exemption bill discussed earlier, was almost totally inactive in seeking to rollback OSHA's field enforcement program. One affiliate of the group told me, "We have bigger fish to fry. The ergo[nomics] rule and those sorts of new burdens are a much bigger concern than the way OSHA enforces [existing rules]."

was that it sacrificed relatively few of OSHA's leaders' goals while securing important political ends. To show this, it is first useful to contrast OSHA's early enforcement efforts, and their political implications, with this later approach to enforcement. Doing so helps to reveal that while some change was necessary to avoid political opposition, agency leaders made strategic choices about how to accommodate political opposition with minimal disruption.

OSHA's early enforcement efforts differed substantially from the centrally managed and hazard-focused system described above.[38] Area offices in different parts of the country varied dramatically in their aggressiveness, with some seeking to issue as many serious violations as possible while others sought only to document any violation without concern for its severity. The agency's targeting system was similarly variegated, with individual area offices often relying only on telephone books and intuitions about workplace danger to select establishments for inspection. Perhaps most perniciously, the agency was also laden with the baggage of adopting and enforcing numerous existing consensus safety and health standards that included provisions related indirectly, if at all, to workplace safety (e.g., requirements for split-front toilet seats).[39]

Moe aptly described the agency's political fortunes during these early years:

[M]uch of [OSHA's regulatory structure] was designed to ensure that the regulatory policy everyone agreed upon in principle would be a miserable failure in practice. And so it was. . . . True to its agency-forcing mandate, OSHA immediately acted to promulgate over 4,000 consensus standards as mandatory rules – many of them later turning out to be trivial, absurd, or hopelessly complex. Small business, especially, became apoplectic as thousands of penalties were issued by discretionless inspectors compelled to enforce a ridiculous body of rules. (1989: 302)

This sentiment was echoed by Lane Kirkland, the president of the AFL-CIO: "[T]his hodgepodge collection of standards and OSHA's early efforts to enforce them probably did more to damage the initial acceptance of the entire program than any other single action."[40]

---

[38] Information about previous field enforcement efforts was provided by interviews with OSHA officials who had been with the agency since the early to mid-1970s. See also Hearings before the Subcommittee on Labor of the Committee on Labor and Public Welfare, United States Senate, November 1974.

[39] Formerly 29 CFR 1910.141(c)(3)(iii).

[40] Testimony before the Senate Committee on Labor and Human Resources on Oversight on the Administration of the Occupational Safety and Health Act, March 18–28, 1980, pp. 730–731.

Throughout the 1970s, numerous efforts were initiated in Congress to either reduce OSHA's authority or repeal the OSH Act entirely. These efforts included bills that would have formally exempted certain classes of employers from inspection or prohibited the issuance of citations the first time a violation was detected by a government inspection. Often, the publicly stated rationale for these measures was the perceived inefficiency and ineffectiveness of OSHA's enforcement efforts. By the early 1980s, however, OSHA's enforcement program had largely come to resemble the one described in general terms here (and in greater detail in Chapter 3). The three significant characteristics of this program were centralized control of planned inspection targeting decisions to send inspectors first to workplaces in dangerous industries, formal efforts to achieve consistent treatment (classification of violations and amounts of fines) across firms and geographic areas (after accounting for firm size and compliance efforts), and efforts to document many violations of standards directly related to workplace hazards while minimizing citations for violations of standards weakly related to workplace conditions.

Overall, OSHA did not step back from enforcement in the face of opposition to its early implementation of the act. Rather, the agency changed how it enforced the law to embrace the rhetoric of efficiency (finding many real hazards with scarce government resources) while carefully calibrating enforcement efforts to undermine the basis of much of the early opposition to the OSH Act, including aggressive enforcement of unimportant standards, geographic and firm-by-firm variation, and large monetary penalties for small and safe businesses. According to longtime agency officials, these sorts of "errors" had arisen, in part, because of OSHA's lack of central direction of the newly established field enforcement apparatus. By establishing careful control of field operations through centralized selection of inspection targets and giving greater attention to local productivity, classification of violations, and issuance of penalties, the agency's leadership was able to defuse some of the opposition that might have led the agency's opponents to persist in seeking reductions in OSHA's authority or budget. Similarly, the increasing professionalism of the agency's field staff lessened many concerns about incompetent, inconsistent, or intransigent field enforcement.

Some of this evolution undoubtedly resulted from the simple process of bureaucratic maturation (e.g., Perrow 1986). Even in the absence of political concerns, agency managers likely would have learned of the limitations of early field enforcement efforts and sought to improve and standardize them. Similarly, field inspectors and their direct supervisors were acquiring information about the efficacy of different targeting procedures. But two key elements of the agency's adopted enforcement process were uniquely driven by political concerns unrelated to the idea of professional enforcement, according to agency officials. The first was the reduced focus on "paperwork" violations (such as failure to post the OSH Act poster, poor record keeping of injuries, and lack of safety instructions or plans) because of the impression that OSHA was unnecessarily penalizing employers who did not in fact endanger workers. Paperwork violations, as distinct from unimportant standards (e.g., toilet seat regulations), however, often reflected real hazards to workers. As one regional official who had been in the field in the mid-1970s commented,

Paperwork violations aren't "ticky-tack" fouls. . . . they can be a sign than an employer is negligent or malicious, and so workers [there] are endangered. . . . But since we [OSHA] couldn't show negligence, the [political] price [of fining those employers] was too high. . . . [It made for] very good committee hearing fodder.

Politics therefore demanded changes that diverged from simple policy efficacy.

The second was the implementation of aggressive reductions in penalties for small businesses. The OSH Act originally authorized penalties of up to $1,000 for serious violations, though most penalties were far less than this amount. But because of perceptions that the agency's regulatory burden was unfairly borne by small business, agency leaders moved to grant generous reductions to small businesses rather than to seek an increase in the penalty cap above $1,000. "Small employer" was also defined expansively as fewer than 200 employers. These reductions essentially gave many unsafe small (and not-so-small) businesses penalty reductions that diminished their likelihood of contesting the OSH Act. (One official described this as "the beginning of our 'special sensitivity' to the political power of small business.") This occurred despite the continued belief by most OSHA officials that small businesses present a greater threat, on a per-worker basis, than larger and more professional establishments.[41]

But the fact that these changes served the agency's political goals does not indicate that the political environment expressly required them.

[41] Source: Author interview. See also Marsh 1994: "Most small companies don't have any medical staff, trained supervisors and professionals who track health and safety regulations," and, quoting an OSHA official, "We have seen more deplorable conditions in small business [than in large ones]."

OSHA could have done different things, choosing to exempt whole industries (perhaps those that were politically powerful but still dangerous to workers) through informal targeting decisions. Instead, focusing on "high-quality" inspections allowed agency leaders to continue their commitment to worker protection without having to give up much. They abandoned planned (but not complaint) inspections in small businesses in safe industries and the enforcement of rules only marginally related to worker protection. Additionally, they stopped assessing large penalties against small and safe employers. In return, the agency demobilized significant opponents of the agency.

3.2. *The Political Benefits of Strategic Neutrality*

The benefits to OSHA's leadership of embracing this strategic neutrality are apparent in the agency's ongoing public interactions with Congress in the thirty-plus years since the agency was created. I examined all of the public interactions between OSHA's leadership and members of Congress in congressional hearings during the period 1972–2002 and identified three ways in which OSHA blunted early criticism by adopting the enforcement system described here.

First, OSHA has been able to demonstrate its political efficiency by focusing on "real" hazards. Carefully targeting unsafe establishments, which also helped to lessen the agency's burden on small business and in many safe industries, helped to improve the agency's violations yield rate *per inspection*. As early as 1972, for example, OSHA's leadership refuted claims that it was issuing citations for "paperwork" violations or those unrelated to worker safety:

If I may, Mr. Chairman, we have heard more about split toilet seats, coat hangers in the back of the toilet door, height of partitions, and ice in the water than anything else. We recognize that [these citations] are wrong.... If indeed a compliance officer even pays attention to them, they are de minimis and not subject to citation.[42]

---

[42] Testimony of George C. Guenther, Assistant Secretary of Labor, before the Subcommittee on Environmental Problems Affecting Small Business of the Select Committee on Small Business, House of Representatives, June 20, 21, 22, 27, and 28, 1972, p. 314. See also testimony by Assistant Secretary Joseph A. Dear about paperwork violations in 1995 (The Administration and Congressional Initiatives to Reform OSHA, and Their Impact on Small Businesses. Hearing before the Committee on Small Business, House of Representatives, July 26, 1995).

Similarly, even in 1975 OSHA was publicly advertising its efforts to target dangerous industries and those areas with known hazards:

> I could not agree with you more on the desire to pick the most pressing targets for inspection.... [W]e have developed a computerized model.... designed to allocate resources so that inspections can be directed to the work establishments with the most serious problems in terms of injuries and illnesses.... This is intended to focus on a high hazard target, while bringing to bear all of the ingredients of what I call in quotes a 'professional utilization of OSHA's services.'[43]

OSHA also claimed that this focus on real hazards would directly lessen the burden on small employers:

> In order to confront the most serious workplace problems...I have begun to redirect the priorities of this agency....We intend to focus 95 percent of the inspection resources on those industries with the most serious safety and health problems.... Thus, for 80 percent of the small business establishments in the less dangerous industries, OSHA's inspection rate will decrease from approximately one inspection in every 500 work establishments to one in every 1,300 work establishments, and this is on a per-year basis.[44]

More generally, the benefits for OSHA of focusing on inspections likely to generate substantial yields of violations are apparent from bipartisan

---

[43] Statement of Dr. Morton Corn, Ph.D., Assistant Secretary of Labor for Occupational Health and Safety, before the Subcommittee on Manpower, Compensation, and Health and Safety of the Committee on Education and Labor, House of Representatives, April 17, 21, 23; May 7; September 10; November 4; December 8, 1975; May 3, 1975, p. 604.

   See also Scannell in his 1990 testimony (Gerard F. Scannell, Assistant Secretary of Labor, Occupational Safety and Health Administration, testimony before the Subcommittee on Health and Safety of the Committee on Education and Labor, House of Representatives, August 1, 1990).

[44] Testimony of Eula Bingham, Administrator, Occupational Safety and Health Administration, before the Subcommittee on Energy, Environment, Safety and Research of the Committee on Small Business, House of Representatives, May 23, 24, 25, and 26, 1977, p. 382.

   Note that despite this willingness to lessen the regulatory burden for small and safe employers, OSHA has consistently maintained that it is nonetheless necessary for it to have the right to inspect all businesses and has rebuffed efforts to obtain outright exemption of small businesses and those in low-hazard industries. For example, OSHA head Pendergrass in 1987: "Thus, although some employers are less likely to be inspected than others, all larger employers can be subject to a programmed OSHA inspection, and all employers to an OSHA inspection of some kind." (Prepared Statement of Mr. Pendergrass. Oversight Hearing on Occupational Safety and Health Administration. Hearing before the Subcommittee on Health and Safety of the Committee on Education and Labor, House of Representatives, April 29, 1987, p. 22/5.)

criticism of the agency's early enforcement practices. For example, in 1974 Democratic Senator Harrison Williams (NJ) wrote to OSHA that

The low number of serious violations being cited would seem to indicate either that (1) there is haphazard selection of establishments to be inspected which, consequently, bears little or no relationship to the serious accidents and illnesses which are occupationally related; or that (2) serious hazards are, in fact, being found but are not being cited as serious violations; or that (3) OSHA is devoting an inordinate amount of time to non-serious violations.[45]

By contrast, in 1980 Republican Senator Richard Schweiker (PA) acknowledged OSHA's shift toward (politically) efficient resource use:

First, Mr. Secretary, I do want to acknowledge that I think you have made some progress since the original days of OSHA, in that we are not arguing about Mickey Mouse regulations. We are arguing about the real meat of the program, which is targeting and utilizing resources. I think that is a compliment to you and to what has been done in some of these areas. . . . [46]

In fact, while OSHA's annual inspection and penalty outputs have varied considerably over the period from 1980 to the present, the agency's leadership has repeatedly sought to emphasize that it is more efficiently using OSHA's resources to locate serious hazards. For instance, in 1980 the agency cut back on conducting inspections in response to worker complaints that did not allege a serious hazard, with a result that the overall number of inspections declined. But the agency was able to tout a higher violation yield rate *per inspection* after the move:

[T]wo out of three [inspections] find hazards. The response has to be that we are not there yet. . . . We should note, however, that the inspection yield figure I am quoting reflects the influence [of] . . . over the last 3 or 4 years . . . when the agency responded with an inspection to anyone who came in over the phone or off the street with any kind of allegation regarding unsafe conditions, and the efficiency of those inspections was relatively low.[47]

---

45 Senator Harrison A.Williams, Jr.'s, letter to Secretary Peter J. Brennan, September 5, 1974. In Hearings before the Subcommittee on Labor of the Committee on Labor and Public Welfare, United States Senate, November 1974, p. A-2.

46 Oversight on the Administration of the Occupational Safety and Health Act, 1980. Hearings before the Committee on Labor and Human Resources, United States Senate, March 18, 21, and 28, 1980.

47 Testimony of Basil Whiting, Deputy Assistant Secretary, Occupational Safety and Health Administration, during Hearings on Oversight on the Administration of the Occupational Safety and Health Act before the Committee on Labor and Human Resources, United States Senate, March 18, 21, and 28, 1980, p. 322.

Similarly, in 1981 OSHA's head had this exchange with Republican Senator Orrin Hatch (UT):

Senator Hatch: The AFL-CIO charges, among other things, that the number of inspections are down, and the inspections have been reduced in scope, thus supposedly indicating a reduction in compliance efforts. . . .
    Mr. Auchter: As a matter of fact, our targeted inspections, general scheduled inspections, which statistically pay off much greater than any other sort that we do, are up 15 percent.[48]

Second, OSHA has muted criticism that it is overbearing by demonstrating its willingness to discriminate in setting penalties on the basis of business size and employer commitment to safety. This graduated penalty policy, as well as the targeting efforts discussed earlier, has blunted criticisms of the agency as imposing unnecessary costs on small and safe businesses. In the late 1970s, for example, OSHA's leadership openly touted its expanded penalty reduction for small businesses as a way to "consider the financial burden on small business employers without sacrificing employee protection."[49] Similarly, the agency stressed that it would reduce penalties for "good faith effort in the attempts by the employer to clean up the workplace."[50] Overall, OSHA has consistently used its efforts to distinguish between "good" and "bad" employers to argue that it is not overbearing: "[B]y treating employers differently, we are according responsible employers penalty reductions, limited scope inspections, and a variety of other incentives and rewards."[51]

See also Whiting's testimony on abandonment of pure inspection quotas ("We have removed every vestige of such a quota system, and concentrated on quality inspections in those places we inspect" [p. 259]) and 1988 testimony by OSHA head Wachtman on efficient use of agency resources (Statement of Greg Watchman before the Small Business, Advocacy Review Panels, Joint Hearing before the Subcommittee on Government Programs and Oversight Subcommittee on Regulation Reform and Paperwork Reduction of the Committee on Small Business, House of Representatives, March 18, 1998).

[48] Oversight on the Administration of the Occupational Safety and Health, Joint Hearing before the Subcommittee on Investigations and General Oversight and the Subcommittee on Labor of the Committee on Labor and Human Resources, United States Senate, September 23, 1981, p. 53.

[49] Testimony of Eula Bingham, Administrator, Occupational Safety and Health Administration, before the Subcommittee on Energy, Environment, Safety and Research of the Committee on Small Business, House of Representatives, May 23, 24, 25, and 26, 1977, p. 385.

[50] Testimony of Dr. Eula Bingham, Assistant Secretary of Labor for Occupational Safety and Health, before the Committee on Labor and Human Resources, United States Senate, April 15, 17, and 25, 1980, p. 60.

[51] Statement of Gregory R. Watchman, Acting Assistant Secretary for Occupational Safety and Health, U.S. Department of Labor, before the Subcommittee on Public Health and

Finally, OSHA has successfully addressed persistent criticism of the agency's enforcement program as inconsistent, and therefore unfair or simply inefficient, by emphasizing centralized control of the field offices. The typical criticisms of OSHA's early field enforcement efforts often noted the vast discretion delegated to local offices. For example, Senator Williams (D-NJ) claimed in 1974 that "OSHA inspection officials have been permitted to classify violations according to individual views as to how the Act should be applied.... Little attempt has been made to coordinate the inspection policies of the various areas into a single comprehensive enforcement effort."[52] OSHA responded by noting, "[We are] constantly identifying those standards which have presented enforcement or interpretative difficulties."[53] Later, the agency also touted its expanded monitoring of the field offices:

First, a directive was sent to the field emphasizing that there should be no failure to classify violations as serious.... Second, a case file review in area offices has been made to determine if proper classification has been made.... Third, a study of the percent of violations in different area offices is being made; and last, revisions are being made in the field operations manual clarifying the factors to be considered in the classification of violations as serious.[54]

Ironically, the greatest ongoing opposition to OSHA's enforcement posture has emerged because of tensions among the components of the agency's efforts to demonstrate its political efficiency. Specifically, conflict has emerged among the goals of reasonableness (targeting and punishment of unsafe businesses), efficiency (safety provided per dollar spent),

Safety of the Committee on Labor and Human Resources, United States Senate, July 10, 1997, p. 19.

Additionally, OSHA head Dear in 1997: "At times the old OSHA was too confrontational with employers, often failing to distinguish between responsible employers and those who were neglectful of their work force. The new OSHA rewards responsible employers with cooperative programs, penalty reductions, and other incentives. Serious violators of the law, however, receive serious penalties." (Testimony of Joseph Dear, Assistant Secretary for Occupational Safety and Health, before the Committee on Small Business, House of Representatives, September 25, 1996, p. 4.)

[52] Senator Harrison A. Williams, Jr.'s, letter to Secretary Peter J. Brennan, September 5, 1974. Hearings before the Subcommittee on Labor of the Committee on Labor and Public Welfare, United States Senate, November 1974, p. A-37.

[53] Statement of John H. Stender, Assistant Secretary of Labor, before the Subcommittee on Labor of the Committee on Labor and Public Welfare, United States Senate, July 22, 30, and 31; August 13 and 14, 1974, p. 224.

[54] Statement of Dr. Morton Corn, Ph.D., Assistant Secretary of Labor for Occupational Health and Safety, before the Subcommittee on Manpower, Compensation, and Health and Safety of the Committee on Education and Labor, House of Representatives, April 17, 21, 23; May 7; September 10; November 4; December 8, 1975, May 3, 1975, p. 605.

and consistency (equal treatment of equals).[55] This tension has arisen because of claims that OSHA uses inspection and penalty quotas for field offices to motivate inspectors, but that inspectors are therefore inclined to sacrifice quality inspections for quantity or to behave unreasonably by citing unimportant violations. OSHA's response before Congress to allegations arising in 1988 that the agency was trading quantity for quality illustrate how OSHA has justified the focus on inspector productivity as nonetheless necessary to maintain control of field operations:

Inspection *quotas* are not assigned to OSHA Regional and Area offices. Inspection *goals* are set for each region as a management tool to ensure that all field offices are contributing to the agency's enforcement objectives. The *quality* of inspections is stressed in the agency's Field Operations Manual, in the standards against which the performance of individual compliance officers is measured, in the agency's periodic internal audits of its Regional and Area Offices, and in frequent, often informal, exhortations by national and field managers at all levels.

The balance between productivity and quality is always of concern to management. It is always possible that some of our employees may have misunderstood our policy and even that a few among them may have perverted our system to focus on the quantity of inspections conducted rather than on what was accomplished in the course of those inspections.[56]

Likewise, in a 1988 exchange with Republican Senator Hatch (UT), OSHA's head stated:

In the management of the agency, you have to set goals. These are overall goals for the agency, overall goals for each region and area office. However, we have stressed in writing that there should be no sacrifice for quality in order to achieve a set of numbers.... A director of an area office said that in the past... he frequently did not make the number of inspections that were called for. The circumstances are different from one office to another, and we recognize this. This did not hamper his career one bit; in fact, he has received two promotions since he was an area director. So it is a matter of judgment.[57]

In sum, OSHA's enforcement efforts, which produce a regular stream of serious violations, help demonstrate to the agency's supporters the agency's efficacy. Simultaneously, they minimize opposition on the

---

[55] For evidence of similar value conflicts in the area of tax enforcement, see Scholz and Wood 1998 and 1999.

[56] Letter from Mr. Pendergrass regarding Oversight of the Occupational Safety and Health Administration. Hearings before the Committee on Labor and Human Resources, United States Senate, April 18, 19, and 20, 1988. Emphasis in original.

[57] Statement of Mr. Pendergrass before the Committee on Labor and Human Resources, United States Senate, April 18, 19, and 20, 1988, p. 913.

grounds that OSHA imposes unnecessary costs on business, is unfair to small and safe businesses, or is inconsistent.

3.3. *Purely versus Strategically Neutral*
How does OSHA's "strategically neutral" enforcement posture differ from what one would expect in the absence of the political and management concerns highlighted here? In addition to the politically motivated reduced focus on paperwork violations and penalty reductions for small businesses just discussed, another indication of how OSHA's leaders were constrained was the effort to channel subordinates to generate regular allotments of serious violations. At the most basic level, subordinate bureaucrats in the field were forced to standardize their efforts. The clearest way to accomplish this goal was to emphasize the production of many violations for serious hazards while discriminating among employers via strong central control of inspection targets and penalty policies.

This move accomplished two ends. First, it allowed managers to control these subordinates and direct their behavior toward specific actions. Many of the administrators I interviewed noted that while OSHA did not need enforcement quotas, it did require some means for ensuring that the field offices worked toward the collective goal of effective enforcement. Basic professionalism, backed by strong management expectations about aggressive enforcement in the field, helped to focus OSHA on these enforcement outputs. Second, these outputs helped as demonstrations of the agency's efficiency, with sufficient standardization that the agency could also mitigate concerns about fairness and discrimination (other than for firm size and safety) across geographic areas and types of businesses. In the words of one administrator I spoke with, "We [OSHA] got very good at playing the numbers game, where we demonstrated that there were lots of serious hazards and violations out there and we could find them."

On the one hand, if OSHA's leadership had confronted only political concerns, they might have done more to carefully calibrate enforcement to the political strength of enforcement targets or to allow greater discretion in enforcement to distinguish among employers on the basis of perceived cooperativeness. In these circumstances, the agency might have been able to be more aggressive (in the aggregate) while simultaneously discriminating so as to avoid opposition from other politically powerful or high-compliance businesses. Implementing either approach in the field and away from headquarters, however, risked a dangerous destabilization of OSHA's enforcement apparatus. It is not at all clear that officials in Washington were confident in the judgments of field-level personnel about the political power or blameworthiness of individual employers. Management concerns, in other words, interfered with greater devolution of discretionary authority to the field-level bureaucrats.

On the other hand, had it only been for management concerns, OSHA's leadership would still have implemented some means to harness subordinate effort. But it is not at all clear that this would have focused solely on producing inspections and violations. Nor would the agency have offered such extreme penalty reductions to small and safe businesses. To do otherwise, however, was political suicide, especially during the late 1970s. More interestingly, the agency might have pulled back on enforcement in workplaces with known but less severe safety hazards in place of greater enforcement of health standards in other businesses. That is, OSHA might have given up trying to produce regular allotments of safety violations, particularly in industries where hazards are well recognized but difficult to remedy completely at a reasonable cost (e.g., the intrinsic danger of working on scaffolding, even with proper safety equipment), and instead sought out less readily identified but potentially dangerous situations. This shift in priorities could easily have been managed from Washington, but it would not have served the agency politically.

Shifting attention to hazards with long latency periods (e.g., health hazards resulting from exposure to potential carcinogens [see Mendeloff 1988]) and risks with low probabilities but catastrophic outcomes (e.g., large-scale explosions at petroleum refineries) might seem counterintuitive, but it would have allowed OSHA to focus on areas where other mechanisms, especially workers' compensation and wage premiums, are least effective in deterring employers from endangering workers owing to the inability of workers to identify these hazards, the propensity for employers to discount heavily the future occurrence of low-probability events, and the inability of either mechanism to internalize hazards with long latency periods (see appendix 2.3). At least in the short run, however, such a move would likely have left the agency open to criticism because it would have substantially diminished (or created variation in) the agency's yield of serious violations. Without a steady stream of serious violations to tout before outsiders, OSHA would have had difficulty demonstrating to supporters and opponents alike that the agency was both necessary and effective in enforcing the law.

Similarly, OSHA might also have loosened its control of field enforcement efforts by devolving more authority to local offices to implement its partnership programs. This would have allowed field offices greater discretion to sort out those employers who could be trusted to cooperate with OSHA from those who likely required the traditional regulatory approach (Scholz 1991). (Currently, OSHA's partnership program is run out of headquarters. While OSHA has experimented with expanding its partnership program through the local offices [see Chapter 5], these efforts were ultimately attacked because they pressed all field offices to enlist employers, even when there was no suitable pool of cooperative local businesses.) Were OSHA to let local offices decide whether an employer was sufficiently trustworthy, it might allow the agency as a whole to maximize its improvement of working conditions by targeting scarce enforcement resources on employers unwilling to cooperate with the agency *ex ante*. But, in the current context, devolving that authority to local offices would likely run afoul of opposition from both those who doubt OSHA's competence and those who believe the agency's employees cannot be trusted to fairly implement a set standard. Additionally, it would substantially increase the management burden on headquarters staff to oversee the field offices. It is much more difficult to assess the reasonableness of partnership outreach efforts in the field that it is to monitor inspector productivity and violation yields.

In summary, political and management constraints led OSHA's leadership to reject both targeting arrangements less likely to yield regular outputs of inspections and violations as well as the devolution of greater authority to OSHA's lower-level bureaucrats to differentiate among employers on the basis of commitment to improving working conditions. The larger implications of this move are that OSHA's enforcement program duplicates many functions of the private labor market and may unnecessarily limit subordinate discretion. Reforms that would address either limitation, however, seem largely untenable.

APPENDIX 2.I. DEFINING AND MEASURING
WORKPLACE SAFETY AND HEALTH

A necessary prerequisite for understanding the effect of OSH Act enforcement on workplace safety and health is developing a common understanding of the phrase "worker safety and health." Defining and measuring "worker safety and health" is difficult, however, because it is hard to quantify the hazards that workers face. Any measure of observed injuries and illnesses is an imperfect quantification of actual workplace hazards for two reasons. First, counts of observed injuries and illnesses poorly measure hazards with long latency periods or cumulative effects. Cancer, for instance, usually occurs many years after exposure to carcinogens. Similarly, lifting heavy boxes may damage an employee's back, but might not result in an injury until the employee performs additional lifting. Second, observed injuries and illnesses are only probabilistic manifestations of underlying workplace hazards. Sometimes events will make a workplace appear safer than it "really" is, and sometimes it will appear more dangerous. The term "really" is used because, while a worker is either injured or she is not, the underlying hazard may remain the same (e.g., a 1/6 chance of death is a constant danger, but on average results in death in only 1/6 of cases of exposure).

The most widely used measure of workplace hazards, the workplace lost-workday injury and illness incidence rate (LWDII), illustrates these and additional difficulties in choosing among measures of workplace hazards. The LWDII is calculated as the number of injuries and illnesses that cause an employee to miss at least one day of work relative to the number of employee hours of work.[58] Using data gathered from an annual nationwide survey of employers, the Bureau of Labor Statistics (BLS) in the Department of Labor reports the LWDII as well as the incidence rate for injuries and illnesses that do not result in missing at least a day of work (the injury and illness incidence rate [IIR]).[59] The limitation of

[58] OSHA often incorrectly refers to the lost-workday injury and illness *incident* rate as the lost-workday injury and illness rate. The incident-rate measure is a calculation of the relative frequency of lost-workday incidents, not days of work lost.

[59] These incident rates are calculated annually for each business as (N/EH) × 200,000, where N is the number of observed injuries and illnesses, EH is the total number of hours worked by all employees, and 200,000 is a standardization constant. The BLS reports that among all manufacturing employers surveyed the average LWDII was 2.4 in 1997 (BLS: April 22, 1999, Table 6) and the average IIR was 9.7 in 1998 (BLS: December 1999, Table 7). These figures correspond to approximately one out of every forty employees losing at least a day of work due to injury or illness and one out of every ten employees suffering a reportable injury or illness in 1998.

these incident-rate measures, however, is that they equate serious and nonserious events. An injury that forces a worker to miss a day of work has the same weight in the LWDII as an injury that results in the worker being hospitalized for a month. Likewise, all injuries are weighted equally in the IIR.

The lost-workday rate (LWR) is one attempt to account for differences in the severity of injuries and illnesses. The LWR is calculated as the number of workdays lost due to injury or illness per employee hour worked.[60] However, the BLS does not use the data it gathers to calculate this figure and instead reports only the median number of days away from work for each injury and illness that results in time away from work (BLS: April 1999, Table 7). Like the LWDII and IIR, the LWR misses injuries and illnesses with long latency periods or cumulative effects. Along with the LWDII, it also ignores injuries and illnesses that do not force an employee to miss a day of work. Additionally, the LWR is very susceptible to the stochastic variation problem discussed earlier. A hazard that only rarely manifests itself as an egregious accident will result in a very high LWR when an accident occurs and a very low LWR when it does not. Similarly, in small workplaces a single serious injury can inflate the LWR by large amounts.

Table 2.2 shows the LWDII, IIR, and LWR for several incident severity and duration scenarios. These results show that the IIR overlooks differences in injury and illness severity and that the LWDII succeeds only in distinguishing incidents that do not result in days away from work from those that do. The LWR, however, more effectively measures injury and illness severity by accounting for the amount of time that workers are actually incapacitated due to injury or illness. Thus, the LWR assists in identifying greater danger at a workplace where each injury or illness incapacitates a worker for a longer period of time, even if another workplace has an identical LWDII or IIR.

While it is difficult to produce a single accurate empirical measure of workplace hazards that captures differences in both hazard probability

---

[60] One problem in calculating the lost-workday rate is deciding how to treat fatalities and injuries that result in very long periods of time away from work. Obviously, someone who is deceased will never return to work, and this fatality will contribute solely to the numerator in the calculation of D/EH, where D is the number of days away from work and EH is defined as in note 59. The most straightforward solution to this problem is to include in the denominator the number of hours that an employee would have worked had he or she not been away from work D/(EH+(D × 8)) and then to arbitrarily truncate the length of time used to count injuries and illness that permanently keep workers home.

TABLE 2.2. *Comparison of different measures of workplace safety and health*

Workers	Annual Injuries and Illnesses	Injuries and Illnesses Resulting in Days Away from Work	Average Number of Days Away from Work for Each Incident	IIR[a]	LWDII[b]	LWR[c]
100	10	0	1	10	0	0
100	10	5	1	10	5	5
100	10	10	1	10	10	10
100	10	0	5	10	0	0
100	10	5	5	10	5	25
100	10	10	5	10	10	50
100	10	0	10	10	0	0
100	10	5	10	10	5	50
100	10	10	10	10	10	100

[a] Calculated according to the BLS formula $(N/EH) \times 200,000$, where N is the number of incidents and EH is the total number of hours worked by all employees assuming that all employees work 2,000 hours per year.

[b] Calculated according to the BLS formula $(N/EH) \times 200,000$, where N is the number of incidents resulting in days away from work and EH is the total number of hours worked by all employees assuming that all employees work 2,000 hours per year.

[c] Calculated according to the formula $D/(EH + (D \times 8)) \times 200,000$, where D is the number of employee days away from work and EH is the total number of hours worked by all employees assuming that all employees work 2,000 hours per year.

and severity, it is still useful to think of "workplace safety and health" as an aggregation of all the hazards a worker faces. This aggregation should take into account the likelihood that a worker will be injured or made ill and the severity of this injury or illness. Therefore, "workplace safety and health" or hazards as used throughout this book means, roughly, the sum of the hazards a worker faces where each hazard is weighted by its probability of occurrence and severity of impairment.

APPENDIX 2.2. OSH ACT ENFORCEMENT AND WORKPLACE SAFETY AND HEALTH

The OSH Act empowers OSHA to issue standards governing workplace hazards and to enforce these standards through workplace inspections. OSHA's field enforcement may deter businesses from endangering workers or inform employers about previously unidentified hazards. Additionally, OSHA's enforcement activities may influence only the specific businesses subject to OSHA inspections or the general business community.

OSHA enforcement may therefore protect workers in three ways: specific deterrence, general deterrence, and awareness.

Specific deterrence occurs when an employer remedies workplace hazards in response to an OSHA penalty. Gray and Scholz (1993) find there is a 22 percent decline in workplace injuries in the few years following an OSHA inspection in which penalties are imposed. This finding supports a rational-deterrence model of employers' decisions about whether to comply with OSHA standards.[61] An OSHA penalty raises the cost of noncompliance with OSHA standards because there are large penalties for failing to abate recognized hazards and because after having been "caught" an employer is subject to further review.[62]

Thus, specific deterrence improves workplace safety both by encouraging employers to rectify violations of OSHA standards and (perhaps) by encouraging a general attention to safety matters that are unrelated to OSHA standards.[63] Whether specific deterrence improves workplace health is less certain. Because of the long latency periods of most occupational illnesses, it is hard to measure decreases in occupational illnesses. If the rational-deterrence model is correct (if OSHA enforcement encourages employers to remedy violations of OSHA standards to avoid a penalty), then employers presumably correct violations of both safety and health standards. If the behavioral model is correct, however, employers may

---

[61] A rational-deterrence model states that employers will comply when noncompliance is more costly than compliance (see Becker 1968 and Block and Heineke 1973 for overviews of rational-compliance models). Generally, the risk-neutral cost of noncompliance is calculated as the probability of being caught multiplied by the penalty if caught. For example, if my chance of being caught jaywalking is 1 in 10 and the penalty if I am caught is $1.00, then I will jaywalk only when it is worth at least $.10 to me. If I am certain I will be caught, I may still jaywalk if doing so is worth at least the amount of the penalty, $1.00. Also, see Scholz and Gray 1990 for a review of criticisms of OSHA's deterrent effect.

[62] Gray and Scholz also contend, however, that this finding supports a behavioral model of specific deterrence. The behavioral model asserts that employers choose to devote more attention to safety and health concerns in response to OSHA penalties because penalties provide notice that safety and health concerns are important. In support of this theory, they note that the greatest decrease in accidents occurs one to two years after a penalty is imposed and that this effect subsequently decays over time. This would seem to show that employers respond to OSHA penalties by paying more attention to all safety and health matters, but that this attentiveness fades over time. In either case, the data support the claim that inspections with penalties are necessary to cause employers to invest in reducing workplace hazards.

[63] This finding also suggests that the claim that OSHA enforcement would draw resources away from other employer efforts that might improve workplace safety *more* than compliance with OSHA standards is unfounded (Mendeloff 1979: 92). Instead, employers make more general efforts to improve safety and health in response to an OSHA penalty.

correct only hazards that attract their attention. Because some health hazards are less likely to manifest themselves in immediate illness, enforcement may encourage employers to abate only certain health hazards.

General deterrence occurs when an employer removes workplace hazards in response to OSHA's punitive enforcement activities in other workplaces. By increasing the perceived cost of violating OSHA standards, OSHA's field enforcement program discourages employers from flaunting OSHA's rules.[64] As a result, a business may take action to indemnify itself against the future cost of an OSHA inspection.

OSHA's simple existence and its outreach efforts may also help employers to identify new hazards in the workplace and provide guidance on ways to reduce injuries and illnesses. This process is called "awareness." Awareness occurs when an employer improves workplace safety and health in response to OSHA, rather than because of any potential penalties. (One way awareness occurs is when an OSHA inspection leads employers to improve worker protection by assisting employers in identifying hazards unrelated to OSHA standards.)

Empirical analyses of both the general-deterrence and the awareness mechanism are rare because it is difficult to account for all of the other factors that may encourage a business that has not been visited by OSHA to reduce workplace hazards. For instance, rising workers' compensation premiums or union activism may lead employers to reduce workplace hazards. Additionally, the OSH Act has probably increased the accuracy of record keeping, so that injury and illness rates before and after the passage of the act are not comparable. Finally, it is very hard to disentangle employer efforts undertaken in response to OSHA's punitive threats from those made because of OSHA's informational role. Nonetheless, it is undoubtedly the case that some employers take immediate action to come into compliance with new OSHA standards because they fear OSHA penalties. General deterrence plays some, as yet undetermined, role in encouraging employers to reduce workplace hazards. However, given that OSHA inspections without penalties do not reduce workplace accidents, it seems unlikely that this effect is very large. Finally, some businesses may also comply with OSHA standards because they are industry best practices or because compliance is required by collective bargaining agreements.

---

[64] General deterrence rests on the *perceived* cost of noncompliance. Empirical evidence generally shows that perceptions of the likelihood and severity of punishment only somewhat reflect true shifts in these variables (Scholz 1985).

APPENDIX 2.3. LABOR MARKETS, WORKERS' COMPENSATION,
AND WORKPLACE SAFETY AND HEALTH

Before the passage of the OSH Act in 1970, state workers' compensation systems and liability litigation were the primary means by which the government regulated workplace hazards. This appendix describes the implications of the private labor market, as supplemented by contemporary workers' compensation programs, for workplace safety and health conditions. It focuses on the variation, across employers and classes of workers, in the effectiveness of these systems.

1. The Historical Liability System and Private Labor Markets[65]

Prior to the enactment of the first state workers' compensation laws in 1911, the damages arising from workplace illnesses and injuries were assigned to different parties through a liability system based on fault. Under this system, employers were obligated to meet a standard of due care for employee safety. Despite the absence of direct regulation of working conditions, however, employers were not free to ignore all matters of workplace safety and health. The assumption-of-risk doctrine and the concept of contributory negligence were critical efficiency-inducing components of this liability system.

The assumption-of-risk doctrine allowed employers to forego the abatement of workplace hazards if workers were informed and accepted these hazards. The assumption-of-risk doctrine allowed each employer to turn to the labor market to decide whether or not to abate a particular hazard. Risk-seeking workers – those who were willing to choose a job where they were more likely to be injured – could accept a "risk premium" in the form of greater salary or benefits in place of a less dangerous but lower-paying job. Theoretically, this arrangement promoted efficiency because employers were free to decide both which hazards to remedy and how to remove them. The concept of contributory negligence also promoted efficiency by encouraging workers to exercise due care in the workplace. If a worker's carelessness contributed to an accident, the worker could not seek compensation. An important benefit of this method for allocating responsibility for worker injuries was that employees had a large incentive to avoid impairment.

However, there were two limitations of using the labor market to manage and allocate workplace risk. First, workers who were injured at work

---

[65] This section draws heavily on Chelius 1977, Chapter 2.

could be left destitute. Second, labor markets did not work as hypothesized. The core assumptions of the liability approach to the management
of risk were that workers received premiums for workplace hazards and
that employers mitigated any hazard that cost more in wages than it cost
to remove. Several conditions, however, left workers less well off than
hypothesized.

First, the employment contract did not fully internalize the cost of
worker disability. Numerous sources of aid for disabled workers lessened
the impact to a worker of being injured on the job. Workers therefore
demanded a smaller wage premium than they would have if being injured
guaranteed poverty, and employers consequently did not have a sufficient
incentive to reduce workplace hazards.

Second, workers were unable to force employers to offer the wage-risk
package they most desired. In general, the balance of risk and wages will
tend toward the preferences of the marginal worker (Kahn 1987). Established workers are generally less geographically mobile, face higher costs
(such as lost pensions) in moving to new jobs, and prefer less workplace
risk than younger workers (Herzog and Schlottmann 1990). The higher
cost of exit for these established workers limits their ability to threaten
exit in order to extract higher levels of workplace safety and health in the
face of changing demands by more risk-accepting marginal workers. In
this respect, unions restructure the intrafirm labor market by empower-
ing the median worker vis-à-vis the marginal worker (Moore and Viscusi
1990: 8). In nonunion workplaces, however, the level of safety and health
will tend to disproportionately represent the demands of more marginal
workers (Kahn 1987). Empirical studies show that most workers are willing to pay more in lost salary than it would cost their employers to provide a safer workplace, further evidence that employers are not responsive to the average employee's preferences (Herzog and Schlottmann
1990).

Third, workers were unable to accurately identify and measure risks
and therefore were unable to request adequate compensation for their
exposure to these hazards. A well-developed literature in labor economics
attempts to deduce the value of a human life from the observed wage
premiums that workers in more hazardous jobs earn (e.g., Rosen 1974;
Viscusi 1993). The problem with this method for deducing preferences
from observed wages and fatality rates is that workers may misestimate
the likelihood of death. *Ex ante*, when choosing among employers offering different wage-risk packages, workers do not have the retrospective
information about actual risks necessary to pick the workplace that best
suits their preferences.

Moore and Viscusi argue that although workers are not perfectly informed, they do learn about job hazards in the course of their employment. But, as the aforementioned evidence about worker immobility suggests, workers are not completely free to leave unsafe jobs. Additionally, there are systematic biases in the types of health and safety risks that workers learn about while employed. If a hazard has a sufficiently low probability of occurrence, a worker is unlikely to observe an injury or illness that "signals" to them the true hazard they face. This claim is supported by the fact that nonunion workers receive higher pay in workplaces where they are more likely to suffer a nonfatal injury, but lower pay in workplaces where the risk of death is higher (Dickens 1984). Similarly, injuries and illness with cumulative effects or long latency periods are hard for workers to link to on-the-job hazards.

2. Workers' Compensation

Workers' compensation provides guaranteed support to injured and ill workers regardless of whether or not a worker's impairment was attributable to employer negligence, employee carelessness, or a hazard intrinsic to the workplace. This support is financed by insurance premiums paid by employers. In return for the promised support of all disabled workers, employers are indemnified against claims of negligence. All fifty states and the District of Columbia have wide-ranging workers' compensation programs.

Theoretically, this compensation system is as desirable for workers and employers as is reliance on wage premiums and employer liability to counterbalance workplace risk. Because workers' compensation decreases the cost to a worker of injury, workers accept lower wages in the short term in return for the future promise of support if they are injured. Workers' compensation simply redistributes the payment for risk from all workers to those who are actually unlucky enough to suffer impairment. Workers' compensation, like labor market–induced risk premiums, also encourages the efficient management of risk because of the way employer premiums are assessed. When premiums are "experience-rated," when they take into account the injury and illness history of a particular employer and the resulting claims for worker support, they give the employer an incentive to remedy a workplace hazard that costs less to fix than it would cost the employer to compensate the injuries and illnesses that result from the hazard.

Two problems of "moral hazard," the tendency of insured persons to behave differently than they would in the absence of insurance, undercut the efficiency of any workers' compensation system (Haynes 1895: 445). First, workers may exaggerate the extent of their impairment in order to receive greater support or may report nonwork impairments as originating at work.[66] The net result is that workers' compensation is more expensive to employers than actual workplace hazards would warrant. In response, employers have an even larger incentive to reduce workplace hazards in order to minimize their workers' compensation premiums.[67]

By contrast, the second moral hazard problem associated with workers' compensation may lead to less workplace safety and health than is considered optimal. Workers' compensation may cause workers to devote less attention to their own safety and health because their injuries and illnesses will be compensated regardless of whether they were at fault (Rea 1981). Paradoxically, then, workers' compensation may leave workers worse off because employers devote more attention to safety and health but workers are simultaneously more careless.

The common solution to each of these problems of moral hazard is to keep workers' compensation benefits from becoming "too generous." The waiting period for disability benefits, for instance, is comparable to the deductible in most other insurance policies. Similarly, disabled workers receive only a portion of their full salary and benefits. Unfortunately, decreasing the benefits provided to injured workers may also discourage employers from taking steps to reduce workplace hazards. Workers' compensation programs are generally self-financing systems in which employer premiums have to be large enough to cover the costs of the benefits provided to workers. Decreasing benefit levels lowers the premium that employers pay per accident and therefore weakens the incentive for employers to prevent workplace accidents.

3. The Limitations of Workers' Compensation

Workers' compensation is only a partial solution, however, to one limitation of using the labor market to manage risk: workers' inability to

---

[66] Recent research suggests that more generous payments lead to more frequent claims of injury and also lengthen the time that workers spend away from work following an injury (Ruser 1993; Meyer et al. 1995). This evidence is consistent both with workers exaggerating their impairment and with workers choosing to seek care for more marginal injuries. See Card and McCall 1996 for a summary of the evidence in support of the "Monday effect" as well as their own rejoinder.

[67] The logic here is that because the workplace appears more dangerous than it really is, employers will have a financial incentive to reduce workplace hazards to make it appear safer. Employers may end up making the workplace safer than workers would choose if they knew that the costs of safety and health improvements were being passed along to them in the form of lower salary and benefits (Rea 1981).

properly identify and measure workplace hazards. Because this system functions effectively only when employers can reasonably anticipate that their costs will increase if they expose their employees to workplace hazards, workers' compensation is unlikely to deter employers under many of the same circumstances that render workers unable to appraise workplace hazards accurately. Specifically, when an occupational disease or injury has a long period of latency after exposure, an employer's premiums are unlikely to take into account the costs of these future injuries. By the time a worker becomes ill, it may be impossible to attribute the illness to the exposing employer, the worker may have moved on to another job, or the company may have gone out of business.

Similarly, low-probability hazards are problematic for workers to measure accurately enough to demand appropriate compensation. Workers' compensation provides some incentive for employers to mitigate these hazards, but because the employer pays the cost in increased premiums only after the fact, it also allows an employer to gamble that an accident will not occur. Accentuating this problem is the large discount that employers may give to future liabilities. Even if it is possible ten or twenty years in the future to identify the employer responsible for endangering a worker, the present value to the employer of that future insurance premium may be so small as to eliminate its effectiveness as a deterrent. Furthermore, when an employer is facing an uncertain financial future, exposing a worker to greater risk may be more acceptable that it otherwise would be. If the firm fails, future workers' compensation premiums are not a concern; if it succeeds, the problem can be dealt with later. As a rule, employers are not concerned with profit maximization in all cases. Rather, their foremost concern is avoiding insolvency (Cyert and March 1963).[68] Thus, workers' compensation may fail to deter employers from exposing workers to excess risks if the employer can rely on bankruptcy to avoid future liability (Heyes 1998).[69]

---

[68] The avoidance of insolvency actually encourages employers to gamble on the same hazards that workers have the hardest time observing because the probability that an "event" of worker impairment will occur in the short term is low. If the employer is unlucky enough to lose this "bet," then insolvency and bankruptcy ensue, but the employer is shielded from the full cost of this gamble.

[69] Even under the best financial circumstances, employers are strategic in recognizing potential liability and will develop corporate structures to indemnify themselves against future costs (Ringleb and Wiggins 1990). In the most common scenario, a parent corporation oversees the creation of a nominally independent surrogate corporation to undertake hazardous work. Because these independent surrogates have relatively few assets, they are, for all practical purposes, judgment-proof. In one extreme case, officials in a state workers' compensation program that I interviewed identified a single individual who kept dissolving and reforming his construction corporation to avoid the increased workers'

There is also evidence that workers' compensation premiums are too low to adequately deter employers from endangering workers.[70] Specifically, workers' compensation systems seem to provide insufficient benefits for the more serious risks of death and long-term disability (Boden 1995; Weiler 1986). Because these are the same risks workers have a hard time recognizing in the labor market, these data suggest that workers' compensation systems are limited in rectifying the limitations of using labor markets to manage risk. More generally, as Herzog and Schlottmann (1990) have shown, the average worker is willing to pay more for a safer workplace than it would cost to provide it. Workers' compensation systems therefore do little to represent the preferences of the median, rather than the marginal, worker. Finally, despite the importance of experience-rated premiums in deterring workplace risk, premiums are not experience-rated for most businesses with fewer than 200 workers as well as for most new employers (Chelius and Moscovitch 1996).[71] Many states also place floors and caps on workers' compensation premium rates, further interfering with true experience rating. Overall, low-risk employers often subsidize the coverage of high-risk employers. While these problems are not intrinsic to the use of economic incentives, they occur in most state systems.

compensation premiums that would have followed from a series of accidents at businesses he ran.

Nor is this problem attributable only to nefarious business owners who knowingly gamble with their workers' safety. Rather, avoidance of accidents is just one of many concerns that managers must attend to on a regular basis. Future employer costs are effective at deterring workplace hazards only when employers are forward-looking enough to realize that allowing a hazard to persist in the present will cost them in the future. Scholz and Gray (1990) show that employer attention to safety and health matters is episodic: Employers devote energy to remedying workplace hazards when enough injuries and illnesses occur to make management aware of the costs associated with these hazards. This behavior is consistent with models of firm decision making in which the search for problems and solutions are both costly (e.g., Simon 1947). When injuries and illnesses have long latency periods or when the probability of occurrence is low, both managers and employees may overlook these risks.

[70] See Moore and Viscusi 1990, Chapters 3 and 4, for a summary of the debate about whether premiums are too low.

[71] Smaller firms have great variability in observed injury rates, while new firms do not have an accident and illness history from which to calculate appropriate premiums. In these cases, premiums are often calculated based on industry-averaged claim rates, so that a firm pays premiums based on the safety and health record of all firms in a particular industrial category. This assessment system unfortunately discourages investment in safety and health because employers do not reap the rewards of their own efforts to reduce workers' compensation claims.

3

From Regulatory Search to Enforcement

The previous chapter argued that OSHA's leadership has chosen a strategically neutral enforcement posture. But actual enforcement in the field, seeking out and punishing those who violate the law, may differ substantially from this ideal vision proffered by agency leaders in Washington. This chapter examines OSHA's field enforcement program from start to finish, considering separately OSHA's deployment of resources (staffing of regions and local offices), search for violators (inspection targeting and inspector productivity), and punitiveness. Thus, it takes an "inside the agency" look at how agency leaders attempt to structure and manage the agency's field enforcement efforts, successfully or not, in order to secure their larger political goals.

An additional motivation for this inquiry is to reconcile the arguments made in Chapter 2 about OSHA's geographic neutrality with previous scholarship that portrays OSHA's field enforcement efforts as heavily affected by a variety of local political concerns – the preferences of locally elected members of Congress, business and labor advocacy group strength, and local constituency preferences (Scholz and Wei 1986; Scholz, Twombly, and Headrick 1991). These arguments are hard to dismiss given the aggregate association between state-level politics and OSHA's enforcement efforts. For example, there is a strong positive correlation between statewide Democratic Party support and OSHA's enforcement efforts. Table 3.1 shows that in states where support for Clinton was greater in the 1992 presidential election, OSHA inspected a larger proportion of businesses than in states where Bush did better. In the seven most Democratic states, OSHA conducted, on average from 1993 to 1996, 105 inspections per 10,000 businesses, while in the 7 most Republican states, the agency

TABLE 3.1. *State partisanship and OSHA inspection rate, sorted by Democratic Party strength*

State[a]	Democratic Presidential Vote 1992[b]	Annual Inspections per 10,000 Businesses[c]
Nebraska	0.39	49.23
Idaho	0.40	91.52
North Dakota	0.42	101.26
Oklahoma	0.44	90.33
Mississippi	0.45	102.20
Alabama	0.46	82.90
Kansas	0.46	63.30
South Dakota	0.48	57.69
Texas	0.48	89.12
Florida	0.49	41.96
Georgia	0.50	60.72
New Hampshire	0.51	96.18
Ohio	0.51	93.17
New Jersey	0.51	78.25
Montana	0.52	122.99
Louisiana	0.53	67.30
Wisconsin	0.53	98.26
Colorado	0.53	73.76
Connecticut	0.54	104.15
Delaware	0.55	65.98
Pennsylvania	0.56	91.75
Maine	0.56	118.39
Missouri	0.57	70.30
West Virginia	0.58	131.84
Illinois	0.59	71.84
New York	0.59	66.53
Arkansas	0.60	98.08
Rhode Island	0.62	124.16
Massachusetts	0.62	102.43
District of Columbia	0.90	143.05

[a] Listed states are those where OSHA retains primary enforcement authority for private sector workplaces.

[b] *Source:* Bureau of the Census, USA Counties Database. Reported figure is the Democratic share of the 1992 two-party presidential vote.

[c] *Source:* OSHA IMIS database and County Business Patterns Reports. Number of businesses as of 1995; inspection counts are averages across four years, 1993–96.

TABLE 3.2. *Planned manufacturing inspections and violations and penalties per planned inspection in four states*

State	Number of Inspections	Average Number of Serious Violations per Inspection	Average Penalty per Inspection
Massachusetts	555	5.45	$2,610
New York	629	4.62	$2,756
North Average		5.01	$2,688
Alabama	327	2.80	$1,862
Mississippi	62	2.73	$1,046
South Average		2.79	$1,732

Source: OSHA IMIS database. Completed planned safety inspections of private manufacturing facilities, 1993–95.

performed only 83 inspections. Overall, OSHA inspected businesses 25 percent more frequently in the most Democratic states than in the least Democratic states.[1]

Additional data suggest that the stringency of OSHA's field enforcement may also be related to local politics. Table 3.2 displays the average number of violations and penalties that OSHA issued per planned manufacturing inspection in two northern states, Massachusetts and New York, and two southern ones, Alabama and Mississippi. Both Alabama and Mississippi are "right-to-work states" that prohibit unions from negotiating closed-shop contracts, have relatively low rates of unionization,[2] and are ideologically conservative. Massachusetts and New York, by contrast, have stronger unions and are generally more liberal. Thus, these two sets of states vary widely on two generic correlates of support for OSHA, and the outcome of OSHA inspections in the two regions seems to mirror local demand. OSHA inspects more frequently in the two more industrialized northern states, but the more striking disparity is in the *outcomes* of OSHA inspections in the two regions. On average, OSHA issues about 2.2 more serious violations per inspection in the northern states than in the southern ones. Similarly, the average penalty per inspection is more than $950 greater in the northern states. In other words, OSHA issues 80 percent more violations and 55 percent greater penalties *per inspection* in

[1] The bivariate correlation between the Democratic share of the two-party presidential vote and the number of inspections per business is .50 ($p = .005$). Excluding the District of Columbia, it is .31 ($p = .10$).

[2] Using data derived from the Current Population Survey, I estimated the proportion of each state's labor force that was unionized in 1996: Alabama, 12 percent; Mississippi, 6 percent; Massachusetts, 16 percent; and New York, 28 percent.

the two northern states than in the southern ones. Across all northern and southern states, there are 60 percent more violations and 40 percent greater penalties per inspection in the North.

More generally, public administration and political science scholars have long noted the ability of local political actors to influence field enforcement despite administrative efforts to the contrary.[3] In the case of strip mining regulation, Shover and colleagues (1986) find that Office of Surface Mining agents adopted a more conciliatory approach in their interactions with larger firms that employed safety and health professionals in the West than in their interactions with smaller and less professional mining operations in the East. Hedge and Jallow argue that such local differentiation can allow regulatory agencies to mitigate political opposition:

Agencies that uniformly adopt a vigorous approach to regulation will sustain opposition from industry sources, while a moderate approach is likely to draw attacks from consumer or environmental groups. An alternative strategy would allow regulation to vary with the political and economic climate of each of the regulated states. . . . [R]egulatory agencies will be able to maximize political support and minimize political fallout by allowing regulation to vary with the political and economic climates of the states. (1990: 790–791)

Likewise, Hutter (1989) argues that pollution control agents in Great Britain resorted to punitive sanctions only when factory managers resisted inspectors' less coercive efforts to rectify noncompliance. In a more explicitly political analysis, Gordon (1999) argues that Environmental Protection Agency officials in regions that were more hostile toward government regulation were less likely to file charges because they imposed a higher "burden of proof" on claims of noncompliance. Do OSHA's enforcement efforts exhibit similar strategizing?

In answering this question, the remainder of this chapter proceeds in three broad parts. The first examines OSHA's field enforcement program and how politics affects, sequentially, the staffing of local offices, the selection of inspection targets, inspector productivity, and the stringency of regulatory enforcement. Disaggregating the analysis of OSHA's field enforcement practices allows me to diagnose the particular ways in which politics influences enforcement of the OSH Act. Aggregate counts of inspections broken down by geographic area, for example, reveal little about how individual bureaucrats make decisions in the face of political

---

[3] On the influence of local politics on policy implementation more generally, see Pressman and Wildavsky 1973 and Lipsky 1980.

demands and how OSHA's leadership has sought to shape responsiveness to local politics.[4]

Two points about the analysis that follows are worth noting outright. First, during the period studied in this chapter, roughly 1990–98, OSHA generally exercised tight control over field-level enforcement. Briefly during the Clinton administration, however, OSHA's leadership (acting under the rubric of Vice President Gore's reinvention efforts) decreased its relative focus on inspector productivity. This "natural experiment" provides an observed counterfactual to the claim made earlier that bureaucratic leaders generically, and OSHA's leadership in particular, have an incentive to control their subordinates. It also allows me to test whether strong central control of subordinate behavior affects the linkages between local politics and field enforcement.

Second, unlike much previous work on bureaucratic decision making in enforcement, the analysis that follows takes into account *the behavior of regulated parties*. My concern is with measuring determinants of enforcement *relative to the ideal of fair treatment*. Obviously, OSHA's appropriate behavior following an inspection will depend on how many violations actually exist at a workplace. Furthermore, if noncompliance is dynamic, it will be affected by previous OSHA enforcement efforts. Fortunately, I have obtained information about earlier enforcement activities and workplace conditions prior to the initiation of certain OSHA inspections. Thus, I can compare OSHA's observed behavior to what one would expect in the absence of political pressures. (This is akin to having an actual measure of traffic violations and drivers' race when seeking to measure racial disparity in enforcement behavior by police officers.) More generally, understanding the nature of bureaucratic decision making necessitates distinguishing variation in outcomes arising from differences in OSHA's behavior from disparity originating in private actor behavior.

[4] This is true for two reasons. First, the number of inspections that OSHA conducts and the number of citations it issues (and penalties it imposes) in a particular locality are the ultimate product of the assignment of inspectors to local area offices, the selection of a list of workplaces for inspection, and the relative productivity and punitiveness of inspectors in completing inspections. To identify the source of the linkage between political geography and OSHA's local enforcement efforts, one needs to ascertain where (and if) local politics enters the regulatory search process. Second, identifying the bureaucrats who make each of these important decisions and the factors that shape their decisions is critical for choosing among different explanations for these outcomes. If local bureaucrats conduct more inspections in areas where workers file more complaints because an OSHA-wide policy instructs local offices to respond to worker complaints, this is fundamentally different from a finding that field-level bureaucrats in these areas have and use their discretion to conduct additional inspection.

Part two of this chapter reconciles the results of my analysis of contemporary OSHA Act enforcement with previous research on OSHA.
Unlike earlier characterizations of OSHA's field enforcement during the
late 1970s and early 1980s as directly affected by local political forces, I
find little evidence that contemporary OSHA bureaucrats take local political conditions into account when choosing how to enforce the law. This
does not mean that local politics does not matter in shaping enforcement
outcomes. As will be shown, the decisions of businesses and workers have
direct effects on the nature and efficacy of OSHA's enforcement efforts.
Still, this finding is distinct from, and has national political implications
distinct from, the claim that OSHA's field enforcement personnel consider local political preferences when implementing the law in different
geographic areas.

Finally, part three of the chapter relates these findings about OSHA's
implementation of the law to OSHA's efforts to secure national political
support and embrace the logic and language of strategic neutrality. Supporting my general contention that OSHA has sought to mitigate localism
in enforcement, I find additional evidence that OSHA has tried to compensate for variation in private actor behavior that makes enforcing the
law easier in some areas than in others.

PART I. UNPACKING OSHA'S FIELD ENFORCEMENT EFFORT

1. Fielding an Enforcement Bureaucracy

OSHA's first step in enforcing the rules governing workplace safety and
health is inspecting workplaces. Where OSHA goes – which businesses it
visits and in what localities – affects both the aggregate level of enforcement and the distribution of this effort across geographic areas and different classes of businesses. OSHA's staffing of local offices and choice of
inspection targets therefore determines, in part, who bears the costs (and
receives the benefits) of regulation.

1.1. Deploying the Troops: Staffing Local Offices

How OSHA staffs local offices has a large effect on the geographic distribution of the agency's regulatory efforts. The size of a local office establishes an upper boundary on the number of inspections the agency can
complete in that area. No matter how aggressively a poorly staffed office
seeks to enforce the law, having too few inspectors available to conduct
regular inspections limits the stringency of enforcement. The assignment

of enforcement resources to localities is one general mechanism through which interested parties can shape local regulation.

For actors who are interested in influencing OSHA's regulatory efforts in a particular locality, altering the allocation of staff seems to provide an ideal way to strengthen or weaken local enforcement. Manipulating staff assignments should have a straightforward effect on regulatory policy. More inspectors allow for more aggressive enforcement; fewer inspectors constrain enforcement. Additionally, monitoring the allocation of staff is relatively easy. Outside parties need only count agency employment and the size of the regulated community in different localities. Finally, reallocating staff resources is less burdensome than direct efforts to influence field-level enforcement. Rather than having to change bureaucrats' behavior, one simply increases or decreases the number of bureaucrats available to enforce the law.

Despite the apparent opportunities for strategic manipulation of enforcement via inspector allocation, OSHA assigns staff in a way that demonstrates a remarkable disregard for local politics. OSHA's national office instead simply allocates staff positions to the regional offices proportionally to the number of business facilities OSHA oversees in each region.[5] In deciding which regional offices receive the authority to hire new inspectors, OSHA's leadership relies on a simple measure of the number of inspectors in each region relative to the number of workplaces overseen by the agency. Each region contains several states, and in states where OSHA retains enforcement authority, the number of facilities OSHA oversees is the sum of the number of private and federal workplaces. (Table 3.3 lists these states in each region.) In states that have been delegated enforcement authority, OSHA regulates federal workplaces and certain maritime operations.[6] In practice, OSHA's leadership, acting under imposed budgetary limits, first gives the right to hire new inspectors to the regions with the lowest number of inspectors relative to the number of regulated employers.[7]

Within each region, however, the devolution of decisions about staffing local offices to regional administrators presents an opportunity for crafting enforcement in response to local pressures. Indeed, the regional

[5] Source: author interviews with regional and headquarters staff.

[6] In these states, OSHA also allocates additional staff to oversee state enforcement efforts.

[7] I verified this claim by repeating the econometric analysis reported in Panel B of Table 3.5 for area office staffing at the regional level, and found no evidence of political influence on regional staffing. I also discussed the matter with national union groups, who verified this staffing rule.

TABLE 3.3. OSHA *federal enforcement states, by region*

Federal Region	Federal Enforcement States
I	New Hampshire, Massachusetts, Maine, Connecticut, Rhode Island
II	New Jersey, New York
III	District of Columbia, Delaware, West Virginia, Pennsylvania
IV	Mississippi, Georgia, Florida, Alabama
V	Wisconsin, Ohio, Illinois
VI	Texas, Louisiana, Arkansas, Oklahoma
VII	Nebraska, Kansas, Missouri
VIII	North Dakota, South Dakota, Colorado, Montana
IX	None
X	Idaho

administrators I interviewed acknowledged that the allocation of staff to local offices takes into account additional factors beyond the ratio of inspectors to businesses. (Details about the interviews I conducted with OSHA officials appear in appendix 3.1.) First, regional administrators attempt to assign staff in order to ensure an adequate number of personnel trained as health inspectors in each area office. Traditionally, a larger proportion of OSHA's inspectors have been safety inspectors than health inspectors. Consequently, retirement, promotion, or reassignment can leave an office without a single health inspector. In this case, administrators will assign new staff to an office that is already comparatively well staffed if this is necessary in order for it to continue health inspections.

Second, regional administrators consider a more broadly defined measure of regulatory need in assigning staff. OSHA's national office relies on the County Business Patterns Reports of the Bureau of the Census in calculating the ratio of inspectors to regulated workplaces. This ratio, however, does not account for differences in workload attributable to other factors. In an urban area, for instance, inspection sites are relatively close to one another, while in rural areas traveling between businesses requires a greater proportion of an inspector's time. Urban and suburban areas, however, are more likely to have ongoing construction work that does not appear in the County Business Patterns Reports. The County Business Patterns data that OSHA uses are also only a measure of the number of facilities in different geographic areas. They do not take into account how hazardous these facilities are or their size. If one area in a region has proportionally more facilities on OSHA's national targeting list, then the regional administrator can allocate more staff to this office.

TABLE 3.4. *1994 staffing levels and allocation of new inspectors in 1995 for OSHA Region I area offices, sorted by 1994 staffing levels*

Area Office[a]	Inspectors per 10,000 Businesses 1994[b]	New Inspector Hires in 1995[c]		
		Total	Safety	Health
South Boston	1.52	3	1	2
Bridgeport	1.59	3	0	3
North Boston	1.83	2	1	1
Concord	2.19	1	1	0
Hartford	2.35	0	0	0
Providence	2.57	0	0	0
Springfield	2.76	0	0	0
Bangor	2.79	0	0	0

[a] This list excludes one office that closed at the end of 1994 and one new office that opened in 1995.
[b] *Source:* OSHA IMIS database and County Business Patterns Reports.
[c] *Source:* OSHA IMIS database.

These considerations appear to trump any strategic political calculation by regional administrators in their assignment of staff. The regional and national administrators I spoke with largely viewed staff assignment as a technical administrative task governed overwhelmingly by limited resources and a uniform need for more inspections. (As one administrator noted, "we need a health CSHO [inspector] in every office, and we have to compensate for the distribution of service and industrial employers...[but mostly] what we need is more inspectors.") My analysis of staffing practices confirms this presentation. The allocation of new inspectors to OSHA area offices in Region I in 1995 and each office's relative staffing level in 1994 are shown in Table 3.4. From this table it appears that, at least in Region I, neutral measures of workload – the number of facilities – dominated the calculation concerning staff placement. All nine of the new hires in the region were assigned to the four most understaffed offices, and two-thirds were assigned to the two most understaffed offices.

I also examined staffing of local offices in all of OSHA's regions for 1994 and 1995. Table 3.5 reports the results of this analysis. Panel (A) of the table shows the results from statistical models in which the dependent variable is the number of inspectors, per business, in each local office in 1994. Because regional administrators have to choose which of their local offices to allocate staff to, I compare staffing within a region by both including an indicator (fixed effect) for each region and scaling all variables relative to the average for the region. The measure of the dangerousness of the businesses that an area office oversees (the proportion

TABLE 3.5. *Political and task explanations for OSHA's staffing of local offices within regions*

(A) *Local Office Staffing Levels, 1994*

	1994 Inspectors per Facility				
	(1)	(2)	(3)	(4)	(5)
Proportion high-hazard facilities	0.0017***	0.0018	0.0013**	0.0019***	0.0017***
	(0.00049)	(0.00102)	(0.00041)	(0.00042)	(0.00093)
Complaints per facility		−0.0067			−0.0104
		(0.04157)			(0.04109)
Democratic two-party vote share (1992)			−0.0003**		−0.0003*
			(0.00014)		(0.00016)
Unemployment rate			0.0012***		0.0009**
			(0.00033)		(0.00029)
Congressional conservatism				0.0000	−0.0001
				(0.00004)	(0.00004)
Labor subcommittee conservatism				0.0012**	0.0010
				(0.00047)	(0.00071)
Appropriations subcommittee conservatism				0.0006***	0.0005
				(0.00013)	(0.00028)
Constant	0.0000***	0.0000***	0.0000***	0.0000***	0.0000***
	(0.00000)	(0.00000)	(0.00000)	(0.00000)	(0.00000)
Observations	69	69	69	69	69
R-squared	0.19	0.19	0.23	0.24	0.27

Note: OLS estimates with robust standard errors in parentheses, clustered by region. Region indicators not reported. All dependent and independent variables are scaled relative to region average. * denotes $p < .10$; ** denotes $p < .05$; *** denotes $p < .01$.

(B) *Allocation of New Inspectors, 1995*

	1995 New Inspector Hires				
	(1)	(2)	(3)	(4)	(5)
Inspectors per facility 1994	−5,774.41**	−5,134.53*	−5,385.33**	−5,016.54*	−4,483.23**
	(2,560.59)	(2,647.75)	(2,658.76)	(2,586.08)	(2,707.45)
Proportion high-hazard facilities	−6.90	−8.09	−10.69*	−10.56*	−12.83*
	(5.68)	(5.83)	(6.25)	(6.31)	(6.61)
Health inspector shortage 1994	0.35	0.42	0.41	0.30	0.41
	(0.26)	(0.27)	(0.26)	(0.29)	(0.31)
Complaints per inspector 1994		0.03			0.03
		(0.03)			(0.04)
Democratic two-party vote share (1992)			−2.23		−2.81
			(2.15)		(2.55)
Unemployment rate			−3.74		−2.05
			(10.99)		(11.06)
Congressional conservatism				1.08	−0.08
				(0.87)	(1.15)
Labor subcommittee conservatism				0.23	−1.47
				(7.87)	(7.87)
Appropriations subcommittee conservatism				−3.26	−2.72
				(4.22)	(4.34)
Constant	0.88**	0.87**	0.88**	0.86**	0.87**
	(0.39)	(0.38)	(0.38)	(0.38)	(0.37)
Observations	69	69	69	69	69
Log-likelihood	−59.36	−59.06	−57.95	−58.41	−57.33
Chi squared	28.16	28.76	30.99	30.07	32.23

Note: Tobit estimates with standard errors in parentheses. Region indicators not reported. All independent variables are scaled relative to region average. * denotes $p < .10$; ** denotes $p < .05$.

of high-hazard facilities, as defined later in the discussion of OSHA's targeting efforts) is therefore scaled relative to the businesses that all the
area offices in the region oversee and not relative to other regions' local
offices, to which an administrator cannot assign staff. The results shown
in column (1) demonstrate that the intrinsic dangerousness of a locality's
businesses has, as expected, a positive and statistically significant effect on
the allocation of inspectors to area offices within regions. It also confirms
my interview evidence that regional administrators consider the distribution of hazardous workplaces in allocating staff.

In addition to this "neutral" measure of regulatory need, the estimated models also include a series of variables that measure local political support for vigorous OSH Act enforcement. These measures are used
throughout this chapter, so I discuss them at length here. First, I examine whether administrators allocate additional inspectors to area offices
where complaints are more frequent. As will be shown, the complaint
rate is a good proxy for both the relative dangerousness of workplaces
and worker support for OSHA. Column (2) shows that regional administrators do not allocate additional staff to offices with high complaint
rates once one accounts for the relative dangerousness of the businesses
in an area office's jurisdiction (the coefficient on complaints per business
is negative, but not statistically significant).

Next I examine whether regional administrators consider citizen preferences more generally in allocating inspectors. Two measures of citizen
preferences are used: the Democratic share of the two-party presidential vote in 1992[8] and the local unemployment rate.[9] If regional administrators consider constituency support in allocating staff, one would
expect them to assign additional staff to more Democratic and lower-
unemployment areas where, respectively, individuals are more supportive
of OSHA and the political costs of OSH Act enforcement are less onerous. Neither prediction is supported in the column (3) results. Regional
administrators do not appear to allocate staff to reward Democratic constituencies or to avoid angering Republican ones. In fact, there is a negative relationship between Democratic support and staffing. Nor do they

---

[8] Because of concern about the effects of Perot's presence on the ballot, I also estimated the
model using the raw 1992 Democratic vote share as well as the 1988 and 1996 Democratic
vote shares. In none of the models reported in this chapter did changing these measures
produce substantially different results.

[9] Unfortunately, no reliable measure of unionization is available below the state level.
Repeating this analysis by imputing local unionization rates using average unionization
by industry in a state produces similar results.

appear to tailor staffing to weaken enforcement in areas where unemployment is higher.[10]

Column (4) displays the results from a model testing for the effects of the preferences of locally elected members of Congress.[11] My measure of congressional preferences is the Poole (1998) common-space transformation of the Poole and Rosenthal (1991) "W-Nominate" ideology scores derived from the votes of members on all measures considered in each session of Congress. These scores range from -1 to 1, with a positive score indicating a more conservative member.[12] Because of the disproportionate power of committee members, I also calculated a conservatism score for membership on the House Education and Labor subcommittee and the House Appropriations subcommittee with responsibility for OSHA matters. Each of these bodies has substantial authority over OSHA policy and budgets.[13] For areas represented by members serving on either committee, the value of the variable is the conservatism score of that member. For all other areas, it is coded 0 (neither conservative nor liberal).

I find no evidence that OSHA allocates additional inspectors to area offices overseen by more liberal members of the House, either generically or specifically for those on the relevant oversight committees. The only statistically significant effects that appear show that offices in areas with more *conservative* members on the two relevant oversight committees are better staffed than areas with more liberal members. Finally, column (5)

---

[10] Here the positive coefficient is perhaps not surprising, because in areas that have high unemployment OSHA's previous staffing decisions will have created a surplus of inspectors relative to a now shrinking workforce.

[11] I confine my analysis in this chapter to House member's preferences. Including measures of senator's preferences (members generally or those on relevant committees) produced null findings. I used data supplied by Blodgett and CIESIN (1998) to map counties to congressional districts. I then took a population-weighted average of the ideology scores for all of the counties overseen by the area office. If more than one member of Congress represented a single county, I calculated a constituency-weighted average of the ideology scores across all members who represented the county.

[12] These scores have three advantages over alternative measures of preferences. First, they are consistent across time, so that a high (very conservative) score in one session is equivalent to a high score in another session. Second, unlike ADA scores and other measures based on a sample of votes, they are highly discriminating and based on preferences as they are revealed by votes on the hundreds of issues considered by Congress in any given session. (Nonetheless, they are highly correlated with industry and labor groups' scores for legislators.) Third, they are good predictors of how members of Congress vote on matters of OSHA policy (Poole and Rosenthal 1991).

[13] Information on committee assignments was gathered from Congressional Quarterly's Washington Alert database. I also tried using information about entire committees, rather than subcommittees, for this analysis and found fewer instances in which committee preferences were statistically significant.

displays the estimates from a unified model, which confirms that simultaneously estimating the effects of complaint rates and citizen and House member preferences does not produce evidence that staffing is tailored to local support. The measure of hazardousness remains statistically significant, as do the findings indicating more inspectors in higher unemployment and more Republican areas. (In this specification, the previous findings regarding committee preferences are no longer statistically significant.)

Of course, it may be the case that there are unobserved factors that explain the baseline allocation of staff across area offices. In this case, a simple cross-sectional analysis might miss the discretionary use of regional administrators' authority in those cases where they have resources to allocate to individual area offices. For this reason, in panel (B) of Table 3.5, I report the results from an analysis of the allocation of *new inspectors* to area offices in 1995 after accounting for the ratio of inspectors per business in the area offices in 1994.[14] Once again, since I am interested in regional administrators' decisions, the models include indicators for each region (fixed effects, to account for variation in the availability of new hires) and the independent variables are scaled relative to regional averages.

Column (1) displays the results of an estimate that includes only simple task measures of area office responsibility. Across all specifications, offices that were better staffed in 1994 are less likely to receive new inspectors in 1995, and this effect is consistently statistically significant. Area offices that had a more dangerous set of businesses to oversee were less likely to receive new inspectors, a finding that is probably due to OSHA's slight decline in overall inspector strength in 1995. Forced to cut back on inspectors, regional administrators first reduced staffing in those area offices with the most inspectors, some of which were likely to be highly staffed (per the results in panel [A] of the table) owing to the relative dangerousness of the workplaces they oversaw. Finally, area offices that had a shortage of health inspectors were more likely to receive additional new inspector hires, further confirming the earlier interview evidence.[15]

The results shown in columns (2) through (5), mirroring the earlier results, also suggest that regional administrators give little weight to local

---

[14] I also examined the sources of new openings in area offices to discern whether or not inspectors were more likely to leave the field in less supportive areas and found no relationship between complaint rates or local constituency preferences and staff turnover. This is perhaps not surprising given the self-selection of individuals to become OSHA inspectors in the first place.

[15] The health inspector shortage variable was coded 2 if the area office had no health inspectors and 1 if they had only a single health inspector. All other cases were coded 0.

political concerns when considering the allocation of new resources to area offices. In the column (2) specification, including a measure of complaint rates has a negligible and statistically insignificant effect on inspector allocation. In the column (3) specification, including the measures of local support for OSHA produces insignificant results. Nor, per the column (4) results, do the preferences of House members, even those on powerful committees, explain the allocation of new staff. Finally, in the unified model shown in column (5), the earlier results persist.

At the national level, OSHA's leadership has difficulty in mirroring the distribution of inspectors to the distribution of workplaces reported in the County Business Patterns data because staffing decisions persist over time. OSHA inspectors are protected by civil service rules. Consequently, administrators are relatively powerless to reassign staff to different geographic regions to account for changes in the distribution of employment. Limitations on reassignment powers are particularly important because OSHA's inspection force has not grown since the Carter administration. Apart from voluntary transfers, administrators must therefore rely on promotions and retirement to free additional slots that are then reallocated to areas that have greater need than in the past. The regional allocation of OSHA inspectors reflects this limitation. Table 3.6 shows the average number of OSHA safety inspectors relative to the number of businesses in each federal region during the period 1992–95. The table also includes the percentage of all workplaces that OSHA oversees that are located in each region in 1995, a historical figure for 1977, and the change in the contribution of each region to the nation's total business community from 1977 to 1995.

Three of the four most poorly staffed regions have grown in national economic importance since 1977. In particular, Region IV, encompassing Mississippi, Georgia, Florida, and Alabama, has increased the most in economic importance but remains, comparatively, the second least well-staffed. By contrast, four of the five regions that have shrunk in economic importance are overstaffed.[16] Overall, OSHA's regions that encompass the "Rust Belt" are comparatively overstaffed relative to those in the "Sun Belt," although this problem is likely to moderate with the expected boom in retirement among federal employees over the next decade.[17]

[16] The one exception is Region VII, which shrank in importance but remains understaffed. From 1990 to 1993, Region VII lost thirty of about forty inspectors due to retirement, promotion, or transfers to other regions.

[17] "Within five years, about 30 percent of the government's 1.6 million full-time employees will be eligible to retire. An additional 20 percent could seek early retirement" (Barr 2000).

TABLE 3.6. *OSHA regional staffing and size of the regulated community, sorted by current staffing levels*

Federal Region[a]	Average Inspectors per 10,000 Businesses, 1992–95[b]	Total Proportion of Businesses OSHA Oversees		Change in Proportion, 1977–95[c]
		1977[c]	1995[c]	
VII	1.48	7.0%	6.5%	−0.5%
IV	1.52	14.8%	18.5%	3.7%
VIII	1.53	4.3%	4.8%	0.5%
VI	1.60	16.7%	17.1%	0.5%
II	1.72	19.2%	17.4%	−1.8%
V	2.00	18.7%	17.5%	−1.2%
III	2.14	10.2%	9.2%	−1.0%
I	2.15	9.0%	8.9%	−0.1%
OVERALL	1.76	100.0%	100.0%	0.0%

[a] Includes all federal regions where OSHA retains primary enforcement authority in at least two states.

[b] *Source:* OSHA IMIS database and County Business Patterns Reports. Number of inspectors is the average during the period 1992–95. All figures are for states with federal enforcement authority.

[c] *Source:* County Business Patterns Reports.

In sum, this evidence supports the claim that current regional staffing reflects a geographically neutral attempt to align resources with a gross measure of regulatory need as well as inertia generated by civil service rules. The decision-making process within OSHA regions for the allocation of staff to local offices is more complicated, however, accounting for measures of task responsibilities linked with the concept of strategic neutrality (more frequent inspections and more aggressive regulation of dangerous firms). There is no evidence, however, that OSHA's national or regional offices reward particular subnational constituencies, business or labor groups, or elected officials by allocating more or fewer enforcement resources. (Most telling in this regard is the finding that complaints, the clearest manifestation of local support for aggressive OSH Act enforcement, are not associated with greater staff allocation.)

1.2. Targeting Inspections: Planned and Complaint Inspections

While differences in staffing of local offices are one potential source of geographic variation in OSHA enforcement, the selection of inspection targets is another important determinant of enforcement outcomes across localities and individual businesses. Within an area office's jurisdiction, which businesses OSHA's inspectors visit affects which workplace hazards are remediated and how the costs of regulation are distributed across firms. OSHA's inspection targeting therefore creates opportunities for agency leaders to curry favor with local constituencies, elected officials, and interest groups. This is particularly true because politicians who agree about the merits of the OSH Act in general may still disagree about which businesses should be subject to regular inspections.

OSHA's process for selecting inspection targets, however, places tight limits on local office discretion. OSHA's Field Manual defines OSHA's inspection priorities, in descending order, as (1) imminent danger situations, (2) fatality and catastrophe investigations, (3) complaint and referral investigations, and (4) planned inspections.[18] "Deviations from this priority list are allowed so long as they are justifiable, lead to efficient use of resources, *and* contribute to the effective protection of workers."[19] More specifically, when an area office director is made aware of a situation of imminent danger, he or she must give an inspection of that workplace the highest priority.[20] Likewise, a vast majority of the agency's planned inspections are conducted from numbered lists distributed from Washington. In this case, officials in the local area office choose neither which workplaces to inspect nor the order in which to visit them. Similarly, all formal written complaints by an employee alleging a serious hazard are automatically scheduled for an inspection.

While variation in enforcement efforts introduced by centrally developed inspection lists or patterns of worker complaints reveals little about whether field-level bureaucrats alter their decisions in the face of political pressure, these are important mechanisms through which politics can shape enforcement without affecting the discretionary decisions of individual inspectors. Furthermore, centralized targeting choices reveal the strategic political machinations of bureaucratic superiors in responding to their political environment. Here I examine OSHA's planned and

---

[18] OSHA FIRM, Chapter 1, (B)(3)(a). In the past, OSHA gave first priority to fatality and catastrophe inspections (Mintz 1984: 400).

[19] OSHA FIRM, Chapter 1, (B)(3)(b). Emphasis in original.

[20] OSHA FIRM, Chapter 1, (C)(5)(a).

complaint inspection policies separately and consider whether and how local politics might influence discretionary bureaucratic choices.

1.2.1. PLANNED INSPECTIONS.[21] OSHA's national policy for selecting workplaces for safety inspections places stringent direct limits on local office discretion. Specifically, for the period I study, OSHA's national targeting policy emphasized inspections of businesses in "dangerous" industries.[22] This policy first separated businesses into three categories: high-hazard, low-hazard, and exempt. High-hazard businesses were defined as those operating in the 200 most dangerous industries as reported by the Bureau of Labor Statistics annual summary of occupational injuries and illnesses.[23] Low-hazard businesses were businesses operating in any industry not in the top 200. Finally, exempt businesses were those outside of OSHA's statutory scope or for which inspection had been limited by Congress (e.g., small business in industries with injury rates below the national average).

OSHA's national office then generated random lists of businesses for inspection by each area office, weighting each business so as to draw high-hazard businesses 90 percent of the time, low-hazard businesses 5 percent of the time, and high-hazard nonmanufacturing businesses an additional 5 percent of the time.[24] These lists were then transmitted to the area office,

---

[21] As elsewhere in this book, I restrict my discussion in this section to the targeting procedure for planned safety inspections.

[22] See OSHA Instruction 2.25H, Scheduling System for Programmed Inspections (December 31, 1990). The 1990 targeting system is similar to the systems in place throughout the 1980s.

[23] High-hazard industries are also defined so as to include all maritime and construction activities. In the past, OSHA also considered the number of violations found in previous inspections in the industry in rating dangerousness, but for safety inspections during the period I study it relied instead on the BLS survey.

[24] The courts have also placed indirect limits on OSHA's system for selecting workplaces through their review of private lawsuits challenging agency enforcement actions. In *Marshall v. Barlow's Inc.* (1978), the Supreme Court confirmed that a business could refuse entry to an OSHA inspector if the inspector did not have a search warrant. The Court also ruled, however, that

A warrant showing that a specific business has been chosen for an OSHA search on the basis of a general administrative plan for the enforcement of the Act derived from neutral sources such as, for example, dispersion of employees in various types of industries across a given area, and the desired frequency of searches in any of the lesser divisions of the area, would protect an employer's Fourth Amendment rights. (321)

This interpretation of the OSHA Act and the Constitution allows OSHA to obtain a search warrant and compel entry so long as OSHA's targeting system is based on "reasonable . . . administrative standards" (*Camara v. Municipal Court* [1967], quoted in

which had to begin at the top of the list and work its way as far down the list as resources allowed.[25] In 1991, these national lists accounted for 95 percent of OSHA's planned inspections.[26]

Even this seemingly neutral targeting policy, however, yields surprising variation in enforcement efforts across OSHA's regions when combined with the agency's allocation of staff. Because dangerous businesses are

Marshall v. Barlow's at 320). Although Mr. Barlow's business was chosen for inspection under just such a neutral administrative plan, the broader implication of this decision is that the Court would likely view with suspicion the arbitrary choice of inspection targets. An area office director cannot send an OSHA inspector to a business simply because it is owned by a personal enemy and expect to be granted a warrant to compel entry. In general, however, the courts have deferred to law enforcement agencies in choosing which instances of illegality to pursue. So, for instance, there have been no successful challenges to OSHA targeting systems that prioritize inspections for certain local hazards or industries above other potential inspection targets. Rather, the *Barlow's* decision would simply seem to prevent the agency from singling out individual businesses for reasons completely unrelated to working conditions.

[25] For certain industries (e.g., logging and construction) the national office did not have establishment location information and instead relied on third-party reports (in the case of construction) or information collected by the area office (logging) to identify potential inspection targets. The area office then randomly selected from these lists at predetermined rates.

Area office administrators do retain the discretion to assign inspectors to individual inspections. This assignment process generally takes into account other obligations an inspector has in a geographic area (to minimize time lost to travel), experience (newer inspectors are assigned less difficult inspections), and expertise (inspectors, especially those who have previously worked in the private sector, often have areas of specialization). Inspectors and administrators I interviewed thought these factors, rather than any other political concerns, affected which inspectors were assigned individual inspections. I tested whether there was any relationship between inspection assignment and inspector punitiveness or productivity and found no effects.

[26] The remaining 5 percent of planned inspections are conducted according to regional and local emphasis programs (REP/LEP). "LEPs are generally based on knowledge of local industry hazards or knowledge of local industry injury/illness experience" (OSHA CPL 2-0.102A). All LEP and REP programs are subject to mandatory review by OSHA's regional and national offices. In 1991, more than 87 percent of LEP and REP inspections were directed at construction or construction-related hazards (e.g., trenching hazards, fall protection, and tunnel construction). This is consistent with my interviews with OSHA officials, who argued that the LEPs and REPs were used largely to target hazards, often in temporary workplaces, that would otherwise be missed by OSHA's industrywide targeting of fixed workplaces. In addition to the construction inspections, an additional 5 percent of LEPs and REPs were targeted at logging and oil and gas exploration. No other category accounted for even 1 percent. There was no evidence of political strategizing about which types of firms or industries were to be targeted in the emphasis programs. Rather, in reviewing proposed emphasis programs, OSHA focused on whether or not the program would detect hazards more efficiently than the industry-based targeting system.

TABLE 3.7. *High-hazard businesses and relative workload by OSHA region, sorted by proportion of high-hazard businesses*

Federal Region[a]	Proportion of Business in High-Hazard Category[b]	Relative Workload[c]
II	15.1%	−12.3%
VI	15.4%	−10.0%
IV	16.5%	−2.1%
III	16.7%	−1.4%
I	17.1%	1.0%
VIII	17.9%	5.7%
V	18.0%	6.3%
VII	18.5%	8.9%
OVERALL	16.9%	n/a

[a] Includes all federal regions where OSHA retains primary enforcement authority in at least two states.

[b] *Source:* County Business Patterns Reports 1995 and Bureau of Labor Statistics Survey of Occupational Injuries and Illnesses 1993. High-hazard businesses are the top 200 most dangerous by lost-workday incidence rate plus construction and maritime.

[c] Calculated as 1 minus the proportion of businesses in the region categorized as high-hazard divided by the average proportion in the entire country.

concentrated in certain areas relative to the overall number of businesses in the region, OSHA's inspectors in some areas have a harder time inspecting the businesses on their targeting list. In "safer" regions, by contrast, dangerous businesses are inspected with greater regularity. For each federal region, Table 3.7 shows the number of private businesses OSHA oversees and the proportion of these businesses that would have been classified in 1995 as high-hazard establishments.[27] Businesses in Regions IV and VI, encompassing the Deep South and more politically conservative areas of the country, are comparatively less dangerous than businesses in the Midwest (Region V). Earlier I found that the Midwest and other

[27] High-hazard classification is based on the 1993 BLS survey because the survey results are generally reported after a two-year lag.

Rust Belt OSHA regions are overstaffed relative to the Sun Belt. Because businesses in the Midwest are more dangerous, however, the net effect is to leave OSHA better staffed in the regions where OSHA's national targeting policy identifies greater need. Coincidentally, overstaffing generated by inertia in personnel placement is mitigated by the nonrandom distribution of dangerous workplaces.

OSHA's handling of planned inspections both denies subordinate OSHA officials opportunities to consider local politics and is devoid of considerations for local support for the agency. That is not to suggest, however, that the choice of planned inspection targets is politically unimportant. Rather, as I discussed more fully in the previous chapter and will show in part 3 of this chapter, it is a strategic political decision too important to be left to subordinate bureaucrats.

1.2.2. COMPLAINT INSPECTIONS. Like OSHA's national policy for targeting planned inspections, OSHA's policy for handling worker complaints (and the OSH Act [Moe 1989]) seeks to prevent local offices from choosing which workplaces to inspect. The OSH Act grants workers the right to complain, and OSHA gives inspections that result from complaints a higher priority than planned inspections. Specifically, the OSH Act states that, "[i]f...the Secretary determines there are reasonable grounds to believe that such violation or danger [as is specified in an employee's complaint] exists, he shall make a special inspection in accordance with the provisions of this section as soon as practicable."[28] The right to complain has no effect on where OSHA inspects, however, unless workers exercise this right. Reasonably, workers may vary in their willingness to invoke an OSHA inspection.

First, workers may complain to OSHA more frequently when the benefits of an OSHA inspection are larger. In particular, workers in more dangerous industries, like construction, should have more at stake and should complain more frequently than workers in service industries or office jobs. Second, workers should complain less frequently when the perceived costs of cooperating with OSHA are higher. When the economy is doing poorly,

---

[28] OSH Act, section 8, subsection F, part 1. Area office directors can decide to initiate an inspection in response to unwritten complaints that allege serious violations. In general, if an employee contacts OSHA to report a serious violation, OSHA will prepare a formal complaint and ask the employee to sign it. However, if the employee refuses, the area office director may still initiate an inspection (OSHA FIRM, Chapter 1, (C)(7)(d)(2)). See also part III of this chapter, where I discuss OSHA's complaint investigation (rather than inspection) policy for unsigned complaints.

for instance, workers may be less willing to complain about on-the-job hazards because they fear that OSHA enforcement will lead to their unemployment, either by raising their employer's costs or provoking retaliation. Workers who are uninformed about workplace hazards, who lack the protections of union membership, and who are generally hostile to government activism may also be less likely to invoke an OSHA inspection.[29] (It is also possible that OSHA offices in more supportive areas seek to drum up local complaints, or that workers are more likely to complain in areas where OSHA is more aggressive. I will consider these arguments later.)

In order to ascertain whether or not workers actually respond to these forces, I conducted two sets of analyses of worker propensity to complain to OSHA. First, I examined annual complaints within counties for union and nonunion workers during the period 1990–93. This analysis allows me to assess the effects of underlying features of counties, such as the number of businesses and type of industries, as well as a variety of local political forces, on worker propensity to complain. I analyze union and nonunion worker behavior separately because union workers should be better informed about workplace hazards, less likely to be intimidated by employer threats or worsening economic conditions, and more supportive of government intervention in private businesses. Unfortunately, because no accurate measure of local-level unionization exists, one cannot discern the dominator – the number of union and nonunion workers in a given county – over which a complaint does or does not take place. Nor can a simple cross-sectional analysis account for any underlying and unmeasured differences in counties that might explain aggregate variation in complaint rates. For this reason, I also conducted a panel analysis in which I examine variation in union and nonunion complaint rates over time after accounting for all other static characteristics of each county.

[29] Employer opposition to OSHA can also play a large part in reducing worker willingness to complain. Employers can explicitly threaten their employees (although this is contrary to statutory language), keep them from learning about workplace hazards, or simply misrepresent the effects of an OSHA inspection in order to quell employee concerns about safety. These actions raise the perceived costs (or lower the perceived benefits) to workers of complaining to OSHA. Many OSHA inspectors I interviewed suggested that much of the variation in worker willingness to cooperate with OSHA stemmed from employers' efforts to persuade their employees. (As one inspector stated, "The big difference between union and nonunion workplaces isn't always the workers, it's the fact that the union rep[resentative] won't let the boss pressure the employees. A lot of the time it is the employer who shapes how workers behave.") Later I will examine the direct effect on inspection outcomes of worker cooperation during an inspection.

Results from these analyses appear in Table 3.8. The left and right sides of panel (A) display, respectively, the results of the cross-sectional analysis of union and nonunion complaints by county.[30] Not surprisingly, for both union (column [1]) and nonunion workers (column [5]), complaints are more frequent in counties with many dangerous businesses, although once one accounts for the number of dangerous businesses, the raw number of businesses (irrespective of type) has a negative effect on the frequency of complaints. The effects of Democratic vote share and unemployment are positive and statistically significant for union workers (column [2]), although this result may be due to the high correlation between union strength and both Democratic vote share and unemployment (as a reminder, the measures of the number of facilities does not distinguish between union and nonunion businesses). For nonunion workers, by contrast, neither effect is statistically significant (column [6]).

Finally, for union workers, having a more conservative House member on the House Appropriations subcommittee responsible for oversight of OSHA is associated with fewer complaints (column [3]). This result persists even in the fully specified model shown in column (4), where the opposite effect emerges with respect to the ideology of locally elected member of Congress more generally. In this case, more conservative representation in the House is associated with more complaints. For nonunion workers (column [7]), more conservative representation on the House Appropriations subcommittee is also associated with fewer complaints, but conservative representation on the Labor subcommittee responsible for oversight of OSHA is associated with more complaints. Both results appear also in the fully specified model shown in column (8). There, the effect for the general ideology of the House member is the same as that for union workers.

The results reported in panel (B) of Table 3.8 are estimated using a fixed-effects specification. Unlike the earlier analysis, the fixed-effect model allows me to control for all unmeasured static county characteristics, including the unionization of the labor force, the type and dangerousness of local businesses, and the general political culture. Additionally, this specification also allows me to estimate the relative responsiveness to changing economic conditions of complaints by union and nonunion

[30] The negative binomial specification is appropriate because the number of complaints is a count variable characterized by overdispersion (Long 1997). These results are robust across a wide variety of model specifications, including OLS, tobit, and other count models.

TABLE 3.8. *Union and nonunion workers' complaints by county, 1990–1993*

(A) Negative Binomial Estimates (Pooled Counties)

	Union Complaints				Nonunion Complaints			
	(1)	(2)	(3)	(4)	(5)	(6)	(7)	(8)
Facilities/1,000	-0.047***	-0.060***	-0.047***	-0.058***	-0.059***	-0.062***	-0.059***	-0.062***
	(0.01)	(0.01)	(0.01)	(0.01)	(0.01)	(0.01)	(0.01)	(0.01)
High-hazard facilities/1,000	2.227***	2.244***	2.193***	2.220***	2.201***	2.213***	2.198***	2.211***
	(0.19)	(0.18)	(0.18)	(0.18)	(0.16)	(0.16)	(0.16)	(0.15)
Democratic share of two-party vote (1992)		2.293***		2.367***		0.334		0.391
		(0.41)		(0.43)		(0.31)		(0.32)
Unemployment rate		2.592*		3.659**		0.285		0.581
		(1.46)		(1.45)		(0.92)		(0.90)
Congressional conservatism			-0.236	0.351*			0.110	0.198*
			(0.17)	(0.18)			(0.11)	(0.11)
Labor subcommittee conservatism			-0.079	0.535			1.600**	1.678**
			(1.17)	(1.08)			(0.70)	(0.69)
Appropriations subcommittee conservatism			-2.502***	-2.997***			-1.753***	-1.798***
			(0.70)	(0.78)			(0.54)	(0.55)
Observations	7,856	7,856	5,892	5,892	7,856	7,856	5,892	5,892
Log-likelihood	-8,400.94	-8,332.40	-6,164.93	-6,113.78	-13,778.53	-13,775.66	-10,373.66	-10,370.38
Chi squared	232.087	321.305	237.635	316.897	270.201	284.659	279.903	294.949

Note: Negative binomial estimates with robust standard errors, clustered by county, in parentheses. Constant and year indicators not reported. Estimates include all counties. * denotes $p < .10$; ** denotes $p < .05$; *** denotes $p < .01$.

(B) *Fixed-Effect (County) Negative Binomial Estimates*

	Union Complaints				Nonunion Complaints			
	(1)	(2)	(3)	(4)	(5)	(6)	(7)	(8)
Unemployment rate	-3.287** (1.55)	0.020 (6.52)	-6.230*** (2.03)	8.577 (10.61)	-1.802 (1.18)	-5.778 (4.62)	-0.800 (1.59)	-17.584** (7.25)
Unemployment * Democratic share of two-party vote (1992)		-5.761 (11.06)		-26.124 (18.44)		7.222 (8.10)		30.863** (12.94)
Unemployment * conservatism of locally elected member of congress			-4.603* (2.44)	-5.285** (2.47)			0.485 (1.72)	1.312 (1.76)
Unemployment * Labor subcommittee conservatism			-0.638 (7.41)	-0.477 (7.45)			11.132 (6.78)	9.987 (6.61)
Unemployment * Appropriations subcommittee conservatism			-2.366 (10.93)	-2.777 (11.14)			19.074* (10.68)	20.910** (10.56)
Observations	3,468	3,468	2,406	2,406	3,340	3,340	2,286	2,286
Log-likelihood	-3,278.96	-3,278.83	-2,037.04	-2,036.01	-4,454.22	-4,453.83	-2,750.53	-2,747.70
Chi squared	76.60	76.56	27.83	30.05	17.44	18.22	17.42	23.43
Groups (Counties)	867	867	802	802	835	835	762	762

Note: Negative binomial estimates with standard errors in parentheses. Constant and year indicators not reported. Estimates include all counties with at least one union complaint during the period 1990–94. * denotes $p < .10$; ** denotes $p < .05$; *** denotes $p < .01$.

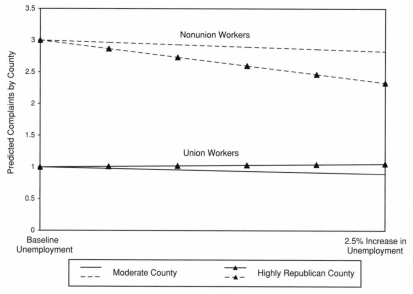

FIGURE 3.1. Predicted changes in worker complaints given rising unemployment, by union status of workers.

workers without measuring county labor force characteristics directly. For both union and nonunion workers, higher levels of unemployment are associated with a decline in complaints, although the relative magnitude of the effect is highly sensitive to model specification. Additionally, the relative responsiveness of union and nonunion workers to changing economic conditions appears to be affected by different elements of the political context. Figure 3.1 shows (for the full model specification reported in columns [4] and [8]) that in an average county a one-standard-deviation increase in unemployment (about 2.5 percent) is associated with a predicted decline in union complaints of about .10 (solid line, from the observed median of one union complaint per county) and a .16 decline in nonunion complaints (dashed line, from the observed median of three nonunion complaints per county).[31]

In more Republican areas, this effect is mitigated for union complaints but enhanced for nonunion workers. Using the scenario just outlined but

---

[31] Because these are interactive models, it is important to recognize that the magnitude of these effects is sensitive to the values of other model parameters. I assume that this hypothetical county also had sample median values of Democratic vote share, about .50, and the congressional conservatism measures, 0.

in a highly Republican county (Democratic vote share .25), the lines with triangles in Figure 3.1 show that a one-standard-deviation increase in unemployment is predicted to *increase* union complaints by about .05 (from the baseline of 1) and decreases nonunion complaints by about .66 (from a baseline of 3). The union response to unemployment is less affected by local partisanship than the response of nonunion workers, a finding that is not surprising when one recognizes that union workers are already members of advocacy organizations designed to protect their interests. By contrast, nonunion workers seem to be likely to exercise their rights under the OSH Act in worsening economic conditions only in areas populated by supportive Democratic constituencies.

The results for the interaction between congressional ideology and unemployment are starkly different. Union workers complain less as unemployment increases in areas represented by more conservative members (although only the effect of generic House member conservatism is statistically significant), while nonunion workers complain more frequently as unemployment increases in areas represented by more conservative members of the House (here, only the effect of Appropriations subcommittee conservatism is significant). There is no convenient theoretical explanation for this result, although it does suggest that there are important correlations between worker behavior and congressional ideology that must be accounted for in trying to measure OSHA's discretionary decision making.[32]

The central insight provided here is that the inclusion in the OSH Act of a mechanism for workers to initiate an OSHA inspection allows local politics to enter the calculus of where the agency inspects despite the fact that local offices and field inspectors do not have the discretion to choose which workplaces to inspect. The right to complain is exercised more frequently by union workers (although only about 16 percent of American workers were unionized in 1993, they accounted for 26 percent of OSHA's complaints in 1993) and workers in more dangerous industries. Complaints appear to be depressed by poor economic conditions, especially for nonunion workers, but these effects are offset in areas with constituencies already supportive of OSHA. For field-level OSHA bureaucrats, whose hands are largely tied in the matter, however, the complaint

---

[32] One data-driven explanation is that counties with Republican representatives are likely to have low Democratic vote shares, which (per the column [4] results) are associated with more union complaints.

policy is simply another "rule of the game" that advantages some workers more than others.

One might wonder if these results, rather than being caused by natural variability in worker behavior, instead reflect either the willingness of OSHA field offices to encourage complaints or the responsiveness of workers to the aggressiveness of OSHA field enforcement efforts. In my interviews with OSHA regional administrators and field office supervisors, however, the opposite pattern was more apparent. In area offices with high levels of complaints, area office officials felt overwhelmed and said that "too many" complaints prevented them from conducting planned inspections of high-hazard businesses. For example, one area office director whose inspectors had recently devoted about two-thirds of their field time to complaint inspections commented,

[I'd like to be able to handle] more complaints for less-severe hazards "informally" [without inspection] . . . because complaint inspections prevent my inspectors from having time to complete important planned inspections.

By contrast, in areas where complaints were less frequent, area office administrators expressed an interest in more "high-quality" complaints. (As one regional official from a "low-complaint" region noted, "You [high-complaint areas] come close to being overwhelmed, but we wish we had more high-quality complaints from industrial workplaces.") Field office effort, if it affected complaints, would therefore most likely counteract the results shown here, with OSHA officials in low-complaint areas seeking to drum up high-quality complaints.

Similarly, it seems unlikely that worker complaints are affected by OSHA's aggressiveness in an area. For one, OSHA is more likely to seek out complaints in hostile areas. Additionally, as I will show, OSHA's stringency and productivity are generally not affected directly by local political conditions. Finally, while willingness to complain to OSHA might be affected by citizen preferences and the behavior of businesses (for example, if they threaten their employees), there is no direct evidence that workers perceive variation in OSHA's aggressiveness in different parts of the country.[33]

---

[33] Members of a national OSHA–labor union task force I interviewed generally seemed surprised by my raising this concern. As one member noted, "All the action is at the national level, we don't worry about field-level problems at OSHA anymore [relative to the 1970s]." Rather, it was their belief that workers were far more affected by citizen support for OSHA and the willingness of employers to (illegally) threaten employees for cooperating with OSHA.

2. Counting Beans: Inspector Effort and Productivity

OSHA's lower-level bureaucrats appear to lack much discretion to choose where to inspect. How hard these field-level bureaucrats work, however, is more fully under their own control and is something that bureaucratic superiors cannot control as easily from afar. Here I examine variation in inspector productivity in the field. This allows me to observe individual-level variation in regulatory effort over time and across geographic areas.

Within OSHA and at other agencies, the systematic pursuit of agency targets for regulatory outputs is labeled, at times derisively, "bean counting." At OSHA, bean counting of inspections is formalized through an agencywide process for identifying a desired annual inspection goal and then assigning a portion of this total to each region. In this way, OSHA's leadership tries to direct field-level operations. Among the administrators I interviewed, the importance of centralized inspection goals was clear. Regional administrators monitor their region's progress toward annual goals and the relative productivity of their area offices. As one regional official noted after showing me the monthly spreadsheet of area office productivity in the region,

[T]here is not a "hard quota" at work, but rather [the] numbers [area office productivity figures] are used to raise questions about potential problems. Are the numbers down, if so why? It might be because of a staffing problem, or something else.... [But] these are [only] management tools, not a ruler, there is no knife to the throat here.... Everything is geared toward the agency's strategic plan.

Likewise, area office directors observe whether they are ahead of or behind the rate of inspections necessary to meet annual production goals. In one local area office manager's words,

The area office has goals [set by the region], and we constantly monitor how we are doing in meeting those goals. If we slack off, you better believe that we'll hear "you're not meeting your goals." ... [A]nd you know what? Congress, the unions, and business groups have those same numbers.

According to the field inspectors I interviewed, these management imperatives percolated down to the field. With the notable exception of the reinvention experience, to be discussed later, perceptions that the agency would not meet these goals often led to pressure to "up the inspection count."

Efforts to increase inspection counts within the constraints of OSHA's budget take two forms. First, OSHA can devote greater staff time to workplace inspections. In the area office, for instance, supervisors who normally do not conduct inspections might be assigned inspections and sent into the field. Alternatively, inspectors can simply work harder, devoting more time to inspections relative to their other official activities (including meetings, training, and documentation) and periods of free time. Second, OSHA can alter the mix of inspection activities it undertakes to favor "lower-cost" inspections, thereby increasing the number of inspections the agency can complete without altering the overall level of resources devoted to field operations. This is an effective strategy because not all types of OSHA inspections are equally time-consuming for the agency.[34] For instance, construction inspections are "cheaper" for OSHA because construction workplaces are smaller and often located close to one another. This comparative efficiency is not solely a theoretical concern. The OSHA officials I spoke with recognized that the agency could conduct more inspections in any year simply by increasing the proportion of planned construction inspections.[35] They also stressed, however, that regional and national administrators, and even interest groups, could easily detect such behavior. As one regional administrator commented, "With computers, everyone can crunch the numbers and see exactly what we [the agency] are doing [in the field]. Things are very transparent."

Centralized control of field-level enforcement via emphasis on inspections demonstrates the long-identified capacity of agency leaders to direct field-level operations. How effective is this central control in monitoring field-level bureaucrats and insulating them from local political concerns? A unique "natural experiment" involving variation in oversight of field operations, which occurred at OSHA during the period I study, allows me to answer this question directly. Specifically, as part of agency reinvention activities, OSHA reduced the pressure on field operations to conduct inspections and reorganized certain field offices. These reinvention activities created administrative "slack" in OSHA's regulatory apparatus. This variation in the slack available to lower-level bureaucrats is useful for determining why (and if) bureaucratic leaders are successful in eliminating local variation in enforcement. Did OSHA's subordinate bureaucrats

---

[34] Olson (1995) finds similar strategizing at the FDA, where agency leaders substituted low-cost enforcement actions for higher-cost activities to meet Congressional demands for greater enforcement.

[35] Officials in Virginia's state OSHA program even go so far as to adjust measures of inspector productivity to account for the relative ease of construction and nonconstruction inspections. By their tabulations, three construction inspections are equivalent to one manufacturing inspection.

behave differently when the focus on inspections waned? Was this effect contingent on local political conditions?

Before proceeding to answer these questions directly, it is useful to review how OSHA's leadership and policy relating to the importance of inspections changed during the period I study. During the first Bush administration, OSHA was perceived as relatively aggressive despite being headed by Republican appointees (*BNA Occupational Safety and Health Daily*, March 9, 1993). At that time, the Democratic Congress was supportive of a revived post-Reagan OSHA, and the agency regained funding lost during the prior administration (Victor 1989). After taking office in 1993, Clinton appointed Joseph Dear, formerly the head of Washington state's delegated OSH Act program, as OSHA's head. Dear's tenure was marked by a forceful message, communicated through OSHA's hierarchy, that high inspection counts and frequent violations were not in and of themselves agency goals:

Dear said that . . . the agency has traditionally counted the number of inspections and citations issued to measure agency performance. Now said Dear, "I have to put a stop to this practice." Stanley, OSHA's deputy administrator, agreed. "OSHA, for the past 25 years, has basically done business the same way. Congress gave us money, and we gave them inspections." "We finally realized," said Stanley, "that the number of inspections doesn't change the behavior of anyone. . . ." (Yuill 1995)

Dear's message coincided with, and was part of, OSHA's agencywide reinvention program initiated in early 1994. This reinvention effort contained many components, including several directly relevant to field-level operations. Most significantly, the agency changed the area offices themselves by undertaking efforts at process improvement, reducing the number of administrative and support staff, and delegating greater authority to the area offices to engage in "creative problem solving" by developing new local outreach, partnership, and targeted inspection programs. (The most extensive redesign of individual area offices was limited to a subset of all OSHA field offices.) Perhaps not surprisingly, reinvention activities and the reduced emphasis on inspection counts led to a decrease in the frequency of OSHA inspections:

Current OSHA chief Joe Dear says his agency stopped playing this "shell game" in 1995, and that's one reason for the decline in inspections. Dear has said repeatedly that inspectors would no longer be evaluated by "cranking up the inspection numbers." "There are easy explanations for the decline in inspections," says OSHA spokeswoman Cheryl Byrne. She says "reinventing" the agency by putting area office personnel through intensive training lasting several weeks "takes up a lot of time." So do problem-solving projects. . . . (Johnson 1996)

TABLE 3.9. *OSHA inspections by year, 1990–1999*

Year	Number of Inspections	Percentage Change from 1992
1990	44,975	5.0%
1991	41,432	−3.3%
1992	42,839	0.0%
1993	39,987	−6.7%
1994	40,780	−4.8%
1995	26,402	−38.4%
1996	25,852	−39.7%
1997	35,889	−16.2%
1998	37,644	−12.1%
1999	38,442	−10.3%

Source: OSHA IMIS database.

Particularly during 1995 and 1996, the number of OSHA inspections plummeted from earlier levels. Table 3.9 shows OSHA's annual inspection totals for the period 1990 to 1999 and how these totals compare to OSHA's output in 1992. In 1993 and 1994, OSHA conducted about 5 percent fewer inspections than during the last year of the Bush administration. In 1995 and 1996, by contrast, OSHA's production was almost 40 percent below the 1992 figure. In December 1996, Dear resigned as head of OSHA. Around this time, many reinvention activities, including the field office redesign, were put on hold and subsequently revamped. In 1997, OSHA's inspection numbers rebounded to about 15 percent below the 1992 level, and by 1999 they seem to have stabilized at about 10 percent below the 1992 level.

Of course, this period also coincides with the Republican takeover of Congress following the 1994 midterm election. OSHA faced intense opposition in the new Congress, and numerous bills were introduced to cut the agency's funding and reduce its authority. OSHA also stopped conducting inspections during the government shutdown of late 1995–early 1996 and delayed filling vacancies because of budgetary uncertainty (Scott 1996). Undoubtedly, the government shutdown and Congress' threats to OSHA's budget contributed to the fall in inspections during this period, but inspections began to decline prior to the congressional attacks. Additionally, the Clinton administration ultimately prevailed in defending OSHA's budget, and Dear's successors successfully returned to the traditional emphasis on inspection productivity. Still, this period of turmoil at OSHA provides an ideal circumstance in which to observe the effectiveness of a centralized focus on inspections as a way to control field-level behavior.

Reinvention and congressional threats had two effects on enforcement. First, they restricted the resources available for enforcement. In the OSHA-wide reinvention, staff inspectors were assigned additional administrative tasks because the ratio of supervisors to inspectors was reduced. (One official said reinvention was "making management worse by giving [inspectors] more [administrative] responsibilities and having [them] do things [they're] not trained to do.") Congressional action similarly constrained enforcement by forcing OSHA's bureaucrats to spend time testifying before Congress and because budgetary uncertainty led the agency to delay hiring new inspectors.

Second, and more importantly for my analysis, reinvention introduced slack into the regulatory production process. Agencywide, reinvention reduced the emphasis on informal inspection quotas as a way of evaluating field inspectors and instead stressed quality of inspections and improving workplace safety. As one inspector noted, "The perception was that we were getting out of the numbers game." In redesigned field offices, inspectors were free to consider creative approaches to reducing workplace hazards. As a result, inspectors spent more time in meetings and developing programs than they had in the past.[36] On repeated occasions I was told the same joke about how OSHA's new "strategic teams" acted given their discretion to consider new creative problem-solving techniques: "OSHA's field offices are now split into two teams, one is the strategic team, or SiT. Well, the SiTs sat." Several local area office directors noted that teams were much harder to monitor than individual inspectors. ("It is hard to assign blame in a team [without individual numbers]. The only thing we really have is peer pressure.") One regional official described the entire local office reinvention process as ignoring basic tenets of management by "putting the cart before the horse . . . [and embracing] too much employee empowerment."

These changes, which gave local offices and inspectors greater discretion to choose between inspections and alternative tasks, allow me to examine how inspectors with newfound freedom altered their behavior as oversight weakened. Furthermore, I can distinguish the generic agencywide effect of diminished oversight from the more extensive

---

[36] To be fair, OSHA's field office redesign required inspectors to develop and implement new local problem-solving approaches. Area offices were free, however, to decide the appropriate mix between program development and inspection activity in the field.

reduction in the pressure to conduct inspections in the redesigned field offices.

When OSHA was running all out to produce violations prior to Dear's tenure, there was precious little slack to allow the tailoring of enforcement to local support. Enforcement in any given area was simply the maximization of inspections using all available resources and the inspection targets determined by OSHA's national targeting list and by worker complaints.

But the agency's rejection of concern for local political support seems to be more fundamental than a simple focus on inspector productivity. My interviews with inspectors and their direct supervisors suggest that there were no differences in agency rewards for conducting frequent inspections in different localities. Similarly, regional administrators stressed that while they monitored the productivity of local offices, this was to ensure the agency's overall productivity, not local targeting. More generally, OSHA seems to have effectively eliminated any basis of exchange between individual field-level bureaucrats and interest groups, particular firms, or elected officials. The individual inspectors and field officials I interviewed perceived having nothing to gain by tailoring enforcement to local politics. Also, a general norm of professionalism and a strong sense that enforcement was neutral law enforcement necessary to protect workers appear to have undercut any propensity for inspectors to seek out rewards, either within OSHA or outside of the agency, by shaping regulation to gain local support.

More than 80 percent of the inspectors I interviewed described their role as one of "law enforcement," where the relevant criterion for assigning a violation was generally "legal sufficiency." (Suggesting that the phrase is used in training, I repeatedly heard nearly the same sentence: "Is there a harm that violates an OSHA standard and can you prove it [exists and workers were exposed]?") The remaining 20 percent of inspectors described themselves most often as "consultants" or some fusion of consultant and law enforcement, but even these inspectors saw the need for aggressive enforcement to generate compliance: "Unlike a private sector consultant, the [fact that I assign] penalties mean[s] that they pay attention to me." One OSHA official who had served in three areas of the country with vastly different political climates best summed up my impression, noting that while there are important differences in "worker culture," "OSHA inspectors are basically the same everywhere." This was followed by an incredulous response to a query about inspector responsiveness to local pressure: "We're OSHA inspectors, not the local sheriff.... We know that our job is the same everywhere, even if employees and employers don't feel that way." Agency inspectors, in short, appear to have embraced this sense of neutrality.

To test whether these characterizations of inspector neutrality, either in general or during the reinvention experience, are accurate, I constructed a dataset that contains information about the inspections each OSHA inspector undertook during the period 1991–96 and the political environment in which the inspector operated. Specifically, I identified inspectors who were actively in the field in a given month and calculated the number of inspections they conducted. Because inspections vary in the time they take to conduct, I also gathered information about the characteristics of the inspections that each inspector performed. I calculated the proportion of inspections conducted in OSHA's high-hazard classified businesses; the average number of employees overseen during the inspections; the average number of serious violations issued; and the proportion of inspections that were fatality or catastrophe investigations, accident investigations, of construction or manufacturing facilities, had violations that were contested by employers, and were planned or complaint inspections. All else being equal, inspections in more dangerous industries that cover more employees and yield more violations should take longer to complete and document. Likewise, fatality or catastrophe and accident investigations, where OSHA is inspecting after an accident, should be substantially more time-consuming than other inspections. Construction inspections, by contrast, should be less time-consuming than inspections of other types of businesses, particularly manufacturing establishments. When employers contest violations, inspectors have less time in the field to conduct inspections. Lastly, planned and complaint inspections should be more time-consuming than other inspections because OSHA is visiting workplaces that are more likely to contain hazards.

I also determined whether or not the inspector was operating in an area office that had been "reinvented." (Data about reinvention, including the month in which local field offices were reinvented, was obtained from OSHA's national reinvention office.) On average, field offices that have been reinvented should have lower levels of inspection outputs for the reasons discussed earlier. In my subsequent model, year indicator variables serve as controls for headquarters' inspection prioritization. To test for political influence on inspector effort, I gathered information about the local strength of the Democratic Party, the health of the local economy, and the ideology of the locally elected member of Congress.[37]

---

[37] Out of concern that these results might be influenced by the strategic assignment of inspectors to more or less supportive counties, I tested whether inspector assignment

TABLE 3.10. *OSHA inspector productivity, 1991–96*

	Inspections				
	(1)	(2)	(3)	(4)	(5)
Proportion of inspections in high-hazard industries	-0.05*	-0.05**	-0.05*	-0.06**	-0.06**
	(0.027)	(0.027)	(0.027)	(0.027)	(0.027)
Average number of employees in workplace/1,000	-0.28***	-0.28***	-0.28***	-0.28***	-0.28***
	(0.046)	(0.046)	(0.046)	(0.046)	(0.046)
Average number of employees in workplace squared/1,000,000	0.02***	0.02***	0.02***	0.02***	0.02***
	(0.003)	(0.003)	(0.003)	(0.003)	(0.003)
Average number of serious violations issued	-0.04***	-0.04***	-0.04***	-0.04***	-0.04***
	(0.004)	(0.004)	(0.004)	(0.004)	(0.004)
Proportion of inspections by category					
Fatality or catastrophe	-1.18***	-1.18***	-1.18***	-1.18***	-1.18***
	(0.050)	(0.049)	(0.049)	(0.049)	(0.049)
Accidents	-0.05**	-0.05**	-0.05**	-0.05**	-0.05**
	(0.025)	(0.025)	(0.025)	(0.025)	(0.025)
Construction	0.44***	0.45***	0.45***	0.45***	0.45***
	(0.040)	(0.040)	(0.040)	(0.040)	(0.040)
Manufacturing	-0.16***	-0.15***	-0.15***	-0.15***	-0.15***
	(0.037)	(0.036)	(0.036)	(0.036)	(0.036)
With contested violations	-0.23***	-0.23***	-0.23***	-0.23***	-0.23***
	(0.032)	(0.031)	(0.031)	(0.031)	(0.031)
Planned	0.02	0.02	0.02	0.02	0.02
	(0.028)	(0.028)	(0.028)	(0.028)	(0.028)
Complaint	-0.66***	-0.65***	-0.66***	-0.65***	-0.65***
	(0.034)	(0.034)	(0.034)	(0.034)	(0.034)
Democratic Party strength		0.08	0.11	0.04	0.04
		(0.135)	(0.136)	(0.149)	(0.149)
Unemployment		-0.04	-0.05	0.27	0.27
		(0.641)	(0.645)	(0.663)	(0.663)
Congressional conservatism		0.08	0.09	0.11	0.11
		(0.091)	(0.092)	(0.101)	(0.101)

	(1)	(2)	(3)	(4)	(5)
Labor subcommittee conservatism		−0.63 (0.524)	−0.58 (0.548)	−1.11* (0.637)	−1.01 (0.822)
Appropriations subcommittee conservatism		0.07 (0.293)	0.11 (0.293)	0.15 (0.302)	0.14 (0.302)
Reinvented field office		−0.18*** (0.050)	−0.33 (0.907)	−0.19*** (0.051)	0.39 (0.909)
Area office slack interactions					
Reinvented*Democratic Party strength			−0.49 (1.698)		−0.69 (1.702)
Reinvented*unemployment			−3.14 (3.944)		−2.32 (4.010)
Reinvented*congressional conservatism			−0.53 (0.519)		−0.46 (0.533)
Reinvented*Labor subcommittee conservatism			−0.13 (1.739)		−1.19 (1.843)
Reinvented*Appropriations subcommittee conservatism			−25.74*** (9.888)		−25.80*** (9.888)
Agency slack interactions (base effect in year indicators not reported)					
Dear*Democratic Party strength				0.11 (0.207)	0.22 (0.204)
Dear*unemployment				−0.91 (0.820)	−0.99 (0.831)
Dear*congressional conservatism				−0.11 (0.122)	−0.09 (0.125)
Dear*Labor subcommittee conservatism				1.23 (0.795)	1.45* (0.827)
Dear*Appropriations subcommittee conservatism				−0.24 (0.454)	−0.11 (0.453)
Constant	2.11*** (0.046)	2.07*** (0.087)	2.05*** (0.088)	2.07*** (0.095)	2.07*** (0.095)
Observations	23010	23010	23010	23010	23010
Log-likelihood	−5,698.20	−5,671.00	−5,652.50	−5,664.10	−5,644.20

Note: Robust (clustered by inspector) standard errors in parentheses. *** denotes $p < .01$; ** denotes $p < .05$; * denotes $p < .10$. Dependent variable is number of inspections per month per inspector. Analysis is restricted to inspectors who conducted fewer than 10 percent of their inspections as health inspectors. Year indicators not reported.

131

Both the reduced emphasis on inspections during Dear's tenure and the redesign of the field offices created administrative slack. Did this slack allow local politics to affect how hard field-level bureaucrats worked? To test for greater responsiveness during Dear's tenure, with its reduced focus on inspections, and in reinvented field offices I constructed two sets of interaction terms. First, I interacted each of the measures of the local political environment with a new indicator variable that was coded 1 in 1995 and 1996, the period during which Dear's effort to shift the agency away from a focus on enforcement outputs was strongest (and 0 otherwise). Second, I interacted the political environment variables with the reinvented field office indicator variable. This technique allows me to examine whether or not central oversight promotes neutrality, and to contrast how local politics affects enforcement during periods of strong and weak central office oversight of inspection outputs.

In the resulting dataset there are individual observations for each inspector in each month he or she was active in the field. Model estimates appear in Table 3.10. Column (1) reports the results from a baseline apolitical model of inspector effort. Ten of the eleven variables have the expected effect on inspector productivity and are statistically significant. The remaining variable, proportion of inspections that were planned, has a very small but positive effect on inspector productivity, perhaps reflecting the fact that once one accounts for the proportion of inspections that were in dangerous businesses and yielded violations, the proportion of inspections that were planned (most of which are targeted at dangerous facilities) has little or no additional effect.

Column (2) reports the results from a model that tests for the average effect of constituency preferences, congressional ideology, and area office reinvention on inspector productivity. Among the task variables also included in the column (1) specification, the signs and indications of statistical significance are nearly identical. Democratic Party strength, unemployment, and congressional ideology (generically and on the relevant oversight committees) all have very small and statistically insignificant effects on inspector productivity. Being in a reinvented field office, as expected, has a negative and statistically significant effect on inspector productivity. Per this specification, with all variables held constant at their sample means, shifting an inspector to a reinvented field office decreases

---

was independent of local political conditions and could find no effects. Not surprisingly, therefore, if I reestimate these models weighting the political variables according to the counties in which an inspector conducted inspections, the results are nearly identical.

her predicted monthly inspection output by about 18 percent, from 6.4 to 5.3 inspections per month. This is a large effect that may explain, in the aggregate, part of the decline in overall agency inspections during 1995 and 1996.

The results reported in column (3) allow me to examine the relationship between local political support and inspector behavior in reinvented field offices. Note that the task variables from the original specification still have their expected effects and that the baseline effects of local politics remain small and insignificant. There is suggestive evidence, however, that introducing slack into the regulatory process increased the effect of local politics on inspector behavior. Specifically, the interaction between House Appropriations subcommittee member conservatism and being in a reinvented field office is negative and statistically significant. As is shown by the solid line in Figure 3.2, this effect is substantively large. Holding all other variables constant at their sample means, inspectors in a reinvented field office represented by a House Appropriations subcommittee member one standard deviation more conservative than the mean were predicted to become 47 percent less productive than inspectors in a reinvented field office represented by an average member on that committee (predicted inspections per month of 3.2 versus 6). The dashed line in the figure shows

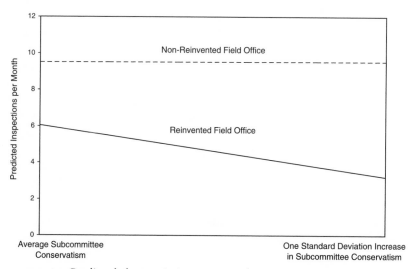

FIGURE 3.2. Predicted changes in inspector productivity given increasing conservatism of House Appropriations subcommittee member in reinvented and non-reinvented field offices.

that a similar shift in House Appropriations subcommittee conservatism has a nearly zero effect in nonreinvented field offices.

Rather than focusing on the specific area office reforms, the estimation results reported in column (4) examine the agencywide effects of a diminished focus on inspections during Dear's tenure. None of the interaction terms between Dear's leadership and local support for OSHA have statistically significant effects on inspector effort. Inspectors in more Democratic areas, those having lower unemployment rates, and those with more conservative representation in Congress were more productive, but these effects are very small and none is statistically significant. Nor do these effects appear in the unified model reported in column (5). By contrast, the interaction between reinvented field office and House Appropriations subcommittee conservatism has roughly the same magnitude as in the column (3) specification.[38]

The finding from columns (2) through (5) that field-level bureaucrats do not tailor their enforcement effort to local political support during periods of strong central office oversight of agency productivity is perhaps unsurprising. After all, prior to Dear's arrival at OSHA, inspectors had little time to devote to conducting more inspections in supportive areas (or discretion to conduct fewer in hostile areas). Agencywide, however, I find little evidence that Dear's focus on "quality inspections" encouraged greater responsiveness to local politics (per columns [4] and [5]). In part, this may reflect Dear's emphasis on different types of inspections and the generic effects of agencywide reorganizations that increased the managerial responsibilities of inspectors, thereby keeping them out of the field for longer periods of time.

But the results reported in columns (3) and (5) suggest that the area office reinvention activities had a substantially different effect by allowing local political conditions to shape inspector effort. Generically, inspectors in reinvented offices conducted fewer inspections. From a management perspective, inspectors reacted to a decreased emphasis on inspection counts in a predictable way – by conducting fewer inspections. As one inspector I interviewed put it, "given the chance, who wouldn't rather attend meetings or sit in an office than get yelled at [by an employer] for issuing citations?" More interestingly, however, bureaucrats seemed less willing to engage in this unpleasant task in those areas where they were

---

[38] Additionally, there is a marginally significant relationship between Labor subcommittee conservatism and inspector productivity during Dear's tenure, but this is not substantively significant because it merely offsets the baseline (and insignificant) effect of Labor subcommittee conservatism.

less likely to find support because of hostile representation on the House Appropriations committee responsible for oversight of OSHA (and more willing in areas represented by supportive members).

Central oversight of field office productivity therefore appears to help field-level bureaucrats remain neutral by making sure that they uniformly work hard. Bureaucrats may convert slack resources into personal gain, in this case by avoiding an unpleasant task in especially unsupportive areas. Prior to the field office reinvention initiative, however, inspectors didn't have the discretion to make this choice.[39] More broadly, these results suggest that ongoing oversight of field operations productivity is important for maintaining a "stubborn consistency" in the face of variation in local support for enforcement, despite the strong professionalism of OSHA's field enforcement staff. Perhaps this pattern is also indicative of the value of professional norms. While inspectors continued to profess a belief in equal treatment, and while "going easy" on employers during an inspection in areas represented by hostile members of Congress would clearly violate this norm, avoiding unpleasant fieldwork did not create such an obvious norm violation. Management was therefore still necessary to compel inspectors to devote greater time to field inspections.

3. Inspector Stringency: Information or Influence?

The final step in my examination of OSHA's field enforcement program is to test whether the stringency of OSHA enforcement, conditional on inspection, is responsive to local political conditions. To do so, I examine the outcome of individual OSHA inspections across local political conditions and firm characteristics. The dependent variable in this analysis is the number of serious, willful, and repeat violations that OSHA issued following the conclusion of each planned safety inspection of a private manufacturing firm the agency completed in 1996 and 1997.[40] All else

---

[39] Of course, inspectors who reacted to local hostility by conducting fewer inspections did not abandon their goal of protecting workers in reinvented field offices. Rather, inspectors attended meetings to develop new programs and sought new ways to protect workers. But this choice – attend meetings to consider creative ways to protect workers or persist in conducting inspections – was apparently shaped by the reaction that inspectors anticipated in the field.

[40] Unfortunately, I cannot repeat my earlier analysis of changing enforcement in reinvented field offices because the data necessary to measure workplace dangers are not available for the period during OSHA's reinvention efforts.

Additionally my analysis is restricted to OSHA's planned safety inspections of private manufacturing facilities completed in 1996 and 1997 for three reasons. First, I was concerned that the selection of complaint inspections is nonrandom and highly correlated

being equal, more aggressive inspections should yield more violations. I tabulate only serious, willful, and repeat violations in order to exclude paperwork violations and other violations that would not otherwise result in a financial or criminal penalty.[41]

A critical feature of the OSH Act is the provision allowing workers to participate in the inspection by walking through the workplace with the investigating OSHA official. Based on my interviews with OSHA officials and previous research (Weil 1991, 1992), I expect to find that when workers exercise their right to participate in an inspection, OSHA will have an easier time locating and proving violations of OSHA standards. (As one inspector explained, "Workers are your eyes and ears. What has the employer done since the accident [that led to the inspection]? Is there any [safety] equipment broken? [They can tell you] 'The guard on the machine that was moved into the closet is broken.'") OSHA records in the agency's inspection database whether or not workers elected to participate in an inspection. The worker participation variable is coded 1 if workers participated in the inspection and 0 otherwise.

The model also includes five sets of control variables. First, I constructed a measure of noncompliance for each workplace in my dataset. The lost-workday injury and illnesses incidence rate, or injury rate, is

with the variables I use to explain inspection outcomes. The evidence reported earlier in this chapter shows that worker willingness to invoke an OSHA inspection varies across the country. Thus, the pool of workplaces inspected in unplanned inspections is different in different local area offices. By contrast, local offices use neutral targeting lists developed by OSHA's headquarters to initiate planned inspections. Second, I limited my analysis to safety, rather than health, inspections because my measure of noncompliance is a more accurate measure of occupational injuries than of illnesses. Illnesses often have long latency periods such that noncompliance during one time period will not result in an increase in the observed injury rate. Third, I included only inspections of private facilities because OSHA does not issue fines following some inspections of public facilities. Without the force of monetary penalties, I was concerned that inspectors would have less incentive to document violations. Finally, I limited my analysis to manufacturing facilities because my proxy measure of noncompliance, the workplace injury rate, was primarily available for manufacturing facilities and because it is more readily comparable across fixed-location manufacturing facilities than it is between, for instance, manufacturing and construction businesses. OSHA has different standards for different industries, and confining my analysis to manufacturing facilities also eliminates any potential bias in using the injury rate as a proxy measure of noncompliance across industries with different standards.

[41] I used the number of violations issued instead of the penalty imposed as my dependent variable because the issuance of a violation is independent of employer size and compliance history. By contrast, penalties are calculated according to formulas published in OSHA's Field Manual and take into account the size of the company, the employer's previous compliance history, and specific details of a violation. The previous chapter examined the political origins of OSHA's penalty policy.

a proxy measure of compliance with OSHA standards.[42] By law, most regulated businesses are required to keep logs of workplace injuries and illnesses and employee hours worked. These logs allow an OSHA inspector to calculate the injury rate for each workplace at the beginning of an inspection. Unfortunately, OSHA does not systematically record injury-rate data in the agency's inspection database. Since OSHA's founding, however, the Bureau of Labor Statistics (BLS) in the Department of Labor has conducted an annual survey of injury and illness rates from a nation-wide sample of businesses. These data are gathered under an agreement that they will not be used for enforcement purposes and with a promise of anonymity.[43]

In 1997, however, OSHA began collecting injury-rate information to improve agency procedures for targeting dangerous workplaces. In 1997 and 1998, under the auspices of the OSHA Data Initiative, OSHA collected accident and employment information for the previous year from approximately 45,000 workplaces nationwide in conjunction with the BLS survey.[44] Unfortunately, these data were not linked to OSHA's own inspection records. In order to overcome this limitation, I wrote a computer program to automate the matching of OSHA's inspection records to these injury-rate data.[45] The program assigned each potential match an "accuracy score." Preliminary matches with low accuracy scores were checked by hand, and any suspect entries were deleted. Table 3.11 displays the performance of this matching algorithm. Of OSHA's approximately

---

[42] For a full discussion of this measure, see Chapter 2, appendix 2.1. One concern about using injury-rate data to measure compliance is that OSHA's enforcement actions may decrease the observed injury rate. However, the best empirical evidence is that the effect of an OSHA inspection on the observed injury rate is lagged, taking more than a year to appear (Gray and Scholz 1993). In other words, an OSHA fine this year does not reduce this year's observed injury rate, only next year's.

[43] In a few cases (e.g., Gray and Scholz 1993), the BLS has shared these data with researchers under restrictive conditions.

[44] Approximately 80 percent of the surveyed businesses were manufacturing establishments. OSHA actually collected this data for the first time in 1996 (for calendar year 1995) but was unable to use it because of a successful court challenge based on OSHA's failure to abide by necessary rule-making requirements. OSHA did not try to use these data to select inspection targets until 1998. At that time, the agency's new targeting policy was challenged in court and subsequently revised.

[45] The computer code necessary for this matching is available from the author. The computer algorithm uses business name, location, industry, Dunn & Bradstreet identification code, size, and other characteristics to match the two datasets. The largest barrier to successful matching was inconsistent naming (e.g., Smith Company might appear as Smith Co., Smith & Company, or Smyth Company), poor address information (e.g., 124 Main Street might appear as 130 Main Street, Main and Union, or PO Box 100), and mobile employers (e.g., construction contractors).

TABLE 3.11. *Matching algorithm performance*

Year	All Planned Manufacturing Inspections		Planned Manufacturing Inspections with Matching Injury Data		
	Inspections	Average Number of Employees Covered	Inspections	Average Number of Employees Covered	Percentage of All Planned Manufacturing Inspections
1996	1,704	100	443	201	26%
1997	2,507	78	547	168	22%
OVERALL	4,211	86	990	182	24%

Note: Completed planned safety inspections of private manufacturing facilities, 1996–97.

4,200 planned safety inspections of manufacturing facilities conducted in 1996 and 1997, I was able to find matching injury-rate data for 990 cases, or approximately 24 percent. On average, the inspections with matching injury data cover about 100 more employees per inspection than the inspections for which the injury rate is unavailable. This is not surprising as OSHA's Data Initiative was designed to gather data from larger employees first. Additionally, because the injury-rate data is an imperfect measure of noncompliance and is subject to greater variability in smaller firms, the limited number of smaller firms should increase the probity of this proxy measure of noncompliance.

Second, I constructed a measure of the scope of the OSHA inspection. The number of workers that an inspection covers provides a rough measure of the potential scope of noncompliance. For instance, a workplace of 1,000 employees provides approximately 10 times as many opportunities for worker endangerment as a workplace of 100 employees. Therefore, to account for variations in facility size, I included the number of employees overseen by the inspection as reported in OSHA's inspection database and that number squared.[46] Inspections that cover more employees should yield more violations than more limited inspections.

Third, to account for additional unobserved heterogeneity in employer practices (compliance efforts, previous inspection history, etc.) and working conditions that might explain variation in inspection outcomes, I also included lagged measures of inspection and violations activity in each workplace (the last two years and years three and four for each measure) and indicator variables for each two-digit Standard Industrial Classification code in the manufacturing sector. While prior compliance activity might create bias in my results if many facilities in my analysis had recently been inspected, I found that fewer than 2.6 percent of the workplaces in my dataset had been inspected in the prior four years, and only 1.6 percent had been issued a serious or willful violation. (In part, this occurs because OSHA will not conduct a planned safety inspection in workplaces where it has recently conducted a comprehensive inspection.)

Fourth, I constructed a measure of the inexperience of the inspector who conducted each inspection. For each OSHA inspection in my dataset,

[46] Not every OSHA inspection covers an entire plant. Therefore, I chose to use the number of employees covered, rather than the number of employees in the plant. For instance, if OSHA chooses to inspect only part of a 5,000-worker manufacturing facility, I use the reported inspection scope, perhaps 2,500 employees. For most of the cases in my dataset, OSHA inspects the entire workplace. Inspection scope does not appear to be related to any of the political variables used in my analysis.

I determined which inspector conducted the inspection as well as when the inspector first began conducting inspections, based on both his or her unique OSHA identification number and reports in OSHA's inspection database. I then calculated a proxy measure of inspector inexperience by subtracting the number of years the inspector had been in the field from five. All inspectors who had been in the field longer than five years were coded 0. I chose the five-year cutoff because OSHA officials said that five years was about how long it took a new inspector to become fully trained and effective in the field. Inexperienced inspectors should be disadvantaged in finding OSHA violations because of their more limited knowledge of OSHA standards and less frequent interaction with workers in the field.[47]

In order to measure the effect of each of these independent variables on the number of violations OSHA issues following an inspection, I estimated a negative binomial regression model.[48] Results are shown in Table 3.12. Across specifications, the control variables largely behave as expected. I find that OSHA issues more violations in less safe and larger facilities. Per the column (6) specification, a one-standard-deviation increase in the injury rate increases the predicted number of violations by about 8 percent (from 3.46 to 3.72) in a nonunion workplace where workers did not participate in the inspection and all other variables are held constant at their sample means.[49] Facilities inspected in the last two years are less likely to be issued violations, which is consistent with prior work finding that inspections motivate firms to remedy workplace hazards. Workplaces inspected three or four years ago, however, are more likely to be found in violation of the law, although this effect appears to diminish if violations were issued at that time. Additionally, less experienced inspectors issue fewer violations, although this effect is not statistically significant. At first glance, then, the model seems to conform to "nonpolitical" expectations for enforcement outcomes.

Looking next at the measure of worker behavior and characteristics, worker participation in an inspection has a large and positive effect on the number of violations issued, and this coefficient estimate is statistically

---

[47] Source: author interview.

[48] This specification is appropriate because the dependent variable in my analysis is a non-negative count variable with overdispersion. The reported results are consistent across different specifications, including a pure Poisson model and a Tobit specification where I parameterize the dependent variable as the number of violations per employee.

[49] These predictions are calculated for a firm in the modal two-digit SIC category (34, Fabricated Metal Products).

TABLE 3.12. *Predicting inspector punitiveness*

	Violations					
	(1)	(2)	(3)	(4)	(5)	(6)
Workplace injury rate	0.014***	0.013**	0.012**	0.013**	0.011**	0.012**
	(0.005)	(0.005)	(0.005)	(0.005)	(0.005)	(0.005)
Number of employees/1,000	0.706***	0.638***	0.635***	0.618***	0.714***	0.701***
	(0.209)	(0.208)	(0.208)	(0.209)	(0.208)	(0.209)
Number of employees squared/1,000,000	−0.043	−0.041	−0.041	−0.038	−0.055*	−0.053
	(0.033)	(0.033)	(0.033)	(0.033)	(0.033)	(0.033)
Inspections, prior 2 years	−0.974**	−0.848**	−0.845**	−0.864**	−0.842**	−0.869**
	(0.394)	(0.407)	(0.408)	(0.409)	(0.408)	(0.411)
Inspections, 3–4 years ago	0.831**	0.800**	0.790**	0.791**	0.802**	0.808**
	(0.369)	(0.360)	(0.362)	(0.365)	(0.360)	(0.366)
Violations, prior 2 years	0.265	0.181	0.192	0.198	0.204	0.214
	(0.292)	(0.294)	(0.298)	(0.299)	(0.298)	(0.300)
Violations, 3–4 years ago	−0.100*	−0.106*	−0.105*	−0.104*	−0.106*	−0.105*
	(0.057)	(0.055)	(0.055)	(0.055)	(0.055)	(0.055)
Inspector inexperience	−0.027	−0.031	−0.030	−0.026	−0.037	−0.032
	(0.027)	(0.027)	(0.027)	(0.028)	(0.027)	(0.028)
Employee participation in inspection	0.300***	0.253***	0.259***	0.240**	0.247**	
	(0.078)	(0.098)	(0.098)	(0.099)	(0.099)	

(continued)

TABLE 3.12 (continued)

	Violations					
	(1)	(2)	(3)	(4)	(5)	(6)
Union workplace			0.079	0.074	0.102	0.093
			(0.099)	(0.098)	(0.099)	(0.099)
Democratic Party strength				−0.295		−0.405
				(0.334)		(0.459)
Unemployment				1.755		2.432
				(1.760)		(1.794)
Congressional conservatism					−0.080	−0.139
					(0.148)	(0.201)
Labor subcommittee conservatism					1.449**	1.506**
					(0.661)	(0.665)
Appropriations subcommittee conservatism					−1.581***	−1.562***
					(0.515)	(0.536)
Constant	−0.040	−0.117	−0.125	−0.051	−0.143	−0.050
	(0.698)	(0.784)	(0.794)	(0.821)	(0.793)	(0.830)
Observations	967	967	967	967	967	967
Log-likelihood	−2,314.100	−2,305.590	−2,305.270	−2,304.690	−2,298.240	−2,297.210

Note: Dependent variable is number of serious and willful violations issued following planned safety inspections of private manufacturing facilities where other measures were available. Coefficients for nineteen two-digit SIC categories not reported. Robust standard errors in parentheses. *** denotes $p < .01$; ** denotes $p < .05$; * denotes $p < .10$.

significant (columns [2] through [6]). Worker participation is sufficient to lead OSHA to issue almost an entire extra violation (using the same assumptions as used earlier, predicted violations increase by .98, from 3.46 to 4.42). This represents a 28 percent increase in inspection stringency. Once one accounts for worker participation, however, whether or not a workforce is unionized has a negligible and statistically insignificant effect on enforcement outcomes (columns [3] through [6]).

There is mixed evidence that local political conditions influence inspector stringency. Per the column (4) and (6) results, inspections yield *more* violations in Republican and high-unemployment areas, although again neither effect is significant. Whether a business is in an area represented by a member on one of the two important OSHA oversight committees does appear to have an effect on inspection stringency. Despite the fact that the overall effect of House member conservatism is small and statistically insignificant, a business in an area represented by a conservative (liberal) member of the House Labor subcommittee responsible for oversight of OSHA is predicted to experience more (less) stringent enforcement than a business represented by a moderate member on the committee. This effect is large and unexpected by any theoretical account, because it suggests that OSHA is more aggressive when locally elected and powerful committee members are hostile to the agency, and less aggressive when they are supportive. The effect of being represented on the House Appropriations subcommittee responsible for OSHA is of the opposite sign (and nearly the same magnitude), however, and statistically significant. A business in an area represented by the average House member (slightly conservative) would, if that member were placed on the Appropriations subcommittee, experience a predicted decrease of .23 violations per inspection, or about 7 percent.

This last set of results is something of a puzzle. No theory predicts that the stringency of OSHA enforcement will respond one way to the preferences of House Labor subcommittee members but the opposite way to the preferences of House Appropriations subcommittee members. Given the general lack of evidence of localism in enforcement stringency, this conflicting evidence is perhaps best regarded as an aberration. More generally, two concerns with the results presented here remain. First, while I argue that OSHA enforcement is enhanced by worker participation, one might argue that OSHA is responding to the signal of worker participation in calibrating enforcement to worker preferences. Second, it might also be the case that unobserved variation in worker cooperation affects the outcome of OSHA's inspections, but that my analysis misattributes this variation to OSHA's discretionary behavior. I consider each argument in turn.

3.1.1. DOES WORKER PARTICIPATION TRANSMIT INFORMATION OR INFLUENCE? An alternative interpretation of the finding that worker participation leads to more stringent enforcement is that worker participation is merely a signal to the OSHA inspector that a particular inspection is important to OSHA's labor constituency. According to this argument, rather than informing the inspector about workplace hazards, worker participation indicates to the OSHA inspector that any deference to business will damage the agency politically. When workers do not participate and appear uninterested in the inspection outcome, however, OSHA inspectors may simply assume that "keeping their heads down" and not antagonizing business groups is the safest strategy.

Four tests help to resolve this uncertainty. First, if worker participation really signals to the OSHA inspector whether a particular inspection is important, union status should be a stronger signal than worker participation. Union workers, by virtue of their membership in a labor advocacy organization, form OSHA's core supporters. But the results presented in Table 3.12 show that enforcement is no more stringent in union workplaces than in nonunion workplaces. Second, if worker participation is a signal, it should lead to more stringent enforcement regardless of the underlying level of workplace safety. The results reported in Table 3.12 show that actual workplace conditions matter. Additionally, I estimated an expanded version of this model that included an interaction between worker participation and the injury rate. I found that worker participation has *less* effect on the number of violations issued in more dangerous workplaces than in less dangerous workplaces.[50] In other words, worker participation is important because it helps the OSHA inspector to locate hazards when they are less obvious. When a workplace is very dangerous, the OSHA inspector can easily locate violations without worker support.

My third and fourth tests of whether worker participation provides information or influences inspectors compare the importance of worker participation across inspection types. In complaint inspections, the OSHA inspector is already notified of the exact nature of an alleged hazard. In this case, worker participation should be less important than during a planned inspection, where it conveys new information. When I estimated the model shown in Table 3.12 for complaint (rather than planned) inspections, I

---

[50] The coefficient on the worker participation and injury rate interaction term is negative, while the coefficients for the separate injury-rate and worker-participation variables remain positive and statistically significant. The net effect of worker participation is positive for lower injury rates and decays toward zero for the top 20 percent most dangerous workplaces.

found that worker participation no longer had a statistically significant effect on the number of violations issued. Finally, if worker participation is a political signal, it should matter as much in construction inspections as in manufacturing inspections. By contrast, if worker participation provides information, it should matter more in manufacturing inspections because manufacturing violations are harder to identify than construction violations. For example, in a manufacturing plant, one common violation is that a machine's lockout feature or safety guide has been disabled. This may not be immediately apparent to an inspector walking through a shop floor. On a construction site, by contrast, it is comparatively easy for an inspector to observe whether workers are wearing hardhats or if fall protection is in place. In fact, I found that employee participation had almost twice as much effect on the number of violations issued following a manufacturing inspection than following a construction inspection.[51]

Overall, the preponderance of the evidence presented here suggests that worker participation is a mechanism by which workers provide information to the OSHA inspector about workplace hazards, rather than a political signal to OSHA that a particular inspection should be more stringent. OSHA inspectors do not appear to mold their behavior to accommodate worker demands. Instead, they seem to be relying on workers to help them identify, document, and sustain violations.

3.1.2. DOES CONGRESS AFFECT WORKERS OR OSHA? The statistical findings reported in Table 3.12 about the influence of House Appropriations subcommittee members are at odds with the characterizations of inspector neutrality provided in my interviews with OSHA officials. What then explains the apparent relationship between House Appropriations subcommittee members' (and House Labor subcommittee members') preferences and OSHA inspection stringency? Perhaps workers are really responding to variation in congressional preferences, but my results emerge because I cannot measure variation in worker cooperation beyond whether workers participated in the inspection.

Interviews with OSHA inspectors and their supervisors provide suggestive support for the argument that OSHA inspectors are not tailoring

---

[51] Injury-rate data are not available for many construction establishments. Instead, I examined the effect of worker participation in construction and manufacturing businesses on the number of citations issued following a planned inspection while controlling for the scope of the inspection and the type of workplace. In this model, the coefficient estimates for worker participation in manufacturing inspections and construction inspections are individually statistically significant, and the coefficient for worker participation in manufacturing is twice as large as the coefficient for worker participation in construction.

enforcement to congressional preferences. In addition to the aforementioned evidence about the experience of inspectors who had served in different field offices and the general norm of professionalism, I also asked inspectors directly about whether members of Congress sought to influence their decisions. No inspector could recount an instance where a member of Congress had sought to influence a specific OSHA inspection or local field operations. Instead, several inspectors pointed out that they were shielded from political conflict in Washington by OSHA's national and regional offices. In simple terms, "This is all over our heads." One local administrator recounted that in a high-profile case he had dealt with, a request for information by a member of Congress was answered with a simple response that "OSHA cannot comment on ongoing investigations," and the member pushed no further. A regional official whose responsibilities included responding to outside inquiries described these interactions as follows:

We make sure that complaints about OSHA are investigated and documented very carefully. . . . [M]embers of Congress may receive pressure from their constituency to do something . . . [but we respond,] "the matter is under review or the case is under investigation." [Basically we state,] "We looked into it, we did everything properly." We know this is an attempt to squeeze the agency, but we resist and do our best to keep it out of the field.

More broadly, there is also no evidence of anticipatory action by OSHA inspectors to account for the preferences of locally elected members of Congress.

Perhaps it is not surprising that OSHA officials describe the agency as immune to local political concerns. The labor group leaders I interview expressed a similar lack of concern, however. Moreover, my interviews revealed not that OSHA officials are naïvely ignorant of politics, but rather that they are highly aware of the national nature of conflict over enforcement of the OSH Act. That is, inspectors frequently emphasized that OSHA's field operations were scrutinized nationwide, not by local interest groups or elected officials, but by national labor and business groups. Throughout the country, I repeatedly heard the same story about "Judy's Bakery," a 1994 case in which OSHA had issued $13,000 in penalties after inspecting a small Illinois bakery for (among other things) failing to have material safety data sheets on hand for common cleaning products and not providing sufficient fall protection on a set of stairs. This case, which generated substantial negative coverage of OSHA as overbearing, was discussed by the inspectors I interviewed as an example of the failure to recognize that "nit-picking" in the field would invite widespread opposition to the agency:

> [OSHA] should have been more discrete. [The] penalties for trivial violations bring back the toilet seat violations [memory] and undercut everything else good we do. This [assigning penalties for unimportant violations rather than just issuing citations without monetary penalties] is not a popularity contest we are going to win.

Two additional features of how OSHA officials interpreted this case are interesting. First, inspectors and administrators recognized that the outcry about the case had little to do with the preferences of the locally elected member of Congress. As one administrator stated, "It [the Judy's Bakery case] just shows that they [members of Congress who are opposed to OSHA] are just looking for one case, anywhere in the country, to drag us through the mud." Second, when pressed about whether the opposite were true, if going "too easy" on a business for a serious violation would invite opposition to the agency, most inspectors said that it posed the same risk of being exposed after the fact and thereby yielding negative publicity for the agency. "If we let something [a serious hazard] go [without a fine] and they [unions] find out or an accident takes place, we could lose an important ally."

However, the inspectors I interviewed did agree that local politics and labor market conditions affected how willing workers were to cooperate during an inspection. In particular, the inspectors I spoke with emphasized two factors that influenced worker support for vigorous OSHA enforcement. First, they stated that union employees were far more willing to cooperate with an OSHA inspector. Second, they argued that nonunion employees were more likely to be cowed, both by employers who threatened them and by the possibility that OSHA enforcement would endanger their jobs (see footnote 29). The results reported in Table 3.12 are consistent with this explanation. More conservative representation and weaker unions may undercut worker cooperation, but this cooperation is imprecisely measured by whether or not employees participate in an inspection.[52] While there is no available direct measure of worker cooperation

---

[52] OSHA's guidelines for field inspectors allow nonunion workers to participate in the walk-around phase of the inspection only when certain conditions are met concerning whether workers can reasonably select an appropriate representative. If these conditions are not met, the inspector is supposed to interview employees during the inspection. Unfortunately, no information is available on whether these conditions were met and workers subsequently declined to participate, or whether workers were simply ineligible under OSHA's guidelines.

apart from whether or not workers exercised their right to participate in the inspection, an analysis of workers' willingness to exercise their walk-around rights provides one way to assess the validity of the claim that workers behave differently in different environments.

Table 3.13 reports the results of six statistical models predicting how likely workers are to exercise their walk-around rights. The dependent variable is coded one if workers exercised their rights, and zero otherwise. There are separate models for union and nonunion workers for all the planned manufacturing cases for which I also have workplace injury rate data. The estimated models include the same independent variables as the models reported in Table 3.12 (absent union membership and exercise of walk-around rights). The estimates in columns (1) and (4) consider the effect of local constituency preferences, while columns (2) and (5) estimate the effects of differences in formal representation in Congress. Finally, columns (3) and (6) integrate these models. Because the coefficients for the integrated models are similar to those for the reduced form models, I focus on these results.

In both union and nonunion workplaces, I find that workers are more likely to exercise their rights in larger and more dangerous businesses and when a less experienced inspector conducts an inspection. (The latter finding provides additional evidence that workers are not responding to OSHA behavior, because if they were, they would be less likely to cooperate with newer inspectors, who I show are less likely to issue citations than more experienced inspectors.)[53] Beyond these variables, however, the results diverge for union and nonunion workers. As the leftmost part of Figure 3.3 shows, Democratic Party strength marginally decreases the probability that union workers (black bar) exercise their walk-around rights, but substantially increases the probability that nonunion workers (white bar) do so.[54] However, the center of the figure shows that higher unemployment diminishes the probability that nonunion workers participate in the inspection, while having the opposite effect for union workers. (In the unified models, only the coefficients for the nonunion workers are statistically significant.) Finally, the rightmost portion of the figure shows union workers are more likely to exercise their rights in areas

---

[53] The coefficient estimates are not statistically significant, but this is not surprising given the small number of observations.

[54] All percentages shown in Figure 3.3 are proportional shift in predicted probability, calculated as $(X_1 - X_0)/X_0$, where X_0 is calculated with variables held constant at their sample means and modal SIC category and X_1 is calculated under the same scenario with the relevant independent variable incremented by one standard deviation.

TABLE 3.13. *Predicting worker exercise of walk-around rights*

	Union Worker Participation			Nonunion Worker Participation		
	(1)	(2)	(3)	(4)	(5)	(6)
Workplace injury rate	0.011	0.009	0.012	0.011	0.009	0.010
	(0.015)	(0.015)	(0.015)	(0.010)	(0.010)	(0.010)
Number of employees/1,000	0.986	0.907	0.921	0.917*	0.693	0.891*
	(1.432)	(1.467)	(1.510)	(0.538)	(0.529)	(0.539)
Number of employees squared/1,000,000	0.374	0.450	0.453	−0.558	−0.383	−0.522
	(1.764)	(1.887)	(2.011)	(0.361)	(0.360)	(0.365)
Inspector inexperience	0.070	0.077	0.079	0.053	0.064	0.056
	(0.077)	(0.074)	(0.075)	(0.042)	(0.042)	(0.043)
Democratic Party strength	−2.296**		−0.075	2.336***		1.667*
	(0.896)		(1.146)	(0.682)		(0.890)
Unemployment	5.519		6.223	−7.980***		−7.327**
	(5.290)		(5.449)	(3.008)		(3.041)
Congressional conservatism		1.406***	1.596***		−0.775***	−0.475
		(0.412)	(0.558)		(0.243)	(0.320)
Labor subcommittee conservatism		4.325	4.335		1.036	0.877
		(3.407)	(3.392)		(1.133)	(1.142)
Appropriations subcommittee conservatism		−1.592	−1.858		−0.026	−0.309
		(1.576)	(1.654)		(0.934)	(1.006)
Constant	1.309	0.263	−0.050	−1.771**	−1.039	−1.440*
	(0.899)	(0.776)	(1.006)	(0.748)	(0.650)	(0.796)
Observations	289	289	289	670	670	670
Log-likelihood	−129.150	−125.230	−124.550	−304.381	−305.994	−302.538

Note: Dependent variable is whether workers exercised walk-around rights during planned safety inspections of private manufacturing facilities where other measures were available. Coefficients for nineteen two-digit SIC categories not reported. Sample is the same as reported in Table 3.12. Robust standard errors in parentheses. *** denotes $p < .01$; ** denotes $p < .05$; * denotes $p < .10$.

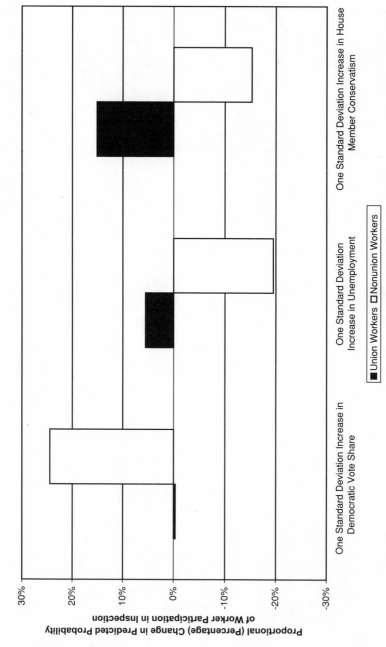

FIGURE 3.3. Effect of changing local political conditions on worker exercise of right to participate in inspection, by union status of workers.

represented by hostile House members, while nonunion workers are less so. Although neither effect is statistically significant, I also find that both union and nonunion workers are more likely to participate in inspections in areas represented by conservatives members of the House Labor sub-committee, but less likely to do so in areas represented by conservatives on the House Appropriations subcommittee. This suggests that there may be independent variation in worker cooperation that is correlated with the ideology of representation on these two powerful committees. Insofar as observed participation is an imperfect measure of worker coopera-tion, this (unobserved) variation in worker cooperation may explain the opposing effects on enforcement stringency of representation on these two powerful committees, as shown in Table 3.12.

This analysis offers additional suggestive evidence that workers, and not OSHA inspectors, are the conduits by which local politics influences inspection outcomes. Based on these results, a reasonable interpreta-tion for the effect of House Appropriations subcommittee membership on enforcement stringency is variation in private actor behavior. Given the self-selection of members to this committee, committee membership may be correlated with unmeasured variation in local constituencies that explains both worker and business behavior. Net, the evidence in sup-port of inspector neutrality seems stronger than the evidence of inspector responsiveness to local members of Congress, whether on committees or not.

PART 2: RECONCILING THESE FINDINGS
WITH PREVIOUS RESEARCH

The findings presented in part 1 of this chapter suggest that OSHA enforcement personnel are, by and large, not directly responsive to local political influences in choosing how to implement the law. (The one notable exception is bureaucratic effort in reinvented field offices.) Rather, taken as a whole, this evidence depicts an agency that has done a rea-sonable job of moving from the abstract idea of "strategically neutral enforcement" to a field effort that largely mirrors the priorities of agency leaders in Washington.

Of course, this in-depth examination has also revealed many instances in which local conditions affect OSHA enforcement outcomes, but these arise largely because variation in business and worker behavior affects noncompliance and the ability of OSHA inspectors to detect and punish violations of the OSH Act. Putting aside for the moment the question of exactly how these local pressures (and the resulting variation in local enforcement) affect OSHA's political fortunes, this empirical work portrays OSHA in a starkly different light than some previous scholarship that diagnoses substantial *direct* responsiveness by OSHA bureaucrats to local political conditions. How can one reconcile these findings with previous portrayals of OSHA as directly responsive to local political concerns?

4. OSHA Enforcement and Political Influence Recapitulated

In answering this question, it is useful to first review the evidence presented earlier in this chapter that disaggregates the OSHA enforcement process into four component parts: staffing local offices, targeting inspections, inspector productivity, and inspector punitiveness. Table 3.14 summarizes those findings by enforcement activity and the sources of variation in enforcement outcomes. Specifically, it reports separately how national political concerns affect centralized OSHA decisions, how politics affects local OSHA decisions in the field (regional and area offices), and how workers and employers (and other private actors) shape OSHA enforcement activities indirectly.

First, for the staffing of both regional and local offices (the first row of Table 3.14), there is little evidence of any direct concern for local political conditions on the part of OSHA officials in the national or regional offices. Within the regions, area offices with more dangerous businesses (those more heavily targeted by OSHA's national office) receive more inspectors, but this is almost entirely without regard for the preferences of local constituencies.[55] Nor is there any evidence that workers or businesses (apart from their very existence) are able to influence OSHA's staff allocation.

Targeting of inspections is more clearly affected by external political forces, but again there is not much evidence of concern for local political support on the part of OSHA officials. The national office's targeting list compels the local offices primarily to conduct inspections of the nation's most dangerous businesses. Local offices, meanwhile, largely lack discretion to choose where to inspect. The complaint procedure included in the OSH Act does, however, provide a direct means for external actors

---

[55] There is weak evidence that OSHA's regional administrators allocate more inspectors to less-Democratic and higher-unemployment areas, although this finding probably emerges because of the high correlation between the dangerousness of businesses OSHA targets for inspection and partisanship and unemployment.

TABLE 3.14. *Summarizing the sources of political influence on enforcement outcomes, by source*

Enforcement Activity	Source of Political Influence over Enforcement Outcomes		
	National Politics	Local Politics	Worker/Firm Behavior
Staffing regions and local offices	None	More inspectors per business in areas with more dangerous businesses. (Weak evidence of greater allocation of inspectors to *less* Democratic areas and areas with *worse* local economic conditions.)	None
Targeting inspections	More frequent inspections of more dangerous businesses	None	Complaints affect enforcement outcomes. Source of variation in complaint rates: (1) More complaints in less-safe businesses. (2) More hostile political conditions associated with greater decline in nonunion complaints than in union complaints.
Inspector productivity	Uniform focus on productivity. (Exception is reinvention experiment.)	Persistent focus on productivity, except during local office reinvention. (During reinvention, decreased productivity in hostile areas, particularly those with higher unemployment and less support in Congress.)	(1) Employer behavior can slow OSHA inspectors (contesting violations, frequent noncompliance). (2) Worker complaints change focus of OSHA's inspections.
Inspector punitiveness	Formal penalty policy decreasing penalties for small, safe, and previously compliant businesses.	Conflicting evidence about influence on enforcement stringency of congressional representation on crucial House committees. (Evidence that responsiveness to preferences of locally elected member of Congress may simply reflect variations in worker cooperation with OSHA.)	(1) Employer noncompliance affects OSHA behavior. (2) Worker cooperation during inspections affects efficacy of OSHA inspections.

to affect the geographic allocation of OSHA's inspection effort. Specifically, I find that workers are more likely to complain where more dangerous businesses are more common, and that nonunion workers complain less frequently during economic downturns in more Republican areas. OSHA's hands are largely tied in this matter, however, since the agency must respond to these complaints.

Inspector productivity, one of the areas in which OSHA's national office is likely to have the hardest time controlling OSHA officials in the field, presents a more interesting pattern. Except for a brief period under the leadership of Joseph Dear, OSHA's national office has sought to maximize the productivity of its field offices in producing "high-quality" inspections yielding many violations. My analysis suggests that this pressure limited local OSHA officials' discretion to respond to local political pressure. When OSHA's national office experimented with redesigning the local enforcement programs of some area offices to give them more discretion, however, this uniformity disappeared. OSHA's inspectors in hostile areas (high unemployment, conservative representation in the House) working in reinvented field offices conducted fewer inspections.

Private actors do seem able to influence the productivity of OSHA inspectors, but again this appears to be because their actions change the tasks of inspectors in the field. When noncompliance is more frequent and employers contest OSHA citations, inspectors conduct fewer inspections because they must spend more time documenting and defending violations of OSHA rules. Likewise, worker complaints can change what types of inspections OSHA conducts by substituting complaint inspections for planned inspections.

Finally, variation in the punitiveness of OSHA inspections potentially presents the strongest evidence for direct responsiveness to local politics on the part of OSHA officials. At the national level, OSHA's penalty policy discriminates among businesses by rewarding small, safe, and previously compliant employers relative to similar firms that are larger, have poor safety records, or have previously been cited for violations of the OSH Act. This discrimination is without regard for local political support for OSHA, however, and is related to OSHA's efforts to target persistent violators of the OSH Act while mitigating claims of overregulation of small and safer businesses. At the local level, there is some evidence that OSHA inspectors in areas represented by members on the House Appropriations subcommittee with responsibility for oversight of OSHA tailor enforcement to be less aggressive in areas represented by conservatives. But this evidence is offset by data showing the opposite effect for representation on the House Labor subcommittee with oversight of OSHA. A careful examination of when workers cooperate with OSHA during an inspection hints that both findings may be due to variation in worker cooperation with OSHA, cooperation that appears to be correlated with the preferences of locally elected members of Congress for both complaint rates (Table 3.8) and workers choosing to participate in OSHA inspections (Table 3.13).

Workers and employers are more clearly able to indirectly influence the stringency of OSHA enforcement. Less-safe businesses are more likely to be cited by OSHA, and whether workers cooperate with OSHA affects the ability of an OSHA inspector to detect violation of the OSH Act. Workers' cooperation, however, is likely to be affected both by workers' own desires for strong OSH Act enforcement *and* the willingness of employers to threaten workers who exercise their statutory rights. As a consequence, nonunion workers are less likely to exercise their rights in Republican areas or when the economy is poor, while union workers are not similarly affected. (Union workers may even participate more frequently, per Table 3.13, in areas represented by conservative members of Congress.) Once again, this finding is evidence that variation in private behavior can shape enforcement outcomes without altering the discretionary behavior of local OSHA bureaucrats.

5. Previous Studies of OSHA Responsiveness

In contrast to this portrayal of OSHA officials as unaffected directly by local political conditions (with the notable exception of the period of the reinvention experiment), previous work has found important correlations between local political support and OSHA's enforcement efforts. The two most prominent works in this regard are Scholz and Wei (1986) and Scholz, Twombly, and Headrick (1991). Scholz and Wei (1986) present a pooled cross-sectional analysis of state-level federal and state OSH Act enforcement for the period 1976–83. The primary theoretical argument in their work is that "task factors" (injury rates and the number of businesses) will affect substantive OSHA activities (OSHA inspections with penalties), while political factors will lead bureaucrats to take symbolic actions (manipulating inspections without penalties).

In support of their theoretical propositions about the effects of local politics, they find that federal inspections were more frequent in states with strong labor unions, while inspections with penalties were more likely in states represented by more liberal members of Congress, states with stronger unions, and states where unemployment was lower.[56] How can one reconcile these findings with my own? Obviously, it may simply be the case that OSHA has changed since 1983. Putting this argument aside for the moment, however, are there other explanations for these differences? Two seem most likely. First, Scholz and Wei's work may attribute to OSHA differences in enforcement activity caused by variation in private actor behavior. Second, their aggregate analysis of state-level data may overstate the effects of local politics because of unmeasured variation in workplace conditions that is correlated with their measured political variables.

Regarding the first point, Scholz and Wei measure union strength as the number of complaints per industrial worker in the state. As I argued earlier, however, given a valid complaint, OSHA has little choice but to respond. Moreover, variation in complaint rates arises for a number of reasons, including variation in the relative danger of workplaces and changing political and economic circumstances. It seems inappropriate to claim that OSHA officials discretionarily change their behavior in the presence of more complaints. Rather, OSHA local officials must act differently in areas with more complaints because they do not have the discretion to do otherwise. Similarly, the unemployment effects documented by Scholz and Wei, with higher unemployment associated with a decrease in serious violations but no change in the number of inspections, may reflect variation in worker behavior. When workers are less willing to cooperate with OSHA (which is less likely when unemployment rises), OSHA inspectors will have a harder time finding violations. Unemployment therefore has an effect on factors outside of the control of local OSHA officials that nonetheless shape enforcement outcomes.

The second explanation for the disjuncture between my own findings and those of Scholz and Wei concerns their use and analysis of state-level data to test the effects of local political conditions on OSHA behavior.[57]

---

[56] Scholz and Wei classify unemployment as a task factor, although their assumption is that it affects the willingness of private actors and OSHA officials to enforce the OSH Act. Thus, I label it a political factor. Scholz and Wei report finding no effects of representation on OSHA oversight committees.

[57] An important technical concern is that Scholz and Wei use a Parks regression model, which Beck and Katz (1995) have shown understates substantially the imprecision of model coefficients in panel data. This leads to finding statistically significant results where none should exist. More troubling, Scholz and Wei implement the Parks approach even though their dataset has more cross-sections (states) than units of time (years). Beck and Katz and Beck and colleagues (1993) have shown that Parks models cannot be estimated under these conditions and argue that the results reported in these circumstances are due

Because there is a positive correlation between local support for OSHA and the presence of the types of businesses OSHA is likely to inspect and penalize even in the absence of political influence, their analysis may overstate the effects of local political factors. During the period of their study, industrial states in the Midwest and Northeast tended to elect more liberal members of Congress relative to the less industrial South and West. Additionally, manufacturers in both the Midwest and Northeast were more likely to be engaged in the most dangerous types of manufacturing relative to other areas of the country.[58] Consequently, it is not surprising that Scholz and Wei find a positive association between liberal representation in Congress and aggressive OSHA behavior after controlling for the number of manufacturing workers, because liberals were more likely to hold office in states that had more dangerous manufacturing pools. Similarly, these areas also had stronger unions than the less-dangerous manufacturing sectors in other states. The higher rates of unionization and the more dangerous nature of the workplaces in these areas probably contributed to more enforcement for reasons unrelated to OSHA's concern for local political support.

A later analysis by Scholz, Twombly, and Headrick (1991) addresses this concern about unmeasured variation in industry composition across geographic areas. In a panel study of federal OSHA enforcement in thirty New York counties for the period 1976–85, they examine variation in enforcement over time after accounting for baseline differences in enforcement in each county by using a fixed-effects approach. They find that enforcement was more aggressive in counties where the Democratic Party was strong and in those areas represented by liberals in the state assembly and U.S. House. (House member ideology affects all phases of enforcement, whereas local party strength and state assembly representation affect only penalties and inspections with penalties.)

---

entirely to computational errors produced by the statistical software used to estimate their models. "It is impossible to use the Parks method if the length of the time frame, T, is smaller than the number of units, N. Several published studies, therefore, present results that are either logically impossible to obtain or are completely the result of numerical inaccuracies" (Beck and Katz 1995: 644).

[58] Table 3.7 shows the current ratio of dangerous businesses to businesses. For 1977, Regions I, II, and V score even higher for the ratio of dangerous manufacturing businesses to manufacturers. Scholz and Wei do control for the number of injuries per worker, but not for manufacturing injuries per manufacturing worker. Thus, they account for the rough variation between manufacturing businesses and other types of less-dangerous workplaces, but not for differences across states in the nature of manufacturing processes.

Once again, these results depict OSHA as far more responsive to local politics than does my own analysis. What explains this difference? Again putting aside the question of whether OSHA has changed since 1985, the two sets of concerns raised regarding Scholz and Wei (1986) also apply here.[59] First, these results indicate covariation between local politics and inspection outcomes, but do not show that OSHA officials actually made discretionary decisions differently in the face of more (or less) supportive local politics. If changing local politics was correlated with changes in worker (and firm) behavior, this alone could produce the results reported in their analysis.[60] Second, there is important covariation between changes in economic conditions and changes in political conditions during the period of their study. Specifically, New York (like many other Rust Belt states) lost a substantial number of manufacturing establishments during the period they study (from 1976 to 1985). Throughout the state, the percentage of all businesses that were manufacturers declined by over 20 percent. Scholz and colleagues, however, account only for the overall number of businesses in each county in their analysis. Consequently, they overestimate the natural level of enforcement in the later part of their study period (when fewer businesses were engaged in dangerous manufacturing activity) relative to the natural level earlier in the period. This may produce bias, because simultaneously the state shifted in the Republican direction, so that the Democrats held 20 percent fewer of the state's congressional House seats by 1985 relative to 1976. (In state offices too, Republicans recovered somewhat from their post-Watergate losses.) For this reason, the measurement error in regulatory need induces too low a predicted baseline level of enforcement in the 1970s and too high a level in the 1980s. This prediction error is correlated with representation in the House, so the model attributes diminished enforcement that is actually a result of measurement error in regulatory need to the shift toward a more Republican House delegation.[61]

---

[59] Also, like Scholz and Wei, Scholz, Twombly, and Headrick use the Parks method that both produces too-small standard errors and cannot be estimated for their data (because the number of counties in their analysis exceeds the number of years). In the non-Parks specifications reported in their work (Table 2), only the effect of House member ideology and local partisanship remain statistically significant.

[60] Scholz and colleagues acknowledge this fact, suggesting that local support might simply affect the ease with which inspectors can go about their jobs, an interpretation my data analysis supports. See the following discussion.

[61] This problem is even more acute at the county level, because the counties that deindustrialized most (had the biggest decline in the ratio of manufacturers to overall businesses) were many of the suburban counties around New York City that became more

These concerns aside, it may also be the case that the results reported by Scholz and Wei and Scholz, Twombly, and Headrick accurately reflected OSHA's responsiveness to local political pressures during the period of these studies. Building an enforcement bureaucracy from scratch is not an easy task, and while OSHA was well established by the mid-1970s, its system for targeting inspections using centrally generated lists disseminated to the field offices was not fully in place until the 1980s. Local area offices therefore had somewhat greater discretion in choosing inspection targets than they do now, at least during the beginning of the period studied in both articles. Furthermore, prior to the widespread computerization of field offices and centralized record keeping, it was arguably more difficult for OSHA's leaders to carefully monitor field office productivity.

But this explanation seems less likely when one considers that OSHA's leadership was already very aware of the dangers of geographically variable enforcement during this period (see Chapter 2). The agency as a whole was less sophisticated, but agency leaders were nonetheless aware that perceptions of partisanship in enforcement would have serious political consequences. Field office activities were carefully monitored, and OSHA already had in place a system of auditing field office files to look for instances of favoritism and variable enforcement. Agency leaders were also highly motivated to have the field offices conduct many inspections and detect many serious violations in order to demonstrate both the need for OSHA and its efficiency in punishing violations of the OSH Act.

If one were to rank the three explanations I have provided for the divergence between my results and those of earlier work (attributing to OSHA variation in private actor behavior, the correlation between local politics and private actor behavior, and changes at OSHA), the first two seem clearly to dominate the last. My own findings in the first part of this chapter are that variation in private actor behavior (of workers and firms) has a large independent effect on enforcement outcomes despite largely successful efforts to weed out politically motivated variation in

Democratic during the post-Watergate period but then reverted to Republican hands by the 1980s. For example, for Westchester County (just outside of New York City), the Democratic vote share in the 1980 presidential election dropped about 10 percent from 1976 levels, 2 percent greater than the 8 percent drop statewide. At the same time, the percentage of businesses that were manufacturing establishments in the county dropped 23 percent, or about 3 percent more than the average statewide drop. Thus, at the county level, measurement error in the natural level of regulatory enforcement is correlated with partisanship, with areas that became more Republican having the most overpredicted levels of enforcement due to the changing mix of manufacturing employment relative to all other work.

discretionary bureaucratic behavior. Additionally, variation in worker and employer behavior is correlated with the very independent variables that previous scholarship has relied on to measure political pressures on OSHA officials. Consequently, it is not that politics does not matter, just that it does not matter by directly affecting the discretionary decisions of OSHA officials.

This conclusion reveals that a more general source of the disagreement between my own work and this previous scholarship may be the interpretation of the linkage between local politics and private actor behavior. Scholz and Wei argue that

A pragmatic agency, however, is likely to respond to the more subtle concerns of congressmen for their particular districts by initiating more intensive enforcement efforts in areas and industries where congressmen hope to maintain strong labor support.... [Variation in enforcement] may also reflect the local enforcement official's inclination to take advantage of an elected official's willingness to provide local leadership and implementation resources. (1252)

Similarly, Scholz and colleagues state that

Local leadership activities of representatives may influence OSHA enforcement efforts through the provision or denial of negotiating resources needed for these enforcement tasks. Political leaders can meet with local businesses to iron out OSHA-related problems, thereby minimizing enforcement resources tied up in a special problem.... Alternatively, the official could be a catalyst for efforts by business to tie up OSHA enforcement by requiring warrants for all inspections and by appealing all citations.

Such leadership activities may have a broader effect on the perceived legitimacy of the agency's actions among local groups important to the agency.... For OSHA inspectors, such responses may change the boundaries within which they can operate without concern for complaints about overzealousness on the one hand or complacency on the other.... Local leadership activities can also directly affect policy preferences of bureaucrats by changing their beliefs and loyalties. (835)

These authors therefore posit three different ways in which local politics can influence OSHA behavior. First, it can alter the strategic behavior of agency field personnel seeking to please local officials. Second, it can directly affect the beliefs of field personnel about acceptable behavior. Third, it can be correlated with variation in private actor behavior.[62] I

---

[62] There is sparse evidence to support the conclusion that workers or firms change their behavior in response to the preferences of elected officials. Far more compelling is the argument that elected officials are products of their local environments, so that pro-OSHA officials are elected in areas where citizens support OSHA and anti-OSHA officials are elected in areas where citizens are hostile to the agency.

find little evidence to support the first two mechanisms, however. Once one accounts for differences in private actor behavior in individual workplaces, OSHA officials are not any more or less aggressive in supportive areas or hostile ones (however measured).

Even if local politics affects the cooperation of local workers and businesses, the simple fact that private actors can make it easier or harder for OSHA to enforce the law is not evidence for the stronger claim that OSHA officials change their behavior in light of this variation. Rather, when workers complain frequently to OSHA or cooperate with OSHA inspectors, OSHA officials will simply have an easier time detecting violations. By contrast, in areas where businesses challenge OSHA inspectors, threaten workers, and appeal OSHA citations, OSHA will be slowed despite its best efforts. There is strong evidence that local politics affects enforcement outcomes, but next to none that it affects discretionary OSHA decisions. Rather, the evidence is more consistent with a portrayal of an agency engaged in the largely geographically neutral enforcement of the law.

In the conclusion of their work, Scholz and Wei note that their data contrast with OSHA's own description of its sensitivity to local politics:

It should be noted that OSHA officials firmly deny any informal influence of elected officials at the local level, but the pervasive influence of local interest group actions combined with the likely influence of local electoral networks indicate the need for further studies of the complex, subtle interactions between political and bureaucratic institutions at the local level. (1262)

The analysis here perhaps resolves this apparent puzzle. OSHA officials are not lying; they just cannot overcome all sources of variation in worker and firm behavior that are correlated with salient measures of local support for OSHA. The mechanism of this influence, however, is different than previous work has suggested. The remaining question, which I take up in the chapter's final section, is what are the implications of this generic commitment to neutral enforcement coupled with local variation originating in private actor behavior?

PART 3: STRATEGIC NEUTRALITY AND THE CONTROL
OF FIELD ENFORCEMENT

6. Politics and Bureaucratic Decision Making

My examination of OSHA's field enforcement program reveals that the agency eschews active localism in seeking out and punishing those who violate the law. What are the theoretical implications of this finding for understanding bureaucratic decision making? In the aggregate, OSHA's nationally uniform enforcement effort allows agency leaders to engage in geographically uniform enforcement in exchange for support from prominent national political groups. This is a not a bargain between individual inspectors (or area offices) and local groups or members of Congress. At the same time, the national calibration of enforcement efforts to business size and real workplace dangers allows the agency to minimize the likelihood of mobilization by potential agency opponents. In other words, as I argued in Chapter 2, a consistent OSHA is a strategic response by the agency's leadership to national interest groups and congressional concerns about agency policy. National political conflict effectively trumps local politics, removing the primary mechanism for interest groups and members of Congress to shape the stringency with which individual inspectors enforce the law in different areas of the country.

Clearly, then, OSHA is not immune to political influence. Additionally, while OSHA is constrained by the political environment, its leadership has chosen to become strategically neutral. Supporting this decision requires the agency to mitigate local responsiveness among subordinates and to maintain productivity in order to attract support and defuse criticism. At the same time, this neutrality is at odds with portrayals of the agency as simply responding to external stimuli or having been captured by either labor or business interests. Rather, OSHA has embraced a strategy that is less confrontational than labor would like (especially toward small business), but substantially more confrontational and aggressive than the business community would prefer. Manipulating enforcement to target dangerous businesses while shrinking penalties for small and safe businesses has therefore allowed the agency to minimize the chances of being overwhelmed by opposition from either end of the political spectrum. Thus, the external political environment is a constraint on OSHA's behavior, but does not directly predict which course of action the agency will take (or when).

Furthermore, the direct linkage between interest group preferences and field-level behavior proposed in previous work is not supported in the OSHA case. OSHA inspectors do not internalize the wishes of powerful local groups when deciding how hard to work or how vigorously to enforce the law. OSHA's field-level bureaucrats are generally tightly controlled and discouraged from considering local politics when going about their jobs. This insulation is accomplished by broadly inculcating norms of uniform enforcement, by making explicit efforts to remove any basis of exchange between individual bureaucrats and local political actors, and finally by management efforts that leave field-level bureaucrats without the option of avoiding uncomfortable confrontations with hostile employers. This last component, in combination with general professional norms of aggressive enforcement and fair treatment, is perhaps most important, because I find that local politics had a larger effect on local enforcement efforts when OSHA reorganized field offices to grant local officials greater discretion to decide how to enforce the law. Overall, I show that aggressive central control can, if properly implemented, mitigate localism in enforcement.

Nor do OSHA's field enforcement efforts appear to respond to the wishes of powerful congressional committee members (or House members more generally) about how to enforce the law in their individual districts. This is evidence not that OSHA ignores the preferences of powerful committee members, but just that the agency (and its field staff) is not bound by the wishes of committee members when those committee members make demands about local enforcement that are not supported by the rest of the Congress. (By contrast, the agency has clearly been bound by the appropriations riders passed by the entire Congress, and by the threat of similar viable political initiatives.)

Still, the procedural requirements imposed on OSHA in the OSH Act clearly have had a large effect on the agency's field enforcement program. The obligation for the agency to respond to a worker complaint by conducting an inspection creates a direct route for workers to initiate agency inspections. As my analysis shows, worker variability in invoking this procedure has large effects on the geographic distribution of the agency's regulatory effort. Similarly, variation in worker cooperation with OSHA during an inspection affects the stringency of field inspections. But these rules alone explain only some of the variation in OSHA's enforcement, not the main thrust of the agency's efforts to ignore local political support and tailor enforcement to workplace safety and business size.

The cumulative evidence presented in this chapter describes an agency that is pursuing a strategy of neutrality because doing so serves agency leaders' political and management needs as documented in Chapter 2. Because enforcing the OSH Act requires fielding an enforcement program, this national effort necessarily intertwines management of field activities with these national political concerns. OSHA's leaders have therefore taken extraordinary steps to ensure that subordinates do not take actions that will hurt the agency's political standing or detract from agency leaders' efforts to demonstrate their effectiveness in detecting real safety violations. (On alternative enforcement strategies that would not serve these political goals, see Chapter 2.)

The clearest evidence linking tight control of field operations and the agency's political standing is the reaction to changes in enforcement undertaken during Dear's tenure as OSHA head. Agency reforms diminished the focus on frequent inspections. But this did little to insulate the agency from hostile forces in the newly Republican Congress. Rather, to OSHA's opponents, lower productivity strengthened claims that the agency was inefficient and, as fewer inspections produced fewer violations, unnecessary. (As one official at the U.S. Chamber of Commerce put it, "What we want is an agency that helps us reduce injuries and illness. What we see is an agency talking out of both sides of its mouth" [Finnegan 1998].) Among OSHA's supporters, diminished productivity likewise weakened the payoffs of fighting for the agency's survival vis-à-vis fighting for other programs. (As one administrator noted, "Opponents said we [a reinvented OSHA that didn't conduct as many inspections or assess as many penalties] were ineffective, while supportive members of Congress wanted to know what their hard-fought money was buying." An AFL-CIO representative was more critical: "There has been more of an emphasis on the agency and how it should operate, than on safety and health problems facing workers" [Finnegan 1998].)

More perniciously, my data suggest that local politics began to affect directly the decisions of individual bureaucrats in reinvented field offices. OSHA quickly shelved this program after the extensive negative reaction to it, further evidence that even a generic decline in enforcement would do little to protect the agency. Of course, OSHA's reinvention program might have, in the long run, yielded more extensive improvements in worker safety and health than a focus on traditional enforcement. In the short run, however, the decline in visible agency productivity was too costly politically. It emboldened traditional critics of the agency and thereby endangered the agency's budget and its statutory authority.

7. Does Worker- and Firm-Induced Variation in Enforcement Help or Hurt OSHA?

While my data suggest that OSHA is consistent across different political environments, I nonetheless find evidence that variation in worker and firm behavior affects the ease with which OSHA can enforce the law in different areas of the country. Specifically, in areas where workers cooperate with OSHA by complaining and participating in inspections, OSHA has an easier time detecting noncompliance than in areas where workers are unwilling to work with the agency. Perhaps this "accidental" variation, through no fault of OSHA's, has helped the agency to avoid becoming too aggressive in hostile areas while becoming more aggressive in supportive ones. Thus, one might argue that (this ecologically induced) localism helps the agency, even if the agency is not the source of localism.

But this argument is not supported by the nature of political conflict surrounding OSHA or by the agency's own behavior. OSHA is not helped in national conflicts by evidence of geographic variation in enforcement outcomes. While my analysis shows that such variation arises largely for reasons outside of OSHA's control, previous scholarly work has contended that OSHA is calibrating enforcement to local politics. The congressional testimony reviewed in Chapter 2 shows that members of Congress in fact perceive negatively any evidence that enforcement is different in their own districts than in other areas. This arises because the national interest groups most active on matters of OSHA policy are concerned with enforcement throughout the country, and because individual members of Congress risk complaints from workers (firms) if enforcement in their own districts is less (more) strict than in other districts. Because of the interrelationship among local labor markets, enforcement has externalities that extend beyond individual districts and place competitive pressures on other geographic areas.

Nor has OSHA sought to allocate resources so as to respond to local demands for enforcement. In fact, OSHA's allocation of staff to regions and local offices is without regard for the receptivity of the area to vigorous enforcement. If OSHA were really trying to defuse opposition by cutting back on enforcement in hostile areas (or beefing it up in supportive ones), it would make much more sense to allocate additional inspectors to those areas where workers complain more frequently or cooperate with inspectors more often. OSHA has, however, explicitly avoided such a move. Similarly, my analysis of inspector productivity shows that in areas where inspectors have a harder time locating violations (in part because of lower levels of worker cooperation) the agency has not responded by becoming less aggressive, but instead simply conducts more inspections. If OSHA field personnel were being encouraged to pull back in these areas, one would expect the opposite effect.

Finally, in my interviews with senior OSHA regional officials, it also became clear that they view the inspection-forcing mechanism of worker complaints as a political liability, and not as a strength. (See also the earlier discussion of low- and high-complaint areas.) OSHA field offices have at times been overwhelmed with handling complaints that OSHA managers perceive as less important than conducting planned inspections.

At the same time, OSHA officials have been leery of ignoring these apparently weak (uninformative) complaints out of fear that subsequent events would reveal a hazard that OSHA should have reacted to. This fear had previously been realized in the 1975 "Kepone incident," in which a former employee complained about health hazards at a plant that manufactured Kepone, a dangerous pesticide, but OSHA did not initiate an inspection because it classified the complaint by a *former* employee as a matter of job discrimination. Subsequent events revealed widespread worker exposure and environmental damage. In reaction, OSHA enacted a policy of responding to nearly every type of complaint with an on-site inspection.

In 1996, OSHA adopted a policy of conducting "investigations" rather than on-site visits for complaints that did not meet the long set of requirements for a formal complaint inspection under the text of the OSH Act.[63] Under this policy, complaints that were signed, that involved a business with a poor compliance record, or that alleged a serious hazard, injury to workers, or imminent danger would continue to trigger on-site inspections, while other complaints would be handled by contacting the employer and requesting evidence that the alleged hazard had been abated. OSHA officials stressed to me that the complaining employee was told that the employer would be contacted if they did not sign the complaint and it did not meet the other criteria. They reported that many workers did not want a physical inspection, but just felt more comfortable talking to OSHA than to their boss directly about workplace hazards. ("Many of these are relatively minor hazards that workers just want taken care of, but they are afraid if they complain they'll look like trouble makers. This way, everyone is happy.") If OSHA received evidence that the hazard had been corrected (or did not exist), OSHA then randomly conducted follow-up inspections to verify compliance. If the employer did not respond, OSHA scheduled an inspection.

This policy allowed the agency to save substantial enforcement resources so that inspectors could spend more time conducting targeted inspections in high-hazard industries. Eight years later the Government Accountability Office endorsed the policy as allowing OSHA to conserve its scarce enforcement resources for the search for serious hazards.[64] (The policy also received bipartisan support in Congress and from labor and

---

[63] See OSHA Instruction CPL 2.115, published June 14, 1996.
[64] OSHA's Complaint Response Policies, June 2004, GAO-04-658.

business groups.) It also further confirms that OSHA's leaders sought to minimize the disruptions to their normal enforcement efforts caused by variability in worker behavior, rather than embracing strong local support for the agency by conducting widespread inspections where minimal hazards were alleged. (Furthermore, OSHA tested the policy in those high-complaint areas [Cleveland and Peoria] where agency officials felt most overwhelmed by complaints, despite the strong labor communities in those areas. See BNA *Occupational Safety and Health Daily*, February 1, 1995.)

8. Conclusion and Implications

Returning then to the question posed at the beginning of this section, what do these findings reveal about the broader contours of bureaucratic decision making? Most forcefully, they repudiate arguments that presume a direct linkage between local political concerns and bureaucratic decision making. OSHA constrains subordinate bureaucrats and demonstrates a stubborn consistency in seeking out those who violate the law. Local groups and elected officials are unable to affect how OSHA behaves in their localities (except through worker complaints). Congress affects the aggregate level of enforcement through its oversight of OSHA's budget and through the passage of laws limiting which businesses to inspect, but these are a far cry from strategic localism by an agency in response to the pressures of local interest groups or elected officials acting on their behalf.

These findings provide two lessons for political leaders responsible for the design and oversight of bureaucracies with field enforcement programs. First, geographically neutral bureaucrats may not be able to guarantee uniform compliance with the law if regulators must rely on cooperation from third parties to enforce the law. The evidence in this chapter shows that workers play a critical role during an OSHA inspection, and that workers vary in their willingness to cooperate with OSHA's inspectors. If uniform compliance is desired, there must be greater protections for the independent parties who determine the stringency of regulatory enforcement. Second, a unitary federal agency may, despite contentious national politics, develop and maintain a geographically neutral enforcement apparatus. While opponents of OSHA have, over the years, succeeded in reducing the agency's budget, overturning proposed rules, and conducting intensive investigations into agency procedures, OSHA has nonetheless developed and maintained a fair-minded and consistent field-enforcement staff.

Additional confirmation of this argument is provided by a limited examination of OSHA's informal process for negotiating penalty and citation reductions. Unfortunately, the agency does not accurately enter negotiated penalty and citations records into its inspection database.[65] Consequently, it is impossible to conduct a systematic analysis of these patterns. Nonetheless, this was a frequent topic in my interviews with local, regional, and national administrators. As a whole, OSHA faces a difficult problem in choosing whether or not to negotiate with employers following issuance of a citation. On the one hand, the agency can simply tell a business that it will "see it in court," when the formal contest of an OSHA citation is heard by the Review Commission. But cases with formal contests can take years to make their way through the many levels of review. Furthermore, OSHA officials must spend time defending their decisions in a formal contest. Finally, formal contests often result in reductions in imposed penalties, in part because of the general tendency of the Review Commission's administrative law judges (according to OSHA officials) to "split the difference" and reduce imposed penalties.

On the other hand, OSHA can negotiate with employers prior to a formal contest so as to avoid this uncertain route. Informal negotiations allow the agency to save resources that would otherwise be spent on litigation and also give the agency a sure, if smaller, win. Additionally, OSHA officials can often extract concessions from employers in return for offering reductions in penalties. Employers may agree, for instance, to implement a safety and health program or provide additional employee training to reduce their liability to OSHA.

But does this process allow local political concerns to shape enforcement outcomes? Across all of my interviews with OSHA's managers, every official denied the possibility that OSHA officials are concerned about the local ramifications of their decisions. Of course, OSHA does not delegate this authority to regular field inspectors. Rather, area office directors (and their assistants) are responsible for negotiating with employers. These officials repeatedly acknowledged that the administrative costs of formal contests lead them to seek quick resolution through informal settlements. They rejected the assertion that the perceived clout of any particular firm

---

[65] This point was made to me several times by OSHA officials, who claimed that computerized record-keeping of negotiated settlements was improving but still relatively inaccurate.

or the fear that a local interest group or elected official would complain about their behavior affected their bargaining. Insofar as businesses in one area of the country might be more likely to exercise their right to contest OSHA citations or were more recalcitrant in their dealings with the agency, however, variation in business behavior might translate into variation in negotiated outcomes.[66]

While OSHA's managers dismissed the direct concern for local political forces, they did acknowledge that national political factors might come into play in the resolution of informal contests. Specifically, they recognized that one single case in which OSHA was perceived as unnecessarily punitive *or* overly lenient could affect the agency's national political fortunes. In other words, agency officials again linked their local performance to the agency's national political fortunes. This is yet another example of OSHA's success in weakening the linkages between local political pressures and local officials' standing and success. Local OSHA officials simply have little to gain from making local businesses, groups, or elected officials happy. Far more important is how field decisions are perceived in Congress at large.

In sum, OSHA's process for negotiating penalty reductions is similar to the rest of the agency's field enforcement program in its limited consideration of local political concerns. Local politics matters, if at all, only as it affects the behavior of workers and employers who can choose how aggressively they participate in settlement negotiations. Agency-wide, OSHA has taken steps to mitigate local concerns. Nonetheless, the agency's efforts to avoid angering potential small business coalitions and their elected allies reflect the strategic decision making of OSHA's leadership. Rather than risk attacks from this coalition, OSHA has chosen to give these businesses a break. The agency has not, however, chosen to shape enforcement to accommodate local concerns.

---

[66] OSHA also provides opportunities for workers to participate in informal settlement negotiations, although OSHA officials stated that even union workers rarely bother to send a representative to participate in the face-to-face meetings between agency officials and cited employers. Rather, they stated, worker review is primarily an *ex post* phenomenon.

APPENDIX 3.1. OSHA INTERVIEW SELECTION AND PROCEDURE

From 1998 to 2000, I conducted interviews with approximately sixty OSHA officials across OSHA's national, regional, and local offices. Each subject was interviewed under the condition that no material would identify him or her by name (or by position, where that would reveal his or her identity). All interviews were conducted without a tape recorder. Individuals were also given the opportunity to speak "off the record" or without any attribution to their general position. In general, very few of the lower-level bureaucrats I interviewed seemed concerned about speaking openly. (Where possible, individuals were interviewed away from their supervisors, either outside the OSHA office or in private conference rooms.) Among the regional and national officials, however, subjects frequently made clear that they wished to be identified without reference to their specific programmatic or regional affiliation. In general, however, once these conditions were met, I detected almost no unwillingness to speak openly about working at OSHA or the political conflicts surrounding the agency.

To select individuals for interviews, I relied on several contacts at OSHA's headquarters to obtain permission to contact the local and regional offices. I then arranged interviews (where possible) with a selection of regional officials. (In several cases I also contacted former OSHA officials identified by those still with the agency.) I also contacted randomly selected area offices directly to arrange interviews with area office supervisors and a selection of field inspectors. (In most cases this also necessitated contacting the regional administrator to garner his or her approval.) Where possible, I requested a list of inspectors in the area office and asked to speak with a random selection of inspectors.

For both managers and field inspectors, the interviews were semistructured. I developed an evolving set of standard questions that I used to initiate the discussion, beginning with relatively apolitical matters of internal agency rules for implementing the OSH Act and then touching more directly on potentially controversial questions of politics and agency reform. For management officials, the topics covered in the interviews included management of subordinates and field operations, field office discretion, oversight of individual inspectors and cases, negotiation and litigation of contested citations, interactions with superiors in the regional and national offices, OSHA's reinvention initiative, and interactions with national politicians and interest groups.

Field inspectors were queried on many of the same management topics, although I generally began by asking them semitechnical questions about field operation to demonstrate my familiarity with OSHA's field operation procedures. Inspectors were also questioned about their general approach to enforcing the OSH Act (did they perceive their role as one of law enforcement, consultant, etc.), their interactions with individual firms and workers (did they distinguish between employers on the basis of commitment to safety, etc.), and their interactions with their superiors about appropriate field behavior.

4

Federal Oversight and State OSH Act Enforcement

The scope of federal regulation has increased dramatically during the last 100 years. Many of these national efforts involve the states in implementing federal policy. The EPA, for instance, relies heavily on the states to enforce both the Clean Water and Clean Air Acts. For many scholars, this arrangement is one benefit of the American system of federalism, in which power is not concentrated exclusively in the national government (Buchanan 1996). At the same time, other scholars are suspicious of state regulation, noting that states face pressures to reduce the level of regulation in order to attract businesses (Fesler 1949). In this scenario, a "race to the bottom" ensues, and the result is less regulation vis-à-vis unitary federal oversight.

Hybrid federal-state enforcement is perhaps an ideal solution to these trade-offs. States are free to pursue innovative policies or to provide extensive regulation, but the federal government ensures a minimum level of stringency and therefore prevents destructive interstate competition. Shared enforcement is a viable solution to the problem of state competition, however, only if state enforcement is as least as vigorous as its federal alternative. To achieve this end, federal agencies must either avoid delegating power to states that will subvert their statutory mandate or discipline state transgressions.

In the case studied here, the OSH Act allows states to replace OSHA in enforcing the law within their borders. The act also places a "floor" on state enforcement, however, by requiring that it be "at least as effective [as OSHA] in providing safe and healthful employment"[1] and by imposing

---

[1] OSH Act, section 18, subsection C, part 2.

additional procedural requirements. According to Noble (1986) and others, this state enforcement provision was nonetheless widely viewed as a "safety valve" that would transfer regulatory authority from OSHA to the states, where business has more influence. For instance, one steel lobbyist was quoted as saying, "Everyone knew that the state commissions were in bed with industry and everyone expected that the states would start up plans as soon as this passed" (Noble 1986: 97). This assertion raises interesting empirical and theoretical questions.

Foremost, does delegation lead to a loss of control? This question can be broken down into two parts. First, are the states that chose to enforce the law themselves (with OSHA's permission) the ones where business reasonably could anticipate less-aggressive regulation? Did only "low-demand" states try to assume enforcement authority, and did OSHA approve these delegations? Second, in practice, has state enforcement been less aggressive than federal enforcement? Does federal oversight constrain the ways in which state officials and interest groups can affect the tenor of state regulation?

This inquiry is particularly important because of the implications of weak state enforcement for the maintenance of OSHA's posture of "strategic neutrality." Up to now, this book has suggested that OSHA has taken steps to enforce the law without concern for local support for the agency. State delegation, however, if it allows some states to provide a less-regulated business environment, threatens to upset this delicate balance. Primarily, why should any business (or member of Congress) have to put up with overly aggressive federal regulation when their counterparts operating under a state program face lower costs? How state enforcement agencies have performed (in light of OSHA oversight) therefore has important consequences for OSHA's ability to claim in national political debates that it is not overly aggressive in enforcing the law. (Additionally, an examination of state enforcement provides another window into the imperative of agency leaders to seek to control and guide their subordinates.)

In answering these questions, the remainder of this chapter is divided into four sections. The first describes the statutory and historical foundations of state participation in enforcement of the OSH Act. Of critical import are the provisions of the OSH Act requiring state enforcement to be "at least as effective" as OSHA and the allowance of federal funding of up to 50 percent of state enforcement efforts. In light of these rules, the second section examines the state choice to participate in enforcing the OSH Act. On the one hand, if "low-demand" states are most likely to request authority to enforce the law, OSHA must carefully police state activity. On the other hand, if state performance is equivalent to federal enforcement, one explanation may be that OSHA successfully weeds out states that would be likely to provide lower levels of enforcement than OSHA. (In the language of principal-agent relationships, OSHA may have solved the problem of adverse selection, thereby obviating the need to police moral hazard.) The data presented here show that there are indeed systematic biases in the states implementing a state enforcement program, but that both "high-demand" and "low-demand" states are most likely to enforce the law.

The third section examines contemporary federal and state enforcement of the OSH Act in light of federal oversight. Comparing enforcement effort across regulatory agencies, however, is difficult. I develop a new set of measures of state enforcement effort. These measures are then used to describe interstate and temporal variation in enforcement. The noteworthy result here is that although state enforcement is occasionally inferior to OSHA's, it is often far better. This section also includes a more detailed review of the process of federal oversight and the ways in which states can seek to circumvent federal control.

Additionally, this section provides an in-depth review of state management efforts in one state where support for OSH Act enforcement should be strong, Washington, and in one where it should be weak, Virginia. Each state's experience demonstrates that, in shaping state enforcement efforts without incurring OSHA's wrath, manipulation of agency resources and internal management efforts are more important than statutory changes or overt political attacks on state enforcement agencies. The section concludes by demonstrating that, in most cases, OSHA has little to gain by revoking state delegation. Few states are such poor performers that stepping in with fewer but potentially more punitive federal inspectors would be worth the loss of state resources. Finally, the last section relates these findings to OSHA's efforts to pursue "strategically neutral" enforcement. By ensuring that, in most cases, state enforcement is as aggressive as federal enforcement, OSHA has mitigated one reason businesses might attack OSHA's field enforcement efforts as unduly onerous.

1. The Statutory and Historical Foundations of State Enforcement

The statutory foundations for state enforcement of the OSH Act are laid out in the OSH Act itself. Specifically, section 18 of the act provides that "Any State which ... desires to assume responsibility for development and enforcement therein of occupational safety and health standards ... shall submit a State plan."[2] OSHA "shall approve the plan"[3] if it

1. "provides for the development and enforcement of safety and health standards... [that will be] at least as effective in providing safe and healthful employment"[4] as OSHA's enforcement of these standards;

2. provides the state enforcement agency with sufficient statutory authority, including "a right of entry and inspection of all workplaces subject to the Act";[5]

3. "contains satisfactory assurances that such agency or agencies have or will have... qualified personnel necessary for... enforcement"[6] and "gives satisfactory assurances that such State will devote adequate funds to the administration and enforcement";[7] and

4. extends OSH Act protections to state and local employees.[8]

Once OSHA determines that an operating state plan meets these requirements, the agency is authorized to suspend concurrent federal enforcement in the state and grant the state final approval.[9] (Under OSHA rules, a state may also operate a "certified state plan" in which OSHA agrees to suspend enforcement but does not grant the agency final approval.) If, subsequent to this point, OSHA is made aware of state deficiencies, it "shall notify the state agency of [OSHA's] withdrawal of approval"[10] and resume federal enforcement. Significantly, OSHA is authorized to fund *up to* 50 percent of any state enforcement program. States wishing to assume enforcement authority must therefore commit substantial resources to enforcing the act in order to garner OSHA's approval.

During the Nixon and Ford administrations, forty-five states submitted state plan applications.[11] Ten state applications were rejected outright, and six states withdrew their applications prior to approval. Additionally,

---

[2] OSH Act, section 18, subsection B.
[3] OSH Act, section 18, subsection C.
[4] OSH Act, section 18, subsection C, part 2.
[5] OSH Act, section 18, subsection C, part 3.
[6] OSH Act, section 18, subsection C, part 4.
[7] OSH Act, section 18, subsection C, part 5.
[8] OSH Act, section 18, subsection C, part 6.
[9] OSH Act, section 18, subsection E. OSHA retains enforcement jurisdiction for federal establishments and certain maritime activities.
[10] OSH Act, section 18, subsection F.
[11] Only Kansas, Louisiana, Nebraska, Ohio, and South Dakota failed to submit an application to assume enforcement authority.

eight states voluntarily closed down approved programs. The remaining twenty-one states had private sector enforcement programs in place in 1981.[12] Today, the same twenty-one states have state programs in place. The great disparity between the forty-five applications and the twenty-one approved programs reflects the contentiousness of OSHA oversight and approval of state plans during the 1970s. The following section examines in greater detail conflict over the approval of particular state programs. Prior to turning to this subject, however, it is important to review one important historical episode from this period concerning state agency staffing levels.

After passage of the OSH Act, OSHA initially required states to submit state plans that specified staffing levels equal to OSHA's in order to satisfy the "at least as effective as" provision of the OSH Act.[13] In 1974, the AFL-CIO sued OSHA, arguing that the part of the OSH Act requiring the states to provide "qualified personnel necessary for... enforcement" imposed a higher burden on the states and that this section of the act was separable from the "at least as effective as" provision. In *AFL-CIO v. Marshall* (1978), the district court agreed. This decision led OSHA in 1980 to issue a series of staffing benchmarks that required the states to field many more inspectors than OSHA itself could provide. Most states did not meet these guidelines and consequently were ineligible for final approval of enforcement delegation. In the meantime, OSHA continued temporary delegation to states that could not meet the original benchmarks if they nonetheless provided substantial staff beyond what OSHA could commit to the area.[14]

The statutory foundation for state enforcement helps to illuminate the broader institutional framework in which battles over state enforcement are fought. States must apply to OSHA to assume enforcement authority, and the agency must accept state proposals that meet the extensive procedural rules laid out in the OSH Act (as interpreted by the courts and OSHA). OSHA is therefore a limited "veto player," with the ability

---

[12] New Jersey, New York, and Connecticut have state enforcement authority only for state and local employees and are not included in the twenty-one-state count.

[13] For a more extensive discussion, see Mintz 1984, Chapter 19.

[14] Over the next two decades, OSHA revised the benchmarks downward, although they still require the states to provide more inspectors than OSHA does in comparable areas. I interviewed one official who had been at OSHA when the initial "equal staffing" decision had been made, and he suggested that the equality constraint had been set at a time when many individuals anticipated that the agency's workforce would be more than twice its previous highest level. This implies that, at least at the time it was made, it was not seen as allowing the states to shirk their responsibilities.

to reject state programs and proposals that do not meet these statutory standards (Tsebelis 1995). The states also offer an important potential benefit to supporters of aggressive OSH Act enforcement: more extensive enforcement. For every dollar OSHA provides for state enforcement, the states are required to put forth at least one of their own. Of course, if state agencies are less punitive or otherwise poorly run, the states may still offer a "safety valve" for groups seeking to avoid aggressive federal enforcement. Which of these outcomes prevails depends on how OSHA interacts with and oversees state agencies.

2. The State Plan Approval Battle

Are the states that chose to share in enforcing the OSH Act somehow different from those that did not? More specifically, did the state enforcement provision of the act allow "low-demand" states to substitute less vigorous state enforcement for federal enforcement, as Noble and others allege? This section examines in greater detail the process by which states applied for and were granted initial OSHA approval of state plans. Contrary to earlier research, this inquiry shows that it was not just "low-demand" states that implemented state OSH Act programs. Instead, the pool of states with delegated OSH Act programs is a mix of states where (historically) support for OSHA was highest and lowest.

Previous analysts argue that states with weak unions and strong Republican parties should be more likely to implement state programs because these programs provide a safety valve for business (e.g., Thompson 1983; Thompson and Scicchitano 1985a and 1985b). These analysts, however, find little support for their argument. Thompson and Scicchitano report that states with strong Republican Parties were more likely to adopt state programs, but also show that there is no relationship between union strength and state participation. This finding is not surprising in light of existing research on delegation, which shows that delegation decisions depend on the likely behavior of subordinates to whom authority is delegated (e.g., Brehm and Gates 1997). In the OSH Act case, the simple assertion that delegation implies abdication to business ignores the fact that states vary considerably in their susceptibility to business influence. While business may have preferred state OSH Act programs to federal OSHA in states with weaker unions, unions may have preferred state enforcement in states where they were politically dominant. In these states, in fact, local OSH Act enforcement might have been seen as a threat to business, not labor.

More generally, while business and labor could probably predict the outcome of state enforcement in areas where either was dominant, delegation in contested states was less certain.[15] If unions and business groups (and state politicians acting on their behalf) were strategic, one would therefore expect that they would be most likely to pursue state enforcement programs when either business or unions were dominant. In the former case, states would apply because local enforcement would seem to promise less aggressive enforcement. In the latter case, however, states would apply because local enforcement would be more aggressive.[16]

In light of this prediction, I estimated a series of models to identify the factors affecting actual state adoption of a delegated OSH Act enforcement program. The dependent variable in this analysis, whether or not a state had a delegated private sector OSH Act enforcement program in place in 1981, was also used by Thompson and Scicchitano.[17] Results of the statistical estimation appear in Table 4.1.

The three models share four independent variables. The first is a measure of union strength, operationalized as the proportion of private sector workers in the state who belonged to a union in 1972.[18] The second is a measure of business strength in those industries most threatened by federal enforcement. It is calculated as the proportion of employees in the state who worked in manufacturing in 1977.[19] Manufacturing was chosen because OSHA's detailed safety and health standards have the greatest effect on these firms vis-à-vis, for instance, service industries and agriculture.

---

[15] Additionally, state enforcement was not free. Undertaking a state OSH Act program required a state to provide at least half of the funding for enforcement of the act within its borders. In light of this, business was likely to view the additional tax burden of state enforcement with skepticism if diminished enforcement was not certain.

[16] That unions were willing to pursue aggressive enforcement in states where they were strong relative to competing states suggests that union workers were more concerned about hazards in their own workplaces or competition from nonunion labor within their state than they were about competition from less-regulated employers in other states.

[17] One might be tempted to differentiate among whether a state (1) failed to submit a proposal, (2) was rebuffed by OSHA, or (3) voluntarily withdrew an approved plan. But the strategic nature of applications, withdrawals, and approvals suggests that these data are better considered in the aggregate. States that failed to apply might have anticipated being rebuffed or might have strategically chosen not to apply. Similarly, withdrawals could have been precipitated by state political concerns or the threat of more vigorous OSHA oversight of state operations. As a whole, whether a state plan was in place in 1981 best captures internal state dynamics in light of OSHA's evolving oversight of the states throughout the 1970s.

[18] This is the same measure employed by Thompson and Scicchitano.

[19] The year 1977 was chosen because 1972 data are not available.

TABLE 4.1. *Predicting state adoption of a delegated OSH Act program*

Variable	(1) Coefficient (Std. Error)	(2) Coefficient (Std. Error)	(3) Coefficient (Std. Error)
Union strength	12.71**	16.37***	17.09***
	(5.97)	(6.19)	(6.44)
Manufacturing sector size	9.97*	13.60***	14.54***
	(5.18)	(5.34)	(5.34)
Union strength * manufacturing sector size	−38.89**	−56.21***	−55.10***
	(19.66)	(20.45)	(20.41)
State and local government employment as share of all nonfederal state employment	24.45*	24.44*	40.21***
	(13.40)	(14.97)	(16.51)
Republican control of state government		2.54**	2.14
		(1.21)	(1.67)
South			−1.02
			(1.02)
Republican control of state government * South			8.30**
			(3.85)
Constant	−6.53**	−8.22***	−10.72***
	(2.91)	(3.15)	(3.47)
Chi squared	6.60	11.64**	20.59***
Log-likelihood	−30.226	−27.869	−24.721

Dependent variable is whether a state had a delegated OSHA program in 1981 (1 = yes, 0 = no). Functional form is probit. Number of observations is 50. *** denotes $p < .01$, ** denotes $p < .05$, * denotes $p < .10$. Robust standard errors.

Union strength from Bureau of Labor Statistics, Directory of National Unions and Employee Associations, 1975. Manufacturing sector size from Bureau of the Census, County Business Patterns data, 1977. State and Local government employment from Bureau of Economic Analysis, Regional Economic Accounts, 1972. Republican control from Bureau of the Census, Statistical Abstract of the United States. South denotes states of the Confederacy.

The third variable is an interaction between union strength and business strength. To reiterate, I argue that state adoption should be more likely in states with strong unions and a weak anti-OSHA business lobby, as well as in states with weak unions and a powerful anti-OSHA industry lobby. In the former case, this is because union strength and weak opposition presages more aggressive state enforcement; in the latter, it is because the threat of stringent federal regulation entices businesses in the state to seek a less aggressive state enforcement agency despite the costs.

The final common variable is a measure of state fiscal and administrative capacity. It is measured as state and local government employment as a proportion of all employment in the state in 1972. States with a larger public sector should have had an easier time shouldering the fiscal load of an additional program, should have been more likely to have state employee unions lobbying for a state enforcement agency to provide additional state jobs (and union members), and should have been more likely to have in place pre–OSH Act state occupational safety and health programs that would readily transform into formal OSH Act programs.

Additionally, the supplementary models incorporate three additional variables. The column (2) specification includes a measure of state Republican Party strength from 1970 to 1980.[20] This variable is used to test the assertion of previous analysts that Republican administrations were more likely to adopt state programs to replace aggressive federal enforcement. Because of the strong correlation during this period between party and region, the column (3) model adds an indicator variable for whether a state was in the South and an interaction between Republican Party strength and the South variable.

The dependent variable in this case is dichotomous. Consequently, a probit specification is used. For a model with only fifty cases, the results are impressive. In the column (1) specification, all four of the independent variables of interest and the constant receive statistically significant coefficients ($p < .10$). Both states with strong unions and weak business lobbies and states with strong business lobbies and weak unions are more likely to adopt state programs than states where unions and business are equally matched. (The magnitude of this effect will be discussed later.) With the inclusion of the measure of Republican strength, column (2) presents the same basic findings and suggests that Republican governments were more likely to adopt state programs.

The column (3) specification also confirms the core result about union and business strength, but it calls into question the assertion about the effect of Republican control. While the four original independent variables are highly significant, Republican control no longer has a statistically significant effect on state program adoption in any region except the South. There, states with Republican administrations were more likely to implement state programs than other states. Examining an electoral map from the period helps to explain the substance of this finding. Virginia and Tennessee both implemented state programs and were the most Republican of the "Old South" states during this period. Both were also weak

---

[20] This is calculated as the average across all years of the proportion of seats held by Republicans in the upper legislative chamber in the state (one-third), plus the proportion of seats held in the lower legislative chamber (one-third), plus whether the governor was a Republican (one-third). (Because of Nebraska's nonpartisan legislature, only the governor's party is used in that state.)

TABLE 4.2. *State adoption and predicted adoption of delegated enforcement program, sorted by predicted probability of adoption*

State	State Program?	Predicted Probability of Adoption[a]	State	State Program?	Predicted Probability of Adoption[a]
AR	No	0.019	ME	No	0.359
AL	No	0.029	CO	No	0.380
TX	No	0.041	ID	No	0.381
RI	No	0.046	CA	Yes	0.445
PA	No	0.057	NH	No	0.515
GA	No	0.069	KS	No	0.537
LA	No	0.074	DE	No	0.560
CT	No	0.108	NM	Yes	0.578
MA	No	0.114	IA	Yes	0.579
OH	No	0.117	OR	Yes	0.582
FL	No	0.139	NV	Yes	0.608
OK	No	0.152	UT	Yes	0.623
NJ	No	0.190	VT	Yes	0.628
NE	No	0.196	HI	Yes	0.649
IN	Yes	0.205	MT	No	0.658
MS	No	0.217	NY	No	0.678
ND	No	0.237	NC	Yes	0.704
KY	Yes	0.239	MO	No	0.718
IL	No	0.253	SC	Yes	0.726
MD	Yes	0.267	WV	No	0.787
MI	Yes	0.293	WY	Yes	0.876
WI	No	0.313	WA	Yes	0.927
SD	No	0.332	TN	Yes	0.975
MN	Yes	0.338	VA	Yes	0.990
AZ	Yes	0.341	AK	Yes	1.000

[a] Errors of prediction are shaded. Results of estimation reported in Table 4.1, column (3).

union states with relatively large manufacturing sectors. In other words, the importance of Republican government in predicting state programs is magnified in an environment in which business was already likely to press for state programs.[21] Predicted probabilities of state plan adoption for the column (3) estimates and actual adoptions are reported in Table 4.2. The

[21] I also estimated a model incorporating the interactions between union and business strength and Republican control of the government to test for strategic lobbying and conditional influence of this lobbying. If state programs were more threatening to unions when the Republican Party was dominant, they should have opposed state delegation more in states with stronger Republican parties. Likewise, business should have succeeded in pursuing state programs in favorable states when they were allied with supportive Republican administrations. However, neither interaction term is statistically significant

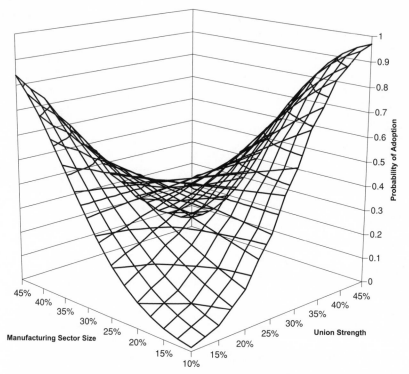

FIGURE 4.1. Predicted probability of state plan adoption for different levels of union and business strength. *Note:* Predicted probabilities are derived from column (3) specification reported in Table 4.1. See text for details.

model correctly predicts the status of thirty-six of the fifty states. This is a 24 percent reduction in error compared to simply choosing the dominant outcome (no state program).

Because the interaction between union strength and business advocacy is difficult to interpret directly from the coefficients reported in Table 4.1, Figure 4.1 displays the predicted probability of state plan adoption for the observed range of manufacturing business and union strength. (The other variables are held constant at their sample means.) Here, the strategic behavior of unions and business is easily observed. When unions are strong and manufacturers are weak (the right side of the figure), state adoption is almost certain. This is the case in Hawaii and Nevada. By contrast, when unions and business are both weak (the front center part

when included in the model. This may be a result of the small sample size. Alternatively, it may reflect Democratic dominance in the South or the fact that, outside of the South, states with strong unions tended to have moderate Republican governors.

of the figure), state adoption is predicted less than 2 percent of the time. This is the case in North and South Dakota, Florida, and New Mexico. (New Mexico is a prediction error.) Holding constant a weak anti-OSHA business coalition, increasing union strength makes state adoption more likely, in line with the earlier argument that in these cases unions anticipated being able to rely on state enforcement to provide greater protection than OSHA enforcement.

The opposite pattern appears when business is strong (the left side of the figure). In this case, increasing union strength decreases the probability of state plan adoption. With very weak unions, the probability of state adoption when business is strongest exceeds 80 percent (e.g., North and South Carolina), while with strong unions it is less than 5 percent (e.g., Ohio, Michigan, and Pennsylvania [Michigan is a prediction error]). This is also consistent with the earlier argument that unions and business are strategic in opposing state delegation. When the pressure for a state to "cheat" by implementing a less aggressive state enforcement program is highest, union strength is important for preventing state adoption of an OSHA program. (In these cases, a powerful business lobby might also feel that the risk of a state program dominated by unions is too great and opt for a "sure thing" in federal enforcement.)

In the aggregate, state adoption is likely both in states where enforcement is likely to surpass OSHA's and where (in the absence of effective federal oversight) it is likely to be less stringent than OSHA's. In the latter case, when unions are weak and the anti-OSHA manufacturing lobby is strong, OSHA must contend with state agencies that are likely to face pressures to reduce the stringency of state enforcement. Why did OSHA approve these state proposals in the first place, knowing they might constitute a threat to uniform nationwide enforcement?

Most significantly, OSHA had little choice about whether or not to approve state proposals that met the procedural obligations of the OSH Act. Initial approval only required a state to submit an application that detailed forthcoming lawmaking and implementation plans. Once a plan meeting these requirements was in place, OSHA had little discretion to reject the application.[22] For this reason, lobbying by business and union groups in the states was critically important. Groups that could influence whether a credible application was submitted and implemented were able

---

[22] That is not to suggest that this was merely a cursory review. Many state applications were rejected or revised because of OSHA concerns about insufficient statutory authority, procedures for review of contested citations, and administrative sufficiency. Rather, my point is that initial approval concerned the plan in the abstract rather than the plan as implemented.

to alter the pool of plans available for OSHA review. Of course, this largely procedural review of submitted state plans simply enhanced the importance of subsequent federal monitoring of state implementation efforts, the topic of the following section.

3. Federal Oversight and State Management

The previous section suggested that some states that were inclined to offer less aggressive enforcement than OSHA-implemented state programs. Did OSHA fulfill its mandate to ensure that these state programs were "at least as effective as" its own? What explains how OSHA responds to (real or apparent) weaknesses in state enforcement? Comparing how state agencies enforce the OSH Act, relative to one another and to OSHA, requires a common metric of agency performance. Section 3.1 presents several measures of agency performance and uses these measures to evaluate state performance. Section 3.2 examines the particular tools of federal oversight and of state management efforts to shape enforcement without evoking a federal response. Section 3.3 then explores OSHA's central dilemma in the oversight of state enforcement: when to "pull the plug" on state enforcement programs that lag behind OSHA's. Because of the relatively high level of state performance and the fact that OSHA can recoup, at most, 50 percent of state enforcement spending, this analysis shows that even though OSHA has a desire to ensure aggressive state enforcement, it is rarely in OSHA's interest to revoke state delegation.

3.1. *State Enforcement Vigor*

Previous attempts to quantify OSHA Act enforcement by the states have relied on a variety of measures of enforcement behavior. Analysts have used (1) the number of inspectors that agencies employ (relative to the size of the regulated community), (2) the number of inspections agencies conduct, and (3) the average penalty (or number of citations) assessed per inspection (see Scholz and Wei 1986; Thompson 1983; Thompson and Scicchitano 1985a and 1985b). These measures may misrepresent the effectiveness of state programs, however, because they do not account for the dynamic nature of compliance or the full complexity of the regulatory process.

For instance, some agencies may issue many citations per inspection, but this apparent punitiveness may indicate either an aggressive agency or one so woefully understaffed that noncompliance is ubiquitous. Overall, because assessed citations and violations reveal little about latent noncompliance (see Chapter 3), using them alone to measure agency punitiveness is suspect. Similarly, the number of inspectors that an agency employs does not reveal how these inspectors go about their jobs. While some inspectors are well trained and aggressive, others may be ill-prepared and lax. Furthermore, agencies may vary substantially in the types of businesses they oversee. Consequently, aggregate or per-inspection variation in inspection outputs may simply reflect variation in the industrial mix of different states.

Chapter 3 used facility-level information about workplace safety and health to estimate actual levels of noncompliance in different workplaces. Unfortunately, no comparative compliance data exists for state-regulated facilities. Furthermore, because the states (unlike OSHA's regions) vary considerably in their staffing levels relative to the size of the regulated community, even observed injury and illness rates may reflect the deterrent effect of larger and better-funded agencies rather than natural variation in compliance.

For the purposes of the comparative inquiry here, an ideal measure of agency enforcement effort would instead identify the actual deterrent effect of different enforcement programs. In other words, this type of measure would allow one to estimate the likely cost to a regulated party of violating the law and the resulting level of noncompliance. The core assumption of this measure is that deterrence is a function of the probability that noncompliance is detected and the degree of punishment conditional on detection.[23] Here I calculate a single estimate of an agency's deterrent effect by combining information about the size of the regulated community, agency resources, and the use of these resources into a single statistic summarizing how aggressively an agency enforces the law. This measure is then used to compare the performance of state OSHA agencies to one another and to OSHA. Effectively, this statistic provides an outside analyst with a standardized measure of enforcement vigor, capturing the expected number of violations a noncompliant business in any locality might face in any given period. The measure is derived from two components: a measure of relative agency resources and a measure of inspector stringency.

3.1.1. AGENCY RESOURCES. Agency resources are measured as the size of a state's (or OSHA's) inspection workforce relative to the size of the regulated community. The inspection workforce is a count derived from

[23] See Chapter 2, appendix 2.2, for a review of research supporting this assumption. This assumption will be discussed in greater detail later.

OSHA's Integrated Management Information System (IMIS) database of state and federal activities and identifies, on a monthly basis, inspectors who are actually active in the field.[24] This measure relies on active inspectors rather than reported staffing because inspectors are often detailed to management positions while still classified, for accounting purposes, as inspectors. In addition, an inability or unwillingness to fill authorized positions in the states makes annual reports of active inspectors and authorized slots unreliable measures of actual enforcement resources.[25]

The size of the regulated community is calculated as the number of private sector businesses in the geographic area overseen by the agency in 1993.[26] This figure is highly correlated with the number of private sector workers.[27] The number of private sector businesses was chosen because OSHA and the states regulate businesses rather than employees. The final standardized measure of agency resources is 10,000 multiplied by the number of active inspectors divided by the number of private sector businesses. Higher scores indicate more inspectors per regulated business. This standardized measure is reported in Table 4.3 for each enforcement agency from 1990 to 1996. Notice that almost every state enforcement agency had, relative to the number of businesses in the state, more resources than OSHA. The only exceptions were California in 1990, North Carolina in 1990–91, and New Mexico in 1990–92.

Table 4.3 also demonstrates that most of these agencies had relatively stable resource levels during this period. The most notable exception is North Carolina, one of the worst-staffed agencies in 1990. By 1996, it was better staffed than all but three other agencies. Part of the explanation for this turnaround is the 1991 fire at a poultry processing plant in Hamlet,

---

[24] An inspector is coded as active if he or she conducts two or more inspections in any given month, and is coded as half-active (.5) if he or she conducted one inspection. In the OSHA case, inspectors in area offices located in states with their own enforcement programs were excluded because these inspectors primarily oversee state enforcement efforts or conduct inspections of maritime activities and federal facilities. Inspectors active outside the fifty states and the District of Columbia were also excluded. I experimented with different cut-offs for labeling inspectors active. Doing so does not alter the basic results presented here.

[25] Source: author interview.

[26] I use the term "business," although the County Business Patterns data is actually a count of facilities. A business can have multiple facilities – e.g., a plant in county X and a plant in county Y. These data do not account for state and local government employment (regulated only by delegated states) or federal employment and maritime activity (regulated only by OSHA).

[27] The bivariate correlation between the number of private sector workers and the number of private sector businesses in a state is .9999 ($p = .0001$).

TABLE 4.3. *Agency resources by year*

Agency	1990	1991	1992	1993	1994	1995	1996	Average
OSHA	1.62	1.64	1.66	1.64	1.62	1.31	1.28	1.54
AK	6.33	8.91	7.97	6.53	5.37	5.64	3.52	6.32
AZ	1.86	1.98	1.97	1.67	1.91	1.61	1.61	1.80
CA	1.17	2.43	2.14	1.97	2.17	2.25	2.01	2.02
HI	6.83	5.51	6.27	4.02	4.38	5.15	3.94	5.16
IA	2.39	2.34	2.18	2.13	1.96	1.65	1.79	2.06
IN	2.75	2.81	3.54	3.35	3.12	2.79	2.94	3.04
KY	2.89	3.19	2.72	2.61	2.68	2.92	3.15	2.88
MD	3.45	3.17	2.78	2.84	2.65	2.99	2.95	2.97
MI	2.92	3.33	2.97	3.07	2.89	2.88	2.84	2.98
MN	3.06	2.92	2.71	2.69	2.80	2.65	2.48	2.76
NC	1.46	1.23	1.89	2.56	3.52	3.94	4.47	2.72
NM	1.36	1.43	1.64	1.91	1.81	1.98	1.88	1.72
NV	5.16	4.69	4.59	4.16	4.79	4.58	5.23	4.74
OR	5.43	7.21	7.66	7.54	7.14	6.95	7.10	7.00
SC	2.50	2.38	1.94	2.11	2.10	1.98	2.00	2.14
TN	2.96	2.73	2.53	2.66	2.73	2.82	2.81	2.75
UT	2.53	2.39	3.10	3.03	3.28	3.26	3.06	2.95
VA	2.33	2.24	2.54	2.76	2.67	2.43	2.20	2.45
VT	3.95	4.13	3.47	3.58	4.07	3.78	3.14	3.73
WA	5.74	5.96	6.08	5.20	4.90	5.56	5.82	5.61
WY	4.10	4.28	3.18	3.56	3.10	3.56	2.79	3.51

Table entries are calculated as 10,000 * the number of active inspectors divided by the number of private sector businesses overseen. Shaded entries are agencies that, in a given year, had fewer resources than OSHA.

North Carolina, in which twenty-five people died (Smothers 1991). Later investigation revealed that the exit doors at the plant had been chained shut and that North Carolina's state OSHA had not inspected the facility in several years. Subsequently, the AFL-CIO filed a petition with OSHA to force the agency to revoke the state's enforcement delegation.[28] North Carolina responded by reforming its enforcement agency and infusing it with additional resources. California's resource level increased sharply after 1990 as the state resumed enforcement authority from OSHA. OSHA took over enforcing the law in California from 1988 to 1991 after California's governor used his line-item veto power to remove all funding for OSH Act enforcement from the state's budget.

[28] 56 CFR 49444, September 30, 1991: "Notice of Petition to Withdraw Approval of North Carolina State Plan."

Hawaii declined from being the state with the highest level of resources, with around 7 inspectors per 10,000 businesses in 1990, to around 4 in 1996. This decrease, while substantial in absolute terms, still left the state with well-above-average staffing levels. Finally, Iowa's staffing declined and New Mexico's grew. Both states are relatively poorly staffed, and both are small agencies overseeing relatively small industrial bases. In part, this variation may simply show how smaller state agencies are more likely to display larger apparent resource fluctuations because the loss of a single inspector (to retirement, promotion, the private sector, etc.) will have a bigger proportional effect on relative agency resources while that position remains unfilled.

3.1.2. AGENCY STRINGENCY. The second component of the aggregate enforcement effort measure is agency stringency. Stringency is a measure of the punishment that is likely to arise from an enforcement inspection. It is measured as the standardized number of serious violations issued following an inspection.

Any measure of stringency will be inaccurate if it does not take into account the characteristics of the businesses inspected, worker behavior, and the type of inspection performed. In this case, therefore, enforcement outputs (serious violations) are modeled as a function of a vector of independent variables including the number of employees covered by the inspection (and that number squared), whether or not the workforce was unionized, whether workers exercised their right to participate in the inspection, and what type of business the facility was engaged in.[29] As in Chapter 3, my analysis is restricted to planned safety inspections of manufacturing facilities in order to overcome the limitations caused by nonrandom worker complaints, the distinction between safety and health violations, innate differences in the dangerousness of different industries, and the differing incentives to issue citations or penalties following public sector inspections. Agency stringency was then measured through the inclusion of a vector of indicator variables for each agency-year combination in the dataset. An inspection was coded 1 for the appropriate indicator variable (e.g., OSHA 1994 or Michigan 1996) and 0 for the remainder of the categories (Wyoming 1996 is the excluded category).

---

[29] There are substantial differences in business practices that should affect the innate dangerousness of different workplaces even within the manufacturing sector. Consequently, I analyzed inspection outcomes in 139 different 3-digit Standard Industrial Classification (SIC) codes for which there was substantial inspection coverage across states and included indicator variables for each of these categories.

TABLE 4.4. *Predicting agency stringency – serious violations*

Variable	(1) Without Agency-Year Variables: Coefficient (Std. Error)	(2) With Agency-Year Variables: Coefficient (Std. Error)
Number of employees/1,000	18.164** (25.557)	10.197** (15.459)
Number of employees squared/1,000,000	−118.765** (18.997)	−59.671** (10.389)
Employee participation in inspection	0.102** (5.287)	0.021 (1.175)
Union workplace	−0.124** (7.760)	0.020 (1.277)
138 3-digit SIC industrial categories	Rejected all zero with chi squared (138) = 4,562.46; $p < .0000$	Rejected all zero with chi squared (138) = 2,517.00; $p < .0000$
153 agency-year dummy variables	Not included	Rejected all zero with chi squared (153) = 11,695.90; $p < .0000$
Constant	−0.363** (16.227)	0.309 (0.970)
N	48,513	48,513

Dependent variable is the number of serious, willful, and repeat violations. Functional form is negative-binomial regression. Robust standard errors in parentheses. *** denotes $p < .01$, ** denotes $p < .05$, * denotes $p < .10$.

Results from the model predicting the number of serious violations issued following an inspection appear in Table 4.4. The column (1) model excludes the agency-year indicator variables. The model as a whole is statistically significant, and the hypothesis that industrial category has no effect on enforcement outcomes is easily rejected. The column (2) specification is estimated with the inclusion of agency-year indicator variables. Of the 153 agency-year indicator variables, 105 are significant at the $p < .10$ or better level. One can also handily reject the hypothesis that all of the agency-year coefficients are simultaneously zero.

Violation stringency scores for each agency and year are reported in Table 4.5. These figures are derived from the results reported in Table 4.4 and are calculated by assuming that all inspections took place in a nonunion private sector manufacturing business with twenty-five employees in which workers did not participate in the inspection.[30] Before

---

[30] Table entries calculated for the modal 3-digit SIC category 201. Note that since these scores are derived in a regression framework, they have associated degrees of imprecision (not shown here).

TABLE 4.5. *Agency stringency (violations) by year*

Agency	1990	1991	1992	1993	1994	1995	1996	Average
OSHA	2.78	2.38	2.43	2.50	2.57	1.49	1.54	2.24
AK	0.47	0.75	0.81	1.48	1.87	1.09	1.40	1.12
AZ	0.59	0.59	0.52	0.36	1.52	0.74	0.62	0.71
CA	0.07	0.15	0.34	0.29	0.83	1.48	1.49	0.67
HI	0.16	0.42	0.98	0.79	1.02	1.43	0.57	0.77
IA	1.12	3.07	3.36	2.53	1.59	1.86	1.04	2.08
IN	1.23	2.24	1.86	1.47	1.63	1.58	1.34	1.62
KY	0.59	0.68	0.91	0.69	0.73	0.48	0.46	0.65
MD	0.72	1.16	1.90	1.46	1.88	1.49	0.85	1.35
MI	0.90	0.89	2.44	2.87	2.75	2.21	2.05	2.02
MN	0.54	0.60	0.52	0.77	1.48	2.52	1.92	1.19
NC	1.26	0.98	1.66	1.63	1.50	1.84	1.48	1.48
NM	0.83	2.69	1.91	1.07	0.79	0.31	0.26	1.12
NV	0.40	0.25	0.53	1.00	1.57	0.60	0.25	0.66
OR	0.80	0.82	1.09	0.94	0.99	0.92	0.74	0.90
SC	1.57	1.66	2.27	2.15	2.41	1.59	1.57	1.89
TN	0.27	0.43	0.59	0.76	0.90	1.04	0.66	0.66
UT	0.10	0.44	0.43	0.42	0.65	0.55	0.26	0.41
VA	1.52	2.02	2.30	2.57	2.07	1.37	1.62	1.92
VT	1.24	1.37	1.03	1.20	0.89	0.98	0.89	1.09
WA	0.39	0.56	0.64	0.53	0.50	0.53	0.49	0.52
WY	0.05	0.21	0.29	1.57	1.37	1.10	1.69	0.90

Table entries are calculated as predicted number of violations per inspection. See text for details. Shaded entries are agencies that, in a given year, were *more* stringent than OSHA.

proceeding further, it is important to reiterate an earlier point about the interpretation of these numbers. A high stringency score does not necessarily indicate an effective agency, nor does a low score indicate a weak one. This is because the observed stringency score reflects both agency punitiveness *and* underlying levels of noncompliance. Despite this caveat, the contrast with Table 4.3 is stunning. In all but 19 of the 147 cases, OSHA is more likely than a state agency to issue citations following an inspection. Overall, OSHA enforcement on a per-inspection basis is more stringent than state enforcement almost 90 percent of the time.

3.1.3. OVERALL AGENCY ENFORCEMENT VIGOR. With separate estimates of resources and stringency in hand, calculating each agency's overall enforcement vigor is straightforward. Table 4.6 displays one overall measure of enforcement vigor for each agency for each year from 1990 to 1996. Each entry is calculated by multiplying the appropriate resources score by the stringency score. Individual table entries are best understood

TABLE 4.6. *Overall agency enforcement vigor (violations)*

Agency	Violations							Average
	1990	1991	1992	1993	1994	1995	1996	
OSHA	4.49	3.89	4.03	4.08	4.17	1.96	1.97	3.51
AK	2.95	6.65	6.42	9.64	10.04	6.17	4.93	6.69
AZ	1.10	1.16	1.01	0.60	2.91	1.19	1.00	1.28
CA	0.08	0.37	0.73	0.58	1.80	3.32	3.00	1.41
HI	1.06	2.31	6.15	3.18	4.49	7.39	2.25	3.83
IA	2.68	7.18	7.31	5.39	3.11	3.07	1.86	4.37
IN	3.39	6.29	6.59	4.93	5.07	4.40	3.94	4.94
KY	1.71	2.18	2.47	1.80	1.95	1.39	1.45	1.85
MD	2.50	3.67	5.30	4.15	4.98	4.46	2.51	3.94
MI	2.63	2.97	7.24	8.80	7.96	6.36	5.82	5.97
MN	1.66	1.74	1.40	2.07	4.16	6.67	4.75	3.21
NC	1.83	1.21	3.15	4.17	5.30	7.25	6.61	4.22
NM	1.13	3.84	3.14	2.04	1.43	0.62	0.49	1.81
NV	2.04	1.15	2.41	4.18	7.53	2.74	1.30	3.05
OR	4.36	5.88	8.34	7.06	7.08	6.39	5.24	6.34
SC	3.93	3.95	4.41	4.53	5.06	3.13	3.13	4.02
TN	0.80	1.17	1.49	201	2.47	2.94	1.85	1.82
UT	0.25	1.05	1.32	1.27	2.14	1.78	0.79	1.23
VA	3.54	4.53	5.85	7.10	5.53	3.32	3.56	4.78
VT	4.90	5.67	3.57	4.31	3.64	3.71	2.81	4.09
WA	2.25	3.33	3.87	2.76	2.45	2.93	2.85	2.92
WY	0.20	0.89	0.93	5.57	4.24	3.91	4.73	2.92

Table entries are calculated by multiplying resources * stringency (violations). Shaded entries are agencies that, in a given year, had less enforcement effort than OSHA. Shaded and reversed entries had less than 50 percent of the enforcement vigor of OSHA in that year.

as representing the expected number of serious violations that a business in that state (or, in the OSHA case, in all of the states that OSHA oversees) is likely to have imposed upon it in a year scaled upward by a factor of about 100.[31] Shaded entries are state agencies that were less vigorous in enforcing the law than OSHA was in that year. Reversed entries are agencies that were less than 50 percent as vigorous as OSHA in that year. To reiterate, it is more important to pay attention to the relative scores than to the absolute scores, because the absolute scores are calculated after making assumptions about the types of businesses that each agency inspects.

[31] The appropriative scaling factor is 100 because the raw resources score is multiplied by 10,000 and because the average inspector conducts about 100 inspections in a given year: 10,000/100 = 100.

Note the decline in OSHA enforcement vigor during the period studied, from about 4.5 in 1990 to 2.0 in 1996 (a 56 percent decrease). OSHA's resources decreased by about 21 percent in these six years (see Chapter 3 for more about this pattern), while the agency's stringency diminished by a more substantial 44 percent. Part of this decrease in observed stringency is due to the revision of the OSH Act's penalty structure in late 1990, which increased the penalties that OSHA could assess per violation. Under the 1990 law, maximum penalties for willful and repeat violations increased from $10,000 to $70,000, and maximum penalties for other violations increased from $1,000 to $7,000. According to OSHA officials, this gradually led the agency to reduce the number of violations it issued while increasing assessed penalties per violation. Prior to this time, agency officials had encouraged the issuance of many violations to allow the agency to impose substantial penalties.[32]

A closer examination of the penalties accompanying citations confirms this claim. Table 4.7 displays agency enforcement vigor scores for all agencies adjusted for the size of assessed penalties and average inspector productivity. Table entries are calculated by multiplying the appropriate Table 4.6 score by the observed per-violation penalty assessed by the agency in that year (after accounting for differences in the size of the businesses that different agencies inspected) and a standardized measure of the number of inspections that agency personnel conducted.[33] In support of OSHA's claim about penalties, OSHA's standardized enforcement vigor score adjusted for penalties and productivity (Table 4.7) was nearly the same in 1996 as in 1990.

If deterrence is a function of the probability of being inspected multiplied by the conditional likelihood of being penalized, agencies with similar enforcement vigor scores will produce the same amount of deterrence. In other words, agencies can have a similar deterrent effect by inspecting frequently or by issuing many violations conditional on inspection. For 1995, Figure 4.2 displays each agency's resources and stringency score and additional data. The dashed curves indicate constant

---

[32] For instance, by issuing a separate violation for each employee exposed to a given hazard. Further supporting this characterization, while the average number of violations per inspection declined, the average penalty per inspection was nearly unchanged.

[33] Regression analysis confirms that penalties are strongly affected by business size. The per-inspection penalty figure is therefore divided by the number of employees and then multiplied by twenty-five. Per-inspection penalties are calculated using the same data used for the Table 4.4 estimates. The estimation of agency productivity is identical to that reported in Chapter 3 for federal OSHA officials, except that it excludes violations as a predictor of productivity, since violations are already measured directly here.

TABLE 4.7. *Overall agency enforcement vigor, adjusted for penalties and agency productivity*

| Agency | Violations*Penalty*Productivity | | | | | | | Average |
	1990	1991	1992	1993	1994	1995	1996	
OSHA	1,239	2,015	2,359	2,499	2,761	1,069	1,291	1,891
AK	1,346	3,846	5,574	11,012	6,454	7,584	3,902	5,674
AZ	517	1,205	2,565	7,883	9,463	1,220	762	3,374
CA	5	345	3,474	2,957	8,964	11,929	10,450	5,446
HI	215	458	8,987	1,982	6,444	5,712	2,712	3,787
IA	402	2,079	7,457	1,885	932	1,017	460	2,033
IN	788	2,970	4,320	2,634	3,075	2,187	1,860	2,548
KY	391	694	894	1,034	1,076	1,680	1,515	1,040
MD	1,132	1,802	2,746	2,584	3,025	3,443	2,008	2,391
MI	1,862	2,253	5,454	5,019	7,174	4,840	3,293	4,271
MN	554	739	963	1,512	2,278	2,043	2,016	1,444
NC	758	1,370	2,156	2,077	8,603	6,398	3,916	3,611
NM	145	3,887	1,114	690	843	506	339	1,075
NV	5,110	1,005	14,978	4,416	314,434	11,155	5,840	50,991
OR	7,114	7,927	9,682	10,334	8,964	7,649	6,677	8,335
SC	5,347	5,279	16,983	4,927	3,391	6,262	6,617	6,972
TN	263	586	403	549	884	956	816	637
UT	133	2,932	1,963	3,092	6,135	4,994	2,515	3,109
VA	773	1,295	2,753	3,649	2,410	1,440	1,328	1,949
VT	1,360	2,215	2,060	1,274	1,604	1,229	860	1,515
WA	2,673	4,095	6,050	3,472	3,175	5,138	4,757	4,194
WY	25	560	508	2,647	1,498	1,317	1,926	1,212

Table entries are calculated by multiplying Table 4.6 entries by expected standardized penalty and agency productivity scale. See text for details. Shaded entries are agencies that, in a given year, had less enforcement effort than OSHA. Shaded and reversed entries had less than 50 percent of the enforcement vigor of OSHA in that year.

resources*stringency scores of (from top to bottom) 3, 2, and 1. Agencies that lie on the same curve have, roughly, the same deterrent effect. (As a reminder, resources*stringency scores are also reported directly in Table 4.6.)

An additional assumption of this measure of an agency's deterrent effect is that noncompliance is relatively static in response to relatively static agency enforcement efforts. For this reason, agencies that have experienced large increases (decreases) in resources will end up inspecting businesses with higher (lower) levels of noncompliance than if they had static resource levels. Over time, businesses will probably adapt to an agency's new enforcement posture, but in the short run, compliance will

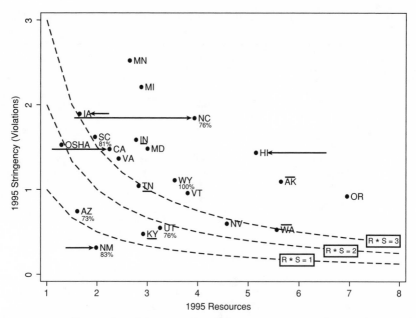

FIGURE 4.2. Inspector stringency and agency resources, 1995. *Note:* Horizontal lines indicate 1990 resources for agencies with large changes, 1990–95. Dashed lines indicate resources*stringency equal to 1, 2, and 3. Percentages indicate staff turnover, 1990–95, for agencies with turnover greater than 70 percent. Overbars indicate agencies with inspector salaries greater than 75 percent of private sector salaries. Underbars indicate agencies with inspector salaries less than 50 percent of private sector salaries.

be affected by previous enforcement efforts.[34] For this reason, Figure 4.2 also includes horizontal lines demarking 1990 resource levels for agencies with substantial changes during the period 1990–95.

With these additional data in hand, Figure 4.2 allows for a direct comparison of agency enforcement vigor. Two patterns are apparent. First, in 1995, seventeen of the twenty-one state agencies have a more vigorous enforcement program than OSHA's (OSHA lies just below the resources*stringency = 2 line). Those agencies lying farthest to the upper right in the figure are the most vigorous relative to OSHA, including Minnesota, Michigan, Hawaii, Alaska, and Oregon. North Carolina is also substantially more vigorous, but it experienced a sharp increase in resources relative to 1990 that may explain a (temporarily) high level of

[34] See Chapter 2, appendix 2.2, for evidence on the lag between enforcement and changes in workplace injury rates.

apparent stringency, because business noncompliance would be likely to lag behind the equilibrium level for the newly invigorated agency.

Second, not all agencies are as vigorous as OSHA. New Mexico is nearly 70 percent less vigorous than OSHA. This state both has a low stringency score and is relatively poorly staffed (like OSHA). Arizona is also a poor performer with a low stringency score. Utah and Kentucky have higher resource levels than OSHA, but make up for this with much lower levels of per-inspection stringency. In both of these agencies, however, the infrequent issuance of serious violations is largely made up for by greater agency productivity and the magnitude of penalties assessed in conjunction with these violations. After accounting for these factors, as in the Table 4.7 estimates, Nevada and Utah appear substantially more vigorous than OSHA, while Kentucky is only marginally less vigorous than OSHA. (Note also that New Mexico still fares poorly relative to OSHA. Additionally, Tennessee and Iowa appear less vigorous than OSHA, although by smaller amounts.) Overall, only New Mexico is a poor performer on both measures of agency enforcement vigor.

Averaging across all six years, the states that are less vigorous than OSHA on the Table 4.7 measure, which accounts for both relative penalties and agency productivity, are an interesting mix. On the one hand, New Mexico and Wyoming are among the least industrial states in the nation, ranking forty-sixth and forty-ninth, respectively, in the proportion of state workforce engaged in manufacturing. In these states, the apparent low ranking probably reflects the roughness of the measure of staffing, which does not account for the danger of local workplaces. On the other hand, Kentucky, Minnesota, Tennessee, and Utah are more industrial states where weaker enforcement is perhaps more threatening to OSHA's national standing.

Part of the reason these states may appear inferior to OSHA is that the measure of overall enforcement vigor reported here assumes that penalties and probability of detection are perfect substitutes. That is, enforcement vigor is calculated as the probability of inspection (resources) multiplied by the expected penalty (violations per inspection), so that an agency can inspect half as frequently but twice as punitively and achieve the same amount of deterrence. There is evidence, however, that businesses heavily discount future costs relative to current ones (see Chapter 2, appendix 2.3). In this case, frequency of inspection would matter far more than the prospect of a more punitive (but much delayed) future inspection. Similarly, in behavioral models of compliance, inspections with penalties are shown to have a temporary effect on compliance, so that the frequency of inspection matters far more than the degree of punitiveness (e.g., Gray and Scholz 1993; see also appendix 2.2). For this reason, the vigor scores reported in Tables 4.6 and 4.7 probably understate substantially the deterrent effect of the better-staffed state inspection programs.[35]

Finally, reviewing Tables 4.6 and 4.7 across all years reveals the relative variability of state enforcement. Across the seven-year period, all the states but Tennessee have larger standard deviations in resources than OSHA, while six have bigger shifts in stringency (California, Iowa, Michigan, Minnesota, New Mexico, and Wyoming). Also, in fourteen of the twenty-one states, the standard deviation of the overall enforcement vigor score is greater than OSHA's. In addition to this raw variability, it is also clear that the states are performing better, relative to OSHA, in the later part of this period than in the beginning. In part, this is due to a decline in OSHA's observed enforcement vigor in 1995 and 1996 (although this drop does not appear in the penalty- and productivity-adjusted estimates). It is also due, however, to an overall increase in the vigor of state enforcement. From 1990 to 1996, only one state, Vermont, experienced a drop in both Table 4.6 and Table 4.7 measures of agency vigor. In other words, all but one of the states increased the overall vigorousness of their enforcement programs during the period studied.

3.2. *The Tools of Federal Oversight*

So far, this section has shown that the vigor of state enforcement occasionally falls below OSHA's. The discussion has neglected, however, the details of federal oversight and state management. Specifically, it has not examined the tools federal regulators have available to monitor and pressure state officials or the ways in which state officials can (try to) subvert federal oversight. This section rectifies this deficiency and includes a more detailed examination of management practices and changes over time in two states with delegated enforcement programs, Washington and Virginia.

OSHA's monitoring of state programs takes three forms. First, OSHA requires states to abide by the procedural rules specified in the OSH Act

---

[35] For example, under the simple assumption that deterrence is affected by the product of resources squared and expected stringency, only New Mexico and Arizona are less vigorous than OSHA. Similarly, the states look even better if one estimates a model in which the measure of stringency is whether *any* violation is issued, which previous analysts have shown is sufficient to cause employers to devote attention to worker safety (e.g., Gray and Scholz 1993).

concerning program sufficiency. Second, the agency requires states to meet the staffing benchmarks, discussed earlier, in order to be granted final program approval. Third, OSHA reviews actual state enforcement practices. OSHA conducts accompanied inspections with state officials, examines selections of state case files, collects complaints about state enforcement, and uses computerized reports of agency activities to monitor state actions. OSHA's use of computerized reports, officially labeled the Computerized State Plan Activities Measures (C-SPAM), is significant because it provides OSHA with monthly updates on state activities.

A C-SPAM report is generated from data entered into OSHA's IMIS database and provides comparisons between state and federal enforcement on a wealth of measures. For instance, the report lists the proportion of inspections that are planned, the number of inspections per 100 hours of inspector work, the proportion of inspections with violations issued, and the average penalty per inspection. State programs are designated "outliers" for any measure if they deviate from OSHA's performance during the same period by some predetermined amount. The C-SPAM reports are useful in identifying agencies that are clearly neglecting enforcement, but they take no account of actual compliance or other legitimate factors that might explain observed variation in enforcement outputs. More significantly, they monitor only outputs, not actual safety and health outcomes, and then only relative to OSHA's performance. In effect, this creates a moving bar that the states must exceed to avoid being classified as deficient.

Until very recently, OSHA monitored state performance on a regular basis and issued annual reviews of state programs. These reports reference all forms of federal oversight and often include the C-SPAM report for the period reviewed. The evaluation of Wyoming's enforcement program for 1992 and 1993 provides a general sense of these reviews:

The Wyoming program continues to improve. None of the case files reviewed showed evidence that violation classification has continued to be a problem. Abatement assurance procedures have also improved. Most case files contained abatement photographs to support abatement. The number of violations identified in not-in-compliance inspections continues to be below federal numbers, especially in health. Favorable comparisons are becoming more evident in other measures. Enhancing the Wyoming enforcement effort is their success in meeting their goal of maintaining a well trained and more experienced staff. (OSHA 1993. "Evaluation Report of the Occupational Safety and Health Program State of Wyoming October 1, 1992 through September 30, 1993")

During the Clinton administration, OSHA began to reform federal oversight of state programs by adopting biennial instead of annual reviews and by moving to establish more flexible performance agreements to replace the relatively rigid annual reviews. The performance agreements provided OSHA with a way to negotiate with the states to monitor and meet particular outcome goals – real improvements in worker safety and health – rather than focusing purely on agency outputs. In practice, however, OSHA's reviews of state programs with negotiated performance agreements still rely heavily on the traditional monitoring tools but supplement them with reference to policy outcomes. As one administrator noted,

Even with performance agreements, we have to monitor state program outputs on a regular basis, because changes in real performance [in deterring safety violations] wouldn't show up for several years. We can't wait that long to find out [if things are going badly].

State plan administrators I interviewed in six states seemed pleased with the reduced paperwork under the new system, especially the end to the practice of designating states as outliers relative to OSHA's changing performance (the "outliers game," in their words). They acknowledged, however, that little of substance had changed in OSHA's monitoring of state activities because the agency continued to calculate and monitor state staffing, productivity, and punitiveness. The OSHA officials I interviewed on this topic pointed out that the big advantage was not getting rid of the monitoring of state program activities, but instead using the performance agreements to negotiate with individual states about how to tailor monitoring to particular state conditions:

Some states, by virtue of their access to workers' compensation and other data, can target individual employers more readily than we can. We shouldn't try to standardize that achievement away. In others states, I've heard, we've got to worry much more about basic staffing and training.

Additionally, they recognized the fact that the states had more resources than OSHA, even if they are less punitive on a per-inspection basis: "[The states] are less aggressive in their enforcement programs, with fewer violations and lower penalties, but their overwhelming numbers make up for it." In light of the trade-off between frequency of inspection and penalties in achieving deterrence, this view is not surprising.

3.2.1. STATE MANAGEMENT UNDER FEDERAL OVERSIGHT: THE VOSH AND WISHA CASES. In light of this type of federal oversight, how can state politicians and agency leaders shape state enforcement? Specifically, how can state enforcement be diminished, contrary to OSHA's wishes, without triggering an OSHA response? An in-depth review of two state enforcement programs provides a first step in answering these questions. The first agency is Virginia's Occupational Safety and Health Agency (VOSH), and the second is Washington's Industrial Safety and Health Agency (WISHA). These two states provide interesting grounds for comparison for several reasons. First, relative to each state's industrial base, VOSH's staffing is less than half of WISHA's. Second, Virginia's population is relatively conservative, while Washington's is relatively liberal. Clinton secured, on average, 57 percent of the two-party presidential vote in Washington in 1992 and 1996, but only 48 percent in Virginia. Washington had a Democratic governor throughout the 1990s, while a Republican held the office in Virginia from 1994 to 2002.

Despite these somewhat stark differences, the approximately twenty-five inspectors and administrators I interviewed in each state shared a strong commitment to enforcement. (Details of the interview selection process and procedures appear in appendix 4.1). There were no discernible differences in the expressed beliefs of VOSH and WISHA inspectors (relative to OSHA or to one another) about the role of government inspectors, how to handle recalcitrant employers, the fairness of OSHA standards, or the effects of OSH Act enforcement on small business. Nor did inspectors report any pressure to tailor enforcement to particular industries or political concerns.

Like their federal OSHA counterparts, I found that state inspectors usually perceived themselves as law enforcement agents or as a fusion of law enforcement agents and consultants. Additionally, much like the shared national stories told by the federal inspectors, many state inspectors (and administrators) told shared stories about enforcement activity by their agency in other parts of the state. State inspectors thus had a strong sense of state action, rather than perceiving themselves as agents of local offices or particular geographic areas. (This last point is particularly important in light of the regionalization reforms in both agencies [to be discussed].) More generally, the enforcement practices in the states are remarkably similar to those at OSHA, including the reliance on the field manuals for guidance on questions of enforcement policy. OSHA's reports on state plan performance paint a similar picture. In none of the more than fifty reports I examined did OSHA find that state inspectors were too sympathetic to businesses or too lax in their commitment to worker protection.

While there are occasional references in these reports to state failure to adopt new standards or necessary program revisions, there are few references to state legislative actions to amend the statutory foundations of state delegation. In fact, a search for state legislative activity on OSH Act matters for the years 1990 through 1997 revealed that in only three of twenty-one states were more than four matters relating to OSHA policy passed into law.[36] In California, twenty-seven such bills were enacted, and the governor vetoed an additional twelve measures passed by the legislature. In Utah, seven measures were enacted, and in Virginia eight. The average number of laws enacted in the remaining states was slightly more than two. The OSH Act itself was amended in 1990 to allow for increased penalties, a move that led most states to adopt similar statutory changes to comply with OSHA's mandates for state plan performance. With California as the clear outlier, this lack of state action is not completely surprising. Revoking the foundation of state authority for enforcement would force OSHA to take action to rescind state delegation. It is a far too visible and crude mechanism to undercut state enforcement without evoking a federal response.

However, the OSHA reports do reference an inability to fill funded inspector positions, inspector turnover, and inspector inexperience as barriers to more effective enforcement. Federal OSHA officials I interviewed were well aware of this issue, labeling turnover in state agencies as "the bodies problem." Table 4.8 reports the starting inspector salary level, the comparable private sector wage, and inspector turnover for the period 1990 to 1995 for each state agency and OSHA. These figures make clear that inspector turnover is a problem, reaching a stunning 100 percent in Wyoming over six years. OSHA clearly has the lowest turnover among all the agencies studied, at only 40 percent (there are only two states with turnover less than 50 percent). Low pay may contribute to high state turnover, although there is no statistically significant correlation between the magnitude of inspector turnover and the generosity of state wages relative to the private sector.

Turnover is significant because, as the results concerning OSHA presented in Chapter 3 demonstrate, inexperienced inspectors enforce the law less stringently than more senior inspectors. Additionally, turnover creates unfilled inspector positions, which do not contribute to an agency's field

---

[36] These figures were calculated by examining the Lexis-Nexis archive of state legislative activity for each state for each year from 1990 to 1997 and searching for all matters that include references to OSHA or the OSH Act.

TABLE 4.8. *Enforcement agency salaries and turnover*

Program	Government Inspector Salary[a]	Average Private Sector Salary[b]	Government Salary Relative to Private Sector Salary	Observed Inspector Turnover 1990–95[c]
OSHA	N/A	N/A	N/A	40%
AK	$45,000	$51,900	87%	55%
AZ	$29,000	$48,000	60%	73%
CA	N/A	$51,180	N/A	46%
HI	$26,000	$48,400	54%	64%
IA	N/A	$42,220	N/A	48%
IN	$21,000	$44,700	47%	67%
KY	$22,000	$44,500	49%	50%
MD	$26,000	$46,280	56%	65%
MI	N/A	$51,440	N/A	52%
MN	$30,000	$48,500	62%	51%
NC	$30,000	$45,180	66%	76%
NM	$27,000	$36,780	73%	83%
NV	$30,000	$49,400	61%	48%
OR	$26,000	$47,380	55%	67%
SC	$20,000	$40,360	50%	81%
TN	$19,000	$43,820	43%	43%
UT	$25,000	$37,160	67%	76%
VA	$27,204	$48,400	56%	56%
VT	N/A	$51,720	N/A	55%
WA	$35,000	$45,200	77%	55%
WY	$25,000	$42,400	59%	100%

[a] Starting (nontrainee) safety inspector salary. Source: author survey. Average OSHA starting inspector salary greater than $40,000 (GS-11).

[b] Average safety manager salary derived from Bureau of Labor Statistics Occupational Earnings Survey, 1997. Annual income imputed using hourly wage and assuming a 2,000-hour work year for employment category 13005 – Personnel, Training, and Labor Relations Manager.

[c] Turnover calculated as proportion of inspectors reporting in 1990 and no longer reporting in 1995. Derived from OSHA IMIS system.

enforcement at all. In Figure 4.2, agencies with low and high pay (relative to the private sector wages in the state) and high levels of turnover are labeled. Among the states near the bottom in relative enforcement vigor, New Mexico, Arizona, and Utah have high levels of turnover. Additionally, Kentucky and Tennessee pay poorly.

For state leaders seeking to weaken state enforcement, low wages for enforcement personnel are a useful tool for restricting enforcement. First, they contribute to high turnover. Conversations with state officials revealed that individuals often take positions with state OSHA agencies in order to garner training and experience that will improve their future employment opportunities in the private sector. After a few years, inspectors then leave government for higher-paying private sector positions. (As one state official put it, "We hire them right out of college, train them, and then they leave to go into corporate work where they make more and work less.") They may also move into state consultation agencies, positions without the stress of being a field enforcement agent. ("Some people can't take the confrontation, so they move into consultation. It takes a certain kind of personality to keep this [field inspection] up.") Here the contrast with OSHA was sharp. None of the OSHA inspectors I interviewed acknowledged considering a job outside the agency in the field of industrial safety or health, while several state inspectors stated that they had considered moving from enforcement to consultation or leaving the public sector altogether.

Second, low salaries discourage qualified personnel from taking government jobs. In some cases, slots remain open for more than a year because there are no qualified personnel willing to fill them. Also, because in most agencies salaries increase with tenure, even maintaining a static enforcement presence requires a growing budget. Thus, mere budgetary uncertainty may cause managers to leave funded positions unfilled because the prospect of hiring and then having to fire someone (or being unable to provide promised salary increases) is unattractive. The third advantage of state manipulation of wages is that it does not trigger immediate OSHA action. OSHA's reviews of compliance with staffing benchmarks usually reference funded, rather than filled, staffing positions.[37]

In addition to setting salaries, state politicians also control the level of agency funding. For states that exceed the required staffing benchmarks, decreases in funding are beyond the scope of federal review. For the remaining states, OSHA may be willing to tolerate failure to meet the required benchmarks if moving to rescind state delegation would require the agency to step in and enforce the law (see the following discussion). A state can also decrease enforcement of the OSH Act, at least in the short run, if it follows California's move and withholds all funding for state enforcement, but this guarantees the return of federal enforcement.

---

[37] Why OSHA chooses to examine allocated rather than filled slots is not clear. The OSHA officials I interviewed all readily recognized the disjuncture between allocated and filled slots. They also noted that the CSPAM reports track active inspectors.

More generally, OSHA's provision of matching funds gives the states an incentive, up to a point, to exhaust the federal grant because it subsidizes state enforcement and employment.

The last, and perhaps most important, mechanism for state leaders, specifically governors, to influence state enforcement is through direct administrative control of the state enforcement apparatus. The heads of most state enforcement agencies are career bureaucrats protected by civil service laws. Unlike their federal counterpart, who is a presidential appointee, they therefore serve across gubernatorial administrations. This largely prevents a governor from simply appointing a less aggressive administrator to head a state agency as a way to undercut enforcement outside of the legislative process. But governors are not powerless. State enforcement agencies are often situated within the state equivalent of the federal Department of Labor, and governors usually appoint the heads of these agencies. In this case, reorganizing the relevant state department or relying on an anti-OSHA ally as the head can provide a governor with a simple way to shape enforcement policy.

Virginia's Occupational Safety and Health Agency's history from 1990 to 1997 shows these dynamics of state administration. VOSH's approved enforcement staffing level was constant at about 103 full-time equivalents (FTEs) for fiscal years (FY) 1990–95.[38] In FY 1996, VOSH's approved enforcement staffing fell to 100 FTEs, and from FY 1996 onward it has been around 91 FTEs. Likewise, VOSH's enforcement budget increased in each year from 1990 to 1994, but fell in FY 1995. In FY 1996, however, VOSH's enforcement budget rebounded to well above the level it would have reached if the increases prior to FY 1995 had been maintained. This increase in spending, however, was not associated with an increase in staffing. As was the case in many other state enforcement agencies, the aging of VOSH's enforcement staff as well as the need to recruit new workers required the agency to devote more resources, per inspector, to a shrinking enforcement staff.

Figure 4.3 displays the number of active VOSH field inspectors and the number of agency inspections for each quarter from 1990 to 1997. (In Figures 4.3 through 4.7, all figures are three-quarter moving averages of the previous, current, and next quarter.) Despite the relatively constant

[38] This FTE figure is for all enforcement personnel and support staff, not just field inspectors. The figures may not be comparable before and after the regional reorganization (to be discussed). Data supplied by VOSH.

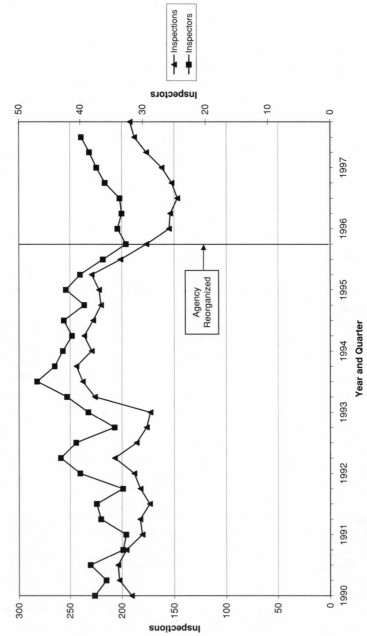

FIGURE 4.3. VOSH staffing and inspections. *Note:* All data points are moving averages across three quarters.

resource level for VOSH enforcement efforts during the period 1990–95, the number of inspectors active in the field increased in 1993 and 1994 to about forty from around thirty-five. In 1995, however, the number of active inspectors began to decrease, reaching a low of about thirty-three in 1996. Obviously, budgetary factors played a role in this decrease, but so did a significant management reform undertaken by the state.

Virginia's Department of Labor and Industry (DLI), of which VOSH is one division, was reorganized in late 1995. This reorganization region-alized all of DLI's operations in each part of the state. Whereas before the reorganization VOSH field offices reported directly to their superiors in Richmond, after the reorganization they (and the other DLI divisions) reported first to a regional administrator, who in turn dealt with the DLI leadership in Richmond. The overall effect of this reorganization was to transfer day-to-day management authority from VOSH headquarters to the regional administrators.[39] Not surprisingly, VOSH administrators reported that this changed the nature of their oversight. The VOSH field personnel were now beholden to two masters: first to the regional admin-istrator, and then to the VOSH administrators in Richmond.

The indirect effects of this reorganization are apparent in Figures 4.3 and 4.4. Not only did the number of personnel active in the field decrease after the reorganization, so did their relative productivity. The top line (black diamonds) in Figure 4.4 is a standardized measure of inspector productivity for the agency for each quarter from 1990 to 1997.[40] After the reorganization, real inspector productivity declined about 20 per-cent, from about 6.5 inspections per month to around 5.2 inspections per month. (As a reminder, the apparent decrease prior to the reorgani-zation is attributable to the fact that each data point is a three-period moving average.) This demonstrates not that inspectors were conducting fewer inspections merely because of some artifact in the types of busi-nesses inspected, but that they were simply less productive. The other data shown in Figure 4.4 confirm this finding. VOSH's relative attention to planned inspections and construction inspections are the same in the two years before and after the reorganization. The proportion of health

[39] The stated reason for this reorganization was to rationalize the services provided to businesses (and labor) by providing a "one-stop" agency in each region. As a practical matter, the newly empowered regional administrators could be more or less supportive of VOSH's mission vis-à-vis the rest of the DLI's programs.

[40] This figure is derived in the same way as the results concerning OSHA inspectors reported in Chapter 3.

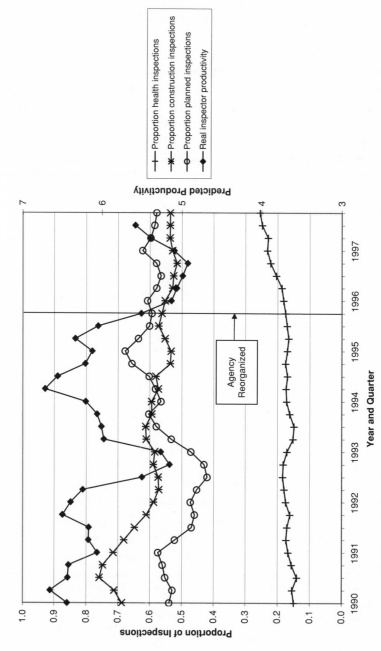

FIGURE 4.4. VOSH inspection characteristics and inspector productivity. *Note:* All data points are moving averages across three quarters.

inspections did increase, although mostly because the decrease in productivity was largest among the safety inspectors. Additionally, the standardized measure of productivity accounts for the more time-consuming nature of health inspections.

Two interrelated factors explain this decline in productivity following the reorganization. First, in the reorganized DLI, VOSH field offices shouldered a greater administrative burden. With fewer personnel and more "regionwide" tasks, inspectors had less time available to conduct inspections. (The inspectors I interviewed acknowledged greater attention to regional outreach efforts after the reorganization.) Second, VOSH administrators in Richmond lost their ability to drive their subordinates to concentrate on conducting inspections. The VOSH field offices now had to balance demands placed on them by regional administrators against demands from headquarters. Subsequently, the VOSH administrators I interviewed reported being successful in restoring some of their administrative tools for encouraging field-level productivity. For instance, VOSH's administrators used productivity reports for each individual inspector to monitor how many inspections he or she conducted. These expectations were communicated to the inspector at the beginning of each year, and follow-up reports were disseminated to the field throughout the year to ensure that inspectors knew of their relative success in meeting these productivity goals. The increase in inspector productivity beginning with the second quarter of 1997 is probably attributable to this type of management effort.

Unfortunately, the information necessary to calculate individual inspector productivity is not available after the third quarter of 1997. Nonetheless, I would predict that after VOSH adapted to the new institutional arrangements, it could recover a great deal of the loss of control caused by the added levels of hierarchy between VOSH headquarters and the field offices. The loss associated with new regional tasks, however, is unlikely to diminish because the regional administrators can still place demands on field-level staff, and these demands are unlikely to be ignored absent action by the overall head of DLI. Overall, regionalization decreased the vigor of VOSH enforcement by reducing inspector attention to enforcement (Figure 4.3) and by decreasing inspector stringency (Table 4.5). While VOSH administrators adapted to these changes and were able to counteract some of them, the net effect, at least in the short term, was an unequivocal decrease in enforcement vigor (Tables 4.6 and 4.7).

The experience of Washington's Industrial Safety and Health Agency (WISHA) during the same period is also informative of the nature of state administration. WISHA is located within Washington State's Department of Labor and Industries (DLI). Unlike VOSH and most other state agencies, however, WISHA has an independent source of funding. WISHA is funded by premiums collected by the state workers' compensation system, although the legislature must subsequently authorize WISHA's use of these funds. The administrators I spoke with confirmed that this funding mechanism shielded the agency from most budgetary uncertainty brought about by economic fluctuations and also from the "zero-sum" conflict for general revenues. In fact, during the period studied, WISHA's underlying budget never decreased, and there were no large cuts in formal enforcement resources.

Despite WISHA's relative financial security, the agency's field enforcement presence, shown in Figure 4.5, decreased between 1990 and 1994. The number of WISHA inspectors active in the field, however, rebounded to 1990 levels by 1996. During the same period, the average number of inspections conducted by the agency, and per inspector, plummeted, and then recovered partially. Why, despite relative resource security, did WISHA's enforcement activities diminish? My investigation suggests that two related factors explain this pattern. First, while the agency's resources did not diminish during the period studied, the agency lost many inspectors to the private sector and to retirement. While slots were being filled, the number of active inspectors decreased. Additionally, new inspectors were required to undergo training that kept them out of the field. Thus, part of the decline in the agency's enforcement presence is due simply to turnover.

The second explanation for the decline in the agency's enforcement presence and its subsequent resurgence is internal agency management. Joseph Dear was the head of DLI from 1987 until 1993, when he left to become the head of federal OSHA. Beginning in the early 1990s, Dear oversaw a round of management reforms at WISHA similar to those he would later implement at OSHA. The central thrust of these reforms was to deemphasize enforcement outputs – the number of inspections completed and the penalities imposed – as measures of agency success. Instead, administrators were asked to evaluate the effectiveness of their enforcement activities and to consider tools other than inspections and penalties to provide greater worker protection. As at OSHA, raw productivity, measured simply as the number of inspections conducted per inspector, declined following the decreased emphasis on inspections. In fact, from 1990 to the third quarter of 1993, raw agency outputs fell by almost 50 percent.

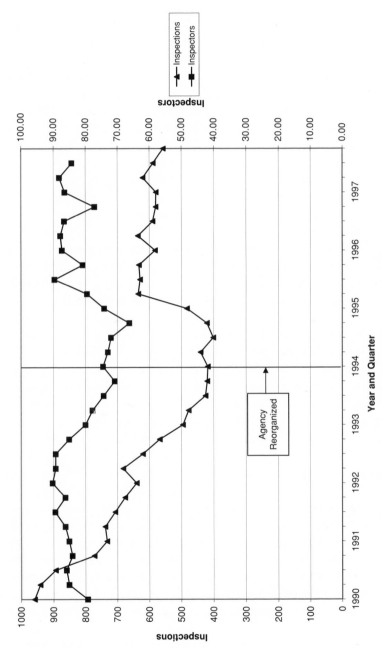

FIGURE 4.5. WISHA staffing and inspections. *Note:* All data points are moving averages across three quarters.

Soon after Dear's departure, Washington's DLI was reorganized in a manner similar to Virginia's. WISHA's local offices were now required to report to a regional administrator who oversaw all DLI activities in a defined geographic area. WISHA's headquarters staff then had to navigate an additional administrative hurdle in securing the cooperation of the field staff as the regional administrator now oversaw their daily activities. WISHA administrators identified the reorganization as a strong impediment to effective management, but one to which they (like VOSH's managers) were able to adapt over time by securing cooperation from the regional administrators (with the help of the DLI leadership) and by reestablishing informal means for centralized coordination. These improvised tools included the use of existing regular interregional and regional meetings to clarify expectations for field offices and the dissemination of annual performance expectations (through the regional administrator) to local WISHA offices.

The bottom line in Figure 4.5 shows that the sharp decline in agency inspection outputs that began in 1991 stabilized in mid-1993 and that agency numbers had rebounded (partially) by mid-1995. Thus, administrators were able to overcome both the centrifugal tendencies brought about by regionalization and, following Dear's departure, the earlier deemphasis of inspection outputs. Figure 4.6 reveals, however, the more complicated nature of changes at WISHA during this period. Specifically, while raw productivity decreased and then rebounded during this period, real productivity – accounting for both the types of businesses inspected and inspection outcomes and shown as the top line (black diamonds) on Figure 4.6 – was relatively constant beginning in 1992. How can real productivity stay constant while raw productivity declines?

Here the answer has to do with the complicated effects of Dear's deemphasis of inspection numbers. Under Dear's leadership, WISHA's raw productivity decreased because, beginning in 1992, the agency conducted fewer low-cost inspections. The proportion of all agency inspections that were planned safety inspections declined beginning in 1990, and fell again beginning in 1992. Also in 1992, the proportion of construction inspections declined. In a sense, then, Dear's reforms succeeded in devoting WISHA's resources to more substantial targets (nonconstruction and health inspection), but the cost was a simultaneous decrease in the proportion of inspections that were the strategically targeted planned inspections.

Additionally, Figure 4.6 illuminates the way that the regionalization reform initially reduced the focus on quality inspections. Immediately

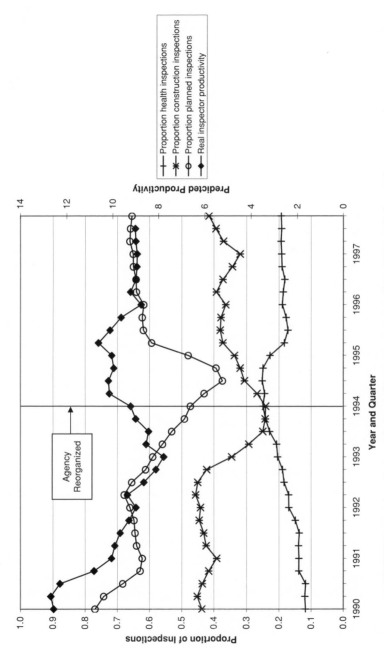

FIGURE 4.6. WISHA inspection characteristics and inspector productivity. *Note:* All data points are moving averages across three quarters.

after the agency was reorganized, the proportion of inspection resources devoted to construction inspections increased, and the proportion of planned inspections declined even further. The net effect was that, without strong mechanisms for centralized control, the field offices engaged in more frequent low-cost inspections, neglecting the more strategic planned manufacturing inspections. As the central office reasserted control, these anomalies disappeared and the allocation of inspector effort returned to the 1992 patterns.

Looking back at Tables 4.5, 4.6, and 4.7 provides further insight into the way in which these reforms also affected the stringency of inspections in the field. As a reminder, Table 4.5 stringency scores are calculated by looking only at planned safety inspections. These are targeted inspections that should yield (if agency enforcement programs and business noncompliance are relatively static) a relatively constant return of violations. During the period studied, there is no clear change in WISHA's enforcement stringency. (In fact, WISHA had the lowest standard deviation in observed punitiveness of all the agencies.) Although per-inspection violations fell in 1993 and 1994 relative to 1991 and 1992, this decline was more than made up for by a rise in penalty- and productivity-adjusted violations. WISHA adopted OSHA's increased penalty structure in 1991, which accounts for the increase in penalty-adjusted vigor score (Table 4.7) the following year.

Dear's deemphasis of inspection numbers at WISHA thus had a different effect than at OSHA. As at OSHA, inspectors conducted fewer inspections. But WISHA's regionalization reform was not associated with a real decrease in inspector productivity. Unlike at OSHA, where the more extensive field office redesign caused inspector productivity to plummet, WISHA inspectors were still active in the field. They conducted different inspections, but worked no less hard. This suggests that, relative to the redesign of field office operations, regionalization is a far less disruptive reform.

3.3. OSHA's Central Dilemma: When to Revoke State Delegation

After examining a selection of OSHA reports of state program performance and discussing state oversight with OSHA officials, it became clear that OSHA regularly finds state enforcement deficient along one dimension or another. States are frequently classified as outliers on the C-SPAM reports. Additionally, states often fail to meet the staffing benchmarks imposed by OSHA. But OSHA has never chosen to act on this type of evidence in order to resume complete enforcement authority on its own volition. OSHA initiated revocation proceedings against Indiana during the Carter administration, but this move was subsequently quashed by the Reagan administration. On other occasions, most recently in North Carolina from 1991 to 1995, OSHA has temporarily resumed concurrent enforcement, whereby the agency conducts inspections at the same time as the state. Why this unwillingness to forgo state enforcement?

Perhaps the most enticing explanation is that OSHA prefers weak state enforcement. I believe this explanation is wrong because it overlooks two important facts about state enforcement. First, state enforcement is usually not that bad. In fact, state enforcement is usually more vigorous than OSHA's. While state inspectors are less punitive, they make up for that deficiency with their greater numbers. In order for even the most pro-enforcement OSHA officials to be willing to resume enforcing the law, they must believe that doing so is a good deal. These cases turn out to be rare. OSHA pays *up to* 50 percent of each state program's enforcement budget. Consequently, if OSHA wanted to step in and enforce the law without state assistance, it would probably have to live with at least a 50 percent cut in staff in affected states (see Thompson 1983: 76 for a similar argument). Furthermore, assuming that OSHA maintained its broad commitment to geographic neutrality in staffing allocation, it would have to reallocate staff from other areas to equalize the staffing levels in the newly overseen jurisdictions.

Table 4.9 displays a per-jurisdiction analysis of the effect of OSHA revocation of *all* state enforcement programs. It is calculated by assuming (1) that OSHA maintained its relative stringency as reported in Table 4.5, (2) that OSHA translated rescinded state funds into federal inspectors at the same rate as for the remainder of its enforcement budget, and (3) that OSHA allocated its inspection workforce to equalize staffing per workplace in the areas overseen by the agency. In this scenario, the first column displays the predicted change in the number of inspectors in each jurisdiction. Note that in all cases the number of inspectors decreases, by a minimum of 4.4 percent in states currently overseen by OSHA to nearly 80 percent in Oregon.[41] Among the states that currently enforce the law, only in New Mexico and Arizona is the figure less than 20 percent.

The last two columns in the table display the predicted effect of this move on overall enforcement vigor. Only in one state, New Mexico, is

---

[41] These estimates are calculated to favor OSHA because they rely on observed state inspectors in the field, despite the fact that the states have a harder time filling funded inspection slots. If these slots were filled, the figures would favor state enforcement even more.

TABLE 4.9. *Comparative state performance under pure federal enforcement*

Agency	Predicted Change in Inspectors versus Observed Inspectors if State Programs Withdrawn[a]	Change in Predicted Agency Vigor, 1995 (Table 4.7)[b]	Change in Predicted Penalty- and Productivity-Adjusted Agency Vigor, 1995 (Table 4.8)[b]
OSHA	−4.4%	−4.4%	−4.4%
AK	−76.4%	−69.7%	−86.5%
AZ	−15.6%	56.9%	−16.2%
CA	−29.2%	−43.7%	−91.4%
HI	−72.6%	−74.7%	−82.1%
IA	−29.6%	−39.0%	0.5%
IN	−51.4%	−57.4%	−53.3%
KY	−49.2%	34.8%	−39.2%
MD	−50.8%	−58.0%	−70.3%
MI	−50.5%	−70.6%	−78.9%
MN	−46.1%	−72.0%	−50.0%
NC	−44.8%	−74.2%	−84.0%
NM	−13.3%	201.0%	102.0%
NV	−66.9%	−31.7%	−90.8%
OR	−78.4%	−70.7%	−86.6%
SC	−30.5%	−40.3%	−83.7%
TN	−45.8%	−36.3%	6.9%
UT	−46.7%	4.9%	−79.5%
VA	−39.5%	−43.6%	−29.0%
VT	−61.2%	−49.5%	−16.8%
WA	−73.6%	−36.2%	−80.1%
WY	−57.3%	−52.1%	−22.4%

[a] Based on observed inspectors, average 1990–96. Predicted federal inspectors based on assumption that OSHA's share of state enforcement budgets is used to hire inspectors at same rate that current OSHA enforcement budget is used to hire inspectors and that all federal inspectors are allocated to equalize inspectors per overseen business facility (see Chapter 3).

[b] Shaded entries are agencies that replacing with OSHA would increase enforcement vigor.

enforcement predicted to increase on both the violations and penalty- and productivity-adjusted violations measures. To reiterate the point made earlier, New Mexico is a small state encompassing less than 2 percent of the nation's workplaces and 1.8 percent of the manufacturing facilities. In sum, for the observed period, state enforcement is rarely so bad that OSHA would improve enforcement by stepping in to replace even a weak state agency. (As a reminder, these numbers probably overstate OSHA's effectiveness relative to the states, because although OSHA inspectors are highly punitive, they inspect much less frequently than state inspectors. See footnote 35.) Despite this relative strength, every OSHA official I interviewed who was willing to express a position stated that he or she would prefer uniform OSHA enforcement to the state plans. They also acknowledged, however, that there was no political support for amending the OSH Act to remove the state plan provision.

The second reason OSHA is unwilling to act against all weak state programs is that stepping in to replace marginal state enforcement is an extreme and taxing step. When California's budget cuts compelled OSHA to enforce the law in the state from 1988 to 1991, it severely disrupted the agency's operations elsewhere in the country. New inspectors were hired, existing staff was reassigned, and office space was procured. But OSHA's field enforcement in the state was still minimal. Furthermore, there was nothing to stop the state from reapplying to enforce the law, which it did in 1990. OSHA then had to reverse its temporary moves, again with substantial disruption.

OSHA faces the same dilemma in its dealings with other states. If it revokes delegation, it must contend with the administrative hassle of enforcing the law on its own. It must also recognize that states can reapply and that OSHA is compelled to accept applications meeting the rules laid out in the OSH Act. In light of these difficulties, for OSHA bureaucrats to be willing to rescind enforcement delegation, state enforcement must represent a substantial and persistent failure. Of course, the weak threat of a federal response might encourage state transgressions. Here OSHA's interactions with North Carolina's enforcement program in the early 1990s are informative. State enforcement personnel were poorly paid, and turnover was rampant. But OSHA did not force the state to rectify these abuses, and labor unions did not seek to initiate program revocation until after the Hamlet fire. Subsequently, the threat of program revocation led the state to dramatically reform the agency, but OSHA (and labor unions) tolerated a poorly performing program prior to this reform.

Still, the states do not in general function as a mechanism to provide less aggressive regulation. A weak OSHA threat to revoke delegation and the 50 percent funding rule seem sufficient to force most states to rectify poorly performing state programs. In fact, the states perform better than one might expect given the unwillingness of OSHA to exercise its threat to rescind state delegation.

4. Conclusion

The evidence presented in this chapter provides new insights into federal oversight of the states that share in enforcing the OSH Act. It started with a question: Does delegation lead to a loss of control? This chapter demonstrates that state enforcement is, in the vast majority of cases, at least as vigorous as OSHA's. While on a *per inspection* basis OSHA's field inspectors are often more punitive than their state counterparts, the states largely make up for their (apparent) laxness with greater staffing levels. Moreover, this outcome is not an artifact of some screening process used by OSHA in choosing which programs to approve. Instead, states where OSHA supporters are strongest and states where they are weakest are more likely than other states to adopt delegated programs.

In the aggregate, state enforcement is a good deal for supporters of vigorous OSH Act enforcement. The level of enforcement is higher than it would be in the absence of the state agencies because of state assistance in funding enforcement. Clearly, however, shared federal/state enforcement is not a panacea. States may choose to provide regulation at a level that exceeds that of the federal government, but this is not a natural consequence of shared enforcement. In the OSH Act case, the 50 percent funding mechanism provides competing incentives for state leaders and OSHA officials. On the one hand, the 50 percent rule almost guarantees that state agencies are better staffed than federal OSHA. On the other hand, this same funding mechanism decreases the incentive for federal OSHA officials to penalize less effective state regulators. Rescinding state enforcement authority would require OSHA to step in and enforce the law with many fewer inspectors. States occasionally provide a level of enforcement below that which OSHA provides elsewhere. Were OSHA to step in and replace the states, however, it would come at the cost of an overall reduction in OSH Act enforcement and substantial administrative hassles.

This pattern of reasonably aggressive state enforcement has had substantial implications for OSHA's efforts to secure political support for its own regulatory efforts. Because state enforcement is largely as vigorous as OSHA's, businesses cannot accuse OSHA of being too aggressive relative to its state counterparts. (In fact, as one OSHA administrator I interviewed noted, "a complaint that they [the states] are too aggressive is a problem for those [state] officials, but not OSHA.") So long as state regulation is at least as onerous, OSHA is therefore protected from some complaints by business that OSHA regulation disadvantages them relative to state regulation. Members of Congress who might similarly advocate against OSHA on the grounds that its field program is too costly for their constituencies are also less likely to do so when state programs are just as aggressive. For labor, less aggressive state regulation would present similar risks. But, by and large, state regulation is weak only where unions have little at stake.[42] In short, because of the success of OSHA in ensuring that state enforcement is not a less-punitive alternative to federal regulation, OSHA is less likely to attract opposition as it pursues its own strategically neutral enforcement efforts.

In discussing the overall vigor of state enforcement, I have purposely sidestepped the important question of the consistency across individual employers and industries of state OSH Act enforcement. This is largely because I was unable to find any evidence, in either quantitative analysis or my interviews with state and federal officials and labor and business groups, of concerns about this sort of variation. Much like their federal counterpart, state agencies (and their inspectors) seem largely insulated from political pressures by individual elected officials, industries, and employers. (In the aggregate, state inspectors turn over more quickly than their federal counterparts, and for this reason they are less professionalized as government safety inspectors, but they are certainly not corrupt.) In both Virginia and Washington, state administrators devote substantial attention to overseeing their field offices to ensure that the classification of violations and amounts of penalties are consistent across employers. The oversight of the field mimics the agencies' federal counterpart and includes ongoing training, centralized guidance memoranda, and a review of case files by central auditors. As at OSHA, state inspection targeting and penalty policies are generally calibrated to business (and industry) safety history and employer size. The state enforcement agencies, like their federal counterpart, have also sought to institutionalize differences across classes of employers. In general, they seem to have been relatively successful in forgoing more individualized political bargaining over enforcement behavior and in avoiding local political pressures. In the aggregate, the twin imperatives of controlling subordinates

---

[42] In this light, the AFL-CIO's lawsuit in the 1970s concerning state staffing was farsighted, because it compelled OSHA to require the states to substantially expand the staffing of their enforcement programs in order to be granted final approval. The state programs continued to operate (without final approval) with fewer inspectors than required by the benchmarks, but nonetheless with more than OSHA would have provided in the same area. The 50 percent funding rule appears to have been the most important reason for this relatively high level of state staffing.

and guiding policy to secure political support are apparent in the efforts of state bureaucratic leaders to control their subordinates. On balance, the states have implemented policy in a strategically neutral manner that seems, in many ways, to mirror that of federal OSHA.

Finally, OSHA has arguably enjoyed a more general political benefit from being seen as both competent in its oversight of the states and willing to work with state administrators. Insofar as OSHA can document that the states are doing a reasonably effective job in enforcing the OSH Act, the likelihood increases that labor groups (and their supporters) will see OSHA as trustworthy in overseeing implementation of the OSH Act without extensive outside intervention. Regarding the latter point, conflict with state administrators threatens to provide fodder for groups on the right seeking to demonstrate that OSHA is overbearing and unnecessarily punitive in its dealings with both businesses and the states.

More generally, the hybrid federal/state enforcement mechanism put in place by the OSH Act has performed better than one might have expected given businesses' prospective beliefs about their political influence at the state level. The state enforcement option has not proven to be a means to a less aggressive state substitute for federal regulation. For this very reason, federal OSHA has managed to sidestep yet another potential threat to its political support.

APPENDIX 4.I. STATE INTERVIEW SELECTION AND PROCEDURE

I conducted interviews with approximately twenty-five officials in Virginia's and Washington's OSH Act enforcement agencies for this chapter. (Additionally, I interviewed state plan administrators in four other states.) As with the interviews of federal OSHA officials described in appendix 3.1, each subject was interviewed under the condition that no material would identify him or her by name (or by position, where that would reveal his or her identity). The topics of the interviews are discussed in appendix 3.1.

The smaller size of the state agencies, where titles would easily identify individuals, led me to group all administrators together in the descriptions in this chapter and to forgo many direct quotations in the text. All interviews with inspectors were conducted away from their supervisors. Where possible, interviews were also conducted away from the office (often at nearby eating establishments). In no case did I detect any reticence to share negative feelings about agency management or OSHA oversight of the states. (As with my interviews with federal OSHA officials, interviews were conducted without a tape recorder.)

To select inspectors and regional officials for interviews, I contacted state administrators and received permission to contact each agency's local offices. I then randomly selected individual local offices and arranged to make a one- or two-day visit to conduct interviews. Where possible, I requested a list of inspectors and supervisors in the area office and asked to speak with a random selection of inspectors. Additionally, during the course of my visits, I arrived early in the morning and stayed late in the afternoon so as to catch inspectors arriving for work and returning from the field.

For the interviews with headquarters staff, I used an organizational chart to identify important agency officials and then conducted follow-up interviews with others in headquarters. I spent a total of four days in the headquarters office of Washington's agency, and three in Virginia's.

5

Conclusion

Bureaucrats are policy-minded entrepreneurs who make strategic choices governed by both the constraints imposed by the political environment and the need to control their subordinates. Bureaucratic leaders can use their authority to change policy so long as they can avoid being rebuked by coalitions sufficiently powerful to compel changes in their behavior. Given this ongoing threat, bureaucratic leaders have incentives to seek politically efficient solutions in pursuit of their policy goals. In the enforcement context, a strategy that achieves these ends with minimal disadvantage is strategic neutrality, which combines the careful calibration of centrally directed discretionary decisions with tight control of subordinates.

In the case of the OSH Act, despite pressure from individual industries, businesses, and localities (and the politicians acting on behalf of them), OSHA has managed to implement the law with remarkable geographic and firm-by-firm consistency. OSHA does not tailor local or individual enforcement to the wishes of powerful elected officials or to the demands of any single interest group. This neutrality persists despite the strong local pressures on the agency and its dispersed workforce. This outcome points to the capability of bureaucratic leaders to insulate their subordinates from external political pressures. OSHA both recruits those motivated to police employer behavior and actively seeks to disrupt potential linkages between inspectors and interest groups or elected officials. The agency also pushes its subordinates to work hard, creating incentives that motivate uniform law enforcement.

Theoretically, strategic neutrality bridges the gap between ideal visions of bureaucratic professionalism in implementation and political theories of bureaucratic leadership. Centrally directed particularism allows agency leaders to shape policy toward desired ends to both fulfill policy ends and build political support. At the same time, agency leaders can seek to standardize how subordinate bureaucrats behave through general management efforts and the inculcation of profession norms. Strategic neutrality therefore shows how the language and practice of depersonalized Weberian bureaucracy is fully compatible with visions of bureaucracies as independent political actors. In order to achieve their desired policy ends, bureaucratic leaders must skillfully guide policy and ensure that their subordinates implement those desires. Policy choices that fail to attract supportive coalitions, either by design or because of an inability to harness subordinate bureaucrats to those ends, are, by contrast, politically inefficient. A theory of bureaucratic power must therefore recognize that bureaucratic leadership is contingent on both internal control and external support.

In the OSHA case, despite the agency's explicit commitment to neutrality in enforcement, there is still substantial variation in enforcement outcomes across local political environments and individual workplaces. This pattern persists for two reasons. First, variation arises because of centralized discrimination on the basis of businesses size and dangerousness (at both the industry and firm level). Second, additional variation arises because of differences in the behavior of private actors. These deviations persist, therefore, *despite agency neutrality* and not because of some failings on OSHA's part. Because OSHA must rely on workers both (1) to learn about hazards at workplaces not subject to planned inspection and (2) to assist inspectors in identifying hazards during an inspection, the willingness of workers to cooperate with OSHA (and of employers to threaten their employees) shapes how the law is enforced. The agency, however, is powerless to alter worker or employer beliefs except through aggressive enforcement. Because it must partially rely on outsiders to implement the law, OSHA must contend with variation in worker willingness to assist the agency in enforcement. This empirical finding – that OSHA outcomes vary with local support for the agency – is similar to that reported in earlier research. But the inference this earlier work draws – namely, that OSHA's leadership and field-level bureaucrats strategically tailor enforcement to local political conditions or embrace this unavoidable localism – appears incorrect.

OSHA's centralized discernment between small and large businesses and between safe and unsafe establishments (and industries) is politically wise because it defuses criticism from small and safe businesses. OSHA's enforcement program is therefore "strategically neutral," and its particular choices about how to enforce the law persist because outsiders have been unable to compel the agency to abandon them. Significantly, these are not the same choices that any external interest group would make if it were running the show. Nor are these choices completely determined by the external political environment; the agency makes choices.

Furthermore, OSHA's decisions about how to enforce the law have important consequences for both the distribution of the costs and benefits of government regulation and the political environment in which the agency finds itself. By creating and sustaining an aggressive enforcement bureaucracy that makes important exceptions for safe and small businesses, OSHA has been able to shape political conflict surrounding the agency and therefore what it means to support or oppose it. Outsiders can seek to unbundle the collective structure of OSH Act enforcement, but this is difficult because OSHA has substantial statutory discretion to choose how the law is enforced. While outsiders can control the agency, this control is fundamentally conditional.

The inquiry in this book has so far largely focused on contemporary OSH Act enforcement. The arguments made here have implications across OSHA's entire history, however, both for understanding the public policy consequences of politicized implementation and for specifying the political power of bureaucracy more generally.

1. OSHA, Unions, and Political Agency

My empirical examination of OSHA policymaking has largely focused on a period during the Clinton presidency when OSHA enjoyed support from the president. OSHA's leaders throughout this period mostly sought to enhance the agency's efficacy in diminishing workplace safety and health hazards. The agency as a whole therefore behaved in a way that seemed largely amenable to the interests of OSHA's traditional labor constituency. Is this evidence that OSHA is simply an agent of union pressures that has no choice but to pursue the pro-safety and health agenda apparent here?

My interpretation of this pattern is that OSHA has done things that unions like, but that this is a strategic choice made by agency leaders to support their policy goals and secure support for the agency. But could OSHA pursue another strategy? If it could not have, my reading of the choices made by OSHA's leaders may be a misinterpretation of what is essentially an epiphenomenal manifestation of union influence. In short, are there other politically efficient strategies for OSHA's leaders to choose? Episodes from the Clinton administration and earlier "rightward leaning" reforms implemented during the Reagan administration suggest that OSHA is not forced to pursue a pure pro-union agenda.

1.1. Strategic Choice or Union Influence: The Clinton Years

Even during the Clinton administration, OSHA implemented the law in ways that were not supported by national unions. First, as Chapter 2 elaborates, OSHA pursued a broad commitment to consistent enforcement even in industries and areas where unions had little at stake. Second, OSHA's leaders sought to expand the voluntary protection program (to be discussed), despite union opposition to the extension of inspection exemptions.

Third, OSHA implemented a field-level reinvention program that dramatically reduced the agency's inspection outputs despite opposition from proponents of aggressive field enforcement (see Chapter 3, section 3). As I explain in Chapter 3, the reinvention program was unusual in granting field-level bureaucrats substantial discretion to choose new enforcement efforts. Without extensive control of their behavior, the field offices experimented with many alternatives to traditional inspection- and penalty-based enforcement. Few nontraditional programs were actually implemented, however, and the agency found itself attacked by both traditional supporters and opponents for being unable to demonstrate that the agency was actually doing anything at all worthwhile in view of substantial budgetary outlays.

To reiterate, the reinvention experiment was implemented despite opposition from union groups. It was halted and radically reworked, however, when it failed to shield the agency from attacks by either liberals or conservatives. It was, in short, politically inefficient. What is most surprising about this reform is not that it failed, however, but how it was implemented. Other reforms, including OSHA's partnership initiative, have sought to change OSHA's traditional enforcement system. The reinvention program, however, also granted substantial discretion to field-level bureaucrats to shape the program itself. This is exactly contrary to my argument that demonstrating political efficiency requires tight control of subordinates. That the reform failed to achieve the goals of OSHA's leadership therefore demonstrates the validity of the argument that control of subordinates is essential for defusing opposition. More generally, that it was tried at all shows that OSHA was not compelled to toe the union line.

1.2. The Voluntary Partnership Program

The potential for long-term success of a shift in policy opposed by unions is shown by the history of OSHA's Voluntary Partnership Program (VPP).

The VPP was established by Thorne Auchter, OSHA's head during the early years of the Reagan administration. As part of his general effort to reduce OSHA's reliance on adversarial proceedings, Assistant Secretary Auchter oversaw formulation of the VPP initiative, first publicly announced in 1982.[1] OSHA officials generally describe the VPP as allowing OSHA to "leverage its scarce enforcement resources by encouraging employers to engage in partnerships with OSHA to reduce injuries and illnesses."[2] The VPP program identifies employers who have made a commitment to both comply with OSHA requirements and implement more comprehensive worker protections. Employers who meet these stringent requirements are then exempt from planned OSHA inspections.[3]

Efficiency is the primary justification for the partnership approach to enforcement. OSHA's limited inspector corps can visit only a small subset of employers every year. Additionally, inspectors may miss violations of OSHA standards during an inspection or find hazards that are not attributable to violations of these standards. In the former case, violations go undetected, while in the latter case OSHA is relatively powerless to force employers to remedy these hazards. By contrast, a partnership program requires employers to monitor their own compliance with OSHA standards and to correct many unregulated hazards. This allows OSHA to conserve its limited inspection resources for workplaces where noncompliance is more likely. In totality, the VPP's supporters assert that this tactic enhances OSHA's deterrent effect by allowing OSHA to attack the worst cases of noncompliance.

To date, OSHA's VPP has shown promising results. There were more than 450 employers participating in the VPP in 1999 (OSHA: February 29, 2000). These employers have experienced large and sustained reductions in observed injuries and illnesses (OSHA VPP: n.d.). As a political strategy, the VPP has also been a solid success. OSHA can now respond to critics who contend that the agency is unnecessarily punitive by stating that employers have a choice between providing safe workplaces (and working cooperatively with OSHA) or maintaining the status quo (and facing regular OSHA inspections).[4] The VPP therefore allows the agency to back away from a purely confrontational approach to enforcement without

---

[1] 47 Federal Register 29, 025–26, July 1982.
[2] Source: author interview.
[3] For a useful summary of the VPP process, see BNA *Occupational Safety and Health Daily*, September 17, 1998.
[4] Source: author interview. See also BNA *Occupational Safety and Health Daily*, September 17, 1998, for an example of the positive appraisal of OSHA by VPP participants.

abandoning a general commitment to protecting workers. (Indeed, in 1995, then OSHA head Dear appealed to VPP members to lobby Congress on its behalf: "I can't tell you to lobby. But I know hundreds of you are going on the hill." [BNA *Occupational Safety and Health Daily*, September 28, 1995])

This is not to suggest that unions were supportive of the VPP. In fact, when the program was proposed, unions lumped it together with other Reagan administration proposals under the general rubric of deregulation.[5] (One union associate told me, "If we could have killed it [VPP] at the beginning, we would have.") Nonetheless, the VPP allowed OSHA to garner some support in the business community and demonstrated, even to OSHA's critics, that investments in the agency could be efficient in promoting worker safety and health without automatically hassling and penalizing businesses. The VPP therefore separated questions about OSHA's effectiveness and importance from questions about the agency's reasonableness.

OSHA has continued to blunt most criticisms of the VPP through careful national oversight of the implementation of partnership agreements. In order to qualify for the VPP, employers must demonstrate a commitment to safety and health that extends beyond simple compliance with OSHA standards. A business accepted into the VPP, therefore, has already shown that it is willing to take costly action to improve working conditions. Furthermore, VPP employers are unlikely to renege on their commitment to safety and health without being caught, because employee participation is a critical part of the VPP program. "Empowered employees" thus provide an independent source of information about business compliance to OSHA and can use OSHA's complaint process to trigger an inspection if they fear their employer is taking advantage of its exemption from planned inspections.

More dramatic shifts toward partnerships, however, have not been as politically successful. As part of the aforementioned Clinton administration reinvention program, OSHA devolved problem-solving authority to local offices. Whereas prior to this point OSHA's national office had tightly controlled VPP participation, reinvention encouraged local offices to develop alternatives to traditional enforcement. With this newfound authority, OSHA's East Atlanta office negotiated a partnership agreement with the local poultry industry, where safety and health records were poor and where workers were less likely to be organized.

5 See also Mintz 1984: 363, footnote 52.

The national response was unequivocally negative. "The partnership OSHA has envisioned for the poultry industry essentially would have given an industry with a questionable safety and health track record VPP perquisites without the required effort to become eligible for the program."[6] An OSHA official noted, "[In the] Atlanta case [they] left the national union out of the picture, which really pissed them off. From afar, it looked like a giveaway to local industry." By contrast, one of the reasons the VPP has not engendered this type of opposition is the strong requirement for employee participation that renders the program effectively a tripartite OSHA-employer-employee cooperative agreement. While OSHA exempts VPP employers from regular inspections, it expects workers at these facilities to participate actively in safety and health programs and to audit continued compliance with OSHA standards on behalf of the agency. Not only did the poultry initiative reward employers who had failed to comply with OSHA standards, it did nothing to guarantee that employees would serve as effective monitors of employer performance. In the ensuing storm of negative publicity, OSHA's national office quickly rescinded the agreement.

Two lessons are apparent from the history of the VPP. First, bureaucratic leaders have a strong incentive to control their subordinates. Even Auchter, the conservative, restricted the discretion of field-level bureaucrats to decide how to implement the VPP. Instead, the program was conceived and coordinated from OSHA's national and regional offices. By contrast, when the Clinton-era reinvention reforms devolved substantial discretion to the field, the outcome for OSHA's leaders was politically damaging. Partnerships and nontraditional enforcement as a bargain between local OSHA officials and local advocacy groups was locally tenable, but it was damaging to the agency's national standing. The local implementation of the program upset the fragile pro-VPP balance that allowed the agency to both appease some businesses and avoid substantial labor opposition.

Second, the VPP also shows that pro-business shifts in policy, even for an agency with a traditional support base in labor, are tenable. Why did VPP succeed initially and continue to succeed even in the face of opposition from labor groups? The simplest answer is that it allowed the agency to demobilize a component of the agency's opposition by giving high-performing businesses (and their political allies) an option to partner with OSHA and thereby opt out of the traditional adversarial enforcement

---

[6] A representative from the United Food and Commercial Workers Union quoted in *BNA Occupational Safety and Health Daily*, October 23, 1995.

process. (One OSHA official related a story in which a VPP participant described the program as having "taken OSHA off our lobbying agenda. With VPP we get good PR, our unions are happy, and our shareholders are happy.") Labor groups opposed the move, but lacked sufficient support (even later, with Clinton as president and a unified Democratic Congress) to force OSHA to withdraw the program. OSHA, in other words, shaped the political environment by creating a program that differentiated among businesses based on their commitment to worker protection.[7]

1.3. Records-Check Inspections

The brief history of OSHA's "records-check" inspection program similarly demonstrates the importance of political efficiency. Records-check inspections were another Auchter initiative designed to move OSHA away from a reliance on traditional confrontational enforcement efforts.[8] Under the records-check program, OSHA altered how it conducted planned safety inspections. Whereas prior to this point all planned safety inspections involved a complete examination of a workplace, the records-check procedure required the OSHA inspector to first examine the selected business's workplace injury and illness logs and calculate the facility's injury and illness rate. For businesses with injury and illness rates below a certain threshold – the average rate in manufacturing according to the Bureau of Labor Statistics annual survey – OSHA would not conduct a physical examination of the workplace. (The program did not apply to unplanned or health inspections.)

Like the VPP, the records-check initiative met with strong criticism from labor groups, who argued that it simply exempted large numbers of businesses from planned inspections. These critics also argued that calculating only observed injuries and illnesses would miss health hazards with long latency periods and would do little to protect workers who had, by

---

[7] Once the VPP was in place, it was hard even for liberal Democrats to criticize it absent evidence that it was ineffective.

Of course, a remaining question is whether an OSHA administrator backed by a Republican president and a supportive Republican Congress could go further than Auchter by replacing all traditional OSHA enforcement activities with a VPP-like program with weak standards. Such a move seems unlikely for two reasons. First, if opposition to OSHA were really so uniform that the Congress and the president supported dismantling OSHA, they could do so directly by repealing the OSH Act or gutting the agency's budget. Second, it is not clear that a weak partnership program would demonstrate the agency's political efficiency even to opponents of traditional enforcement practices. If VPP participation didn't protect workers any better than (or at least as well as) traditional enforcement, why would any investment in OSHA attract legislative support? In short, a dramatically weakened VPP would be politically inefficient.

[8] OSHA CPL 2.25B, October 1, 1981.

sheer good luck, avoided being injured by latent but unrealized hazards. Furthermore, unions and other outside analysts argued that because the records-check procedure relied on employer-generated reports of workplace dangers, it encouraged employers to fraudulently alter records in order to avoid inspection.

The political justification for the records-check initiative was very similar to that espoused for the VPP program.[9] OSHA argued that the agency had too few resources to inspect every business. Consequently, it should concentrate on performing the very time-consuming wall-to-wall inspections of workplaces with demonstrated, rather than potential, hazards to workers. While labor groups criticized the initiative from the start, they were unable to generate sufficient legislative support to overturn the decision. As with VPP, business groups supported the move, in part because it seemed to move OSHA in a direction of "reasonableness" by differentiating between poorly performing businesses and those with exemplary safety and health records.

Unlike the VPP, however, the records-check program subsequently lost a great deal of its luster when evidence supporting outside criticism of the initiative surfaced. For one, research began to support the contention that businesses were underreporting injuries and illnesses in order to avoid full inspection (GAO 1988, Pollack and Keimig 1987).[10] Additionally, a series of cases became public in which employees died at facilities that OSHA had earlier visited and deemed the business sufficiently safe, on the basis of observed injury and illness records, to exempt it from physical inspection. These criticisms weakened the agency's claim that records-check inspections were efficient – that they properly differentiated between safe and unsafe businesses. In 1988, OSHA head John Pendergrass rescinded the records-check program.

The records-check experiment again shows that rightward shifts in OSHA policy are possible despite the agency's traditional labor constituency. Unlike the VPP example, however, the claim that records checks were efficient was undercut both by evidence that showed employers could misrepresent their safety records and by the growing realization that even valid records might not accurately demonstrate a workplace's safety. Taken together, these decreased the support the agency enjoyed for the program, even from those officials who were seeking to mitigate OSHA's

---

[9] See, for instance: Department of Labor press release, September 23, 1981.

[10] This finding was subsequently validated in a series of academic studies published by Ruser and Smith (1988, 1991).

traditional reliance on a labor constituency. Absent demonstrated political efficiency and the concomitant generation of new sources of support for the agency, simply undercutting OSHA enforcement did not protect the agency from critics in Congress or elsewhere.

Overall, OSHA's policy-making efforts reveal that the agency does more than serve its primary union supporters. Agency-generated reforms that weaken the agency's dependency on this base of support can succeed. Doing so, however, requires the agency to demonstrate political efficiency, which demands both a skillfully crafted program and effective implementation. All three of the administratively generated reforms considered in this section – the Clinton reinvention experiment, the VPP, and records-check inspections – were couched in the language of political efficiency. They angered OSHA's traditional union support base, but this anger was offset by the potential demobilization of particular elements of the anti-OSHA business community. To sustain these shifts, however, required more than a good idea. OSHA also had to ensure that these reforms lived up to their promise by effectively implementing them. When they did not, the initial political benefits of these moves evaporated along with their perceived efficiency.

2. The Public Policy Consequences of Regulatory Enforcement

2.1. The Political Origins of Suboptimal Regulation

So far, this inquiry has centered on questions of political science and public administration. Are agencies and interest groups powerful and, if so, when? Likewise, how do internal agency management concerns affect an agency's political standing? One might also be concerned, however, with the public policy implications of my arguments about bureaucratic behavior and the nature of strategic neutrality. In the particular case of OSHA, many of these questions are addressed directly in Chapter 2, where I suggest that OSHA has remained remarkably aggressive in enforcing the law despite sustained opposition to the agency. At the same time, however, the agency has stepped back from enforcing (both inspections and penalties) in small businesses and safe industries more than a pure (and unconstrained) effort at worker protection would demand. It is, in short, fundamentally constrained.

More interestingly, politics contributes to a distribution of enforcement effort toward certain hazards at the expense of others. In a quest to guarantee regular allotments of detected violations, I argue that the agency probably inspects more frequently those businesses where violations are readily detectable but unavoidable, while devoting too little attention to low-probability but catastrophic hazards and those hazards with long latency periods (see Chapter 2, section 3.3). This bias further inclines the agency to focus on safety hazards at the expense of health hazards. In the former case, workers' compensation and wage premiums may do a more or less adequate job of compensating for job risk, whereas in the latter case these mechanisms are ineffective. Nonetheless, the problem for OSHA is its inability to demonstrate the continuing necessity of doing otherwise because of the greater difficulty in targeting these sorts of violations.

2.2. Why Professionalism Is Not Enough: The Pathology of Regulatory Reasonableness

Beyond the particular details of OSH Act enforcement, what are the implications of my findings for more general efforts to understand the nature of field enforcement? Most specifically, what do my findings suggest about the pursuit of "regulatory reasonableness?" At least since the 1970s, scholars of public policy have complained of a trend in American regulatory enforcement toward "legalism," the "unreasonable" pursuit by regulators of legally supportable violations even when those violations are only indirectly related to desired outcomes or when coming into compliance is prohibitively expensive. Perhaps the most forceful articulation of this claim is presented by Bardach and Kagan in their 1982 volume *Going by the Book: The Problem of Regulatory Unreasonableness*.

Bardach and Kagan claim that excessive attention to rules (at OSHA as well as more generally) is driven in part by the desire of subordinate bureaucrats and their superiors to make sure their decisions will be upheld in the event of legal challenge. Professionalism, in short, becomes subservient to legalistic maneuvering. As a consequence, unreasonable and inflexible enforcement encourages regulated parties to challenge agency decisions and discourages them from trying to address unregulated harms. Their prescription is greater discretion for field-level enforcement personnel to discriminate among employers on the basis of their professional evaluation of the reasons for violating the law (malice, lack of knowledge, honest mistakes, etc.) and to ascertain whether rules violations in fact constitute real threats.[11]

---

[11] Other analysts have suggested that field enforcement becomes less "cooperative" and more legalistic when regulation itself is more contested (Scholz 1984, 1991; Kagan 1994). That is, the willingness of government inspectors and regulated parties to work together declines when the participants in the regulatory process (both the agency and the regulated firm) fear that their cooperation will lead to being taken advantage of.

My findings, however, call into question both the efficacy of this prescription – greater field-level discretion guided by professionalism – and its
necessity. I show that when centralized pressures on field-level bureaucrats
to aggressively enforce the law declined at OSHA, local politics began to
have a larger effect on local enforcement. OSHA inspectors, despite their
commitment to worker protection, avoided the unpleasant task of conducting inspections at greater rates in politically hostile areas. In other
words, in the absence of the "rules-driven" and output-focused behavior that Bardach and Kagan decry, OSHA enforcement becomes less, not
more, consistent. Professionalism, in short, is not enough to guarantee
fair and reasonable enforcement across diverse political constituencies.

Likewise, the assumption that encouraging field-level bureaucrats to
consider the "reasonableness" of employer justifications for noncompliance would result in fair enforcement that correctly distinguished simple
mistakes from employer malice seems to presuppose an inspector work
environment that is unlikely to exist in all workplaces. In Sweden, Kelman
(1981) finds that safety inspectors engage in highly cooperative enforcement. But the Swedish case, with strong labor control of both the enforcement bureaucracy and the shop floor in nearly all workplaces, is distinctly
different from the American one. The average OSHA inspector does not
enter a workplace where workers are willing to speak openly about hazardous conditions or employer threats. Consequently, in those workplaces
where workers are most at need, OSHA inspectors who try to calibrate
their enforcement to a simple standard of "reasonableness" are likely to
have their work environment dominated by hostile firms. In these cases,
weak enforcement (that is incommensurate with regulatory enforcement
in union firms) seems a far more likely outcome than socially efficient and
reasonable enforcement.

If greater discretion is unlikely to yield more effective enforcement,
it may still be the case that OSHA is highly legalistic. In fact, however,
OSHA's stubborn consistency in inspector behavior is offset by a highly
"reasonable" means for assessing penalties and negotiating citations and
penalties. OSHA's penalty reductions clearly serve political ends, but the
substantial reductions for businesses with good faith compliance efforts
and positive compliance histories are also signs of greater willingness to
engage in the discrimination between "good" and "bad" employers that is
at the core of the search for regulatory reasonableness. What is interesting
is that at OSHA this process for deciding what is reasonable is not left
to the inspector alone, but is instead handled through a calibration of
penalties that takes place in the local office *after the inspection and under*

the supervision of the local administrator. In other words, out of concern that inspectors in the field might feel undue pressure to cut penalties when confronted with a one-sided stream of information about the employer's motivations, OSHA has sought to oversee and standardize the process of discerning reasonableness.

Similarly, OSHA's informal process for negotiating settlements of citations and penalties prior to a formal contest before the Review Commission (see Chapter 3) embodies the substance of reasonableness. If the honest employer agrees to take meaningful steps to improve working conditions, OSHA will often cut penalties. But, just as with initial penalty setting, this process is standardized across workplaces and inspectors by taking place higher up in OSHA's hierarchy.

Overall, the "strategic neutrality" embodied in OSHA's aggressive field inspectors and careful calibration of penalties best seems to serve the aggregate goal of reasonableness while also achieving consistency. OSHA fields a highly professional inspector corps motivated to seek and document violations of safety and health standards that yield real threats to workers (although this represents a shift from OSHA's early "write tickets at any cost" history). Furthermore, when one adds OSHA's partnership programs to the mix (the VPP), the agency is clearly willing to let certain highly cooperative employers opt out of the traditional adversarial enforcement system. OSHA's field enforcement has thus, in its current incarnation, managed to mitigate the pressure toward legalism presumed inherent in agencies operating in highly contested environments (Kagan 1994). It has done so in a way that has not, however, allowed reasonableness to come at the cost of inconsistency. Professionalism alone does not ensure that inspectors will devote themselves to unpleasant tasks, while reasonableness on a case-by-case basis as determined by field inspectors threatens to meld enforcement to power imbalances in individual workplaces.

3. The Nature of Bureaucratic Power

While the empirical focus of this book is federal and state enforcement of the OSH Act, the arguments put forth here have implications for other agencies and the nature of bureaucratic power more generally. How well does my approach explain the experiences of other agencies? Likewise, within this framework, when are bureaucratic actors powerful, and do they warrant the same attention as elected officials and interest groups?

3.1. The Generalized Power of Neutrality

OSHA is permanently authorized. Consequently, the agency operates from a position of relative strength because congressional review of its actions is largely *ex post* and relegated to funding decisions. Additionally, OSH Act enforcement is a policy area with relatively large externalities. Members of Congress, businesses, and labor are all concerned with how the law plays out not only in their areas of responsibility, but across the country as a whole. This makes OSHA's strategic neutrality – targeting of unsafe industries, penalty reductions for small and safe businesses, and geographically uniform enforcement – a particularly useful political strategy for overcoming external political advocacy. How well would my arguments fare in different circumstances, especially for more distributive agencies and during periods of policy creation?

First, even agencies responsible for policy that is not characterized by high externalities appear able to pursue strategies that include geographic neutrality. Kaufman's (1960) classic study of the Forest Service shows how that agency managed forests throughout the country in a consistent and neutral manner unrelated to local support for particular uses of the forests. A critical component of this management was the doctrine of "responsible forestry," which asserted that forests could simultaneously be used to protect natural environments, allow tourism, and provide resources for economic uses (grazing and logging). This ideology of responsible forestry attracted support throughout Congress and from the president by successfully melding together elements of the agendas advanced by conservation movements, loggers, and ranchers. Despite the fact that this was an area of very low externalities – most members of Congress had nothing at stake in how the forests were managed – the Forest Service was able to use the ideal of responsible forestry to defend itself against direct attacks from loggers and ranchers who would have preferred elevating the economic use of the forests above other interests (Kaufman 1960: 226). These forces, however, were unable to generate a sufficiently large coalition in Congress to overturn the agency's commitment to geographic neutrality through responsible forestry.

The Forest Service case also illustrates the relationship between internal agency management and the maintenance of an agency's political support. Responsible forestry was an attractive packaging of competing interests for the Forest Service's national leaders, who had to maintain support in Congress and with the president in order to avoid being overruled. Additionally, as a professional ideology also taught by leading forestry schools, it offered another important benefit: control of subordinates. The

Forest Service's leadership intensively monitored its foresters to ensure the effective and consistent implementation of responsible forestry. But far more importantly, these foresters were self-motivated to implement the doctrine that formed the basis of their professional identity. Thus, the doctrine of responsible forestry was ideal as both an internal agency management technique and an external agency political strategy.[12]

Agencies responsible for other low-externality policy areas, such as the Environmental Protection Agency's oversight of local water pollution programs, have not yielded such a clear commitment to geographic neutrality. Lacking a professional ideology like the Forest Service's around which to build and sustain a geographically neutral approach to enforcement, the EPA appears to have taken a different tack, tailoring local variation in enforcement to avoid direct attacks on the agency (Helland 1998). Such a move, however, is clearly not inevitable in all low-externality policy domains.

Second, reviewing the distributive politics literature through this lens suggests that OSHA is not simply a fortuitous case. Although the imperative to control subordinates often binds less tightly for centralized bureaucracies, the need to demonstrate political efficiency and build sustainable coalitions remains central to sustaining the bureaucracy's power as an agenda setter. For example, consider Arnold's (1979) work on the creation and implementation of the Model Cities program. As originally proposed by the Johnson administration, the program was highly targeted and would have applied to very few cities. Not surprisingly, it met with a cool reception in Congress, which objected to appropriating massive sums of money for the benefit of only a few members' constituencies. Arnold suggests that Housing and Urban Development bureaucrats recognized this limitation and in crafting a program found themselves beholden first to the members of the relevant congressional committees and second to the need to secure majority passage in the House and Senate. But another

---

[12] The subsequent history of the Forest Service (see Tipple and Wellman 1991) is also interesting in that it demonstrates the important relationship between internal agency management and external agency fortunes. As the doctrine of responsible forestry came under greater scrutiny in forestry schools (the primary source for trained foresters), the ability of the agency to use the doctrine to mitigate conflict among tourism, ecology, and economic uses of the forests diminished. Consequently, as foresters began to disagree about how to use the forests, Congress and the president became far less willing to defer to the agency in making such decisions. Pressed by environmental groups, representatives of the tourism industry, and loggers and ranchers, Congress and the president have become involved in specifying which of these relative interests should dominate, both generally and in particular forests.

reading of this history is that in creating the eligibility rules for the program, which prioritized the need for urban renewal, agency leaders structured the choice for members of Congress. Members of Congress then made decisions about how much to fund the program, and thereby how many cities would be eligible.

This was not a matter of allocating money simply to please committee members and floor majorities. Rather, as Rich (1989) has shown, the program (and most Johnson administration initiatives) ended up sending the vast majority of the funds to the cities rated by objective measures as most needy. That Johnson didn't get what he wanted – a small program targeted at a few especially needy cities – is not all that surprising. What is more interesting is that while congressional committees and the need to secure majority approval in the House were important explanations for why the program was not as highly targeted as Johnson would have liked, these variables cannot explain why the program ended up looking largely need-based. Only a theory that recognizes the important role of agencies in packaging the choices for Congress can explain this outcome.

3.2. The Scope of Bureaucratic Power

None of this is to suggest that Congress cannot occasionally overrule agency efforts to redefine the nature of conflict on an issue or to create new political coalitions. But as Carpenter, Rourke, and others have noted, agencies are often the prime source of policy ideas that members of Congress subsequently embrace and expand. Furthermore, when agencies do have discretion to initiate policies and then request congressional support to expand their scope or funding, the agency is already engaged in proactive policymaking that makes it powerful. Agencies that face recalcitrant committees can often turn the tables, seeking allies in the legislature as a whole, outside of the normal committee hierarchy, to achieve these ends.

These cases aside, a more general question is whether bureaucracies ought really to be considered independent political actors on a par with presidents and members of Congress. Contemporary political science tends to focus in much greater detail on the relative power of presidents (Howell 2003) or Congress, for instance, than on independent agency decisions. In part, this is because of an intrinsic interest in the relationships among elected institutions (Congress vs. the president), as well as because of a broader understanding that interest group power or bureaucratic interests alone cannot explain policy. What, then, do agencies do? My claim is that an agency can sometimes structure conflict by crafting and implementing policies that affect the political support it enjoys and the opposition it faces. These policy choices are more complex than simply moving policy left or right along some given and readily identified dimension of choice. In part, agencies craft policies that define dimensions of choice. When elected officials seek to shape bureaucratic decisions, their efforts take place in light of the strategic packaging that agencies initiate. Furthermore, when agencies are able to generate and implement policy on their own, they set the agenda over which outside efforts to shape policy take place.

Carpenter's (2001) work on agency autonomy presents an interesting contrast to the perspective I advance here. His primary argument is that agencies become autonomous when they are able to initiate and implement popular programs that have direct ties to citizen and interest groups outside of normal party coalitions. While my perspective is not incompatible with this vision of agency autonomy, I make a more general argument about agency power. OSHA is not autonomous – it does not have the statutory discretion to implement the sorts of popular programs that would generate direct ties to citizen groups outside of the normal party structures. Nor is the agency held in high esteem by many politicians – it lacks the reputation of many other, more prestigious agencies. Nonetheless, OSHA is clearly able to shape its political environment. The "strategic neutrality" I describe allows the agency to maintain its ties to a traditional union constituency while mitigating the opposition of certain components of the business community. Outside critics of OSHA therefore have a harder time garnering support from elected officials to attack the agency. Its elected supporters also have an easier time justifying their choices to constituents. (In the words of one OSHA official, "OSHA is not a political albatross.") OSHA's leadership, limited by the need to control its subordinates and demonstrate its relative efficiency, has made decisions that affect the ease with which outsiders can direct the agency to perform differently. Congress still regularly denies OSHA's requests for additional resources and authority, but the agency survives and independently shapes how the law is enforced.

There are, of course, cases where agencies seem to have little choice about how to direct policy so as to maintain political support. Take, for instance, the Interstate Commerce Commission (ICC), which was widely perceived as having aligned itself with railroads in setting rules concerning shipping rates and regulations. Two points are in order. First, the mere fact that an agency ends up aligned with one group that has powerful allies in Congress does not demonstrate that agencies are irrelevant in shaping political conflict. To discern alternative patterns of support and opposition, one needs to look beyond observed political conflict to potential choices that agencies could have made. Second, upon closer examination, even the ICC is not such a clear case for the inevitability of agency capture by a monolithic interest group. Rothenberg (1994) has shown that despite the strength of the railroad community, the ICC nonetheless issued decisions that advanced the interstate trucking industry even when that lobby was still politically weak.

Still, I do not claim that agencies are always able to structure conflict and shape policy. An agency needs sufficient discretion to make the initial policy choices that can alter how it garners support. During periods of statutory construction, legislators and presidents can seek to limit bureaucratic discretion so as to make certain coalitions untenable. On an ongoing basis, agencies that are hamstrung by extensive procedural rules, small budgets, and constant meddling by committees or presidential appointees may never gain the political "space" necessary to influence this political environment. Furthermore, even agencies that are able to overcome these initial hurdles may make bad strategic or management decisions, and these miscalculations may reverberate in persistent and extensive external meddling in agency affairs. OSHA, for example, experienced substantial costs as a result of its field office reinvention initiative. Questions about the capacity for agencies to influence the political environment are therefore tied directly to questions of public administration. Poor management or weak policy initiatives can doom an agency, while wisely crafted policies and strong leadership can put an agency in a position where it is difficult for outsiders to undo what the agency initiates.

If agencies can be politically important in shaping policy and limiting opportunities for outside political control of their behavior, what is the degree of this importance? That is, relative to the other actors in the policy-making process, what is the influence of bureaucrats themselves in shaping policy and bureaucratic decision making? In general, existing scholarship provides an incomplete answer to this question. Political scientists have shown conclusively that bureaucracies cannot do as they wish, thereby providing a powerful rejoinder to concerns about unfettered bureaucratic power. At the same time, however, they have largely taken as given the dimensionality and nature of political conflict. In those exceptional studies in which agencies have been recognized as strategic actors (e.g., by Rothenberg), little attention has been given to the way in which problems of implementation limit the range of feasible strategies for bureaucracies to build and sustain political support. (For example, Rourke suggests that bureaucratic power is built on professionalism and expertise or strategic manipulation of policy, without considering how these concerns conflict with one other.) The public administration literature, meanwhile, largely takes as given the power of seemingly neutral administrative leadership without recognizing the crucial ways in which the external political environment constraints the feasible choices of administrative leaders. In short, packaging of policies, and not just their merits, matters.

To accurately assess the way in which elected officials and interest groups can influence bureaucratic decisions one needs to move beyond simple aggregate analyses of agency outputs to a more contextual analysis of the dimensions and uses of agency discretion. But whether discretion yields different bureaucratic decisions than direct mandates of agency behavior through lawmaking depends on the relative influence of other actors (e.g., congressional committees and presidents) in overruling agencies as they initiate and shape policies. As the OSHA case shows, even a relatively constrained agency can insulate itself from some efforts to shape enforcement in response to geographic, industry, and labor pressures.

Finally, one may question whether this holistic approach to policy analysis and bureaucratic decision making is either important or feasible. My analysis has, I hope, demonstrated both the possibility and necessity of this approach. Examining what presidents, Congress, and interest groups do individually misses the way in which bureaucracies create policy choices for these other actors and can play them off against one another. Similarly, looking only at bureaucratic strategy presupposes that agency leaders can overcome their management problems and implement the policy choices they desire. Only by studying carefully what is at stake in a given matter of policy, how agency choices shape political conflict, and what outsiders can do to influence bureaucratic decisions can the full contours of the interactions between agency management and external influence become apparent.

References

Works Cited

Abraham, Katharine G., and James L. Medoff. 1984. "Length of Service and Lay-offs in Union and Nonunion Work Groups." *Industrial and Labor Relations Review* 38(1): 87–97.

Akard, Patrick J. 1992. "Corporate Mobilization and Political Power: The Transformation of U.S. Economic Policy in the 1970s." *American Sociological Review* 57: 597–615.

Arnold, R. Douglas. 1979. *Congress and the Bureaucracy: A Theory of Influence.* New Haven, CT: Yale University Press.

Arnold, R. Douglas. 1990. *The Logic of Congressional Action.* New Haven, CT: Yale University Press.

Bardach, Eugene, and Robert A. Kagan. 1982. *Going by the Book: The Problem of Regulatory Unreasonableness.* Philadelphia: Temple University Press.

Barr, Stephen. 2000. "Retirement Wave Creates Vacuum Series: Empty Pipeline." *Washington Post*, May 7, p. A1.

Bartel, Ann P., and Lacy Glenn Thomas. 1987. "Predation through Regulation: The Wage and Profit Effects of the Occupational Safety and Health Administration and the Environmental Protection Agency." *Journal of Law and Economics* 30: 239–264.

Bawn, Kathleen. 1995. "Political Control versus Expertise: Congressional Choices about Administrative Procedures." *American Political Science Review* 89: 62–73.

Beck, Nathaniel, and Jonathan N. Katz. 1995. "What to Do (and Not to Do) with Time-Series Cross-Section Data." *American Political Science Review* 89(3) (September): 634–647.

Beck, Nathaniel, Jonathan N. Katz, R. Michael Alvarez, Geoffrey Garrett, and Peter Lange. 1993. "Government Partisanship, Labor Organization, and Macroeconomic Performance: A Corrigendum." *American Political Science Review* 87(4) (December): 945–948.

Becker, Gary S. 1968. "Crime and Punishment: An Economic Approach." *Journal of Political Economy* 78: 189–217.

Behrman, Bradley. 1980. "Civil Aeronautics Board." In *The Politics of Regulation*, ed. James Q. Wilson. New York: Basic Books, pp. 75–121.

Bernstein, Marver H. 1955. *Regulating Business by Independent Commission*. Princeton, NJ: Princeton University Press.

Blau, Peter Michael. 1955. *The Dynamics of Bureaucracy*. Chicago: University of Chicago Press.

Block, Michael, and John M. Heineke. 1973. "The Allocation of Effort under Uncertainty: The Case of Risk Averse Behavior." *Journal of Political Economy* 81: 376–385.

Blodgett, John, and the Center for International Earth Science Information Network (CIESIN), Columbia University. 1998. Geographic Correspondence Engine, Version 3.0 [online]. http://plue.sedac.ciesin.org/plue/geocorr.

BNA Occupational Safety and Health Daily, March 9, 1993. "Enforcement, 'Great Swings' in OSHA Policy Documented in Study by DOL Official."

BNA Occupational Safety and Health Daily, February 1, 1995. "Complaints," p. 3.

BNA Occupational Safety and Health Daily, September 28, 1995. "Voluntary Protection," p. 3.

BNA Occupational Safety and Health Daily, October 23, 1995. "OSHA Puts Plans on Hold to Grant Georgia Poultry Companies Exemptions," p. 4.

BNA Occupational Safety and Health Daily, September 17, 1998. "Voluntary Protection," p. 2.

Boden, Leslie I. 1995. "Workers' Compensations in the United States." *Annual Review of Public Health* 16: 208–218.

Brehm, John, and Scott Gates. 1997. *Working, Shirking, and Sabotage*. Ann Arbor: University of Michigan Press.

Buchanan, James M. 1996. "Federalism and Individual Sovereignty." *The Cato Journal* 15(2–3): 259–268.

Burkhauser, Richard V., and T. Aldrich Finegan. 1989. "The Minimum Wage and the Poor: The End of a Relationship." *Journal of Policy Analysis and Management* 8(1) (Winter): 53–71.

Calvert, Randall L., Mathew D. McCubbins, and Barry R. Weingast. 1989. "A Theory of Political Control and Agency Discretion." *American Journal of Political Science* 33(3) (August): 588–611.

Canes-Wrone, Brandice. 2003. "Bureaucratic Decisions and the Composition of the Lower Courts." *American Journal of Political Science* 47: 205–214.

Card, David, and B. P. McCall. 1996. "Is Workers' Compensation Covering Uninsured Medical Costs? Evidence from the 'Monday Effect.'" *Industrial and Labor Relations Review* 49: 690–706.

Carpenter, Daniel. 2001. *The Forging of Bureaucratic Autonomy*. Princeton, NJ: Princeton University Press.

Carpenter, Daniel. 2004. "Protection without Capture." *American Political Science Review* 98(4) (November): 613–631.

Carpenter, Daniel, and Keith E. Whittington. 2003. "Executive Power in American Institutional Development." *Perspectives on Politics* 1(3) (September): 495–513.

Chelius, James R. 1977. *Workplace Safety and Health: The Role of Workers' Compensation.* Washington, DC: American Enterprise Institute.

Chelius, James R., and Edward Moscovitch. 1996. *Toward a Safer Workplace: Reform and Deregulation of Workers' Compensation.* Boston: Pioneer Institute.

Chemical Week, October 11, 1995. "CMA Takes Heat for 'Principled' OSHA Stand," p. 62.

Congressional Quarterly. No date. "Washington Alert Database." Washington, DC: Congressional Quarterly.

Cyert, Richard, and James G. March. 1963. *A Behavioral Theory of the Firm.* Englewood Cliffs, NJ: Prentice-Hall.

de Figueiredo, Rui J. P., Jr. 2002. "Electoral Competition, Political Uncertainty, and Policy Insulation." *American Political Science Review* 96(2): 321–333.

Derthick, Martha, and Paul J. Quirk. 1985. *The Politics of Deregulation.* Washington, DC: Brookings Institution.

Dickens, William T. 1984. "Differences between Risk Premiums in Union and Nonunion Wages and the Case for Occupational Safety Regulation." *The American Economic Review* 74: 320–323.

Diver, Colin S. 1980. "A Theory of Regulatory Enforcement." *Public Policy* 28: 257–299.

Dodd, Lawrence C., and Richard L. Schott. 1979. *Congress and the Administrative State.* New York: Wiley and Sons.

Downs, Anthony. 1967. *Inside Bureaucracy.* Boston: Little, Brown.

Dreazen, Yochi J. 2000. "Government's Proposed Ergonomic Rules Don't Please Employers or Labor Unions." *Wall Street Journal,* May 15, p. A52.

Epstein, David, and Sharyn O'Halloran. 1994. "Administrative Procedures, Information, and Agency Discretion." *American Journal of Political Science* 38: 697–722.

Fairley, Peter. 1998. "Industry Opposes OSHA Legislation." *Chemical Week* 160(4) (January 28): 50–52.

Fesler, James W. 1949. *Area and Administration.* Tuscaloosa: University of Alabama Press.

Finnegan, Lisa. 1998. "Reform and Reinvention." *Occupational Hazards* 60(7): 67–68.

Fiorina, Morris. 1986. "Legislator Uncertainty, Legislative Control, and the Delegation of Legislative Power." *Journal of Law, Economics and Organization* 2: 33–51.

Gilligan, Thomas W., William J. Marshall, and Barry R. Weingast. 1989. "Regulation and the Theory of Legislative Choice: The Interstate Commerce Act of 1887." *Journal of Law and Economics* 32(1) (April): 35–61.

Gordon, Sanford. 1999. "Managing Fairness: Procedural Consistency in Regulatory Enforcement." Ph.D. dissertation, Princeton University.

Gormley, William T., Jr. 1983. "Policy, Politics, and Public Utility Regulation." *American Journal of Political Science* 27: 86–105.

Gormley, William T., Jr. 1989. *Taming the Bureaucracy.* Princeton, NJ: Princeton University Press.

Gray, Wayne B. 1987. "The Cost of Regulation: OSHA, EPA and the Productivity Slowdown." *American Economic Review* 77: 998–1006.

Gray, Wayne B., and John T. Scholz. 1993. "Does Regulatory Enforcement Work? A Panel Analysis of OSHA Enforcement." *Law and Society Review* 27: 177–213.

Hart, David M. 2001. "Why Do Some Firms Give?" *The Journal of Politics* 63(4): 1230–1249.

Haynes, John. 1895. "Risk as an Economic Factor." *Quarterly Journal of Economics* 9(4): 409–449.

Hedge, David, and Saba Jallow. 1990. "The Federal Context of Regulation." *Social Science Quarterly* 71(4): 786–801.

Helland, Eric. 1998. "Environmental Protection in the Federalist System: The Political Economy of NPDES Inspections." *Economic Inquiry* 36: 305–319.

Herzog, Henry W., and Alan M. Schlottmann. 1990. "Valuing Risk in the Workplace: Market Price, Willingness to Pay, and the Optimal Provision of Safety." *The Review of Economics and Statistics* 72(3): 463–470.

Heyes, Anthony G. 1998. "Making Things Stick: Enforcement and Compliance." *Oxford Review of Economic Policy* 14: 50–63.

Hosansky, David. 1998. "Hill Feels the Big Clout of Small Business." *Congressional Quarterly Weekly Report*, January 10, p. 55.

Howell, William G. 2003. *Power without Persuasion: The Politics of Direct Presidential Action*. Princeton, NJ: Princeton University Press.

Huber, John. D., and Charles R. Shipan. 2002. *Deliberate Discretion? The Institutional Foundations of Bureaucratic Autonomy*. Cambridge: Cambridge University Press.

Huntington, Samuel P. 1952. "The Marasmus of the ICC: The Commission, the Railroads, and the Public Interest." *Yale Law Journal* 61: 467–509.

Hutter, Bridget M. 1989. "Variation in Regulatory Enforcement Styles." *Law and Policy* 11: 153–174.

Jacobson, Gary C. 1997. *The Politics of Congressional Elections*. New York: Addison-Wesley.

Johnson, Dave. January 1996. "This Month In Washington." *Industrial Safety and Hygiene News*.

Jones, Bryan D., Saadia R. Greenberg, Clifford Kaufman, and Joseph Drew. 1977. "Bureaucratic Response to Citizen-Initiated Contacts: Environmental Enforcement in Detroit." *American Political Science Review* 71(1) (March): 148–165.

Jones, Bryan D., Saadia R. Greenberg, Clifford Kaufman, and Joseph Drew. 1978. "Service Delivery Rules and the Distribution of Local Government Services: Three Detroit Bureaucracies." *The Journal of Politics* 40(2) (May): 332–368.

Kagan, Robert A. 1994. "Regulatory Enforcement." In *Handbook of Regulation and Administrative Law*, ed. David H. Rosenbloom and Richard D. Schwartz. New York: M. Dekker, pp. 383–422.

Kahn, Shulamit. 1987. "Occupational Safety and Health: Is There a Marginal Worker?" *The Review of Economics and Statistics* 69: 262–268.

Katznelson, Ira. 1981. *City Trenches: Urban Politics and the Patterning of Class in the United States*. Chicago: University of Chicago Press.

Kaufman, Herbert. 1960. *The Forest Ranger: A Study in Administrative Behavior*. Baltimore: Johns Hopkins University Press.

Kaufman, Herbert. 1981. *The Administrative Behavior of Federal Bureau Chiefs.* Washington, DC: The Brookings Institution.

Kelman, Steven. 1980. "Occupational Safety and Health Administration." In *The Politics of Regulation*, ed. James Q. Wilson. New York: Basic Books, pp. 236–266.

Kelman, Steven. 1981. *Regulating America, Regulating Sweden.* Cambridge, MA: MIT Press.

Krause, George A. 1999. *A Two-Way Street: The Institutional Dynamics of the Modern Administrative State.* Pittsburgh: University of Pittsburgh Press.

Krehbiel, Keith. 1991. *Information and Legislative Organization.* Ann Arbor: University of Michigan Press.

Krehbiel, Keith, and Douglas Rivers. 1988. "The Analysis of Committee Power: An Application to Senate Voting on the Minimum Wage." *American Journal of Political Science* 32: 1151–1174.

Krizan, William G. 1994. "Unions and Nonunion Hunt for Market Edge." *Engineering News-Record*, May 2, p. 6.

Lafont, Jean-Jacques, and Jean Tirole. 1991. "The Politics of Government Decision-Making." *The Quarterly Journal of Economics* 106: 1089–1127.

Lee, Frances E. 2004. "Bicameralism and Geographic Politics: Allocating Funds in the House and Senate." *Legislative Studies Quarterly* 29(2) (May): 185–213.

Levy, Frank, Arnold J. Meltsner, and Aaron Wildavsky. 1974. *Urban Outcomes.* Berkeley: University of California Press.

Lewis, David E. 2003. *Presidents and the Politics of Agency Design.* Stanford, CA: Stanford University Press.

Lind, E. Allan, and Tom R. Tyler. 1988. *The Social Psychology of Procedural Justice.* New York: Plenum Press.

Lipsky, Michael. 1980. *Street-level Bureaucracy.* New York: Russell Sage Foundation.

Long, J. S. 1997. *Regression Models for Categorical and Limited Dependent Variables.* Thousand Oaks, CA: Sage.

Lowi, Theodore J. 1979. *The End of Liberalism.* New York: Norton.

Maloney, M., and R. McCormick. 1982. "A Positive Theory of Environmental Quality Regulation." *Journal of Law and Economics* 25: 99–124.

Marsh, Barbara. 1994. "Workers at Risk." *Wall Street Journal*, February 3, p. A1.

McCraw, Thomas K. 1984. *Prophets of Regulation.* Cambridge, MA: Harvard University Press.

McCubbins, Mathew D., and Thomas Schwartz. 1984. "Congressional Oversight Overlooked: Police Patrols versus Fire Alarms." *American Journal of Political Science* 28: 165–179.

McCubbins, Mathew D., Roger G. Noll, and Barry R. Weingast. 1987. "Administrative Procedures as Instruments of Political Control." *Journal of Law, Economics and Organization* 3(Fall): 243–277.

McGillivray, Fiona. 2004. *Privileging Industry: The Comparative Politics of Trade and Industrial Policy.* Princeton, NJ: Princeton University Press.

McNollgast. 1990. "Positive and Normative Models of Procedural Rights." *Journal of Law, Economics, and Organization* 6: 307–332.

Mendeloff, John M. 1979. *Regulating Safety: An Economic and Political Analysis of Occupational Safety and Health Policy.* Cambridge, MA: MIT Press.

Mendeloff, John M. 1988. *The Dilemma of Toxic Substance Regulation: How Overregulation Causes Underregulation at OSHA.* Cambridge, MA: MIT Press.

Meyer, Bruce D., W. Kip Viscusi, and David L. Durbin. 1995. "Workers' Compensation and Injury Duration: Evidence from a Natural Experiment." *The American Economic Review* 85: 322–340.

Miller, Gary J. 1992. *Managerial Dilemmas: The Political Economy of Hierarchy.* New York: Cambridge University Press.

Mintz, Benjamin W. 1984. *OSHA: History, Law and Policy.* Washington, DC: Bureau of National Affairs.

Mintz, Joel A. 1995. *Enforcement at the EPA.* Austin: University of Texas Press.

Moe, Terry. 1984. "The New Economics of Organization." *American Journal of Political Science* 28: 739–777.

Moe, Terry. 1985. "Control and Feedback in Economic Regulation: The Case of the NLRB." *American Political Science Review* 79: 1094–1116.

Moe, Terry. 1987. "An Assessment of the Positive Theory of 'Congressional Dominance.'" *Legislative Studies Quarterly* 12: 475–520.

Moe, Terry. 1989. "The Politics of Bureaucratic Structure." In *Can the Government Govern?*, ed. John E. Chubb and Paul E. Peterson. Washington, DC: The Brookings Institution.

Moore, Michael J., and W. Kip Viscusi. 1990. *Compensation Mechanisms for Job Risks: Wages, Workers' Compensation, and Product Liability.* Princeton, NJ: Princeton University Press.

Niskanen, William A. 1971. *Bureaucracy and Representative Government.* Chicago: Aldine.

Noble, Charles. 1986. *Liberalism at Work: The Rise and Fall of OSHA.* Philadelphia: Temple University Press.

Ogul, Morris S. 1976. *Congress Oversees the Bureaucracy.* Pittsburgh: University of Pittsburgh Press.

Olson, Mancur. 1965. *The Logic of Collective Action.* Cambridge, MA: Harvard University Press.

Olson, Mary K. 1995. "Regulatory Agency Discretion among Competing Industries: Inside the FDA." *Journal of Law Economics and Organization* 11: 379–405.

Padgett, John F. 1981. "Hierarchy and Ecological Control in Federal Budgetary Decision Making." *The American Journal of Sociology* 87: 75–129.

Peltzman, Sam. 1976. "Toward a More General Theory of Regulation." *Journal of Law and Economics* 19: 211–240.

Perrow, Charles. 1986. *Complex Organizations.* New York: McGraw-Hill.

Pierson, Paul. 2000. "Increasing Returns, Path Dependence, and the Study of Politics." *American Political Science Review* 94: 251–267.

Pollack, E. S., and D. F. Keimig. 1987. *Counting Injuries and Illnesses in the Workplace: Proposals for a Better System.* Washington, DC: National Academy Press.

Poole, Keith T. 1998. "Recovering a Basic Space from a Set of Issue Scales." *American Journal of Political Science* 42: 954–993.

Poole, Keith T., and R. Steven Daniels. 1985. "Ideology, Party, and Voting in the U.S. Congress, 1959–1980." *American Political Science Review* 79(2) (June): 373–399.

Poole, Keith T., and Howard Rosenthal. 1991. "Patterns of Congressional Voting." *American Journal of Political Science* 35: 228–278.

Posner, Richard A. 1974. "Theories of Economic Regulation." *The Bell Journal of Economics and Management Science* 5(2) (Autumn): 335–358.

Pressman, Jeffrey L., and Aaron Wildavsky. 1973. *Implementation*. Berkeley: University of California Press.

Rea, Samuel A., Jr. 1981. "Workmen's Compensation and Occupational Safety under Imperfect Information." *The American Economic Review* 71: 80–93.

Redford, Emmette S. 1969. *Democracy in the Administrative State*. New York: Oxford University Press.

Rich, Michael J. 1989. "Distributive Politics and the Allocation of Federal Grants." *American Political Science Review* 83: 193–213.

Ringleb, Al H., and Steven N. Wiggins. 1990. "Liability and Large-Scale, Long-Term Hazards." *The Journal of Political Economy* 98: 574–595.

Romer, Thomas, and Howard Rosenthal. 1979. "Bureaucrats versus Voters: On the Political Economy of Resource Allocation by Direct Democracy." *The Quarterly Journal of Economics* 93(4) (November): 563–587.

Romer, Thomas, and Howard Rosenthal. 1987. "Modern Political Economy and the Study of Regulation." In *Public Regulation: New Perspectives on Institutions and Policies*, ed. Elizabeth E. Bailey. Cambridge, MA: MIT Press, pp. 73–116.

Rosen, Sherwin. 1974. "Hedonic Prices and Implicit Markets: Product Differentiation in Pure Competition." *Journal of Political Economy* 82: 34–55.

Rothenberg, Lawrence. 1994. *Regulation, Organizations, and Politics*. Ann Arbor: University of Michigan Press.

Rourke, Francis E. 1984. *Bureaucracy, Politics, and Public Policy*, 3rd ed. Boston: Little, Brown.

Ruser, John W. 1993. "Workers' Compensation and the Distribution of Occupational Injuries." *Journal of Human Resources* 28: 593–617.

Ruser, John W., and Robert S. Smith. 1988. "The Effect of OSHA Records-Check Inspections on Reported Occupational Injuries in Manufacturing Establishments." *Journal of Risk and Uncertainty* 1: 415–435.

Ruser, John W., and Robert S. Smith. 1991. "Reestimating OSHA's Effects: Have the Data Changed?" *Journal of Human Resources* 26: 212–235.

Salisbury, Robert, John Heinz, Edward Laumann, and Robert Nelson. 1987. "Who Works with Whom? Interest Group Alliances and Opposition." *American Journal of Political Science* 81: 1217–1234.

Salop, Steven, and David Scheffman. 1987. "Cost-Raising Strategies." *Journal of Industrial Economics* 36: 19–34.

Scholz, John T. 1984. "Cooperation, Deterrence, and the Ecology of Regulatory Enforcement." *Law & Society Review* 18(2): 179–224.

Scholz, John T. 1985. "Coping with Complexity: A Bounded Rationality Perspective on Taxpayer Compliance." In *Proceedings of the Seventy-eighth Annual Conference on Taxation.* Columbus, OH: National Tax Association and Tax Institute of America.

Scholz, John T. 1991. "Cooperative Regulatory Enforcement and the Politics of Administrative Effectiveness." *American Political Science Review* 85(1) (March): 115–136.

Scholz, John T., and Feng Heng Wei. 1986. "Regulatory Enforcement in a Federalist System." *American Political Science Review* 80: 1249–1270.

Scholz, John T., and Wayne B. Gray. 1990. "OSHA Enforcement and Workplace Injuries: A Behavioral Approach to Risk Assessment." *Journal of Risk and Uncertainty* 3: 283–305.

Scholz, John T., and Wayne B. Gray. 1997. "Can Government Facilitate Cooperation? An Informational Model of OSHA Enforcement." *American Journal of Political Science* 41: 693–717.

Scholz, John T., Jim Twombly, and Barbara Headrick. 1991. "Street-Level Political Controls over Federal Bureaucracy." *American Political Science Review* 85: 829–850.

Scholz, John T., and B. Dan Wood. 1998. "Controlling the IRS: Principals, Principles, and Public Administration" *American Journal of Political Science* 42: 141–162.

Scholz, John T., and B. Dan Wood. 1999. "Efficiency, Equity, and Politics." *American Journal of Political Science* 43: 1166–1188.

Scott, Dean. 1996. "OSHA: Repeated Shutdowns, Reduced Funding Forcing OSHA to Rethink Regulatory Priorities." *BNA Occupational Safety and Health Daily*, January 22, p. 2.

Selznick, Philip. 1949. *TVA and the Grass Roots: A Study in the Sociology of Formal Organization.* Berkeley: University of California Press.

Shipan, Charles. 2004. "Regulatory Regimes, Agency Actions, and the Conditional Nature of Political Influence." *American Political Science Review* 93 (August): 467–480.

Shover, Neal, Donald A. Clelland, and John Lynxwiler. 1986. *Enforcement or Negotiation: Constructing a Regulatory Bureaucracy.* Albany: State University of New York Press.

Simon, Herbert A. 1947. *Administrative Behavior: A Study of Decision-Making Processes in Administrative Organization.* New York: Macmillan.

Smith, Mark A. 2000. *American Business and Political Power.* Chicago: University of Chicago Press.

Smothers, Ronald. 1991. "25 Die, Many Reported Trapped, As Blaze Engulfs Carolina Plant." *New York Times*, September 4, p. A1.

Snyder, James M., Jr. 1992. "Committee Power, Structure-Induced Equilibria, and Roll Call Votes." *American Journal of Political Science* 36(1): 1–30.

Stigler, George J. 1971. "The Theory of Economic Regulation." *Bell Journal of Economics and Management Science* 2: 3–21.

Thomas, *an Electronic Database of the Library of Congress.* no date. Washington, DC: Library of Congress. http://thomas.loc.gov.

Thompson, Frank J. 1983. "The Substitution Approach to Intergovernmental Relations: The Case of OSHA." *Publius* 13: 59–78.

Thompson, Frank J., and Michael J. Scicchitano. 1985a. "State Implementation Effort and Federal Regulatory Policy: The Case of Occupational Safety and Health." *Journal of Politics* 47: 686–703.

Thompson, Frank J., and Michael J. Scicchitano. 1985b. "State Enforcement of Federal Regulatory Policy: The Lessons of OSHA." *Policy Studies Journal* 13: 591–598.

Tipple, Terence J., and J. Douglas Wellman. 1991. "Herbert Kaufman's Forest Ranger Thirty Years Later." *Public Administration Review* 51(5): 421–428.

Tsebelis, George. 1995. "Decision Making in Political Systems: Veto Players in Presidentialism, Parliamentarism, Multicameralism and Multipartyism." *British Journal of Political Science* 25(3) (July): 289–325.

Victor, Kirk. 1989. "OSHA's Turnabout." *The National Journal* 21 (November 25): 2889.

Viscusi, W. Kip. 1992. *Fatal Tradeoffs: Public and Private Responsibilities for Risk.* New York: Oxford University Press.

Viscusi, W. Kip. 1993. "The Value of Risks to Life and Health." *Journal of Economic Literature* 31: 1912–1946.

Volden, Craig. 2002. "A Formal Model of the Politics of Delegation in a Separation of Powers System." *American Journal of Political Science* 46(1): 111–133.

Weber, Max. 1946. "Bureaucracy." In *From Max Weber,* ed. H. H. Gerth and C. Wright Mills. New York: Oxford University Press, pp. 196–224.

Weil, David. 1991. "Enforcing OSHA: The Role of Labor Unions." *Industrial Relations* 30: 20–36.

Weil, David. 1992. "Building Safety: The Role of Construction Unions in the Enforcement of OSHA." *Journal of Labor Research* 13: 121–132.

Weiler, Paul. 1986. *Legal Policy for Workplace Injuries.* Philadelphia: American Law Institute Project on Compensation and Liability for Product and Process Injuries.

Weingast, Barry R., and Mark J. Moran. 1982. "The Myth of Runaway Bureaucracy." *Regulation* 6: 33–8.

Weingast, Barry R., and Mark J. Moran. 1983. "Bureaucratic Discretion or Congressional Control? Regulatory Policymaking by the Federal Trade Commission." *Journal of Political Economy* 91: 765–800.

Wilson, James Q. 1989. *Bureaucracy: What Government Agencies Do and Why They Do It.* New York: Basic Books.

Wilson, Woodrow. 1887. "The Study of Administration." *Political Science Quarterly* 2: 197–222.

Wood, B. Dan. 1988. "Principals, Bureaucrats, and Responsiveness in Clean Air Enforcements." *American Political Science Review* 82: 213–234.

Wood, B. Dan, and Richard W. Waterman. 1994. *Bureaucratic Dynamics: The Role of Bureaucracy in a Democracy.* Boulder, CO: Westview Press.

Yuill, Barbara A. 1995. "OSHA: Attorneys Support OSHA Reinvention, but Question Details of New Culture." *BNA Occupational Safety and Health Daily,* March 7, p. 2.

Government Materials Not Cited Fully in the Text

Bureau of Economic Analysis, United States Department of Commerce. 1970. "Regional Accounts Data." Washington, DC: Department of Commerce.

Bureau of Labor Statistics, United States Department of Labor. Washington, DC: Department of Labor.

Multiple Years. "Local Area Unemployment Statistics."

1975. "Directory of National Unions and Employee Associations."

1993. "Survey of Occupational Injuries and Illnesses."

January 1996. "Occupational Safety and Health Statistics."

1997. "Occupational Earnings Survey."

April 22, 1999. "Lost-Worktime Injuries and Illnesses: Characteristics and Resulting Time Away from Work, 1997."

December 16, 1999. "Workplace Injuries and Illnesses in 1998."

Bureau of the Census, United States Department of Commerce. Washington, DC: Department of Commerce.

Multiple Years. "County Business Patterns."

Multiple Years. "Current Population Survey."

Multiple Years. "Statistical Abstract of the United States."

1996. "USA Counties 1996."

Government Accountability Office (GAO) (formerly the Government Accounting Office), Washington, DC.

Occupational Safety and Health: Assuring Accuracy in Employer Injury and Illness Records (GAO/HRD-89-23), December 30, 1988.

Occupational Safety and Health Administration, United States Department of Labor. Washington, DC: Department of Labor.

No Date. "Voluntary Protection Program Overview." Available at http://www.osha.gov/oshaprogs/vpp/.

February 29, 2000. "Chart: Growth of VPP." Available from the author.

Court Cases Cited

Marshall v. Barlow's, Inc. 436 U.S. 307 (1978)

AFL-CIO v. Marshall. 617 F.2d 636 (1978)

Camara v. Municipal Court. 387 U.S. 523 (1967)

Index